D1498887

For Reference Not to be taken from the room.

DISCARDED
FROM
LIU LIBRARY

LONG ISLAND
UNIVERSITY
LIBRARIES

EUROPEAN HISTORICAL DICTIONARIES
Edited by Jon Woronoff

1. *Portugal,* by Douglas L. Wheeler. 1993
2. *Turkey,* by Metin Heper. 1994
3. *Poland,* by George Sanford and Adriana Gozdecka-Sanford. 1994
4. *Germany,* by Wayne C. Thompson, Susan L. Thompson, and Juliet S. Thompson. 1994
5. *Greece,* by Thanos M. Veremis and Mark Dragoumis. 1995
6. *Cyprus,* by Stavros Panteli. 1995
7. *Sweden,* by Irene Scobbie. 1995
8. *Finland,* by George Maude. 1995
9. *Croatia,* by Robert Stallaerts and Jeannine Laurens. 1995
10. *Malta,* by Warren G. Berg. 1995
11. *Spain,* by Angel Smith. 1996
12. *Albania,* by Raymond Hutchings. 1996
13. *Slovenia,* by Leopoldina Plut-Pregelj and Carole Rogel. 1996
14. *Luxembourg,* by Harry C. Barteau. 1996
15. *Romania,* by Kurt W. Treptow and Marcel Popa. 1996
16. *Bulgaria,* by Raymond Detrez. 1997
17. *United Kingdom: Volume 1, England and the United Kingdom; Volume 2, Scotland, Wales, and Northern Ireland,* by Kenneth J. Panton and Keith A. Cowlard. 1997; 1998
18. *Hungary,* by Steven Béla Várdy. 1997
19. *Latvia,* by Andrejs Plakans. 1997
20. *Ireland,* by Colin Thomas and Avril Thomas. 1997
21. *Lithuania,* by Saulius Suziedelis. 1997
22. *Macedonia,* by Valentina Georgieva and Sasha Konechni. 1998
23. *The Czech State,* by Jiri Hochman. 1998
24. *Iceland,* by Guðmundur Hálfdanarson. 1997
25. *Bosnia and Herzegovina,* by Ante Euvalo. 1997
26. *Russia,* by Boris Raymond and Paul Duffy. 1998
27. *Gypsies (Romanies),* by Donald Kenrick. 1998
28. *Belarus,* by Jan Zaprudnik. 1998
29. *Federal Republic of Yugoslavia,* by Zeljan Suster. 1998
30. *France,* by Gino Raymond. 1998
31. *Slovakia,* by Stanislav J. Kirschbaum. 1998
32. *Netherlands,* by Arend H. Huussen Jr. 1998
33. *Denmark,* by Alastair H. Thomas and Stewart P. Oakley. 1998

Historical Dictionary of Russia

Boris Raymond
Paul Duffy

European Historical Dictionaries, No. 26

The Scarecrow Press, Inc.
Lanham, Md., & London
1998

SCARECROW PRESS, INC.

Published in the United States of America
by Scarecrow Press, Inc.
4720 Boston Way
Lanham, Maryland 20706

4 Pleydell Gardens, Folkestone
Kent CT20 2DN, England

Copyright © 1998 by Boris Raymond

All rights reserved. No part of this publication may be reproduced,
stored in a retrieval system, or transmitted in any form or by any
means, electronic, mechanical, photocopying, recording, or otherwise,
without the prior permission of the publisher.

British Library Cataloguing in Publication Information Available

Library of Congress Cataloging-in-Publican Data

Raymond, Boris, 1925–
    Historical dictionary of Russia / Boris Raymond and Paul Duffy.
        p. cm.—(European historical dictionaries ; no. 26)
    Includes bibliographical references.
    ISBN 0–8108–3357–3 (cloth : alk. paper)
    1. Russia—History—Dictionaries. 2. Soviet Union—History—
Dictionaries. 3. Russia (Federation)—History—1991—
Dictionaries. I. Duffy, Paul, 1958– . II. Title. III. Series.
DK36.R39   1997
947′.003—dc21   97–22659
                                                 CIP

ISBN 0–8108–3357–3 (cloth : alk. paper)

∞ ™ The paper used in this publication meets the minimum requirements of
American National Standard for Information Sciences—Permanence of Paper
for Printed Library Materials, ANSI Z39.48—1984. Manufactured in the United
States of America.

Contents

Ref.
DK
36
.R39
1998

Editor's Foreword

Few countries have had as eventful a history as what is presently called Russia, which once was called the Union of Soviet Socialist Republics, and before that the Tsarist Empire, and yet further back Kievan Rus. Even today, shorn of some of its republics (now independent states) and of the territories that were ruled over by the tsar, Russia is an exceedingly important country. It is the world's largest in area, among the largest in population, despite everything an impressive military force, potentially an economic giant, and too close to too many other countries to be ignored by its neighbors or those further afield. These facts mean that it remains a country that must be reckoned with and that must be better known, a not entirely simple task even under a more democratic regime.

One path to knowing Russia is to consider its history, especially when the past seems to be making a comeback. Such knowledge can be facilitated by this *Historical Dictionary of Russia*. In a multitude of succinct entries this work covers many of the crucial events, significant persons, and basic insitutions that have shaped Russia over the ages. While most of these relate to politics, a fair number deal with culture, society, and the economy. The path is easier to negotiate thanks to both a chronology of events and a chronology of rulers. These chronologies are followed by a list of acronyms, then by the dictionary proper, and finally by a selective bibliography to direct those who want to delve further into Russia's past and present to other sources of information.

The main author of this book is Boris Raymond (born Boris Romanov), who would probably have been born in Russia if not for some of the dramatic events sketched in this book. Still, although he grew up in the United States, he maintained links professionally, studying library science and then Russian history and becoming a Russian bibliographer and, later, also a professor of library science. This enabled him to follow Russian events more closely and keep abreast of the literature. He was helped by Paul Duffy, who works at Dalhousie University's Killam Library. The result is a very handy guide to a very important country.

Jon Woronoff
Series Editor

Acknowledgments

The authors wish to thank Dr. Valentina Agaeva of the Institute of Scientific Information on the Social Sciences (INION) for her major contribution to this effort. Dr. Agaeva wrote many of the longer articles included in this dictionary. We are also indebted to Dr. David Jones of the Russian Research Center of Nova Scotia for his bibliographic advice and his generosity in permitting us to make use of the center's extensive library. Others of the Dalhousie University community were also very helpful, especially members of the Dalhousie University Library, Ms. Donna Edwards of the University's Department of Sociology and Social Anthropology, and the staff of the Computer Centre. Finally, we wish to thank Janice Raymond and Dr. David Jones for their editorial contribution to this project.

Map

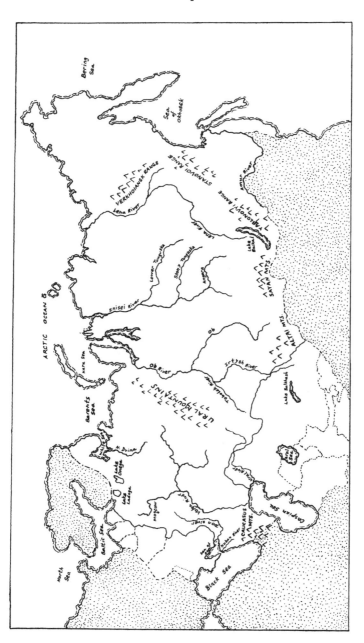

User's Notes

Although this is a historical dictionary, a fair number of living people have been included, in particular figures such as Mikhail Gorbachev and Boris Yeltsin, without whose mention major events of the 1990s would remain obscure. Likewise, because this is intended to be a dictionary of Russia, care was taken not to include material that primarily concerns the other former republics of the USSR or their nationals. With regard to dating: until 1918 the Russian Empire used the Julian calendar rather than the Gregorian calendar used in the Western world. The Gregorian calendar is 13 days ahead of the Julian calendar. Consequently, such events as the revolution, which occurred on October 26, 1917, on the Julian calendar, occurred 13 days later by Western reckoning, on November 7, 1917. However, in order to keep the historical designation of events in Russia before its calendar was modernized after the revolution, this volume will retain the old designation for all events prior to 1918.

One further note: In transliterating from Russian into English, the Library of Congress system was used. However, in cases of such familiar names as Nicholas II or Trotsky, the traditional spelling was retained, that is, Nicholas II, rather than Nikolai II.

Because of its size and economic, political, and military power, as well as its rich and varied culture, Russia has been the subject of countless publications that would be impossible to survey. Just in the area of English-language reference works, the listings number in the hundreds. The present dictionary is an attempt to gather into one compact volume all of the salient historical and geographical data for the non-Russian-speaking user who is not a specialist in this field. The appendixes are intended to furnish such a user primarily with major English-language reference sources for additional data.

Library of Congress Transliteration (Modified) for Cyrillic

With the exception of conventional spellings, Russian words in this book appear transliterated in accordance with the Library of Congress system, but without diacritical marks, ligatures, or the *tverdyi znak* and *miagkii znak* (hard sign and soft sign). These features do not affect filing or indexing.

Also, to avoid awkwardness, if a Cyrillic letter which is transliterated by two combined Latin letters is meant to be in upper case, only the first of the two Latin letters is capitalized. For example, "Iakir" rather than "IAkir." In an initialism, the second element has been left out: for example, the patronymic "IAkovlevich," if reduced to an initial, is written "I." rather than "Ia."

А а	**A a**	Р р	**R r**
Б б	**B b**	С с	**S s**
В в	**V v**	Т т	**T t**
Г г	**G g**	У у	**U u**
Д д	**D d**	Ф ф	**F f**
Е е	**E e**	Х х	**Kh kh**
Ё ё	**E e**	Ц ц	**Ts ts**
Ж ж	**Zh zh**	Ч ч	**Ch ch**
З з	**Z z**	Ш ш	**Sh sh**
И и	**I i**	Щ щ	**Shch shch**
Й й	**I i**	Ъ ъ	**" "** [*tverdyi znak* (hard sign)]
К к	**K k**	Ы ы	**Y y**
Л л	**L l**	Ь ь	**' '** [*miagkii znak* (soft sign)]
М м	**M m**	Э э	**E e**
Н н	**N n**	Ю ю	**Iu iu**
О о	**O o**	Я я	**Ia ia**
П п	**P p**		

Common Acronyms

AES	Nuclear power station (*Atomnaia elektrostantsiia*)
AN	Academy of Sciences (*Akademiia nauk*)
AO	Autonomous oblast (*Avtonomnaia oblast*); investment group (*Aktsionernoe obshchestvo*)
ASSR	Autonomous Soviet Socialist Republic (*Avtonomnaia sovetskaia sotsialisticheskaia respublika*)
BAM	Baikal-Amur railway (*Baikalo-Amurskaia magistral*)
ChK	Extraordinary Commission for the Fight against Counterrevolution and Sabotage (*Chrezvychainaia kommissiia po borbe s kontrrevoliutsiei i sabotazhem*, or "*Cheka*")
DOSAAF	Voluntary Society for Collaboration with the Army, Air Force, and Navy (*Dobrovolnoe obshchestvo sodeistviiaarmii, aviatsii i flotu*)
DSO	Voluntary Sports Society (*Dobrovolnoe sportivnoe obshchestvo*)
EVM	Computer (*Elektronno-vychislitelnaia mashina*)
GAI	State motor vehicle inspection (*Gosudarstvennaia avtomobilnaia inspektsiia*)
GES	Hydroelectric power station (*Gidroelektrostantsiia*)
GITIS	State Institute of Dramatic Art (*Gosudarstvennyi institut teatralnogo iskusstva*)
GLAVLIT	Main Administration for Literature and Publishing (*Glavnoe upravlenie po delam literatury i izdatelstv*)
GPU	State Political Directorate (*Gosudarstvennoe politicheskoe upravlenie*)
GULAG	Main Administration for Corrective Labor Camps (*Glavnoe upravlenie ispravitelno-trudovykh lagerei*)
GRU	Main Intelligence Directorate (*Glavnoe razvedyvatelnoe upravlenie*)
GUM	State department store (*Gosudarstvennyi universalnyi magazin*)
IML	Institute of Marxism-Leninism (*Institut marksizma-leninizma*)
KGB	State Security Committee (*Komitet gosudarstvennoi bezopasnosti*)

KONR	Committee for the Liberation of the Peoples of Russia (*Komitet osvobozhdenie narodov Rossii*)
KP	Communist Party (*Kommunisticheskaia partiia*)
KPRF	Communist Party of the Russian Federation (*Kommunisticheskaia partiia rossiiskoi federatsii*)
KRO	Congress of Russian Communities (*Kongres russkikh obshchin*)
KVZhD	Chinese Far Eastern Railroad (*Kitaiskaia Vostochnaia Zheleznaia Doroga*)
LEF	Left Front of Arts (*Levyi front*)
LGU	Leningrad State University (*Leningradskii gosudarstvennyi universitet*)
MGB	Ministry of State Security (*Ministerstvo gosudarstvennoi bezopasnosti*)
MGU	Moscow State University (*Moskovskii gosudarstvennyi universitet*)
MID	Ministry of Foreign Affairs (*Ministerstvo inostrannykh del*)
MKhAT	Moscow Arts Theater (*Moskovskii Khudozhestvennyi akademicheskii teatr*)
MO	Ministry of Defense (*Ministerstvo oborony*)
MVD	Ministry of Internal Affairs (*Ministerstvo vnutrennykh del*)
NEP	New Economic Policy (*Novaia ekonomicheskaia politika*)
NKVD	People's Commissariat for Internal Affairs (*Narodnyi komissariat vnutrennykh del*)
NTS	Popular Labor Alliance (*Narodno-trudovoi soiuz*)
OGIZ	Central State Publishing House (*Obedinenie gosudarstvennykh izdatelstv*)
OGPU	Unified State Political Directorate (*Obedinennoe gosudarstvennoe politicheskoe upravlenie*)
OMON	Special Forces (*Otriad militsii osobennogo naznacheniia*)
OON	United Nations (*Organizatsii obedinennykh natsii*)
OViR	Department of Visas and Registration (*Otdel viz i registratsii*)
OZU	Random access memory (*Operativnoe zapominaiushchee ustroistvo*)
RAPP	Russian Proletarian Writers' Association (*Rossiiskaia assotsiatsiia proletarskikh pisatelei*)
RKKA	Workers' and Peasants' Red Army (*Raboche-krestianskaia krasnaia armiia*)
ROA	Russian Liberation Army (*Russkaia osvoboditelnaia armiia*)
RSDRP	Russian Socialist Democratic Labor Party (*Rossiiskaia sotsial-demokraticheskaia rabochaia partiia*)

RSFSR	Russian Soviet Federal Socialist Republic (*Rossiiskaia sovetskaia federativnaia sotsialisticheskaia respublika*)
SEV	Council for Mutual Economic Aid (*Sovet ekonomicheskoi vzaimopomoshchi*)
SNG	Commonwealth of Independent States (*Sodruzhestvo nezavisimykh gosudarstv*)
SPb	Saint Petersburg (*Sankt-Peterburg*)
SPID	AIDS (*Sindrom priobretennogo immunnogo defitsita*)
SShA	USA (*Soedinennye Shtaty Ameriki*)
SSR	Soviet Socialist Republic (*Sovetskaia sotsialisticheskaia respublika*)
SSSR	USSR (*Soiuz sovetskikh sotsialisticheskikh respublik*)
SU	Soviet Union
SVR	Foreign Intelligence Service (*Sluzhba vneshnei razvedki*)
TASS	Telegraph Agency of the Soviet Union (*Telegrafnoe agentstvo Sovetskogo Soiuza*)
TsAU	Central Archive Administration (*Tsentralnoe arkhivnoe upravlenie*)
TsK	Central Committee (*Tsentralnyi komitet*)
TsGALI	Central State Archives of Literature and Art (*Tsentralnyi gosudarstvennyi arkhiv literatury i iskusstva*)
TsGIA	Central State Historical Archives (*Tsentralnyi gosudarstvennyi istoricheskii arkhiv*)
TsRU	CIA (*Tsentralnoe razvedyvatelnoe upravlenie*)
UK	Criminal Code (*Ugolovnyi kodeks*)
USSR	Union of Soviet Socialist Republics
VDNKh	Exhibition of Economic Achievements (*Vystavka dostizhenii narodnogo khoziaistva*)
VGIK	All-Union State Cinematography Institute (*Vsesoiuznyi gosudarstvennyi institut kinematografii*)
VINITI	All-Union Scientific and Technical Information Institute (*Vsesoiuznyi institut nauchnoi i tekhnicheskoi informatsii*)
VKP(b)	All-Union Communist Party (Bolsheviks) (*Vsesoiuznaia Kommunisticheskaia partiia bolshevikov*)
VLKSM	All-Union Leninist Communist Youth League (*Vsesoiuznyi Leninskii kommunisticheskii soiuz molodezhi*)
VMF	Navy (*Voenno-morskoi flot*)
VO	Military district (*Voenny okrug*)
VPSh	Higher Party School (*Vysshaia partiinaia shkola*)
VTsIK	All-Russian Central Executive Committee (*Vserossiiskii tsentralnyi ispolnitelnyi komitet*)
VUZ	Institution of Higher Education (*Vysshee uchebnoe zavedenie*)

VVS	Air Force (*Voenno-vozdushnye sily*)
ZAGS	Registry of Civil Status ([*biuro*] *Zapisi aktov grazhdan-skogo sostoianiia*)
ZIM	Molotov factory [type of automobile] (*Zavod imeni Molo-tova*)

Chronology of Major Events

860	Byzantium is raided by the northern Slavic tribes
862	Three Varangian princes are invited by the Slavs to rule over them. The eldest, Riurik, establishes his capital at Novgorod.
882	One of Riurik's descendants, Oleg, unites Novgorod with Kiev and transfers his capital to that city.
941–44	Grand Prince Igor leads the Slavs against Byzantium.
955	Olga, grand princess of Kiev, is baptized into the Greek Orthodox faith.
978–89	Grand Prince Vladimir adopts his mother's Orthodox faith and proclaims it the official religion of his principality.
1097	Kievan Rus is partitioned into patrimonial estates, each belonging to a prince of the Riurik dynasty.
1113	The *Primary Chronicle*, the basic historical document of Rus, is composed.
1147	Moscow is first mentioned in a document.
1167	Kiev is destroyed in the fighting between the Riurik princes by the prince of Vladimir-Suzdal.
1169	The capital is transferred from Kiev to Suzdal.
1221	Nizhni-Novgorod is established.
1223	Mongols invade and defeat the Slavs at the Battle of the Kalka River, then withdraw to their homeland in Siberia.
1237–38	Led by Khan Batu, the Mongol hordes return.
1240	Prince Alexander Nevsky defeats the Teutonic Knights in their invasion attempt.
1241	Mongols conquer Rus.
1243	The victorious Mongols establish the Khandom of the Golden Horde on the lower Volga. They make all of northeastern Rus their tributary.
1252	Moscow becomes an independent principality by permission of the Mongol khan.
1302	The grand prince of Moscow annexes several surrounding towns including Mozhaisk and Koloma.
1325–40	Ivan I Kalita becomes grand prince of Moscow and of Vladimir.

xxi

1328	Ivan I moves his seat from Vladimir to Moscow.
1340	Saint Sergius establishes the Troitsa-Sergeeva Lavra.
1378	Grand Prince Dmitrii Donsko defeats the Mongol Khan Mamay at Kulikovo.
1392	Moscow conquers and annexes Suzdal and Nizhni-Novgorod.
1439	A final attempt is made to reconcile the Roman and Orthodox churches at the Council of Florence in Italy. Its decisions are promptly rejected by the Russian church.
1450	The Golden Horde disintegrates into the khanates of Astrakhan, Kazan, and Crimea.
1462–1505	Ivan III the Great, becomes ruler of the Moscow principality.
1463	Moscow annexes Yaroslav principality.
1472	Moscow annexes Perm.
1474	Moscow annexes Rostov.
1477	Moscow annexes Novgorod.
1480	Ivan III finally breaks the Mongol yoke.
1485	Moscow begins construction of the Kremlin.
1505	Tsar Vasilii III ascends the Moscow throne.
1510	Moscow annexes Pskov.
1514	Moscow annexes the Smolensk region.
1533–84	Reign of Ivan IV the Terrible.
1550s	Moscow begins to colonize the southern steppes.
1550–51	The Stoglav church synod meets in Moscow.
1552	Moscow annexes the khanate of Kazan.
1556	Moscow annexes the khanate of Astrakhan.
1564	Ivan Fedorov prints the first book in Russia.
1565–84	Ivan the Terrible begins a reign of terror.
1582	Cossacks under Ermak conquer the khanate of Sibir, which is annexed by Moscow.
1589	The metropolitan of Moscow is raised to the rank of an independent patriarch of the Russian Orthodox Church.
1597	The tsar issues orders granting the nobility power to apprehend and detain their peasants during the first five years of their flight.
1598	The Riurik dynasty ends with the death of Ivan IV's son, Feodor.
1598–1605	Reign of Boris Godunov.
1605–13	The "Time of Troubles" begins with Boris Godunov's death; Russia is invaded by Poland and Sweden.
1610–12	Polish troops occupy Moscow.
1613	Michael Romanov is elected Tsar of All the Russias by a zemskii sobor (land assembly).

1627	Cossacks take Azov which is annexed by Moscow.
1648	Ukrainian Cossacks rebel against Polish rule.
1652–59	Church reforms are initiated by the patriarch Nikon.
1654	Bogdan Khmelnitskii, hetman of the autonomous Orthodox Zaporozhskii Sech (the Ukrainian Cossacks), swears allegiance to Tsar Aleksei in exchange for protection from the Catholic Poles.
1654–57	War between Poland and Russia over possession of the Ukraine.
1666	Patriarch Nikon is deposed by a church council, but his reforms are confirmed and a church split begins.
1667	At the peace treaty of Andrusevo, Russia obtains from Poland the cities of Smolensk and Kiev.
1670–71	Stenka Razin leads a peasant revolt against the tsar.
1682	Peter the Great and his half-witted brother Feodor are proclaimed corulers; their sister Sophia becomes regent.
1687	The Slavo-Greek-Latin Academy is established in Moscow.
1689	Russia signs its first peace treaty with China at Nerchinsk, allowing it to send a permanent delegation to Beijing.
1696	Russia captures Azov and begins the construction of a seaport there.
1697–98	Peter the Great travels to Western Europe to study its industry and commerce.
1699	Major expansion of metal and industrial production is begun in the Urals on Peter's command.
1700	Peter abolishes the patriarchy; war with Sweden begins.
1703	Peter the Great lays foundations for his new capital, St. Petersburg, on the Baltic Sea.
1708	Peter moves his capital from Moscow to St. Petersburg.
1709	Russian armies defeat the Swedes at Poltava.
1718	Peter executes his son Alexis for treason.
1721	A peace treaty is signed between Sweden and Russia at Nystad. Peter assumes the title of emperor; a holy synod is established to replace the patriarchate as the supreme governing body of the Russian Orthodox Church.
1725	Peter dies after having named his second wife, Catherine, as his empress and heir.
1727	Empress Catherine II dies and is succeeded by Peter II, grandson of Peter the Great.
1730	Peter II dies and is succeeded by Peter's daughter Anna.
1740	Empress Anna dies and is succeeded by Ivan VI.
1741	Ivan VI dies and is succeeded by Empress Elizabeth.
1755	Moscow University is established.

1761–62	Reign of Peter III.
1762	The *dvorianstvo* (gentry) class is exempt from obligatory state service imposed on it by Peter the Great.
1762	Catherine the Great is placed on the throne after a coup by officers of the guard who murder her husband, Peter III.
1772	Poland is partitioned between Prussia, Austria and Russia.
1773–75	Pugachev leads a dangerous but unsuccessful peasant serf rebellion.
1787–91	War with the Ottoman Empire.
1793–95	Second and third partitions of Poland.
1796–1801	Reign of Paul I, Catherine the Great's son.
1801	Court cabal overthrows and murders Paul I. It places his son Alexander I on the throne.
1804	The establishment of Kazan and Kharkov universities.
1807	Alexander I signs the peace treaty with Napoleon at Tilsit.
1812	Napoleon invades Russia, occupies Moscow, and is then defeated during his army's long winter retreat to France.
1814	Alexander I enters Paris at the head of the Russian army.
1816	The first conspiratorial prodemocratic organization from among high-ranking guards officers comes into being.
1825	Alexander I dies and is succeeded by his brother, Nicholas I. The Decembrist revolt, an attempt made by army officers to prevent his coronation, fails and the leaders are either executed or sent into exile.
1825	Pushkin publishes his drama *Boris Godunov*.
1828–29	War with the Ottoman Empire ends with the Treaty of Andrianopole.
1830–31	Poland rebels against Russian rule; the rebellion fails and Poland's constitution is abolished.
1834	Herzen, a leading dissident, is banished from the capital and a century-long conflict between the Russian intelligentsia and the government begins.
1837	Pushkin is killed in a duel.
1849	Russian armies intervene to prevent a revolution in Hungary; Dostoevsky is sentenced first to death, then to exile.
1851	Russia opens its first railroad between Moscow and St. Petersburg.
1853–56	The Crimean War begins between Russia and an alliance of France, Britain, and Turkey. It is ended by the treaty of Paris.
1855	Nicholas I dies and is succeeded by his son, crowned Alexander II.

1858	Russia acquires the Maritime and Amur provinces from China.
1859	Russian armies complete the occupation of the Caucasus.
1860	The port of Vladivostok is opened on the Pacific ocean.
1861	Emperor Alexander II issues the decree abolishing serfdom in Russia.
1862	Major reforms of the legal system, education, and local government are inaugurated.
1863	A rebellion in Poland is crushed.
1864–80	Russia conquers Central Asia and Turkestan.
1864	Chernyshevski, a radical journalist, is exiled to Siberia.
1866	Dostoevsky publishes his *Crime and Punishment*.
1867	Russia sells Alaska to the United States.
1868	Count Leo Tolstoy publishes *War and Peace*.
1880	A bomb is exploded under the Winter Palace but Tsar Alexander II escapes injury.
1881	Tsar Alexander II is assassinated by members of a terrorist organization. His son, as Alexander III, becomes emperor and begins a period of severe repression of political dissidents.
1890	A severe famine breaks out in central and southeastern Russia.
1891	Construction begins of the Trans-Siberian railroad to link European Russia with the Far East.
1892	Finance Minister Witte initiates a decade of growth in Russian industry, commerce, and transportation.
1894	Alexander III dies. His son ascends the throne as Nicholas II.
1896	Russia acquires extraterritorial rights in Manchuria and begins the construction of the Chinese Far Eastern Railroad linking Siberia with Vladivostok.
1898	The Russian Socialist Democratic Labor Party is established.
1902	The Russian Socialist Revolutionary party is organized. It recognizes the use of individual terror to promote its ends.
1903	The Russian Socialist Democratic Labor Party holds a congress in London at which it splits into two rival factions: the Bolsheviks under Lenin, and the Mensheviks under Martov.
1904	Minister of the Interior Plehve is assassinated.
1904–05	The Russo-Japanese war.
1905	The "Bloody Sunday" massacre of petitioners in St. Petersburg; defeat of the Russian army in the Battle of Mukden; establishment of the Soviet (Council) of Workers'

Deputies in St. Petersburg; Nicholas II issues the October Manifesto, which grants a Duma—an assembly of elected representatives empowered to discuss and write laws.

1906   Meeting and rapid dissolution of the first Duma.

1906   Prime Minister Stolypin begins a five-year period of major agricultural and industrial reforms.

1906   The Siberian elder Gregory Rasputin is introduced to the tsar's family and succeeds in alleviating the suffering of Prince Aleksei, who is a hemophiliac.

1909   Publication of *Vekhi*, a revisionist document questioning the basic revolutionary assumptions held by the majority of the Russian intelligentsia.

1910   Count Leo Tolstoy dies.

1912   Massacre of striking workers at the Lena goldfields; *Pravda*, the Bolshevik newspaper, begins publication.

1914   World War I begins. Russia and the Allies confront Germany, Austria, and Turkey.

1916   Rasputin is murdered by a group that includes a grand duke.

1917   Nicholas II abdicates in February (the February revolution); the Duma forms a Provisional government; Lenin and Trotsky organize the seizure of power in October (old style).

1918   Soviet authorities murder former Tsar Nicholas II, his family, and remaining retainers in Ekaterinburg.

1918   Soviet Russia signs a separate peace treaty with Germany; civil war between the procommunists ("Reds") and the anticommunists ("Whites") begins.

1921   Lenin inaugurates the New Economic Policy (NEP) as a temporary concession to the peasantry and small urban entrepreneurs.

1922   The last White armies are forced to leave the Russian Far East, and the civil war is effectively over.

1923   The Union of Soviet Socialist Republics is established.

1924   Vladimir Lenin dies.

1925   Trotsky is defeated in the interparty struggle and is dismissed from his post as commissar of war.

1927   Stalin confronts and defeats the left coalition within the Communist Party with the help of Bukharin and other rightists.

1928   Stalin confronts the Bolshevik "right wing" and launches a massive five-year plan to industrialize the USSR. He also begins the forcible collectivization of the peasantry.

1934	Sergei Kirov, second only to Stalin in popularity among the Communists, is assassinated.
1936–38	A period of mass purges of the party and Soviet government begins, during which over one million individuals are sent to concentration camps or executed on Stalin's orders.
1939	Soviet-German non-aggression pact signed.
1940	Trotsky assassinated in Mexico.
1941	Germany invades the Soviet Union in June. In December it suffers its first defeat at the gates of Moscow.
1942	Soviet victory at Stalingrad (Volgograd).
1943	Soviet victory in the Kursk tank battle.
1945	The Allied victory and occupation of Germany.
1946	The beginning of the Cold War.
1953	Stalin dies; Malenkov becomes general secretary of the CPSU.
1955	Khrushchev replaces Malenkov as general secretary.
1956	At the 20th Congress of the Communist Party, Khrushchev reveals some of Stalin's crimes.
1957	Russia places the first successful satellite into space.
1961	Russian cosmonaut Gagarin is the first man in space.
1962	Khrushchev permits the publication in the Soviet Union of *One Day in the Life of Ivan Denisovich*, Solzhenitsyn's novel about Soviet concentration camps.
1964	Khrushchev is dismissed as general secretary of the Communist Party and replaced by Brezhnev.
1968	Beginning of illegal publications (samizdat), by Soviet dissidents.
1974	Soviet Union expels Solzhenitsyn for publishing the *GULAG Archipelago* abroad.
1979	Soviet invasion of Afghanistan.
1980	Olympic games were held in Moscow and boycotted by the United States.
1982	Brezhnev dies; Andropov becomes general secretary.
1984	Andropov dies; Chernenko is elected in his place.
1985	Chernenko dies and is replaced by Gorbachev, who names Shevardnadze as his foreign minister.
1986	An atomic reactor in Chernobyl melts down, polluting the earth's atmosphere with radioactive dust.
1987	A treaty regulating nuclear weapons of the two superpowers, the United States and the USSR, is signed.
1988	The Soviet Union agrees to remove its troops from Afghanistan.

1989	The Soviet Union acquiesces to the dismantling of the Berlin Wall.
1990	Gorbachev is elected president of the Soviet Union by the Supreme Soviet. He pushes through the removal of the constitutional clause giving the Communist Party the exclusive right to power in the country. Yeltsin is elected president of the Russian Republic and resigns from the Communist Party. The Soviet Union agrees to the reunification of Germany and to pull its troops out of the country.
1991	Lithuania votes for independence from the Soviet Union. Leningrad is renamed St. Petersburg. Gorbachev signs the Strategic Arms Reduction Treaty. In August, an unsuccessful coup attempts to overthrow Gorbachev. Russia, Belarus, and Ukraine secede from the Soviet Union and form the Commonwealth of Independent States. Gorbachev resigns as president of the USSR, which ceases to exist in December 1991, and is replaced by the Commonwealth of Independent States.
1992	The government of the Russian Federation lifts price controls, Presidents Bush and Yeltsin sign the Start II nuclear arms pact, a power struggle begins in Russia between President Yeltsin and the Congress of People's Deputies. Reformer Gaidar is appointed acting prime minister. The Supreme Court upholds the ban on the outlawed national Communist Party but allows its local branches to operate legally. Yeltsin appoints Chernomyrdin in place of Gaidar as prime minister.
1993	A conflict arises between President Yeltsin and the Chamber of Deputies. Yeltsin survives a vote of no confidence and begins large-scale privatization of state-owned means of production. Group of Seven promises Russia a $28 billion aid package and the rescheduling of its debt. President Yeltsin wins a 58 percent approval in a nationwide referendum and drafts a proposed new constitution. The United States and Russia extend the ban on nuclear bomb tests. Russia removes its troops from Lithuania and signs a treaty of friendship with Germany. President Yeltsin and the Russian parliament escalate their confrontation with each other until troops are forced to put down an armed revolt against the president led by parliament and the vice president. Parliament is dissolved and a new constitution is approved by voters. A new state Duma is elected with the ultranationalist parties winning a plurality.

1994   Reformers resign from Yeltsin's cabinet. Russia signs an economic union with Belarus and a cooperation pact with Georgia. A dispute between Russia and Ukraine over the partition of the Black Sea fleet is not resolved. The Duma pardons the leaders of the 1991 coup. Solzhenitsyn returns to Russia. Russian troops are pulled out of Latvia and Estonia, but fighting begins in Chechnia.

1995   Assault on Chechnia continues, and its capital, Groznyi, is occupied. Russia accelerates its rate of privatization and signs an agreement to sell a nuclear reactor to Iran. Ethnic conflicts continue in countries of the former Soviet Union; Duma elections show support for Zyuganov's Communist Party and comparatively little interest in the numerous factions.

1996   A peace agreement is reached with Chechen leaders, months after Jokhar Dudayev is killed and shortly before the presidential election; polls indicate that Yeltsin is still somewhat favored over his rivals, despite widespread criticism. President Yeltsin wins runoff elections. He vows to end the war in Chechnya, but fighting does not stop. In July Yeltsin is hospitalized with a heart attack. Genetic tests in Ekaterinburg confirm that the bones found there were those of former Tsar Nicholas II.

Chronology of the Rulers of Russia

Ancient Rus: The Grand Princes of Novgorod, Kiev, and Vladimir

862–79	Riurik the Varangian, ruler of Novgorod
879–912	Prince Oleg, Grand Prince of Kiev
912–45	Igor, Grand Prince of Kiev
945–55	Saint Olga (Igor's widow), Regent
955–72	Sviatoslav, Grand Prince of Kiev
972–77	Yaropolk, Grand Prince of Kiev
977–1015	Saint Vladimir, Grand Prince of Kiev
1015–19	Sviatopolk, Grand Prince of Kiev
1016	Yaroslav, Grand Prince of Kiev
1017	Sviatopolk, Grand Prince of Kiev (second reign)
1019–54	Yaroslav, Grand Prince of Kiev (second reign)
1054–73	Iziaslav, Grand Prince of Kiev
1073–76	Svyatoslav I, Prince of Kiev
1093–1113	Sviatopolk Iziaslavich, Grand Prince of Kiev
1113–25	Vladimir II Monomakh, Grand Prince of Kiev
1125–32	Mstislav I, Grand Prince of Kiev
1132–39	Yaropolk II, Grand Prince of Kiev
1139–46	Vsevolod II, Grand Prince of Chernigov
1146–54	Izaslav II, Grand Prince of Kiev
1154	Rostislav, Grand Prince of Smolensk
1154–57	Yuri Dolgoruki, Grand Prince of Vladimir
1157–75	Andrei Bogolubski, Grand Prince of Vladimir
1176–1212	Vsevolod III, Grand Prince of Vladimir and Novgorod
1212–18	Konstantin, Grand Prince of Vladimir and Novgorod
1218–38	Yuri II, Grand Prince of Suzdal and Novgorod
1238–46	Yaroslav II, Grand Prince of Tver
1246	Svyatoslav III, Grand Prince of Vladimir and Novgorod
1248	Mikhail Khorobrit, Grand Prince of Moscow
1249–52	Joint rule by Andrei II, Prince of Peryaslavl, and Aleksandr Nevsky, Prince of Novgorod

1253–63	Aleksandr Nevsky, Grand Prince of Vladimir and Novgorod
1263–72	Yaroslav III, Prince of Tver
1272–76	Vasily, Prince of Kostroma
1276–93	Dmitrii, Prince of Peryaslavl
1293–1304	Andreii III, Grand Prince of Vladimir and Novgorod
1304–18	Mikhail I, Prince of Tver
1319–26	Yuri III, Prince of Moscow
1326–28	Alexander, Prince of Tver

Grand Princes of Moscow

1328–41	Ivan I Kalita
1354–59	Ivan II
1359–89	Dmitrii II Donsko
1389–1425	Vasily I
1425–62	Vasily II the Blind
1462–1505	Ivan III the Great
1505–33	Vasily IV
1533–47	Ivan IV the Terrible

Tsars of Russia

1547–84	Ivan IV the Terrible proclaimed in 1547 Tsar of All the Russias
1584–98	Fedor I
1598–1605	Boris Godunov
1605	Fedor II
1605–1606	"False" Dmitrii
1606–10	Vassily Shuisky
1610–13	Interregnum with several pretenders and a son of the king of Poland

House of Romanov

1613–45	Mikhail I
1645–76	Aleksei
1676–82	Fedor III
1682–89	Sophia, Regent
1682–1721	Peter I the Great (as Tsar)
1721–25	Peter I (as Tsar and Emperor of Russia)

1725–27	Catherine I, Tsaritsa and Empress
1727–30	Peter II
1730–40	Anna
1740–41	Ivan IV
1741–62	Elizabeth
1762	Peter III
1762–96	Catherine II the Great
1796–1801	Paul I
1801–25	Alexander I
1825–55	Nicholas I
1855–81	Alexander II
1881–94	Alexander III
1894–1917	Nicholas II

1917: Abolition of the Russian Monarchy and Declaration of a Republic

1917, February	Prince Lvov, Prime Minister of the provisional government
1917, March	Kerensky, Prime Minister of the provisional government

November 1917 to December 1991: The Soviet Period

Heads of the Communist Party of the Soviet Union

1917–24	Lenin
1924–25	A triumvirate of Stalin, Kamenev and Zinoviev
1925–53	Stalin, General Secretary of the CPSU
1953–55	Malenkov, General Secretary of the CPSU
1955–64	Khrushchev, General Secretary of the CPSU
1966–82	Brezhnev, General Secretary of the CPSU
1982–84	Andropov, General Secretary of the CPSU
1984–85	Chernenko, General Secretary of the CPSU
1985–91	Gorbachev, General Secretary of the CPSU

Chairmen of the Council of Peoples' Commissars and Prime Ministers of the USSR

1917–24	Lenin, Chairman of the Council of People's Commissars

1924–30	Rykov, Chairman of the Council of People's Commissars
1930–41	Molotov, Chairman of the Council of People's Commissars
1941–46	Stalin, Chairman of the Council of People's Commissars
1946–53	Stalin, Chairman of the Council of Ministers
1953–55	Malenkov, Chairman of the Council of Ministers
1955–58	Bulganin, Chairman of the Council of Ministers
1958–64	Khrushchev, Chairman of the Council of Ministers
1964–80	Kosygin, Chairman of the Council of Ministers
1983–84	Andropov, President of the Presidium of the Supreme Soviet
1984–85	Chernenko, President of the Presidium of the Supreme Soviet
1985–88	Gromyko, President of the Presidium of the Supreme Soviet
1988–91	Gorbachev, President of the Presidium of the Supreme Soviet

The Russian Republic

1991–	Yeltsin, President of Russia

Introduction

The Russian Federation is a republic that straddles the Eurasian continent from the Baltic and Black seas to the west and south and to the Pacific Ocean in the east. It occupies a territory of some 6.6 million square miles and is the largest country in the world in area, comprising a vast mixture of ethnic and linguistic groups. Its present population is approximately 147,500,000. Until 1917 it was known as the Russian Empire and was governed by an emperor or tsar (Russian for "caesar"). Following the October 1917 Communist revolution and until December 1991 it was known as Soviet Russia (alternatively, as the Soviet Union or the Union of Soviet Socialist Republics). Since 1991 its official name is the Russian Republic.

On the whole, the climate of Russia is a moderate continental one and only in the extreme northern regions does it lie in the cold zone. In the south, especially in the Black Sea region of the Caucasus, the climate is subtropical. The average annual temperature of continental Russia is highest in July and lowest in January. The lowest average temperature in winter is in Verkhoiansk, Siberia.

According to the 1989 census, the population of Russia totalled 147,386,000. Over the previous 30 years it had increased by 26.5 percent, with an average annual growth rate of 0.5 percent. The urban population has increased while the rural one has dropped. In 1989 there were 30 cities in Russia with a population of over half a million, compared with only 14 such cities in 1959. The country's birthrate slowly declined from the 1950s to the 1980s and then sharply accelerated in the 1990s. Average life expectancy in 1992 was 62 years for males and 73.8 years for females. The rapid industrialization that began in the mid- to late nineteenth century caused an internal migration from the rural areas to the urban centers, but this flow has almost stopped. The only significant flow of migrants today is that of ethnic Russians returning home from the former Soviet republics. Since the emigration restrictions were lifted in 1989, departures from Russia increased rapidly, mainly to Israel, Germany, and the United States.

Early History of Russia

The history of Russia begins in the ninth century, in the area of eastern Europe that was inhabited by a Slavic people who called themselves

1

the Rus. The great rivers of this region—the Don, the Volga, and the Donets—were the principal channels used to transport goods from the Scandinavian region to the Byzantine empire.

The Kievan State

The establishment of an Eastern Slavic state occurred in A.D. 862 when residents of the northern city of Novgorod are said to have invited the Varangian (Viking) Prince Riurik to become their grand prince. They did so, it is believed, in order to obtain his protection from attacks by nomadic tribes that lived to their east and south. After Riurik's death in 879, his throne was inherited by a relative, Oleg. Through a series of armed expeditions Oleg succeeded in unifying the lands of Novgorod with those of Kiev and made the latter capital of Kievan Rus. In A.D. 907 he led a large body of armed men in an attack on Byzantium. Although it failed to breach the city's defenses, Oleg's expedition resulted in an advantageous trade agreement with the Greek empire.

During the following decades Kievan princes were able to subdue a number of neighboring tribes, including the Pechenegs and the Khazars. Grand Prince Yaroslav's rule (1019–54) was especially notable. He concentrated all state powers into his own hands, including the conduct of foreign affairs and the maintenance of internal tranquility. Yaroslav depended on a large body of armed men who were his personal followers. With their help, he gathered state taxes and enforced the fulfillment of civil and military obligations from his subjects.

In the 10th century ancestral land ownership by private families became the dominant form of the Kievan state. Until the second half of the 13th century, peasants were not attached to the land and paid taxes only to the grand prince. The old structures of tribal democracy remained mostly intact: the population met in local assemblies to elect their village leaders. The armed forces of Kiev consisted of the bodyguards of the grand prince and of those of his dependent nobles. Peasants were drafted into service only during times of war. On average about 60,000 armed men were available to the grand princes.

At the end of the 10th century Christianity was introduced to Kievan Rus. This helped to consolidate the Slavic tribes and broadened Kiev's relations with the West European and Greek worlds. The conversion of the Kievan state to Orthodox Christianity laid the foundation for a melding of the secular authority of the prince with the church hierarchy along the Byzantine model. It also established the identification of Russian nationality with Orthodoxy.

By the 12th century separatist tendencies began to manifest themselves as individual princelings asserted their independence. As this characteristic feudal scattering process took place, the unified state broke into numerous warring principalities, each ruled by a scion of the Riurik dynasty. Among the smallest of these was the northern principality of Moscow.

In the 1220s the first Mongol invasion occurred. Like numerous other cities, Kiev itself was destroyed and the regions surrounding it were depopulated. An alien Mongol rule over a large part of the territory was installed by the khans of the Golden Horde, who established their capital on the lower Volga. The subject princes collected heavy taxes, which they were then forced to bring in person to the khan, who confirmed them on their thrones.

The Russian Middle Ages

The Battle of Kulikovo Field in 1380 was an important event in the struggle against the Mongols. There Prince Dmitrii Donskoi, the prince of Moscow, for the first time succeeded in defeating a Mongol army. However, their final overthrow did not occur until 100 years later, under Ivan III. This grand prince unified many of the small principalities and was the first ruler to call himself Lord of All the Russias. During his reign a centralized state emerged around Moscow, and in 1492 he promulgated a single set of laws for the whole of his principality. Ivan III gave the lands taken from the Mongols to his retainers as a reward for their service and in exchange for their undertaking to furnish him with armed men in times of war.

The creation of a unified Russian state was prompted by the necessity to ensure its independence from external foes. This process began at the end of the 15th century and was centered around Moscow. Being located in the middle of the East European landmass, with no easily defensible frontiers and an abundance of hostile neighbors, (the expansionist Order of the Livonian Knights and the powerful Kingdom of Poland to the west, the Ottoman empire to the south, and the Tatar khandoms to the east), Moscow was forced to rely for its security on a highly centralized state structure and on an all-powerful ruler who commanded a strong army. By the middle of the 16th century its princes had succeeded in defeating the Kazan and the Astrakhan khandoms, and by the end of that century they had also acquired all of the thinly populated Siberia.

In the middle of the 16th century, Ivan IV the Terrible carried out major reforms. He established two separate forms of military service: one for the children of the gentry and the higher *boiar* aristocracy and another for the rest of his free subjects. A single unified system of taxation was instituted, and government departments (the *prikaz*) were organized to carry on the affairs of state. Simultaneously, local elective bodies were created to gather taxes. During this period a gradual imposition of limitations on the freedom of movement of the peasantry occurred. Initially, peasants had been allowed to leave their landlord only at certain times of the year. Later, such movement was forbidden altogether. Eventually, landlords received the right to initiate searches and to apprehend peasants who moved away without permission.

On the death of Ivan IV, there occurred what historians refer to as the "Time of Troubles." The internal conflicts between the different layers of society, peasant uprisings, wars with neighboring countries, and the Polish invasion all weakened the Muscovite state and led to its economic collapse. Several pretenders to the throne appeared, and Polish troops occupied Moscow and placed a puppet on the Russian throne. These disorders came to an end in 1611, when a coalition was formed in Nizhni-Novgorod by Minin, one of the city elders, and Prince Pozharskii. It succeeded in ridding Moscow of Polish troops, and in February 1613 a land council (zemskii sobor) was convened to elect a new tsar, Mikhail Romanov.

In the 17th century Russia fought successful wars against Poland, Sweden, and the Crimean khans and reached the coast of the Pacific Ocean. It established relations with countries in Central Asia and the Far East. In 1654 a union took place between Russia and the Orthodox Christian Zaparozhie Cossacks, who had rebelled against their Polish Catholic overlords. The leader of the rebellion, Bogdan Khmelnitskii, asked Tsar Aleksei Romanov for protection from the Catholic Poles and the Muslim Turks and negotiated the union at the Pereiaslav Rada. Also in the 17th century the first manifestations of capitalism appeared, and a countrywide market began to form. However, the country remained far behind Western Europe in its industrial and mercantile development.

The Rise of Modern Russia

The origin of modern Russia is associated with the names of Peter I, Catherine II, and Alexander I. Peter sought to Europeanize Russia, while retaining such feudal institutions as serfdom and an autocratic system of government. During his rule a number of important industries, primarily textile and leather, were developed. New metallurgical enterprises were initiated in the Ural region, and major relief from taxation was granted to the growing merchant class. Peter also reformed the structure of the state. In 1711 he created the State Senate as the highest organ of government and, between 1718 and 1721, replaced the former *prikaz* or chancelleries with 13 collegiae, which were responsible for administering government business. In 1721 he established the Most Holy Synod to govern the affairs of the Orthodox Church in lieu of a patriarch. Under

Peter the country was divided into eight provinces (*guberniias*), which were subdivided into counties (*uezds*). In the cities, the urban magistracies became organs of administration. He also instituted military reforms, changing the recruiting system. Peter was victorious in his war with Sweden. As a consequence of this success, Russia obtained a window on the Baltic Sea and Peter was able, in 1703, to begin building his new capital—St. Petersburg—on the River Neva. It was during this war that Hetman Mazepa attempted to free the Ukraine from Russian rule. Mazepa rebelled and went over to the Swedish side in 1709. After the defeat of the Swedes at Poltava he was forced into exile.

Following several relatively insignificant reigns, Catherine II came to the imperial throne in 1769 after a palace coup against her ineffectual husband, Peter III. During her reign the frontiers of the empire spread to the littoral of the Black Sea and into the northern Caucasus. In 1783 Irakli II, king of the ancient Christian state of Georgia, recognized Russia's suzerainty as the price for Russia's military protection from Moslem Persia. Catherine granted a number of privileges to the nobility, including freeing them from the obligation to serve the state in exchange for their land and serfs. At the same time, she restricted entry into their class. The power of the landlords over their peasant serfs was increased by giving landlords the right to exile serfs and by forbidding them to complain against their masters. Despite these measures, her reign saw a flowering of Russian literary, artistic, and academic culture and the creation of the foundation of a national education system.

Her grandson, Alexander I, granted the State Senate ultimate civil, judicial, and administrative powers in 1802, and he replaced the administrative collegiae with ministries. In 1812, he formed a cabinet of ministers responsible directly to himself. He also initiated changes in the system of serfdom by allowing serfs to purchase their own freedom. During his reign wars were frequent, the most significant one being the 1812 war against Napoleon. The French invasion of Russia was defeated, and in 1814 Paris was occupied by Russian troops.

Nicholas I (1825–55) began his reign by crushing a rebellion of guards officers during his coronation in December 1825 (the Decembrist rebellion). The reign was characterized by the extensive militarization of the country's life, the growth of state bureaucracy, and the increased role of the secret police.

One of the most important events of the 19th century in Russia was the abolition of serfdom by Alexander II (1855–81). During his reign rapid development of commercial and industrial activity took place in the country. Russia's defeat in the Crimean War (1853–56) against Great Britain, France, and Turkey was caused by its cultural, political and industrial backwardness, and this event convinced the new tsar of the need for fundamental reforms. He instituted a series of changes, including the emancipation of the serfs, land reform, military and judicial reforms, and reforms in the fields of education and the press. It was during his reign that a new phenomenon took shape—the rise of a radicalized intelligentsia in the country.

The modern Russian revolutionary tradition began with the Decembrist revolt. At first it was limited mainly to aristocratic army officers. After the revolt's defeat in 1825, this prodemocratic movement gained the sympathy of such civilians as the poet Pushkin and such aristocrats as Herzen. In essence, it was a movement that opposed the unlimited autocracy of the Russian Tsars, as well as the enserfment of the Russian peasantry. During the reign of Alexander II, the movement acquired a socialist ideology and spawned such anarchists as Bakunin and Kropotkin. In 1873 and 1874 a large number of university students "went to the people" during their summer vacation, in order to educate the peasants and to propagandize them against the land reforms of the previous decade. Most of these students were arrested by local police authorities, tried, and condemned to jail terms. Their frustration led to the formation of the secret Land and Freedom (Zemlia i Volia) society in 1876. Three years later, the group split into two factions, the majority opting for the use of individual terror against members of the tsarist establishment—the People's Will (Narodnaia Volia) and the minority advocating a long-range effort of education and propaganda among the peasantry—the Black Soil Repartition (Chernyi Peredel). After members of the Executive Committee of the People's Will succeeded in assassinating Alexander II in 1881, a period of severe reaction followed. Under his son, Tsar Alexander III, revolutionaries were kept under strict control, and efforts at individual terror were punished by summary execution. These years were characterized by a rapid growth of capitalism in Russia, led by the textile industry. Metallurgy, mining, and oil extraction were significant areas of entrepreneurial growth. Nationwide markets were opened up, and private property rights became firmly entrenched.

After the death of Alexander III in 1895, his son Nicholas II became Tsar and Emperor of All the Russias. His reign, from 1895 to 1917, saw two unsuccessfully waged wars—the Russo-Japanese war of 1904 and World War I—as well as resurgence of the revolutionary movement in Russia. In 1898 and 1902, respectively, the Russian Socialist Democratic Labor (Marxist) Party and the Socialist Revolutionary Party were founded. The latter group had a secret "combat organization" that carried out terrorist activities against major government figures. In addition to the discontent that was caused by both of the military defeats and by the strains on the social fabric due to rapid industrialization, Nicholas's authority was undermined by a restive intelligentsia that had come into being since the Crimean War. It sought participation in the governing of the country through some form of representative government that would be responsible to an elected parliament. These demands, however, were resisted by the tsar and especially by his spouse, the Empress Alexandra. The 1905 revolution forced Nicholas II to make a partial concession to these pressures and to grant an elected Duma, but he strictly circumscribed its powers and granted it no control over the cabinet. His concession helped temporarily to quell the revolutionary movement, which did not revive until after Russia suffered severe losses during World War I.

Russia's leading governmental and industrial circles well understood that without a strongly developed industry the country would not be able to maintain its status as a great power. To this end the government provided substantial aid to industry by creating the necessary infrastructure by means of high protectionist tariffs and by simultaneously helping to finance enterprises with resources obtained from foreign loans. The government also initiated a series of agrarian reforms directed at strengthening the peasant economy and at creating a capital-based rural economy. However, political reforms in Russia lagged behind economic ones. This situation was manifested in such policies as the prevention of even mildly liberal statesmen from attaining influential positions in the government, despite the promises contained in the October Manifesto of 1905.

The European system of national security at the end of the 19th century combined unbridled imperialism by the Great Powers with a precarious balance of power among them. Austro-Hungary, Italy, Germany, Russia, France and Great Britain strove to maximize their wealth, prestige and strategic advantage at the expense of others. This competition provided the precondition for the outbreak of war in 1914. The leaders of Austria, seeking to check the rising nationalism of their Slav subjects, saw the destruction of a resurgent Serbia as a condition for the survival of their empire. When the Austrian heir to the throne was assassinated by a Serb national in July 1914, they used the murder as a pretext for crushing Serbia's independence, which Russia was committed to protect. This obligation led Nicholas II to decree mobilization, a step that prompted Germany to declare war on Russia and, in turn, made France come to the aid of its Russian ally. Within a few days Great Britain was also drawn into the conflict. There followed three years of inconclusive slaughter on the eastern front, during which there were millions of Russian casualties and a rapidly deteriorating internal political situation. Tsar Nicholas's prestige was deeply undermined by unscrupulous partisan attacks from liberal and socialist Duma delegates, as well as by Empress Alexandra's dependence on the "holy man" Rasputin, who was able to stop the pain of the hemophiliac heir, Aleksei. Rasputin's personal sexual and financial behavior caused constant nationwide scandals.

At the end of February 1917 a temporary shortage of bread led to street disturbances in St. Petersburg. Several days later the garrison of the city refused to continue putting down the demonstrators and went over to the side of the rebellious workers and students. Within a week the movement spilled over from the capital into Moscow and other urban centers of the empire. On the advice of his army commanders, Tsar Nicholas II signed the instrument of abdication, giving up his throne for himself and his son, the ailing Prince Aleksei.

Amid chaos in the city, the Duma established a Provisional government that tried to restore order in St. Petersburg and prepared for the election of a Constituent Assembly that would determine the future government of Russia. Simultaneously, the Petrograd Soviet (council) of Workers and Soldiers came into being, forming an alternate center of political power. Between February and October 1917, these two parallel channels of authority managed to coexist in an uneasy truce. After the followers of Lenin won a majority of seats on the Soviet Central Executive Committee, cooperation became impossible, and Russia experienced a new revolution.

Soviet Russia

The history of Soviet Russia begins with the October (November) 1917 overthrow of the Provisional government by the Communist Party (Bolsheviks), under the leadership of V.I. Lenin, and the transfer of state power to the All-Russian Congress of Soviets. In the following months the new Soviet government promulgated a series of fundamental laws that aimed to transform Russia economically, politically and socially. In July 1918 the first constitution of the Russian Soviet Federal Socialist Republic (RSFSR) was confirmed by the All-Russian Congress of Soviets. These Communist measures met with resistance from large sections of the population, resulting in a full-scale civil war in late spring of 1918.

The Soviet government countered with a policy of "war communism." It nationalized all land and real property, as well as large and middle-sized industrial enterprises. It also created a centralized administration for industrial production, the Council of National Economy. A universal labor service obligation was introduced, and a law was passed forbidding the leaving of one's employment without official permission. After January 1919 compulsory delivery of agricultural produce to the state by peasants was mandated, and a state monopoly on the distribution of both industrial and agrarian commodities was proclaimed. All private trade in bread was forbidden and a system of rationing was instituted.

The civil war came to an end on the principal fronts in late 1920. This enabled the Soviet government to begin stabilizing its external relations. Between 1921 and 1922 it signed trade agreements with Britain, Germany, Norway, and Italy. In 1922 Soviet Russia participated in the Genoa Conference and reestablished relations with Germany. By 1924 it had diplomatic ties with many of the European powers.

In 1921 the Council of National Economy issued its decree introducing a New Economic Policy—the NEP. This decree formalized Lenin's demand that the government abandon its policy of "war communism" in favor of conciliation with the peasantry. His intention was to provide the peasants with incentives to raise their production, thereby increasing the availability of foodstuffs to the population. Forcible confiscation of produce was replaced by taxation in kind, and the peasants were allowed to sell their surplus production. Free trade in agricultural and handicraft products was permitted once again, as was the renting of farm land and the hiring of a limited amount of labor. Small-scale entrepreneurial activity was legalized. At the same time, all large-scale enterprises and banks were retained by the state, as was its foreign trade monopoly. Within two years, Russia's agricultural and industrial output reached the pre-World War I level. However, this free enterprise system could not long coexist with a totalitarian state. Within the Communist Party factional struggles increased. By the end of 1927 Stalin's faction had triumphed over the group led by Trotsky, who denied the possibility of building socialism in one country.

The program of rapid industrialization of Soviet Russia was initiated at the 14th Party Congress in 1925. Its objective was to transform the country, in as short a period as possible, from an agrarian to an industrial nation and thereby to make it possible to establish socialism in the Soviet Union. This was to be accomplished by the introduction of the latest technologies developed in Western Europe and North America. Industrialization was to be financed with resources obtained from the agrarian sector. In 1928 Stalin ordered a sharp rise in the rate of industrial growth, arguing that this step was required in order to protect the country from the danger of foreign intervention by surrounding capitalist countries. To pay for this increase he demanded that a supertax be levied on the agrarian sector of the economy. Bukharin, his hitherto ally against Trotsky, resisted these proposals, arguing for a simultaneous growth of both agrarian and industrial sectors.

Stalin won this intraparty struggle because of his support from the regional party secretaries at the 16th Party Congress in 1930. His method of carrying out the industrialization of the Soviet Union was accompanied by reverting to the confiscation of grain from the peasantry, to fanning the class warfare between the poorer and the wealthier peasants (the so-called kulaks, or "fists"), and forcible collectivization of individual peasant households into state-controlled collective farms (kolkhoz). Other aspects of Stalin's methods included setting ever higher individual production quotas and sharply reducing real wages. Major resources were taken from social consumption and channeled into enforced savings, which were then used to finance industrialization. Once again, as during the period of "war communism," the state became the sole employer in the country. The secret police was expanded, and individuals were made to inform on each other. The Communist youth organization (Komsomol), the schools and mass media were required to help transform the population into "New Soviet Men"— collectivist in mentality, submissive to authority, and faithful to their leader, Stalin. This indoctrination was reinforced both by fear of repression and by the offering of attractive careers to those who faithfully complied with prescribed norms.

Despite the many failures and hardships that Stalin's economic policies produced, a major transformation of Russian society occurred between 1929 and the involvement of the USSR in World War II in June 1941. The country reached, and in many cases surpassed, the total volume of production of the largest European countries in such commodities as steel and coal. Another change was a demographic one: the majority of the Soviet population was shifted from a rural to an urban life.

The strains created by these changes gave rise to an opposition to Stalin within the top layer of the Communist Party. Although on the surface, at the 17th Party Congress in 1934 delegates unanimously supported him, many secretly questioned his leadership. They were aware of what forced collectivization had brought to the villages of the richest grain-producing regions of the Soviet Union—the Ukraine, the Don basin, and Western Siberia—regions in which several million peasants had perished from starvation. Stalin too was aware of this opposition, and in the fall of that year he initiated purges and arrests of leading party members. Staged trials of his most prominent opponents, such as Zinovev and Bukharin, followed. During these trials, the accused confessed to sabotage and treason. Hundreds of thousands of innocent individuals were either shot or condemned to concentration camps between 1934 and the beginning of World War II, including most of the top military commanders and three of the five marshals of the Soviet Union. Soviet foreign policy during the decade of the 1930s saw a continuation of its previous effort to expand diplomatic and commercial relations with the capitalist world. In 1934 the USSR joined the League of Nations, and in 1935 it signed mutual defense treaties with France and Czechoslovakia. In 1937 it concluded a nonaggression pact with China. Unable to arrive at a mutually satisfactory agreement with Great Britain, Poland or France, in the late summer of 1939 Stalin and Molotov reversed years of hostility toward Hitler and signed a nonaggression pact with Germany. Its secret protocols defined spheres of influence between the two countries, allowing the Soviet Union freedom of action in Eastern Poland, Bessarabia, Northern Bukovina and the Baltic states. This arrangement did not last long, however. In June 1941 Germany invaded the Soviet Union. Initially, the Red Army suffered very heavy casualties and sustained serious defeats. Much of the western part of the country, including all of the Belorussian and Ukrainian republics, was occupied by the Germans, who reached the Volga River at Stalingrad (Volgograd) in late summer 1942. However, by the beginning of 1943 the tide of war turned in Russia's favor, and in April 1945 the red flag of the Soviet Union flew over the Reichstag in Berlin.

After the end of World War II the foreign policy of the Soviet Union was guided by hostility toward the United States and Great Britain. This was the period referred to as the Cold War. The Western powers sought to contain Soviet expansionism abroad, while the USSR actively promoted the extension of its socialist system into eastern Europe and parts of Asia and Africa.

The Soviet population had expected major improvements in their lives after the war's end. However, almost as soon as victory was achieved, the Cold War began, and with it came a new wave of repressions. In 1947 Zhdanov, Stalin's chief ideological lieutenant, initiated a campaign to tighten controls over the artistic and cultural life of the country. He demanded that Soviet artists and writers become "engineers of the human soul," that is, to act as propagandists for Communist ideology. In 1953, the Soviet press gave wide publicity to a "Doctor's Plot" against Stalin's life—a fictitious conspiracy that was to serve as a prelude for renewed staged trials and mass executions. Only the sudden death of the dictator in March of that year prevented a repetition of the events of the 1930s.

After Stalin's death and the ascension to power of Khrushchev, substantial changes in the internal policy of the Soviet Union occurred. The new Communist leadership criticized the personality cult of Stalin and condemned the mass repressions that had taken place under him. Khrushchev propounded the thesis that peaceful coexistence with the capitalist world was possible, and he made serious efforts to deescalate the Cold War. This endeavor received the approval of U.S. president Kennedy, and in 1963 the first treaty between the USSR and the United States regulating the nuclear arms race was signed. The Soviet government initiated other foreign policy moves as well, including the restoration of relations with Yugoslavia, which had been broken off after Stalin's 1948 quarrel with Marshal Tito. Diplomatic ties were reestablished with West Germany and Japan. Alongside positive developments, there occurred such negative ones as the Soviet intervention in Hungary in 1956 and the construction of the Berlin Wall in 1962.

At the 22nd Congress of the Communist Party in 1962, a new party program was adopted. It promised that the construction of "full communism" would be completed by the 1980s. This utopian assertion soon proved to be an empty one. Attempts by the government to institute fundamental economic reforms were likewise unsuccessful. The government bureaucracy, with its innumerable functionaries, continued to grow exponentially. In the 1960s the monetary income of the population increased, but since production of consumer goods failed to keep pace with the rise in the money supply, inflation occurred. Inexpensive goods disappeared from the shelves; queues became normal. At the same time the consumption of alcohol grew rapidly compared to that in the 1950s. The gap between party propaganda and reality became ever more apparent while, in the face of a lack of economic progress, party spokesmen continued to praise the triumphs of a "developed socialist" society. In the 1970s, renewed tendencies toward enforced conformity appeared. Trials took place in which dissidents—citizens who dared to protest against government policies—were automatically convicted.

In the area of foreign relations, Soviet policy was contradictory. On the one hand, the creation of a European Security System was achieved and a treaty regulating strategic atomic armament was signed. On the other, Czechoslovakia was invaded by Soviet-led Warsaw Pact forces in 1969, and the Afghanistan war was started a decade later. In an effort to achieve military parity with the United States and its NATO allies, the Soviet government diverted ever more of its resources to the military sector, thereby causing a near collapse of the civilian economy and further exacerbating internal political tensions.

Following the death of Brezhnev in 1982, the need for fundamental change became apparent to a large section of the Communist leadership. Andropov, the new general secretary of the Communist Party and a former head of the secret police, tried to introduce some improvements in the country's economy. However, his campaign to tighten worker discipline failed to produce significant results. Following his death in 1984, his short-lived successor Chernenko did not attempt any reforms. Chernenko's death in 1985 was followed by the election of Gorbachev as general secretary. He began a series of economic initiatives but kept them strictly within the framework of the existing centralized socialist state system. He first attempted to place greater emphasis on improving heavy industry and to further centralize the agrarian sector. These measures did not bring about significant improvement because the Soviet economy continued to be handicapped by old methods of administrative command and by a bloated bureaucracy. The option of legalizing private ownership of the means of production and distribution—an anathema to orthodox Marxists—was not considered.

Despite the timidity of his economic reform efforts, Gorbachev's actions threatened an important segment of the Communist leadership, thus creating the basis for a split within the Communist Party. This was especially true of reforms that allowed a gradual democratization of Soviet society. Most threatening of all to the bureaucracy was the abolition of political repression and the removal of preventive censorship in 1989. This "glasnost" (openness) policy led to an outpouring of data that hitherto had been kept from the Soviet public. For the first time, broad layers of the population learned the truth about Stalin's crimes. In 1987 Gorbachev proclaimed the legitimacy of ideological pluralism, as well as the possibility of accepting values other than those held by Marxist-Leninists. In 1988, because of his leadership, the Communist Party acknowledged the need to establish a Soviet government based on laws. Gorbachev also transformed the existing rubber-stamp Supreme Soviet into a functioning parliament. A new post of president of the USSR was created, to which he was elected by the Supreme Soviet in 1990.

Under Gorbachev a series of positive changes took place in Soviet foreign policy, including the recognition of the importance of universal human values and of the impossibility of victory in an atomic confrontation. The interdependence of all countries, regardless of their economic system, was recognized, as was the necessity of their mutual cooperation. Soviet troops were withdrawn from Afghanistan and a normalization of relations with China was achieved. Finally, an agreement was reached with the United States concerning a staged destruction of medium- and close-range rockets.

Toward the end of the 1980s, a marked drop in the influence of the Communist Party occurred in the Soviet Union, and Gorbachev began increasingly to rely on the Supreme Soviet. Relatively free elections were held that year for the highest state organ—the Congress of People's Deputies of the USSR. At the first session of this congress a parliamentary opposition to the Communist majority was formed by a group of deputies. Organized by this newly formed democratic opposition, numerous meetings were held across the country to pressure the government for even more democracy. The next year, a wave of labor unrest swept the country. The largest outbreak was the coal miners' strike, which was led by a labor union no longer controlled by the Communist Party. In February 1990, the clause in the Soviet constitution that guaranteed sole political power to the Communist Party was repealed.

At the same time, in such outlying union republics as the Baltics and Georgia, strong nationalist movements developed. In 1988 a full-fledged war flared up between Armenians and the Azeris over the territory of Nagorno-Karabakh. Gorbachev authorized harsh measures to be taken in order to dampen these nationalistic movements. Nevertheless, in Estonia, Latvia, Lithuania, Georgia and Moldavia, demands for independence continued to grow. Russia itself declared independence from the Soviet Union in 1990, and in a free election in June Yeltsin won the presidency of the republic. That same summer, Gorbachev had prepared a proposal to reorganize the structure of the USSR and create a new federative union. Before the agreement could be signed, an attempt was made to overthrow him. The coup leaders, all high-ranking members of the Communist Party and of the Soviet government, intended to restore the Communist Party to its previous position of power. While the coup failed, it did prevent the signing of the new union agreement and thus paved the way for the final dissolution of the USSR in December 1991. Most of the former Soviet republics entered the newly created Commonwealth of Independent States (CIS), which was formed to replace the Soviet Union. Among them were the four largest republics, Ukraine, Belarus, Kazakhstan and Russia.

In the Russian Republic a new series of economic reforms began in 1992. These were, in the main, attempts to open up opportunities for private entrepreneurial initiative, for strengthening property rights, for privatizing state enterprises, and for removing state subsidies on items of consumption. The reforms have thus far been accompanied by a sharp fall in the standard of living for most of the population, as well as a drop in production. Unemployment has occurred for the first time since before World War II. Such negative developments have given rise to an antireform movement and to the growth of pro-Communist organizations. In October 1993 these forces united within the Supreme Soviet in an attempt at a violent overthrow of the government of President Yeltsin. This attempt was put down by army units loyal to him.

New parliamentary elections were held in December 1993 concurrently with a vote to ratify a post-Soviet Russian constitution. Instead of a Supreme Soviet, the new fundamental law established two chambers: the Council of the Federation and the Duma. At present (late 1996), the split that exists within the prodemocracy forces, as well as the discontent of the population with the social and economic situation, has given rise to an extremist right-wing party—the Liberal-Democratic Party—as well as to the resurgence of the Communist Party. Since the elections, the economic situation in Russia appears to be improving, and a gradual drop in the rate of inflation has taken place. Balancing this positive development is a sharp increase in organized criminal activity and a continuing drop in the standard of living of the average Russian.

The Dictionary

A

ABAKUMOV, VIKTOR S. (1894–1954). Abakumov worked in the state security system during the early 1930s. At first a member of Stalin's (q.v.) personal secretariat, he became deputy to Lavrentii Beria (q.v.), the head of the secret police and then head of Smersh (q.v.), the Soviet counterespionage organization. In 1951, while minister of state security, Abakumov organized the so-called Leningrad Affair (q.v.). After Beria's fall in 1954, he was tried and executed.

ACADEMY OF FINE ARTS. In 1757 an Academy of Fine Arts was established in St. Petersburg (q.v.). Over time its orientation became increasingly conservative and academic, until in the middle of the 19th century students began to withdraw in protest. The academy was abolished in 1918. In 1933 the All-Russian Academy of Fine Arts was opened in St. Petersburg, and in 1948 was renamed the Academy of Fine Arts of the USSR.

ACADEMY OF SCIENCES. The Russian Academy of Sciences was established by Peter the Great (q.v.) in 1724. In 1934 its headquarters were moved from St. Petersburg (q.v.) to Moscow (q.v.). It is now divided into nine sections: physics and mathematics, chemistry, geology and geography, biology, technology, history, economy, philosophy and law, and literature and linguistics. It has over 200 separate institutes employing more than 150,000 individuals engaged in research in all sectors of the natural and social sciences. The academy publishes numerous scientific journals and maintains a large number of libraries. In October 1986 a series of reforms was introduced, including the use of the secret ballot to elect the president and the placing of a 75-year age limit on membership. Since 1990, the academy has been independent of direct control by the government.

ACMEISTS. This movement of Russian poets was started in 1912 by Gorodetski and Gumilev (q.v). It rejected mysticism and the "art for art's sake" philosophy and strove to restore clarity and precision to poetry. Its most prominent members were Osip Mandelshtam (q.v.) and Kuzmin (q.v).

ADMINISTRATIVE AND TERRITORIAL DIVISIONS OF THE RUSSIAN FEDERATION. The administrative structure of Russia has not been changed in its essential characteristics from what it was during the existence of the Soviet Union. It is still based on the territorial-ethnic principle, where each sizable ethnic group that is settled in a contiguous territory is given a territorial-administrative base, depending on its size: an autonomous republic, an autonomous oblast (region), or the smallest local unit of government, the *raion* (district). This structure differs from that which existed in pre-1917 Russia, when the country was divided into *guberniias* (provinces), uezds (counties), and *volosts* (rural districts).

Today, each territorial unit is entitled to its own elected soviet (council). Under the Communist system these councils were elected in a way that ensured their control by the Communist Party. The territory of the Russian Soviet Federated Socialist Republic (q.v.) is administratively divided according to the ethnic and nationality principle. Each major national group within the Russian Federated Republic (q.v.) had its own autonomous republic.

These republics have remained essentially unchanged since the collapse of the Soviet Union. They were the largest territorial administrative units that existed during the Soviet period and were designed to provide a measure of local self-rule to ethnic groups large enough to warrant such a designation. Each such republic has its own constitution, a supreme soviet, and representation in the Supreme Soviet (q.v.) of the USSR. At the time of the abolition of the Soviet Union in 1991 there were 16 such republics in Russia: Bashkortostan (q.v.), Buryatia (q.v.), Chechnya (q.v.), Chuvashia (q.v.), Dagestan (q.v.), Kabardino-Balkaria (q.v.), Kalmykia (q.v.), Karelia (q.v.), Komi (q.v.), Mari-El (q.v.), Mordovia (q.v.), North Ossetia (q.v.), Sakha (q.v.) Tatarstan (q.v.), Tuva (q.v.) and Udmurtia (q.v.).

Each of these republics is in turn divided into smaller territorial subdivisions: oblast, or region, and *raion* or district. The term *krai* is equivalent to oblast, the distinction being a matter of historical usage. There are also a few *okrugs* within the Russian Republic, a term likewise equivalent to oblast, but reserved for areas that have an ethnic distinction from their surrounding populations.

The autonomous *krai* is a district level division, the smallest of the territorial divisions in Russia that have a measure of autonomy from central authorities. It is a component part of an oblast. The autonomous oblast is larger than a *krai* and smaller than a republic. Autonomous oblasts were introduced under Soviet rule and designed to administer ethnic populations not large enough to warrant the establishment of an autonomous republic; they were represented in the Council of Nationalities of the USSR.

ADRIAN, PATRIARCH (1627–1700). He was the last of the Russian Orthodox Church (q.v.) patriarchs before the post was abolished by Peter the Great (q.v). His attempt to stop Peter's reforms resulted in the subordination of the Russian Orthodox Church to governance by secular authorities.

ADRIANOPOL, TREATY OF (1829). A treaty concluded between Turkey and Russia after the end of the Russo-Turkish Wars (q.v). It resulted in the Ottoman Empire granting autonomy to Serbia, the recognition of the independence of Greece, and Russia obtaining an unlimited right to pass its shipping through the Dardanelles.

ADYGEI (Adygei Autonomous Oblast). An area of some 1,740 square miles on the Kuban River, its administrative center is the city of Maikop. Its population is around 130,000. The Adygeians are composed of several related ethnic groups, sometimes collectively referred to as Circassians (*see* Circassia). The dialects spoken by the Adygeians belong, with those of the Kabardinans and Cherkess, to the Northwestern group of Caucasian languages (*see* Language).

AEROFLOT. Founded in 1923 and reorganized in 1991, it is the state-owned Russian national airline. Until its reorganization, Aeroflot could boast of being the largest single airline system in the world in terms of passengers carried and the length of its routes.

AFANASII, BISHOP OF KOVNO (b. SAKHAROV) (1887–1962). A graduate of the Moscow Theological Academy in 1912, he was ordained bishop in 1921. Several years later Bishop Afanasii refused to submit to Soviet authorities and became leader of the underground catacomb church. He was kept in prison until after Stalin's (q.v.) death in 1953.

AGAGINSK BURIAT NATIONAL DISTRICT. Located in the Chita (q.v.) oblast, its principal city is Aginskoe. The economy consists of mixed cattle and grain farming. The population is close to 50,000.

AGRARIAN REFORMS. Between 1906 and his assassination in 1911, Prime Minister Stolypin (q.v.) initiated a series of major reforms of Russian agriculture. Among these were removal of restrictions on the movement of peasants, the abolition of the common land tenure system, and legalization of private land ownership among the peasantry. He also encouraged the voluntary resettlement of peasants from European Russia to fertile, but empty, regions of Siberia (q.v.) by granting them land ownership on favorable terms.

AGRICULTURE. The development of Russian agriculture has always been associated with considerable difficulties, even as it has been of major importance to the country. Agricultural production in 1992 constituted approximately one-third of the total gross national product.

After the reorganization of Russian agriculture following the emancipation of serfs in 1864, some major problems remained. The total amount of land that had been allocated to the peasantry was inadequate, the mandatory redemption payments to the state for this land were excessive, and the peasants, while free from their erstwhile bondage to landlords, remained legally bound to their village communes. Annual allocations of arable land to individual households by the communes changed from year to year, providing little incentive for making improvements. All members of the commune were held collectively responsible for the repayment of the land debt and were therefore not free to leave it without special permission, and then only at a substantial financial cost (*see* Peasantry—pre-revolutionary).

The 1906 reforms removed most of these negative provisions and a new era of Russian agriculture began. By 1916 most of the Russian peasants owned their own plots, which amounted to nearly three quarters of all privately held land in the country. Gross agricultural output rose sharply, even during World War I (q.v.). After the October 1917 revolution the Soviet government decreed the expropriation of private estates and nationalized all land. However, individual small peasant households were temporarily allowed to keep and cultivate the land that they had acquired. An exception to this policy were the rich peasant households of the kulaks (q.v.), whose farms were often confiscated.

In 1918 forcible requisitions of agricultural produce were instituted by the Soviet government in order to enable it to feed the urban population (*see* War Communism). In 1921, responding to a famine and a massive peasant resistance, Lenin (q.v.) instituted his New Economic Policy (*see* NEP). It replaced requisitions with a monetary tax and opened a limited free market to the peasantry. These measures resulted in a rapid increase in productivity and quickly increased the availability of food.

After the 1928 victory of the Stalin (q.v.) faction within the Communist Party leadership, the new agricultural policy of collectivization was inaugurated. It was designed to maximize the extraction of an economic surplus from the agricultural sector. The intention was to use this surplus in order to initiate a rapid industrialization of the country. This program met with fierce resistance on the part of a large part of the peasantry, and the Soviet government unleashed a rural class war (*see* Collectivization of Agriculture).

Using the poor peasants as their principal ally, detachments of urban Communists were sent to the villages to liquidate the prosperous peasants, the kulaks, as a class. Over five million of them were deported to the northern and eastern areas of the country. Individual households of the poorer peasants were forcibly herded into collective farms (kolkhoz, q.v.), which were administered by Communist managers appointed by the government. Everything except for their cottage, one cow, and a small plot of land had to be turned over to the collective farm. Obligatory labor was instituted, and all large agricultural equipment was taken over by state-owned machine-tractor stations.

Even in the 1980s the productivity of labor in collective and state farms remained low. One of the causes was a lack of material incentives for the agrarian population to work harder because they were not adequately rewarded for such efforts. The top-down bureaucratic control that prevailed in this collectivized system caused numerous faulty decisions to be made by remote administrators who had only the haziest notion of the actual conditions that prevailed in any given locality, which resulted in low levels of agrarian productivity and low incomes. This, in turn, caused a large migration of labor from the countryside into the cities and a gradual abandonment of productive lands.

The system persisted with some alterations until after the dissolution of the Soviet Union. In some of its aspects it remains a major factor in Russian agriculture today. New problems inevitably occurred after the introduction of the reforms that followed the collapse of the Soviet state.

However, with the rise in the market price of wheat and cereals that the state is currently paying, there has been a substantial increase in the amount of produce that is being placed on the market. There has also been a significant increase in the availability of vegetables supplied by the collective and state farms to the food distribution network. As of January 1993 there were close to 80,000 enterprises engaged in Russia's agro-industrial complex. In comparison with 1985, the total number of rural families that cultivated their own vegetable or fruit gardens in 1993 has doubled.

In general, there is noticeable if slow improvement in Russian agriculture. The number of private farmers is growing and their labor productivity is significantly higher than in the collective or state farms. In 1991 there were, in the whole of Russia, only some one hundred such farm units, whereas in the autumn of 1993 their number had grown to over 270,000. Estimates are that in 1993 there were over a million independent farmers. However, they still face significant obstacles, especially due to a lack of a firm legislative base, a shortage of farm technology, and hostility from the surrounding collective farmers.

AGROPROMBANK. A state agrarian bank was established in September 1991 to provide credit and promote the development of a rural market economy.

AKADEMGORODOK. This scientific research settlement was built during the Soviet era near the Siberian city of Novosibirsk (q.v.). Today it is the headquarters of the Siberian Division of the Russian Academy of Sciences (q.v.).

AKADEMIK. This is the official title of a full or a corresponding member of the Russian Academy of Sciences. The membership of the academy fluctuates between one hundred and two hundred individuals with an additional three hundred to four hundred corresponding (or associate) members.

AKHMATOVA, ANNA A. (b. GORENKO) (1889–1966). A major poet who first began publishing in 1911, she married Gumilev (q.v.), a fellow poet and member of the Acmeist (q.v.) literary movement. After the early 1920s, her work was seldom published in the Soviet Union, and in the 1930s her son was arrested and sent to a concentration camp. In 1946, Stalin's (q.v.) cultural lieutenant, Zhdanov (q.v.), had her expelled from the Union of Soviet Writers (q.v.). She was rehabilitated only after Stalin's death. In 1965 Oxford University awarded her an honorary doctorate.

AKHROMEEV, SERGEI F. (1923–1991). Marshal of the Soviet Union and former chief of staff of the armed forces under Gorbachev (q.v.), he worked closely with Western military leaders during disarmament negotiations in the late 1980s. Akhromeev resigned in 1988 to become President Gorbachev's personal defense advisor but committed suicide in August 1991 during the attempt to overthrow the president.

AKSAKOV, IVAN (1823–1886). Slavophile and journalist, Aksakov spent his career in the Ministry of Justice investigating religious problems in the provinces. On his retirement, he devoted himself to journalism and propagating his pan-Slavic and nationalist ideas. In 1858

he edited the paper *Russkaia beseda* (*Russian Colloquium*) and, in
the period between 1861 and 1865, edited and published *Den* (*Day*);
he came out strongly on behalf of the peasants and encouraged the
government to take a tougher line with foreign powers; toward the
end of his life his views became more extreme and, at times, antise-
mitic. In 1866 he married Tiutchev's (q.v.) daughter; he continued
with journalism but met with censorship because of his more critical
views.

AKSELROD, PAVEL (1850–1928). As a university student he first became a populist and then a Marxist. In 1883, together with Plekhanov
(q.v.) and Zasulich (q.v.), he organized the group known as the Osvobozhdenie Truda (q.v.), or Liberation of Labor. He was one of the
editors of the newspaper *Iskra* (q.v.) and in 1903 became leader of
the Mensheviks (q.v.). He supported the Provisional government
(q.v.) after February 1917 and strongly opposed the Communists.
After October 1917 he emigrated from Russia to Germany.

AKSENOV, VASILII (1932–). A writer whose parents were both arrested and sent to labor camps, he was not to see his mother again
until he was 16. From then on he lived with her in exile in Magadan
(q.v.) before studying medicine and working as a doctor. In 1960 he
published *Kollegi*, a novel that brought him fame. He has written
steadily since then but had to emigrate to the United States in 1980,
where he also began teaching Russian literature.

ALASKA. First explored by a Russian naval expedition in 1741, several
of the coastal locations were settled by fur trading companies. The
Russian American Company (q.v.) under Baranov (q.v.) held a monopoly in Alaska after 1799 until the territory was sold to the United
States in 1867 for seven million dollars.

ALATYR. A town on the Sura River in the Chuvashia Autonomous
Republic (q.v.), its economy consists of woodwork production, flour
milling and distilleries. The population is approximately 40,000.

ALDANOV, MARK A. (b. LANDAU) (1886–1957). A writer of historical fiction, he emigrated from Russia first to France, then the United
States. One of his best-known series of novels deals with the French
revolution and its aftermath.

ALEICHEM, SCHOLEM (1859–1916). This Ukrainian-born writer's
stories of Jewish village life in the Russian empire became enor-

mously popular. He is among the best-known of Yiddish-language writers.

ALEKHIN, ALEKSANDR A. (1892–1946). This Russian pre-World War I chess champion emigrated to France and became a French citizen after the October 1917 revolution. He won the world championship in 1927 and held it until 1946.

ALEKSANDROV. This is a village close to Moscow (q.v.) to which Ivan the Terrible (q.v.) retreated during his struggle against the old Russia boiar (q.v.) aristocracy. Its present economy is based on the production of leather and woven goods. The population is just over 33,000.

ALEKSEEV, MIKHAIL V. (1857–1918). A general and a professor at the Academy of the General Staff, he served in the Russo-Japanese war (q.v.) and became chief of staff during World War I (q.v.). In February 1917 he was appointed supreme commander by the Provisional government (q.v.). Alekseev tried unsuccessfully to effect a reconciliation between Kerensky (q.v.), the minister of war, and General Kornilov (q.v.), leader of a right-wing attempt to suppress the revolution. After being dismissed from his post, he became head of the first of the White Armies (q.v.) in the Don River (q.v.) area of Russia.

ALEKSEI, PATRIARCH OF MOSCOW (b. SIMIANSKII) (1873–1970). A graduate of the Moscow University (*see* Universities), he served in the Russian army before taking his monastic vows and undertaking theological studies at the Moscow Theological Academy. After graduating he was made Bishop of Tikhvin in 1913. After the 1922 execution of Metropolitan Veniamin (q.v.) by Soviet authorities, Patriarch Aleksei was placed in charge of the Petrograd (St. Petersburg, q.v.) diocese and in 1933 was made Metropolitan of Leningrad (St. Petersburg). He was one of the Orthodox Church (q.v.) leaders who backed the policy of supporting the Soviet state in exchange for government tolerance of the Church. In 1955 Aleksei was elevated to the Patriarchate of Moscow.

ALEKSEI ROMANOV, PRINCE (1690–1718). The son of Peter the Great (q.v.) by his first wife, he lived in exile during his youth. After being sent to study in Germany he turned against his father's reform efforts in Russia. Lured back to Russia, Aleksei was imprisoned on Peter's orders and accused of conspiracy. He was interrogated and died under torture.

ALEKSEI ROMANOV, TSAR (1629–76). The second tsar of the Romanov dynasty (q.v.), and son of Tsar Michael Romanov (q.v.), he conducted an expansionist foreign policy in Western Ukraine (q.v.) and favored the landowning classes by strengthening the institution of serfdom among the Russian peasants. Tsar Aleksei survived several revolts by Cossacks (q.v.), the Ukrainians and the peasantry.

ALEKSEI ROMANOV, TSAREVICH (1904–1918). Son of Tsar Nicholas II (q.v.) and heir to the Russian throne, he suffered from hemophilia. In July 1918 he was shot by local Communists in Ekaterinburg (q.v.) while in the arms of his father.

ALESHKOVSKII, IUZ (1929-). This writer composed the song "Comrade Stalin" ("Comrade Stalin, you are a great scholar"), which became part of folklore in the late 1950s. The author of several novels and a number of stories characterized by flamboyant use of colloquial language and a penetrating view of extreme, intense characters, his early work was known chiefly through samizdat (q.v.). He emigrated in 1979 to the United States, where he continued to write and publish.

ALEUTIAN ISLANDS. This chain of volcanic islands stretches between Siberia (q.v.) and Alaska (q.v.) and separates the Bering Sea (q.v.) from the Pacific Ocean. They were discovered by a Russian expedition led by Bering. They were sold to the United States in 1867 together with Alaska.

ALEXANDER I ROMANOV, TSAR AND EMPEROR (1775–1825). Ruler of Russia after his father Paul I (q.v.) was murdered in 1801, he showed liberal and reformist tendencies. In later life, after Russia's victory over Napoleon, Tsar Alexander became increasingly conservative and abandoned earlier plans for abolishing serfdom and for granting a constitution. By the time of his death there had arisen significant military (mostly aristocratic) opposition to his policies.

ALEXANDER II ROMANOV, TSAR AND EMPEROR (1818–81). Known as "the Tsar Liberator," he ascended the throne in 1855 on the death of his father, Nicholas I (q.v.). Reacting to Russia's defeat in the Crimean War (q.v.), Alexander implemented a series of major reforms beginning with the emancipation of the serfs in 1861. Despite these measures, discontent among the Russian intelligentsia mounted during the last part of his reign, especially after his repression of the Polish uprising of 1863. Tsar Alexander was assassinated in 1881 by members of the Narodnaia Volia (q.v.) (People's Will) party, a terrorist organization.

ALEXANDER III ROMANOV, TSAR AND EMPEROR (1845–94). He became emperor in 1881, after the assassination of his father. His policies were aimed at reversing many of his father's reforms and putting a stop to the incipient revolutionary movement that was spreading among Russian university students and the intelligentsia. To this end, counterreforms were implemented under the aegis of his closest advisor, Pobedonostsev (q.v.). Among these were attempts to Russify national minorities and to place additional restrictions on Jews living within the empire. Under Alexander III's rule, a protectionist national economic policy led to a rapid industrialization of the country.

ALLILUEVA, NADEZHDA S. (1901–32). The daughter of an old Communist and a Communist herself, she married Stalin (q.v.) in 1921. She was the mother of Svetlana Allilueva and Vasilii Stalin. Allilueva's sudden death has been judged a suicide following a violent quarrel with her husband.

ALL-RUSSIAN CONGRESS OF SOVIETS, FIRST (JUNE 1917). The congress met in St. Petersburg (q.v.) (then called Petrograd), with representatives of some 350 districts of the empire attending, and elected a Central Executive Committee (q.v.). It was at first dominated by the Mensheviks (q.v.) and the Socialist Revolutionaries (q.v.) Party, but came under the control of Lenin's (q.v.) followers after September 1917.

ALMA-ATA AGREEMENT. This was a treaty that, in 1991, replaced the former structure of the Soviet Union with the present Commonwealth of Independent States (q.v.). All of the former Soviet republics signed the agreement except Georgia (q.v.), Estonia (q.v.), Latvia (q.v.), and Lithuania (q.v.). The treaty text was based on a previous agreement, the so-called Belovezhsk accord, arrived at by the presidents of the Russian Federated Republic (q.v.), Ukraine (q.v.) and Belarus (q.v.).

ALTAI. This *krai*, or region, of south Siberia (q.v.), which is rich in diamonds, gold and fertile agricultural lands has a population of close to three million. Its principal city is Barnaul (q.v.).

ALTAI MOUNTAINS. These mountains stretch in two parallel chains across Siberia (q.v.) and are the source for both the Ob (q.v.) and the Irtysh (q.v.) rivers, which flow into the Arctic Ocean.

AMALRIK, ANDREI A. (1938–80). A post-Stalin dissident, his plays and essays received a wide circulation in samizdat (q.v.), the illegal "self-publications" that Soviet dissidents resorted to in order to communicate their ideas. Amalrik was sentenced to a brief jail term in 1965 for "parasitism" and rearrested in 1970 for a book he published in the West in which he predicted the proximate dissolution of the Soviet Union. He left the country after his release in 1976.

AMFITEATROV, ALEKSANDR V. (1862–1938). A Russian journalist, he was exiled in 1902 for writing a satire about the imperial family. While in Western Europe, he published a radical periodical. Returning to Russia before World War I (q.v.), Amfiteatrov continued his publishing activities until he again emigrated after the October 1917 revolution.

AMTORG. This Russian acronym designates a Soviet state-owned trading company that was created in 1924 to handle Soviet foreign trade transactions. It was particularly active before and during World War II.

AMUR COSSACK. These are Cossacks (q.v.) who inhabit the Amur River (q.v.) region in Eastern Siberia (q.v.). Before the 1917 revolution, they had their own administrative structure.

AMUR OBLAST. This region in Eastern Siberia, traversed by the Amur River (q.v.), produces a large amount of grain and other agricultural and forestry products and is rich in mineral deposits. Its administrative center is Blagoveshchensk (q.v.), and has a population of over 700,000.

AMUR RIVER. This river enters the Sea of Okhotsk (q.v.). It forms a large part of the border between the People's Republic of China and the Russian Federation.

ANARCHISTS. Beginning with the end of the Crimean War (q.v.), there arose a strong anarchist movement in Russia. Its primary exponents were Bakunin (q.v.) and Prince Kropotkin (q.v.). Count Leo Tolstoy's (q.v.) philosophy of nonresistance to evil was a variation on the ideology of Russian anarchism: distrust of the state, emphasis on individual liberty, and opposition to industrial capitalism. At the time of the 1905 and 1917 revolutions there were numerous groupings of anarchists, most of whom, with the exception of the followers of Tolstoy, advocated the use of individual terror as an instrument for the attainment of their political and social goals.

After the Communist seizure of power in October 1917, the anarchists split on the question of their relationship with the Soviet government. In 1919 an anarchist organization exploded a bomb that killed a number of Communists who were attending a meeting in Moscow. By 1921 Soviet authorities had arrested and executed the majority of anarchists in Russia.

ANASTASIA ROMANOVA, GRAND DUCHESS (1901–18). Youngest daughter of Tsar Nicholas II (q.v.), she was murdered along with the rest of her family by the Communists in Ekaterinburg (q.v.). Over the years since, a number of women claiming to be Anastasia have fed the legend that she survived the assassination and escaped to the West. These claims were proven false by genetic tests carried out in 1994 on the remains of the imperial family, which were disinterred after the fall of Communism in Russia.

ANASTASII, METROPOLITAN (b. GRIBANOVSKII) (1873–1964). A graduate of the Moscow Theological Academy, he was consecrated bishop in 1906 and emigrated during the civil war (q.v.) to become the presiding bishop of the Russian Orthodox Church in Exile. Bishop Anastasii attempted to create an anti-Communist movement in Germany during World War II. After the war he settled in the United States.

ANDREEV, ANDREI A. (1885–1971). After joining the Communist Party in 1914, he took an active part in the October revolution in the Ural Region and in the Ukraine (q.v.). In 1920 he was elected Secretary of the Trade Union Council and member of the Central Committee of the Communist Party. He chaired the Central Control Commission from 1930 to 1931, was commissar of agriculture and deputy chairman of the Council of Ministers from 1946 to 1953, and then served as head of the commission charged with reviewing the cases of individuals who had been sentenced during the purges of the 1930s and 1940s.

ANDREEV, LEONID N. (1871–1919). Born in Orel (q.v.), he was a law student at the St. Petersburg University (see Universities), then worked as a journalist until he was helped by Gorky (q.v.) to begin writing short stories. His novels and plays frequently have dark themes; notable among the latter is *He Who Gets Slapped* (1915). After the October revolution he became a bitter enemy of the Soviet government and moved from Russia to Finland.

ANDRUSOVO, TREATY OF (1667). This was the treaty that ended the Russo-Polish War of 1654–67 and set the frontier between the two countries at the Dnepr River (q.v.). It divided what became the

Ukraine (q.v.), allocating the Polish cities of Kiev (q.v.) and Smolensk (q.v.) to Russia.

ANDROPOV, YURI V. (1914–84). Born into a worker's family, his university education was interrupted by World War II. Andropov rose in rank within the Komsomol (q.v.) and joined the Communist Party in 1938. As the Soviet Union's ambassador to Hungary between 1953 and 1957 he was directly involved in the crushing of the Hungarian uprising in 1956. He became head of the KGB (q.v.) in 1967 and in 1982 succeeded Brezhnev (q.v.) as the general secretary of the Communist Party. Andropov attempted to introduce reforms into the Soviet system by promoting the careers of such younger men as Gorbachev (q.v.) but died of kidney failure before he could accomplish any lasting improvements in the structure of Soviet society.

ANGARA RIVER. A Siberian river that begins at Lake Baikal (q.v.) and flows north, it becomes a tributary of the Enisei River (q.v.). It boasts one of the largest hydroelectric dams in the world, at Bratsk (q.v.).

ANGARSK. A city in the Irkutsk (q.v.) oblast, it is important for its chemical industries and oil-refining facilities. The population is close to 200,000.

ANGLO-RUSSIAN ENTENTE. This was a reconciliation between these two expanding colonial powers in 1907 that came about as a result of their mutual fear of German incursions into Persia and the Near East, where both countries had major interests.

ANNA ROMANOVA, EMPRESS AND TSARITSA (1693–1740). Daughter of Tsar Ivan V (q.v.) and Peter the Great's (q.v.) niece, she was the empress of Russia from 1730 to 1740 and temporarily agreed to an aristocratic constitution that limited her powers. During her reign Russia captured the strategic region of Azov (q.v.) from the Turks.

ANNENKOV, IURII P. (b. TEMIRZAEFF) (1889–1974). He grew up in St. Petersburg (q.v.), then studied painting and design at the St. Petersburg University (*see* Universities) and in Paris. In the 1920s he became one of Russia's avant-garde artists and illustrators, as well as a professor at the Academy of Fine Arts (q.v.). During this period Annenkov drew portraits of leading Russian revolutionaries, including Lenin (q.v.). In 1924 he moved to France, where he played an important role in the life of the Parisian artistic elite. Before his death he wrote his memoirs.

ANNENSKII, INNOKENTII F. (1856–1909). A poet known primarily for his translations of Euripides, his own poetry focused on sadness, death, and other negative aspects of existence. He was also the author of several plays and a collection of articles.

ANTONOV, ALEKSANDR S. (1885–1922). A member of the Socialist Revolutionaries (q.v.) party, he participated in the storming of the Winter Palace (q.v.) during the October 1917 revolution, then served as a commissar with the Red Army (see Armed Forces, Soviet). He was dismissed in 1925 for being a follower of Trotsky (q.v.) but was given a post as an ambassador. He was active in Spain during the Spanish civil war on the side of the republic, faithfully carrying out Stalin's (q.v.) policies. On his return to Russia in 1938 he was arrested and executed.

APPARAT. This is the term coined by Lenin (q.v.) to refer to the main executive groups, such as the secretariat of the Central Committee of the Communist Party (q.v.) and the top commissariats of the Soviet state that were responsible for implementing policies arrived at by the Politburo (q.v.).

APRIL THESES. This was a set of propositions published by Lenin (q.v.) on his return from exile in April 1917. They expressed nonconfidence in the Provisional government (q.v.) and called for the transfer of all state power to the soviets (q.v.) and an immediate peace treaty with Germany.

ARAKCHEEV, COUNT ALEXIS A. (1769–1834). Advisor to both Paul I (q.v.) and his son, Alexander I (q.v.), he was a lifelong conservative and virtual ruler of the Russian empire during Alexander's frequent absences caused by the Napoleonic wars (q.v.). Arakcheev was responsible for establishing military colonies that were inhabited by soldiers on active duty, together with their families.

ARCHAEOLOGY, RUSSIAN. The most ancient archaeological edifices on Russian territory go back to the Paleolithic period in Siberia (q.v.) and other regions of the republic. There, weapons have been found that date to that time—knifelike sharp shards and stone cairns, as well as beads made out of mammoth tusks, bone pins and stone daggers and spearheads.

Findings from the Mesolithic period have been discovered in the middle Volga region. During this period there is a noticeable change in the form of the stone weapons. There now appear small adzes, cutters, and arrow points. At the end of this age the central Russian region was already populated and remnants of semiunderground habitations have been found. Their centers usually have oval holes for a hearth. During the Neolithic period the techniques of working with stone were perfected and one also finds clay pottery and weaving. Neolithic settlements were established from the Ural (q.v.) region all the way to the Pacific Ocean.

In the fourth century B.C. humans learned to smelt metal and to prepare metal weapons as well as tools. They had a developed animal husbandry. In the steppe regions of Russia traces of such a culture have been found. These findings include bones of domesticated sheep, cattle and horses. The culture was characterized by a large assortment of bronze objects such as spear points, kettles, axes and knives, as well as such decorative objects as silver and nephrite earrings and rings.

The middle of the first century B.C. was the early iron age, traces of which were found in the Povolgia, Ural (q.v.) and southern Siberian regions. These areas were then peopled by the Scythian (q.v.) (Skif-Siberian), culture. The Scythians were primarily occupied with animal husbandry. They worshipped the sun and had begun to develop a rudimentary state organization. They lived in houses that were half subterranean, with mud floors and built-in furnaces. All of their homes had underground storage areas for grain. Their art is characterized by representations of fantastic animals. They also used carpets and four-wheel wagons.

The end of the second and beginning of the first millennium saw the formation of a Slavic culture. By the eighth and ninth centuries A.D. this culture covered the vast territory of the Eastern European plains. These East Slavic tribes formed a single ethnic population characterized by a series of common traits of material culture as well as of a common Slavic language (q.v.).

In the 10th century A.D. these tribes formed a single state that was converted to Byzantine Christianity in 989. They practiced plow-based agriculture and, in the forested areas, slash and burn (*otsechnoe*) agriculture. They also had a developed artisanry and practiced smelting, pottery and jewelry crafts. These East European tribes were closely tied to Scandinavia in the north and Transcaucasia (q.v.) and the Byzantine Empire through the trade that followed the rivers that ran through their territories: the Dnestr and the Dnepr (q.v.).

By the end of the first millennium after Christ, an active era of city building occurred. Each of these cities had three separate parts: a kremlin, or inner fortress; a *pos ad*, or the artisan sector; and the *torg*, or trading sector. In the cities were located the courts of the princes, the nobility and their armed retainers. The majority of the population were artisans who practiced jewelry work, smithing, weaving, pottery and other crafts. The earliest Russian coins date back to the tenth century. In ancient Russia literacy was widespread. In Novgorod (q.v.) documents have been found that date back to the 13th and 14th centuries. These documents contain legal matters, complaints, testaments, private letters and merchant accounts. The south Russian, the Crimean (q.v.), and the Black Sea (q.v.) littoral are especially rich in archaeological finds. Russia's many past civilizations—the Scythians (q.v.), the Mongols and the Turks—have left a wealth of burial sites and ancient ruins.

ARCHITECTURE, RUSSIAN. Originally based on wooden construction, it was greatly affected by Byzantine designs of churches shaped as cubes with domes resting on the four walls. Large buildings were constructed in Russia as early as the 11th century, at the end of which the great cathedral of Kiev was finished, as was the Novgorod cathedral some years earlier. These buildings were covered with numerous cupolas and their interiors decorated with frescos and mosaics.

From the 12th to the 13th centuries there were numerous palaces built for the ruling princes, as well as churches and some stone houses for the wealthier urban inhabitants. In the 14th and 15th centuries, during the reign of Tsar Ivan I Kalita (q.v.), the Moscow (q.v.) Kremlin and the churches within it were built out of stone. At the end of that century residential construction of private stone dwellings in Moscow became prevalent. However, until the end of the 16th century wooden buildings continued to predominate even in the capital. The richer inhabitants decorated them with carvings and paint.

In the 16th century domes began to take on an onion shape brought to Russia by Italian architects. Peter I the Great (q.v.) introduced a deliberately West European baroque architectural style. The 18th century saw a greatly accelerated development of Russian architectural art as a result of the building of St. Petersburg (q.v.). In the process of its construction a unique style began to evolve—it was referred to as the St. Petersburg baroque and was characterized by simplicity of line combined with picturesque colorfulness. The best-known architect who worked in this style was the Italian Resterelli. At that time a classical style developed in juxtaposition to the baroque, but by the middle of the 19th century architectural classicism began to undergo a crisis because of the emergence of a monumental style—the so-called Russian Imperial style. Examples are the building of the Admiralty in St. Petersburg and the Bolshoi Theater (q.v.) in Moscow. By the beginning of the 20th century, the Russian modern style began to emerge. The large Moscow hotel, the Metropole, was built in this style, as were multistoried buildings in St. Petersburg. After the 1917 revolution, thanks to a number of talented architects who remained in Russia, modernistic buildings started being built in Moscow. In the 1920s these architects undertook an active search for new solutions for theaters, clubs, and residential buildings. However, during this time numerous historically significant buildings, especially churches, were also destroyed. This style was replaced in the 1930s by the "wedding cake" structures favored by Stalin (q.v.).

A major disaster to Russian architecture occurred during World War II, when hundreds of thousands of buildings were destroyed. In the 1950s the principal focus of architects in Russia was the designing of mass-produced multistoried apartments. This process led to a major improvement of the housing situation for the population of the country and to the solution of the previous severe housing shortage. However, this Soviet-modern style introduced a standardization of apartment constructions and greatly increased urban anonymity. From 1949 to 1953 the new Moscow university complex and several other large Moscow buildings such as the hotels Rossiia and Ukraina were erected in what is now referred to as Stalin's rococo style. During this period new theaters were also constructed—the Moscow Artistic Theater and in 1980 the Children's Musical Theater.

ARCHIVES, RUSSIAN AND SOVIET. The systematic keeping of Russian state records was begun in 1852, following the establishment of the Archives of the Ministry of Justice. After the October 1917 revolution, the Soviet government established a complex system under the Central Archives Board, now renamed the Chief Archives Board.

ARCOS. This was an organization established in England by the Soviet government to promote trade between the Soviet Union and Britain. Its role was also secretly to help the British Communist Party and its sympathizers to carry out Communist propaganda.

ARCTIC, RUSSIAN. Russia, within the Arctic circle, is mainly an uninhabited tundra with the exception of the Kola Peninsula where numerous mining operations are located, and the city of Murmansk (q.v.), a major port north of the Arctic circle. The largest of the rivers that flow from the south into the Arctic Ocean in European Russia and Siberia (q.v.) are the Lena (q.v.), the Ob (q.v.), the Enisei (q.v.) and the Kolyma (q.v.). This Arctic region is inhabited by several ethnic populations among whom are Russian settlers, the Komi, the Chukchis (q.v.), the Iakutiia (*see* Sakha), the Lapps (q.v.) and the Nenets (q.v.).

ARKHANGELSK. This is the name of a city and also a region in the northern part of the Russian Federation. The city was established in 1584. It is the principal Russian port on the North Sea (q.v.) and serves as a base for both naval forces and the Atlantic fishing fleet. The economy of the region is based mainly on forestry.

ARKHANGELSKII, ALEKSANDR A. (1846–1924). A composer of religious music and choir master at the court cappella and a Guards' regiment, he organized his own choir in 1880 and gave concerts both in Russia and abroad. Arkhangelskii left Russia following the October 1917 revolution.

ARKHIPOV, ABRAM Y. (1862–1930). A student of art in St. Petersburg (q.v.) and Moscow (q.v.), his main interest was in painting scenes from the life of Russian peasants. He became a member of the Academy of Fine Arts (q.v.) and was awarded the title of People's Artist by the Soviet government.

ARMAND, INESSA F. (b. STEPHEN) (1875–1920). Of French parentage, she was brought up by a wealthy Moscow family of factory owners and married one of the sons. Armand became a revolutionary at an early age, joined the Socialist Revolutionaries (q.v.) party, and took part in the 1905 revolution. Arrested and exiled, she emigrated from Russia to Paris after her release. There, in 1909 she met and, it is said, had a romantic liaison with Lenin (q.v.). Armand lived in Switzerland during World War I and represented the Communists at several peace conferences. Returning to Russia after the 1917 revolution, she became a member of the Soviet government and organized the first conference of women Communists in 1920.

ARMED FORCES, CURRENT. During the 1970s and 1980s a number of problems accumulated in the Russian armed forces. Among these were the marked drop in military preparedness and the lack of social security for members of the forces and of their families. Surveys found that over one-third of the professional officers were suffering from either apathy or insecurity and that approximately 50 percent did not trust the country's political leaders. From 1985 to 1992, reforms in the army were constantly postponed.

With the beginning of perestroika (q.v.), the forward strategic policy of the armed forces began to change to a defensive conception.

However, during this period the military capability of the armed forces continued to drop. Only 40 percent of officers and generals considered that the units that they commanded were capable of effectively carrying out military tasks.

Condemnation of the war in Afghanistan also gave rise to a fear of utilizing the armed forces even for the defense of the citizenry or in the interests of the country. Conversion of the defense industry to civilian use was fraught with difficulties, occasionally causing some harm to the scientific and industrial potential of such enterprises. The Russian army also underwent a complete deidealization. However, among the remaining inherited elements of the Communist period are a number of negative ones. Existing regulations are not enforced strictly enough among the majority of army units. This is especially true of day-to-day life in the barracks, where new recruits are often mistreated and subjected to numerous insults that they in turn perpetrate on more recent enlistees. Many of these recruits become chronically ill and very often even need psychiatric attention.

ARMED FORCES, IMPERIAL. The history of its armed forces is inextricably linked with the economic and political life of the Russian state. The military has played a major role in defending the country against foreign attacks as well as serving as an instrument of its expansion to territories adjoining it.

Until the 15th century, Russia's army consisted of armed units supplied to the tsar by his feudal aristocracy. These units were made up of volunteers and by the peasants dependent on their lords. The principal type of soldier was the infantryman; cavalry was used only for secondary tasks. By the end of the 14th century firearms had been introduced. From the 15th to the 17th century, the core of Russia's armed forces consisted of "the servants of the Tsar," units of cavalry manned by the *dvoriane* (q.v.), or minor nobility.

In the middle of the 16th century Ivan the Terrible (q.v.) carried out a series of military reforms aimed to regulate the manner in which the armed forces were recruited and maintained. A permanent army was established. These troops were called the *streltsy*, or sharpshooters. Supply and administration were centralized by Peter the Great (q.v.), and artillery was made into an independent branch. Also, a permanent armed border guard was placed on Russia's southern frontier.

The reforms that were carried out by Peter the Great in the early 18th century created a regular army and navy. These two services were manned by draftees who were for the most part peasant serfs. They belonged to landlords, each of whom had a quota of men they were obliged to supply. In 1719 Peter issued a decree that mandated a unified system of training and strengthened the administration of all military matters. He established a military collegium as well as an admiralty; military schools were opened for the preparation of an officer cadre; and the military justice system was reformed. By the end of his reign the total number in the Russian armed forces had risen to over 220,000 regular troops. Another 110,000 irregular troops consisted mainly of Cossacks (q.v.). In 1769 the military order of Cavaliers of St. George (q.v.), the most prestigious military decoration of imperial Russia, was established.

The system created by Peter lasted without major changes until Russia's defeat in the Crimean War (q.v.). After the war's conclusion in 1856, new military reforms were undertaken along with reforms in other spheres of Russian life. A universal system of military obligation was instituted in 1874 that replaced the previous method of selective recruiting. All individuals, on reaching the age of 21, were subject to call-up and selected by a lottery; those who were not drafted were placed in the reserves. For the infantry, the length of service was established at six years instead of 25, as it had been previously. For the navy, the term was seven years. Individuals with a higher education were taken on active service for only six months while those with a secondary education were enlisted for up to a year and a half.

These reforms also created 15 military districts and mandated a special course of education for all officers. As well, an armaments industry began to be established. The next stage of the evolution of the Russian armed forces occurred in 1904 after the unsuccessful Russo-Japanese War (q.v.). Military administration was further centralized: a territorial recruiting system was introduced, the length of service was reduced, efforts were made to rejuvenate the officer corps, and new regulations concerning the Cadet Corps schools were issued. By the beginning of World War I, as a result of these efforts, Russia was able to put into the field five million well-armed and well-trained men.

ARMED FORCES, SOVIET. On January 15, 1918, soon after the Communist Party captured state power, Lenin (q.v.) signed a decree to organize a workers' and peasants' Red Army, and at the end of that month he signed another decree creating the Red Navy. Russia was still in a state of war with Germany, and on the day that the formation of the Red Army was decreed, Germany violated the existing armistice and began an advance into Russian territory. The Soviet government was compelled to sign an unfavorable peace treaty with Germany and Austria at Brest-Litovsk (q.v.) in March 1918.

In the spring of 1918, in several parts of the country, spontaneous revolts occurred against the Soviet government and soon merged into a nationwide civil war (q.v.). Beginning in May 1918 the Soviet government began to carry out a mass mobilization of workers and peasants into the Red Army. As a result of these levies, its numbers grew rapidly to three million men. (By 1920, it had reached five million.) The mobilization, however, was carried out only with great difficulty; between 20 percent and 30 percent of those called up managed to avoid the draft.

These new Red Army units, which consisted primarily of peasants, frequently retreated, and some even went over to the side of the White Army. This largely explains the initially successful advances of the White Armies (q.v.) in the summer of 1919. The operational leadership of the Red Army units was controlled by the Revolutionary Military Council (q.v.), presided over by Trotsky (q.v.). From the very first days, finding experienced commanding staff for the army was a problem. To solve it, the Red Army recruited over 75,000 former officers of the old tsarist army. Many of them came to occupy high positions of command. By the end of 1918, some 65 military schools had been established to educate Red Army officers.

The Communist Party focused a great deal of ideological work on the Red Army. In all of the military units it created party groups and assigned political commissars who were directly responsible to the party's Central Committee. In August 1920 there were about 30,000 Communists in the ranks of the Red Army.

The repressive measures that were conducted in the middle of the 1930s hit the Red Army very hard. Among those repressed were three of the five marshals of the Soviet Union. Between May 1937 and December 1938, more than half of all the regimental commanders, and nearly all brigade and division commanders were arrested. The total number of arrested officers exceeded 40,000 men. As a result, at the time of the German invasion in June 1941, almost 75 percent of the army commanders had occupied their posts for less than a year and did not understand modern principles of warfare. The remaining top military leadership was not up to its task either. Thus, the People's Commissar of Defense Voroshilov (q.v.) actively supported increases in the number of cavalry divisions, while at the same time breaking up the existing mechanized corps into small units that were assigned to the infantry.

The Soviet experience of the war with Finland in the winter of 1939–40 proved that it was necessary to reunify these mechanized forces. This lesson came too late to prepare the Red Army for the German attack in June 1941. Immediately after the start of the German invasion of the Soviet Union in June 1941, the Red Army began to expand. The July 1941 mobilization brought it up to 5.3 million men. At the same time its administrative structure was changed by the creation of the General Headquarters of the Supreme Command (*see* Stavka) and by the establishment of the State Committee for Defense, which had unlimited power to conduct military operations and control all activities related to the war effort. During the summer and autumn months of 1941, the Red Army suffered very serious losses, and by November, the Germans were at the gates of Moscow. Dozens of the Red Army's best divisions were destroyed. And although orders were given by Stalin (q.v.) forbidding retreats and commanding the execution of retreating units, these failed to help.

The political leadership, and especially Stalin, showed their incompetence in military questions and their inability to conduct military operations. However, it was at this time that several talented professional soldiers emerged. By August 1942, a deputy of Stalin had become the actual director of military operations—Marshal Georgii Zhukov (q.v.). The first victories of the Red Army were during the winter of 1941. As the war progressed, the ability of the Red Army commanders, as well as the level and quality of its technical supplies, improved rapidly, until it captured Berlin in April 1945. The German High Command was forced to accept unconditional surrender from the Soviet Union, Great Britain, and the United States. After 1946 the military forces of the USSR were renamed the Soviet Army.

ART, RUSSIAN. Russian art has its roots in folk traditions, primarily woodworking. Wood carvers specialized in making devotional objects such as crosses and figurines of saints. Icon painting began to flourish after the 14th century, inspired by Byzantine prototypes. After Peter the Great (q.v.), Russian portrait and landscape paintings, like those of Ilia Repin (q.v.) began to acquire West European characteristics. At the turn of the 20th century, a flowering of abstract, symbolist and other avant-guard genres produced such outstanding painters as Kandinskii (q.v.) and Malevich (q.v.). After the 1920s, these experimental movements were replaced in the Soviet Union by the officially sponsored style of socialist realism (q.v.).

ARTIST'S UNION. This is a cultural organization of Russian artists designed to implement Communist Party policies in matters of art. As one of the most conservative cultural organizations in the Soviet Union, it strongly opposed exhibitions of such artists as Malevich (q.v.) and Kandinskii (q.v.) and long resisted *glasnost* (q.v.) and perestroika (q.v.), which were initiated by Gorbachev (q.v.) in the late 1980s.

ARZAMAS-16. The Russian equivalent to Los Alamos in the United States is a closed city some 200 miles east of Moscow centered on the town of Sarov. Its development began in 1946. It was here that Russia's first atomic and hydrogen bombs were constructed. "Arzamas" is the name of a separate town nearby that is famous for its monastery, founded in 1654, and its best-known inhabitant, St. Seraphin (1759–1833).

ASPIRANT. The Russian term designating a graduate university student who is preparing for the candidate of science degrees, which under the Russian system of higher education precedes the doctorate. In comparison with advanced North American degrees, it is generally viewed as falling between the master's and the Ph.D. degrees.

ASTRAKHAN. Located at the estuary of the Volga River (q.v.) on the Caspian Sea (q.v.), this city belonging to the Khanate of Astrakhan was conquered in 1556 by Ivan the Terrible (q.v.). Today it is an important trade center for oil, fish, lumber and grain products that are shipped to central Russia.

ATOMIC ENERGY. From the time of the organization of the State Committee for the Problems of Uranium in 1940, Russian atomic scientists have had state support to study the nature of atomic fission. The first efforts at a peaceful utilization of atomic energy began in 1948 because of the initiative of Kurchatov (q.v.). This research was accelerated under the leadership of General Vannikov. In 1947 the Soviets began operating their first atomic reactor. In September 1950 the construction of the first atomic station began, and in June 1954 it began to produce energy. The Soviet Union exploded its first atomic bomb in 1949 and tested its first hydrogen weapon in 1953. The atomic power station at Obinsk was the first such unit in the world to become fully operational. By 1959 an atomic icebreaker was launched. It had a displacement of 17,000 tons and shortly thereafter two more such icebreakers entered into service, guaranteeing uninterrupted year-round navigation in the Arctic. In the 1960s, several large atomic energy plants were constructed.

In the 1970s a new program of construction of atomic energy stations was begun and a series of large stations came into production. By the end of the 1970s there were ten atomic stations in the Soviet Union. In 1976 construction began of a factory in Volgograd (q.v.) for the production of atomic reactors. During the late Brezhnev (q.v.) years, there was an influx of some relatively poorly trained personnel into the atomic industry of the country. Such individuals were frequently guilty of hiding existing defects under the pretext of national security. As a result of such practices a major disaster occurred in the Soviet Union in April 1986, when the Chernobyl (q.v.) atomic explosion took place and where the danger of the accident was initially understated. By the beginning of the 1990s power produced by atomic energy has reached the billion kilowatt level in Russia, and atomic electrical stations are currently playing a major role in the production of electrical energy. In 1993 they produced 12.7 percent of the total electrical energy of the country, and in certain regions almost half of the required amount. Current opinion polls show that the majority of the Russian population is unhappy with their inability to influence such atomic policy matters as setting levels of radiation. These polls also indicate that the majority of the population does not believe the official statistics that the government issues concerning atomic energy matters.

AVARS. Originally a group of related nationalities but treated as one since the 1930s, the Avars (or Ma'arulul) number around 500,000 and speak a varied group of languages of the Northeastern Caucasian group. They live in western Dagestan and are largely Sunnite Moslem.

AVERBAKH, LEOPOLD L. (1903–39). A literary critic and a vigorous advocate of proletarian literature in the early 1920s, he was one of the most influential Soviet literary officials until he was brought down by Stalin's (q.v.) change of policy in 1932.

AVKSENTIEV, NICHOLAS D. (1878–1943). A Socialist Revolutionary (q.v.), he participated in the 1905 revolution and served as minister of the interior in the 1917 Provisional government (q.v.) After the Communist seizure of state power, he played an active role in the anti-Communist Ufa (q.v.) government until he was expelled by Admiral Kolchak (q.v.). He took part in the civil war (q.v.) on the side of the White Armies (q.v.), then emigrated from Russia to France where he lived until 1940, when he moved to the United States.

AVVAKUM, ARCHPRIEST (1621–82). He reacted against the religious reforms initiated by Patriarch Nikon (q.v.) during the reign of Peter the Great (q.v.) and became the leader of the Starovertsy (q.v.), or Old Believers, a sect that refused to accept changes to ancient Orthodox Church (q.v.) religious practices. First exiled to Siberia (q.v.), Avvakum was later burned at the stake.

AZEF, EVNO F. (b. RASKIN) (1869–1918). Born into an impoverished Jewish tailor's family, he joined the Socialist Revolutionaries (q.v.) party in 1899. In 1903 he became director of its terrorist branch, and was responsible, in 1904, for the assassinations of Plehve (q.v.), the chief of the security forces, and, in 1905, of Grand Duke Sergei (q.v.), the governor of Moscow (q.v.). He was employed by the secret police as an informer and is known to have betrayed numerous party comrades before being unmasked in 1908. Subsequently, he lived in Germany until his death in Berlin.

AZERBAIJAN. A republic of 33,425 square miles on the Caspian Sea (q.v.) bordering on Georgia, Armenia, Iran and Turkey. The capital is Baku (q.v.). The principal river is the Kura, which has been used to irrigate the otherwise dry Kura Plain. The Azeris, who constitute 67 percent of the population of Azerbaijan, speak a language very similar to Republican Turkish; relations with Turkey have also been fairly close. The population is around 4,200,000. In 1991 Azerbaijan became a member of the Commonwealth of Independent States (q.v.).

AZOV. A river port, it is located some 20 miles away from the Black Sea (q.v.) estuary of the Don River (q.v.). It was established as the Greek colony of Tanais before the Christian era, and was acquired by Russia from Turkey in 1774.

B

BABEL, ISAAC E. (1894–1941). Born to a Jewish merchant family, he started writing short stories at an early age. In 1916 Babel met Gorky (q.v.), who became his mentor. During the civil war (q.v.) he joined General Yudenich's (q.v.) White Armies (q.v.), then went over to the Soviet side and volunteered for the cavalry. After the end of the civil war he published a book about his experiences. In 1935 Babel took part in the International Congress of Writers held in Paris, then disappeared during the purges.

BAGRATION, PRINCE PETR (1765–1812). A Russian general of Caucasian descent, he served in the Napoleonic campaigns. He won a victory at the battle of Eylau but was killed in 1812 at the Battle of Borodino (q.v.).

BAIKAL, LAKE. One of the largest fresh water lakes in the world, it is located in Siberia (q.v.). It is over 5,500 feet deep and contains nearly 2,000 unique animal and plant species.

BAIKAL-AMUR MAGISTRAL (BAM). This northern railroad line links the Lake Baikal (q.v.) region with the Pacific Ocean ports of Vladivostok (q.v.) and Nakhodka (q.v.). It was completed in the late

1980s, despite great difficulties caused by climatic and geographical conditions. It contains over 3,200 bridges, culverts and tunnels.

BAKALEINIKOV, VLADIMIR R. (1885–1953). A Russian orchestra conductor and viola player, as well as a member of several string quartets he was a professor of music at the Moscow Conservatory from 1917 to 1924. Bakaleinikov emigrated in 1925 to the United States.

BAKHMETEFF, BORIS A. (1880–1951). Professor of hydraulics at the St. Petersburg Polytechnic Institute from 1908 to 1917, he became, during World War I, a member of the powerful War Industries Committee, which had the task of ensuring the adequate provisioning of the Russian army. After the February 1917 revolution (q.v.) Bakhmeteff was appointed Russian ambassador to the United States, a position he surrendered when the Communists took power in Russia. He then took the post of professor of engineering at Columbia University.

BAKHTIN, MIKHAIL (1895–1975). One of the leading literary theorists of Russia, Bakhtin proposed the idea of polyphony as opposed to a single authoritative voice in the novels of Dostoevsky. He elaborated this and similar ideas in a number of works, many of which were not published under his own name in the Soviet period. Since the 1960s his ideas have become current and widely influential.

BAKST, LEON S. (1866–1924). A stage designer, he was responsible for many of the sets at the Imperial Theater in St. Petersburg (q.v.) and later for those in Diaghilev's (q.v.) ballet productions.

BAKU. The capital of Azerbaijan (q.v.), Baku is a port on the Caspian Sea (q.v.) with a population of 1,780,000. It is a center of the oil industry; related industries such as chemical processing and textiles are also found there, as are shipbuilding and machine building. Baku has a long history of independence in the Middle Ages; it came under Persian influence in the 16th century and was annexed by Russia in 1806.

BAKUNIN, MIKHAIL A. (1814–76). An aristocrat turned anarchist, he exiled himself from Russia in 1840 and took part in the Dresden uprising of 1848, during which he was arrested and deported back to Russia. Bakunin was first jailed, then sent to Siberian exile, but escaped to London in 1861. In England he continued to be actively involved in the revolutionary movement, and in 1872 Bakunin briefly collaborated with Karl Marx in setting up the First International.

After a disagreement with Marx, he left the organization. His writings were very influential among Russian radicals in the latter part of the 19th century.

BALAKIREV, MILII A. (1837–1910). A successful musician and pianist, he was the pupil of Glinka (q.v.) and leader of a group of Russian nationalist composers. Balakirev was also the teacher of Cui (q.v.) and Mussorgskii (q.v.).

BALANCHIN, GEORGE. (1904–1983). Born into the family of a minor St. Petersburg (q.v.) composer, he studied music at the St. Petersburg Conservatory. From 1914 until 1921 he was a member of the Mariinskii Theater (q.v.) school. After emigrating to France in 1924, Balanchin worked as a choreographer with Diaghilev (q.v.). In 1933 he moved to the United States and became the artistic director of the New York City Ballet.

BALLET. The first ballet in Russia, *Orpheus and Eurydice,* was performed at the court of Tsar Aleksei (q.v.) in 1673. By the middle of the 18th century ballet had won a place for itself as an independent art form in Russia. A choreographic school was opened in 1738 in St. Petersburg (q.v.) and another one in Moscow (q.v.) in 1773. In 1811, the French choreographer Didelot brought to the Imperial Ballet of St. Petersburg the classical tradition that became its trademark in subsequent years.

The development of the ballet in the first half of the 19th century is connected with the name of I. I. Valberkh. In his spectacles he attempted to expose the inner world of his protagonists and give free reign to pantomime. In Moscow A. P. Glushkovskii became the first historian and theoretician of the Russian ballet. His own productions were romantic in style. At the beginning of the 19th century, ballets on mythological themes became very popular, and entertaining spectacles with moral themes also enjoyed great vogue. After the war of 1812 a number of ballets on patriotic themes were staged. When the Bolshoi Theater (q.v.) was opened in Moscow in 1825, new possibilities for the staging of ballet productions became available and the Bolshoi Ballet Company was formed. A major influence on the development of the Russian ballet was provided by Tchaikovsky (q.v.), who brought dance and symphonic music closer together with such classics as *Swan Lake.* Ballet in Russia is also closely tied to such outstanding masters as Perrot and Marius Petipa (q.v.), both of whom attempted to make this dance form capable of expressing character, thought, and feelings. At the same time they sought to create beauty in their productions and to exhibit inventiveness.

At the beginning of the 20th century Russian ballet came to occupy an outstanding place in the world of dance. Ballet troupes from Moscow and St. Petersburg boasted highly professional corps-de-ballets. The Ballets Russes (q.v.), organized by the impressario Diaghilev (q.v.), opened in Paris in 1909 and consisted for the most part of dancers trained at the Mariinskii Theater (q.v.), such as Vaclav Nijinsky (q.v.) and Tamara Karsavina, together with composer Igor Stravinskii (q.v.) and choreographer Fokin (q.v.). This company enjoyed tremendous success in Paris before World War I (q.v.).

After the 1917 revolutions the Imperial Ballet was renamed the Kirov Ballet Company (q.v.) and continued the classical traditions of Russian dance. During the 1920s, Russian ballet was enriched with populist themes drawn from sports and acrobatics. In the 1930s and 1940s the leading direction of choreographic drama was exemplified by such productions as *Romeo and Juliet*, set to the music of Prokofiev (q.v.). Some 17 new ballet groups were organized during this period, but the mainstay of their repertoires remained the classical ballets of the 19th century. In the 1960s the ballet master Grigorievich produced such outstanding ballets as *Spartacus*, which was set to the music of Khachaturian (q.v.). By the middle of the 1970s there were six ballet schools in the USSR, as well as numerous ballet troupes. During this period the prima ballerina Plisetskaia (q.v.) created a spectacular role in the Carmen Suite to the music of Bizet, and Russian ballet troupes once again were permitted by the government to travel abroad.

BALLETS RUSSES. Founded by Sergei Diaghilev (q.v.) with dancers from the Imperial Mariinskii Theater (q.v.), and appearing first in Paris in 1909, this company drew together the talents of Nijinsky (q.v.), Pavlova (q.v.), Cherepnin, Fokin (q.v.), Bakst and Stravinskii (q.v.); it also attracted others such as Debussy and Picasso. The company performed mainly in Europe and disbanded with the death of Diaghilev in 1929.

BALMONT, KONSTANTIN D. (1867–1943). Son of a landowner, he began his studies at the University of Moscow (*see* Universities), but was expelled for revolutionary activities. By the turn of the century Balmont had gained a fashionable reputation in Russia as a symbolist poet. In 1920 he emigrated to France and continued to write poetry and to translate French and English poets into Russian.

BALNEV, BORIS V. (1902–65). Grandson of an Englishman who had settled in Russia, he became a film director in 1926 and created a unique genre of silent films. After Stalin's (q.v.) ascendency Balnev was unable to continue his career; he became an alcoholic and ended his life by suicide. His films received international recognition in the late 1970s.

BALTIC SEA. This body of water is connected to the Atlantic Ocean by the straits between Denmark and Sweden. It is partially frozen in the winter but is a rich fishing area and a vital maritime link for commerce between Central Europe, Scandinavia, the Baltic countries and Russia.

BANKING. Banks first appeared in Russia at the end of the 18th century. In the middle of the 19th century there were only two functioning banks, a central one owned the government and a second one belonging to a private joint-stock company. By the time of the 1917 revolution, nearly 50 banks with hundreds of branches in most of the large cities of the empire had come into being. After the Communist seizure of power in 1917, all banks were nationalized and restructured so as to integrate their activities into the centralized national economy. Separate banks were established under the direction of the State Bank (Gosbank) for each of the principal economic activities: a trade bank (Torgbank); an industrial bank (Prombank); an agricultural bank (Selkhozbank); a municipal bank (Tsekombank); and a foreign trade bank (Vneshtorgbank).

The primary mission of these banks was the financing of sectorial activities called for by the national economic plans. In January 1988 the banking system of the country was reorganized. In addition to the continuing functioning of the State Bank, five specialized state banks were established. These were the foreign trade bank, the industrial construction bank, the agricultural bank, the communal residential bank, and a savings and credit bank. The State Bank remained the single center for currency distribution. It also had the function of administering the central monetary and credit system of the country, implementing the credit policy of the state, coordinating the activities of the other banks of the USSR, and settling their mutual accounts. In addition, it was charged with controlling the activities of specialized banks and regulating all currency questions. Specialized banks were charged with providing credit and financing capital investments in their specialized areas, organizing savings and handling cash and noncash transactions. The overcentralization of the Russian banking system, as well as its relative inflexibility, created a need for privately owned commercial banks.

Between 1988 and 1990 these new banks were divided into commercial and cooperative ones. There were some 140 of them registered in the country. By the end of 1990 the government issued a series of decrees that set down a new legal basis for the banking system. This system envisaged two levels of activity. At the top level there was the central bank of Russia, which carried out the credit and monetary regulations of the country and controlled the activity of commercial banks. At the lower level were the commercial banks, which worked on the basis of licenses issued by the central bank. These commercial banks were allowed to attract deposits and to provide credit required to finance capital investments and to issue, sell, and keep valuable documents.

After the collapse of the Soviet Union in 1991, major reforms were initiated for the Russian banking system. These included privatization and the severing of bank activities from direct guidance by the government. These reforms are still in their infancy. By October 1992 the total number of commercial banks in the Russian Federation was over 1,600. However, the size of their capital is not very large, and at present their main function is to provide credit to individuals and small firms, carry out various credit and commercial transactions, accumulate savings, and provide advice regarding financial questions.

BARANOV, ALEKSANDR A. (1746–1819). A merchant, he became the explorer of Siberia (q.v.) and director of the Russian American Company (q.v.), which was granted a monopoly for trading in Alaska (q.v.). He was also the founder of Sitka (q.v.) and established Fort Ross, a Russian colony on the coast of California, north of San Francisco Bay.

BARCLAY DE TOLLY, PRINCE MIKHAIL B. (1761–1818). A field marshal in the Russian army of Alexander I (q.v.), as well as minister of war, his family was of Scottish descent. He commanded the Russian army at the beginning of Napoleon's invasion of Russia in 1812, until he was replaced by Field Marshal Kutuzov (q.v.). De Tolly commanded the Russian army that occupied Paris in 1815.

BARDIN, IVAN P. (1883–1960). A graduate of the Kiev Polytechnical Institute in 1910, he worked in a U.S. steel plant in 1911 before returning to Russia. Following the October 1917 revolution, Bardin occupied several high positions in the Soviet steel industry and headed a major research institute on ferrous metallurgy. In 1955 he was chairman of the Soviet Committee for the International Geophysical Year. Bardin was the recipient of several Stalin (q.v.) and Lenin (q.v.) prizes.

BARENTS SEA. Murmansk (q.v.) is the principal port on this mostly ice-free northern body of water, which lies between the islands of

Novaia Zemlia (q.v.), Spitzbergen (q.v.), and northern Russia. Besides being an outlet for shipping, it also has rich fishing grounds.

BARMIN, ALEXANDER G. (1899–1987). He served in the Red Army (*see* Armed Forces, Soviet) during the civil war (q.v.) and, having reached the rank of general, he was transferred to the diplomatic service with the rank of ambassador. In 1937, in order to escape the purges that were taking place at home, Barmin abandoned his post and fled to Paris, where he denounced Stalin (q.v.). In 1940 he moved to the United States and served as a private in the United States Army. After his discharge he worked for the Voice of America.

BARNAUL. A city on the Ob River (q.v.), this is an important industrial center in western Siberia (q.v.). Its economy is based on machine works, textiles and food processing. Its population is over 300,000.

BARSHCHINA. Before the emancipation of the serfs in 1861, this was the unpaid, or corvée, labor, customarily three days each week, that was due to the landlord, or *barin*, by his serfs.

BASHKORTOSTAN. Situated in the western foothills of the Ural Mountains (q.v.), its capital is Ufa (q.v.). The population is just under 4,000,000.

BATU KHAN (d. 1255). Leader of the Mongol invaders of Russia, he was the grandson of Genghis Khan (q.v.). In 1236 his hordes destroyed the armies of the Russian princes and reached into Poland and Hungary. Following these victories, he led his forces to the lower Volga (q.v.) region where he established Sarai, the capital of his state, which was called the Golden Horde (q.v.).

BAZHANOV, BORIS (1900-). Member of the Communist Party from 1919, he first worked in the party's Central Committee (q.v.) under Lazar Kaganovich (q.v.) as his ghostwriter. His articles drew Stalin's (q.v.) attention, and in 1923 he was appointed Stalin's personal secretary. In 1926, having secretly become disillusioned with the Soviet regime, he changed his work to that of editor of a financial periodical and in 1928 fled to Western Europe through Persia. After World War II (q.v.) he moved to England, where he published his memoirs, which describe Stalin's rise to power.

BAZHENOV, VASILII I. (1737–99). Born into the family of a priest, he studied in Moscow (q.v.) and at the Academy of Fine Arts (q.v.), where he earned a scholarship to continue architectural studies in

Western Europe. On his return to Russia in 1765, Bazhenov was elected a member of the Russian Academy of Sciences (q.v.) and given the assignment of redesigning the Moscow Kremlin (q.v.). He was very influential in the creation of a uniquely Russian architectural tradition.

BEDNYI, DEMIAN (pseud. of PRIDVOROV) (1883–1945). Highly popular in Russia for his antireligious poetry during the twenties, he was called the chief proletarian poet. Later, Bednyi displeased Stalin (q.v.), despite his attempts to flatter the dictator, but managed to escape arrest during the purges of the 1930s.

BEKHTEREV, VLADIMIR M. (1857–1927). A graduate of the Medical and Surgical Academy in 1878, he went on to specialize in psychiatry and neuropathology, particularly the activity of the higher nervous system, and promulgated the study of reflexes as the foundation of human behavior. Bekhterev was professor of psychiatry at the University of Kazan and at the Military Academy of Medicine, and in 1908 he helped found the Institute of Psychoneurology.

BELARUS. A well-forested land to the east of Poland, its capital is the city of Minsk. Its area is 80,134 square miles, and the population is around 10,259,000. Belarus was variously part of the Kievan and Lithuanian duchies and was acquired by Russia in the late 18th century. It was an independent republic between 1918 and 1922. In addition to timber, it has important mineral deposits. Belarus was one of the first to join the Commonwealth of Independent States (q.v.) in 1991.

BELGOROD OBLAST AND CITY. Located in the center of the Russian Federation, this area, with its capital by the same name, is surrounded by rich agricultural soil and mineral iron deposits.

BELINSKII, VISSARION G. (1811–48). A leading Russian literary and social critic and a westernizer (q.v.), he was highly popular with the progressive intelligentsia during the middle of the 19th century.

BELNIKOV, ARKADII V. (1921–70). A student at the Gorky Literary Institute, he was arrested by Soviet authorities in 1943. Belnikov served eight years in the Karaganda (q.v.) concentration camp. After his release in 1956, he became a lecturer at the Gorky Institute and began publishing numerous works on Russian writers. In 1968 he defected from the Soviet Union to settle in the United States, where he became a university professor.

BELOBORODOV, ALEKSANDR G. (1891–1938). He joined the Communist Party in 1908 and after the October revolution (q.v.) became chairman of the Ural soviet (q.v.). Beloborodov was personally responsible for organizing the execution of the tsar and his whole family in Ekaterinburg in June 1918.

BELOMORSK. This small town in the Karelian Autonomous Republic (q.v.) is situated at the terminus of the Belomorsk Canal that links the Baltic Sea (q.v.) to the White Sea (q.v.). Its population is just under 12,000.

BELORUSSIA see BELARUS

BELOVEZHSK ACCORD see ALMA-ATA AGREEMENT

BELY, ANDREI (pseud. of BUGAEV). (1880–1934). A major Symbolist (q.v.) poet, he is most commonly known now for his innovative novel about the 1905 revolution, *St. Petersburg*. In 1921 he turned against the Soviet government and emigrated to Western Europe. He returned to the Soviet Union in 1923 and remained there until his death.

BENOIT, ALEKSANDR N. (1870–1960). Born into an artistic family of French origin, he became the protege and collaborator of Diaghilev (q.v.) and wrote extensively on art history and stage design. In 1927 Benoit moved to Paris, where he worked as a stage designer and painter.

BERBEROVA, NINA N. (1901–). A minor author, she emigrated from Russia after 1917 and married the poet Khodasevich (q.v.), a close friend of Gorky's (q.v.). Before World War II (q.v.) she lived in Paris and wrote short stories and biographies. At the end of the war Berberova became a journalist, working on the staff of a Russian newspaper. She moved to the United States in 1950 and taught the history of Russian literature at Princeton, Yale and Columbia universities.

BERDIAEV, NIKOLAI A. (1874–1948). Having been involved in revolutionary activities as a student, he was exiled in 1898. On his release, Berdiaev left for Germany, where he continued his studies. He returned to Russia in 1904 and associated himself with Sergei Bulgakov (q.v.), whose philosophy drew him away from Marxism and toward a religious viewpoint that stressed personal liberty. In 1922 Berdiaev was expelled from the Soviet Union after an interview with secret police chief Dzerzhinskii (q.v.). During World War II (q.v.) he lived in France.

BEREZINA RIVER. This river runs through Belarus (q.v.) to join the Dnepr (q.v.). It was the site of a major disaster that overtook the retreating Napoleonic army in 1812. Today, a canal that was built during the Soviet era links it with both the Baltic Sea (q.v.) and the Black Sea (q.v.).

BERGHOLTS, OLGA F. (1910–75). Born in St. Petersburg (q.v.), she was a minor poet who used that city as the subject of much of her work. Bergholts was a member of the Communist Party and received the Stalin Prize (q.v.) for literature in 1950.

BERIA, LAVRENTII P. (1899–1953). A graduate of the Baku Technical College in 1919, he was active in the revolutionary underground of Azerbaijan (q.v.) during the civil war (q.v.), then in 1921 joined the ranks of the Soviet secret police. By 1931 Beria was first secretary of the Georgian Communist Party, and in 1934 Stalin (q.v.) summoned him to Moscow (q.v.). Beria replaced Ezhov (q.v.) in 1938 as head of the NKVD (q.v.), a post he retained until 1953. At the end of World War II he was promoted to the rank of marshal. Beria directed the administration of Soviet forced labor camps as well as the development of Soviet atomic weaponry. He failed in his attempt to succeed Stalin in 1953 and was arrested and executed by his Politburo (q.v.) colleagues.

BERING SEA. Located between Siberia (q.v.) and Alaska (q.v.), it forms part of the northern seaway around both the Eurasian continent and North America. It was named after Vitus Bering, the Danish explorer who led the Russian expedition that discovered Alaska.

BERIOZKA STORES. These were special government stores where one could make purchases only with foreign currency. They were designed primarily for tourists and for those few Soviet citizens who possessed such funds.

BERZIN, JAN K. (pseud. of PETERIS). (1889–1938). A member of the Communist Party since 1905, he was imprisoned in 1907, released, then rearrested again in 1911. Conscripted during World War I (q.v.), Berzin went underground and moved to St. Petersburg (q.v.), where he worked in a war factory under an assumed identity while continuing to take an active part in the revolutionary movement. He began his career as a secret police officer in 1919 and advanced to the position of chief of the Red Army's Military Intelligence, the GRU (q.v.), in 1924, a post he filled until 1935. It was during this period that Kim Philby began his career as a Soviet spy. During the Spanish civil war Berzin acted as the principal Soviet advisor to the Republican government. Recalled to Moscow (q.v.) in 1937, he was arrested and shot.

BESSARABIA. An area of roughly 17,100 square miles between the rivers Dnestr and Prut, part of Bessarabia now lies in Moldova (q.v.) and part in Ukraine (q.v.). Authority over the region has been contested for centuries, the latest exchanges having been between Romania and the Soviet Union.

BESTUZHEV, ALEKSANDR A. (1797–1837). A leading member of the Decembrist (q.v.) society, he was also coeditor of its publication, the *Polar Star.* He escaped execution after the unsuccessful Decembrist-led army rebellion in 1825. As punishment Bestuzhev was enrolled in the Russian army as a private and sent into combat in the Caucasus (q.v.). He died there in 1837 during the seige of a Circassian (q.v.) town.

BIROBIDZHAN AUTONOMOUS AREA. This Jewish autonomous area in the Russian Federation was established by the Soviet government in 1934. Only a very small number of Soviet Jews (q.v.) were willing to move to the area because of its lack of historical significance to them, as well as because of its remoteness. Today only a small percentage of its population is Jewish.

BLACK HUNDREDS. These political organizations of the extreme right came into being with police assistance after 1905. They were monarchist in persuasion and generally anti-Semitic. The most important of these groups was the Union of Russian People (q.v.) and the Union of Archangel Michael (q.v.).

BLACK REPARTITION see CHERNYI PEREDEL

BLACK SEA. A large body of salt water, it is almost completely landlocked. It abuts the southern shores of Russia and Ukraine (q.v.). It is connected to the Mediterranean by the narrow Kerch (q.v.) strait and the Bosporus. As it is ice-free, it is an important year-round water passage for Russian shipping to the Mediterranean.

BLAGOVESHCHENSK. A city on the Amur River (q.v.), it is the administrative center of that region and an important railroad and industrial center that provides shipbuilding and ship repair facilities. The population is close to 100,000.

BLAT. The Soviet term for "influence," it can be obtained by providing someone with special services, favors, or friendship or by family ties. Within a rigidly centralized and hierarchically structured system such as that which existed in the Soviet Union, *blat* was an indispensable ingredient in most bureaucratic and managerial interactions.

BLIUKHER, VASILII K. (1890–1938). The son of a peasant, he became a metal worker and participated in revolutionary activities before World War I (q.v.). An outstanding commander of the Red Army (*see* Armed Forces, Soviet) on the Volga (q.v.) front during the civil war (q.v.), he rose rapidly in rank and by 1924 was entrusted with the post of chief Soviet advisor to the Chinese Communists. He was sentenced to death and executed during the purges of the 1930s.

BLOK, ALEKSANDR A. (1880–1921). A leading Symbolist (q.v.) poet, he began publishing his poetry in 1903. During the 1917 revolutions Blok chose to remain in Russia and wrote the celebrated poem, *The Twelve*, which glorified the revolution. He cooperated with Gorky (q.v.) on a number of projects but shortly before his death complained that artistic freedom was being taken away in the Soviet Union and that life had lost its meaning for him.

BLOODY SUNDAY. On Sunday, January 9, 1905, an attempt was made by a crowd of some 150,000 workers to present a petition to Tsar Nicholas II (q.v.) at the Winter Palace (q.v.). They were led by a priest, Father Gapon (q.v). On orders of the governor-general of St. Petersburg (q.v.), the crowd was fired on, resulting in numerous casualties and permanently damaging the reputation of the tsar. This event served as a signal for a general strike that became the prelude to the revolution of 1905 (q.v.).

BLUMKIN, IAKOV G. (1899–1929). A left Socialist revolutionary and the murderer of the German ambassador to Russia in 1918, he became Trotsky's (q.v.) military secretary during the civil war (q.v.), after which he served in a series of high posts in the GPU (q.v.). In 1929 Blumkin secretly met with Trotsky and agreed to carry a message from him to his supporters in the Soviet Union. This message was transmitted to Radek, who betrayed Blumkin to Stalin. For this act Blumkin was executed in December 1929.

BOGDANOV, ALEKSANDR A. (1873–1928). After graduating from Kharkov University in 1899, he became a revolutionary and joined

Lenin's (q.v.) faction of the Russian Socialist Democratic Labor Party (q.v.). He was a member of the party's Central Committee from 1905 to 1907 and organized the party's school at Capri, which was financed by Gorky (q.v.). During this period he clashed with Lenin on a number of philosophical issues. After the October 1917 (q.v.) revolution, he became a member of the Communist Academy and a lecturer in economics at Moscow University (*see* Universities). He was also one of the leading ideologists of the Proletkult (q.v.) movement in Russian literature.

BOGLIUBSKII, PRINCE ANDREI Y. (1111–74). The grand prince of Suzdal (q.v.) and later of Vladimir (q.v.), he failed in his attempt to conquer Kiev (q.v.). However, he did succeed in subordinating Novgorod (q.v.) to his rule before being murdered by his own courtiers.

BOGOLEPOV, ALEKSANDR A. (1885–1980). A graduate of the University of St. Petersburg (*see* Universities) in 1910, he became a legal advisor in the Ministry of Finance in 1915. On Lenin's (q.v.) orders he was exiled to Germany in 1922 with other leading Russian intellectuals. There, Bogolepov was invited to work at the Russian Scientific Institute. In 1945 he moved to the United States and in 1951 became professor of law at the St. Vladimir Orthodox Seminary.

BOGOSTROITSY. The literal meaning of this Russian term is "god-builders." They were an influential group of Russian intellectuals that included Zinaida Gippius (q.v.), Merezhkovskii (q.v.), and Lunacharskii (q.v.). Their credo was that God is the product of the human collective striving for self-perfection. Their theories were strongly criticized by Lenin (q.v.).

BOIARS. This rank of the Russian medieval nobility originated in the 10th century. Boiars were large landowners and served the tsar (q.v.) as councilors and military officers. They received their titles directly from the grand princes and, later, the tsars.

BOLOTNIKOV, IVAN I. (d. 1608). In his youth he was captured and enslaved by Turks. After his escape to Russia he led a large peasant rebellion during the Time of Troubles (q.v.). Eventually Bolotnikov was captured by the tsar's (q.v.) forces and executed.

BOLSHEVIK. Literally, this term means a member of the majority. It was the label adopted by Lenin's (q.v.) faction after it won a narrow majority at the 1903 Congress of the Russian Socialist Democratic Labor Party (q.v.) in London. After the October 1917 revolution (q.v.), the group changed its name to the Russian Communist Party (Bolsheviks [q.v.]).

BOLSHOI THEATER. Established in 1776, this building has housed the prime theatrical and musical productions of Moscow (q.v.), as well as the world-famous Bolshoi Ballet Company.

BORODIN, ALEKSANDR P. (1833–87). A professional chemist, he was also a self-taught musician who became a composer of symphonies and opera. A strong nationalist, Borodin was a follower of Glinka (q.v.).

BORODINO. The village of Borodino is located a short distance west of Moscow (q.v.) and was the site of a major but inconclusive battle against Napoleon during the French invasion of Russia in 1812.

BRATSK. A town on the Angara River (q.v.), it was founded as a fortress in the 1630s. Bratsk is located at the site of one of the world's largest hydroelectrical dams, which produces vast amounts of electrical energy that supports the local manufacture of wood products and cellulose. Its population is over 200,000.

BRESHKO-BRESHKOVSKAIA, EKATERINA K. (1844–1934). A famed Socialist Revolutionary (q.v.), she was known as the "Grandmother of the Russian Revolution." Having supported Kerensky (q.v.), she left Soviet Russia after the Communists seized power in 1917 and settled in Czechoslovakia.

BREST-LITOVSK. This city in the western part of the Soviet Union, in Belarus (q.v.), was the site of the 1918 peace treaty between the young Soviet state and the German empire.

BREST-LITOVSK PEACE TREATY (1918). A peace treaty forced on Soviet Russia by imperial Germany early in 1918, it was negotiated on the Russian side by Leon Trotsky (q.v.). By its provisions, Russia lost the Ukraine (q.v.), its possessions in Poland, and its Baltic provinces. Considered by many Russians as an act of treason and a disgrace to Russian arms, this treaty was one of the catalysts for the formation of anti-Communist White Armies (q.v.), composed in large part of former tsarist officers. It also provoked a major factional fight within the Communist Party (q.v.). However, Lenin (q.v.) believed that it was only a temporary concession to German imperialism and his view prevailed.

BREZHNEV see NABEREZHNYE-CHELNY

BREZHNEV, LEONID I. (1906–82). A member of the Communist Party (q.v.) since 1931, he graduated from a metallurgical institute in 1935 and became the secretary of a regional party organization in 1939. During World War II (q.v.) Brezhnev held the post of senior political officer in the Soviet army. After the war he became first secretary of the Moldovian (q.v.) Communist Party and, after Stalin's (q.v.) death, the deputy head of the Chief Political Administration of the Armed Forces (*see* Armed Forces, Soviet). In 1953 Khrushchev (q.v.) gave him the task of supervising his Virgin Land (q.v.) project in Kazakhstan (q.v.), which was designed to extend vastly the cultivated grain-growing area of the Soviet Union. Brezhnev fulfilled this task successfully and was elected a member of the Politburo (q.v.) in 1956. He also became secretary of the Communist Party and chairman of the Presidium of the Supreme Soviet after Khrushchev was forced into retirement in 1964. In 1968 he had the Communist Party newspaper *Pravda* (q.v.) publish an article that declared the sovereignty of the USSR's East European allies limited insofar as any abandonment of their socialist systems was concerned—the "Brezhnev Doctrine." Under Brezhnev the Soviet Union greatly expanded its involvement with local revolutionary movements in Africa and Latin America and invaded Afghanistan in 1979 to support one of its clients. At the same time, however, Brezhnev participated in successful negotiations with U.S. president Nixon on controlling the atomic armaments of both superpowers. After General Secretary Gorbachev (q.v.) came to power in the middle 1980s he blamed Brezhnev's leadership for what he termed a period of *zastoi*, or stagnation.

BRIANSK. A port on the river Desna some 210 miles southwest of Moscow (q.v.), it has a population of 458,900. In 1956 it was merged with the city of Bezhitsa to form a large industrial area with significant steel and timber industries.

BRIUSOV, VALERII I. (1873–1924). Born into a wealthy merchant family and educated in Moscow (q.v.), he became a poet and edited numerous Symbolist (q.v.) publications. Briusov was lionized by the prewar Russian intelligentsia. After the October 1917 revolution (q.v.) he joined the Communist Party (q.v.) and wrote mostly propagandistic verses.

BRODSKII, IOSIF see BRODSKY, JOSEPH

BRODSKY, JOSEPH (1940–96). One of the most highly regarded poets of his age, Brodsky was born and raised in St. Petersburg (q.v.), where, toward the end of the 1950s, he had already earned recognition among his fellow poets and had become friends with Anna Akhmatova (q.v.). In addition to writing, Brodsky worked at a great variety of day jobs, but in 1964 he was arrested and sentenced to five years in prison for parasitism; he was released the following year. In 1972 he left Russia and settled in the United States, where he continued to write poetry and also a number of essays. In 1987 he was awarded the Nobel Prize for literature.

BRUSILOV, ALEKSEI A. (1853–1926). A member of a Russian military family, he became commander of a cavalry division in 1906. During World War I (q.v.) he commanded an army front against the Austrians and was one of the top generals who advised Tsar Nicholas II (q.v.) to abdicate. Made supreme commander of the Russian army by the Provisional government (q.v.) in 1917, he mounted an unsuccessful offensive against the Central Powers that summer. Brusilov sided with the Communist government after the October 1917 revolution (q.v.) and served as Inspector of the Red Army Cavalry.

BRUSILOV OFFENSIVE. During the summer of 1917 the Provisional government (q.v.) made an unsuccessful effort to break through the Austro-German front. Its defeat signaled the beginning of the disintegration of the Russian army.

BUBNOV, ANDREI S. (1883–1940). A member of the Communist Party (q.v.) since 1903, he played an active part in the 1917 revolutions and the civil war (q.v.). He supported Trotsky (q.v.) in an intraparty dispute in 1923 but then rejoined the majority in the party. He was made a member of the Politburo (q.v.) and, in 1929, commissar of education of the RSFSR. Bubnov was executed during the purges in 1940.

BUDENNYI, SEMEN M. (1883–1973). Having served in a Don Cossack (q.v.) cavalry regiment during the Russo-Japanese war (q.v.), his bravery in the field during World War I won him numerous medals and promotion to sergeant major. He joined the Communists in 1918 and gained fame as commander of the First Cavalry Army. After the civil war (q.v.) he served as inspector of cavalry and was one of Stalin's (q.v.) most loyal followers. His loyalty was rewarded with the rank of marshal of the Soviet Union. Completely ineffective as a commander at the beginning of World War II (q.v.) because of his lack of understanding of modern warfare, he was nevertheless retained as a revolutionary symbol and was given the sinecure post as head of Soviet horse breeding.

BUKHARIN, NIKOLAI I. (1888–1938). Son of a schoolteacher, he studied economics at the University of Moscow (*see* Universities) and joined the Communist Party (q.v.) in 1906. Arrested in 1909, he was soon released but was rearrested in 1910. He escaped from Russia in 1911 and moved to Germany where he remained until the beginning of World War I (q.v.). He then lived in Switzerland, Sweden and the United States. In New York, he coedited with Leon Trotsky (q.v.) a radical Russian-language newspaper. He returned to Russia after the February 1917 revolution (q.v.) and occupied a number of high party posts. He was a member of the Politburo (q.v.) until his break with Stalin (q.v.) in 1928 over the forced collectivization of the peasantry. Demoted, he was made editor of the official government newspaper, *Izvestiia* (q.v.), which post he occupied until his arrest in 1937. Tried at a Moscow (q.v.) show trial, he was executed in 1938 as a traitor and a spy.

BULGAKOV, MIKHAIL A. (1891–1940). A prominent literary figure, he remained in Russia after 1917. His work initially received Stalin's (q.v.) approval because of his belief in the inevitability of the revolution. However, his most memorable work, *The Master and Margarita*, was written in secret and was published only after his death.

BULGAKOV, SERGEI N. (1871–1944). The son of a priest, he graduated from the University of Moscow (*see* Universities) in 1894 and became a Marxist. He served as a professor at the Moscow Institute of Commerce and was a member of the second Duma (q.v.). He participated in the 1909 Vekhi (q.v.) movement, which attempted to steer the Russian intelligentsia away from political activism and toward religion. Bulgakov was ordained a priest in 1918. After he was expelled from Russia in 1923, he moved to France and served as dean of the St. Sergius Theological Institute in Paris. He also played an active intermediary role between Protestant and Catholic circles in Europe.

BULGANIN, NIKOLAI A. (1895–1975). An early member of the Cheka (q.v.) and a member of the Central Committee of the Communist Party (q.v.) since 1934, he was the Soviet defense minister between 1953 and 1955 and then prime minister. After Bulganin joined the "Anti-Party" group in 1957 against Khrushchev (q.v.), he was forced to retire.

BUND. This organization was established in 1897 by Jewish workers in the western part of the Russian empire. It was affiliated with the Russian Socialist Democratic Labor Party (q.v.).

BUNIN, IVAN A. (1870–1953). His poetry was first published in 1891. Beginning in 1909, Bunin traveled abroad and was acknowledged as a master of Russian prose. He emigrated to France after the revolution and remained a strong opponent of Communism. Bunin received the Nobel Prize for literature in 1933.

BURLIUK, DAVID D. (1882–1967). After studying art in Russia and abroad, he began exhibiting his paintings in Munich in 1910 at the invitation of Kandinskii (q.v.). In 1919 Burliuk left Russia permanently and moved to the United States, where he settled on Long Island and continued painting.

BURTSEV, VLADIMIR L. (1862–1942). A member of the People's Will terrorist group in the late 1880s, he was arrested and exiled to Siberia (q.v.). From exile he fled to England and Switzerland, where he was active in editing Russian revolutionary publications. In 1905 Burtsev returned to Russia to edit a St. Petersburg (q.v.) historical periodical and gained fame for unmasking such police provocateurs as Azef (q.v.) and Malinovskii (q.v.). Burtsev left Russia again after the October 1917 revolution (q.v.) and published a newspaper in Paris, acquiring a reputation for being the "conscience of the revolution."

BURYATIA AUTONOMOUS REPUBLIC. Located between the Mongolian People's Republic (q.v.) and Lake Baikal (q.v.), its economy is based on cattle raising. The population is just under one million.

BUTLEROV, ALEKSANDR M. (1828–86). A graduate of Kazan University in 1849, he was first a professor there and then head of the chemistry department at the University of St. Petersburg (*see* Universities). Butlerov discovered the formaldehyde polymer and proposed a theory to explain the structure of organic matter that became the basis of organic chemistry. He is the author of several major works in the field of chemistry.

BUTURLIN, COUNT ALEKSANDR (1694–1767). He rose in rank during the reign of Empress Elizabeth (q.v.) and in 1760 became commander of the Russian armies during the Seven Years' War (q.v.) with Prussia.

BYELORUSSIA see BELARUS

BYLINY. These are ancient Russian epic poems, some dating from before Russia's conversion to Christianity in the 990s. They recount events in Kievan Rus (q.v.).

C

CADET. This name is used for a student at one of the 27 Cadet Corps schools founded beginning in 1733. These were military training institutions maintained by the Russian state. They had a seven-year curriculum with a heavy emphasis on preparation for military service as officers. Students began their studies at eight or nine years of age and, after graduation, usually entered one of the military academies.

CADRES. This was the official Soviet designation of the leading members of the Communist Party (q.v.) and the Soviet government. A great deal of attention was paid to the training of such individuals, beginning with their participation and performance in the Communist youth organizations—Pioneers (q.v.), followed by the Komsomol (q.v.). The cadre department of the Communist Party's Central Committee had jurisdiction over all important party and state appointments.

CASPIAN SEA. The largest inland body of salt water in the world, it lies between Asia and Southwest Europe. The Volga River (q.v.) flows into it at its northern end.

CATHERINE I, EMPRESS AND TSARITSA (1684–1727). She was the second wife of Peter the Great, whom she married in 1712. She was born into a Lithuanian peasant family and taken as prisoner of war by the Russian army. Peter encountered her at the house of Prince Menshikov and made her his mistress. Crowned empress-consort in 1724, Catherine was declared empress-regent after Peter's death in 1725.

CATHERINE THE GREAT, EMPRESS AND TSARITSA, (1729–96). Born in Stettin, Germany, she converted to Orthodoxy in 1744 and married the future Tsar Peter III (q.v.) in 1745. After her husband was murdered by Prince Potemkin (q.v.) and, probably, Count Orlov (q.v.), she became Empress of Russia. A 1773 peasant rebellion led by Pugachev (q.v.) was put down after great difficulty and her regime grew increasingly repressive. During her reign, Russia expanded its territory to the south and annexed the Crimea (q.v.) from Turkey, as well as fully absorbing the Ukraine (q.v.), or "borderlands," and a part of the kingdom of Poland, which was partitioned between Russia, Prussia and Austria. Catherine's plans for educational and legal reforms were not completed by the time of her death, and the lot of the serf peasantry had grown worse.

CAUCASUS. A chain of mountains that separates the Black (q.v.) and the Caspian (q.v.) seas. The area is inhabited by a large number of ethnic groups. Its northern region is part of the Russian Republic and includes several autonomous areas inhabited by such peoples as the Ossets (q.v.), the Ingush (q.v.) and the Chechens (*see* Chechnya).

CAVALIERS OF ST. GEORGE. The highest military decoration awarded in Imperial Russia, it was established in 1769.

CENTRAL COMMITTEE OF THE COMMUNIST PARTY OF THE SOVIET UNION. This was the supreme organ of the party and carried out the work of the party congresses and conferences. Its committees, the political bureau (*see* Politburo), the organizational bureau (Orgburo), and the secretariat, constituted the primary organs of executive power not only in the Communist Party, but also in the Soviet government.

CENTRAL EXECUTIVE COMMITTEE OF THE CONGRESS OF SOVIETS. This was the central organ of state power established by the Soviet regime after the October 1917 revolution (q.v.). It was kept in the Soviet Union after 1927, but following adoption of the 1936 Stalin Constitution, (*see* Constitutions of the USSR and Russia), its functions were assumed by the Supreme Soviet (q.v.) and its Presidium.

CHAADAEV, PETR (1793–1856). A Russian author who, after he graduated from the university, joined the Russian army during the Napoleonic wars. Living in Moscow (q.v.) after the end of the war, Chaadaev wrote philosophical letters about Russia's backwardness and advocated Russia's conversion to Roman Catholicism. For this act the government authorities declared him to be insane, and he was placed under house arrest by Tsar Nicholas I (q.v.).

CHAGALL, MARC (b. SEGAL). (1887–1985). Born into a working class Hasidic family in Vitebsk (q.v.), he moved to St. Petersburg (q.v.) and studied art while working as a sign painter. In 1910 he moved to Paris, where he was strongly influenced by the Cubist school of painters. Chagall returned to Russia in 1914 and, in 1917, was appointed the commissar of fine arts in the city of Vitebsk, where he established an art academy. In 1922 Chagall left Russia for Berlin and then moved to Paris, where he lived until 1941, when he moved to New York. Chagall remained in the United States until the end of World War II (q.v.), then returned to France. Very much in demand, he received commissions from the Paris Opera as well as from the government of Israel.

CHAIKOVSKII, NIKOLAI V. (1852–1926). Son of a government official, he studied at the St. Petersburg University (*see* Universities) where in 1869 he organized a group of populists into a secret circle. The members of this circle were soon arrested by the Tsar's police and placed on trial. Chaikovskii escaped and emigrated to the United States in 1875, where he founded a commune in Kansas. In 1878 he went to Paris, then moved to London to become an active participant in the British labor movement. In 1904 Chaikovskii returned to Russia. After the October 1917 revolution he opposed the Communists and became the prime commissar of the Arkhangelsk (q.v.) territory, which was at that time under the control of a British expeditionary force. After the British pulled their troops out, Chaikovskii once again emigrated to France.

CHAIKOVSKII, PETR I. see TCHAIKOVSKY

CHALIAPIN, FEDOR see SHALIAPIN

CHAPAEV, VASILII I. (1887–1919). Famous (and largely apocryphal), this Soviet partisan leader during the civil war (q.v.) was a simple laborer who was elevated to the status of a hero by the 1934 film *Chapaev.*

CHECHEN-INGUSHIA AUTONOMOUS REPUBLIC see CHECHNYA

CHECHNYA. One of the autonomous republics of the Russian Federation in the Soviet period, it is located on the northern slopes of the Caucasus (q.v.) mountains. Its population is mainly Muslim and numbers approximately 1.2 million. Chechnya was conquered by Russia in the 19th century. During World War II a large part of the Chechen population allegedly collaborated with the German occupation troops, and the Chechens were deported on orders from Stalin (q.v.) to Central Asia.

   In 1991, after the breakup of the Soviet Union, Chechen leader, Jokhar Dudaev (q.v.) proclaimed himself the president of an independent Chechen republic. After months of unsuccessful negotiations, Russian president Yeltsin (q.v.) ordered the army to invade this territory and restore it as an autonomous republic within the Russian Federation. In June 1992 Ingushetia decided to separate from Chechnya to avoid further trouble. In April 1996, after bitter fighting and several hostage-taking incidents, Dudaev was killed in a rocket attack while talking on a cellular phone. He was succeeded by Vice President Zelimkhan Yandarbiev, and, in anticipation of presidential election in Russia in June of that year, Yeltsin managed to sign a ceasefire agreement with Chechen rebels.

CHEKA. The Russian acronym stands for the security police organization known initially as the All-Russian Extraordinary Commission for the Struggle against Counterrevolution and Sabotage. It was established in December 1917 by a decree of the Council of People's Commissars (q.v.) one month after the Communist seizure of power.

The head of this first Soviet security service was Feliks Dzerzhinskii (q.v.), a fanatical Communist who had been a political prisoner for over ten years in tsarist jails. The acronym has become the Russian colloquial expression for secret police. Later, the organization was renamed several times: GPU (q.v.), OGPU, NKVD (q.v.), and KGB (q.v.). One of the first serious tests of the Cheka was its ability to handle the anti-Communist rebellion of the Left-Socialist Revolutionaries (q.v.) in June 1918.

Since part of the organization's staff was made up of non-Communists, a purge of its employees was instituted, and anyone suspected of involvement with the rebellion was shot. The leadership of the Cheka under Dzerzhinskii was merciless in its handling of the Left-Socialist Revolutionary Party. By February 1919 over fifty of its leaders had been arrested, as well as numerous rank-and-file members. A widespread network of local Cheka offices was established in all the regions of the country, as well as in railroad and army units. These offices had the power to conduct arrests, carry out investigations, pronounce judgments, and execute their prisoners on their own recognizance.

The cruelty of the Cheka increased especially in the autumn of 1918, after the killing of one of the local Cheka representatives in Petrograd (q.v.) and after the attempt by Fanny Kaplan (q.v.), a young Socialist Revolutionary, on Lenin's (q.v.) life. Hundreds of individuals were shot without trial or investigation and terror became the principal political tool of the Soviet state. Wide use was made of hostages—innocent individuals who had been arrested by the Cheka and held as a guarantee for the behavior of the local population.

All actions against the Communist regime, including retreats by Red Army (see Armed Forces, Soviet) units, served as a basis for the shooting of these hostages. In the case of Red Army officers who defected to the White Armies (q.v.) side, the Cheka arrested their families and frequently executed them.

Another responsibility of the Cheka was to search for and eliminate individuals who did not agree with Communist Party (q.v.) policies.

From the first months of its existence, secret Cheka circulars urged the necessity of keeping lists of all counterrevolutionaries. Some of the most outstanding representatives of the Russian intelligentsia were placed into this category. The Cheka arrested workers as well as intellectuals, especially those who spoke out openly against such Soviet actions as the closing down of the Constituent Assembly (q.v.) in 1918 and the signing of the Brest-Litovsk Peace Treaty (q.v.) with Germany. In time, Cheka's repression of political deviants expanded. Even the local committees of the Communist Party were obliged regularly to provide it with information about the opinions of individual party members as well as about the mood of industrial workers.

Beginning in the summer of 1918, the Cheka started placing individuals in concentration camps. Initially, these were mainly people who had served in the White Armies, but later the contingent of those sent to the camps was widened to include all who appeared to be suspicious politically.

In the first years after the revolution there was a sharp increase in the number of criminal groups and thieves who robbed passersby or committed armed attacks on individuals. In February 1919 the Cheka began implementing measures to fight against banditry. Half of all actions of the Moscow Cheka dealt with criminal rather than political activity. During the initial period of Soviet rule, from 1917 to 1919, the Cheka's activities were hardly regulated at all. However, by the beginning of the 1920s, the government began to centralize the administration and control of its repressive organs and implemented a series of formal procedures.

In 1922, the Cheka formally ceased to exist; however, its staff was not dispersed. A new repressive police organization, the GPU, or Chief Political Administration, was established in its place, attached to the Commissariat of Internal Affairs.

CHEKHOV, ANTON P. (1860–1904). Born in Taganrog (q.v.) on the Black Sea (q.v.), he studied medicine at Moscow University (*see* Universities) and graduated in 1884. After his graduation Chekhov turned to writing and soon became well known for his plays and short stories. For most of his adult life Chekhov was ill with tuberculosis and lived in the Crimea (q.v.) as well as at health resorts abroad.

CHELIABINSK. A major city in the Ural mountains (q.v.), it is the capital of the region of the same name. It is situated on the Trans-Siberian Railroad (q.v.) and has an industrial base of iron and steel, as well as manufacturing agricultural equipment. Its population is over 1,000,000.

CHERKASSOV, NIKOLAI K. (1903–66). A distinguished film actor of the 1930s, he began his career as a vaudeville comedian, then moved to films where he played leading roles in such Eisenstein (q.v.) films as *Ivan the Terrible* and *Aleksandr Nevskii*, as well as the 1939 film, *Lenin*.

CHERNENKO, KONSTANTIN U. (1911–85). Born into a peasant family, he joined the Communist Party (q.v.) in 1930 while serving in the border guards. In the 1950s Chernenko moved to Moldova (q.v.), where he began his close association with Brezhnev (q.v.), who at the time was first secretary of that republic. Chernenko followed Brezhnev to Moscow (q.v.) and was elected a member of the Central Committee of the Communist Party (q.v.) and its Politburo (q.v.) in 1978. In 1984, after the death of Andropov (q.v.), Chernenko was selected as the general secretary of the Communist Party but he died a year later.

CHERNOBYL. This Ukrainian city north of Kiev (q.v.) is where a serious nuclear accident occurred in April 1986, when a reactor exploded, killing at least 30 people at the site and covering much of Europe with fallout. The exact extent and gravity of the damage is still curiously obscure.

CHERNOMYRDIN, VIKTOR (1938–). A strong and loyal supporter of Boris Yeltsin (q.v.), Chernomyrdin studied engineering and worked in the Orsk oil refinery and later became manager of the Orenburg gas refinery. From 1978 to 1982 he was a member of the Central Committee of the Communist Party (q.v.), then deputy minister of the gas industry, and finally head of the ministry of oil and gas industries. In 1992 Boris Yeltsin appointed him prime minister; in 1995 he gained attention for his successful negotiations with Chechen rebels during a hostage-taking incident in Budennovsk, caused by Russian military intervention in Chechnya (q.v.). In that year he founded "Our Home Is Russia" (Nash dom-Rossiia), which presented a middle-of-the-road, even conservative, profile. In the 1995 Duma (q.v.) elections it won 9.89 percent of the total party-list vote and acquired ten Duma seats, for a total of 45 seats.

CHERNOV, VIKTOR M. (1876–1952). The political leader of the Socialist Revolutionaries (q.v.) party, which he helped found in 1902, Chernov was a strong opponent of Marxism-Leninism and of the Russian Socialist Democratic Labor Party (q.v.). He served in the Provisional government (q.v.) as minister of agriculture, and in January 1918 he presided over the short-lived Constituent Assembly (q.v.).

He left Russia in 1920 and moved first to Paris, then to the United States.

CHERNYI PEREDEL. This Russian phrase is usually translated as "Black Repartition." It was the name of a revolutionary organization formed in Switzerland by Russian emigres such as Plekhanov (q.v.), Zasulich (q.v.) and Akselrod (q.v.). It was the antiterrorist splinter of the populist Zemlia i Volia (q.v.) party, whose majority advocated individual terror in order to achieve their political aims. The primary demand of Chernyi Peredel was the repartition of tillable soil among the working peasantry.

CHERNYSHEVA, LIUBOV P. (1890–1976). A world-famous ballerina and graduate of the St. Petersburg (q.v.) Theater School in 1908, she was a pupil of Fokin (q.v.) and became a member of Diaghilev's (q.v.) ballet troupe in Paris. Chernysheva settled in France in 1912, where she danced with the Ballets Russes (q.v.) and worked with Fokin and Ballanchin (q.v.). She choreographed ballets for La Scala and Saddler Wells and in 1938 moved to London, where she taught ballet.

CHERNYSHEVSKII, NIKOLAI G. (1828–89). Born in Saratov (q.v.), he became the intellectual leader of the radicalized Russian youth in the middle of the 19th century. An author and journalist, he was employed by the progressive journal *Sovremennik* (q.v.). Chernyshevskii spent nearly 20 years in Siberian exile after his arrest by the tsarist police. His political novel, *What Is to Be Done?* (q.v.) was a major influence on Lenin (q.v.) and other Russian revolutionaries.

CHICHERIN, GEORGI M. (1872–1936). The son of a nobleman and graduate of St. Petersburg University (*see* Universities), he joined the Russian Socialist Democratic Labor Party (q.v.) and emigrated from Russia in 1904. After the revolution, Chicherin returned to Russia, joined the Communist Party (q.v.) and became the commissar of foreign affairs. He resigned all his government posts in 1930 because of illness.

CHIEF PROCURATOR OF THE MOST HOLY SYNOD. The main administrative officer of the Most Holy Synod (q.v.) was introduced in 1722. His authority began to grow in the later 18th century, culminating in the right to exclusive access to the emperor by the beginning of the 19th century. In the early part of that century, however, government ministries began to encroach on various areas of the chief procurator's interest; this was remedied by giving the chief procurator ministerial authority in 1824. The last chief procurator was A. V. Kartshev, under whom the position was renamed minister of confessions in 1917, shortly before its abolition.

CHINESE FAR EASTERN RAILROAD (KVZhD). This was a railroad built by Russia during the 1880s within a zone of exclusion across Manchuria granted to Russia by the Chinese government. It provided a rail connection to the Pacific Ocean port of Vladivostok (q.v.) from eastern Siberia. After 1917 it was taken over by the Russo-Asiatic Bank and administered by its general director, engineer B. V. Ostroumoff. In 1927 the Soviet government abrogated the former tsarist treaty, and the ownership of the railroad reverted to the Chinese republic. (*See* Trans-Siberian railroad)

CHITA. A south Siberian town, population 375,000, it is an important rail center on the river Chita. The town was founded in 1653, and served as an exile post for the Decembrists (q.v.).

CHKHEIDZE, NIKOLAI S. (1864–1926). The leader of the Social Democrats (*see* Russian Socialist Democratic Labor Party) in the Duma (q.v.), he was chairman of the Petrograd soviet (q.v.) after the February 1917 revolution (q.v.). Chkheidze returned to Georgia after the Communists overthrew the Provisional government (q.v.) in October 1917 and became the president of the Georgian Republic (*see* Georgia). After the occupation of Georgia by Soviet armed forces, he escaped to France.

CHORNYI, SASHA (b. GLIKBERG) (1880–1932). A humorist and satirical poet and short-story writer, he wrote parodies of other poets and, in later years, verses for children. After emigrating to France in 1920 he published a number of anti-Communist works.

CHRISTIANITY, CONVERSION TO. The conversion of the Eastern Slavs—the Rus (q.v.)—occurred in 988 after Prince Vladimir (q.v.) of Kiev (q.v.) chose the Byzantine Orthodox Christianity (*see* Orthodox Church) as his state religion. He had himself baptized and married the sister of a Byzantine emperor. Following the prince's conversion, the entire population of Kiev was baptized en masse.

CHRONICLES. These were annals written over a period of several centuries by monks and lawyers. They constitute the most extensive surviving literature of ancient Rus (q.v.) and include the Primary Chronicle (q.v.), which covers the period until 1110, as well as the Kievan Chronicle, which takes history up to 1200.

CHUBAR, V. I. (1891–1939). A member of the Bolshevik (q.v.) faction since 1907, Chubar was a leader of the St. Petersburg workers during 1917. After the October revolution (q.v.) Chubar became a member of the presidium of the supreme council of the national economy of the Ukraine (q.v.) and then a member of the Politburo (q.v.) of the Ukrainian Communist Party. In 1939 he was executed by Stalin (q.v.).

CHUDSKOE LAKE, BATTLE OF (1224). This battle was fought by Prince Aleksandr Nevskii (q.v.) against invading Teutonic knights on Peipus Lake (q.v.), the larger of two lakes that are located between Estonia and the Russian Republic.

CHUKCHIS. Nomadic hunters and reindeer herdsmen living on the Chukhotsk Peninsula, at the northeasternmost tip of Siberia (q.v.), they are one of the Paleoasitic peoples, related to the Koryaks. The languages spoken by these groups are possibly related to Yupik and Inuktitut.

CHURCH SLAVONIC. This was a language used by the Byzantine missionaries, Sts. Cyril and Methodius (q.v.), in their conversion of the Eastern Slavs. A modified version of this language continues to be employed by the Russian Orthodox Church (q.v.) in its offices.

CHUVASHIA AUTONOMOUS REPUBLIC. An autonomous republic of the Russian Federation located on the Volga River (q.v.), its principal industries are lumber, farming, chemicals and textiles.

CINEMA. The first cinefilms and news chronicles were shown in Russia at the end of the 19th century. After the turn of the century Russian cinematography grew rapidly, and some 2,000 films were produced before World War I (q.v.).

The film industry was nationalized by the Soviet government in 1919 and placed under the Commissariat of Education. In 1922 Goskino was established as the centralized organization for Soviet cinema. In 1924 it was renamed Sovkino. During the civil war (q.v.) cinematography was widely used for propaganda purposes, with this trend continuing through the 1920s with documentary films. In this period Russian cinema acquired a worldwide reputation, primarily as a result of the work of Pudovkin (q.v.) and Eisenstein (q.v.). These outstanding directors produced such film classics as *Battleship Potemkin*, *October* and *The Mother*.

Toward the end of the 1920s new, well-equipped studios were built, and the Soviet Union began to produce its own cinematographic equipment. A large network of film theaters was also constructed. At the same time, Soviet cinematography began to undergo a crisis provoked by the pressure from the Communist Party (q.v.) to produce politically correct films. During the Stalin (q.v.) period especially, Soviet cinema was largely transformed into a propaganda instrument. However, a number of films were made of outstanding Russian literary classics, such as *Anna Karenina*.

With the coming of World War II (q.v.) Soviet cinema redirected its efforts to create documentary films and newscasts. After the end of the war, the state-initiated campaigns against cosmopolitanism and the tightening of censorship had a negative impact on further development of art, until the death of Stalin and the beginning of the "thaw" (q.v.).

New growth in Soviet filmmaking occurred in the 1960s, after Moscow began hosting international film festivals. The Brezhnev (q.v.) period saw Soviet studios producing a large number of mediocre films. There was also an intensification of government pressure on the film industry to conform to state political demands. Thus, in 1962 the film director Tarkovskii (q.v.) was severely criticized by Soviet film critics for his *Andrei Rublev*, primarily for political reasons.

With the beginning of perestroika (q.v.) in the middle 1980s, many previously forbidden films, some of which had lain on the shelf for over 20 years, began to be publicly shown, and new films such as *Little Vera* received large popular acclaim because they showed for the first time in Soviet history many of the ills of Soviet society, such as alcoholism and mass cynicism. In 1987 the film *Repentance*, directed by Georgian Tengiz Abuladze, was seen by over 4,000,000 viewers in the Soviet Union. Its theme was the rise and fall of the Stalin dictatorship and the evils of totalitarianism.

CIRCASSIA (KARACHAEVO-CHERKES AUTONOMOUS REGION). Much of this North Caucasus region is now in the Stavropol oblast. "Circassians" are now commonly identified with the Adygeians, Abkhazi and other groups of speakers of northwest Caucasian languages.

CIVIL WAR (1918–22). The Communist seizure of power in October 1917 was opposed by a portion of the Russian population and resulted in a civil war that lasted until the end of 1922. The dissolution of the Constituent Assembly (q.v.) by Baltic fleet sailors in January 1918 was a signal for unification of all democratic elements of the country. Resistance to the Soviet government policy of war communism, with its forcible requisitioning of farm produce grew in intensity. In response, the Communist Party mobilized urban workers into armed detachments charged with confiscating the peasants' harvest.

Initially localized in the south of Russia and the Don Cossack (q.v.) regions, the anti-Communist movement soon spread eastward to Siberia (q.v.), north to the Arkhangelsk (q.v.) region, to the Far Eastern Republic (q.v.), and even to the vicinity of St. Petersburg (q.v.). At first it bore a local character, but in the spring of 1918 some 40,000 men, led by General Krasnov (q.v.), began military activities in southern Russia. This was one of the first of the anti-Communist White Armies (q.v.).

At the same time the Czech Legion (q.v.), composed of Austro-Hungarian prisoners of war, was retreating eastward through Siberia toward the Pacific Ocean. This body of armed men also joined the struggle against the Soviets.

Both of these anti-Soviet groups initially made substantial progress. Soviet power was overthrown in a number of places, including the Volga (q.v.) and the Ural (q.v.) regions and in Siberia (q.v.). In the territories that were freed, new governments were formed, consisting primarily of Socialist Revolutionaries (q.v.) and other prodemocratic elements that had led the February 1917 revolution (q.v.). Their aim was to transfer state power to a reconstituted Constituent Assembly. However, there was a conspicuous lack of unity among them, and very soon White Army officers in Siberia instituted a military dictatorship under a supreme leader, Admiral Kolchak (q.v.), who established his headquarters in Omsk (q.v.). Lack of a united political program played a large role in the eventual defeat of the White movement. Another factor was its inability to win the support of the Russian peasantry, the country's most numerous layer. The peasants viewed the White forces as being on the side of the former landlords and preferred the Soviets to them.

A further factor in the eventual triumph of the Soviets was their implacable use of mass terror through the Cheka (q.v.), including the wholesale incarceration of their opponents in concentration camps. These measures proved effective, and by 1920 the Red Army recaptured the initiative. Admiral Kolchak was taken prisoner and executed. The northern front was liquidated in 1920 after the departure of the intervening British expeditionary force. In the south, first General Denikin (q.v.) and then his successor, General Wrangel (q.v.), were defeated and forced to evacuate their last stronghold, the Crimean (q.v.) peninsula, in 1920. Also by 1920 the Red Army had succeeded in recapturing the Ukraine (q.v.) and Belarus (q.v.) from occupying Polish troops. The final act of the civil war (q.v.) was the defeat of the White armies in the Far East and their forced evacuation to China in 1922.

CLIMATE, RUSSIAN. On the whole, Russia has a moderate continental climate. Only the extreme northern region lies in the cold zone. In the south, especially in the Black Sea (q.v.) region of the Caucasus (q.v.), the climate is subtropical. The territory of the country is extensive, in both the north-south and the west-east directions. There are significant variations in climate depending on the width of the landmass from sea to sea.

Moving west to east from St. Petersburg (q.v.), one moves from relatively mild winters and moderate summers to Siberia (q.v.), which is characterized by heavy frost in winter and a short, hot, and humid summer. The annual temperature of continental Russia is usually highest in July and lowest in January. The lowest average temperature in winter is in Verkhoiansk (q.v.), Siberia, where it can drop to -50 degrees centigrade in January. In the south of the country the summer temperature reaches +24 degrees.

The climate of the Far Eastern Republic (q.v.) is quite different. In this region there are frequent strong winds, the monsoons, that flow from the continent toward the ocean in winter and from the opposite direction in summer. As a result of these winds, the average January temperature of the Kamchatka (q.v.) peninsula is almost the same as that of Moscow (q.v.), even though Kamchatka is on the same latitude as mainland Siberia, where the cold drops to -35 degrees.

In the western regions of European Russia precipitation reaches 600mm to 700mm, then gradually drops as one moves east, north and southeast. Thus in Sakha (formerly Iakutiia), Siberia, precipitation is less than 100mm per annum.

In winter, almost all of the Russian Federation is covered by snow. The length of time that snow remains on the ground varies from an average of 60 days in central European Russia to 260 days in the extreme north. The deepest layers of snow occur in the Ural (q.v.) region, in western Siberia and in Kamchatka, where its depth reaches up to 80cm. In the Russian Far East, the depth of snow is considerably less, but the thin layer, combined with heavy frost, creates a condition in which the soil is permanently frozen. Such zones are also found in the European tundra areas of western Siberia. In the southernmost areas of Russia, on the Black Sea coast, snow is infrequent and melts rapidly.

COLLECTIVIZATION OF AGRICULTURE. In 1929 Stalin (q.v.) initiated a forcible integration of the Russian peasantry into large communes, or collective farms, which were rigidly regulated by the state. This transformation of Russian agriculture was accompanied by a mass deportation of kulaks (q.v.), or rich peasants, because they resisted this measure. Russian agriculture suffered very heavy losses, especially in livestock, that resulted in a period of severe famine in several regions of the Soviet Union, including the Russian Volga (q.v.) region, large areas of the Ukraine (q.v.), the Don River (q.v.) region, and western Siberia, during which millions of peasants died of starvation.

COMECON. This acronym refers to the Council for Mutual Economic Assistance, which was established in 1949 by the Soviet Union to link the economies of the USSR with the eastern European countries it dominated. It is now disbanded.

COMINFORM. This was the name by which the Communist Information Bureau came to be known. It was established in 1946 in Belgrade, Yugoslavia, and took on some of the functions of the Communist International (*see* Comintern), which had been dissolved by Stalin (q.v.) in 1943. The Cominform published a newspaper and sought to coordinate the activities of its European satellites, as well as those of the Communist parties of Western Europe. After Stalin's break with Yugoslavia in 1948, its headquarters were moved to Bucharest, Romania.

COMINTERN. This was the term used to designate the Communist, or Third, International, an organization established by Lenin (q.v.) in 1919 to act as the "general staff" of the world revolution. During its existence, it directed the activities of all of the member Communist parties from its Moscow (q.v.) headquarters. Nominally superior to any national party, including that of the USSR, it was in fact an instrument of Soviet foreign policy.

The idea of creating a new International had been discussed by Lenin's followers at the beginning of World War I (q.v.). The core of the new organization was made up of Russian Bolsheviks (q.v.) and the members of the German Spartak Union. Around them, representatives of the left socialist movements in many countries united and, in March of 1919, the birth of the Communist Third International was announced in Moscow. Its constituent congress proclaimed the thesis that the "dictatorship of the proletariat" was a form of proletarian democracy and a distinctive characteristic of Communist revolutionary strategy.

The prestige of the Russian revolution during this period was very high among the workers of North America and Western Europe, and many of the delegates to this first congress believed in the proximate coming of a world socialist revolution. They considered it essential to institute an iron discipline in the various national Communist parties in order to protect the International from the influence of socialists, whom they considered to be mere reformists. For this purpose they proclaimed a set of 21 conditions for admission. These conditions included the acceptance of the necessity of proletarian dictatorship as the main principle of revolutionary struggle, as well as an ideological adherence to Marxism. Another of the conditions was the acceptance of the structure of "democratic centralism" as the organizational basis for individual Communist parties.

In 1920/1921, Communist parties came into being in the majority of Western countries, as well as in some Asian states. However, they never succeeded in becoming the majority parties within their respective working classes. In 1921 the Comintern consisted of over one million supporters outside of Russia, while the various socialist parties (which were members of the Second, or Socialist, International) had some eight million adherents.

In the summer of 1921 the third congress of the Communist International took place in Moscow. By this time it had become clear that it was futile to count on a world revolution, and the congress called for Communists around the world to change tactics that had been designed primarily to foment an immediate revolution and to participate in the struggle of workers for the improvement of their living conditions. This policy aided the growth of a number of Communist front organizations: the Committee for International Workers' Aid, the Trade Union International (Profintern), the Peasant International (Krestintern), and the Communist International of Youth.

At the fifth Congress of the Comintern in 1924, Zinovev (q.v.), who was then the head of the Comintern, defined social democrats as the left wing of fascism. To the extent that there was no possibility of a world revolution taking place, the defense of the USSR from external intervention and the building of socialism there became in fact the first order of business of the Comintern.

In 1927 Stalin declared that Europe was entering a new era of revolutionary upheavals. Basing itself on this thesis, the Comintern initiated a struggle against the "right-wing opportunists" of the socialist parties, on the ground that they were preventing Communists from utilizing the sharpening of the class struggle in Germany and other countries to take power.

In 1928, the sixth congress of the Comintern once again predicted the proximate sharpening of the "contradictions of capitalism" and the growth of class warfare. From this time on, social democrats were referred to as "social fascists." Those members of the Comintern who did not agree with Stalin's line were expelled.

The seventh congress of the Comintern took place in August 1935. It was dominated by Dmitrov, the Bulgarian Communist who had distinguished himself as a defendant in the Reichstag fire mounted by the Nazi government in Germany. In his report Dmitrov emphasized the desirability of "united front" policies in order to prevent further fascist advances and declared that it was essential to unify with all other socialist parties in the struggle against fascism. He also underscored the need for Communists to protect democratic achievements, to respect national feelings, and to understand the specifics of the revolutionary struggle within each country. This congress was a turning point in the history of the Third International. The struggle against war and fascism became the basic direction of its activities.

In 1938 Stalin initiated a major repression against those members of the International who had moved to Russia in order to escape fascism in their own countries. Such outstanding foreign Communists as the Hungarian Bela Kun and the German Eberlein were arrested, and the Communist party of Poland was abolished. The 1939 nonaggression pact between Germany and the USSR was a major blow to the Comintern, with national Communist Parties suffering major losses of membership because of it. In 1943, in order to placate the United States and Great Britain, Stalin unilaterally abolished the Comintern.

COMMAND-ADMINISTRATIVE SYSTEM. This is the name given to the Soviet system of top-down state administration characterized by centralized planning carried out by a hierarchical bureaucracy. Since the collapse of Communism a number of Russian commentators have blamed this system for most of the economic shortcomings of the former Soviet Union.

COMMISSAR see KOMMISSAR

COMMONWEALTH OF INDEPENDENT STATES (SODRUZHES-TVO NEZAVISIMYKH GOSUDARSTV). With the collapse of the Soviet Union in 1991, a new organization was established at a meeting of the leaders of Russia, Belarus and Ukraine near Minsk. On December 12, at a meeting in Ashkhabad, Turkmenistan, leaders of Kazakhstan, Kirghizstan, Tajikistan, Turkmenistan and Uzbekistan also decided to join. Moldova, Azerbaijan and Armenia joined on December 21 on the occasion of the formalization of the establishment of the CIS in Alma-Ata, Kazakhstan.

COMMUNIST INTERNATIONAL see COMINTERN

COMMUNIST PARTY OF THE SOVIET UNION (CPSU). In March 1898 in Moscow, the Russian Socialist Democratic Labor Party (q.v.) was established. This was to become the official name of the Communist party of the Soviet Union. The party was very small and weak, and its program was not formulated until 1903, during its second congress held in London. At this congress a serious ideological difference occurred between Lenin (q.v.) and Martov (q.v.), its two principal leaders. A slim majority of the delegates approved Lenin's stance, and from that time his supporters began to be known by the Russian term "Bolsheviks" (q.v.), or "majoritarians," whereas the minority was labelled "Mensheviks" (q.v.), or "minoritarians." Lenin's thesis concerning the necessity of overthrowing the tsarist autocracy by force was accepted, as were his demands for the abolition of all private land ownership and the establishment of a "dictatorship of the proletariat" (q.v.) as a precondition for the building of a socialist society in Russia. Tied directly to these propositions was his insistence on a revolutionary party of a new type, one in which the lower units would be subordinate to the higher levels of the party hierarchy and in which all members would be obligated to support decisions made by a majority of the party. Lenin envisaged that the principal form of party activity would be political agitation and propaganda as well as publishing newspapers.

During the February 1917 revolution (q.v.) the Communist (Bolshevik) Party numbered fewer than 350,000 individuals throughout the whole of the Russian empire. However, after Lenin's return from Switzerland in April of that year, its influence grew rapidly, especially among the workers of St. Petersburg (q.v.) and Moscow (q.v.) and within the army at the front. Lenin came out for a socialist revolution and against a coalition with any other party. After lengthy hesitations, in October 1917 the Central Committee of the Communist Party approved Lenin's demand for an armed insurrection against the Provisional government (q.v.). The Bolsheviks thus became the main organizers of the October 1917 revolution (q.v.). The coming to power of the Communist Party in Russia signaled the beginning of the stifling of the democratic freedoms that had been won during the February 1917 revolution. As early as October 1917 the Constitutional Democratic (KD) party (*see* Kadet Party) was declared illegal, and other parties were also soon outlawed. The liquidation of the Socialist Revolutionaries (q.v.) party in the middle of 1918 led to the final consolidation of a one-party system in Russia and the establishment of a power monopoly by the Communist Party (Bolsheviks). As it evolved, the party came to be based on a territorial/industrial structure, with its primary units (cells) located in territorial or work units. These units were subordinated to a hierarchy that culminated with the party's Central Committee, dominated by its Politburo (q.v.). The Politburo in turn, was controlled by the party's general secretary (q.v.)— first Lenin, then Stalin (q.v.), then Malenkov (q.v.), Khrushchev (q.v.), Brezhnev (q.v.), Andropov (q.v.), Chernenko (q.v.), and finally Gorbachev (q.v.).

By the summer of 1918 the Communist Party completely controlled the government of the USSR. The members of its political bureau (Politburo) and its Central Committee occupied all of the leading positions within the Central Executive Committee of the Supreme Soviet (q.v.) and the Council of People's Commissars (q.v.)—the ruling state institutions of the Soviet Union. At the 17th congress of the Communist Party in 1934, some of the "Old Bolsheviks," as those who had joined it before the revolution were known, seem to have attempted to reduce the personal power of Stalin (q.v.). In this they failed. Some months later, Stalin, with the help of the secret police as well as of the party's bureaucracy, began to eliminate all those within the party who had opposed, or potentially could have opposed his policies.

In 1952, at the 19th congress of the Communist Party the party's name was changed to the Communist Party of the Soviet Union.

After the death of Stalin, the first tentative attempts to democratize the internal life of the party were undertaken by Khrushchev. Party congresses and the plenums of the Central Committee began to be held on schedule, and opponents of the top leaders, instead of being automatically executed, were merely expelled. The role of the republican and regional party committees was also increased. During the Brezhnev period, from 1964 to 1982, efforts to democratize the internal regime of the party were stopped and corruption and nepotism flourished. In 1985 Gorbachev was elected to the post of general secretary of the Communist Party of the Soviet Union. From the very beginning of his rule he began to carry out reforms. At the January 1987 plenum of the Central Committee, the process of democratization of Soviet society received his strong endorsement. At the party conference of June 1988 political openness (*see* glasnost) was proclaimed. Then at the 28th party congress the critical situation of Soviet society was given open recognition. By this time the role of the Communist Party had been considerably reduced and that of the country's elected councils (soviets) heightened. Their role in the economic life of the country was likewise enhanced. However, these changes displeased members of the Communist establishment, who saw their basis of power being reduced. Many of these individuals supported the August 1991 coup that attempted to overthrow President Gorbachev and restore the old party regime. This coup failed and resulted in the Communist Party being declared illegal. Soon thereafter, in December 1991, the collapse of the USSR took place. The Communist Party that exists today in Russia, notwithstanding its general ideological agreement with Leninist doctrines, is quite different from the former party insofar as it endorses free elections and pluralism of political power.

CONCENTRATION CAMPS see GULAG

CONGRESS OF BERLIN. An international conference of European powers, it met shortly after the conclusion of the Russo-Turkish War (q.v.) in 1878. At that conference, many of Russia's gains from the war, and from the San Stephano treaty that had concluded it, were nullified.

CONGRESS OF THE COMMUNIST PARTY OF THE SOVIET UNION. These were irregularly held meetings of delegates of the Communist Party from the whole of the Soviet Union at which Central Committee (q.v.) and other governing party bodies were elected. Although nominally the supreme authority of the party, after the 1920s these congresses rubber-stamped policies of the party leadership.

Dates of the congresses are as follows:

First	March 1898
Second	July-August 1903
Third	April-May 1905
Fourth	April-May 1906
Fifth	May 1907
Sixth	August 1917
Seventh	March 1918
Eighth	March 1919
Ninth	March-April 1920
Tenth	March 1921
Eleventh	March 1922
Twelfth	April 1923
Thirteenth	May 1924
Fourteenth	December 1925
Fifteenth	December 1927
Sixteenth	June-July 1930
Seventeenth	January-February 1934
Eighteenth	March 1939
Nineteenth	October 1952
Twentieth	February 1956
Twenty-first	February 1959
Twenty-second	October 1961
Twenty-third	March-April 1966
Twenty-fourth	March-April 1971
Twenty-fifth	February 1976

Twenty-sixth   February-March 1981
Twenty-seventh   February-March 1986

CONGRESS OF VIENNA. This series of meetings between the rulers of Great Britain, Austria, Russia, and France followed the downfall of Napoleon Bonaparte in 1814–15.

CONSTITUENT ASSEMBLY. The democratically inclined groups in Imperial Russia had contended that the fundamental structure of Russian society should be decided by a constituent assembly. This was true even for the followers of Lenin (q.v.) during the period after the February 1917 revolution (q.v.). They too had called for the convocation of such an assembly. The Second Congress of Soviets had likewise called for a constituent assembly in October 1917, after the Communists had overthrown the Provisional government (q.v.) and had transferred all state power to the Soviets.

At the beginning of October Lenin had tried to postpone elections to the Constituent Assembly, fearing that his party would not receive a majority of the votes, but he was unable to get enough support for such a step. The hope of his supporters was that together with the Left-Socialist Revolutionaries (q.v.) and the Menshevik Internationalists, they would have enough votes to control this assembly. They proceeded to convene it, fearing that not to do so would unite all opposition forces against them. The elections that were held in the whole of the former empire in November 1917 resulted in a loss for the Communists, who won only 24 percent of the seats, whereas their opponents, the Socialist Revolutionaries, won a majority of representatives. These elections reflected a general turn of the country toward socialism but not toward the Communists. Having suffered this defeat, Lenin's followers began to prepare for the abrogation of the assembly by concentrating over 10,000 of the highly radicalized Baltic Sea (q.v.) fleet sailors in the capital. To further counterbalance the Constituent Assembly, they convened a session of the All-Russian Congress of Soviets (q.v.), which they controlled, for January 8, 1918.

On January 5, 1918, the opening session of the Constituent Assembly met and elected Chernov (q.v.), the leader of the Socialist Revolutionary Party, as chairman. The assembly also refused to endorse the Communist motion approving of the forcible transfer of state power to the soviets (q.v.), as well as the Communist-authored declaration of the rights of workers. Instead, it condemned the armed Communist takeover of power. At this point the Communists and their only allies, the Left-Socialist Revolutionaries, left the hall. Following their walkout, guards forced the assembly to adjourn. No further meetings of the Constituent Assembly were allowed, and on January 7, 1918, the All-Russian Central Executive Committee ordered its dissolution. This dispersal of the very first fully democratically elected governing body in Russian history signaled the start of a policy of repressions against all political parties hostile to the Communists. It was the first step toward the civil war (q.v.), which broke out a few months later, in the summer of 1918.

CONSTITUTIONAL DEMOCRATS (KDs) see KADET (KD) PARTY

CONSTITUTIONS OF THE USSR AND RUSSIA. The first Soviet constitution was adopted in July 1918 by the All-Russian Congress of Soviets (q.v.). According to this constitution, the supreme organ of state power of the RSFSR was declared to be the All-Russian Congress of Workers, Peasants and Soldiers. Between meetings of the congress, the All-Russian Central Executive Committee (VTsIK), elected by the congress and responsible to it, were to be the highest organs of state power. The lowest organs of executive power were the city and village councils, followed by their district, regional, and provincial equivalents.

The fundamental law of 1918 deprived entrepreneurs, receivers of rents, tradesmen and former policemen of their electoral rights, and decreased the relative electoral strength of the peasantry by fixing an unequal number of electors in urban and rural areas of the country: each rural district was to contain five times as many voters as an urban one. This constitution declared the Russian republic to be a federation of national republics and to be socialist in its nature. From this came the title: Russian Federative Socialist Republic (RSFSR). It also guaranteed freedom of conscience, of speech, of assembly, and of trade unions, although these guarantees were never implemented in practice. Work was declared to be mandatory for all citizens, as was a universal mandatory service in the armed forces of the country for all men. The dictatorship of the proletariat was defined as totally depriving the bourgeois class of state power.

A second constitution for the Soviet state was adopted by the All-Russian Congress of Soviets in January 1924 and included a declaration concerning the establishment of the Union of Soviet Socialist Republics (q.v.). According to this document, the federal government was to have control over foreign policy, the right to declare war and conclude peace, the borders of the USSR and of its constituent republics, admission of new republics into the union, the command of the military forces of the country, transportation and communication and the planning of the national economy. The jurisdiction over all questions was given to the union republics, each of which had the right to a free secession from the USSR. The supreme organ of power was to be the Supreme Congress of Soviets and, in the intervals between congresses, the Central Executive Committee of the Congress of Soviets (q.v.), which was to consist of two equal chambers: the Council of Nationalities and the Council of Union. The executive and administrative organ of the Central Executive Committee was to be the Council of People's Commissars (q.v.) of the USSR. The election system under this second constitution continued the disproportionate weighting of urban and rural voters that had been instituted by the first constitution, as well as the deprivation of certain categories of the population of their voting rights.

The third, or "Stalin," constitution, was proclaimed in 1936. In its content it appeared very democratic, because it abolished the voting prohibitions placed by the two previous documents on several categories of Soviet citizens and guaranteed all citizens the rights to the security of their homes; secrecy of correspondence; freedom of press, assembly, and meetings; employment, rest, and education; and material security in old age or in case of inability to work. This constitution proclaimed the USSR to be a socialist society of workers and peasants. The old Central Executive Council was replaced by the Supreme Soviet (q.v.), which consisted of the two chambers. However, almost all of these clauses remained on paper. Instead, the principal impact of this document was its declaration that the Communist Party was the "leading nucleus of all organizations" in the country.

In 1977 the fourth Soviet constitution was adopted. It declared that the USSR was a "people's socialist state" in which "all power belongs to the people," with the Communist Party occupying the leading political role. According to this constitution, the economic basis of the USSR was socialist ownership of the means of production in the form of state and collective farm property. The rights to health care and housing were added to the list of rights contained in the first three constitutions.

The currently effective constitution was promulgated in December 1993 and is sharply different from the previous four. According to this (fifth) Russian constitution, the Russian Federation is declared to be a democratic federal government based on the rule of law, with a republican form of state. It guarantees both the separation of the executive, judicial and legislative branches of government and their independence from each other. State power is to be implemented by the president, the federal Duma (q.v.), and the court of the Russian Federation. Ideological differences, full freedom of speech, and a multiparty system are recognized as legitimate by this document, as is the right to private property. The constitution defines the Russian state as a federal one, in which each citizen is guaranteed security, free medical services, and free preschool and secondary education. Among the responsibilities placed on citizens are the obligations of defending the country, the carrying out of military obligations, the safeguarding of nature, and the payment of taxes. The judiciary is guaranteed independence, and the powers of the Constitutional Court of the Russian Federation are spelled out.

CONSTRUCTIVISM. A school of Russian art that emphasized science and technology in art, it was especially influential in the fields of architecture and industrial design. Its members sought to free art from bourgeois influence.

CORRECTIVE LABOR CAMPS. Concentration camps were established by the Soviet government after the October 1917 revolution (q.v.). They evolved from camps where political prisoners were supposedly reeducated, into slave labor camps charged with the construction of large-scale projects such as canals, hydroelectric dams, and railroads. The chief administration of these camps was known by its Russian acronym, GULAG (q.v.).

COSMONAUT. This term is the Russian equivalent of the American astronaut and refers to an individual who was part of the Soviet corps of space explorers. The first of the Russian cosmonauts was Iurii Gagarin (q.v.).

COSMOS. The first serious theoretical efforts concerned with the possibility of sending cosmic instruments into space took place at the beginning of the 20th century. An important role in their development was played by Tsiolkovskii. He gathered around him a small group of enthusiasts who, in the 1920s and 1930s, united into a group for the study of the phenomenon of reactive movement. In 1933 they organized the Reactive Scientific Experimental Institute and in the 1930s began attempting to create a prototype of a ballistic rocket that would be capable of overcoming Earth's gravitational pull. In October 1957 the Soviet Union sent the first artificial satellite into orbit in preparation for a manned flight into the cosmos. In April 1961 Gagarin (q.v.) accomplished the first human flight around the earth. In 1967 a cosmic spaceship was launched for the purpose of carrying out scientific space experiments, and in 1971 the orbital station Saliut was launched with the mission of carrying out medical and biological research. It was equipped with a docking system to enable it to receive supply rockets. From that time on, the duration of the stay of human navigators has continued to lengthen, until the present record of over a year in space was reached by Russian cosmonauts. In addition to sending men into space, a number of unmanned satellites were launched for meteorological observations, and in 1961 a robot was landed on the Moon. Other automatic cosmic stations were sent to study Mars and Venus. In 1970 a self-propelled vehicle traveled on the surface of the Moon and studied it. The Soviet government funded this area of scientific activity generously because it perceived successes in cosmic research as helping to heighten the prestige of the socialist system. In the 1990s the various cosmological activities began to suffer from serious financial shortages. However, Russia continues to exploit its unique cosmic station *Mir* (*see* Mir) and has created the Russian Cosmic Space Agency, which is attempting to expand its international cooperative activities.

COSSACKS. These were groups of settlers on the outskirts of the Russian state in the 15th and 16th centuries. The tsars (q.v.) gave them special privileges and tax exemptions, as well as considerable self-government in exchange for supplying the state with contingents of troops (mostly cavalry). Traditionally very loyal to the tsar, the Cossacks were the mainstay of the imperial government until the 1917 revolution and the civil war (q.v.). Besides the Zaporozhnye Cossacks in the Ukraine, there were other Cossack groupings: the Don (q.v.), Kuban, Terek (q.v.), Orenburg (q.v.), Ural, and Amur (q.v.) Cossacks.

COUNCIL OF PEOPLE'S COMMISSARS (SOVET NARODNYKH KOMMISSAROV, or SOVNARKOM). The main executive body of the Soviet government was established by the All-Russian Congress of Soviets in 1917 and renamed the Council of Ministers in 1946.

CRIMEA. A peninsula that juts out into the Black Sea (q.v.), Crimea is joined to its northern shore by the Perekop (q.v.) Isthmus. Originally occupied by Tatars (q.v.), it was acquired for Russia by Empress Catherine the Great (q.v.). Cities such as Simferopol and Sebastopol (q.v.) were established in the 18th and 19th centuries. It was the battleground for the Crimean War (q.v.) between the Russian empire and a coalition of France, Turkey and Great Britain in the middle of the 19th century. Khrushchev (q.v.) gave the Crimea to the Ukrainian Soviet Socialist Republic (*see* Ukraine) in 1953 as a "birthday present" without consulting its predominantly Russian inhabitants. It is now an autonomous area within the Ukrainian Republic.

CRIMEAN TATARS. In 1239 Tatars (Mongols) of the Golden Horde (q.v.) occupied the Crimean peninsula. In 1475 it was conquered by the Turks, who established their rule over the Crimean khanate a few years later. With the Russian conquest of Crimea (q.v.) in the 18th century, most of the Tatars and the defeated Turks were expelled. In 1921 the Soviet government established the Tatarstan Autonomous Republic (q.v.). This republic was abolished following World War II (q.v.) as the result of allegations of Tatar collaboration with the German occupation troops. The Tatar population was evacuated to Central Asia and was not included in the 1957 Soviet government decree of the rehabilitation of deportees.

CRIMEAN WAR (1853–56). This war between the Russian empire and Great Britain, France and Turkey started because of a dispute over the control of holy places in Palestine. Most of the fighting took place on the Crimean (q.v.) peninsula, hence the name of the war. Russia was defeated and by the Treaty of Paris it agreed to make the Black Sea (q.v.) area a neutral zone.

CUI, CAESAR A. (1835–1918). A specialist in military engineering who reached the rank of general in the Russian imperial army, Cui served as professor at the Academy of Engineering in St. Petersburg (q.v.). He was also a highly regarded composer and music critic.

CYRILLIC ALPHABET, REFORM OF. The alphabet used in the Russian empire was originally developed by Sts. Cyril and Methodius (q.v.). Before it was modernized in 1917, the alphabet consisted of 36 letters; after the reform this number was reduced to 32.

CZECH LEGION. The Czech legion was formed in Russia during World War I (q.v.) from Autro-Hungarian prisoners of war who were ethnic Czechs and Slovaks. In 1918, after the Soviets signed a peace treaty with the German empire, these soldiers began making their way to the Western (French) front by moving east on the Trans-Siberian Railroad (q.v.) and then to North America. After they were attacked by Soviet troops, they began aiding local anti-Communist Russians. They occupied most of the towns on the railroad all the way to Vladivostok (q.v.). With their aid the anti-Communists were able to organize themselves into an army and begin a civil war (q.v.) against the Soviet government.

D

DACHA. This the Russian term for a summer country house. During the Soviet period the government provided such residences for leading political, state, and artistic figures.

DAGESTAN AUTONOMOUS REPUBLIC. Located in the Caucasus (q.v.), its population is close to two million, and comprises such ethnic groupings as the Kumyks (q.v.), the Dargwa (q.v.), and the Avars (q.v.). The main industries are farming and ranching. There is also some oil production and textile manufacturing and a woodworking industry.

DALIN, DAVID I. (b. LEVIN). (1889–1962). Having joined the Russian Socialist Democratic Labor Party (q.v.) in 1907, he became a member of the Menshevik Party Central Committee after 1917. He was expelled from Soviet Russia in 1921 and after 1939 lived in the United States, where he wrote extensively on Soviet affairs.

DAN, FEDOR I. (b. GURVICH) (1871–1947). A medical doctor by profession, he became a revolutionary at an early age and joined the Russian Socialist Democratic Labor Party (q.v.) in 1894. While an immigrant in Germany, he sided with the Menshevik (q.v.) faction. In 1917, after the February revolution (q.v.) he returned to Russia and strongly supported the Provisional government (q.v.). He remained in Russia following the October 1917 overthrow by the Communists, working as a doctor until he was expelled in 1922 as an enemy of the Soviet government. He participated in the work of the Second (Socialist) International after 1923.

DANIL ALEKSANDROVICH, GRAND PRINCE (1261–1303). Son of Aleksandr Nevskii (q.v.), he was grand prince of Moscow (q.v.), a principality created for him by his father in 1276. Under him, the city's domains were extended to the mouth of the Moscow River (q.v.) He was succeeded by his son Yuri.

DANILOVA, ALEKSANDRA (1904–). Trained at the Imperial Ballet, she became a member of Diaghilev's (q.v.) Ballets Russes (q.v.) company in France in 1924 and a prima ballerina. She later choreographed for Balanchin (q.v.) at the New York City Ballet.

DARGOMYZHSKII, ALEKSANDR (1813–69). This composer began as something of a dilettante but became an important songwriter and composed several operas. His *Stone Guest* (1872), based on the Pushkin work, was left to be finished by Cui (q.v.) and Rimskii-Korsakov (q.v.); it fully reflected Dargomyzhskii's favoring of dramatic impact over musical display in opera and became something of a textbook example for Russian opera.

DARGWA (also DARGIN). This is a collection of peoples who speak related though disparate northeast Caucasian languages. They number some 100,000 and inhabit southern Dagestan; they are mostly Sunnite Muslim.

DARUGA. This term denotes a Mongol official who governs a conquered territory, chiefly for purposes of census taking, assessment, and taxation, but also to administer law more generally. In the early years of the Mongol Yoke (q.v.) he was usually a powerful member of the emperor's circle, but later there were non-Mongol appointees. Compare modern Mongolian *darga*, a governor or ruler.

DASHKOVA, PRINCESS EKATERINA (1743–1810). A major patron of the arts, she married Prince Mikhail Dashkov in 1759. She helped install Catherine the Great (q.v.) on the throne of her murdered husband, Peter III (q.v.), and subsequently was appointed by the empress to the presidency of the Russian Academy of Arts (q.v.).

DEBORIN, ABRAM M. (b. IOFFE) (1881–1963). He joined the Russian Socialist Democratic Labor Party (q.v.) in 1903 and became a Menshevik (q.v.) in 1907. After the revolution he joined the Communist Party (q.v.) and worked as the editor of its theoretical journal. He was also the secretary of the historical section of the Academy of Sciences (q.v.) of the USSR from 1935 until 1945.

DECEMBRISTS (DEKABRISTY). This was the term applied to participants of the uprising against Emperor Nicholas I (q.v.) on December 14, 1825. It was led by young officers of the Imperial Guards. The uprising was suppressed, five of its leaders were executed, and close to one hundred others were exiled to Siberia (q.v.). Survivors were pardoned by Alexander II (q.v.) in 1856.

DEITCH, LEV G. (1855–1941). Cofounder with Plekhanov (q.v.) of the first organization of Russian Marxists, the Emancipation of Labor Group, he joined the Menshevik (q.v.) faction in 1903. After the February 1917 revolution he edited a Russian socialist newspaper, retiring from politics after the Communists came to power.

DEKABRISTY see DECEMBRISTS

DEMOCRATIC CENTRALISM. This was the ideological principle imposed on the Communist Party (q.v.) and the Comintern (q.v.) by Lenin (q.v.). It required a rigid subordination and support by individual party members of all the decisions arrived at by the majority of their party unit. It also required that lower units of the party obey all orders from those above them.

DEMOCRATIC CONFERENCE. This conference of political leaders of all prodemocratic parties of Russia was convened by Kerensky (q.v.) in late September 1917, after the failed coup by General Kornilov (q.v.). Kerensky's objectives were to strengthen the Provisional government (q.v.) against the Communists and to prepare for the convocation of the Constituent Assembly (q.v.). The conference appointed a council, the Pre-Parliament (q.v.), that was designed to act as the national representative body until the convocation of the Constituent Assembly.

DEMOGRAPHY. During the 1990s a sharp drop occurred in the country's birthrate, coinciding with an elevation of the death rate. As a result, in 1992, for the first time since World War II (q.v.), the number of deaths exceeded the number of births. According to the 1989 census, the population of Russia totaled 147,386,000. Over the 30 previous years, it had increased by 26.5 percent, with an average annual growth of 0.5 percent. There had also taken place an increase in the urban population and a drop in the rural one. Starting with 1959 and up to 1989, the urban population, as a percentage of the total, grew from 52.4 percent to 73.3 percent, while the proportion made up by the rural population decreased from 47.6 percent to 26.7 percent. In 1989 there were 30 cities in Russia with a population over half a million, compared with only 14 such cities in 1959.

The number of males is now growing at a faster rate than that of females, narrowing the numerical disproportion caused by high death rates among men during World War II (this disproportion still exists among the older population). In general, there is an observable process of aging in the Russian population as a whole. The proportion of individuals 60 years of age and older has grown from nine percent in 1959 to 16.5 percent in 1989. The tendency of the country's birthrate during the last 30 years was one of slow decline, sharply accelerating in the 1990s. According to several surveys, the proportion of women who use some form of birth control in Russia approaches 100 percent. The majority of them today plan the number of children they wish to have.

Average life expectancy for males in 1992 was 62 years and for females, 73.8 years. (In 1988 it was 64.7 for males and 74.3 for females.) The drop in the average longevity of the Russian population is connected with the rise in chronic illnesses and traumas and to the general deterioration of the population's health associated with the events through which the country passed during the 20th century: two major wars, three violent revolutions, several famines and a number of ecological disasters. Other contributing factors include environmental pollution from experiments with atomic weapons, the low quality of food, and the unhygienic habits of the population. Russian surveys have indicated that as the level of education increases, life expectancy improves.

According to the 1989 survey, the number of families in Russia was 40.2 million. Almost 90 percent of its inhabitants were members of families. Approximately 12 percent of the population consisted of single individuals, or those who lived apart from their families. These single individuals were concentrated, as a rule, in larger cities. The proportion of large families, consisting of seven or more persons, is decreasing, while the proportion of small families of two to four individuals is increasing. Approximately 13 percent of families consist of single mothers with children. Internal migration was, since the middle of the last century, a movement from rural areas into urban centers. This is explainable by the industrialization of the country, which began in the late 19th century. The migration was relatively slow until the 1930s, when it increased rapidly because of Stalin's (q.v.) five-year plans (q.v.) of national development. Today, this flow has almost stopped; there has been a noticeable decrease of migration into cities and industrial regions. The only significant flow of migrants today is that of ethnic Russians returning home from the former Soviet republics. In 1992, this group comprised over 925,000 individuals. (In 1989, 17.4 percent of all Russians living in the Soviet Union resided outside the borders of the Russian Republic.)

While migratory flows are determined by political or economic circumstances, the decisive factor in the last five years has been the ethno-cultural factor. Over 70 percent of those who were asked about the reason for returning to Russia stated that it was because of interethnic conflicts and the deteriorating attitudes toward Russians in the non-Russian republics of the former Soviet Union. Emigration was for a long time restricted by the Soviet government, but after the restrictions were lifted in 1989, it increased rapidly. The main flow was to Israel (44 percent), to Germany (38 percent), and to the United States (12 percent). This emigration also exhibited an ethnic factor: the repatriation of Jews to their historical homeland, Israel. Economics has been a minor factor in the last decade. Further emigration from Russia depends on the speed with which the existing domestic political and social crisis is resolved, as well as on the limitations placed on it by foreign governments.

DENIKIN, ANTON I. (1872–1947). A general during World War I (q.v.), he was imprisoned by the Provisional government (q.v.) for supporting General Kornilov's (q.v.) attempted coup d'état in the autumn of 1917. In 1920, he became commander in chief of the White Armies (q.v.) in southern Russia. He emigrated from Russia to Western Europe after the defeat of the Whites, and died in the United States.

DESNA RIVER. This river rises close to Smolensk (q.v.) and flows for some 700 miles to the southwest, where it merges with the Dnepr River (q.v.) just above Kiev (q.v.).

DE-STALINIZATION. This is the designation of the policy adopted by the 20th congress of the Communist Party of the Soviet Union (q.v.) in 1956. It was sponsored by Khrushchev (q.v.) and designed to "overcome the cult of the personality," a Soviet euphemism for ending the glorification of Stalin (q.v.). Among other measures, it involved the renaming of cities that had been named after him—for example, Stalingrad became Volgograd (q.v.)—and the removal of Stalin's body from the Lenin (q.v.) mausoleum.

DIAGHILEV, SERGEI P. (1872–1929). A son of a landowner born near the city of Novgorod (q.v.), he graduated from the University of St. Petersburg (*see* Universities) in 1896 and continued to study music under Rimskii-Korsakov (q.v.). He edited an art journal from 1898 to 1904, and mounted art exhibitions all over Russia. After 1905 he moved to Paris, where he became an impresario and the organizer of Russian musical concerts. From 1911 to 1929 he was director of the Ballets Russes (q.v.), which gained fame throughout the world.

DIALECTICAL MATERIALISM. The colloquial Soviet term for this philosophy was *diamat*. It referred to the school of philosophy founded by Karl Marx and Friedrich Engels and added to by Lenin (q.v.). It became the keystone of the Communist worldview. *Diamat* stressed the primacy of the observable, material universe in human thought and the primacy of economic relations among men, especially the relationships that are entered into during the process of producing the essentials of life. This philosophy was labeled "dialectic" because it stressed the complex interactions between phenomena, rather than simple, unicausal explanations, and perceived external reality as being in a constant state of flux produced by the contradictions between internal aspects of phenomena. It became a mandatory subject of study in all Soviet schools.

DICTATORSHIP OF THE PROLETARIAT. As postulated by Marx and by Lenin (q.v.), this was to be the initial stage of the transformation of society from capitalism to socialism. During this stage, the state would remain necessary and the rule (dictatorship) of the bourgeoisie (capitalist class) would be gradually replaced by the rule (dictatorship) of the working class (proletariat).

DISSIDENTS. This name was given to writers, artists and other intellectuals who expressed their dissent from Soviet government policies following the easing of controls initiated by Khrushchev (q.v.) in 1956. After Khrushchev's dismissal in 1964, these dissenters were subjected to harassment, arrests, imprisonment, and forcible exile until political reforms (*see* glasnost) were inaugurated by Gorbachev (q.v.) in 1986.

DMITRII DONSKOI (1350–89). He was the victor at the battle of Kulikovo (q.v.), near the Don River (q.v.) in 1380. There, for the first time, Russians were able to defeat the Mongols of the Golden Horde (q.v.). This triumph made him the preeminent prince of the Riurik (q.v.) dynasty and heightened the prestige of his Moscow (q.v.) principality.

DMITRII, FALSE. After the death of Ivan the Terrible (q.v.) and of his son Fedor I (q.v.), three pretenders emerged to claim the throne of Russia. Each asserted that he was Dmitrii (*see* following entry), the youngest son of Ivan who had died under suspicious circumstances in 1591. These pretenders emerged during and after the reign of Boris Godunov (q.v.), who succeeded Fedor to the throne in 1598. The first False Dmitrii's claim was supported by Poland, and he was placed on the Russian throne after Godunov's death in 1605, only to be murdered a year later. The second False Dmitrii appeared in 1607 and attracted massive support in southern Russia, primarily from the discontented peasantry. He died of a wound inflicted by a follower in 1610. The final False Dmitrii emerged in 1611 and, with the support of Cossacks (q.v.), plundered the plains around Moscow (q.v.). He was captured by government forces and executed.

DMITRII OF UGLICH, PRINCE (1581–91). Youngest son of Ivan the Terrible (q.v.), this prince resided in Uglich (q.v.) and is believed to have been murdered during the rule of his elder brother, Fedor I (q.v.). With his death the Riurik (q.v.) line of Russian rulers came to an end. He was canonized as a martyr by the Orthodox Church (q.v.) after his death.

DNEPR RIVER. Emerging from the Valdai Hills (q.v.) west of Moscow (q.v.), this river flows south for some 1,400 miles. It passes through Belarus (q.v.) and past Kiev (q.v.) before entering the Black Sea (q.v.) below Kherson (q.v.).

DOBROLIUBOV, NIKOLAI A. (1836–61). Born into the family of a priest in the provincial town of Nizhnii Novgorod, Dobroliubov studied at the University of St. Petersburg (*see* Universities) before meeting the radical publicist Chernyshevskii (q.v.), who became his mentor and who helped him obtain a position on the staff of the periodical *Sovremennik* (q.v.) as a literary critic. Dobroliubov's principal concern was to convince his readers that art had to have a social value. He was strongly opposed to the "art for art's sake" philosophy.

DOBRZHANSKII, FEODOSII G. (1900–75). A leading Soviet geneticist and lecturer at Leningrad University (*see* Universities), he published a number of major works in zoology. During a trip abroad in 1927, he defected and settled in the United States to become professor of genetics at the California Technological Institute. In 1940 he was made professor of zoology at Columbia University. Dobrzhanskii was one of the founders of experimental population genetics.

DOBUZHINSKII, MSTISLAV V. (1875–1957). A student of art in St. Petersburg (q.v.) and Munich between 1899 and 1901, he worked on a number of Russian art journals before World War I (q.v.), and was also a stage designer for the Moscow Art Theater (q.v.) and for some Diaghilev (q.v.) ballet productions. In 1929 Dobuzhinskii emigrated from Russia to Lithuania and, at the beginning of World War II(q.v.), to England. Later he lived in the United States.

DOCTORS' PLOT. A plot manufactured by Stalin's (q.v.) secret police in 1953, its purpose was to implicate a number of prominent Soviet doctors, mostly Jewish, in a supposed attempt to assassinate leaders of the Soviet Union, including the dictator himself. This plot is commonly considered to have been intended as a prelude for a new period of purges of the Soviet leadership that was aborted only by the death of Stalin in March 1953. Two of the accused doctors were killed during incarceration, but the rest were released soon after the dictator's death.

DOLGORUKAIA, EKATERINA (PRINCESS IUREVSKAIA) (1847–1922). This was the morganatic wife of Alexander II (q.v.), whom he married after the death of his first wife in 1880 and with whom he had children. It was after a visit to her palace that the tsar was assassinated while he was returning to the Winter Palace (q.v.).

DON COSSACKS. This name applies to the Cossack (q.v.) host that was settled in the Don River (q.v.) region. It played a major role

during the civil war (q.v.) on the side of the White Armies (q.v.), led
by its elected generals, the Atamans Kaledin (q.v.) and Krasnov.

DON RIVER. Rising some 100 miles southeast of Moscow (q.v.), the
Don flows for about 1,200 miles, first to the city of Voronezh (q.v.),
then into the Sea of Azov (q.v.). It has served as a major waterway
for trade from ancient times to the present.

DONSKOI, MARK S. (1901–81). A graduate of Simferopol University
in 1925, he published a book of stories based on his experiences as a
prisoner of the White Armies (q.v.) in the Crimea (q.v.). After 1926
he began working in films as an actor, writer and director. During
the 1930s he directed a Gorky (q.v.) trilogy, which became a Soviet
classic.

DOSTOEVSKY, FEDOR M. (1821–81). One of the greatest novelists
of the 19th century, he disliked both socialism and the aristocracy.
Dostoevsky was distinguished by a deep religiosity and compassion.
His father was a landlord and a doctor who was murdered by rebellious serfs on his estate. Dostoevsky intended to become a military
engineer but instead turned to literature and to writing. Arrested in
1849 for peripheral participation in a radical discussion group, he was
condemned to death but was later reprieved and exiled to Siberia
(q.v.) for four years. Dostoevsky became an inveterate gambler and
had to flee abroad to avoid his creditors. With the help of his second
wife he was able to return to Russia and begin a decade of intense
work on his most important novels.

DUDAEV, JOKHAR (1944–96). Charismatic leader of the Chechen independence movement, Dudaev was a graduate of the Gagarin Air
Force Academy and commanded nuclear bombers in Estonia; he became a member of the Communist Party (q.v.) in 1968. He retired in
1990 and became president of the Checheno-Ingushia Autonomous
Republic, and in 1991 he proclaimed Chechnya's (q.v.) independence
from Russia. The military reaction caused thereby turned into a bitter
struggle in which Dudaev himself was eventually killed in April
1996. In June of that year tentative accords were signed by Yeltsin
(q.v.) and Dudaev's successor, Zelimkhan Yandarbiev.

DUKHOBORY. Members of a Russian religious sect, "the Fighters of
the Spirit," they fled from persecution by church authorities to North
America in the early part of the 20th century. They left Russia with
the financial help of Count Leo Tolstoy (q.v.), and many of them
settled in Canada.

DUKHONIN, NIKOLAI N. (1876–1917). Commander in chief of the
Russian armed forces at the time of the October 1917 revolution
(q.v.), he refused to obey orders from the Soviet government to open
peace negotiations with the German Kaiser and was shot by Red soldiers in November 1917.

DUMA. During the medieval period this was the name of a deliberative
body of the tsar's councilors. In 1905 Nicholas II (q.v.) issued a manifesto establishing a State Duma (*Gosudarstvennaia Duma*) with legislative powers and chosen through an indirect electoral process.
There were four Dumas before the revolution of February 1917 (q.v.).
After the Communists seized power in October 1917 they dispersed
the institution. The Duma was revived only after the collapse of Communist rule in Russia.

DVINA RIVER. This river flows from its point of formation at the confluence of the Yug and Sukhona Rivers to the White Sea (q.v.) near
the city of Arkhangelsk (q.v.); it is navigable only in the summer
months.

DVORIANE. The gentry: these were members of a legally defined
upper social stratum of the Russian population. The designation goes
back to the 12th century, when this appellation was applied to individuals living at the court of a prince and later expanded to include
all those holding state lands. Peter the Great (q.v.) opened access to
this stratum for all military officers and civil servants who attained a
high rank. In the 19th century, *dvorianstvo* was divided into personal
and hereditary categories, with the latter being awarded to the families of military officers who attained the rank of colonel and to the
highest civil servants.

DYBENKO, PAVEL E. (1889–1938). The Communist organizer of the
rebellion in the Baltic (q.v.) fleet in 1917, he later became commissar
of the Soviet navy. He was arrested and executed on Stalin's (q.v.)
orders during the purges of the 1930s.

DZERZHINSKII, FELIKS, (1877–1926). Born in the Vilna province
of Polish gentry, Dzerzhinskii was named head of the Cheka (q.v.)
(Extraordinary Committee for Fighting the Counterrevolution; later
OGPU) in 1917. He had been active in revolutionary circles in Poland
and Russia and was imprisoned several times. In 1917 he became a
member of the central committee of the Bolshevik (q.v.) party, and,
in addition to his lifelong duties as a chekist, he streamlined Russia's
railway system as people's commisssar for transport (1921) and orga-

nized heavy industry as chairman of the supreme council of national economy (1924).

DZHUGASHVILI, IAKOV I. (1922–1943). The eldest son of Stalin (q.v.), he volunteered for the front at the beginning of World War II (q.v.) in 1941. He was captured by the Germans near Smolensk (q.v.), but Stalin refused a German offer to exchange him for Field Marshal von Paulus. He is said to have deliberately thrown himself on the barbed wire of the concentration camp where he was being held.

DZHUGASHVILI, IOSIF V. see STALIN, I. V.

E

ECONOMY, IMPERIAL RUSSIA. Russia began industrializing while still possessing significant remnants of feudalism. Accumulation of capital by private individuals began before the reforms of the 1860s. By the end of the 1880s, transformations in the manufacturing sector became significant and the tempo of the country's industrialization began to accelerate rapidly. The production of manufactured goods grew sevenfold between 1861 and 1900. A significant role in this process was played by foreign investments, primarily French, English and German. This was particularly true for large-scale industry, which was responsible for over two-thirds of total national production.

By the beginning of the 20th century, 200 of the country's largest factories employed over 1,000 employees each, while over four million were employed by independent, small-scale enterprises. Toward the end of the 19th century the most industrially developed areas of Russia were St. Petersburg (q.v.), Moscow (q.v.) and the Ural (q.v.) region.

Almost half of the total value of manufactured goods consisted of wool, linen and paper products. Metal manufacturing amounted to approximately 20 percent of total national production, while woodworking, clothing and the processing of animal products constituted the major part of the balance.

The protectionist policies under Alexander III (q.v.) favored a speedy development of industry in Russia. One of its landmarks was the 1891 tariff that raised custom duties on many categories of imports. This helped to increase the profitability of capital invested in industry and was among the principal reasons for the rapid rates of industrialization that were realized at the turn of the century. Another factor was the government's success in decreasing currency fluctuation. A further aspect supporting industrialization was the state's participation in the construction of railroads and in the creation of large-scale metallurgical enterprises that produced transport machinery. During the second half of the 19th century, the system of taxation in the empire was altered from indirect taxation on consumption goods to a system in which the main tax burden was placed on incomes derived from mercantile and industrial activities. The new tax structure was designed to take advantage of the profitability of entrepreneurial and trade activities and to lessen the tax burden on small and medium-sized businesses.

By the beginning of the century the role of banks in Russia had increased significantly. The 12 largest banks controlled approximately 80 percent of all banking resources. These banks began to shift their portfolios from short-term loans to large enterprises toward providing them with long-term credit in exchange for shares of their stock. For small businesses, financing was provided by credit cooperatives. The Stolypin (q.v.) reforms of 1906–11 played a very important role in the development of the Russian economy. These reforms focused on replacing the existing peasant communes with rural entrepreneurs and on moving the excess agrarian population from overcrowded regions of central Russia to eastern Siberia (q.v.), where fertile land was plentiful. As a consequence of these measures, individual peasants were allowed to leave their communes, sell their share of the land, and move to another region or into the towns. These changes greatly accelerated the pace of the country's industrialization by increasing the available labor force. By the beginning of the 20th century Russia had begun to be transformed from an agrarian state to a substantially industrialized one.

ECONOMY, SOVIET ERA. Among the first initiatives of the newly formed Soviet government in 1917 was the nationalization of all land, industries, banks, and the means of transportation. Workers' control was introduced in all industrial enterprises, but it soon became apparent that this type of management could not produce adequate results: industrial production dropped sharply in 1917 and continued to drop further in 1918. To replace worker control, a rigid centralization of authority was introduced. Decrees were issued by the government that envisaged the total elimination of private property and the centralized management of the nationalized economy, as well as the abolition of all monetary relationships, an egalitarian distribution of food and consumer goods, and compulsory enrollment of peasants in cooperative producers' societies.

The majority of peasants were not affected by the nationalization of land ownership; they were allowed to continue cultivating their plots as before. However, they were now obliged to sell their produce at artificially low prices to the Soviet government, something they were not interested in doing. Their refusal to comply with the government's procurement policies led rapidly to a famine in the urban centers. In order to counter this threat, the Soviet government turned to compulsion. It organized a system of forced requisitioning and to the confiscation of land from the more prosperous peasants, the so-called kulaks (q.v.), who led the resistance to the forcible sale of their crops. As a result of these industrial and agrarian policies, now referred to as War Communism (q.v.), there occurred a major downturn in the national economy, which led to a drastic fall in production and to a sharp shortage of food to feed the urban population.

In 1921, seeking to find a way out of this crisis, Lenin (q.v.) proposed the New Economic Policy, or NEP (q.v.). It replaced compulsory deliveries of agricultural produce with a land tax, thereby allowing the peasantry to keep the surplus after payment of taxes and to sell it for their own profit. Attempts to promote the creation of agricultural cooperatives by force were discontinued, thus allowing the independent households to remain intact. This return to a market-based system brought rapid improvements and within two years resulted in a major revival of Russian agriculture. By December 1921 all industrial enterprises with fewer than 20 employees were denationalized; foreign investment capital was permitted, and decentralization in industry and trade was introduced, as was cost accounting. Attempts to totally equalize were abandoned. These measures soon produced positive results. By 1928 the country had surpassed its prewar levels of production in agriculture by 24 percent and in the manufacturing industry by 32 percent, and there occurred a considerable rise in the population's standard of living. A fully convertible and stable monetary unit, the *chervonets*, was introduced and allowed to be traded in the London money market.

The attitude of the top Soviet leaders to the new economic policy was divergent, and in 1928 the struggle among the several factions ended with a victory for Stalin (q.v.) He formulated the theory of the historical leap—the construction of socialism under conditions of the dictatorship of the proletariat—in a minimal period of time. Urging necessity imposed by the danger of war, Stalin proposed to force the agricultural sector to bear the brunt of financing the country's industrialization. During the period between 1929 and 1940, a sequence of five-year Plans (q.v.) transformed the USSR into an industrialized country. Russia became the leading country of Europe and the second in the world after the United States in terms of total industrial output. Metallurgy and energy were rapidly developed.

However, these successes were attained through a feudal-like exploitation of the country's peasantry, forced loans to the government, an increase in the sales of alcohol, and a massive employment of concentration camp labor. The growth of light industry was far slower than that of heavy industry. The mass collectivization of individual peasant households begun in 1929 had, in effect, transformed them into serfs. World War II (q.v.) had delivered a severe blow to the country's further development. During the postwar period major efforts at restructuring the country's economy were attempted. In 1953 economic incentives for agriculture were introduced in order to increase production. The prices received for compulsory deliveries to the government were raised, and taxes were lowered. A gradual introduction of a guaranteed annual payment to collective farmers occurred, and direct financial help to the rural population was augmented. In 1954 the government also began the reclamation of unused agricultural lands. Toward the end of the 1950s a major construction effort was initiated, designed to provide the population with hundreds of thousands of new housing units. Investment in light industry was likewise increased, and attempts were made to focus economic activity on the needs of individual consumers.

During the first years of Brezhnev's (q.v.) rule these changes continued. In 1965 a decision was made to provide adequate material incentives and to decrease compulsory production targets for individual factories and enterprises. However, after the middle of the 1970s, growth in the Soviet Union came to a halt. This was mainly caused by the enormous strains placed on the economy by the armaments race that it was engaged in with the West. It was also caused by the excessive growth of the administrative bureaucracy composed of salaried managers with little incentive to take risks or to innovate in order to improve productivity. The productivity of the Soviet industrial labor force in the 1980s was only 55 percent of that of the United States, and its agricultural labor productivity only 25 percent. What economic development did occur during the 1980s was based on exports of primary resources such as oil, gas, and forestry products. By the middle of the decade there occurred a major drop of both industrial and agricultural production, which led, in turn, to growing shortages of essential goods.

The country's political leadership attempted to reduce the impact of this crisis by importing meat, grain, sugar and other consumer products. Nevertheless, social stress increased. In April 1985, Gorbachev (q.v.), the new general secretary of the Communist Party (q.v.), publicly admitted the need for a fundamental transformation of the country's economy and of its social relations, and he initiated the process of perestroika (q.v.), or rebuilding. However, the first steps that he took did not affect the basic structures of the country because they remained based on the administrative-command system of management and on nationalized property controlled by party and state bureaucracies. Laws were passed in 1986 to improve labor discipline. Other laws were designed to regulate the activity of the collective and state farms, but they provided only a limited scope for individual initiative. While they did allow individuals to set up their own businesses or earn a living through self-employment, these new rights remained strictly circumscribed by a government that continued to regiment the activities of private entrepreneurs. Crisis symptoms continued to grow.

Attempts to change the management system from an administrative/command system to a market-based system continued to be blocked by the party/state bureaucracy which stood to lose much of its power and privilege. Transition was also hindered by a lack of laws that clearly established private ownership of the means of production. The Gorbachev reforms lasted from 1990 through 1991. During this period several important pieces of legislation were passed, and a number of ideologically based limitations on economic activity were removed. The concept of private enterprise was partially accepted. On the whole, however, the old administrative/command system continued unchanged.

ECONOMY, TODAY'S RUSSIA. A new stage of reforms began after the breakup of the Soviet Union at the end of 1991. At that time, under President Yeltsin (q.v.), the government began to implement a series of radical changes aimed at a rapid transition to a market economy. The first step taken was the liberalization of prices in January 1992. The result was that Russia's prices began to be determined almost entirely by the laws of supply and demand. This achievement has eliminated the previous shortage of consumer goods, while raising the cost of living. The current value of the ruble, Russia's basic currency unit, is now determined on the free exchange market and commercial banks are involved in financial transactions.

Privatization is one of the key elements of the reforms under Yeltsin. By September 1993 over 80,000 enterprises had been privatized, among them 8,300 large-scale ones employing some 16 million workers. Over two-thirds of these privatized enterprises are in the trade or service sectors. Enterprises that are still owned by the state have had to accommodate to this new situation and are now actively participating in free enterprise commercial transactions. At the beginning of 1994, 42 percent of all employees were working in the nongovernmental sector. The state is currently attempting to include in its privatization program as many individuals as possible. The Yeltsin administration sees this as the basic guarantee for the nonreversibility of its reforms. Another major program issues to the population ownership shares to land and to a variety of enterprises that are being privatized.

Notwithstanding the continuing successes of these reforms, the economic situation of the country remains severe. The fall in production has not been stopped. Consumption of foodstuffs by the population has dropped by 15 to 20 percent between 1989 and 1993. Housing construction has been cut in half, and there are not enough funds to support science or culture adequately. The collapse of the existing technical and scientific complexes has led to a reduction in the technological innovation that is essential for further industrial growth.

One of the reasons for these difficulties is the slow growth of the new legal and economic systems. As well, the majority of enterprises that were given a measure of autonomy did not have either the necessary commercial connections or the experience to operate in a market economy, nor did they have sufficient operating or investment capital. These circumstances have led to a drop in production and have given rise to an inability of many enterprises to continue payments on their obligations.

After the collapse of the old socialist system, production in many of the areas that provided the population with clothing, fuel, and transport services became economically unprofitable. The high cost of fuel, which has been raised by the government to the international market price, often inhibits the harvesting of crops; the cost of transportation makes it uneconomical for coal suppliers to provide coal to electrical stations. The ineffectiveness of the existing tax-gathering system has reduced state revenues.

Slow progress in legislation needed to secure private enterprise has prevented the normal development of entrepreneurial activity and frightened off foreign investment capital. The first half of 1994 saw signs of some economic improvement, including a reduction in the inflation rate and a slowing of the decline in the standard of living. However, there is as yet no economic stabilization in sight.

EDUARDOVNA, EVGENIIA T. (1882–1960). A graduate of the St. Petersburg (q.v.) Theater School in 1901, she danced at the Mariinskii Theater (q.v.) until 1917, when she emigrated to Germany. There, she ran her own ballet school until 1925, when she moved to Paris and continued teaching ballet. Eduardovna settled in the United States in 1935.

EDUCATION. During the Soviet period, Russian education underwent several major changes. In the 1920s and 1930s the government's main objective was to create a countrywide system of schools that would provide universal elementary education for all children and eliminate illiteracy in the adult population. During this period, elementary seven-year and nine-year schools were established in the cities alongside the seven-year factory schools, while in rural areas elementary schools were opened for peasant youth. By 1932, the number of literate individuals had reached 89 percent of the population. Starting in the middle of the 1930s and lasting until the end of the 1950s, a new stage in the development of the country's education occurred. During this period the stress was on providing a secondary-level education, at first on a seven-year, then on an eight-year basis. After World War II (q.v.) secondary schools began to issue certificates of maturity to students who passed exit examinations and to award their best graduates silver and then gold medals. During the 1960s and 1970s secondary schools lengthened their hours of instruction. As well, the country's network of schools was expanded with the view of achieving a universal mandatory secondary education, a goal that was largely reached by the beginning of the 1980s. In 1985 over four million individuals received an eight-year education. Of these, over two million individuals continued on to a ninth year, while more than one million were accepted into postsecondary professional schools. Another half a million entered universities and higher educational institutes (VUZ). But for all this progress, critics of the former Soviet system of education draw attention to the fact that its principal aim was to inculcate a Communist worldview and that it tended to breed a type of student who was obedient, easily led, and dependent on external rather than internalized systems of control.

By the late 1980s Soviet government expenditures on education had become insufficient to meet the requirements of the country's economy. Thus, while there was still an adequate supply of engineers and metallurgists for industry, there was a severe shortage of financial managers, economists and lawyers. During the period since 1990, the educational choices of Russian students has begun to change. The former prestige of such fields as engineering, science and education has shifted sharply in favor of training in commerce, and especially banking. At the beginning of the 1992/93 academic year there were in Russia 587 gymnasiums and 343 lyceums, as well as some 300 private educational institutions, with a total enrollment of over 20 thousand. The number of students in the secondary school network was approximately 20 million. There were 40 universities and more than 500 institutes of higher education. However, since 1990, for the first time ever, the problem of finding jobs for graduates of the institutes of higher education has arisen. Out of the total graduates in 1991, only 16 percent had searched for employment—the rest had been hired before graduation. In 1992 the number of those having to look for work had more than doubled, to 38 percent. The main difficulty of the country's current secondary educational system is the shortage of classrooms to accommodate the existing student population, forcing classes to be conducted in shifts. The number of students in 1992 who had to attend second (late afternoon) and third (evening) shifts was almost 25 percent.

EHRENBURG, ILIA G. (1891–1967). A noted Soviet author and journalist whose novels were liked by Stalin (q.v.). He began as a student of engineering but soon became a full-time revolutionary. He was arrested in 1908. After being released, Ehrenburg emigrated to France, where he started publishing verse. During World War I (q.v.) he worked as a newspaper correspondent for a Russian newspaper, then returned home in July 1917. In 1921 Ehrenburg went back to Paris, where he remained until 1941, working as a newspaper correspondent. During World War II (q.v.) he served as a war correspondent, then after Stalin's death he published a novel, *The Thaw*, whose name signaled a change in Soviet cultural policy. His memoirs, which came out in the 1960s, describe the lives of the Russian intelligentsia before and after World War I.

EISENSTEIN, SERGEI M. (1898–1948). A world-renowned film director, he first studied to become a civil engineer. In 1919 Eisenstein served as a soldier in the Red Army (*see* Armed Forces, Soviet), then after the end of the civil war, he worked in the art section of a Proletkult (q.v.) theater, as well as giving art classes to the Kremlin (q.v.) garrison and studying theater under Meyerhold (q.v.). In 1924 Eisenstein directed several film masterpieces, traveling extensively in Europe, and collaborated on a film with Charles Chaplin and Walt Disney. In the late 1930s Eisenstein completed his two masterpieces, *Aleksandr Nevskii* and *Ivan the Terrible*.

EKATERINBURG (1924–91: Sverdlovsk). Founded in 1721 by Catherine I (q.v.) and an early center of ironworks, Ekaterinburg became an important location for heavy industry and a junction of the Trans-Siberian railroad (q.v.) in the central Urals. Nicholas II (q.v.) and his family were executed here, and the city's name was changed to Sverdlovsk in honor of I. Sverdlov (q.v.), on whose orders the execution took place. Its population is around 1,300,000.

EKONOMISTY. The Economists were a group of Russian Social Democrats (*see* Russian Socialist Democratic Labor Party) in the late 19th century who opposed the formation of a socialist political party on the grounds that the country was not sufficiently industrialized. Instead, they advocated encouraging the workers to struggle for an improvement of their condition and to seek the support of non-Marxist liberals in extending political democracy to the Russian empire.

ELABUGA. This city in the Tatar Autonomous Republic (q.v.) with a population of 40,000 was founded in the 16th century on the Kama River. Its industries include building materials and oil; in 1995 a joint venture to build automobiles was begun there with General Motors.

ELIZABETH I, EMPRESS AND TSARITSA (1709–61). Daughter of Peter the Great (q.v.) and Empress Catherine I (q.v.), she ascended the throne in 1741. She established the University of Moscow (*see* Universities) and the Academy of Fine Arts (q.v.) and built the Winter Palace (q.v.) in St. Petersburg (q.v.). Never married, Elizabeth left no direct successors. During her reign Russia took part in the Seven Years' War (q.v.) against Prussia, which resulted in the first Russian occupation of Berlin.

EMANCIPATION EDICT. Tsar Alexander II (q.v.) issued an edict in 1861 that abolished serfdom in Russia. It gave the serfs freedom from their landlords, to whom they had been chattel. They were, however, obligated to repay the government for the land it had purchased from these landlords. (*See also* Economy, Imperial Russia.)

EMIGRES, RUSSIAN. The Russian emigration before the revolution provided a stage for the activities of such luminaries as Herzen (q.v.), Bakunin (q.v.) and Lenin (q.v.), but the political importance of the emigration itself might be said to have fluctuated over the years. Following the conclusion of the civil war (q.v.), the very mass of refugees from Russia to Europe, Turkey, China and the United States changed the nature of Russian emigres. The number of emigres was increased by people leaving Russia illegally or being deported, and a second great wave followed World War II (q.v.), when millions of people were displaced or otherwise forced to flee. The very size of the emigration meant that political tendencies of all types were represented, often sharing nothing more than opposition to the Soviet regime, if that. The size of the emigration also meant that communities in cities such as Berlin, Prague and Paris could support Russian language newspapers and journals, book publishing, and even educational and research institutions.

ENERGIIA. The most powerful rocket booster in the world was developed by Soviet aerospace technologists in 1986 for the permanent maintenance of the *Mir* (*see* Mir) space station. It consists of eight liquid-hydrogen motors, generates over 170 million horsepower, and can lift over 100 tons into space.

ENISEI RIVER. One of the major Siberian rivers, it flows north for over two thousand miles from the Sayan mountains to the Kara Sea (q.v.) and the Arctic Ocean.

ENTENTE, THE. This is the name of the alliance between Great Britain, France and Russia that began before World War I (q.v.). It came into being gradually, starting with the Russo-French accord in 1894. It was enlarged by an understanding with Great Britain in 1907–08, after the two countries succeeded in settling their differences over Persia. In September 1914, at the beginning of World War I, the three powers vowed not to conclude a separate peace with their enemies, Germany and Austro-Hungary.

ERMAK TIMOFEEVICH (d. 1584). This Cossack (q.v.) conquered Siberia (q.v.) while in the service of the Stroganov family (q.v.) of merchants.

EROFEEV, VENEDIKT (1938–90). This writer is known chiefly for his tragicomic prose poem *Moskva-Petushki* (1970), a snapshot in the life of a heavy drinker at odds with the world; the protagonist came to be recognized as a characteristic type of Soviet man. Erofeev worked at a number of different jobs for a living and wrote only a few other things.

ESENIN, SERGEI A. (1895–1925). Born into a peasant family, he began writing poetry at an early age. Esenin considered himself a revolutionary, but he never joined the Communist Party (q.v.). During the 1920s he enjoyed great national and international fame as a "peasant poet" and lived a wildly bohemian life. In 1921 he married the American dancer Isidora Duncan. An alcoholic, Esenin was frequently involved in public scandals and in 1925 committed suicide, ostensibly because he was disillusioned with the revolution.

ESTONIA. This Baltic republic has an area of 17,400 square miles and a population of 1,583,000, of whom 62 percent are Estonian. They speak a language related to Finnish. The capital is Tallinn. Estonia was acquired by Peter I from Sweden but enjoyed independence between 1917 and 1939, when the Nazi-Soviet pact of nonaggression gave Estonia to the Soviet Union. In addition to forestry and machine building, Estonia is noted for its dairy products. It became independent in 1991.

EVDOKIIA FEDOROVNA (1669–1731). The first wife of Peter the Great (q.v.), she was forced to become a nun in 1698. Her only son, Aleksei, turned against his father, who condemned him to death. After his execution Evdokiia left the nunnery and took a lover, but soon she was forcibly confined to the Uspensky convent by Peter the Great. She was rehabilitated by her grandson, Peter II (q.v.).

EVENKI NATIONAL OKRUG. Located in eastern Siberia, this region of the Russian Federation has a population of less than 15,000 individuals, who are mostly of Mongolian (*see* Tatar) ethnic origin. Their principal occupations are fur trapping, fishing and coal and graphite mining.

EVLOGII, VASILII G. (1868–1946). Son of a village priest, he graduated from the Moscow Theological Academy in 1892 to become professor of the Kholm Seminary in 1897, then served as bishop of Lublin and Kholm and as a member of the Duma (q.v.) in 1907. In 1914 Bishop Evlogii was elected archbishop of Volhynia (q.v.) but left Russia after the October 1917 revolution to become the temporary head of the Russian Orthodox Church (q.v.) in Western Europe. He lived in Paris between 1922 and 1946, refusing to recognize either the Moscow Patriarchate or the Russian Church in Exile. Bishop Evlogii was the founder of the St. Sergius Theological Institute in Paris.

EVTUSHENKO see YEVTUSHENKO

EXECUTIVE COMMITTEE OF THE ALL-RUSSIAN CONGRESS OF SOVIETS. In theory, the chief administrative organ of the Soviet state, this 300-member committee was elected at periodic meetings of the All-Russian Congress of Soviets (q.v.). In turn, it elected a Council of People's Commissars (q.v.), which was the actual Soviet government.

EZHOV, NIKOLAI I. (1895–1939). Political commissar with the Red Army (*see* Armed Forces, Soviet) during the civil war (q.v.), he became a member of the Central Committee of the Communist Party (q.v.) in 1934 and people's commissar for internal affairs in 1936. Ezhov's name is associated with the worst excesses of the 1930s purges—the "Ezhovshchina." He was removed from all his posts and executed in 1939. At the 20th party congress in 1956 Ezhov was denounced by Khrushchev (q.v.) as a "criminal and drug addict."

F

FABERGÉ, KARL G. (1846–1920). Born in St. Petersburg (q.v.) of a French family, he learned his craft in Germany, Italy and France, then took over his family's jewelry business in 1870. Fabergé became jeweller to the tsar and created world-renowned precious objects for the imperial family, including ornamental Easter eggs, bracelets and necklaces. After the revolution Fabergé emigrated from Russia and died in Lausanne, Switzerland.

FADEEV, ALEKSANDR A. (b. BULYGA) (1901–56). A well-known Russian writer who fought in the civil war (q.v.) on the Soviet side, he became a member of the Communist Party (q.v.) in 1918 and later embraced the official literary doctrine of socialist realism. From 1946 to 1955 Fadeev was the general secretary of the Union of Soviet Writers (q.v.) and denounced a number of writers to the secret police. He committed suicide after Khrushchev's (q.v.) exposure of Stalin's (q.v.) crimes at the 20th party congress in 1956.

FAR EASTERN REPUBLIC. A temporary political unit centered on the Russian Pacific Ocean port of Vladivostok (q.v.), it was created in 1920 to serve as a buffer between the main body of the Russian Republic and the Japanese-occupied Russian Far East. It was reannexed to the Soviet Union in 1922 after the Japanese evacuation of that area.

FEBRUARY REVOLUTION. This was the revolution that overthrew the tsarist regime. It began in St. Petersburg (q.v.) in March 1917 according to the Gregorian calendar and in February according to the Julian calendar (q.v.). The revolution began unexpectedly as a result of bread riots in the capital and within days led to the abdication of Tsar Nicholas II (q.v.) and his heir, Tsarevich Aleksei (q.v.). A Provisional government (q.v.) was formed from members of the Duma (q.v.), with Prince Lvov (q.v.) as its prime minister. At the same time, left-wing political groupings formed a citywide council (*see* soviet), which acted as a parallel political force. In October 1917 a Communist-led coup overthrew the Provisional government and vested all state power in the soviets. (*See also* Revolution of February 1917.)

FEDIN, KONSTANTIN A. (1892–1977). He was a member of the Serapion Brothers (q.v.) literary circle and a novelist sympathetic to the Soviet government. His writings were focused largely on the historical events surrounding the Russian revolution and the civil war (q.v.).

Fedin became the secretary general of the Union of Soviet Writers (q.v.) in 1959.

FEDOR I, TSAR (1557–98). The last descendent of the Riurik (q.v.) dynasty of Russian rulers, this feeble-minded son of Ivan the Terrible (q.v.) was crowned tsar of Russia in 1584. The real power behind his throne was Boris Godunov (q.v.), a powerful nobleman.

FEDOR II, TSAR (1589–1605). Son of Boris Godunov (q.v.), he was proclaimed tsar in 1605 on his father's death. He was murdered by a faction of courtiers who were the enemies of his mother and opposed her attempts to rule in her son's name.

FEDOR III, TSAR (1661–82). Tsar of Russia from 1676 until his death in 1682, he ruled as a figurehead for the powerful noble families of the Likhachevs and the Golitsyns (q.v.). The one important historical event of this reign was the abolition of the ancient practice of *mestnichestvo* (q.v.), or precedence placing, among the tsar's courtiers.

FEDOROV, IVAN F. (1530?-83). The first printer in Russia, he learned his craft from a Dane. He printed the first book in Moscow (q.v.) in 1563, then moved to Lithuania (q.v.).

FEDOROV, NIKOLAI (1828–1903). Born the illegitimate son of Prince P. I. Gagarin (q.v.), Fedorov studied law in Odessa and spent his early life wandering around Russia and working as a teacher. After 1868 he lived in Moscow and worked at the Rumiantsev Library (*see* Russian State Library). He wrote many unpublished works, notably *The Philosophy of the Common Task*, which explained man's purpose as the task of overcoming earthly problems and even death itself. His ideas influenced Dostoevsky (q.v.), Vladimir Solovev (q.v.) and many others.

FEDOTOV, GEORGI P. (1886–1951). Son of a tsarist police official, he became a member of the Russian Socialist Democratic Labor Party (q.v.) and fled abroad to study in Germany, where he lived from 1906 to 1908. On his return to Russia at the beginning of World War I (q.v.), Fedotov graduated from St. Petersburg University (*see* Universities) and taught history there and also at the University of Saratov. Emigrating to France in 1925, Fedotov lectured at the St. Sergius Theological Institute in Paris and from 1931 to 1940 edited a Russian philosophical periodical. Fedotov moved to the United States in 1943 and became a professor at the St. Vladimir Seminary in New York.

FIVE • 103

FIGNER, VERA (1852–1942). Daughter of a wealthy nobleman, she became a revolutionary while studying at Zurich University in Switzerland and joined the Executive Committee of the Narodnaia Volia (q.v.) in 1879. She was one of the few of its members to escape arrest after the assassination of Tsar Alexander II (q.v.) Captured in 1883, Figner was sentenced to death, but her sentence was commuted to life imprisonment. She spent 20 years in solitary confinement in the Schlusselburg Fortress in St. Petersburg (q.v.) and was released only in 1905. After her release Figner lived abroad until she returned to Russia after the February 1917 revolution (q.v.). After the Communist seizure of power in October 1917, she retired from political activity to write her memoirs.

FILARET, PATRIARCH (b. ROMANOV) (1560–1633). A powerful churchman during the Time of Troubles after the death of Ivan the Terrible (q.v.). He lived to see his son Michael (q.v.) selected tsar in 1613 and found the Romanov dynasty (q.v.). During his son's reign, the patriarch was the actual power behind the Russian throne.

FILARET (b. VOZNESSENSKII) (1903–85). Son of a priest, he left Soviet Russia for Harbin (q.v.), China, in 1920 and graduated from the Harbin Polytechnical Institute and from the Harbin Theological Institute where he then became a lecturer. Filaret acquired a high degree of authority among the Orthodox Russians (*see* Orthodox Church) of Harbin. Expelled in 1967 by the Chinese Communist government, he moved to Australia, where he was elected head of the Russian Orthodox Church in Exile. After he moved to the United States, he became the Metropolitan of New York and Eastern America.

FINLAND, GRAND DUCHY OF. The Swedish province of Vyborg, part of which was ceded to Russia in 1721 by the Treaty of Nystad. All of Finland became part of the empire after the Peace of Hamina (1809), and was formed into a Grand Duchy. It remained a semi-independent part of the Russian empire, with its own legislature. Finland declared its independence from Russia in 1917.

FIVE, (THE). This was the name given to the 19th-century Russian group of composers who made it their task to bring Russian music back to its native roots through an emphasis on native folk music and legends. The five were particularly hostile to the music of the Rubinstein (q.v.) brothers and of their pupil Tchaikovsky (q.v.). They were Balakirev (q.v.), Borodin (q.v.), Cui (q.v.), Mussorgskii (q.v.) and Rimskii-Korsakov (q.v.).

FIVE-YEAR PLANS. Inaugurated in 1928–29 by Stalin (q.v.), these were plans for Soviet economic development. They provided the basic framework that guided the country's command economy until the dissolution of the Soviet Union in 1991. Each plan set detailed targets for economic production and growth and was a mandatory guide for all economic and scientific activities of the country.

FLORENCE, COUNCIL OF. The 1439 church council between the Roman and the Orthodox (q.v.) Christian churches, it was designed to bring about a theological reconciliation of the two major branches of Christianity. The Russian representative was Metropolitan (q.v.) Isidor, who eventually acceded to its resolution but was imprisoned for this on his return to Moscow. Among the results of this council was the creation of the Uniate (q.v.) Orthodox Church.

FLORENSKII, PAVEL A. (1882–1939?). A priest in the Orthodox Church (q.v.), a theologian and philosopher, he was a lecturer at the Moscow Theological Academy. After the 1917 revolution Florenskii was arrested and exiled first to central Asia then deported to the Solovetskii (q.v.) labor camp, and finally exiled to Siberia (q.v.).

FOKIN, MIKHAIL M. (1880–1942). A graduate of the St. Petersburg Theater School in 1898, he made his debut as a ballet dancer the same year at the Mariinskii Theater (q.v.). After 1909, Fokin was chief choreographer for the Ballets Russes (q.v.) in Paris. In 1921 Fokin moved to the United States but returned to France to work for the Paris Opera in 1933 and was again associated with the Ballets Russes.

FOMIN, NIKOLAI S. (1895–1980). A graduate of an artillery academy in 1917, he became an officer in the imperial army. In 1919 Fomin joined the Red Army (*see* Armed Forces, Soviet) and in 1937, the Communist Party (q.v.). He graduated from the Frunze (q.v.) Military Academy in 1941 and held several artillery commands during World War II (q.v.), reaching the rank of colonel general. Fomin taught at the Academy of the General Staff from 1956 to 1964.

FORMALISTS. Founded in 1916, this group of literary critics emphasized the problem of form in art. At the end of the 1920s they were subjected to party-inspired attacks and to accusations of "formalism," a Soviet term of abuse. The attacks were based on the grounds that its members separated art from its function as an educational and politically useful activity.

FRANK, SEMEN L. (1877–1950). Expelled from Moscow University (*see* Universities) for distributing Marxist literature, he continued his education in Berlin. After returning to Russia, he graduated from the Kazan University in 1901, then initiated the Legal Marxist (q.v.) movement together with Peter Struve (q.v.). One of the principal authors of *Vekhi* (q.v.), a book that criticized the Russian intelligentsia for its radicalism, Frank urged a revival of religion. He was dismissed by the Soviet government from his post as dean of Saratov University in 1922 and returned to Berlin, where he lived until 1939, when he moved to France and finally to England in 1945.

FRANZ JOSEPH LAND. This is an island archipelago in the Arctic Ocean that belongs to Russia. It was discovered by an Austrian explorer but annexed by the Soviet Union in 1926.

FRIEDLAND, BATTLE OF. The site of the 1807 battle between Napoleon and the Russian army, it resulted in Napoleon's victory over Alexander I (q.v.) and the Treaty of Tilsit (q.v.) between Russia and France.

FRUNZE (1846–1929: PISHPEK). Capital of the Kirghiz Republic, Frunze is located in the Chu River valley, to the west of Alma-Ata on the Turkestan-Siberian railway. It has a largely Russian population of some 533,000; principle industries are textiles and machine building. In 1929 the city was renamed for Mikhail Frunze (1885–1925), the military leader who defeated the White Armies (q.v.) under Kolchak (q.v.) and Wrangel (q.v.).

FRUNZE, MIKHAIL V. (1885–1925). Born into a family of an army sergeant, he studied at the St. Petersburg Polytechnic, where he joined the Communist Party (q.v.). Frunze led several strikes during the 1905 revolution, was imprisoned and exiled, but escaped in 1916 to become an agitator among the soldiers at the front. He was one of the organizers of the Communist takeover in Moscow (q.v.) in October 1917 and served as an army commander in the civil war (q.v.) against Kolchak (q.v.) and Wrangel (q.v.). In 1925 Frunze replaced Trotsky (q.v.) as commissar for military and naval affairs and as chairman of the Revolutionary Military Council (q.v.). He died during an operation for ulcers under suspicious circumstances.

FURTSEVA, EKATERINA A. (1910–74). Born into a working-class family, she worked in a textile mill, then joined the Komsomol (q.v.) in 1924 and the Communist Party in 1930. During World War II (q.v.) Furtseva was secretary of the Frunze district party committee in Moscow (q.v.), and in 1956 she was elected to the Central Committee of the Communist Party (q.v.).

FUTURISTS. This was a group of Russian poets that came into being shortly before World War I (q.v.). Its members admired the wonders of modern technology and praised industrial development in their poetry and were much attracted to the promise of the Soviet industrialization program. They also claimed to be the only true poetic voice of the new order. Vladimir Mayakovsky (q.v.), Stalin's favorite poet, was one of its leaders.

G

GABO, NAUM (1890–1977). A noted sculptor of the Constructivist (q.v.) school, he returned to Russia from Germany after the 1917 revolution. Gabo soon became disillusioned with life in the Soviet Union, and in 1920 he challenged the right of Soviet authorities to interfere in art. Gabo returned to Germany in 1922 and then moved to the United States.

GAGARIN, IURII A. (1934–68). Born into a family of collective farmers in the Smolensk (q.v.) region, he graduated from the Saratov (q.v.) Polytechnic in 1955 and, after finishing at a military aviation school, became a fighter pilot. In 1961 Gagarin was the first man to orbit the earth. He died in a crash during a training flight.

GALICH, ALEKSANDR A. (pseud. of GINZBURG) (1919–77). A Muscovite, he worked at the Stanislavskii Film Studio and, after the end of World War II (q.v.), became a film script writer. During the 1960s Galich was popular for ballads that he wrote and sang himself. Expelled from the Union of Soviet Writers and Filmmakers in 1971, Galich emigrated and began work at Radio Liberty in Munich and Paris. He met with an accidental death in France.

GAPON, FATHER GEORGII A. (1870–1906). An Orthodox priest who cooperated with the tsarist police in organizing a workers' association, he led a march in January 1905 that attempted to petition the tsar in front of the Winter Palace (q.v.). This march resulted in a massacre when police opened fire on the participants.

GARVI, PETR A. (1881–1944). Born in Odessa (q.v.), he joined the Russian Socialist Democratic Labor Party (q.v.) in 1899 and participated in the 1905 revolution. He was active as a Menshevik (q.v.) in St. Petersburg (q.v.) and opposed the Communists. Arrested in 1916, Garvi was released after the 1917 revolution and became the editor of a socialist newspaper in St. Petersburg. He helped organize the

All-Russian Trade Union Congress that year. Because of his hostility to the Soviet government, Garvi moved to Germany in 1922, then to France in 1933, and finally to the United States in 1940, where he continued to be an active leader of the Menshevik party, and a participant in the international socialist movement.

GATCHINA. This small town some 25 miles south of St. Petersburg (q.v.) was a favorite residence of the imperial family. Catherine the Great (q.v.) built a summer palace there. During the coup that overthrew the Provisional government (q.v.) in October 1917, Kerensky (q.v.) attempted to rally anti-Communist forces in Gatchina, but failed.

GENERAL SECRETARY OF THE CENTRAL COMMITTEE. The post of general secretary of the Communist Party's Central Committee (q.v.) evolved shortly after the October 1917 revolution (q.v.). It was first occupied by Krestinskii (q.v.). After the 11th party congress in 1922, Lenin (q.v.) placed Stalin (q.v.) in the post, which he held until his death in 1953. The position of general secretary of the Communist Party (q.v.) continued to grow in power and was not abolished until after the collapse of the Soviet Union under Gorbachev (q.v.) in 1991.

GENERAL SECRETARY OF THE COMMUNIST PARTY (GENER-ALNYI SEKRETAR TSK KPSS). Stalin was the first to fill this post, elected by the Central Committee in 1922. After 1953 the position was termed "First Secretary"; "General Secretary" was reinstated at the 23rd party congress.

GENGHIS KHAN (1162–1227) (b. Temujin). The son of a Mongol chief, he conquered neighboring tribes and consolidated his hold on Mongolia. In 1211 he annexed the North Chinese empire and over the next ten years succeeded in extending his rule over central Asia. His subordinates continued the conquest of ever more distant lands, reaching Russia by way of Georgia in 1238. In his final years he organized the complete subjugation of his acquisitions. His empire was considerably extended by his grandson Kublai Khan (q.v.).

GEOGRAPHY, RUSSIAN. The Russian Federation is located on the eastern edge of Europe, south of the Arctic Ocean. To the east it is bounded by the Pacific Ocean, to the west by the Baltic Sea (q.v.). In the southwest it extends to the Caspian (q.v.), the Black (q.v.) and the Azov (q.v.) seas. Its territory is 6,592,812 square miles in size. Two-thirds of Russia is covered by forests inhabited by numerous and varied fauna, including many species of fur-bearing animals. It has more than 100,000 rivers, including the immense Lena (q.v.), Enisei (q.v.), Ob (q.v.), Irtysh (q.v.), Amur (q.v.) and Volga (q.v.), as well as large freshwater lakes such as Baikal (q.v.) and Lagoda (q.v.).

Its soil contains over 50 different types of minerals, as well as large energy resources from coal, gas and oil. Among these are the gigantic Kuznetsk and the Pecherskii coal basins and the Povolzhia, Ural, and eastern Siberia oil and gas basins. The Russian Federation also possesses large aluminum, copper, and lead deposits. In Siberia (q.v.) and the Ural Mountains (q.v.) there are deposits of diamonds and other precious stones.

The federation is divided into 11 primary regions: the Northern, Northwestern, Central, Central Black Earth, Volga-Viatskii, Povolzhskii, Severnokavkazkii, Uralskii, Zapodno-Sibirskii, Vostochno-Sibirskii, and Dalno-Vostochnyi. The economic conditions of life in these regions are sharply differentiated, and since the early 1990s this differentiation has deepened. The regions that have lost most from the current reforms are Moscow (q.v.) and St. Petersburg (q.v.)—regions that accounted for the largest percentage of military production. On the other hand, the regions that have benefited the most are those that produce natural resources and agricultural goods. The principal machine industry centers are Moscow, St. Petersburg, the Urals, the Povolzhie, and western Siberia. Chemical and oil extraction industries are concentrated in the central regions, the Povolzhie, and the Urals. The forest industry is located primarily in the northern and eastern regions.

GEORGIA. The region anciently known as Iberia is in central Transcaucasia on the east coast of the Black Sea and shares borders with Armenia, Turkey, Azerbaijan (q.v.), and Russia. It occupies an area of 26,900 square miles and has a population of 4,999,000. Georgia is mountainous to the north and south but has a central plain with abundant rainfall and a subtropical climate. Tobacco, tea and citrus fruits grow here, as well as other produce. Besides agriculture, principal industries include oil refining, metallurgy, hydroelectric power and machine building.

Georgia has a long history of statehood, beginning with the campaign of Alexander the Great against the Persian empire, which freed Georgia from Persian control. In the centuries following, Rome, Persia, the Seljuks, and the Mongols interrupted Georgia's sporadic independence; in 1639 Turkey and Persia divided the country between them. A military alliance with Russia in 1783 paved the way for incorporation into the Russian empire in 1801 of those Georgian principalities that were under Persian control. Georgian territories held by the Turks were gradually acquired by Russia throughout the 19th century. After the collapse of the Transcaucasian Federation (composed of Georgia, Armenia and Azerbaijan) in 1918, Georgia was an independent republic with a Menshevik-led (*see* Mensheviks) government. In 1921 the Red Army invaded and Georgia became a Soviet republic. Georgia became independent in 1991.

GERMAN-SOVIET NONAGGRESSION PACT see NAZI-SOVIET NONAGGRESSION PACT

GERTSEN see HERZEN

GESSEN, IOSIF V. (1866–1943). He was one of the founders of the Kadet (KD) party (q.v.). After the October 1917 seizure of power by the Communists, he emigrated to Germany, where he published a series containing massive quantities of archival material dealing with the Russian revolutions of 1917 and edited a Russian-language newspaper.

GILIAKS. This Asiatic people settled at the mouth of the Amur River (q.v.) and on Sakhalin Island (q.v.). Their number is small and they are engaged primarily in fishing and hunting.

GIMNAZIIA. A secondary school, lasting seven or eight years, it emphasized classical instruction in contrast to the *realnoe uchilishche* (Realschule), which stressed science and technology. Its graduates were considered to be qualified to enter a university.

GINZBURG, EVGENIIA S. (1904–77). A dedicated member of the Communist Party (q.v.), she was caught in the net of arrests during the 1930s and sentenced to penal servitude in the labor camps. She was released in 1947 and fully rehabilitated in 1956. Her book on concentration camp experiences was published posthumously.

GIPPIUS, ZINAIDA N. (1869–1945). The daughter of a government official, she grew up in the Caucasus (q.v.) and began publishing in 1888 as a Symbolist (q.v.) poet. She married Merezhkovskii (q.v.). Together they were prominent members of St. Petersburg (q.v.) literary circles before World War I (q.v.). Politically, she was close to the Socialist Revolutionaries (q.v.) party and in 1920 emigrated first to Poland and then to Paris, where she published her diaries.

GLADKOV, FEDOR V. (1883–1958). A Russian writer, he was the author of *Cement*, the first Soviet novel to describe the reconstruction of the country after the devastation of the civil war (q.v.).

GLAGOLITIC ALPHABET. An alphabet used in the oldest extant Slavic documents, its invention is attributed to Saints Cyril and Methodius (q.v.), two Byzantine monks who were posthumously beatified by the Orthodox Church (q.v.).

GLASNOST. Together with perestroika (q.v.), this was the central pillar of Gorbachev's (q.v.) attempts to reform Soviet society before the collapse of the USSR in December 1991. Its intent was to promote openness and to allow full public disclosure of the political and historical issues that had long been kept secret by the Soviet government. Glasnost rapidly acquired a momentum of its own and led to the elimination of most of the totalitarian practices that had characterized Soviet intellectual life since 1917.

GLAVKOSMOS. This is the name of the Soviet space agency that was created in 1986 under Gorbachev (q.v.). It was designed to exploit commercially the superior Soviet space technology.

GLAVLIT. This acronym was used for the Chief Administration for Literature in the Soviet Union, the principal instrument that controlled the literary output of the country's writers by acting as a censorship agency.

GLAZUNOV, ALEKSANDR K. (1865–1936). Born in St. Petersburg (q.v.), he studied under Rimskii-Korsakov (q.v.) and became a major Russian conductor and composer. From 1905 until 1928 Glazunov was the director of the St. Petersburg Conservatory. He then left the Soviet Union to settle in Paris.

GLIERE, REINGOLD M. (1875–1956). He graduated from the Moscow Conservatory in 1900 and went on to study music under Ippolitov-Ivanov (q.v.) and Fried. In 1920 Gliere became professor at the Moscow Conservatory and wrote a number of operas and ballets. He was a teacher of Prokofiev (q.v.), Khachaturian (q.v.), and Miaskovskii (q.v.).

GLINKA, MIKHAIL (1804–57). A student of John Field (piano), Glinka as a youth suffered from poor health and traveled extensively in Italy, where he became acquainted with contemporary Italian opera. After returning to Russia he wrote operas on Russian themes, such as *Ruslan and Liudmila* (1842), and made use of Russian folk motifs.

GODUNOV, TSAR BORIS (1551–1605). Uncle by marriage to Tsar Fedor (q.v.), Ivan the Terrible's (q.v.) son, he was the regent until Fedor's death in 1598, when he was enthroned as tsar. Godunov is suspected of having had Ivan's youngest son, Dmitrii (q.v.), murdered in order to ensure his own accession to the throne. He died near Moscow (q.v.) during the fighting against a pretender who claimed to be Dmitrii.

GOGOL, NIKOLAI V. (1809–1852). Of Cossack (q.v.) origin, he was a major 19th-century writer. Some of his works dealt with such realistic subjects as Russian serfdom, while others were classical political satire, such as his internationally known *Government Inspector.* Still other works border on surrealism and fantasy. Before the end of his life Gogol destroyed a large part of his works.

GOLDEN HORDE. This is the name of the Mongol state that was located on the lower Volga River (q.v.). It came into existence in the 13th century, following the Mongol conquest of most of the Kievan Rus (q.v.). Its rule extended over Russia as well over a large part of Siberia (q.v.). For nearly two centuries it exacted tribute from its vassals, until it was defeated by the grand princes of Moscow (q.v.).

GOLIKOV, FILIP (1900–80). A marshal of the Soviet Union, he joined the Communist Party and the Red Army (*see* Armed Forces, Soviet) in 1918. Golikov graduated from the Frunze military academy in 1933 and during World War II (q.v.) was head of the Soviet military intelligence (*see* GRU) and deputy defense commissar. After the war he headed the Soviet repatriation commission in Germany. From 1958 to 1962 he was chief of the political administration of the armed forces.

GOLITSYN, ANATOLII (1911–). Member of the KGB since 1946, he defected in Finland in 1961 and provided Western intelligence agencies with a framework for understanding the depth of Soviet intelligence operations in the West. He is the author of several books and articles on the topic.

GOLITSYN FAMILY. An ancient Russian princely family with numerous branches, many of its members occupied leading positions in the empire, and a number survived the Russian revolution to continue the family's tradition of service to the nation. Among its early members was Boris Golitsyn (1654–1713), the tutor of Peter the Great (q.v.). Another, Prince Dmitrii Golitsyn (1665–1737), commanded an army in Poland during Russia's war with Sweden.

GONCHAROV, IVAN (1812–91). He wrote the classic novel *Oblomov* (1859) about a landowner named Oblomov whose fantastic laziness prevents him from accomplishing anything. The term "oblomovism" (*oblomovshchina*) was coined to denote the same problem, particularly in relation to the Russian intellectual class's incapacity for action.

GORBACHEV, MIKHAIL S. (1931–   ). He was born to a peasant family in the Stavropol (q.v.) region, where he lived under the German occupation during World War II (q.v.). After the end of the war Gorbachev worked as a manual laborer until 1950, when he was admitted to the faculty of law at the University of Moscow (*see* Universities). In 1952 Gorbachev joined the Communist Party (q.v.). On graduating that year, he returned to his native region and became an active leader, first in the local Komsomol (q.v.) organization, then in the regional Communist Party. In 1968 he became the first secretary of the Stavropol city party committee, and in 1971 Gorbachev was elected to the Central Committee of the Communist Party (q.v.). In 1978 he was made head of its agricultural department and a candidate member of the Politburo (q.v.), and in 1980 he was promoted to full membership. After the death of Chernenko (q.v.) in 1985, he was chosen to be the general secretary of the Communist Party of the Soviet Union, and in 1990 president of the USSR. A year later he was held briefly under house arrest during a coup but was liberated after it collapsed. Gorbachev lost his position as president when the Soviet Union disintegrated in December 1991. He was awarded the Nobel peace prize for his role in de-escalating and then ending the Cold War with the United States. In the period leading up to the 1996 elections, Gorbachev once again appeared in the political arena, offering his own candidacy for president, but was unable to attract a significant vote.

GORKII see NIZHNII NOVGOROD

GORKII, MAKSIM see GORKY, MAXIM

GORKY, MAXIM (b. PESHKOV) (1868–1936). An outstanding Russian writer who, in his youth, worked as an itinerant toiler and first began publishing in 1892. Gorky traveled widely, visiting the United States and Europe. A supporter of Lenin (q.v.), he established a Marxist school on the island of Capri. Although they were friends, Gorky criticized Lenin for his dictatorial policies after the 1917 revolution and tried to protect the lives of many Russian intellectuals during the civil war (q.v.). Gorky left Russia in 1921 but returned in 1931 to become an exponent of socialist realism, the literary philosophy advocated by the Soviet government. He may have been killed on Stalin's (q.v.) orders by the secret police.

GORNO-ALTAI AUTONOMOUS REGION. An autonomous region of the Russian Republic situated on the border of the Mongolian People's Republic (q.v.), its population of under 200,000 is primarily engaged in cattle raising and gold mining.

GOSPLAN. This was the name of the state planning committee of the Soviet Union, the supreme agency for controlling economic development of the country. It had authority to decide all of the significant national economic activities until its functions were eliminated in 1990.

GOSUDAR. The Russian term for "lord" or "great sovereign," it was the formal manner of addressing the tsar. The term *gosudarstvo* (state), is derived from *gosudar* and signifies a state, nation or empire.

GOSUDARSTVENNAIA DUMA see DUMA

GOVERNMENT STRUCTURE, POST-SOVIET. In May and June of 1990, the first Congress of the People's Deputies of the Russian Soviet Federated Socialist Republic (q.v.) approved a declaration asserting the sovereignty of the Russian Republic and established a democratic government based on laws. It envisaged the separation of the state's executive functions from its legislative and its judicial roles. It also established the post of president of the Russian Federation and elected Boris Yeltsin (q.v.) to the office.

During the coup attempt in August 1991, both the executive and the legislative branches of government united against the perpetrators. Shortly thereafter, however, the two branches began to disagree, with legislators increasingly resisting reforms propose by the executive branch. Most members of the legislature were former Communist Party (q.v.) officials who had been elected during the Soviet period when elections were controlled by the party hierarchy. The vast majority of them resisted political and economic reforms because these threatened to undermine their privileges.

This opposition to reforms was helped by a lack of unity within the emerging democratic reform movement. As a consequence, the reformers were unable to obtain majorities either in the local soviets (q.v.) or in the new national Supreme Soviet (q.v.).

At the time, there was no firmly established independent judicial system. The Constitutional Court, which was supposed to adjudicate conflicts between the legislative and executive branches, itself became part of the conflict and openly sided with the antireform forces against President Yeltsin (q.v.). This struggle for power at the highest levels of government ended with an armed confrontation in October 1993.

After a brief but violent clash in the streets of Moscow, President Yeltsin dissolved the Supreme Soviet. New elections for the legislative branch were held in December 1993 concurrently with a nationwide referendum on a new constitution.

The designation of the country as the Russian Federation reflects its national character as well as its federal and republican structure. According to the new constitution, the Russian Federation owns all state property and operates a single monetary system. It possesses an armed force that is responsible for the security and integrity of the state. Its chief executive, the president, is elected for five years by direct, universal, and secret ballot and is limited to two terms of service. The president is the designated highest official of the nation. He represents it externally and is responsible for ensuring the cooperation of the executive, judicial and legislative branches of government. With the consent of the Federal Assembly, he appoints the head of the government (prime minister) and, on request by the prime minister, appoints and dismisses cabinet ministers, directors of state committees, and other state organizations. He also is the head of the state security council, and is authorized to issue mandatory administrative directives.

The highest legislative organ, the Federal Assembly, consists of two houses: the Council of the Federation and the Duma (q.v.). The Council of the Federation is composed of two representatives from each of the political subdivisions of the nation: one from its legislature and one from its executive branch. The Duma consists of 450 deputies elected for four years. The legislature impacts on the executive branch through its control of the budget and through such financial levers as taxation, availability of credit, the issuance of money, and the setting of tariffs.

The judicial branch has a three-layered structure. The first layer consists of a Federal Constitutional Court and the constitutional courts of the autonomous republics. The second layer is the Supreme Court of Arbitration, made up of local arbitration courts. The third is the Supreme Court and its subordinate local courts.

The highest unit of the executive branch is the council of ministers of the Russian Federation. It is subordinate to the Federal Assembly and to the president and consists of the chairman of the council of ministers (prime minister), his deputy, the ministers, and chairmen of the state committees. On the lowest level of the executive branch are local departments that are responsible for acting within their administrative-territorial units.

GOVERNMENT STRUCTURE, SOVIET. Shortly after the Communists overthrew the Provisional government (q.v.) in October 1917, the old governmental institutions began to be liquidated, including the senate, the Most Holy Synod (q.v.), and the various courts of law, and decrees were issued abolishing all titles and legal class distinctions. The sole official designation for adult individuals was henceforth to be that of "citizen." The process of forming the central institutions of Soviet society began. The principal executive organ of state power was henceforth to be the Council of People's Commissars (q.v.).

The first council consisted exclusively of Communists, but soon Lenin (q.v.) co-opted the Left-Socialist Revolutionaries (q.v.), in order to obtain greater support from the Russian peasantry. Seven representatives of that party joined the council in December 1917. Their cooperation with the Communists did not last long, however. By March 1918, the Social Revolutionaries left the government in protest against the Brest-Litovsk peace treaty (q.v.) with Germany, and by July 1918 they were excluded from all Soviet institutions, along with the Mensheviks (q.v.). After this date and until the dissolution of the Soviet Union in 1991, the Communist Party (q.v.) remained the sole legal political party in the USSR.

In December 1917 a criminal investigative unit was created by the Council of People's Commissars. This extraordinary commission— known by its acronym, the Cheka (q.v.)—was headed by Feliks Dzerzhinskii (q.v.) and was established to fight counterrevolution, sabotage, and monetary speculation. Two months later the people's courts and the revolutionary tribunals were established. Other decrees of the Council of People's Commissars created the Red Army and Fleet (*see* Armed Forces, Soviet). All banks were nationalized, and a single state bank was created to replace them.

The country's privately owned industry and businesses were also nationalized, and their administration was placed in the hands of the All-Russian Central Executive Committee (VTsIK). All external government debts were annulled, and a state monopoly on foreign trade was introduced. The People's Commissariat of Education was created, and all matters dealing with education, art, and literature were placed under its purview.

In January 1918, having been unsuccessful in obtaining a majority in the freely elected Constituent Assembly, Lenin dispersed it. In its stead, the Soviet government convened the Third All-Russian Congress of Soviet, Workers', Soldiers', and Peasants' Deputies, which issued a declaration called "The Rights of Toilers and Exploited Peoples." It also decreed that the nation henceforth would be ruled by a "dictatorship of the proletariat," which would be enforced by a Soviet government that was led by the Communist Party.

This congress severely limited the civil and political rights of a significant part of the country's population. It elected an All-Russian Central Executive Committee (q.v.) that consisted of 62 Communists, 29 Socialist Revolutionaries, and two representatives of other socialist parties. In the 1920s, the power of the Communist Party was enlarged. Party functionaries were given the exclusive right to manage all aspects of the country's life, and membership in the Communist Party became the prerequisite for government service. No question of any importance could be decided without its approval. The national and local soviets (councils) were transformed into rubber-stamp organizations, and all other political parties were outlawed. In the 1930s the Soviet dictatorship was further entrenched by total state control over all social organizations.

This system produced the alienation of large sections of the population from the Soviet government. In order to strengthen his hold on power, Stalin (q.v.), who since the late 1920s had dominated the Communist Party, initiated a series of show trials in which accused former rivals were forced to confess to espionage and sabotage. These trials provided scapegoats for the general malfunctioning of the Soviet system.

After Stalin's death in 1953 and the condemnation of the cult of his personality by the new general secretary, Khrushchev (q.v.), an improvement in the political climate of the country began, and the rehabilitation of thousands of political prisoners took place. However, no fundamental changes in the command-administrative system of government were made, and the power of the Communist Party bureaucracy remained intact. An effort at economic reform was undertaken in the middle of the 1960s by Prime Minister Kosygin (q.v.), but no new approach to the Soviet economy proved possible because of the total monopoly of power exercised by the Communist Party.

The role of the party bureaucracy continued to grow, and malfeasance grew at the top of the political pyramid. The atmosphere of flattery, subservience and bribe taking thickened, and acute struggles for power increased among government officials. After the death of General Secretary Brezhnev (q.v.) in the early 1980s, attempts were made to find a remedy for this process of disintegration.

When Gorbachev (q.v.) was elected to the top party post in the mid-1980s, he instituted a two-pronged effort: perestroika (q.v.), or institutional reconstruction, and glasnost (q.v.), or openness in government. Despite five years of effort and some success, by the end of

1991 the rule of the Communist Party was terminated, the Soviet state collapsed, and the USSR broke up into 15 independent republics.

GPU, GLAVNOE POLITICHESKOE UPRAVLENIE. The Russian acronym for Chief Political Directorate, it replaced the Cheka (q.v.) in 1922 as the principal instrument of political control over the Soviet population. It was attached to the Commissariat of the Interior and, in 1923, renamed the OGPU (Unified Chief Political Directorate). In 1926, Stalin (q.v.) began to utilize the Soviet secret police against his inner-party opposition. By the end of the 1920s he had developed the technique of blaming political opponents for all the mistakes for which his own policies were responsible. He ordered the GPU to search for hidden enemies among prosperous peasants and for saboteurs among technical personnel within Soviet industry and to arrest these "enemies of the people."

One of the first public manifestations of this policy was the Shakhty (q.v.) trial of engineers in the Donbas coal fields. Soon thereafter, the OGPU "discovered" a connection between these "saboteurs" and employees of Gosplan (q.v.), the central planning institution of the USSR.

In 1930 the OGPU began arresting individuals working in the commissariat of finances and the Supreme Council of National Economy (q.v.). The arrested individuals were accused of activities designed to harm the Soviet economy and restore capitalism. Another task of the OGPU was the liquidation of the kulaks (q.v.) (prosperous peasants) as a class. This involved mass arrests and forcible deportation to the wastelands of Siberia (q.v.). In order to expedite this program, the OGPU was granted extraordinary quasi-judicial powers. In lieu of regular courts, it was authorized to create judicial committees composed of its own officers who were given the right to investigate, to try, and to pronounce sentences on the accused.

In 1930 the OGPU also carried out a large operation against officers of the Red Army who had served in the imperial forces but had remained in Russia to work within the Soviet government. By 1930, the network of concentration camps covering the country was expanded, and the chief camp administration—the Gulag (q.v.)— was established as part of the OGPU. Over 300,000 individuals, a large number of whom were political prisoners, were incarcerated in these camps. Three years later their number had risen to several million. The OGPU also imprisoned high-ranking members of the Communist Party, such as the group under the leadership of Riutin, a member of the Central Committee who was arrested and eventually shot. In 1934, during the periodic purge campaign within the party, agents of the OGPU frequently dictated the results of individual hearings. In that year the OGPU was placed within the Commissariat of the Interior and renamed the NKVD (q.v.), the Russian acronym for the People's Commissariat of Internal Affairs.

GRACHEV, PAVEL (1948-   ). Graduate of the Frunze Military Academy, Grachev served in Afghanistan in the early 1980s and became commander of airborne troops; he supported Yeltsin (q.v.) during the crucial August 1991 period and was subsequently named deputy minister of defense and later minister of defense of the Russian Federation. He was widely criticized for his handling of the Chechen seizure of the Russian town of Budennovsk and was upstaged by Prime Minister Chernomyrdin's successful negotiation of terms there. Grachev has since been dismissed from his government posts.

GRANOVSKII, ALEKSANDR (1890–1937). He was the founder and director of the Jewish Theater, which initially was located in Leningrad (*see* St. Petersburg) and then moved to Moscow (q.v.), where it was renamed the Moscow State Jewish Theater. Its repertoire was largely based on the works of the Yiddish writer Sholem Aleichem (q.v.).

GRAZHDANIN. This is the Russian term for citizen. In the 18th and 19th centuries, the term referred to a minority stratum of the Russian urban population equivalent to the upper and middle classes. It excluded servants and the peasantry. By a decree of the tsar in 1832, *pochetnye grazhdane* ("honorary citizens"), were defined as persons with a higher education, upper groups of merchants, and children of "personal nobles," that is, those individuals who possessed the status of nobility for themselves but could not transmit it to their children. They enjoyed a number of legal privileges, among which was exemption from corporal punishment.

GREAT RUSSIANS. This is the historic name for that branch of Eastern Slavs that constituted the primary ethnic population of old Muscovy (q.v.), as contrasted with Belorussians (White Russians) and Malorussians (Ukrainians). The former resided on the western borders of Muscovy, around Minsk (q.v.), the latter to the south, around Kiev (q.v.). These three names also refer to geographical areas. All three groups recognized themselves as descendants of the original Kievan Rus (q.v.) state and as members of the Eastern Slav population.

GRECHANINOV, ALEKSANDR T. (1864–1956). He was a student under Arenskii and Rimskii-Korsakov (q.v.) at the St. Petersburg Conservatory of Music. Grechaninov's compositions were primarily in the form of romances on texts by such notable poets as Baudelaire, Lermontov (q.v.) and Pushkin (q.v.). He emigrated from Russia to Western Europe in 1925, then moved to the United States, where he continued to compose.

GRIBOEDOV, ALEKSANDR S. (1795–1829). A well-known Russian dramatist and author of the 19th century, he was a student at the University of Moscow (*see* Universities) before joining the army in 1812. After the war he became a civil servant in the ministry of foreign affairs and served as the Russian ambassador to Persia, where he was murdered by rioting mobs. Griboedov's literary output consists primarily of prose and verse comedies, chief among them *Gore ot Uma* (*Woe from Wit*).

GRIGORENKO, PETR G. (1907–87). Born into an impoverished peasant family, he served in the food requisition detachments during the 1920s and in the Red Army (*see* Armed Forces, Soviet). He rose to the rank of divisional commander during World War II (q.v.). After the war he was promoted to the rank of major general and became the head of the Frunze Military Academy. In 1964 Grigorenko was dismissed from his posts, stripped of rank, and imprisoned in a psychiatric hospital for criticizing the Stalinist system. On his release from the asylum he became a leader of the dissident movement and one of the initiators of the Helsinki Monitoring Group (q.v.). He left Soviet Russia in 1977 and died in the United States.

GROMYKO, ANDREI A. (1909–89). He joined the Communist Party (q.v.) in 1931 and the next year graduated from the Institute of Economics and became head of the American Department of the Soviet Foreign Office. In 1943 he was named ambassador to the United States and in 1946, ambassador to the United Nations, as well as a member of the Central Committee of the Communist Party. By 1957 he was minister for foreign affairs and in 1973 became a member of the Politburo (q.v.). He nominated Gorbachev (q.v.) for the post of secretary general of the Communist Party in 1985, then was promoted to the largely honorific post of chairman of the presidium of the Supreme Soviet (q.v.), the titulary presidency of the USSR.

GROSSMAN, VASILII S. (1905–64). Grossman was educated as an engineer and began working as a mining engineer in the Donbas. He came to the attention of Gorky (q.v.) with his first novel in 1934. During World War II (q.v.) Grossman worked as a war correspondent for the Red Army (*see* Armed Forces, Soviet) newspaper, and after the war he began to write novels and plays, many of which were banned in the Soviet Union.

GROZNYI. Capital of the Autonomous Republic of the Chechen (*see* Chechnya) and Ingush (q.v.) in the north Caucasus (q.v.), it is a region rich in oil. The population is approximately 400,000.

GRU. This is the Russian acronym for the chief military intelligence directorate of the Russian armed forces, which reports directly to the general staff. It was the organization that recruited and ran such Soviet spies in Great Britain as Philby.

GUBERNIIA. This was the largest administrative division of Russia before the revolution. It was established by Peter the Great (q.v.) and headed by a *gubernator* (governor). In 1914 there were 78 such administrative districts in the Russian empire.

GUCHKOV, ALEKSANDR (1862–1936). Founder of the Octobrist Party, he was president of the third Duma (q.v.) in 1910, from which position he resigned the following year. He was critical of the tsarist government and instrumental in the abdication of Tsar Nicholas II (q.v.). He served as war minister in the Provisional government (q.v.) but resigned in May 1917, emigrating to France after the Bolshevik (q.v.) revolution.

GUINS, GEORGE (1887–1971). Graduate of the University of St. Petersburg (*see* Universities), Guins served in the ministry responsible for administering the relocation of landless peasants to free government land in Siberia (q.v.). During the civil war (q.v.) Guins served as a minister in the anti-Communist government of Admiral Kolchak (q.v.). After the defeat of the White Armies (q.v.) he settled first in Harbin (q.v.), China, and then moved to California, where he was editor of a Russian-language newspaper and later professor at the University of California (Berkeley). His memoirs, published by the Regional Oral History Office of the Bancroft Library, provide a rich panorama of Russia during the first half of the 20th century.

GUL, ROMAN (1896–1986). He served as a junior officer in World War I (q.v.), then joined the White Armies (q.v.) of Kornilov (q.v.) in 1917. He moved to Germany after the end of the civil war (q.v.) and lived there until 1933. During the 1920s he began writing novels. With his wife and brother, Gul moved to France after Hitler came to power in Germany. In 1950 Gul went to the United States and took over the editorship of a Russian-language periodical. Before his death Gul published extensive memoirs.

GULAG. *Glavnoe Upravlenie Lagerei*, or Chief Administration of Camps. This organization incarcerated political as well as criminal prisoners in forced labor camps. At its height in the 1930s and 1940s, Gulag was in charge of nearly two million prisoners located in over 50 camps. After 1987, all political prisoners were released.

GUM. This is the Russian acronym for the State Universal Store. During the Soviet era, this state-run Moscow (q.v.) emporium, located close to Red Square (q.v.), featured the most abundant selection of merchandise in the country.

GUMILEV, NIKOLAI S. (1886–1921). A son of a naval doctor, he published his first volume of poetry in 1905. Gumilev studied French literature at the Sorbonne between 1907 and 1908 and married Anna Akhmatova (q.v.) in 1910. He became a well-known figure in St. Petersburg (q.v.) literary circles and was one of the leading members of the Acmeist (q.v.) movement. During World War I (q.v.) he served in the army and was decorated for bravery. After the civil war (q.v.) he was tried by the Soviet government, allegedly for participating in a monarchist plot, found guilty and executed. Gumilev's works were republished in the Soviet Union only after 1986.

GUREV. A town located at the Ural River's (q.v.) mouth to the Caspian Sea (q.v.), its main industries are oil refining and fishing. Its population is just over 100,000.

GUZENKO, IGOR (1919–85). After graduating from the Moscow Engineering Academy, he served as an agent of Soviet military intelligence, the GRU (q.v.). Between 1943 and 1945 Guzenko was posted to Ottawa, Canada, as a cipher clerk, from which post he defected and revealed a great deal of information about Soviet espionage activities in the West. Guzenko published an autobiography as well as a novel, in which he alleged that Stalin (q.v.) had been responsible for the death of Gorky (q.v.).

GYPSIES see ROMA

H

HAGUE CONVENTION (1899). The Russian government sought hereby to limit the growing costs of the technological development of weapons and the expansion of war objectives that would naturally occur in their use, an example being aerial bombardment. Little headway was made on this issue at the first or second Hague conferences, and the third (to have been held in 1915) was postponed because of the war. Innovations in weapon technology by that time made similar undertakings irrelevant.

HANNIBAL, ABRAHIM. The great-grandfather of Pushkin (q.v.), Russia's greatest poet, he was an Ethiopian slave who was presented to Peter the Great (q.v.) by the sultan of Turkey and who became a general in the Russian army.

HARBIN. A city in the middle of Manchuria on the Sungari River, it was built in the 1880s as the administrative center of the Russian-owned Chinese Far Eastern Railroad (q.v.). It was located on a narrow strip of land on both sides of the railroad that the Chinese government had ceded to Russian administration and within which Chinese laws did not apply. This state of affairs lasted until after the October 1917 revolution (q.v.), when Soviet Russia surrendered its treaty rights to China. In the early 1920s several hundred thousand anti-Communist (White) Russians, fleeing from the victorious Red Army (*see* Armed Forces, Soviet) through Siberia (q.v.), settled temporarily in Harbin and, because of the prosperity of the region, earned for it the appellation of "Moscow of the Orient." After the Japanese army occupied Manchuria in 1931 this prosperity rapidly vanished and most of the city's Russian residents moved elsewhere.

HEALTH MAINTENANCE. The development of health maintenance during the Soviet period was uneven. On the one hand it was not adequately financed, even in the most prosperous period, during the 1960s and 1970s. (The index of the total expenditures on health in the USSR did not exceed 4.3 percent of the gross national product, in comparison to the expenditures in many developed countries of up to 10 to 15 percent.) According to data provided by the World Health Organization, in 1991 the life span in the Soviet Union was in 54th place (64.8 years for men) and 47th place for women (73.6 years). The low limits of expenditures of income on health maintenance workers, food and drugs, as well as the lack of any material incentives for improving the level of medical service to the general population led to an inefficient use of available resources.

Alongside the generally low level of medical service, there also existed a number of excellent facilities available only to the privileged members of the Soviet nomenklatura (q.v.). As well, the general population was well supplied with doctors, since there were approximately 50 doctors per 10,000 of population (as compared to worldwide standards of some 30 to 40). The number of beds was also large, some 130 per thousand as compared to 56 in the United States. In addition, Soviet health maintenance covered the whole population as well as providing free services. It was also heavily oriented toward preventive medicine, with a very well-organized system of combating epidemics.

The transition to market relationships has seriously affected those sectors of the economy that produce medicine and medical equipment; the chief Russian supplier of this equipment for medical institutions has recently become a commercial enterprise. As a result of rising prices and the severe financial limitations of the government, the supply of medical equipment to the country has been greatly reduced. The sick frequently do not receive required medicines and food. At the present time the country is experiencing a transition to medical care that is paid for by insurance rather than directly out of general state funds. In June 1991 a law was passed requiring that all medical insurance premiums for employees be paid by the organizations where they work. For those who are not employed, they must be paid for by local territorial administrations. The guaranteed levels of medical services, the amounts of the premiums, and the prices for treatment are established by the government.

HELFLAND, ALEKSANDR L. (pseud. PARVUS) (1867–1924). While a student at Basel University in 1887, he met a number of leading exiled Russian Marxists. After graduating in 1891 Parvus moved to Germany, where he became acquainted with such German Social Democratic leaders as Karl Kautskii and Clara Zetkin. In Munich he edited, together with Lenin (q.v.), the newspaper *Iskra* (q.v.). Parvus was one of the leaders of the 1905 revolution in St. Petersburg (q.v.), for which he was arrested and incarcerated in the Peter and Paul fortress. Exiled to Siberia (q.v.), he managed to escape back to Germany. During World War I (q.v.) he helped the German general staff foment revolutionary subversion in Russia. He helped arrange Lenin's trip through Germany in the spring of 1917 and is believed to have channeled large amounts of German funds to the Communists. He remained in Switzerland after World War I.

HELSINKI MONITORING GROUP. This was a group of Soviet citizens who organized themselves for the purpose of monitoring the Soviet government's promise to honor the commitment made in the treaty it signed at Helsinki. This treaty guaranteed human rights to Soviet citizens.

HERMITAGE MUSEUM. Originally part of the Winter Palace (q.v.) in St. Petersburg (q.v.), it was constructed by Catherine the Great (q.v.) to house her art collection. It later became a center for theatrical and musical activities in St. Petersburg.

HERZEN, ALEKSANDR (1812–70). The illegitimate son of a wealthy nobleman, Herzen was known as the father of the Russian left-wing intelligentsia. He greatly admired the Decembrists (q.v.), who had attempted to overthrow the tsar and create a democracy in Russia. Exiled for taking part in radical conversations, he later served in the Russian army; then, after inheriting a vast fortune, Herzen moved to London, where he became a publicist and the editor of *Kolokol* (q.v.), a Russian-language antigovernment periodical published in England that was widely read inside Russia by the intelligentsia.

HOLY SYNOD see MOST HOLY SYNOD

I

IABLONOVYI KHREBET. This mountain range in Siberia (q.v.) runs east of Lake Baikal (q.v.) between the Amur (q.v.) and Lena (q.v.) rivers for some 700 miles and forms the watershed between the Pacific and Arctic Oceans.

IAGODA, GENRIKH (1891–1938). He headed the NKVD between 1934 and 1936. From 1904 an adherent of the Bolsheviks, and exiled from 1911 to 1913, Iagoda was a member of the commissariat of foreign trade after October 1917; in 1920 he was made one of the heads of the Cheka (q.v.). Iagoda conducted the first two purges but was replaced by Ezhov and made commissar for communications. He was arrested in 1937 and shot as a member of the "Anti-Soviet Bloc of Rightists and Trotskyites."

IAKIR, IONA E. (1896–1937). Later to become a distinguished Soviet general, Iakir joined the Bolsheviks (q.v.) in 1917, and he was active in the October Revolution (q.v.) in Bessarabia (q.v.). Later he was a leader of the Red Guards and a commander on the southwestern front during the civil war (q.v.). In the 1930s he was instrumental in introducing changes to the Red Army. He was arrested and shot in 1937.

IAKOVLEV, ALEKSANDR (1906–   ). As an aeronautical engineer and Soviet general colonel, he was twice made a Hero of Socialist Labor for his work in designing fighter aircraft (the YAK series).

Among them were Russia's first jet fighter (1945) and first supersonic fighter (1952). He was also a recipient of many Stalin prizes (q.v.).

IAKUBOVICH, MIKHAIL (1891–1975). He joined the Bolsheviks (q.v.) before World War I (q.v.), then changed over to the Menshevik (q.v.) party but continued favoring collaboration with the Communist Party (q.v.). He held high posts in the Soviet government until his arrest and trial in 1930. He was sentenced to hard labor and was imprisoned in the Gulag (q.v.) labor camps until 1956.

IAKUTIIA see SAKHA

IAROSLAV (978–1054). Ruler and consolidator of the Kievan state, he is assumed to have compiled the first collection of Russian laws, known as Russian Truth (*Russkaia pravda*).

IAROSLAVL. An important industrial center established in the 11th century, it is located at the confluence of the Kostrol and Volga rivers (q.v.). It is the capital of the Iaroslavl region and produces textile, electrical and rubber products. Its population is just over 600,000.

IAROSLAVSKII, EMILIAN M. (b. GUBELMAN) (1878–1943). He joined the Russian Socialist Democratic Labor Party (q.v.) in 1898, was exiled from 1907 until 1917, and then participated in the October 1917 revolution (q.v.). A strong supporter of Stalin (q.v.), he was the chairman of the Old Bolsheviks Society and a member of the Central Committee of the Communist Party (q.v.). As head of the Union of Atheists, he was in charge of conducting antireligious propaganda. He is often accused of being one of the principal Stalinist falsifiers of the history of the Communist Party (q.v.) and as the man who became a devoted assistant to Stalin and ghostwriter of the latter's *Short Course History of the Communist Party of the Soviet Union.*

IAVLINSKII, GRIGORII see YAVLINSKY, GRIGORY

IAZOV, DMITRII T. (1923–91). He served in the army in World War II (q.v.), then graduated from the Frunze Military Academy in 1956 and from the Academy of the General Staff in 1967. In 1987 Iazov became the minister of defense of the USSR and visited the United States as part of an exchange of military commanders in the late 1980s. Iazov participated in the attempt to overthrow Gorbachev (q.v.) in 1991, then committed suicide.

ICON. An image of either Christ, the Virgin, or saints that had been consecrated in a religious ceremony. It is an object of veneration as well as a channel of prayer for the faithful in the Byzantine tradition of the Orthodox Church (q.v.).

IGOR, GRAND PRINCE (877–945). The second Varangian (q.v.) ruler of the Eastern Slavs, he made Kiev (q.v.) his capital and spent much of his time expanding his power militarily. Although his raid on Byzantium failed, he was able to obtain significant concessions from the Greeks for his merchants. His wife, St. Olga (q.v.), converted to Christianity and was influential in the subsequent conversion of Kievan Rus (q.v.) to Byzantine Orthodoxy (see Orthodox Church).

ILF, ILIA A. (1897–1937). The son of a bank clerk, he graduated from the Odessa Technical School and worked as a designer. Ilf began publishing poetry at a young age, and in 1924 he became president of the Poets' Union in Odessa. After moving to Moscow (q.v.), he worked as a newspaper reporter and, together with Petrov (q.v.), published several satirical novels that gained wide popularity in Russia, among them *The Twelve Chairs*. In the 1930s Ilf was the *Pravda* (q.v.) correspondent in the United States.

ILIN, IVAN A. (1883–1954). He graduated from the University of Moscow (see Universities) with a degree in law in 1906, then studied in Germany and France. Ilin lectured at the University of Moscow between 1912 and 1922, when he was expelled by Soviet authorities from Russia, after which he lived in Berlin from 1922 to 1938, teaching at the Russian Scientific Institute. After being dismissed from this position by Nazi authorities, Ilin moved to Zurich.

ILIUMZHINOV, KIRSAN (1963-). President of Kalmyk Republic since 1993, he is noted for his flamboyance and enigmatic political vision. As a youth he was the republic's chess champion and later became a successful businessman with important Japanese contacts. His administration sought to bring about economic stability through strict, even authoritarian, measures, including the banning of opposition newspapers. He is rumored to have mystical beliefs that he combines with a hard-headed business sense.

ILIUSHIN, SERGEI V. (1894–1977). A Communist since 1918, he served with the Red Army (see Armed Forces, Soviet) during the civil war (q.v.). Iliushin graduated from the Zhukovskii Air Force Academy in 1926, then became an aircraft designer and a major figure in the Soviet aircraft industry. Iliushin was elected to the Academy of Sciences (q.v.) of the USSR in 1968.

ILMEN LAKE. A large body of fresh shallow water near Novgorod (q.v.), this lake is located about 100 miles south of St. Petersburg (q.v.). It is drained by the Volkhov River (q.v.), which then flows into Ladoga Lake (q.v.).

IMAGISTS. This was a literary movement that began in 1919 in Russia as a successor to the Futurists (q.v.). One of their foremost exponents was Sergei Esenin (q.v.), who is known for his use of coarse language and violent imagery in his poems. The movement fell apart because of internal discord before the end of the 1920s.

IMANDRA LAKE. Located some 60 miles south of the city of Murmansk (q.v.), this body of freshwater, which abounds in fish, covers approximately 300 square miles.

IMEMO. This is the acronym for the Institute of World Economy, one of the institutes belonging to the Russian Academy of Sciences (q.v.). It specializes in the study of foreign economies, as well as other external political affairs.

IMPERIAL BALLET COMPANY see KIROV BALLET COMPANY

IMPERIAL GOVERNMENT STRUCTURE. The governmental structure of the Russian empire was formed during the era of Peter the Great, (q.v.) in the late 17th and early 18th century and, with minor changes, it lasted until the revolutions of 1917. Peter divided Russia into provinces (*guberniia*) and made the senate the highest secular institution of the state. This body consisted of individuals who were close to the tsar (q.v.) and who had distinguished themselves in his service. The highest state organ for church affairs became the Most Holy Synod (q.v.). After Peter the Great, the old principle of selection for office based on family lineage ceased to be the sole criterion. Administration of the affairs of state was done by collegia that, after 1802, were transformed into ministries. Each collegium had areas of defined responsibilities, as well as power to carry them out. The three most important ones were foreign affairs, war, and the admiralty. Three separate collegia dealt with finances: the collegium responsible for the gathering of taxes; one for state control, which distributed the funds; and the revision collegium, which supervised the activities of the first two. There was also a collegium responsible for manufacturing and another for internal trade. The mandate that regulated their activities was known as the *Generalynyi Reglament* of 1720.

The Table of Ranks was promulgated in 1722. It was designed to regulate the personnel of the government. All of the state service posts were divided into 14 ranks. Each rank was in turn subdivided into a military, civil or courtly category. The qualification necessary to obtain a position was changed from that of family membership to one's ability to perform the required tasks. In order to control the activities of civil servants, Peter the Great established the office of the procurator, responsible for supervising the civil service. In the course of time an administrative center grew up that was attached directly to the person of the tsar, was independent of the other civil service structures, and wielded real power. At different periods it was called by different names: first, the senior secret council, then the cabinet.

During the reign of Nicholas I (q.v.) (1825–55), the absolutism of the monarchy was strengthened. At the bottom of the hierarchy, Russian society was characterized by a total dependence of the peasants on the state officials or landlords, and at the top, by the unlimited power of the monarch. The dominant principle of administration was subservience of lower organizations to higher ones. Significant administrative changes occurred in the 1860s, during the reign of Alexander II (q.v.), when, together with the elimination of the institution of serfdom, other reforms were carried out: the land reforms, the educational reforms, the judicial reforms of 1864, and the press reforms in April 1865. The reforms of the military occurred in 1874. As a result of these changes in the state administrative structure, the beginnings of a civil society were made possible.

From that time on, appointments to local administrative posts were made on the basis of election for a three-year term. These local administrative organizations—the zemstva (q.v.)—were empowered to make decisions for their localities; the execution of these decisions was vested in a corresponding local administrative board. This restructuring affected both rural localities and urban ones. Another consequence of the 1860s reforms was that the country's courts became relatively independent, and judges could no longer be removed from their posts. A professional organization of lawyers came into being, anticipatory censorship was almost completely eliminated, universities received the right to self-administration, a universal draft liability was introduced, and the period of military service was shortened. By the beginning of the 20th century, the state bureaucracy had grown to a vast size, consisting of some 436,000 civil servants. At its center was the ministry of the interior, which supervised all of the country's

governor-generals, governors, city heads, and other local administrators.

IMPRESSIONISM. Russian impressionism in art was a derivation of
the French movement. It began after 1885 with the work of such artists as Konstantin Korovin (q.v.).

INDUSTRIAL PARTY. An invention of the Soviet secret police in the
early 1930s, it was ostensibly an anti-Soviet organization that was
said to consist of former anti-Communist socialists who remained in
Russia working as experts in Soviet industry. A number of them were
falsely accused of sabotage in one of the earliest Soviet open political
trials.

INGUSH. An ethnic Moslem group living in the Chechen–Ingush Autonomous Republic (*see* Chechnya) of the northern Caucasus (q.v.),
it numbers slightly over 100,000. In 1944 Stalin (q.v.) ordered their
deportation for allegedly collaborating with the German army.

INKERMAN, BATTLE OF. This was the biggest armed encounter between the Franco-British invading armies and Russian defenders during the Crimean war near the fortress of Sebastopol (q.v.).

INTELLIGENTSIA (Russ: *Intelligentsiia*). A 19th-century term used in
Russia to describe individuals of different social backgrounds who
were literate and who shared common attitudes toward politics, culture, and literature. This term began to be used in Russia after the
middle of the 19th century. Originally, it designated individuals who
were engaged in intellectual rather than manual work. Before the turn
of the century, this was a thin layer of society that, according to the
1890 census, did not exceed more than one half of one percent of the
population. The same census shows that there were no more than
290,000 individuals with a middle or higher education in Russia. Politically conscious individuals considered that opposition to the existing imperial government was the defining attribute of the
intelligentsia, irrespective of other social or educational criteria. By
the beginning of the 20th century, the intelligentsia began to differen-
tiate itself into three distinct groupings: the aristocratic-conservative,
the middle-class (bourgeois) liberal, and the revolutionary-demo-
cratic.
    Following the October 1917 revolution (q.v.), most of the Russian
intelligentsia emigrated. However, after the expansion of Soviet industrialization during the late 1920s and the 1930s, a new layer of
technologically educated individuals, coming mainly from the work-

ing and peasant classes, began to be referred to as the "new Soviet intelligentsia." This growth in the number of educated Soviet individuals was subjected to repeated waves of repression. In the 1930s numerous writers, artists and scientists were arrested and executed by the political police for holding views that were considered dangerous. Also, interference by the Communist Party (q.v.) leadership in the creative work of Soviet artists, musicians, and writers placed drastic limits on the activities of the new Soviet intelligentsia.

After the condemnation of the cult of Stalin (q.v.) by Khrushchev (q.v.) in 1956, there was an improvement in the life of Soviet artists and scientists. However, this thaw did not last long. With Khrushchev's fall in 1964, a renewed drive took place to instill a "Soviet unity of thought." Many representatives of the intelligentisa were imprisoned or exiled.

With the inauguration of the policy of glasnost (q.v.) by Gorbachev (q.v.) in 1986, a new era of freedom came to Soviet Russia; censorship was eliminated for all practical purposes, and wide scope was given to artistic and scientific creativity. The intelligentsia is considered to be the principal beneficiary of Gorbachev's glasnost reforms, which permitted freedom of expression and free access to different ideas and political viewpoints and eliminated the ideological dominance of Marxism-Leninism (q.v.) from Russian cultural life. In the post-Soviet period this trend has continued and expanded. However, because of cuts in government expenditure on cultural and artistic activities, the economic well-being of these groups has suffered.

INTERFAX. This Russian national network of journalists, correspondents, and radio broadcasters has replaced the Soviet-era Tass news agency. It was jointly founded by Russian and Franco-Italian interests in 1990.

INTERNATIONAL, THE THIRD. Established by Lenin (q.v.) in 1919, the Third, or Communist, International (see Comintern) was designed to be the general staff of the world Communist movement. It was dissolved by Stalin (q.v.) during World War II (q.v.) as an accommodation to Great Britain and the United States.

INTOURIST. A state-owned and operated agency under the Soviet regime, it controlled all interactions with foreign tourists entering the Soviet Union. After the collapse of the USSR, the agency has continued to operate but without exercising the political surveillance over foreign visitors that it once did, nor has it today any monopoly on the tourist business in Russia.

IOANN, ARCHBISHOP OF SAN FRANCISCO (b. SHAKHOVSKOI) (1902–89). Born into the princely Shakhovskoi family, he was educated at the Lyceum School in St. Petersburg (q.v.) and fought with the White Armies (q.v.) during the civil war (q.v.). He left Russia in 1920 for Belgium and Greece, where he took his monastic vows. He served as a priest in Berlin during the 1930s and 1940s. After World War II (q.v.) he moved to San Francisco and became archbishop of the Orthodox Church (q.v.) in America.

IOANN, ARCHBISHOP OF SHANGHAI (1896–1966). Son of a nobleman, he was educated in a Cadet Corps school. In 1918 he graduated from the Kharkov University (*see* Universities) with a degree in law and emigrated to Yugoslavia after the civil war (q.v.). There, he earned a degree in theology from the University of Belgrade. In 1926 he took monastic vows and in 1934 became the bishop of Shanghai. He came to the United States in 1949 to become the archbishop of San Francisco.

IOFFE, ADOLF A. (1883–1927). Educated as a medical doctor, he became an active revolutionary in the 1890s and participated in the October 1917 revolution (q.v.). He was head of the Soviet delegation to the Brest-Litovsk (q.v.) peace negotiations with Germany in 1918, then in 1922 he was included as part of a delegation to the Geneva Conference. In 1924 he was made Soviet ambassador to Austria. A prominent supporter of Trotsky (q.v.), he committed suicide after the latter's defeat in the power struggle with Stalin (q.v.).

IPATIEFF, VLADIMIR N. (1867–1952). A chemical engineer by profession, he was the chairman of the State Chemical Committee in 1914. He remained in Russia until 1927, when he moved to the United States. During World War II (q.v.) he developed a process of refining high-octane aviation fuel.

IPPOLITOV-IVANOV, MIKHAIL M. (1859–1934). A graduate of the St. Petersburg (q.v.) Conservatory, he began composing and conducting in 1882. Between 1905 and 1922 Ippolitov-Ivanov was the director of the Moscow (q.v.) Conservatory and a conductor at the Bolshoi Theater (q.v.). Influenced by Caucasian and Oriental themes, he is highly regarded for his operas.

IRINEI, METROPOLITAN OF AMERICA AND CANADA (1892–1981). Educated at the Theological Seminary in Kholm in 1914, he was ordained a priest in 1916 and served in German refugee camps during and after World War II (q.v.). In 1952 Bishop Irinei went to the United States to become archbishop of Boston and New England, then of New York, and finally was elevated to the post of metropolitan (q.v.) of America and Canada. He was largely responsible for negotiations that led to the official separation (autocephalia) of the Orthodox Church (q.v.) in America from the patriarchate of Russia (q.v.) in the early 1970s.

IRKUTSK. A major Siberian city, it was established in the middle of the 17th century and is located close to the confluence of the Irkut and Angara (q.v.) rivers, close to Lake Baikal (q.v.). It was the capital of eastern Siberia in the 19th century. Today it is a major industrial and academic center.

IRTYSH RIVER. This major Siberian river flows south to north past the cities of Omsk (q.v.) and Tobolsk (q.v.) until it joins the Ob River (q.v.).

ISHKAN. This acronym stands for the Institute of the United States and Canada, an institute of the Russian Academy of Sciences (q.v.) created in the middle of the 1970s to study the economy and political life of the United States and Canada.

ISKRA (THE SPARK). A newspaper established jointly by Lenin (q.v.), Plekhanov (q.v.), and other exiled Russian socialists in Munich in December 1900. Its original purpose was to act as the organizing center for Russian social democracy. Lenin and the Communists lost control of it in 1903, but it continued to be published by the Menshevik (q.v.) wing of the Russian Socialist Democratic Labor Party (q.v.) until the paper's demise in October 1905.

IUSUPOV see YUSUPOV.

IVAN I KALITA, GRAND PRINCE OF MOSCOW (1304–41). The "moneybag," he became prince of Moscow (q.v.) in 1325 and soon after was elevated to the title of grand prince by his Tatar (q.v.) overlords, whom he served faithfully as a tax collector.

IVAN II, GRAND PRINCE OF MOSCOW (1326–59). He successfully exploited the decline of Mongolian power in order to expand the territory of his small Moscow (q.v.) principality.

IVAN III THE GREAT, GRAND PRINCE OF MOSCOW AND TSAR (1440–1505). Also known as "the gatherer of the Russian lands," he married Zoe Paleologue, the niece of the last Byzantine emperor, in

1472. Ivan thereby created a claim by Moscow (q.v.) to be the Third Rome (q.v.) and acquired the right to use the Byzantine double-headed eagle as his standard, as well as the designation tsar (caesar). Ivan stopped all tribute payments to the Tatars (q.v.) in 1480, thus finally freeing Russia from their yoke. In 1493 he claimed the lands of Kievan Rus (q.v.), which were under Polish and Lithuanian rule, and took the title of Sovereign of All the Russias.

IVAN IV THE TERRIBLE, TSAR (1530–84). He ascended to the Russian throne as a youth of 17 but was kept for a long time under the tutelage of a dominant noble family. Ivan was married early to Anastasia Romanova, the daughter of the head of one of the aristocratic factions. In 1549 Ivan summoned a Zemskii Sobor (q.v.) (Council of the Land), in order to initiate legal and administrative reforms. As a result, a number of changes were made in the administration of the church, the army, and the civil service. Ivan's armies defeated the Tatars (q.v.) of Kazan (q.v.) and the hostile Livonian Order of Knights and occupied Astrakhan (q.v.) on the Caspian Sea (q.v.). After Anastasia's death in 1560, he underwent a change of character, withdrew from all contacts with the nobility, became suspicious of everyone around him and created the *Oprishchnina*, a semimonastic order formed from the lower ranks that functioned as the tsar's bodyguard and enforcer of his orders to arrest, torture and execute. In 1580 Ivan killed his oldest son in a fit of rage.

IVAN V, TSAR (1682–96). The retarded son of Tsar Aleksei (q.v.), he succeeded his brother Fedor III (q.v.) to the throne. He ruled together with his half-brother Peter I (q.v.) under the regency of their sister Sophia Alekseevna (q.v.). After Peter overthrew her in 1689, Ivan continued as nominal coruler but never took part in the affairs of state.

IVAN VI, TSAR (1740–64). Grandson of Ivan V (q.v.), he acceded to the throne as a child. His mother served as regent until she was forced out in 1764 by supporters of Elizabeth (q.v.), the daughter of Peter the Great (q.v.). Ivan was murdered by his guards during the reign of Catherine the Great (q.v.).

IVANOV-RAZUMNIK, RAZUMNIK V. (pseud. IVANOV) (1878–1946). Son of a nobleman, he graduated from the faculty of mathematics at the University of St. Petersburg (*see* Universities), and as a young man became a revolutionary. In 1907 Ivanov-Razumnik published an influential study of the history of Russian social thought. During the February 1917 revolution (q.v.) Ivanov-Razumnik supported the Left-Socialist Revolutionaries (q.v.) and opposed the Communists. After the October 1917 revolution (q.v.) he moved abroad and became leader of the Scythian (q.v.) movement, which stressed Russia's role as a semi-Asiatic society. At the end of World War II (q.v.) he was a displaced person in Germany.

IVANOVO. The capital city of the region of the same name north of Moscow (q.v.). It is a large manufacturing center with a population of nearly half a million.

IVANSKAIA, OLGA V. (1913-   ). This was a close friend of Boris Pasternak (q.v.), the "Lara" in his novel *Doctor Zhivago*. She was arrested in 1949 and sentenced to five years in a prison camp. In 1960 she was rearrested on the charge of having acted as Pasternak's go-between with a Western publisher, but was released in 1964.

IZHEVSK. Founded in the 1760s, this city became the capital of the Udmurt Autonomous Republic (q.v.) after the 1917 revolution. Today it is a major metallurgical and industrial center with a population of over half a million. Named Ustinov in the Soviet period.

IZVESTIIA. A newspaper, formerly the official organ of the Provisional government (q.v.), and later of the Soviet government. Its circulation was over four million before the collapse of the USSR. Today it is an independent publication owned by its staff.

IZVOLSKII, COUNT ALEKSANDR P. (1856–1919). He was Russia's foreign minister, and from 1910 Russian ambassador to France. He concluded the treaty with Great Britain which ended the dispute between that country and Russia over their rivalry in the Middle East.

J

JAWLENSKII, ALEXEI (1864–1941). Trained by Repin (q.v.), he became a noted painter of the experimental school. During his residence in Munich he was strongly influenced by Kandinskii (q.v.) and, later, in France, by Matisse.

JEWS. With the annexation of Eastern Poland during the reign of Catherine the Great (q.v.), Russia acquired a large Jewish population, which resided primarily in its western provinces. Before the revolutions of 1917, the vast majority of Jews in the Russian empire were restricted to residence in the "Pale" (q.v.), which was located in its western regions. In the early 1950s, just before Stalin's (q.v.) death and after the founding of Israel, a massive "anti-cosmopolitan" campaign was organized in the Soviet press and linked with a "Doctors' Plot" (q.v.). Zionism was declared to be an ally of the CIA and other foreign intelligence organizations, and a number of Soviet Jews were either arrested or lost their posts. Those who applied for emigration to Israel were routinely refused exit visas and turned into internal exiles, often losing their jobs and means of livelihood. By the 1980s, under foreign pressure these Soviet emigration policies began to be relaxed until today there exist no restrictions on Jewish emigration, nor is there any evidence of continued state-sponsored anti-Semitism in Russia. By 1990, there were fewer than two million Jews remaining in the former Soviet Union, most of whom lived in Russia, Belarus (q.v.) and Ukraine (q.v.). Only a small percentage of these remain religious believers. As perestroika (q.v.) and glasnost (q.v.) proceeded, the number of synagogues and other Jewish organizations began to increase.

JOB, PATRIARCH. In 1589 he was the first Russian prelate to be raised in 1589 to the rank of Patriarch of Russia by the Patriarch of Constantinople, who was the titular head of the Orthodox Church (q.v.). He was removed by the first False Dmitrii (q.v.) under pressure from his Polish Jesuit advisors in 1605.

JULIAN CALENDAR. Introduced under Julius Caesar into the Roman world, this calendar had 365.25 days in a year, (365 days, plus one additional day every four years). In the West this system was replaced by the Gregorian calendar in 1582, and adopted by most European countries. Until the time of Peter the Great (q.v.) the Russian calendar began the new year on September 1st. In 1700, Peter adopted the Julian system which remained in force until after 1918, when the Gregorian system was adopted by the Soviet government. As a result, Russia's pre-1918 calendar does not coincide with the Western one and the "October Revolution," which took place in October according to the old calendar, actually occurred on November 7th of the Western calendar.

K

KABALEVSKII, DMITRI B. (1904–86). Born in St. Petersburg (q.v.), he completed his musical education at the Moscow (q.v.) Conservatory in 1930 and then became a professor and a composer. Kabalevskii was held in high esteem by the Soviets and made secretary of the

Union of Soviet Composers in 1952, as well as head of the Council on Aesthetic Education in 1969.

KABARDINO-BALKARIA AUTONOMOUS REPUBLIC. This republic borders on Georgia and Stavropol krai, occupying 7,800 square miles, having a population of 700,000. Its capital is Nalchik. Of its principal parts Kabarda joined Russia in 1557, and Balkaria in 1827; the two were combined in 1922 as an autonomous oblast, becoming an autonomous republic in 1936. Industries are mining, stock breeding, and cultivation of corn, hemp, grapes, and other vegetables. The Balkars are a turkic-speaking people, their language belonging to the northwest or Kipchak branch; the Kabardians speak a northwest Caucasian language of the Abkhazi-Adygei group.

KADET (KD) PARTY. This was the common name for the Constitutional Democrats party, a middle-of-the-road political party in the Duma (q.v.) before the 1917 revolutions. The Kadets consisted primarily of representatives of the Russian intelligentsia, a part of the liberally inclined landlords, the urban middle classes, and the higher civil servants. Its Central Committee and its Duma representatives were mainly members of the Russian educated classes, and its leader was the well-known historian Pavel Miliukov (q.v.). In March and April of 1917 the party had over 380 active local committees with a total membership of over 70,000. In the program documents of the Kadets, the future Russian government was envisioned as a parliamentary, constitutional monarchy as in England. The Kadets considered a partial allocation of arable land to the peasants as essential. They also advocated an eight-hour working day, and the right of workers to form unions and to strike. The Kadet Party was outlawed in 1918.

KAGANOVICH, LAZAR M. (1893–1991). Born into a Jewish working-class family, he joined the Communists in 1911 and served as a soldier in World War I (q.v.). After the October 1917 revolution (q.v.) he was elected a member of the Constituent Assembly (q.v.) and served as a commissar in the Red Army (*see* Armed Forces, Soviet) during the civil war (q.v.). In 1924 Kaganovich became a secretary of the Central Committee of the Communist Party (q.v.) and in the early 1930s was placed in charge of the collectivization campaign in the Ukraine (q.v.). Kaganovich was also active during the purges of the late 1930s. In 1935 he became the commissar of transportation and in 1937, commissar of heavy industry. Kaganovich joined Molotov (q.v.) and several other members of the Politburo (q.v.) in 1957 in an attempt to halt Khrushchev's (q.v.) policy of de-Stalinization. For this, he was expelled from the Communist Party.

KALEDIN, ALEKSEI M. (1861–1918). A Cossack (q.v.) from the Don (q.v.), he graduated from the General Staff Academy in 1889 and served as a cavalry commander during World War I (q.v.). In 1917 Kaledin was elected Ataman (commanding general) of the Don Cossacks and led an unsuccessful attempt to overthrow the Communists, committing suicide after the attempt failed.

KALININ see TVER

KALININ, MIKHAIL I. (1875–1946). Born into a peasant family, he joined the Russian Socialist Democratic Labor Party (q.v.) in 1898, and was active in the 1905 revolution (see Revolution of 1905). Kalinin became a member of the Central Committee of the Communist Party (q.v.) in 1919 and of its Politburo (q.v.) in 1925. Beginning in 1938 he held for many years the largely honorific post of chairman of the Central Executive Committee of the USSR, the nominal head of state of the Soviet Union. He had no political power, but served as a symbol of peasant participation in the Soviet government.

KALININGRAD. Formerly Konigsberg, this was once capital of East Prussia. It is an ice-free port on the Bay of Vistula that was annexed by the Russian Republic at the end of World War II (q.v.). Today it is a developed industrial area with a population of nearly 400,000.

KALMYKIA AUTONOMOUS REPUBLIC. This area is part of the Russian Federation, located about two hundred miles west of Astrakhan (q.v.). It is primarily a fishing and cattle breeding area, inhabited by over 300,000 people of predominantly Mongolian ancestry.

KALUGA. An industrial city situated some 100 miles southwest of Moscow (q.v.), it has a population close to 300,000.

KAMA RIVER. Starting in the Udmurt Autonomous Republic (q.v.), it flows in a northerly and easterly direction toward its confluence with the Volga (q.v.) near the city of Kazan (q.v.).

KAMCHATKA. A peninsula, approximately 500,000 square miles in size, which projects from eastern Siberia (q.v.) into the Pacific Ocean. It is rich in fishing, fur and forest products. During the Stalin (q.v.) era it was notorious as a concentration camp area that held hundreds of thousands of convicts. Today its population is just over 300,000.

KAMENEV, LEV (b. ROSENFELD). (1883–1936). An "Old Bolshevik," (q.v.), he became a revolutionary while a student at University of Moscow (*see* Universities), from which he was expelled for political activities. Kamenev joined the Russian Socialist Democratic Labor Party (q.v.) in 1901 and emigrated to Western Europe in 1903, after which date he was closely associated with Lenin (q.v.). On his return to Russia during the 1905 revolution (*see* Revolution of 1905) he was elected to the Duma (q.v.) as a Communist. Arrested in 1914, Kamenev was exiled to Siberia (q.v.). One of the first Communist leaders to return to the capital after the February 1917 revolution (q.v.), Kamenev became editor of the Communist newspaper *Pravda* (q.v.) and a member of the party's Politburo (q.v.). Together with Stalin (q.v.) and Zinovev (q.v.) he was part of the troika, or triumvirate, that ruled the Soviet Union after Lenin became ill in 1922. He was falsely implicated by the GPU in 1934 in the murder of Kirov (q.v.). He remained a close ally of Zinovev, and was tried and executed with him in 1935.

KAMENEV, S. S. (1881–1936). Educated at the Alexander Military Academy and at the Academy of the General Staff, he nevertheless joined the Red Army (*see* Armed Forces, Soviet) in 1918 and commanded the forces that fought against Admiral Kolchak (q.v.) in Siberia (q.v.) during the civil war (q.v.). He was the supreme commander of the Red Army until 1924, and is buried in the Kremlin wall.

KAMENSKII, VASILII V. (1884–1961). He was a Futurist (*see* Futurists) poet who began publishing in 1904 and a close friend of Vladimir Mayakovsky (q.v.). In 1935 Kamenskii was arrested, tried, and sentenced to death as a foreign spy.

KANDINSKII, VASILII V. (1866–1944). One of the founders of the modern movement in Western art, he was born in Moscow (q.v.) and graduated from the University of Moscow (*see* Universities). In the late 1890s he studied art in Germany and did not return to Russia until the outbreak of World War I (q.v.), when he organized the Museum of Painting in St. Petersburg (q.v.). In 1921 Kandinskii left Russia once again and settled in Germany, where in 1922 he became professor at the Bauhaus. He moved to France in 1933 and then to the United States, where he remained until his death.

KANTEMIR, ANTIOCH (1708–44). He was a scholar who introduced syllabic verse in familiar, spoken Russian and thus laid the foundations for literary Russian.

KAPITSA, PETR L. (1894–1984). Born into the family of a military engineer, he studied physics in England in 1921 and then became the deputy head of the Cavendish Research Laboratory at Cambridge. On his return to Russia in 1934 he was made head of the Institute of Physical Problems. He was elected to the Academy of Sciences (q.v.) of the USSR in 1939 and also to the Royal Society in England. Kapitsa was arrested by Stalin (q.v.) for refusing to do military work. After Stalin's death he was released and reappointed head of the institute.

KAPLAN, FANNY (b. ROIDMAN) (1893–1918). A member of the Socialist Revolutionary Party, Kaplan was arrested by the tsarist police for a bombing in Kiev (q.v.) and imprisoned. Freed by the 1917 revolution, Kaplan shot at and seriously wounded Lenin (q.v.) in June 1917, for which act she was arrested and executed.

KAPPEL, VLADIMIR O. (1883–1920). A graduate of the Nikolaevskoe Cavalry School in 1903 and of the General Staff Academy in 1913, he fought against the Red Army (*see* Armed Forces, Soviet) during the civil war (q.v.) as the commander in chief of Kolchak's (q.v.) anti-Communist White Armies (q.v.) in Siberia (q.v.). Severely frostbitten during the army's winter retreat, he lost both legs and finally died of pneumonia.

KARA SEA. A northern sea, it adjoins the Arctic Ocean. Several of the largest Siberian rivers, including the Ob (q.v.) and the Enisei (q.v.), empty into it. It is ice-free only in late summer.

KARACHAIEVO-CHERKESS AUTONOMOUS REGION see CIRCASSIA

KARAGANDA AREA AND CITY. A notorious area during Stalin's (q.v.) rule, it was the center of numerous concentration camps. The city of Karaganda was established in the middle of the last century as a base for coal and copper mining industries. Today it is also a center of steel manufacturing and has a population of close to half a million.

KARAKOZOV, DMITRII V. (1840–66). He is remembered for being the first of the 19th-century Russian terrorists who made an attempt to assassinate a tsar (q.v.). Karakozov, as an impoverished student, shot at, but failed to kill, Emperor Alexander II (q.v.) in 1866.

KARAMZIN, NIKOLAI M. (1766–1826). Born in the Orenburg (q.v.) province, Karamzin studied at the University of Moscow (*see* Universities) and then traveled widely in Western Europe. On his return to

Russia Karamzin began publishing his literary efforts and started work on a history of Russia. Karamzin became the court historian of Nicholas I (q.v.).

KARELIA AUTONOMOUS REPUBLIC. An autonomous republic within the Russian Federation, it was formerly part of Finland. Finland renounced all claims to the territory in 1990. Its population in the early 1990s was approximately 750,000.

KARPOVICH, MIKHAIL M. (1887–1959). A member of the Socialist Revolutionaries (q.v.) party, he graduated from the University of St. Petersburg (*see* Universities) and became a lecturer in history in 1914. In 1917 he was a member of the Russian embassy to the United States and did not return to Russia. He held the post of lecturer in Russian history and head of Harvard's Slavonic department until 1954. He also served as editor of a Russian-language periodical in the United States from 1943 until 1959.

KARSAVIN, LEV P. (1882–1952). He studied history at St. Petersburg University (*see* Universities) and graduated in 1913 to become professor of medieval history. In 1922 Kurasavin was expelled from Russia by the Soviet government and accepted a position first at Kaunas, and then at the Vilno University in Lithuania (q.v.). In 1940 he was dismissed from his post by the Lithuanian Soviet government, arrested, and later sent to a concentration camp.

KARSAVINA, TAMARA P. (1885–1979). She made her debut as ballerina at the St. Petersburg Mariinskii Theater (q.v.). A few years later she helped found the Diaghilev's (q.v.) Ballets Russes (q.v.), where she was the dance partner of Nijinsky (q.v.); she was the principal ballerina in works such as *Petrouchka*, *Giselle*, *Le Spectre de la rose*, and *The Fire Bird*. Based in London after 1917, she also helped found the Royal Ballet of London.

KARTASHOV, ANTON V. (1875–1960). A graduate of the St. Petersburg (q.v.) Theological Academy in 1899, he taught the history of religion at the University College for Women in St. Petersburg from 1906 to 1918. He was appointed procurator of the Most Holy Synod (q.v.) and commissar of religion by the Provisional government (q.v.) in 1917 but was arrested by the Soviet government in 1918. A year later he emigrated to Paris, where he became a professor at the St. Sergius Theological Institute.

KASPAROV, GARRI (1963–   ) (b. WEINSTEIN). A native of Baku, Azerbaijan, Kasparov won his first international chess tournament at

16 and played Anatoly Karpov for the world title in 1984; he was successful in his second bid in 1985, becoming the youngest world champion. A skillful entrepreneur and supporter of reform in Russia, he also helped found the Professional Chessplayers' Association with Nigel Short. In 1996 he managed to defeat the IBM computer Deep Blue in what many believed was to be the last time natural ability would prevail over artificial intelligence in chess.

KATYN FOREST. This forest area on the territory of the Belarus (q.v.) Republic is where the bodies of several thousand Polish army officers were discovered by the Germans during World War II (q.v.). Poland accused the Soviets of being responsible for the massacre, a charge the Soviet authorities denied until President Yeltsin (q.v.) admitted to Soviet guilt for the crime in 1992.

KAVERIN, VENIAMIN A. (b. ZILBER). (1902–). A novelist and member of the Serapion Brothers (q.v.) group of writers during the 1920s in Russia, after Stalin's (q.v.) death he attempted to upgrade Russian literary values in his capacity as an editor of a Moscow (q.v.) literary almanac.

KAVERIN, VLADIMIR A. (1891–1938). A member of the Socialist Revolutionaries (q.v.) party and one of the Left-Socialist Revolutionaries (q.v.), Kaverin served in the coalition government with the Communists as commissar of state property. Kaverin was the organizer of the revolt in July 1918 against the Communists and, after the coup failed, fled abroad.

KAZAKHSTAN. A republic of 1,062,500 square miles with a population of 14,498,000, it is the second-largest of the former Soviet republics. It is situated in north central Asia and borders on China, Siberia (q.v.) and the Caspian Sea (q.v.). Almost two-thirds of the population are non-Kazakh, chiefly Russian, but also deportees such as the Volga Germans. The capital is Alma-Ata (sometimes written Almaata). Industries include metallurgy and coal mining.

KAZAN. Known as Gorkii during the Soviet period, and the capital of the Tatar Autonomous Republic (q.v.) it has a population of about 4.5 million.

KEMEROVO REGION. This region of southern Siberia contains the Kuznetsk basin, measuring some 37,300 square miles. It is rich in coal and iron deposits. Industries include metallurgy and chemical works.

KERCH. A port city in the Crimea on the Kerch peninsula, it was known anciently as Panticapaeum. It has a population of some 158,000 and important shipbuilding and iron industries.

KERENSKY, ALEKSANDR F. (1881–1970). The son of a schoolteacher, he studied law at St. Petersburg University (*see* Universities) and gained early fame as a defense lawyer in political cases. He was a member of the Duma (q.v.) and leader of its Labor Group, (*Trudoviki*). After the February 1917 revolution (q.v.) he was chosen deputy chairman of the St. Petersburg soviet (q.v.), as well as deputy head of the provisional committee of the Duma. In March 1917 he was made minister of justice, and in May, minister of defense. Then, in July 1917, he became prime minister of the Provisional government (q.v.) and commander in chief of the Russian armed forces. Kerensky refused to sign a separate peace with Germany and opposed the efforts of Lenin's (q.v.) followers to capture power by force. After the October 1917 revolution (q.v.), he emigrated from Russia to Berlin, then to France and finally, in 1940, to the United States.

KGB. KOMITET GOSUDARSTVENNOI BEZOPASNOSTI. This is the Russian acronym for the Committee of State Security, the last of a series of names of the Soviet secret police. It was created in March 1954 and grew in number of employees to somewhere close to 500,000 individuals. This organization styled itself as "the punishing sword of the party" and exerted an unlimited amount of force on all Soviet citizens who did not fit into the narrow demands of the ideology of the Communist Party (q.v.).

At the end of World War II (q.v.) there were over 1.5 million political prisoners in the USSR, and by the time of Stalin's (q.v.) death in 1953 this number had almost doubled. This increase was brought about because of the post-1946 party-initiated struggle against "cosmopolitanism," as well as the so-called Leningrad Affair (q.v.), during which all of the party leadership of that city was arrested. In addition, there occurred the so-called doctors' plot (q.v.), a conspiracy of the "doctors-poisoners" who were accused of attempting to kill Stalin. After the trial of former secret police chief Beria (q.v.) in 1954, the worst forms of terror that the KGB and its predecessors had employed—torture and indiscriminate shootings—were stopped, and millions of individuals were freed from the concentration camps of the Gulag (q.v.). However, the Soviet social system continued to be based on the fear generated by the activities of this secret state police. It was only after the 20th party congress in 1956 that a mass rehabilitation of political prisoners was initiated, almost all of those still alive being released and most of the dead ones being rehabilitated posthumously as having been innocent of any crime.

The KGB was the principal source of intelligence for the ruling party hierarchy, and its analytic activities were of the highest professional caliber. As an organization it reached into all aspects of Soviet life and it was capable of controlling all of them. The organization of the KGB was divided into a series of departments. The First Department dealt with international intelligence gathering. The Second Department was responsible for counterintelligence. The Third Department handled counterintelligence within the Soviet armed forces. The Fourth Department dealt with transport security. The Fifth Department struggled against nonconformist thinking of Soviet citizens and was one of the most active departments of the KGB. The Sixth Department was responsible for the economic security of the USSR.

At the end of the 1980s the Fifth Department was renamed the "Z" Department and given the formal responsibility for protecting the existing constitutional structure of the country. Among other tasks, its personnel were charged with the supervision of a series of well-known individuals within the Soviet Union.

Another Department of the KGB had the task of safeguarding the top leadership of the Communist Party (q.v.) and of the Soviet government. A Department of Communications supervised all coded communications of the government and attempted to monitor and penetrate the codes of foreign powers.

In addition, the KGB also commanded large numbers of troops who were charged with maintaining the security of the Soviet frontiers. Local committees of the KGB were active in the regional and union republics as well. Finally, the KGB maintained two schools for the training of its personnel, the Higher School of the KGB and the Andropov Red Flag Institute. After the collapse of the August 1991 coup, the KGB underwent major reforms, being broken up into a series of independent organizations. In November of 1991 the KGB of the R.S.F.S.R. was renamed the Agency for Federal Security of the Russian Republic.

KHABAROVSK, CITY AND OBLAST. This city and region on the Amur River (q.v.) in eastern Siberia (q.v.) is the center of the region's industrial and commercial activities and has a population of just over half a million.

KHACHATURIAN, ARAM (1903–79). This Armenian composer incorporated Armenian folklore themes into his works. His "Sabre Dance" is perhaps most widely known; he also wrote for ballet and film. He was a professor at the Moscow Conservatory beginning in 1951.

KHAKASS. Traditionally nomadic inhabitants of the Kransoiarsk region who speak a Turkic language of the Uigher group, they number around 100,000 and live by herding and some agriculture. They are sometimes called Enisei Tatars.

KHAKASS AUTONOMOUS REGION. The region is inhabited mostly by the Khakass (q.v.), who live on the Enisei River (q.v.) of the Krasnoiarsk (q.v.) territory of the Russian Federation.

KHALIB, IAKOV N. (1908–80). He took his early training in photography and, after 1929, began freelancing as a photographer for Soviet newspapers. In 1938 Khalib took part in the Soviet expedition to the North Pole as its official photographer. Between 1938 and 1941 he traveled throughout the Soviet Union taking photographs for Soviet periodicals. During World War II (q.v.) he served as a war correspondent.

KHALTURIN, STEPAN L. (1856–82). He was a leader of the Northern Union of Russian Workers (q.v.), one of the early trade unions in Russia. Later, Khalturin became a terrorist and smuggled dynamite into the Winter Palace (q.v.) in St. Petersburg (q.v.). The explosion killed 11 individuals but did not harm Tsar Alexander II (q.v.). Khalturin was tried for this offense and executed.

KHANTY-MANSIF NATIONAL AREA. This Siberian national area is situated near the confluence of the Irtysh (q.v.) and the Ob (q.v.) Rivers and is rich in oil and gas deposits. Its population is under 300,000.

KHARKOV. A city in Ukraine (q.v.), it was founded in 1654 and has a population of 1,400,000. It is both an important railway junction and a center of machine building.

KHAVKINA, LIUBOV BORISOVNA (1871–1949). She was a librarian and bibliographer who created Russia's first library science courses and who wrote several works on cataloging.

KHAZARS. A seminomadic people, they lived on the banks of the lower Volga River (q.v.) as late as the 12th century. Their state covered a large area from the Dnepr River (q.v.) to the Ural Mountains (q.v.). The Khazars converted to Judaism, and some writers, among them Arthur Koestler, have argued that they eventually migrated to central Europe and were the ancestors of East European Jewry.

KHERSON. The administrative center of the Kherson oblast in Ukraine (q.v.), with a population of 319,000, it is located on the Dnepr River (q.v.) near the Black Sea (q.v.). Shipbuilding, machinery, textiles and food processing are its chief industries.

KHLEBNIKOV, VIKTOR V. (1885–1922). The son of a scientist, he studied at Kazan (q.v.) and St. Petersburg (q.v.) universities (q.v.). In 1917 Khlebnikov began publishing his poetry and joined the Futurists (q.v.). He supported the 1917 revolutions but refrained from directly engaging in politics. A bohemian, he lived an erratic life and died of hunger shortly after the civil war (q.v.).

KHMELNYTSKYI, BOHDAN (1590?-1657). He was a Ukrainian ataman of the Cossacks (q.v.) who led a rebellion against the Polish administration of the Ukraine (q.v.) in 1648 and again in 1651. In 1654 he signed a treaty with the Russians, bringing about a gradual growth of Russian influence in the Ukraine.

KHODASEVICH, VLADISLAV F. (1886–1939). Born into a family of Polish origin, he studied at Moscow University (*see* Universities) and began publishing his poetry in 1908. In 1922 he emigrated from Russia to Western Europe. Khodasevich was a close friend of Gorky (q.v.) and frequently visited him at his villa in Capri. He is also known for his literary criticism.

KHODYNKA FIELD. This is the location of the disastrous celebration of the coronation of Nicholas II (q.v.), in St. Petersburg (q.v.), which took place on May 18, 1896. During the festivities panic seized a crowd of over half a million people, which resulted in hundreds being trampled to death.

KHORVAT, DMITRII L. (1858–1937). A graduate engineer, Khorvat served in the Lifeguards regiment before becoming the director of the Chinese Far Eastern Railroad (q.v.) in Manchuria in 1902. After leaving this post in 1918, he remained in China until his death.

KHRENNIKOV, TIKHON N. (1913–). He graduated from a musical conservatory in 1936 and then, in 1941, became the director of the Soviet Central Army Theater. He was also head of the Union of Soviet Composers after 1948, and from 1976 a candidate member of the Central Committee of the Communist Party (q.v.), and the recipient of a Stalin prize (q.v.). He is said to have been responsible for the implementation of dictatorial party policies in the field of music.

KHRUSHCHEV, NIKITA S. (1894–1971). Born into a Russian miner's family living in the Ukraine (q.v.), his first work was as a cowherd. In 1918 he joined the Communist Party (q.v.) and served as political commissar in the Red Army (*see* Armed Forces, Soviet) during the civil war (q.v.). In 1929 Khrushchev was a student at the Industrial Academy in Moscow (q.v.) and then worked in that city's political administration department. In 1935 he was made first secretary of the Moscow party committee, and in 1938, the secretary of the Ukrainian Communist Party.

An active supporter of Stalin (q.v.), Khrushchev participated in the purges of the late 1930s. He was elected a member of the Politburo (q.v.) in 1939. After Stalin's (q.v.) death, Khrushchev won the struggle for succession against Malenkov (q.v.) and Beria (q.v.) and, in 1956, at the 20th party congress, he revealed some of Stalin's crimes. As head of state and the Communist Party, he did much to expand friendly relations between the Soviet Union and foreign countries, traveling widely and visiting the United States. Khrushchev came close to an armed confrontation with the United States in 1962 over the deployment of atomic missiles in Cuba.

In 1964 Khrushchev was forced to resign by his colleagues in the Politburo (q.v.) on the grounds of ill health. In retirement, he wrote extensive memoirs that reveal many details of the nature of the Soviet system.

KIAKHTA. This is a town in the Buriat Autonomous Republic (q.v.) near the Mongolian border, about 150 miles from the capital, Ulan-Ude (q.v.).

KIAKHTA, TREATY OF. This was a treaty signed by Russia and China. It established relations between the two countries in 1728 and allowed Russia to maintain an embassy in Beijing.

KIEV. Presently the capital of the Ukrainian Republic (*see* Ukraine), it was known as the "Mother City" of the Slav inhabitants of the plains east of Poland and west of the Ural mountains (q.v.). It was the capital of the Varangian (q.v.) rulers of ancient Rus (q.v.) and cradle of the Russian Orthodox Church (q.v.) after the baptism of Grand Prince Vladimir (q.v.) in A.D. 988. Kiev was conquered and devastated by the Mongol invaders in 1240. It was left nearly uninhabited for decades until it began to recover slowly under the protection first of Lithuanian, then Polish, then the dynastic Riurik (q.v.) princes of

Moscow. During the rule of the Romanov dynasty (q.v.), it was considered to be the third most important city of their empire after Moscow (q.v.) and St. Petersburg (q.v.).

KIEVAN RUS. This region was ruled by the Varangian (q.v.) dynasty that descended from the legendary Riurik (q.v.), with its capital at Kiev (q.v.). The borders of this East Slavic state extended from the Dnepr River (q.v.) north to the Gulf of Finland, and from Lithuania (q.v.) in the west to the realms of the nomadic Turkish tribes in the east. The Varangian dynastic rules of succession were such that the senior members of the Riurik dynasty ruled the most important cities, with Kiev being the foremost, while its lesser members became princes of smaller towns such as Vladimir (q.v.), Suzdal (q.v.), Novgorod (q.v.) and Moscow (q.v.).

Kievan Rus achieved a high level of culture after it was converted to the Orthodox (*see* Orthodox Church) faith by Byzantine missionaries in 988. It prospered because of its exports of forest and agricultural products and also because of its strategic position on rivers that flowed north-south and provided water-based transport between northern Europe and the Mediterranean world. After the Mongol invasions, which resulted in the capture and destruction of Kiev in 1240, the integrity of Kievan Rus was destroyed. Its western regions fell under the rule of Polish and Lithuanian kings; its central regions were practically depopulated for decades; and its northern forest towns, such as Novgorod and Moscow, were reduced to vassaldom to the Mongol khans of the Golden Horde (q.v.)

KIRIL ROMANOV, GRAND DUKE. (1876–1938). A grandson of Alexander II (q.v.) and a naval officer, he fled to Finland in 1917 and settled in France. There, he was proclaimed the official pretender to the Russian throne and head of the Romanov dynasty (q.v.).

KIROV, SERGEI M. (b. KOSTRIKOV) (1886–1934). Educated at the Kazan (q.v.) Technical School, he joined the Communists in 1904 and led a railroad strike in Siberia (q.v.) in 1905. After the February 1917 revolution (q.v.) Kirov became a member of the Vladikavkaz (q.v.) soviet and took part in the October revolution (q.v.). He was one of the principal organizers of the Soviet rule in the northern Caucasus (q.v.) and participated in the defense of Astrakhan (q.v.) against the White Armies (q.v.) in 1919. After Lenin's (q.v.) death in 1924, he joined Stalin's (q.v.) faction in its struggle against Trotsky (q.v.) and was made party leader of St. Petersburg (q.v.) in 1926, as well as a member of the Politburo (q.v.) in 1930. In 1934 he was assassinated by a mentally disturbed party member. Kirov's death, which is thought to have been engineered by Stalin, signaled the beginning of the purges of the 1930s.

KIROV BALLET COMPANY. Formerly the Imperial Ballet of the Mariinskii Theater (q.v.) of St. Petersburg (q.v.), the company was founded in 1735 and is the close rival of the Bolshoi Ballet Company in Moscow (q.v.). Since World War II (q.v.) it has frequently toured abroad, both in Europe and in North America. It is also known as the Mariinskii Ballet Company.

KISELEVSK. This Siberian city of some 125,000 inhabitants is located in the Novosibirsk (q.v.) region. It is a mining equipment manufacturing and coal mining center of the nearby Kuznetsk (q.v.) coal basin.

KITAI GOROD. In the 15th century, this was a trading and artisan center located a short distance from Moscow's Kremlin (q.v.). It was later incorporated into the city of Moscow (q.v.).

KIZEL. An industrial town on the Enisei River (q.v.) south of Krasnoiarsk (q.v.), it is the capital of the Tuva (q.v.) Autonomous Republic and is known for its mining and lumber industries.

KLUCHEVSKII, VASILII O. (1841–1911). A noted Russian historian, he studied philosophy and history at the University of Moscow (q.v.). In 1879 he was appointed chairman of the history faculty of that school.

KNIAZ. The Russian title equivalent to "prince," before Peter the Great (q.v.) it was an inherited title. After Peter, the title was also granted by the tsar to the highest civil servants.

KOKOVTSOV, COUNT VLADIMIR N. (1853–1942). Minister of state and finance to Nicholas II (q.v.), he became prime minister in 1911. He was dismissed in 1914 because of his opposition to Rasputin's (q.v.) corrupt practices. Kokovtsov left Russia after the revolution and died in France.

KOLCHAK, ALEKSANDR V. (1874–1920). Son of an artillery officer, Kolchak graduated from the Naval Cadet Corps in 1894 and took part in Russian polar expeditions and other long sea voyages in the early 1900s. He also served at Port Arthur (q.v.) during the Russo-Japanese war (q.v.) and was taken prisoner. After the war, Kolchak led a reformist group of younger fleet officers. During World War I (q.v.), he commanded the Black Sea fleet. Kolchak left Russia temporarily after the October 1917 revolution (q.v.) but soon returned through Siberia (q.v.) where he was proclaimed supreme ruler in November 1918. After several successful advances against the Red Army (*see* Armed Forces, Soviet), Kolchak's forces were pushed back eastward through Siberia. In February 1920 Kolchak was handed over by Czech troops to the revolutionaries who occupied Irkutsk (q.v.) and then transferred to the local Communists, who executed him.

KOLKHOZ (KOLLEKTIVNOE KHOZIAISTVO). This was the basic unit of the Soviet agricultural system. Theoretically an agricultural cooperative, it was made up of a tightly controlled group of peasant families who worked an assigned area of land belonging to the state and managed by the collective farm administration. Until the Gorbachev (q.v.) era, there were close to 30 thousand such collective farms, comprising more than 12 million members. These agricultural collectives were forcibly created in the Soviet Union in the late 1920s and the early 1930s, a move that caused famine throughout the country and resulted in the deportation of millions of peasant families to Siberia (q.v.).

KOLKHOZ SYSTEM. In the summer of 1929, after Stalin (q.v.) had defeated those in the leadership of the Communist Party (q.v.) who had opposed forcible collectivization of peasant households—Bukharin (q.v.), Tomskii (q.v.), Rykov (q.v.)—the Soviet government initiated a campaign for a total collectivization of Soviet agriculture. The intention behind this action was twofold. It was expected that concentrating the peasantry into large agricultural communes would ultimately increase the efficiency of Soviet agriculture and at the same time eliminate the breeding ground for capitalism in the village. In the short run, collectivization was to enable the government to extract grain and other agricultural produce at minimal prices and thereby provide cheap exports with which to pay for the imports of industrial machinery required by the industrialization drive.

By the beginning of 1930, over 59 percent of peasant households had been gathered into collective farms—the kolkhoz (q.v.). This was accomplished by force through the fanning of a class war between rich and poor peasants. Nevertheless, resistance to the collectivization campaign was so strong that Stalin was forced to retreat from it in March 1930, blaming local authorities for "excesses." By August 1930, only some 20 percent of peasant households still remained in the kolkhoz. However, the respite was a short one; by autumn of that year, the collectivization campaign was renewed.

In 1933 the government issued an order establishing mandatory delivery of bread quotas at artificially low prices. In addition, collective farms were obliged to pay newly established machine tractor stations for their services in plowing and harvesting. These measures left almost no surplus to the collective farms, and peasants were forced to subsist on the meager produce that they could raise on small plots of land reserved for their personal use. By 1937 over 90 percent of peasant households belonged to state or collective farms, and by 1940 the figure reached close to 100 percent. This resolution of the agrarian problem soon led to serious consequences. Productivity of collective farm labor dropped drastically, the rural population began to abandon the land for life in the cities, and agrarian production decreased.

After Stalin's death in 1953, attempts were initiated by the new general secretary of the Communist Party, Khrushchev (q.v.), to improve the agricultural situation. Some taxes on peasants were lowered and some agricultural prices were increased, but the bureaucratic/administrative system of farm management was not changed. The number of agrarian administrators reached one million individuals. As well, the inequality of incomes between the village and the urban areas continued to grow because of a faster rise in the price of manufactured goods than of farm products. There was thus a lack of an incentive for the collective farmers to increase their productivity and improve cost efficiency. A measure introduced in the early 1960s to guarantee a minimum income to all collective farmers led to a mandated equalization of their incomes and failed to provide any stimulus to work harder. In fact, it decreased such motivation. As a consequence, the most qualified individuals and many of the youth left their collectives and moved to the cities. So great was the fall of agricultural production by the 1960s that the government had to make up the shortfall by purchasing grain abroad. After the 1970s, this practice had to be extended to meat, fish and sugar.

KOLLONTAI, ALEKSANDRA M. (1872–1952). The daughter of a tsarist general, she became a revolutionary as a young woman in 1890 and gained fame for her advocacy of free love. Kollontai lived abroad between 1908 and 1917, collaborating closely with Lenin (q.v.). She returned to Russia after the February 1917 revolution (q.v.) to work as an agitator among sailors and soldiers. After the October 1917 revolution (q.v.), Kollontai became the commissar for social security but shortly joined the Left Communist opposition to Lenin and the Brest-Litovsk Peace Treaty (q.v.). Kollontai also headed the Workers' Opposition (q.v.) in 1920, after which she was distanced from internal Russian politics by being appointed Soviet ambassador to Norway, Mexico and Sweden, serving at these posts until 1945.

KOLMOGOROV, ANDREI N. (1903–87). A graduate of the University of Moscow (*see* Universities) he became professor of mathematics in

1925 and was elected to the Academy of Sciences (q.v.) of the USSR in 1939. In 1954 Kolmogorov gained world renown for his theoretical work in the field of the mathematics of probability.

KOLOKOL (THE BELL). This was a highly influential journal founded in 1857 by Herzen (q.v.) in London and smuggled into Russia. It advocated nonviolent reform and attempted to appeal to the enlightened self-interest of the upper crust of Russian society.

KOLOMNA. An ancient town situated on the Moscow River (q.v.), some 60 miles southeast of the capital, it was a distant outpost of Moscow in the early 14th century and is now a center of railroad engineering and machine manufacturing. Its population is close to 150,000.

KOLTSOV, MIKHAIL E. (1898–1942). He joined the Communist Party (q.v.) in 1918 and was an active participant in the 1917 revolution. In the 1920s and 1930s he became an influential journalist and a founder of the satirical Soviet journals *Krokodil* (q.v.) and *Ogonek.* Koltsov served as a news correspondent in Spain during its civil war, acting at the same time as a Soviet security officer. In the late 1930s he was recalled from Spain and sent to a forced labor camp.

KOLYMA MOUNTAIN RANGE. This chain of mountains stretches between the Sea of Okhotsk (q.v.) and the Kolyma River (q.v.) in the Khabarovsk (q.v.) region of the Russian Republic.

KOLYMA RIVER. Rising on the eastern slope of the Verkhoiansk (q.v.) Mountains, it flows for over 1,600 miles through the Iakut Autonomous Republic (*see* Sakha) toward the Siberian Sea. It is famous for its rich deposits of gold.

KOMANDORSKII ISLANDS. This group of islands stretches between the Kamchatka (q.v.) Peninsula and the Aleutian Islands (q.v.) in the northern Pacific ocean. The main settlement is the village of Nikolskoe.

KOMI AUTONOMOUS REPUBLIC. This republic is inhabited mainly by a Finnic-speaking people living in northwestern Russia. They number around 1.5 million and are largely urbanized.

KOMMISSAR. The Russian word for "commissar." This is a rank that existed in prerevolutionary Russia, but it was most widely used under the Soviet system to designate military, political, or civil officials.

The highest *kommissar* ranks were equivalent to those of ministers. The title "commissar" was originally used in France to designate official government positions. It was adopted in Russia after the February 1917 revolution (q.v.) to designate officials of the Provisional government (q.v.) and was retained in the Soviet Union until 1946, when such offices were renamed ministries.

KOMSOMOL. Communist Union of Youth. The first unions of worker and peasant youth were organized shortly after the October 1917 revolution (q.v.) and the coming to power of the Communist Party (q.v.). In October 1918 an All-Russian congress of youth organizations was called in Moscow (q.v.) and created the Russian Communist Union of Youth. All Soviet youth whose parents were not excluded from full citizenship rights because of their social origins and who were between the ages of 14 and 23 were eligible for membership.

Among the principal tasks of the Komsomol was the spreading of the Communist (*see* Marxism-Leninism) worldview and of the philosophy of the dictatorship of the proletariat. The practical activities of the Komsomol organizations included organizing meetings, conferences and assemblies where Communist ideas were presented to youthful audiences. A large amount of attention was directed to sports and military education. There were also efforts at spreading cultural enlightenment and organizing clubs and reader circles for youth.

In the 1920s the Komsomol became the single sociopolitical organization for all of Soviet youth, and in 1922 a parallel Communist organization for children and young adults was created, the Pioneers (q.v.). In 1926 the Komsomol was renamed the All-Union Leninist Communist of Youth League (VLKSM) and became an integral part of the state. In 1936, at the 10th congress of the Komsomol, the existing limitations on membership for children of individuals who had been proscribed from electoral participation because of their social origin was abolished.

In the 1930s most of the initial leaders of the organization were arrested and, in many cases, executed as a result of purges initiated by Stalin (q.v.) and his supporters at the top of the Soviet hierarchy. During this period there were mass searches within the ranks of the Komsomol for "suspicious individuals" and "agents of Trotsky" (q.v.). Nevertheless, members of the Komsomol participated actively in the five-year plans (q.v.) for the industrialization of the country, and helped build the Moscow Metro and develop the mines in the Donbas region. During World War II (q.v.) millions of Komsomol members fought in the ranks of the Red Army (*see* Armed Forces, Soviet), organized underground circles in the German-occupied territories, and helped to restore the economy of the country after the war.

Komsomol members were at the forefront of such Soviet-era mega-projects as the mastering of the empty "virgin" lands of Altai (q.v.), Kazakhstan (q.v.) and Siberia (q.v.) and organized shock brigades for the building of the Baikal-Amur Magistral (q.v.). In 1982 it had 42 million members and had become the principal organization for the preparation of Communists.

Near the end of the Soviet period, attitudes toward the Komsomol deteriorated, and efforts to make it more attractive to young people during the perestroika (q.v.) period by democratizing it had by and large failed. On the other hand, Komsomol experience in economic activities and industrial construction helped many individuals set up private enterprises and commercial structures successfully. With the dissolution of the USSR the Komsomol ceased to exist.

KONDRASHIN, KIRILL PETROVICH (1914–1981). From 1960 onward, he was the conductor and artistic director of the Moscow Philharmonic Orchestra. Kondrashin was born into a family of musicians, and studied at the Moscow Conservatory of Music; he became, successively, assistant conductor at the Nemirovich-Danchenko Musical Theater (1934), conductor of the Malyi Theater in St. Petersburg (1936–43) and conductor of the Bolshoi (1943–56). At the 1958 Tchaikovsky Competition he performed with Van Cliburn. Around this time he began conducting without a baton, relying on a more direct physical rapport between conductor and orchestra. He toured extensively with the Moscow Philharmonic, played with soloists Gilels, Oistrakh, Richter, and others, and premiered works of Shostakovich (q.v.) (Fourth and Thirteenth Symphonies), Khachaturian (q.v.) and others.

KONDRATIEV, NIKOLAI D. (1892–1936). Deputy commissar of food in the Provisional government (q.v.), he was also professor of economics at the Moscow (q.v.) Agricultural Academy and one of the authors of the agricultural five-year plan (q.v.). Arrested in 1934 for "right-wing deviation," Kondratiev was sent to a forced labor camp. His worldwide reputation is based on his theory of economic cycles.

KONEV, IVAN S. (1897–1973). He participated in the civil war (q.v.) on the side of the Red Army (*see* Armed Forces, Soviet), first as a commander of an armored train, then of a division. During World War II (q.v.) Konev was one of the most successful Russian generals and led his armies into Hungary and Czechoslovakia. In 1956 he was given command of the Warsaw Pact forces. Konev was a member of the Central Committee of the Communist Party (q.v.) between 1952 and 1973.

KONOVALOV, ALEKSANDR I. (1875–1948). The son of a rich factory owner, he was educated in England. Konovalov established the Russian Union of Trade and Industry and was a member of the fourth Duma (q.v.), as well as being an ally of Guchkov (q.v.). He became commissar of trade and industry in the Provisional government (q.v.) and deputy to Kerensky (q.v.). Arrested in the Winter Palace (q.v.) by the Communists, Konovalov was soon released and allowed to emigrate from Russia to France, where he spent his last years in poverty.

KONSTANTIN ROMANOV, GRAND DUKE (1779–1831). Son of Tsar Paul I (q.v.) and brother of both Alexander I (q.v.) and Nicholas I (q.v.), he was the commander in chief of the Russian armies in Poland. After the death of his elder brother, Alexander I, Grand Duke Konstantin renounced his rights to succession, making way for his younger brother, Nicholas I. This act helped precipitate the Decembrist (q.v.) revolt by army officers who wanted him, instead of his brother Nicholas, to become tsar.

KORIAK NATIONAL AREA. This is a region of northwest Siberia that encompasses the Kamchatka Peninsula (q.v.). It has a small population of under 50,000. Its principal economic activities are reindeer breeding, hunting and fishing.

KORNILOV, LAVR G. (1870–1918). Son of a Siberian Cossack (q.v.) officer, he was educated at the Mikhailovskoe Artillery School and graduated from the Academy of the General Staff in 1898. He participated in the Russo-Japanese war as well as in World War I (q.v.), as commander of a division. Taken prisoner by the Austrians, he escaped in 1916 to become commander of the southwest front. In September 1917 Kornilov led troops against the Provisional government (q.v.) in St. Petersburg (q.v.). After the failure of this attempt, he was imprisoned for high treason. Kornilov escaped in December 1917 to Novocherkassk (q.v.), where he organized the Volunteer (White) Army of which he was the leader when it was forced to retreat from Rostov-na-Donu (q.v.) to the Kuban (q.v.). Kornilov was killed during one of the numerous battles that ensued.

KORNILOV, VLADIMIR A. (1806–54). A sailor in the Russian navy, he rose to the rank of vice admiral and was placed in command of the Russian naval fortress of Sebastopol (q.v.) during the Crimean War (q.v.). He was killed in action defending the city from the British and French armies.

KOROLENKO, VLADIMIR G. (1853–1921). A graduate of the St. Petersburg (q.v.) Technological College, he was a novelist and writer of short stories before being arrested in 1879 for revolutionary activities. Korolenko was exiled to Siberia but eventually won acclaim for his writings.

KOROLEV, SERGEI P. (1907–66). A graduate of the Moscow (q.v.) Higher Technical School and the Moscow School for Aviators, he became a senior aircraft engineer and designed a series of Russian spacecraft. Korolev was also one of the initiators of the Soviet ballistic missile program. In 1938 he was arrested on charges of selling military plans to Germany but was allowed to continue working in the Soviet defense establishment. After Stalin's (q.v.) death in 1953 he was rehabilitated and in 1959 elected member of the Academy of Sciences (q.v.) of the USSR.

KOROVIN, KONSTANTIN A. (1861–1939). A graduate of the Moscow (q.v.) School of Painting and the St. Petersburg (q.v.) Academy of Fine Arts (q.v.), he became an innovative stage designer for the Imperial Theater in 1910. After the October 1917 revolution (q.v.) he emigrated from Russia to France, where he continued to paint and work in the theater.

KOSTROMA. The adminstrative center of Kostromskaia oblast, it is a port on the river Kostroma some 50 miles northeast of Iaroslavl, where the Kostroma River (q.v.) runs into the Volga (q.v.). The population is around 281,800; textiles are the chief industry and have made the town famous. It was probably founded by Prince Iurii Dolgorukii in 1152; in the 13th and 14th centuries the Kostroma principality enjoyed independence until annexation by Muscovy in 1364.

KOSTROMA RIVER. A tributary of the Volga (q.v.) some 250 miles long, it starts in the swampy environs of Soligach and winds through alluvial valleys. Most of the river is navigable.

KOSYGIN, ALEXEI N. (1904–80). Born into a worker's family in St. Petersburg (q.v.), he served as a soldier in the Red Army (*see* Armed Forces, Soviet) during the civil war (q.v.) and studied at the Leningrad Textile Institute from 1930 to 1935. Kosygin became director of Soviet textile factories after graduation and then commissar for the textile industry in 1939. During World War II (q.v.), he was in charge of evacuating industrial plants to the far rear of the country. In 1948 Kosygin became minister of finance as well as minister for light and food industries. He was also a member of the Central Committee of the Communist Party (q.v.) and the Politburo (q.v.).

KOTZEBUE, OTTO (1787–1846). A Russian naval explorer, he led an expedition to the South Seas between 1815 and 1818. Kotzebue visited Easter Island as well as the Marshall Islands and charted the coast of Alaska (q.v.).

KOUSSEVITZKY see KUSEVITSKII, SERGEI A.

KOVALEVSKAIA, SOFIA V. (1850–91). A student of mathematics in Berlin, Moscow (q.v.), and Heidelberg, she was appointed professor at the University of Stockholm. Kovalevskaia is the author of several novels and plays.

KOVALEVSKII, PETR (1901–   ). After emigrating to Paris in 1920, K. studied classics and literature at the Sorbonne, becoming first a professor at St. Sergius Theological Institute in 1925 and then a lecturer at the Sorbonne in 1930. Throughout his literary work, one finds an abiding interest in Leskov (q.v.).

KOVROV. A town on the Kliazma River south of Ivanovo (q.v.), its principal industries are railway equipment manufacturing and textiles. It has a population of just over 100,000.

KRASIN, LEONID B. (1870–1926). Born into a family of revolutionaries, he studied at the St. Petersburg (q.v.) and Kharkov (q.v.) technological institutes, from the latter of which he graduated in 1900. Krasin was arrested for subversive activities and, after his release, worked as an engineer on the Trans-Siberian Railroad (q.v.) and in the Baku (q.v.) oilfields. He was a member of the Bolshevik (q.v.) central committee in 1903 and the organizer of its newspaper. In 1905 he became a member of the St. Petersburg soviet (q.v.). In 1908 Krasin moved from Russia to the West, returning only after the October 1917 revolution (q.v.). He took part in the peace negotiations with Germany at Brest-Litovsk (q.v.), after which he was made commissar of trade and industry. In 1922 Krasin participated in the Genoa and Hague conferences. He died in London while serving as Soviet ambassador to Britain.

KRASNODAR. Capital of the Krasnodar territory, on the Kuban River (q.v.), it was established under Catherine II (q.v.). Its main economic activities are oil refining, food processing and railway engineering. The population is just over half a million.

KRASNOIARSK. This major industrial and military production center is located in eastern Siberia on the Enisei River (q.v.) and is served by the Trans-Siberian Railway (q.v.). It is near the border of the Mongolian People's Republic (q.v.) close to one of the world's largest hydroelectric plants. Its main economic activities are textile manufacturing, heavy engineering, and cement production. Its population is over 800,000.

KRASNOV, PETR N. (1869–1947). The son of a Cossack (q.v.) general, he was educated in a military school and served in the Lifeguard Cossack regiment from 1910 to 1913. He commanded a Cossack division in World War I (q.v.). In 1918 Krasnov was elected Ataman (commanding general), of the Don Cossacks (q.v.) and helped drive the Communists out of the Don region. After the civil war (q.v.) he emigrated to Germany and began to write historical fiction. During World War II (q.v.) he joined forces with General Vlasov (q.v.) and the pro-German Russian Liberation Army (q.v.), or R.O.A. Captured by the British in May 1945, he was handed over to the Soviets, who tried him for treason and hanged him.

KRASNOVODSK. A port and oil pipeline terminus on the eastern shore of the Caspian Sea (q.v.), it has a population of just under 100,000.

KRAVCHENKO, VIKTOR A. (1905–66). Born into a revolutionary family, he worked as a miner and joined the Communist Party (q.v.) in 1929. In the 1930s Kravchenko became an industrial manager and a member of a Soviet purchasing commission in Washington during World War II (q.v.). In 1944 he defected and wrote an international bestseller denouncing the policies of Stalin (q.v.). In 1948 he won a celebrated slander suit against a French left-wing periodical but later died under suspicious circumstances of a bullet wound in the United States.

KRAVCHINSKII, SERGEI M. (1851–95). He was a member of a revolutionary organization in the 1870s. In order to avoid arrest, Kravchinskii fled to the West, where he pursued a literary career. He is the author of several works on Russian life and politics.

KREMLIN. This is a medieval fortress that forms the center of many Russian cities. The best known kremlin is in Moscow (q.v.) and is the locus of government offices, churches, and former palaces of the tsar (q.v.). The word has come to signify the government of the Soviet Union and now of Russia.

KRESTIANE. Peasants. Before the abolition of serfdom by Alexander II (q.v.), the vast majority of Russian peasants were serfs and were known as *krepostnye liudi*, or bondmen. After their emancipation the peasantry was a legally defined, and the most numerous, category of the Russian population. The word refers to those who cultivate the land.

KRESTINSKII, NIKOLAI N. (1883–1938). An early member of the Communist Party, he was removed from the party's top leadership for his support of Trotsky (q.v.) and sent to Berlin as ambassador. In 1927 he was expelled from the Communist Party and, in 1938, tried and shot.

KRIVITSKII, WALTER (b. GINSBURG) (1899–1941). A ranking officer of the Soviet espionage network in central and Western Europe, he defected to France before World War II in order to escape Stalin's (q.v.) purges. He moved to the United States, where he was later found dead of gunshot wounds.

KRIVOSHEIN, ALEKSANDR V. (1857–1921). Before World War I he served in the ministry of agriculture, heading the program of voluntary resettlement of peasants in Siberia (q.v.). Krivoshein also assisted prime minister Stolypin (q.v.) with his land reform program and attempted to organize a Duma-based government (*see* Duma) during World War I (q.v.). Blocked in this effort by Tsar Nicholas II (q.v.), he retired in 1915. After the October 1917 revolution (q.v.), he resisted the Communists and served as prime minister to General Wrangel (q.v.) in the Crimea (q.v.). After the defeat of the White Armies (q.v.) he went to France and then to Germany.

KROKODIL (*THE CROCODILE*). This is a humorous Russian periodical that was established in 1923 and published by *Pravda* (q.v.). Quite outspoken by Soviet standards, it rapidly became a mass circulation publication. *See* Kolstov, Mikhail E.

KRONSHTADT see KRONSTADT

KRONSTADT. An island just outside of St. Petersburg (q.v.), it is the site of a major Russian naval base. In 1921 it was the locus of the single most dangerous armed uprising against Soviet power. The rebellion was led by sailors of the Baltic fleet and was suppressed with great difficulty by the Red Army (*see* Armed Forces, Soviet). This event was a major contributor to Lenin's (q.v.) decision to inaugurate the New Economic Policy (*see* NEP) in 1921.

KRONSTADT REBELLION. An uprising by the garrison at Kronstadt (q.v.) on the Gulf of Finland, March 7–18, 1921. The sailors had originally supported the revolution, but labor unrest and food shortages caused them to call for greater political freedom. The rebellion was put down by Trotsky (q.v.) with great loss of life.

KROPOTKIN, PRINCE PETER A. (1842–1921). Educated at the Corps of Pages in St. Petersburg (q.v.), he graduated in 1862 and served in the government of Siberia (q.v.). While there, Kropotkin explored parts of eastern Siberia and Manchuria between 1864 and 1866. He resigned from the civil service in 1867 to join followers of the Russian anarchist Bakunin (q.v.) in the First International. On his return to Russia in 1874, Kropotkin was arrested for revolutionary activities but escaped abroad. After being expelled from Switzerland and sentenced to prison in France, he moved to England in 1886, where he lived until 1917. Kropotkin remained a convinced anti-Marxist and after the February revolution (q.v.) opposed Lenin (q.v.) and the Communists. He died of hunger in Soviet Russia.

KRUPSKAIA, NADEZHDA K. (1869–1939). The daughter of an army officer, she joined the Russian Socialist Democratic Labor Party (q.v.) and met Lenin (q.v.) in 1894. In 1896 she was sent to exile in Siberia together with Lenin, whom she married there. After her release in 1901 she moved to Munich and assisted Lenin with his party work. Krupskaia returned to Russia with Lenin during the 1905 revolution but emigrated to Poland and then, during World War I (q.v.), to Switzerland. There she remained until April 1917, when she accompanied Lenin and a group of their comrades in a sealed train through Germany to Sweden and then Russia. After the Communists came to power in October 1917, Krupskaia, as deputy commissar of education, was given the responsibility for reorganizing the Russian educational and library systems. She was at times critical of Stalin (q.v.) and tried to remain a symbol of the humane side of Communism but was unable to help many of his victims.

KRYLOV, IVAN A. (1768–1844). Son of an army officer, Krylov became a critic and playwright. He gained great fame as a fabulist for his collection of tales similar to those of La Fontaine. They were written in colloquial language and usually carried a moral lesson. Having created many enemies in St. Petersburg (q.v.) by his biting sarcasm, Krylov had to leave the city and reside in the provinces, earning his living by giving private lessons.

KSENIA ROMANOVA, GRAND DUCHESS (1875–1960). She was one of the sisters of tsar Nicholas II (q.v.) and wife of Grand Duke

Alexander. Her daughter Irina was married to Prince Feliks Yusupov (q.v.), who was involved in the assassination of Rasputin (q.v.). During the civil war (q.v.) she was rescued by the British navy and taken to England, where she lived for the rest of her life.

KSHESINSKAIA, MATILDA F. (1872–1971). Daughter of a ballet dancer, she graduated from the St. Petersburg Theater School in 1890 and became the mistress of the future Tsar Nicholas II (q.v.). She danced at the Mariinskii Theater (q.v.), then with Diaghilev's (q.v.) Ballets Russes (q.v.) between 1911 and 1912, and after 1920 lived in Paris as the wife of Grand Duke Andrei. In 1929 Kshesinskaia started her own ballet school where many outstanding dancers, including Margot Fonteyn, were trained.

KUBAN COSSACKS. These are Cossacks (q.v.) who inhabited the Kuban River (q.v.) region.

KUBAN RIVER. A river anciently known as the Hypanis, it is some 600 miles long and runs west from the Caucasus (q.v.) to the Sea of Azov and the Black Sea (q.v.) by way of Krasnodar (q.v.).

KUBLAI KHAN (1214–1294). Grandson of Genghis Khan (q.v.), he concentrated his energies in consolidating the Mongolian empire in the east; he assimilated Chinese culture and made his capital at Beijing. It was here that Marco Polo was employed for 17 years.

KUIBYSHEV see SAMARA

KUIBYSHEV, VALERIAN V. (1888–1935). Son of an army officer, he was educated in a Cadet Corps school. He joined the Communists in 1904 and took part in the 1905 revolution (*see* Revolution of 1905), for which he was expelled from the Military Medical School. During the October 1917 revolution (q.v.), Kuibyshev directed the seizure of power in Samara (q.v.) and served there as political commissar. In 1922 he was made secretary of the Central Committee of the Communist Party (q.v.) and chairman of the Supreme Council of National Economy (q.v.). He headed the Gosplan (q.v.) after 1930 and became a strong ally of Stalin (q.v.). He died in Moscow (q.v.) of natural causes.

KULAKS. A term of abuse ("fist") to denote peasants who were considered to be wealthy or mean. It soon came to mean anyone unwilling to join the kolkhozes (q.v.); such people and their families, were liqui-

KURCHATOV, IGOR V. • 161

dated as a class, either being sent to camps or deported to remote regions.

KULESHEV, LEV V. (1899–1970). A pioneering Russian filmmaker who directed his first film in 1917, Kuleshev experimented with different forms of montage and film cuts, as well as training actors and writing a number of works dealing with film directing.

KULIKOVO, BATTLE OF. This was a decisive battle fought in September 1380 between the Mongol overlords under Khan Mamay and the Russian armies led by Grand Prince Dmitrii Donskoi. It took place on the Kulikovo plain near a tributary of the Don River (q.v.). During this encounter the Mongols suffered their first defeat at the hands of their Russian subjects.

KULUNDA. This is a rich agricultural area of western Siberia lying between Kazakhstan (q.v.) and the Altai (q.v.).

KUMYKS. A Turkic-speaking people of Daghestan in the northern Caucasus (q.v.), their lands were annexed by Russia in 1784. They number around 180,000.

KUPRIN, ALEKSANDR I. (1870–1939). Educated in a military school, he left the service in 1894, settled in St. Petersburg (q.v.), and became a professional writer. Kuprin soon gained popularity as the author of novels that were critical of social ills such as prostitution and that described the emptiness of Russian provincial life. In 1919 Kuprin emigrated to France but returned to Russia just before his death.

KUPTSY. Merchants. They were a legally designated segment of the Russian population before the 1917 revolution. This social stratum was divided into three hierarchical categories, or guilds in 1742. In 1863 they were consolidated into two guilds.

KURBSKII, PRINCE ANDREY M. (1528–83). A friend and advisor to Tsar Ivan the Terrible (q.v.) until the early 1560s, he escaped from Russia after breaking with the Tsar. Prince Kurbskii settled in Lithuania (q.v.) but maintained a long correspondence with the tsar. He also wrote a history that was highly critical of the grand duchy of Moscow (q.v.).

KURCHATOV, IGOR V. (1903–60). He graduated from the Crimean University (*see* Universities) in 1923, then taught physics and mathematics in St. Petersburg (q.v.). He was the founder of the Institute of Nuclear Energy in 1943 and was elected to the Academy of Sciences (q.v.) of the USSR. Kurchatov also directed Soviet nuclear research and the construction of an atomic bomb in 1949.

KURILE ISLANDS. A chain of islands running between the Kamchatka Peninsula (q.v.) and the Japanese island of Hokkaido, they form a line separating the Pacific Ocean from the Sea of Okhotsk (q.v.). Owned by the Japanese before World War II (q.v.), they were occupied by Soviet forces at the end of the war and have since become a source of friction between the two countries. Their economy is based on fishing and on hunting fur-bearing animals.

KUROPATKIN, ALEKSEI N. (1848–1925). Son of an officer, he was educated at the Pavlovskoe Military Academy and then graduated from the Academy of the General Staff in 1874. Kuropatkin participated in the conquest of Turkestan (q.v.) in the 1860s and fought in the Russo-Turkish war (q.v.) of 1877–78. He was commander in chief of the Russian army during the Russo-Japanese War (q.v.), but because of his numerous strategic errors, he was forced to resign his command. During World War I (q.v.) Kuropatkin initially commanded the northern front but was then transferred to Turkestan, where he directed the suppression of a rebellion in 1916. Kuropatkin did not take part in the civil war (q.v.), but lived in retirement until his death near Pskov (q.v.).

KURSK. Founded in the ninth century, this ancient Russian town is located on the Seym River. It was destroyed by the Mongols in the 13th century and rebuilt as a fortress in the 16th century. Today it is an important industrial city of close to 400,000.

KUSEVITSKII, SERGEI A. (1874–1951). A graduate of the Moscow (q.v.) Music School in 1894, he was a virtuoso double-bass player and gave concerts in Russia and abroad. In Berlin Kusevitskii established the Russian Music Publishing House. He also founded the Moscow Symphony Orchestra and conducted a symphony orchestra in St. Petersburg (q.v.) between 1917 and 1920. He emigrated during the civil war (q.v.) and settled in the United States, where he conducted the Boston Symphony from 1924 until 1949. Kusevitskii was a teacher of Leonard Bernstein.

KUTEPOV, ALEKSANDR P. (1882–1930). Educated at the St. Petersburg (q.v.) Infantry School in 1904, he served in the Russo-Japanese war (q.v.). Kutepov was a colonel in the Preobrazhenskii Regiment in

1917 and after the October 1917 revolution (q.v.) joined the White Armies (q.v.) and was commander of the First Army in the Crimea (q.v.) under Baron Wrangel (q.v.). When the White Armies were defeated, he moved first to Bulgaria and then to France, where, in 1923, he succeeded Wrangel as head of the Union of Russian Veterans, becoming in effect the leader of the White Russian emigres in France and sending agents into the Soviet Union on underground missions. Kutepov was kidnapped in Paris in 1930 by Soviet secret agents. The circumstances of his death are unknown.

KUTUZOV, PRINCE MIKHAIL I. (1745–1813). He was the commander of the Russian forces at the battle of Austerlitz, which was lost to Napoleon in 1806. Kutuzov was commander in chief of the Russian army during Napoleon's invasion of Russia in 1812. His strategy was to avoid all pitched battles against superior French forces until the battle of Borodino (q.v.). After this indecisive encounter Kutuzov ordered his army to retreat voluntarily from Moscow (q.v.), waited for the coming of winter to force the French to retire from the capital, and then defeated Napoleon's retreating army at Smolensk (q.v.).

KUTUZOV-TOLSTOY, COUNT MIKHAIL P. (1896–1980). A graduate of the Imperial Lyceum in 1915, he married Princess Maria Volkonskaia. After the revolution, Kutuzov-Tolstoy fled to Finland, whence he settled first in Brussels, then in Latvia (q.v.), which the Soviet armies occupied in 1940. He organized an international hospital for wounded soldiers in Budapest, but was arrested there by the Red Army (see Armed Forces, Soviet) in 1944. After his release in 1957, Kutuzov-Tolstoy moved to Ireland, where he established a language school and taught Russian history at Trinity College, Dublin.

KUZBAS. This is a major coalfield region in the Kuznetsk (q.v.) basin that was developed during the 1930s. Its principal city is Novokuznetsk (q.v.).

KUZMICH, FEDOR (d. 1864). A Siberian *starets*, or holy man, he lived near the city of Tomsk (q.v.) after 1825. There was a widespread but unconfirmed belief in Russia that he was really former Tsar Alexsander I (q.v.), who purportedly had not died but had become a monk.

KUZMIN, MIKHAIL A. (1875–1936). Born into a wealthy family, he began publishing his poetry in 1905 while living a bohemian life in St. Petersburg (q.v.). He had a wide knowledge of world culture and art and produced excellent translations from English and Italian.

Kuzmin's poetry was an important part of the silver age of Russian literature.

KUZNETSK (-1780: NARYSHKINO). A city of 97,000, in the Penza oblast. It is known for its leather and textiles.

KUZNETSOV, NIKOLAI G. (1902–74). A son of a peasant, he joined the Red Navy in 1919 and later studied at the Naval Academy. Kuznetsov was posted to Spain as the Soviet military attaché and served there between 1936 and 1937. He commanded the Soviet Pacific fleet and was the commissar of the navy during World War II (q.v.). Arrested on Stalin's (q.v.) orders in 1945, Kuznetsov was demoted but not found guilty of any crime. In 1953, after Stalin's death, he was appointed supreme commander of the Soviet Navy and elected to the Central Committee of the Communist Party (q.v.).

L

LADINSKII, ANTONIN P. (1896–1961). A poet who was born near Pskov, in 1917 Landinskii emigrated to France, where he wrote poetry and historical novels about Kievan Rus (q.v.). He returned to the Soviet Union in the late 1940s.

LADOGA LAKE. One of the largest bodies of freshwater in the world, the lake is located north and east of St. Petersburg (q.v.). During the first winter of World War II (q.v.), the Soviet government built a railroad on its ice in order to supply the city, then named Leningrad, with food and other essential materials.

LAKHOVA, EKATERINA (1948-). A pediatrician by profession, Lakhova was elected as a deputy in 1990 to the state Duma; the following year she left the Communist Party (q.v.), and from 1992 to 1994 she was presidential adviser on women's and family issues. In 1993 she cofounded the Women of Russia party, which generally supported Yeltsin's (q.v.) policies but which failed to exceed the five percent barrier in the December 1995 Duma (q.v.) elections.

LANDAU, LEV D. (1908–68). The son of an engineer and a graduate of the University of Leningrad (q.v.) in 1927, he went on to study physics in Denmark and England and then became head of the theoretical department of the Ukrainian Institute of Physics and Chemistry. Landau received the Nobel Prize for physics in 1962 for his work with Kapitsa (q.v.).

LANGUAGE. The glagolitic alphabet (q.v.), an East Slavonic script, was developed in the beginning of the ninth century and used to record commercial agreements and testaments. In the 10th century another alphabet, which was first used in Bulgaria a century earlier, began to be used by the East Slavic tribes: the *Kirilitsa*, or Cyrillic. Based on the Greek alphabet, it was utilized in the Kievan (q.v.) kingdom and in the Grand Duchy of Moscow (q.v.) until the end of the 18th century with only slight modifications. Abundant examples of both of these scripts are found in manuscripts of conventional materials and also, curiously enough, birch bark. In ancient Russia two distinct languages were in use: Church Slavonic (q.v.) and Old Russian. The former was a liturgical language based on Old Bulgarian. The latter was used for business correspondence and for literary and historical works, as well as in the daily life of people. During the 11th century Byzantine books were fairly widely distributed among the Kievan population, and with them came a considerable enrichment of their vocabulary with Greek-based words.

In the 14th century, paper became available in Russia. This led to a change in writing to accommodate a faster style. By the end of the 16th century, the first Slavic grammars appeared, and during the reign of Peter the Great (q.v.) the Russian language was transformed by the introduction of German, Dutch, French and Polish words, especially in scientific and technical works. One of the most influential individuals in the growth of the Russian language of the 18th century was Lomonosov (q.v.). He produced a new Russian grammar and developed a description of literary styles. Another influential scholar was Karamzin (q.v.), who attempted to bring the literary and colloquial languages closer together.

In Russia at the beginning of the 19th century there was an increased interest in the history of the Russian language, and a number of studies were made into its connection with Greek, Latin, and German. This interest reflected the growth of a Russian national self-awareness. By 1811 the University of Moscow (*see* Universities) could boast of a society of "lovers of Russian linguistics."

It might be said that the language's final formation was aided by the poet Pushkin (q.v.), whose works helped to diffuse modern Russian among tens of thousands of readers. By the middle of the 19th century a growth occurred in the publication of Russian-language as well as Church Slavonic dictionaries.

During the Soviet period, language studies were considerably widened to include specific language characteristics, the connection of language with the process of thinking, and other linguistic topics such as comparative linguistics. According to the 1991 law "On the languages of the peoples of the RSFSR," the Russian language was given the status of the state language of the Russian Federation. At the same time, this law also gave the right of the other nationalities to use, develop, and support their own languages.

LAPPS. A few thousand Lapps, or Sami, live in the Murmansk region of Russia, where they herd reindeer.

LARIN, IURII (b. LUR'E) (1882–1932). Born into a middle-class Jewish family, he became an active revolutionary in 1900. Exiled to Iakutiia (now Sakha, q.v.) in 1902 for his political activities, Larin escaped abroad. Returning to Russia in 1905, he wrote extensively on economic and political subjects. Larin lived abroad during World War I (q.v.), returned to Russia in 1917 and joined the Communist Party (q.v.). He worked in the All-Union Council of the People's Economy after the Communists took power in October 1917.

LARINA, ANNA M. (1914–   ). The daughter of a high-ranking Communist official, she married Bukharin (q.v.) in 1934. After Stalin (q.v.) had him tried and executed in 1938, she was arrested and spent 20 years in concentration camps. Before her husband's arrest she memorized his "Letter to the Future Generations of Soviet Leaders." Since her release, Larina has written a book about his arrest and her own servitude in the camps.

LARIONOV, MIKHAIL FEDOROVICH (1881–1964). He was a painter influenced by impressionism and the founder of a type of abstract art known as rayism (luchism).

LASHEVICH, M.M. (1884–1928). A member of the Russian Socialist Democratic Labor Party (q.v.) since 1901, he served as a member of the Petrograd Military Revolutionary Committee in October 1917. During the civil war (q.v.), Lashevich was given command of the Siberian military district. In 1925 he became deputy commissar for military and naval affairs and then was made chief administrator of the Chinese Far Eastern Railroad (q.v.) from 1926 until 1928. Lashevich committed suicide after his expulsion from the Communist Party (q.v.) for being a supporter of Trotsky (q.v.).

LATVIA. A former Soviet republic on the Baltic Sea, it has a population of 2,500,000 and an area of 24,600 square miles. Its capital is Riga. The main industries are forestry, metalworking and machine building. In the 16th century Latvia was divided between Poland and Sweden. As a result of the Treaty of Nystad (1721), northern Latvia was ceded to Russia; the remaining territories were acquired by Russia as a result of the first and third partitions of Poland (1722 and 1795). Latvia was independent from 1919 until 1940, when, as a result of the Nazi-Soviet nonaggression pact (q.v.) of the previous year, Soviet troops overthrew the Latvian government and Latvia was annexed to the Soviet Union. More than 100,000 Latvians were then deported to central Asia. Latvia became independent in 1991.

LAVRA. This was the name of each of the four most venerated monasteries of Russia: the Troitse-Sergei Lavra near Moscow (q.v.); the Pochevskaia Lavra in Volhynia (q.v.); the Alexandero-Nevskaia Lavra in St. Petersburg (q.v.); and the Kievo-Pecherskaia Lavra in Kiev (q.v.).

LAVRENIOV, BORIS A. (1891–1959). Having served as a cavalry officer in World War I (q.v.), he remained in Soviet Russia after the civil war (q.v.), writing short stories that dealt with the conflict. Lavreniov was at first attracted to the Futurist (q.v.) group, then to the Acmeists (q.v.).

LAVROV, PETR (1823–1900). A major intellectual figure among the populist intelligentsia in the middle of the 19th century, Lavrov left Russia in 1868 and lived in Paris, where he gained a reputation as a radical political theorist. For a time, his works were the bible of the Russian left-wing intelligentsia. In 1872 Lavrov joined Karl Marx's First International.

LAW, IMPERIAL. Peter the Great (q.v.) laid the foundation for all subsequent legislation in the Russian empire. The total of laws and regulations that he promulgated is numbered in the hundreds. In 1720 he issued a "general regulation" that defined the powers of all institutions of the Russian state. Shortly thereafter each government department received a set of specific regulations that covered its particular function. In 1722, Peter promulgated the "table of ranks," which authorized admission of individuals into the service class (*dvorianstvo*) on the basis of past service as well as of heredity. In the economic sphere, Peter's laws regulated the establishment of private factories, the imposition of tariffs, and the exporting of domestic products to foreign countries.

During the 18th century new obligations were placed on the Russian peasantry at the same time that the privileges of the service class were extended. In 1762, and again in 1785, laws were passed that permitted the *dvorianstvo* to own land without obligation to render service to the tsar, as they had had to in the past. In 1785 Russian merchants also received additional privileges. Among these was freedom from per capita taxation, from compulsory military service, and from physical punishment. They also received permission to engage in manufacturing activities.

During the reign of Alexander II (q.v.), between 1860 and 1880, substantial alterations were made to the empire's laws. In 1861 serfdom was abrogated and millions of serfs were set free. In 1864 new laws regulating the nation's courts were passed. They introduced, for the first time in Russia, the concept of the equality of all citizens before the law, and created a separation between the judicial and executive branches of government. In 1865 legislation regulating publishing and press activities was issued. It decreased the extent of censorship in the country. In 1874 the recruitment period for service in the army was reduced from 21 to six years.

In October 1905, under pressure from mass popular demonstrations, Tsar Nicholas II (q.v.) issued a manifesto that proclaimed a series of new democratic freedoms, including the convocation of a Duma (q.v.) (parliament) endowed with legislative rights. The manifesto also authorized the establishment of political parties and granted citizens the right to vote in national elections and to create trade unions.

LAW, POST-SOVIET. The Russian constitution of 1993 establishes a legal framework for federal legislation and for the legislation passed by the autonomous republics and other local units of government.

In June 1990 the "Declaration Concerning the Sovereignty of the RSFSR" was issued, and in November 1991 a law came into effect that defined eligibility for Russian citizenship. In June 1993, this law was amended to give the residents of the federal republic freedom of choice to select their citizenship and to spell out their rights to protection and assistance from the state.

The legal system in Russia encompasses the federal level, the level of the autonomous republics, and the regional level. Federal laws, however, apply to all areas that are within the jurisdiction of the Russian Federal Republic. In March 1992 a decree was issued by the president of the republic that embodied the agreement reached between the various units of government as to the delimitation of the legislative rights between the federal level and the autonomous republics, regions, districts, and large cities. In December 1990, a law was passed regulating possession of private property, and in the same month another law came into effect regulating private enterprises and other entrepreneurial activities. In 1991 a law regulated the privatization of state and municipal enterprises within the Russian Federation.

Post-Soviet legislative activity has also focused on agriculture. In 1990 a law was passed regulating the households of farmers. This law described farms as a form of free enterprise that was based on an expectation of achieving an economic benefit. It guaranteed farmers the private use of agricultural land, as well as ownership of all equipment bought for and improvements made on the land. In December 1991 the federal government also passed legislation dealing with collective and state farms. This law guaranteed members of these agricultural organizations a share of their ownership.

In 1993 the President of the Russian Federation issued a decree that promised to legalize private property of agricultural land and guaranteed owners of shares in the collective and state farms the right to sell them, with the proviso that current members of these organizations would have the first option on them.

The foundation of the Russian Federation's health maintenance policy was laid down in a law passed in June 1991, and that of the educational policy in a law passed in July 1992. Russian cultural policy was defined by legislation passed in October 1991.

In order to implement the legislative structure of the federation, a system of courts was established in Russia. The highest court is the constitutional court. It has the function of adjudicating the constitutionality of legislation and exists as an independent judicial entity of 19 individuals who are collectively responsible for verifying the complaints of citizens as well as of other courts concerning the constitutionality of laws that are being applied in judicial cases.

The flag of the Russian Federation is identical to the old imperial flag: horizontal white, blue and red stripes. The coat of arms contains a double-headed eagle similar to the Tsarist emblem.

LAW, SOVIET. The second congress of the Soviet of Workers', Soldiers' and Peasants' Deputies met in October 1917. It declared the transfer to itself of all state powers of the Russian empire. It also issued decrees on peace and on land. The decree on peace proposed a three-month cease-fire for all warring parties, during which time they could negotiate the conditions of a peace treaty. The decree on land abolished all private ownership of land, forests, waters, and the subsoil. It prohibited the purchase, sale or rental of land, as well as the hiring of agricultural labor. All arable land was subdivided between peasant families, based on the number of labor-capable members in each family. These provisions were formulated in a basic law on the socialization of land issued in January 1918 by the All-Russian Central Executive Committee.

In December 1917 a new codex of Soviet laws was confirmed. Among other topics, it legislated the establishment of workers' control over production and gave the workers' committees the right to manage enterprises. It also made work mandatory for all citizens of Soviet Russia.

In 1918, the first Soviet constitution was confirmed. It stated that the All-Russian Central Executive Committee was the sole institution that had the right to legislate in the RSFSR. A rigid system of hierarchical subordination was mandated whereby all important decisions were to be made at the top of the state organizational pyramid. A decree of the Council of People's Commissars (q.v.) of January 1919 forbade private commerce and authorized confiscation of agrarian produce from peasants. As a result of a resistance to these measures, however, these requisitions were abolished in March 1921 and replaced by taxation in kind. This signaled the beginning of a "New Economic Policy" (see NEP) that lasted until 1929.

Early in 1922 a three-part court system was established. It consisted of the supreme court of the RSFSR, the people's courts, and the provincial courts. A state procurator's office was also created, charged with supervising the implementation of laws.

In June of the same year, the chief administration for publishing (see Glavlit) was set up. Its primary task was to control the content of all published material in the country and to implement Soviet censorship regulations.

A new constitution was introduced in 1924 at the time of the founding of the Union of Soviet Socialist Republics; it was revised by Stalin in 1936 in order to give it a more democratic appearance. During World War II (q.v.) and in the immediate postwar years, a series of laws was passed placing civilian labor under military law. Workers were forbidden to leave their places of work, and technical personnel were subject to compulsory transfers from one place of employment to another. These laws were canceled only in 1956. Three years after the death of Stalin (q.v.), Khrushchev (q.v.) initiated the rehabilitation of political prisoners and the restoration of their citizenship rights. The scope of political repression was lowered and the activity of the secret police was somewhat regulated.

Yet another constitution was introduced in 1977. During the Soviet period, the legal system of the country underwent serious violations. Existing legislation frequently did not correspond at all with accepted norms of behavior by state and Communist Party (q.v.) organizations. Those Soviet institutions that were supposed to safeguard individual rights, including the country's courts, were seriously undermined. In cases where decisions of these organizations contradicted existing laws, such laws were simply ignored.

LEBED, ALEKSANDR (1950-   ). General Lebed gained attention in 1991 for his defence of Yeltsin (q.v.) during the 1991 coup and also for skillfully handling the Moldova-Transdniestr crisis in 1992 as leader of the Fourteenth Army stationed there. On his retirement, Lebed turned his attention to politics and allied himself with the Congress of Russian Communities (KRO); he had already joined the central committee of the Russian Federation's Communist Party in 1990, but his major concern appeared to be ensuring the stability of the country through a reformed, revitalized and strengthened army; his stated admiration for Chile's General Pinochet and France's De Gaulle may be taken as a reflection of this. He opposed the use of Russian troops in Chechnya and was critical of their use in any purely political arena. In the 1995 elections the KRO gained five Duma (q.v.) seats (4.3 percent of the party list). In the period leading up to the presidential elections of June 1996 he modified his tone somewhat and was able to show himself to be tough on corruption yet not fervently nationalistic; he came third after Yeltsin and Zyuganov (q.v.) with 14.71 percent of the vote.

LEBEDEV-POLIANSKII, PAVEL I. (1882–1948). He became involved in revolutionary activities at an early age and in 1908 left Russia to live in Geneva until his return in 1917. After the October 1917 revolution (q.v.) Lebedev-Polianskii was head of the publishing department of the commissariat of education and, from 1918 until 1920 he was chairman of Proletkult (q.v.). He also served as the head of the government censorship commission, the Glavlit.

LEFT OPPOSITION. This term denotes the radical trend in the Communist International or Communist parties to emphasize the revolutionary and proletarian nature of the Communist movement. Lenin used the term to designate those who opposed the Treaty of Brest-Litovsk (q.v.) in 1918; the term later identified opponents of Lenin's 1921 New Economic Policy (see NEP). Bukharin (q.v.), Trotsky (q.v.), Zinovev (q.v.) and Kamenev (q.v.) were all associated with this tendency at different periods.

LEFT-SOCIALIST REVOLUTIONARIES. A semi-independent branch of the Russian Socialist Revolutionaries party, it was the only Russian radical group that agreed to participate in a coalition government with the Communists after the latter forcibly took power in October 1917. This alliance lasted only a short while—until the middle of 1918— when they rebelled against Communist policies such as the signing of a separate peace with Germany. This group's attempt to overthrow Lenin's (q.v.) followers failed, and most of their leaders were arrested by the Cheka (q.v.)

LEGAL MARXISTS. Russian economists and other social scientists, such as Struve (q.v.), Sergei Bulgakov (q.v.), Berdiaev (q.v.), and Tugan-Baranovskii (q.v.), formed a group in 1889 to study and promote the teachings of Karl Marx. Their emphasis was on keeping within the legal parameters of existing Russian laws, and their aim was to improve the conditions of the working class through legal political activity.

LEGAT, NIKOLAI G. (1869–1937). The son of a Swedish ballet dancer, he graduated from the ballet school in St. Petersburg (q.v.) in 1888, and danced in the capital with Pavlova (q.v.) and Kshesinskaia (q.v.). He also performed in Western Europe before World War I (q.v.). In 1920 he became the chief choreographer for the Mariinskii Theater (q.v.) but left Russia for France in 1922. There he became an instructor at Diaghilev's (q.v.) Ballets Russes (q.v.).

LENA RIVER. One of the largest rivers in the world, it rises out of Lake Baikal (q.v.) in Siberia (q.v.) and flows north for over 1,000 miles to the Arctic Ocean.

LENIN, VLADIMIR I. (b. ULIANOV) (1870–1924). The son of a school inspector, he was born in Simbirsk (renamed Ulianovsk, q.v.). After the execution of his older brother, Aleksandr, for the attempted assassination of Tsar Alexander III (q.v.), he became actively involved in revolutionary activities. He graduated with a degree in law from the University of St. Petersburg (*see* Universities) in 1891 and practiced law in Samara (q.v.) from 1891 to 1893 without great success. He then moved to St. Petersburg, where he became prominent in the revolutionary Marxist circles. Lenin went abroad in 1895 in order to contact Plekhanov (q.v.), the senior Russian Marxist and founder of the Union for the Struggle for the Liberation of the Working Class (q.v.). In 1897 Lenin was sentenced to two years in prison and three years of exile in Siberia for illegal political activity.

In 1903 Lenin attended the London congress of the Russian Socialist Democratic Labor Party (q.v.), where he provoked a split of the group into the Menshevik (q.v.) (Social Democratic) and Bolshevik (q.v.) (Communist) factions. He lived in Munich, London, and Geneva between 1900 and 1905, working as a member of the editorial board of the revolutionary newspaper *Iskra* (q.v.). Lenin returned to Russia in 1905 but did not play a major role in the revolutionary events of that year. In 1907 Lenin once again moved from Russia to Switzerland and then to Paris, where in 1911 he organized a party school. At the beginning of World War I (q.v.) Lenin was arrested in Austria as an enemy alien but allowed to leave for Switzerland, where he remained until April 1917. Following the outbreak of the February 1917 revolution (q.v.) he obtained permission from the German government to cross the country in a sealed train to Sweden and then to Russia. On his return, Lenin led his Communist followers in the successful overthrow of the Provisional government (q.v.) in October 1917 and became leader of the new Soviet government. In August 1918 Lenin was wounded by a terrorist but survived to sign the German peace treaty of Brest-Litovsk (q.v.) and to continue to rule Soviet Russia during the civil war (q.v.) against the White Armies (q.v.) and foreign intervention. In 1919 Lenin founded the Communist International (*see* Comintern), and in 1921 he proclaimed the New Economic Policy (*see* NEP). The latter represented a partial retreat from the extremes of War Communism (q.v.) of the previous years. Incapacitated in 1922 by a stroke, he died two years later. After his death he was deified: his body was embalmed and placed in a mausoleum in Moscow's (q.v.) Red Square (q.v.).

LENIN PRIZES. First awarded in 1925, these annual awards were given by the Soviet government for outstanding contributions in arts, literature, science and technology. Renamed the Stalin Prizes during that dictator's rule, they were designated once again as Lenin Prizes after 1956.

LENIN STATE LIBRARY. The former Rumiantsev Library was renamed the Lenin State Library and moved from Leningrad to Moscow by the Soviet government in the middle 1920s. It is now called the Russian State Library (q.v.).

LENINGRAD see ST. PETERSBURG

LENINGRAD AFFAIR. Among other revelations at the famous 20th party congress in 1956, Khrushchev (q.v.) disclosed that after the death of Zhdanov (q.v.) in 1948, leaders of his faction and many prominent officials in Leningrad, Zdhdanov's stronghold, were arrested and shot at the behest of Zhdanov's rival Malenkov (q.v.). The year after this revelation Malenkov was expelled from the Central Committee as part of the "anti-Party group."

LENINGRAD UNIVERSITY see UNIVERSITIES

LEONOV, LEONID M. (1899–1994). He gained fame in the 1920s for his novels depicting peasant life during the revolution and civil war (q.v.) and received the Lenin Prize (q.v.) for literature in 1957. Just before his death, Leonov completed a major work in which he attempted to summarize the moral and philosophical lessons of the 20th century.

LEONTIEV, KONSTANTIN N. (1831–93). He first served as a surgeon during the Crimean War and then joined the Russian diplomatic service. In the late 1880s Leontiev took monastic vows and began his career as an essayist. His views were those of the extreme right.

LEONTII (b. TURKEVICH) (1898–1965). He was a graduate of the Kiev Theological Seminary and served as aid to Bishop Tikhon (q.v.) in the Orthodox diocese of the United States. Bishop Leontii was active in the consolidation of the Orthodox Church (q.v.) in America, as well as in the founding in 1938 of the St. Vladimir Theological Academy of New York. He also helped obtain an autocephalic status for the Orthodox Church in America from the Soviet church hierarchy.

LEONTOVICH, MIKHAIL A. (1903–81). Son of a scientist, he graduated from the University of Moscow (q.v.) in 1923 and taught there from 1929 to 1945. A member of the Physics Institute of the Academy of Sciences (q.v.) of the USSR from 1946 to 1952, Leontovich was one of the leaders in the development of the Soviet atomic industry and participated, along with other prominent Russian intellectuals, in protests against the Soviet government's repression of artists and writers, as well as against its attempts in the late 1970s to rehabilitate Stalin (q.v.).

LEPESHINSKAIA, OLGA V. (1916-). A graduate of the Choreographic School in Moscow (q.v.) in 1933, she became the leading ballerina of the Bolshoi Ballet. After 1963, she taught ballet in Moscow and abroad.

LERMONTOV, MIKHAIL Y. (1814–41). A cavalry officer in his youth, he was exiled to the Caucasus (q.v.) for writing revolutionary poetry. Lermontov is considered to be one of the greatest Russian poets, but outside of Russia he is perhaps best known for his novel *A Hero of Our Time*. Like his fellow poet Pushkin (q.v.), he was killed in a duel.

LESHCHENKO, PETR K. (1898–1954). Born in Bessarabia, he moved to Paris in 1923, where he became a cabaret singer and gained popularity among Russians both in the Soviet Union and abroad. After World War II Leshchenko lived in Romania. In 1951 he was captured by the Soviet counterespionage organization, and died in a Gulag (q.v.) concentration camp hospital.

LESKOV, NIKOLAI S. (1831–95). After first working as a provincial civil servant, Leskov began his career as a journalist in 1860, and then began to write fiction that focused on Russian religious beliefs. An opponent of radicalism, Leskov focused on describing the ordinary lives of Russian people.

LETOPISI. These ancient Russian chronicles, or annals of historical significance, were collected into a complete edition and published in 14 volumes.

LEVITAN, ISAAK I. (1861–1900). A student at the Art School in Moscow (q.v.) from 1873 to 1885, Levitan was considered by contemporary experts to be Russia's greatest landscape painter. His special ability was to render the beauty of the Russian countryside.

LIADOV, ANATOLII K. (1855–1914). A pupil of Rimskii-Korsakov (q.v.), he became a professor at the St. Petersburg (q.v.) Conservatory of Music. Liadov specialized in arranging folk music and children's songs, as well as composing piano pieces and symphonic poems.

LIBERATION OF LABOR see OSVOBOZHDENIE TRUDA

LIBRARIES. The first library of ancient Rus (q.v.) was established in 1037 by Grand Prince Iaroslav (q.v.) the Wise and was attached to the cathedral in Kiev (q.v.). Later, libraries were created at various monasteries and contained not only religious writings but also historical epics. As well, books were owned by many of the aristocratic families. By the 16th century the library of the grand prince of Moscow (q.v.) had grown into a large collection and contained over 800 manuscripts, among them the works of Cicero and Julius Caesar and the collected laws of the Byzantine Empire.

In the beginning of the 17th century, printing became widespread in Russia and libraries began to grow rapidly. The largest Russian printing establishment was located at the Printing Court near the Kremlin (q.v.) in Moscow (q.v.). The first Russian scientific library was established at the apothecary department, while foreign books were collected by the ambassadorial department. Both departments were housed near the Kremlin. In 1725 Peter the Great (q.v.) entrusted the responsibility for purchasing books to the St. Petersburg Library, later to be renamed the Library of the Russian Academy of Sciences (q.v.). Besides books on science and medicine, this library collected works of literature, philosophy, history, and geography. It also acquired the books contained in the ancient Moscow library of the tsars. In 1755 the library of the University of Moscow was opened.

A large reading public had come into being in Russia by the time of Catherine the Great (q.v.), and a number of new libraries were established. Among them was the vast collection of Count Rumiantsev (q.v.), which eventually became the Lenin State Library (q.v.) (now renamed the Russian State Library [q.v.]). The Imperial Public Library was also founded during her reign. Its initial collection consisted of books brought to Russia from Poland as war booty in 1795. It was enriched by the addition of many Russian monastic collections and by the acquisition of Latin manuscripts that had been purchased by her ambassador during the French revolution.

The first public libraries opened in Russia at the end of the 18th century, along with commercial and subscription ones. However, these libraries were severely limited by strict government regulations, police supervision, and censorship laws. It was only after the 1905 revolution that Russian libraries underwent a major expansion. In 1908, the Russian Library Association came into existence; two years later the first Russian library periodical began publication, and in 1911 the first Russian Library Congress took place. In the last years before World War I (q.v.) large amounts of government funds were allocated to public libraries, and regulation of their activities was relaxed. Altogether, by 1914 there were approximately 14,000 public libraries in Russia, as well as several major research libraries.

As libraries multiplied, so did the demand for professionally trained librarians, and in 1913 the first library courses were started in Moscow. With the establishment of Soviet rule in Russia, public libraries were incorporated into the country's educational system and were allotted the task of raising the political, cultural, and literacy level of workers and peasants. In a series of decrees, libraries were centralized, a system of state-controlled acquisition of new books was introduced, and a new system of administration was implemented. During the 1920s and 1930s, Soviet libraries grew rapidly in number and in patrons, but they were increasingly placed under tight ideological supervision by Soviet cultural authorities. During World War II (q.v.), they suffered heavy losses; more than 43,000 were destroyed. In the postwar years Russian libraries were rapidly rebuilt and once again resumed their role as educational, cultural and political centers.

With the introduction of the policy of glasnost (q.v.) in the middle 1980s, some of the major handicaps under which Russian librarians had previously worked began to be removed: censorship was eliminated, books long held in closed collections were made available to the public, and librarians were no longer required to be primarily political propagandists of the Communist Party (q.v.) ideology. However, since the disintegration of the Soviet Union, the drastic reduction of state subsidies to libraries has caused many of them to close their doors or to reduce their acquisitions and services. Severe financial limitations have forced libraries to reduce maintenance. This has resulted in an increase of inundations and fires, with the loss of irreplaceable material.

LIEVEN, PRINCE PAVEL (1875–1963). A graduate of the Institute of Means of Transportation in St. Petersburg (q.v.) in 1899, he became a railroad engineer and took part in the construction of the Trans-Caspian Railway and of the northern link to the Trans-Siberian Railway (q.v.). During World War I (q.v.) Prince Lieven was a Red Cross representative at the front. Taken prisoner by the Germans, he worked to improve the living conditions of Russian prisoners of war. Prince Lieven was a member of the 1915 Stockholm conference concerned with the registration of prisoners of war. He left Russia in 1917 for Sweden and subsequently lived in Germany, Belgium and Ireland. He died in London, England.

LIKHACHEV, DMITRII S. (1906-). A graduate of the University of Leningrad (*see* Universities) in 1928, he was arrested by the Soviet government for his political beliefs and served time in a concentration camp from 1928 to 1931. After his release, Likhachev worked at the Institute of Russian Literature and, from 1946 to 1953, as professor at University of Leningrad. In 1970 he was elected a member of the Academy of Sciences (q.v.) of the USSR, and in 1987 he became chairman of the Soviet Cultural Fund. Likhachev was instrumental in rehabilitating Gumilev (q.v.) and in stimulating a cultural revival in Russia during the late 1980s.

LIPETSK. A town with a population of about half a million, it is located on the Voronezh River. It is an important center of iron and steel manufacturing and is known for its tractor and chemical industries.

LITERATURE, CONTEMPORARY. Currently, Russian literature is undergoing a period of major change of perspective as well as of ideological confusion. After obtaining its long-awaited freedom from government censorship, it has lost its former vigor and mass appeal. As long as it was struggling against totalitarian censorship it was able to play a significant moral role in Russian society because it was able to attract a large following of readers. Today the old ideals have receded, and the commercial slogans that have replaced them do not offer the authors any inspiration. The disillusion with perestroika (q.v.) has led to a traumatization of a part of the Russian reading public.

The special trait of 19th-century Russian literature was its social consciousness. Now the book market is saturated with literature designed primarily for commercial exploitation rather than intellectual or social engagement. Writers are now often inclined to escape from the current Russian reality and to distance themselves from any type of political or ideological position. There remains to them an orientation on the internal psychological world, personality problems, the family and love themes. Many current authors also focus on the unsuccessful hero who rejects accepted social norms of behavior. Another characteristic trait of contemporary Russian literature is the attempt to shock the reader, to produce strong ironic intonations, and to mock the structure of the modern world. The hero-wanderer's search for spirituality is another popular theme. Characteristic of these new literary trends is the mixing of fantasy with realism.

Another trend is the influence of formerly prohibited works such as those of Solzhenitsyn (q.v.), Pasternak (q.v.), and Grossman (q.v.). Major changes have also occurred in Russian poetry, which in the past was at the very epicenter of the country's intellectual life, when authors had read their works in stadiums and city squares to enormous crowds. Today, Russian poetry has turned to individualism and to highly selected segments of readers. Since the fall of the Communist regime, poems have been published that had not been available to Russian readers before, works by Gumilev (q.v.), Khodasevich (q.v.), Brodsky (q.v.) and Galich (q.v.). The "thick" (larger) periodicals are now regularly publishing collections of contemporary poets. However, only a relatively small number of readers are purchasing them. Some contemporary Russian poets have gone into philosophical lyricism, some into total absurdity. Others are returning to traditional styles and to literary conservatism and are rejecting all forms of postmodernism.

LITERATURE, PREREVOLUTIONARY. The decade of the 1890s was the last period of major creative activity for the great Russian writer Leo Tolstoy (q.v.). In 1899 he published his last novel, *Resurrection*, and in 1900 the drama *The Live Corpse*. During this decade Tolstoy frequently turned to theoretical questions of literature and art and stressed that their principal task was to serve the people.

The 1890s and the first decade of the 20th century was also a fruitful period in the life of Anton Chekhov (q.v.). It was at that time that he wrote *My Life*, *The Peasants*, and such well-known plays as *Uncle Vanya*, *Three Sisters*, and *The Cherry Orchard*. This period also saw Korolenko (q.v.) play a major role in the formation of a new social consciousness, which was greatly helped by the writings of Gorky (q.v.), who in 1906 wrote his major novel, *The Mother*, which dealt with the workers's movement. During this period Gorky also helped many young writers, by acting as their mentor and friend. Other important writers of this period were Kuprin (q.v.) and Bunin (q.v.), whose prose and poetry earned him the reputation of a brilliant stylist. The 1890s saw both symbolism and decadence become very popular in Russia. These two literary tendencies were characterized by both extreme individualism and pessimism. The founder of Russian symbolism, Minskii, proclaimed the cult of absolute individuality. Another poet who belonged to the decadence movement was Balmont (q.v.). His writings were characterized by a musicality of verse. A well-known Symbolist (q.v.) was the poet Briusov (q.v.), who was also the chief editor of a Symbolist journal. Blok (q.v.), the poet-mystic, began his creative career at this time also. One of the principal themes of his poetry was that of an idealized and romanticized revolution. Another representative of the mystic and idealistic tendency was Bely (q.v.), whose writings were characterized by complicated language and forms of representation.

A new direction of the decadent spirit known as acmeism (q.v.) had its beginning in the work of Gumilev (q.v.), a poet who advocated a hard, clear and masculine view of life and who came out against mysticism and for the acceptance of this world with all of its beauty and ugliness. The influence of acmeism can be seen in the poetry of Akhmatova (q.v.), whose principal characteristic was intimate lyricism and subtle psychology.

Another direction that was popular during the prerevolutionary years was that of the Futurists (q.v.), who maintained that the content was only a convenient pretext for form and that form was the ultimate goal of literary creation. Mayakovsky (q.v.), who later became the best-known Soviet poet, initially belonged to this tendency. Esenin (q.v.), another major poet of the period, began his creative life as a "peasant" poet, whose work was intimately connected with the popular folklore tradition and was permeated with a deep love for Russia. Other poets of the immediate prerevolutionary period are more difficult to place into any particular school, such as Voloshin and Tsvetaeva (q.v.).

LITERATURE, SOVIET. During the first years of Soviet rule the principal issue for writers was the nature of their relationship to the revolution that had just occurred. Many of them felt that the country Russia was falling apart, as was the Russian culture. Writers such as Bunin (q.v.) and Tsvetaeva (q.v.) were unwilling to accept the Communist regime and emigrated. Even Gorky (q.v.) condemned the forcible overthrow of the Provisional government (q.v.) in October 1917. In a cycle of articles entitled "Not Contemporary Thoughts," he expressed his indignation at the shootings and the closing of opposition newspapers by the Soviet government. In 1921 he went abroad. Among those writers who remained in Russia, a significant number consisted of individuals such as Severianin, Esenin (q.v.) and Mayakovsky (q.v.) who came out of the various modernistic currents that had existed before the revolution and who now claimed to be leaders of the new "revolutionary" art.

Toward the end of the 1920s the Futurists as a group fell apart. At that time the Russian Association of Proletarian Writers (q.v.) was particularly active. Another active group called themselves peasant writers. The principal point of conflict between these groups was the question of what artistic method to follow, what their relationship should be to the Russian literary past, and the nature of the relationship between literature and reality. At the same time there developed a current of realism that attempted graphically to portray the actual atmosphere during these first years of Soviet rule. It was represented by such writers as Zoshchenko (q.v.), Mikhail Bulgakov (q.v.), Ilf (q.v.) and Petrov (q.v.).

During that period a number of new literary periodicals began publication, among them *Molodaia Gvardiia*, *Zvezda*, *Novyi Mir*, and *Oktiabr*. By the beginning of the 1930s the Union of Writers of the USSR came into existence, and in August 1934 the first Congress of Soviet Writers, under the chairmanship of Gorky, took place in Moscow (q.v.). In the future this union was to become part of the administrative structure of the Soviet state and to play an important role in the suppression of artistic innovation and creativity in Russian literature. Success for many members of this union was frequently the result not of literary talent, but of their capacity to praise the Communist Party (q.v.) and its leaders. It was this congress that declared socialist realism to be the only legitimate tendency for Soviet literature.

Nevertheless, during the 1930s a number of writers, such as Aleksei Tolstoy (q.v.), continued to produce significant literary works. Other such writers were Novikov-Priboi and Sholokhov (q.v.). During World War II (q.v.), many Soviet writers worked as war correspondents on the front line. Others, like Bergholts (q.v.), contributed to the cultural life during this period by reading their poems and stories on the radio. Almost as soon as the war was over, the Soviet government began an attack on what it considered to be the incorrect ideological positions of many Russian authors. Two major literary periodicals of Leningrad were used as examples for punishment. In its decree of 1946 the Central Committee of the Communist Party (q.v.) chastised both Akhmatova (q.v.) and Zoshchenko, closed down the literary journal *Leningrad*, and appointed a new editor for the periodical *Zvezda*. After this decree there followed a wave of exposures of the so-called apolitical writers, and Soviet literature began to be filled with protagonists who never questioned the correctness of the party. After the death of Stalin (q.v.) and the condemnation of the cult of personality, a discussion developed within Russian literary circles about the handling of current problems, led by the literary periodical *Novyi Mir* and its editor Tvardovsky (q.v.).

By the end of the 1950s works began to be published that made an attempt to show some of the bad effects of the uncritical praise of Stalin (q.v.), as well as some indirect criticism of the Communist Party's leadership under him. New poets and writers, such as Yevtushenko (q.v.) also began to be published. Their heros were people who had begun to think for themselves and who entertained certain doubts about their existence and did not quite correspond to the Soviet version of the new "socialist man." Because the Communist Party leadership had no intention of surrendering its ideological leadership of Russian literature, it took steps to prevent any loosening of its control over writers, as well as to punish any literary creations that it viewed as negative. Thus Pasternak (q.v.) was expelled from the Writers' Union after being awarded the Nobel Prize for his novel *Doctor Zhivago*, which had not been published in the Soviet Union, and Krushchev (q.v.) criticized Ehrenburg's (q.v.) memoirs for their alleged betrayal of Marxism-Leninism. Grossman's (q.v.) wartime novel, *Life and Fate*, was not permitted to be published. In 1965 two employees of the Institute of World Literature, Siniavskii (q.v.) and Daniil, were arrested. They were tried and condemned to prison terms for anonymously publishing works abroad that were held to be critical of the Soviet system. As well, the editor of *Novyi Mir*, Tvardovsky, was forced to leave his post, and Solzhenitsyn (q.v.) was expelled from the Writers' Union. In 1974 he was exiled from Russia. Others who were forced to leave the Soviet Union were the poets Brodsky (q.v.) and Galich (q.v.).

Nevertheless, even with these major literary losses, Russian literature continued to develop, with truthful novels being written about World War II by Semenov (q.v.) and others. Another important influence on Russian cultural life during the 1970s and 1980s were the poems of Yevtushenko and Voznesenskii (q.v.).

LITERATURNAIA GAZETA. The principal Russian literary publication, it was the organ of the Soviet Union of Writers. At its height its circulation reached over six million.

LITHUANIA. Until 1991 a republic of the USSR, it occupies an area of 25,500 square miles on the Baltic Sea (q.v.) and has a population of

3,364,000. Its capital is Vilnius, and among its chief industries are agriculture and electronics. The Grand Duchy of Lithuania was a successor state to Kiev (q.v.) and was united with Poland in 1569. Russia acquired Lithuania in the third partition of Poland in 1795. Between 1919 and 1940 the country enjoyed a brief independence. The Nazi-Soviet nonaggression pact (q.v.) would have given it to Germany, but the Soviet Union traded the Lublin area of Poland for Lithuania. Many officials and more than 30,000 Lithuanians were then deported to Siberia. Lithuania became independent again in 1991.

LITVINOV, MAXIM M. (b. WALLAKH) (1876–1951). Born in Russian Poland, the son of a Jewish merchant, he served in the Russian army as a clerk. In 1898 he joined the Russian Socialist Democratic Labor Party (q.v.), was arrested for illegal political activities in 1902, but escaped to Switzerland and then moved to London, where he met Lenin (q.v.). During the 1905 revolution (*see* Revolution of 1905) Litvinov helped smuggle arms into Russia. In 1907 he represented the Communists at the 12th international socialist congress. Litvinov was arrested a year later by the French police, having been implicated in the laundering of stolen ruble notes. After his release he moved to England where he married Ivy Low, the daughter of an English journalist. After the 1917 revolution, he was appointed by Lenin to be the Soviet representative to Britain, where he was arrested for illegal political activities, only to be exchanged for the British agent Bruce Hart. In 1921 Litvinov became first the deputy commissar of foreign affairs, and then head of the Soviet delegation to an international conference at The Hague. He chaired the Moscow Disarmament Conference of 1922 and was the Soviet representative at the Geneva Disarmament Conference of 1927. Between 1930 and 1939 Litvinov was the Soviet commissar of foreign affairs and became world famous for his advocacy of collective security at the League of Nations. Replaced by Molotov in 1939, Litvinov was appointed Soviet ambassador to the United States. He was a member of the Central Committee of the Communist Party (q.v.).

LIUBIMOV, IURII P. (1917–). A graduate of the Moscow Theater School, he served in the Soviet Army from 1940 to 1946 and then became an actor in Moscow theaters. In 1964 he was made director of the Taganka Drama and Comedy Theater (q.v.). In 1983, while on a visit to Great Britain, Liubimov defected in protest against harassment by Soviet cultural authorities and began staging Russian productions abroad. He then moved to Israel.

LOBACHEVSKII, NIKOLAI I. (1793–1856). Born in Nizhni-Novgorod, Lobachevskii was the inventor of non-Euclidian geometry. In

1816 he became professor and then rector (1827 to 1846) at the University of Kazan (*see* Universities). Later, Lobachevskii was dismissed from his university post by the government.

LOMONOSOV, MIKHAIL V. (1711–65). The son of a fisherman from northern Russia, he was educated at Moscow's Slavo-Greco-Latin Academy (q.v.) and then in Germany. Lomonosov became professor at the Academy of Science in St. Petersburg (q.v.), where he researched the nature of matter. Lomonosov is the author of a history of Russia and of the first Russian grammar, and was the founder of Russia's first chemical laboratory.

LONSDALE, GORDON see MOLODYI, KONON T.

LOPUKHIN, ALEKSEI A. (1864–1927). The son of a nobleman, he graduated in 1886 from the University of Moscow (*see* Universities), then became the director of the police department. Dismissed after the assassination of Grand Duke Sergei (q.v.) in 1902, in 1908 he exposed Azef's (q.v.) collaboration with the secret police. Lopukhin was arrested for divulging state secrets and sentenced to hard labor for five years. After the 1917 revolution he emigrated.

LOPUKHINA, EVDOKIA F. (1669–1731). The 17-year-old bride of Peter the Great (q.v.), she was dull-witted as well as opposed to the reforms that Peter was implementing. The tsar sent her to a convent on suspicion that she lent her support to an uprising against him. Following her son's execution for treason in 1718, she was imprisoned in a fortress but was freed by her grandson after Peter's death.

LOPUKHOVA, LYDIA V. (MRS. MAYNARD KEYNES) (1891–1981). A graduate of the Theater School at St. Petersburg (q.v.) in 1909, she joined the Mariinskii Theater (q.v.), then in 1910 danced with Diaghilev's (q.v.) Ballets Russes (q.v.). Between 1911 and 1915 she toured the United States, Latin America and Italy. After meeting Dr. Keynes in 1926, she married him, continuing to dance occasionally with British ballet companies.

LORIS-MELIKOV, COUNT MIKHAIL T. (1826–88). A distinguished general of the Russo-Turkish war (q.v.), he became the governor-general of the Volga region and then chairman of a commission to suppress revolutionaries. Loris-Melikov was an advocate of institutional reforms and author of a decree that would have introduced the beginnings of a parliamentary system in Russia. This decree was signed by

Tsar Alexander II (q.v.) on the very day of his assassination but rejected by his heir, Alexander III (q.v.).

LOSSKII, NIKOLAI O. (1870–1965). As a young man he served in the French Foreign Legion, then graduated from the University of St. Petersburg (*see* Universities) in 1902 and became a doctor of philosophy in 1907. In 1916 he was made professor. Loskii is considered one of the most distinguished Russian philosophers of the 20th century. He was dismissed from his post by the Soviet government and expelled from Russia in 1922. He settled in Czechoslovakia, and from 1942 to 1945 he was a professor at the Comenius University in Bratislava. After World War II (q.v.) Losskii moved to Paris and then to the United States, where he taught at the St. Vladimir Theological Seminary.

LUNACHARSKII, ANATOLII V. (1875–1933). The son of a civil servant, he joined the Marxist movement in 1892 and the Russian Socialist Democratic Labor Party (q.v.) in 1895 while studying abroad. On his return to Russia in 1898 he became an active revolutionary and in 1903 joined the Communists. Lunacharskii lived in Europe between 1904 and 1917. Although a devoted Communist, he was criticized by Lenin (q.v.) for some of his philosophical views. After the October 1917 revolution (q.v.) Lunacharskii supported Lenin's policies and became the first Soviet commissar of education. He introduced a number of fundamental changes in Russia's school system. In 1933 he was made Soviet ambassador to Spain. Lunacharskii was the author of plays and a patron of the Soviet intelligentsia (q.v.). He died while on a visit to France.

LUNDBERG, EVGENII G. (1887–1956). As a young man he became interested in religion and philosophy, and after 1910 he wrote articles for Russian liberal newspapers. In 1920 he emigrated and went to Berlin, where he began a Russian-language publishing house. Lundberg returned to Russia in the mid-1920s where he continued to publish. Although arrested during the purges of the 1930s, he was one of the few who were released.

LVOV, PRINCE GEORGII E. (1861–1925). He served in the ministry of internal affairs between 1886 and 1893, then as a member of the Duma (q.v.), where he was associated with the Kadet (KD) Party (q.v.). In February 1917 Prince Lvov became the first prime minister of the Provisional government (q.v.). He went to France after the October 1917 revolution (q.v.) and died in Paris.

LYSENKO, TROFIM D. (1898–1976). A graduate of the Kiev (q.v.) Agricultural Institute in 1925, he was interested in plant breeding. Lysenko is best known for his rejection of modern genetics and for his advocacy of the theory that hereditary changes in plants can be brought about by environmental influences. He claimed that his ideas corresponded to the teachings of Karl Marx and used his influence with Communist Party (q.v.) officials to rise in the academic hierarchy. He became president of the Academy of Agricultural Science in 1938. From this post Lysenko persecuted his academic and political rivals, whom he denounced as being politically incorrect. He became the ideological dictator in Russian biological sciences and was responsible for the death or exile of a number of Soviet geneticists. After Stalin's (q.v.) death Lysenko was criticized by Khrushchev (q.v.) and dismissed from the presidency of the academy.

M

MAGADAN. A port on the Sea of Okhotsk (q.v.), it was for many years one of the principal centers of the Gulag (q.v.) in Siberia (q.v.). Its present population is just over 100,000.

MAGNITOGORSK. A major industrial city and area in the Ural Mountains (q.v.), it was built by the Soviet government between 1929 and 1931 and specializes in metallurgical and chemical production. Its population is just over 400,000.

MAIKOP. Established in 1857 as a fortified city on the Belaia River, southeast of Krasnodar (q.v.), Maikop is the capital of the Adygei (q.v.) Autonomous Region of the Russian Republic. It is rich in oil, and has a population of over 100,000.

MAISKII, IVAN M. (b. LIAKHOVETSKII) (1884–1975). After being expelled from the University of St. Petersburg (*see* Universities) in 1902 he joined the Russian Socialist Democratic Labor Party (q.v.) and emigrated to Switzerland. Maiskii then resided in England until he returned to Russia in 1917 to become a member of the Communist Party (q.v.) and Soviet ambassador to Finland from 1929 to 1932 and then to Great Britain from 1932 to 1943. In 1943 Maiskii again returned to Russia and was appointed deputy commissar of foreign affairs. In 1946 he was elected a member of the Academy of Sciences (q.v.) of the USSR.

MAKARENKO, ANTON, S. (1888–1939). A teacher before the 1917 revolution, after the civil war (q.v.) he specialized in rehabilitating orphans and street waifs in colonies for juvenile delinquents. Makarenko's method was rehabilitation through strict discipline and the stimulation of a strong collective spirit among his pupils, leading to mutual respect among them.

MAKARIUS, METROPOLITAN OF MOSCOW (1482–1563). During the youth of his pupil, Bishop Makarius exercised a strong influence on Tsar Ivan IV the Terrible (q.v.). He was also a strong advocate of the idea that Moscow was the Third Rome (q.v.), whose preeminence was destined to follow the fall of the First Rome in 476 and the demise of the Second Rome, Byzantium, after its conquest by the Turks in 1453.

MAKAROV, STEPAN O. (1848–1904). Commander of the Russian fleet in the Far East during the Russo-Japanese war (q.v.), he died when his flagship was sunk by a mine.

MAKHNO, NESTOR, I. (1889–1935). Born to a peasant family, he played an important role during the civil war (q.v.) as a leader of an anarchist "Green" force, which fought both the Red and the White (q.v.) armies. Makhno is credited with undermining General Denikin's (q.v.) march on Moscow in 1918 by cutting his supply lines. Defeated by the Red Army (*see* Armed Forces, Soviet) in 1921, he emigrated and died in Paris.

MAKLAKOV, VASILII A. (1870–1957). A graduate of the University of Moscow in 1896, he became a lawyer and a leading liberal politician. Maklakov was a member of several Dumas (q.v.), as well as of the Kadet (KD) Party's (q.v.) central committee. In December 1916 he took part in the murder of Rasputin (q.v.). After the February 1917 revolution (q.v.) he was in charge of the reorganization of the ministry of justice, then became the Soviet ambassador to France. There, after the end of the civil war (q.v.), he headed the office of Russian refugees. Following World War II (q.v.) he was involved in the forcible repatriation of Soviet citizens to the USSR, but did not return himself.

MALENKOV, GRIGORII M. (1902–88). A Red Army (*see* Armed Forces, Soviet) commissar during the civil war (q.v.), he became a member of the Communist Party (q.v.) in 1920. In 1925 Malenkov graduated from the Higher Technical Institute in Moscow and began to work in the Central Committee of the Communist Party (q.v.) of the Soviet Union. In the 1930s he was placed in charge of the party's personnel department under Kaganovich (q.v.) and played an important role in the purges (q.v.) of the 1930s. In 1941 he became a member of the Politburo (q.v.) and of the State Defense Committee. By 1946 he was the deputy prime minister of the USSR, occupying a position second only to Stalin (q.v.). In 1955 Malenkov lost the struggle for succession to Khrushchev (q.v.), and in 1957 he was expelled from the Communist Party as an enemy of the party. After his expulsion he served as a manager of a hydroelectric station in Kazakhstan (q.v.).

MALEVICH, KAZIMIR (1878–1935). He was a major Russian abstract painter. After experimenting with various styles of painting—abstraction, impressionism and cubism—he evolved his own style, which he called Suprematism (q.v.). Malevich taught painting during and just after the revolution and then lived in Germany, where he collaborated with another emigre Russian artist, Kandinskii (q.v.), in the publication of an art journal. Malevich died in Leningrad.

MALINOVSKII, RODION I. (1898–1967). During World War I (q.v.) he served as a member of the Russian Expeditionary Force in France, where he was a secret Bolshevik (q.v.) organizer. He fought in the ranks of the Red Army (see Armed Forces, Soviet) during the civil war (q.v.), then graduated from the Frunze Military Academy in 1930. Malinovskii took part in the Spanish civil war as a Soviet military advisor. During World War II (q.v.) he was one of the most successful Soviet commanders, especially distinguishing himself during the defense of Stalingrad (see Volgograd) in 1942. From 1957 to 1967 he served as minister of defense of the USSR and was a member of the Central Committee of the Communist Party (q.v.) of the Soviet Union.

MALORUSSIA (Russ., "LESSER RUSSIA"). This obsolete term denotes the Ukraine (q.v.), in contrast to the "Great Russia" of Russia proper. (Compare such formations as "Asia Minor," "Magna Graeca," and others.)

MALTSEV, VIKTOR I. (1895–1946). Born into a peasant family, he joined the Red Army (see Armed Forces, Soviet) and the Communist Party (q.v.) in 1918. Between 1930 and 1937 he served in the Soviet Air Force, then was arrested during the purges (q.v.) of the 1930s, only to be released in 1939. In 1941 he collaborated with the German occupation forces in the administration of Yalta, and helped organize former Soviet pilots for the Luftwaffe. After being captured by the

United States Army at the end of the war, he was handed over to the Soviet government, which tried and hanged him.

MANDELSHTAM, NADEZHDA I. (b. KHAZINA) (1899–1980). Born on the Volga River (q.v.), she married the poet Osip Mandelshtam (q.v.) in 1919. After his imprisonment in the 1930s, she earned her living as a teacher and succeeded in preserving his poetry. In 1958, she was rehabilitated and allowed to return to Moscow (q.v.), where she wrote her memoirs, covering the period of the 1920s and 1930s.

MANDELSHTAM, OSIP E. (1891–1938). Educated at the University of St. Petersburg (*see* Universities), he first published poetry before World War I (q.v.). One of the greatest poets of his time, he was an acmeist (q.v.) who stressed the importance of culture as a condition of human dignity. In the early 1930s Mandelshtam composed a scathing and angry poem about Stalin (q.v.), which was originally known to only a few people; for this, however, he was arrested and exiled. Released briefly, he was rearrested in 1938 and sent to the concentration camps in Siberia (q.v.), where he died. The time, place and circumstances of his death are unknown.

MANEVICH, L. E. (pseud. ETIEN) (1898–1945). Born into a Jewish family in Belarus (q.v.), he studied in Geneva during World War I (q.v.), then returned to Russia, where he graduated from the Red Army Military Academy in 1924 and from the Air Force Academy in 1929. After graduation he joined the Soviet military intelligence service, the GRU (q.v.), and became one of its top spies. His primary assignment was to kidnap former Soviet citizens who had defected to the West. On being captured by the Gestapo during World War II (q.v.), he was held in the Malthausen concentration camp. After the end of the war he remained in Austria, where he died.

MANUILSKII, DMITRII Z. (1883–1959). He joined the Bolsheviks (q.v.) as a student at the University of St. Petersburg (*see* Universities) in 1903, and was one of the organizers of the sailors' revolt in Kronstadt (q.v.) in 1905. He was arrested for these activities but succeeded in escaping from police custody. Manuilskii lived in France after 1907, where he graduated from the Sorbonne, then returned to Russia in 1912. There, Manuilskii worked briefly in the revolutionary underground but soon returned to France where he spent World War I (q.v.). Returning once again to Russia in 1917, he took an active part in the October 1917 revolution (q.v.). After 1922 Manuilskii worked in the Comintern (q.v.) and in 1944 became foreign minister of the Ukraine (q.v.), which he represented in the United Nations.

MANYCH. This is a vast system of navigable lakes and a major freshwater reservoir northwest of the Caucasus (q.v.) Mountains in the Russian Republic.

MARCHENKO, ANATOLII T. (1938–1987). Born in Siberia (q.v.), he was employed as a construction worker when, in the 1960s, he became a leading Soviet dissident (q.v.). His book, *My Testimony*, was published abroad and exposed the repressive measures used by the Soviet government against those of its citizens who were dissidents.

MARCHUK, GURI I. (1925-   ). A mathematician and expert on nuclear reactors, he was elected president of the Academy of Sciences (q.v.) of the USSR in 1986, in what was the first election of that body to employ the secret ballot system. Marchuk is given credit for establishing an advanced computer center in Novosibirsk (q.v.). He also served as head of the State Committee for Science and Technology (q.v.).

MARI-EL AUTONOMOUS REPUBLIC. Some 400 miles east of Moscow (q.v.), this territory's chief products are metalworks, timber, paper and food processing. Its population is in excess of 700,000.

MARIINSKII THEATER. Known as the Kirov in Soviet times, and home to the Mariinskii (Kirov) Ballet Company, this building was opened in 1860, restored from the original Circus Theater in St. Petersburg (q.v.), which had burned down the previous year. In 1920 it was renamed the State Opera and Ballet Theater and was associated with the name "Kirov" after 1935. Later it was also known as the Leningrad Opera and Ballet Theater.

MARKEVICH, IGOR B. (1912–85). The grandson of a famous historian, he was discovered by the impresario Diaghilev (q.v.) at age 16 and taken by him to Munich. In 1936 Markevich married Nijinsky's (q.v.) daughter. He was a composer of ballets, oratorios and concertos. He also conducted symphony orchestras in Moscow (q.v.) and in Paris. Markevich died in Switzerland.

MARKISH, PERETS D. (1895–1952). A leading Soviet Yiddish poet, novelist and playwright, he was arrested and shot on Stalin's (q.v.) orders in 1952 in connection with the "Doctors' Plot" (q.v.).

MARSHAK, SAMUIL I. (1887–1964). A student at London University between 1912 and 1914, he remained in England during World War I (q.v.), translating English poetry into Russian, but returned home on the eve of World War I. There, he started writing plays for children and organizing children's theaters. Marshak also became known for his translations of Shakespeare and other English poets.

MARSHALS OF THE NOBILITY. Under the system initiated by Catherine the Great (q.v.) in 1785 (the Charter of the Nobility), this was the title of individuals who were chosen by the local and district assemblies of nobles to represent them in dealing with government officials.

MARTOV, IULII O. (b. Tsederbaum) (1873–1923). He became a Marxist as a young man and, jointly with Lenin (q.v.), organized the Union for the Struggle for the Liberation of the Working Class (q.v.). In 1903 the two men parted company. Lenin became the leader of the more radical Bolshevik (q.v.) faction of the Russian Socialist Democratic Labor Party (q.v.), while Martov became the leader of its more moderate Menshevik (q.v.) faction. Martov remained in Russia after the revolution and was elected to the Supreme Soviet (q.v.) but was exiled from the USSR on Lenin's orders in 1922. He settled in Berlin, where he continued to lead the Mensheviks, as well as editing its official organ, *Sotsialisticheskii Vestnik*.

MARX-ENGELS-LENIN INSTITUTE. Formed in 1931 by the amalgamation of the Marx-Engels and the Lenin institutes, this organization served as a focus for the study of the writings and theories of Marx, Engels, and Lenin (q.v.).

MARXISM-LENINISM. Marxist ideology was popularized after the middle of the 19th century in the works of Marx and Engels. In its origins it was based on classical German philosophy (Hegel), English political economy (Adam Smith and Ricardo), and the French utopian socialists (St. Simon and Fourier). The 1870s and 1880s saw the organization of social democratic parties in a number of European countries, parties that were based on the teachings of Marx and Engels. Beginning in the last decade of the 19th century, Lenin (q.v.), together with such Russian socialists as Plekhanov (q.v.), began to adapt Marxism to the conditions that existed in Russia. The result of the changes Lenin introduced was Marxism-Leninism, which became the theoretical underpinning of the revolutionary Communist movement in Russia.

Lenin's version of Marxism stressed that the last and highest stage of capitalism was imperialism and insisted on the necessity of a revolution that would establish a dictatorship of the proletariat, brought about by a political party of a new type. According to Lenin, on its own the Russian working class was capable of developing only a trade union consciousness and would not become revolutionary. He argued that it was therefore essential for a party to implant this revolutionary consciousness into the working class and to then use that class as the striking force with which to overthrow capitalism. Lenin did not tolerate criticism of his theories, which he considered to be based on scientific Marxism, and he built this intolerance into the Marxist-Leninist ideology. Anyone who disagreed with its basic propositions was deemed to be an agent of interests hostile to the working class and, objectively, an agent of the bourgeoisie.

After Lenin and his followers seized power in Russia in October 1917, they treated any disagreements with the general line adopted by the Communist Party (q.v.) as being subject to organizational repression and imprisonment. Lenin and his followers devoted much attention to the propaganda of the Marxist-Leninist ideology among the Russian masses. In 1918 they established the Communist Academy, whose principal task was to develop and propagate Marxism. After 1919 they also established a wide network of Marxist educational institutions, among them the Institute of Marx and Engels in 1921 and, in the same year, the Institute of Red Professors, along with the Communist University of the Toiling Peoples of the East. Classics of Marxism-Leninism, such as *The Communist Manifesto* and *Capital*, were issued in millions of copies and in dozens of languages. In all higher educational institutions of the USSR Marxism-Leninism was made a compulsory course of study.

After World War II (q.v.) the Communist Party of the Soviet Union placed an even greater emphasis on the spread of the Marxist-Leninist ideology. In 1946 the Academy of the Social Sciences, attached to the Central Committee of the Communist Party (q.v.), was opened.

The official philosophy of the Communist Party of the Soviet Union and of the Soviet government was based on a selected set of writings by Marx, Engels and Lenin and, during the period of Stalin's (q.v.) dictatorship, also on the writings of Stalin. Its essence was a belief in dialectical materialism, in historical materialism, and in the inevitable triumph of Communism throughout the world.

MASSINE, LEONID (1894–1979). Massine studied ballet at the Imperial School and began as a dancer for Diaghilev (q.v.) in France before World War I (q.v.). Between 1924 and 1928 he again worked for Diaghilev, then from 1933 for other ballet companies.

MAXIMALISTS. An offshoot of the Socialist Revolutionaries (q.v.) party, this extremist group pursued terrorism as a form of political action. It blew up Prime Minister Stolypin's (q.v.) summer home in

1906. After the 1917 revolution many of its members joined the Communist Party of the Soviet Union (q.v.).

MAYAKOVSKY, VLADIMIR V. (1893–1930). In 1906 he attended school in Moscow, where he became involved in revolutionary activities; then, in 1911, Mayakovsky became a student at the Moscow Art School. After joining the Futurist (q.v.) group of poets, he began writing antiwar poetry. In October 1917 Mayakovsky welcomed the Bolshevik (q.v.) revolution and acted as a propagandist for the Soviet government during the civil war (q.v.). A gifted writer, Mayakovsky was declared by Stalin (q.v.) to be the most talented of Soviet poets. However, in the late 1920s he became disillusioned with Communism and ended his life by suicide.

MEDVEDEV, ROI A. (1925-   ). A graduate of Leningrad University (*see* Universities), he was employed as a researcher by the Academy of Sciences (q.v.) of the USSR until 1970, when he organized an international protest against the detention of his brother, Zhores Medvedev (q.v.), by Soviet authorities; he later published numerous works dealing with the Stalin (q.v.) period of Soviet history.

MEDVEDEV, ZHORES (1925-   ). A graduate of the Moscow Agricultural Academy, he became a critic of Soviet biological theories during the Stalin (q.v.) period. In 1970 he was arrested and placed in a psychiatric hospital. In 1973 Medvedev was allowed to emigrate to Great Britain. He is the author of numerous works dealing with recent Soviet history.

MEKHLIS, LEV Z. (1889–1953). A member of the Communist Party since 1918 when he joined the Red Army (*see* Armed Forces, Soviet), Mekhlis began working in Stalin's (q.v.) personal secretariat in 1922. In 1930 he became editor of *Pravda* (q.v.) as well as the chief of the press section of the Communist Party of the Soviet Union (q.v.). In 1939 he was made head of the main political administration of the Red Army and, in 1940, commissar of state control. In 1939 Mekhlis became a member of the Central Committee of the Communist Party of the Soviet Union (q.v.).

MEMORIAL. Founded in 1988, the aim of this association is to help preserve the memory of the victims of Stalin's (q.v.) purges. Among its activities are efforts to collect information concerning victims in all localities of Russia and to help the surviving families.

MENDELEEV, DMITRII IVANOVICH (1834–1907). After his studies at Heidelberg (under Bunsen and others), Mendeleev returned to Russia to become a virtual polymath, national educator and successful industrialist. He took part in the founding of the Russian Chemistry Society in 1868 and completed the work for which he is celebrated outside of Russia—his discovery of the periodic table of elements—a year later. He wrote on the importance of industrial and technical growth in Russia and applied his analytic powers to practical matters such as directing the work of the Chamber of Weights and Measures. In 1890 he retired from his professorship at St. Petersburg University (*see* Universities) over the refusal of the ministry of education to accept a petition from students, whose part Mendeleev took. He remained a productive scientist and writer until his death.

MENSHAGIN, BORIS G. (1902–80). He served in the Red Army (*see* Armed Forces, Soviet) from 1919 to 1927, then studied at the University of Moscow. Menshagin moved to Smolensk (q.v.) in 1937, remaining there during the German occupation and serving as mayor of the city. He was interned by the United States Army in 1945 and arrested by Soviet authorities. Tried for collaboration with the enemy, he received a 25-year prison sentence. In his memoirs, published posthumously in 1988, he gave an account of the murder of thousands of Polish officers at Katyn (q.v.) by Soviet troops.

MENSHEVIKS. The "minority." This was the moderate faction of the Russian Socialist Democratic Labor Party (q.v.) as it was formed after the split in 1903. It was led by Martov (q.v.) and Dan (q.v.). Most of its members remained in the USSR after the Bolsheviks (q.v.) seized power. In 1922, on Lenin's (q.v.) orders, the Menshevik Party was outlawed and its leadership forced to leave Russia.

MENSHIKOV, PRINCE ALEKSANDR D. (1673–1729). A field marshal of Peter the Great (q.v.), he supported his widow, Catherine I (q.v.), after the tsar's death. As a result of a palace intrigue, he was banished to Siberia (q.v.) toward the end of his life.

MENZHINSKII, VIACHESLAV R. (1874–1934). Born in St. Petersburg (q.v.) of Polish extraction, he graduated from the University of St. Petersburg (*see* Universities) in 1888 and joined the revolutionary movement. Menzhinskii took an active part in the revolution of 1905 (q.v.), was arrested, but escaped to Western Europe and then to the United States. He returned to Russia after the 1917 revolution to serve as an official of the State Bank, then became the first commissar of finance. In 1919 Menzhinksii joined the Cheka (q.v.) and in 1923 became its deputy chief until Dzerzhinskii's (q.v.) death in 1926, when he was made its chairman.

MEREZHKOVSKII, DMITRII S. (1866–1941). The son of a court official, he graduated from the University of St. Petersburg (*see* Universities). He was an early member of the Symbolist (q.v.) group of poets and the husband of Zinaida Gippius (q.v.). As a couple they were prominent in Russian literary circles, where they organized a religious and philosophical society that sought to establish a dialogue between the Russian intelligentsia (q.v.) and the Orthodox Church (q.v.). Merezhkovskii is known primarily as a writer of historical fiction. He condemned the October 1917 revolution (q.v.) and emigrated with his wife to Poland in 1920, then settled in Paris. There they formed a prominent emigre (*see* Emigres, Russian) literary salon.

MESTNICHESTVO. Abolished in 1682, this was a system of determining court and military appointments. It was based on precedent, as established by a family's inherited rank, which, in turn, was determined by its place (*mesto*), at the tsar's table.

METROPOLITAN. This high rank in the Orthodox Church (q.v.) was given to its most important bishoprics: St. Petersburg (q.v.), Moscow (q.v.), Kiev (q.v.), and Minsk (q.v.).

MEYERHOLD, VSEVOLOD Y. (1874–1942). Born into a Russified German-Jewish family, he was baptized early in life into the Orthodox Church (q.v.). Meyerhold began his career as an actor at the Moscow Art Theater (q.v.) in 1898, then in 1918 he joined the Communist Party (q.v.). The commissar of education, Lunacharskii (q.v.), put Meyerhold in charge of all Moscow theaters. In 1920 he organized his own theater, which met with great favor from the public but was criticized by Soviet cultural officials for some of the plays it put on. Meyerhold nevertheless continued as a theater director in Moscow and acquired an enormous popularity with theatergoers. His theater was finally closed by the Soviet government in 1938, and Meyerhold was declared to be alien to Soviet art, arrested, and sentenced to a labor camp.

MEZHRAIONTSY. This term denotes members of the interdistrict grouping of St. Petersburg social democrats led by Trotsky (q.v.). In 1913 they attempted, but failed, to end the quarrel between the Bolsheviks (q.v.) and Mensheviks (q.v.). After the February 1917 revolution (q.v.) this group sided with the Bolsheviks, whom they formally joined in August 1917.

MGB. Ministerstvo Gosudarstvennoi Bezopasnosti (the Ministry of State Security) was one of the names by which the Soviet secret police were known; the organization was renamed several times. (*See* CHEKA, GPU, NKVD, and KGB.)

MIASKOVSKII, NIKOLAI Ia. (1881–1950). The son of a Russian Army general, Miaskovskii was a student of Liadov (q.v.) and Rimskii-Korsakov (q.v.). He served as a military engineer in World War I (q.v.) and became professor of composition at the Moscow Conservatory in 1921. His students included Khachaturian (q.v.) and Kabalevskii (q.v.). He wrote 27 symphonies, among them the *October Revolution* symphony (1923), his sixth, as well as the cantata "The Kremlin at Night," and other works. In style reminiscent of Tchaikovsky (q.v.), he was considered a founder of Soviet musical culture. In 1948 Zhdanov accused Miaskovskii and many others of "formalistic perversion," but the charges were quietly forgotten; Miaskovskii continued to receive prizes toward the end of his life.

MICHAEL ROMANOV, TSAR (1596–1645). He was chosen to be the tsar of Russia in 1613 by a Zemskii Sobor (q.v.), or Land Assembly. Michael's election ended the Time of Troubles (q.v.) that had followed the death of Tsar Fedor I (q.v.), Ivan the Terrible's (q.v.) son. He ruled wisely under the guidance of his father, the Metropolitan Filaret of Moscow.

MICHURIN, IVAN V. (1855–1935). An amateur plant breeder who specialized in crossing fruit trees, he developed the theory of the inheritance of acquired characteristics that contradicted contemporary genetic theories. Michurin's teachings were later adopted by Lysenko (q.v.) and approved by Stalin (q.v.).

MIKHAIL ROMANOV, GRAND DUKE (1878–1918). The younger brother of Tsar Nicholas II (q.v.) and second heir to the imperial throne after the tsar's son Aleksei (q.v.), he married morganatically and against the tsar's orders, for which he was exiled to England. Allowed to return to Russia after the beginning of World War I (q.v.), he served as inspector of the cavalry. When Nicholas II abdicated in March 1917, he did so in favor of Grand Duke Mikhail, who declined to accept the throne unless called on by an elected constituent assembly. His refusal brought the Romanov dynasty (q.v.) to an end. After the Bolshevik (q.v.) overthrow of the Provisional government (q.v.), he was placed under arrest and then shot, together with his wife.

MIKHAILOVSKII, NIKOLAI K. (1842–1904). He was one of the intellectual leaders of the Socialist Revolutionaries (q.v.) party and a strong opponent of Russian Marxists.

MIKHALKOV, NIKITA (1945-   ). This film director made *Oblomov* (1979) and other successful films; in 1995 he won an American Oscar award for best foreign film with his *Burnt by the Sun*. In the 1995 elections in Russia he won a seat for Viktor Chernomyrdin's (q.v.) Our Home Is Russia bloc and lent his personal cachet to the campaign. However, in early 1996 he decided against filling the seat, preferring to start a new film project.

MIKHOELS, SOLOMON M. (1890–1948). A Soviet stage producer and actor, in 1925 he founded the State Jewish theater in Moscow and also taught at that theater's school of acting. Mikhoels was killed in 1948 on Stalin's orders during the anti-Semitic campaign associated with the last years of Stalin's life. His brother, Vovsi, was one of the doctors accused of attempting to poison Stalin and other Soviet leaders.

MIKOYAN, ANASTAS I. (1895–1978). An Armenian revolutionary who became a Bolshevik (q.v.) in 1915, Mikoian was active in the Caucasus (q.v.) during the revolution of 1917 and in the civil war (q.v.). He fell into the hands of the White Armies (q.v.) in 1919 but managed to escape. In 1921 he became a member of the Central Committee of the Communist Party of the Soviet Union (q.v.) and, in 1926, a member of its Politburo (q.v.). He served as commissar of supplies from 1926 to 1930, then as commissar of food industry and of foreign trade between 1930 and 1934. During World War II (q.v.) Mikoian chaired the committee of supply for the Red Army (*see* Armed Forces, Soviet) and was the minister of trade between 1953 and 1955. He was a close ally of Khrushchev (q.v.) and became the titular head of state of the USSR in 1964.

MILITARY EXPERTS. By the summer of 1918 the new Soviet republic had signed a peace treaty with Germany, but military dangers threatened it from the internal uprising of anti-Communist forces, as well as from Russia's former allies—the British, French and Japanese—who were hostile to Lenin's (q.v.) new revolutionary government. Since January 1918 the Soviet government had attempted to reestablish an army but lacked trained military personnel to command it. After Trotsky (q.v.) became chairman of the supreme war council in early 1918, he initiated a policy of recruiting former tsarist officers as specialists to organize the Red Army (*see* Armed Forces, Soviet). In order to ensure the loyalty of these experts, Trotsky placed trusted Communists as military commissars next to these experts, stipulating that all orders of the former officers be countersigned by these commissars before they became valid.

MILITARY SERVICE. Until the military reforms of 1874, Russian soldiers were recruited from the peasant serfs by lot for a 25-year period, later cut to 20 years. After that reform, military service was made obligatory for all men 20 years of age. In 1918 the Soviet government temporarily abolished compulsory service but in 1936 incorporated it into the Stalin constitution (*see* Constitutions of the USSR and Russia) as a basic duty of all male citizens when they reached the age of 17 or 18. The period of service was to last from two to five years and then to continue in the form of membership in reserve units until the age of 50.

MILITIA. This is the postrevolutionary name for the regular police forces in the country. The change of name was primarily a symbolic one, resulting from the acute hatred that much of the population felt for the tsarist police force before the February 1917 revolution (q.v.). The militia was subordinated to the ministry of the interior and to local councils. After the 1990 elections to these councils, many of the cities established police forces completely independent of the central ministry.

MILIUKOV, PAVEL N. (1859–1943). A graduate of the University of Moscow (q.v.) in 1882, he became involved in revolutionary activities and was exiled from 1894 to 1897. He then traveled widely abroad as a lecturer and wrote several major historical works before returning to Russia in 1905. Miliukov was a founder of the Kadet (KD) Party (q.v.) and editor of its newspaper, as well as pursuing a left-of-center policy as one of the leaders of the Progressive Bloc (q.v.) in the Duma (q.v.). After the February 1917 revolution (q.v.) he was minister of foreign affairs in the Provisional government (q.v.). In 1920 Miliukov emigrated to France, where he edited a Russian-language newspaper.

MILLENNIUM. Celebrated in June 1988, this was the thousand-year commemoration of the introduction of Orthodox (*see* Orthodox Church) Christianity into Kievan Rus (q.v.).

MILLER, EVGENII, K. (1867–1937). A graduate of the Cadet (q.v.) Corps and of a cavalry school in 1884, he became a Russian military attaché in Western Europe, then, in 1912, the chief of staff of the Moscow (q.v.) Military District. During World War I (q.v.) Miller served as a general, and during the civil war (q.v.) he participated in the anti-Communist government of Arkhangelsk (q.v.). He was also commander of the northern front under Admiral Kolchak (q.v.). After the evacuation of the White Armies (q.v.) to France in 1920, General Miller became deputy to General Kutepov (q.v.), the leader of the

White civil war (q.v.) veterans. After the latter was kidnapped by Soviet agents, Miller took his place but disappeared from France in 1937 under mysterious circumstances.

MININ (late 16th century-1616). A resident of Nizhnii Novgorod (q.v.), he led the Russian armies against invading Polish forces that were supporting False Dmitrii (q.v.), a pretender to the Russian throne.

MINISTERSTVO VNUTRENNYKH DEL (MINISTRY OF INTERNAL AFFAIRS). Under Sergei Nikiforovich Kruglov, former deputy head of Smersh (q.v.), the MVD was founded in 1946 to look after matters pertaining to the population on a wide scale, including not only police and security (taking over the duties of the former NKVD) but such things as traffic, housing and fire prevention. In 1953 it subsumed the Ministry of State Security (MGB, *Ministerstvo Gosudarstvennoi Bezopasnosti*); but the latter separated a year later to form the Committee of State Security (KGB, *Komitet Gosudarstvennoi Bezopasnosti*).

MINSK. The capital of the Republic of Belarus (q.v.), it was ruled by Lithuania (q.v.) until the end of the 18th century, when it became incorporated into the Russian empire. During both World War I (q.v.) and World War II (q.v.) it was occupied by the German army and in 1920 by the Poles. At the time of its incorporation into the USSR, it became an important center for food processing and for engineering production. Its population is in excess of one million inhabitants.

MIR (1). The literal meaning of the word is "peace" as well as "world," being derived from the root *mei* in the sense of "gentle," "friendly," and thence "friendship," "community." It was also the name of the first and only permanently orbiting space station, placed into orbit by the Soviet Union in 1986.

MIR (2). The basic form of rural peasant self-governing community, it was charged with collecting taxes and with the annual redistribution of cultivated land to each peasant household. Russian Slavophiles (q.v.) and agrarian socialists considered it to be the foundation for a future Russian agrarian socialism.

MIROVICH, VASILI Y. (1740–64). An officer of the guards, he attempted to free the youthful Ivan VI (q.v.) from his incarceration in a fortress and to dethrone Catherine the Great (q.v.) in 1764. His attempt failed when other guards killed the youth. Mirovich was captured and executed.

MIRSKI, DMITRY P. see SVIATOPOLSK-MIRSKII

MOGILEV. This is a 13th-century Belorussian town on the Dnepr River (q.v.). During much of World War I (q.v.) it was the location of the command headquarters of the Russian Army Stavka (q.v.) and residence of Tsar Nicholas II (q.v.). Today it is an industrial city of some 300,000 inhabitants.

MOISEEV, IGOR A. (1906-   ). A graduate of the Bolshoi Ballet school in 1924, he was founder and principal choreographer of the State Folk Dance Ensemble. He stressed folk music and the dances of the different ethnic groups of the USSR.

MOLDAVIA see MOLDOVA

MOLDOVA. This is the former Soviet republic of Moldova SSR, which has an area of 13,011 square miles and a population of over four million. It was established in 1940 by joining part of Bessarabia (q.v.), ceded by Romania, and a part of the Ukraine (q.v.). The capital is Kishinev (alternately written Chiinau). It is a fertile region, with abundant grapes and other fruits. The Moldovan language is practically identical to Romanian, except that it is written in Cyrillic letters.

MOLODYI, KONON T. (pseud. LONSDALE, GORDON) (1923–70). Born in the United States, he went with his family when they returned to Russia in 1938. There he received training as an intelligence officer. In 1955 Molodyi was sent to Great Britain, where, under the pseudonym of Lonsdale, he organized a network to spy on NATO bases. In 1961 he was arrested and sentenced to prison but was exchanged for a British prisoner held by the Soviets.

MOLOKANSTVO. A religious Russian sect that came into existence in the 18th century, it rejected icons (q.v.) and the need for a hierarchy in the Orthodox Church (q.v.).

MOLOTOV, VIACHESLAV M. (b. SKRIABIN) (1890–1986). He joined a Marxist revolutionary circle as a student and became a Bolshevik (q.v.) in 1906. Arrested in 1907, Molotov was soon released and began his studies at the St. Petersburg Polytechnic. In 1915 he became a member of the Russian bureau of the Bolshevik central committee, as well as one of the editors of its newspaper, *Pravda* (q.v.).

After the October 1917 revolution (q.v.) he held a number of important party posts, including that of secretary of the Central Committee of the Communist Party of the Soviet Union (q.v.). A close ally of Stalin (q.v.), he played a leading role in organizing the mass purges of the 1930s. From 1930 to 1941 he served as premier of the USSR and as foreign commissar signed the 1939 Nazi-Soviet nonaggression pact (q.v.) with German Foreign Minister von Ribbentrop. As foreign minister between 1939 and 1949 and again between 1953 and 1957, he participated in the Teheran, Yalta, and Potsdam conferences between the USSR, the United States and Great Britain.

After the 20th congress of the Communist Party in 1956 he opposed Khrushchev's (q.v.) policies and was dismissed from all positions in the Soviet government, along with his allies Kaganovich (q.v.) and Malenkov (q.v.). Molotov was assigned the honorific post of ambassador to the Mongolian People's Republic (q.v.) from 1957 to 1960, then served between 1960 and 1962 as Soviet representative at the International Atomic Agency. In 1962 he was expelled from the Communist Party (q.v.) and retired. He was finally readmitted to the Communist Party in 1985.

MONGOL CONQUEST. In the early 13th century (1240), the Mongol armies led by descendants of Genghis Khan (q.v.) invaded Kievan Rus (q.v.), besieged and sacked a number of towns, including the principal city, Kiev (q.v.), and settled on the Lower Volga River (q.v.). There they established the Khanate of the Golden Horde (q.v.) under Batu Khan (q.v.). From there, the Mongols exercised their suzerainty over the remaining towns of Rus (q.v.) such as Moscow (q.v.) and Vladimir (q.v.). They imposed taxes, controlled the elevation of native princes, and ruthlessly punished any disobedience to their decrees.

Over the next centuries their rule became less certain; some of the westernmost principalities of Rus became protectorates of the grand duchy of Lithuania (q.v.), and the northeastern principality of Moscow (q.v.) was able to consolidate numerous smaller towns under its ruling princes. In 1380, almost 140 years after the initial conquest, these Russian princes, under Dmitrii Donskoi (q.v.), defeated the Mongols for the first time at the battle of Kulikovo (q.v.). It was, however, another 100 years before the princes of Moscow succeeded in freeing themselves completely from the Mongol Yoke (q.v.) and could begin re-establishing contact with Western Europe, from which they had been effectively cut off for two centuries.

MONGOL YOKE. The rule of Rus by the Mongols between the 13th and 15th centuries, it was based on the extortion of tribute maintained through a policy of keeping the several princes at odds with one other. The first governor, or *daruga* (q.v.), was the Mongol emperor's son-in-law Kitat. A turning point in the rule of the Mongols was reached with the battle of Kulikovo (q.v.) in 1380, after which their declining power could demand no more than a casual taxation; it ceased altogether with the outright refusal of Grand Prince Ivan III (q.v.) in 1476. The cumulative effect of the Mongol Yoke was to unite and centralize Russian territories politically, but also to thwart their independent development in other spheres.

MONGOLIAN PEOPLE'S REPUBLIC. A country with a population of 2,185,000 occupying some 604,247 square miles, much of it is grassy plateau conducive to grain growing and cattle raising. The south contains the Gobi Desert. In addition to agriculture, there are deposits of coal and various minerals. The original Mongolian empire was a province of China until 1911, when it became independent. A Communist regime was installed in 1921. In 1990 the ruling Communist Party (q.v.) resigned but was promptly voted back into power in elections. The population of the capital, Ulan Bator (also written Ulaanbaatar), is around 550,000.

MORDOVIAN AUTONOMOUS REPUBLIC. An area at the bend of the Volga River (q.v.) southeast of Moscow (q.v.), its principal city is Saransk (q.v.). Primarily an agricultural area, it produces grain, sugar beets and dairy products. Its population is just under one million.

MOROZOV, PAVLIK (1918–32). A young pioneer in the Sverdlovsk region (see Ekaterinburg), he betrayed his father's hoarding activities to the authorities and was allegedly murdered for the deed by his grandfather and others. For this he was raised to cultlike status as the model of loyalty to the state; the incident was widely publicized.

MOROZOV, SAVVA (end 18th century). This enterprising serf in the 1790s purchased his freedom with the money he made from a ribbon factory at Orekhovo-Zuievo (q.v.). He was the founder of the Morozov family, leading industrialists of Russia. As their wealth grew, the Morozovs became patrons of the arts and of literature. One of the Morozovs became a famous collector of postimpressionist paintings as well as a financier of left-wing political parties.

MOSCOW. The ancient capital of the Russian tsars (q.v.), it was mentioned for the first time in the Primary Chronicle (q.v.). It was one of the smallest and most northerly towns of the Kievan Rus (q.v.). Because of its distance from the seat of the Mongol Khans and the skill of its princes—the junior members of the ruling Riurik (q.v.) dynasty whose senior member ruled in Kiev (q.v.)—it was not sacked by the invaders and managed to enlarge itself during the years of the Mongol Yoke (q.v.). Until Peter the Great (q.v.) moved his government to the newly constructed city of St. Petersburg (q.v.) in the early 18th century, it remained the seat of the tsars of Russia.

After the Bolsheviks (q.v.) seized power in October 1917, the Soviet government moved back to Moscow in order to escape from the menace of a German army advancing toward Petrograd. Since 1918 it has been the capital of the USSR.

Today it is the capital of the Russian Republic and the locus of numerous state, academic and cultural organizations. The population is around 8,967,000.

MOSCOW ART THEATER. The theater was begun by Stanislavsky (q.v.) with funds provided by the Morozov (q.v.) family at the end of the 19th century. It achieved fame for its innovative methods of acting and stage direction. The theater survived the 1917 revolution and civil war (q.v.) and has continued its traditions to the present day.

MOSCOW RIVER. Rising west of Moscow (q.v.), the river flows for over 300 miles eastward to the confluence with the Oka River (q.v.). A canal that was built by forced labor in the 1930s links it with the Volga River (q.v.).

MOST HOLY SYNOD. In 1720 Peter the Great dissolved the patriarchate of Russia and replaced it with the synod in an effort to reform the Orthodox Church (q.v.) and make it more amenable to his own modernizing policies. It ceased to exist after the election of Tikhon as patriarch in 1917.

MUKDEN, BATTLE OF. This site saw a major defeat of Russian arms by the Japanese armies in 1904 during the Russo-Japanese war (q.v.). This disaster, in which Russia lost over 70,000 men, led to the resignation of the commander in chief, General Kuropatkin (q.v.).

MURATOV, PAVEL (1881–1950). Mainly known for his writings on Italy and art, Muratov began his career reporting on the Russo-Japanese war (q.v.). He traveled extensively in Europe to acquire the knowledge he would later put to use in his books. He is also the author of some historical novels. Along with many other intellectuals, he was exiled from Russia in 1922.

MURAVEV, NIKITA (1796–1843). One of the leaders of the Northern Society (q.v.), he had been a student at the University of Moscow (*see* Universities) and later joined the imperial guards as an officer.

After the unsuccessful military coup of December 1825 against Tsar Nicholas I (q.v.), Muravev was sentenced to exile in Siberia (q.v.).

MURAVEV-AMURSKII, NIKOLAI N. (1809–81). As governor-general of Siberia (q.v.), he was instrumental in organizing major exploratory expeditions in the Amur River (q.v.) regions of the country, as well as in obtaining a treaty favorable to Russia from the Chinese empire at the town of Aigun in 1858.

MURAVEV-APOSTOL, SERGEI I. (1796–1826). An officer of the guards, he became a leader of the Southern Society (q.v.) of rebellious officers. During the unsuccessful Decembrist (q.v.) Rebellion against Tsar Nicholas I (q.v.) he was fatally wounded in the fighting in front of the Winter Palace (q.v.) in St. Petersburg (q.v.).

MURMANSK. A northern Russian city on the Kola Bay, it stands on an inlet to the Barents Sea (q.v.), and was occupied by the British Expeditionary Force in 1918 during the civil war (q.v.). Today its principal industrial activities are shipping, the fishing industry, and shipbuilding. The population is just under 400,000.

MUROM. An ancient Russian town, some 200 miles east of Moscow (q.v.) on the Oka River (q.v.), its industries specialize in flax spinning, tanning, and railway works. It has a population of just under 100,000.

MUSCOVY. This principality was founded in 1283 and ruled by Ruricids subordinate to the grand princes of Vladimir (q.v.); eventually, Moscow replaced Vladimir as the capital. Its disposition enabled it to grow relatively unmolested by the Mongols and it annexed Novgorod (q.v.), Tver (q.v.) and other Russian principalities over time; it also replaced Vladimir as the administrative center of the Russian Orthodox Church (q.v.). Under Ivan IV (q.v.), the Mongol khanates of Kazan (q.v.), Astrakhan (q.v.) and Siberia (q.v.) were conquered, making Muscovy a multiethnic kingdom.

MUSIC, RUSSIAN. The folk music of the east Slav tribes received its further development through Orthodox Church (q.v.) liturgy after the tribes' conversion to Christianity at the end of the tenth century. Both forms placed great emphasis on choir singing. In the 16th century strong secular influences on Russian music began to manifest themselves. Everyday songs received special development, and such instruments as the clavichord began to be imported from Western Europe. By the beginning of the 17th century, organ music had also gained popularity in Russia. During the reign of Peter the Great (q.v.), music acquired special significance within court circles in imitation of those in Western Europe, and soon Italian opera could be heard in both St. Petersburg (q.v.) and Moscow (q.v.). These events greatly helped the development of native musicians. During Peter's reign, a court a cappella choir was created, and somewhat later, in 1783, the Mariinskii Theater (q.v.) in St. Petersburg (q.v.) was opened. By the end of that century a Russian national opera had come into existence, and concerts of music composed by Russians were regularly performed.

In the first half of the 19th century Glinka (q.v.) became the founder of modern Russian classical music. His operas still enjoy worldwide popularity. In 1802 the Philharmonic Society was organized in St. Petersburg, and the Bolshoi theater (q.v.) was opened in Moscow in 1825. In 1859 the Russian Musical Society came into existence. By the second half of the century musical education was well established in the country, and concert presentations were a regular feature of life in both the capitals and in larger provincial towns. In the 1850s a group of prominent Russian composers turned to the composition of music that sought to reflect the Russian national character. The leading members of this group were Balakirev (q.v.), Mussorgskii (q.v.), Cui (q.v.), Rimskii-Korsakov (q.v.), and Borodin (q.v.). In 1862, under the directorship of Rubinstein (q.v.), the first Russian musical conservatory was opened in the capital, and in 1866 a similar one was established in Moscow. It was during this period that the best-known Russian composer, Tchaikovsky (q.v.), began his creative activity, producing symphonic, opera and ballet music. At the beginning of the 20th century Rakhmaninov (q.v.) and Scriabin (q.v.) acquired popularity as composers, and the basso Shaliapin (q.v.) gained his international renown.

After the October 1917 revolution (q.v.) the Russian Association of Proletarian Music sought to simplify musical forms and argued that native music should be primarily choral. Musical composition in the Soviet Union in the 1920s and 1930s was primarily connected with the names of Prokofiev (q.v.), Khachaturian (q.v.), and Shostakovich (q.v.). During this period the State Symphonic Orchestra was formed, as well as several chamber music groups. The Union of Soviet Composers came into being in 1932. In 1948 the first All-Union Congress of Soviet Composers took place in Moscow. This meeting was used by Soviet cultural authorities as a platform from which to launch an ideological attack on a number of Soviet composers and to brand them as formalists and as creators of "antipeople music." This congress had a negative impact on the future development of Soviet music and led to the composition of numerous mediocre oratorios on politically correct themes. It was only after Stalin's death that a resolution of the Communist Party (q.v.) rescinded the decisions of the congress.

After a brief thaw under Khrushchev (q.v.), during the Brezhnev (q.v.) era several outstanding musicians were expelled from the Soviet Union for political reasons. Among them were the renowned cellist Rostropovich (q.v.) and the opera singer Vishnevskaia. The symphony conductor Kondrashin (q.v.) was also subjected to severe criticism. However, despite these instances of political interference in the development of music in Russia, in 1993 the country could boast of 22 state opera and ballet companies, as well as 80 symphony orchestras and close to 4,000 schools of music.

Western popular music has always discreetly crept into Russia in one form or another. The availability of relatively inexpensive cassette tape recorders in the 1970s might mark that period as a starting point for its wide appeal there. Around that time rock groups began to appear in urban centers, but their performances were usually restricted to small, underground venues. After the beginning of perestroika (q.v.) Russia was invaded by conventional rock music. This genre became a medium through which the younger generation attempted to express its feelings and aspirations, as well as its attitude toward life.

MUSSORGSKII, MODEST P. (1839–81). An officer of a guards regiment and a severe alcoholic, he resigned his commission in order to have time to compose music. Mussorgskii was forced to work as a clerk in order to support himself. He was a leading member of a group of nationalistic Russian composers. Mussorgskii is primarily known for his operas, which are frequently performed in Western Europe and America, especially his *Boris Godunov*, which is a musical dramatization of Pushkin's (q.v.) play of the same name.

MUZHIK. This term was generally used to designate a peasant, an individual who was a member of the largest social layer of Russia. It also acquired a derogatory connotation as someone who was crude and impolite.

N

NABEREZHNYE-CHELNY. This town on the Kama River (q.v.) near Elabuga (q.v.) is in the Tatar Autonomous Republic (q.v.) of the Russian Federation. In the Soviet period it was known as Brezhnev. Its economy is based on its favorable geographical location as a grain distribution and trade center. It also manufactures metal goods and railroad cars. The town's population is close to 350,000.

NABOKOV, VLADIMIR D. (1869–1922). A graduate of the University of St. Petersburg (*see* Universities) in 1890, then professor of criminal law from 1896 to 1904, he was also a newspaper and law journal editor. Nabokov was a prominent member of the Kadet (KD) Party (q.v.). After the civil war (q.v.) he emigrated to Germany, where he edited a Russian language newspaper in Berlin and where he was assassinated by a right-wing fanatic.

NABOKOV, VLADIMIR V. (pseud. SIRIN) (1899–1977). The son of Vladimir Nabokov (q.v.), he emigrated with his family after the civil war (q.v.) from Russia. Between 1922 and 1937 Nabokov lived in Berlin, then in 1937 he moved to France and from there to the United States in 1940. A graduate of Cambridge University, Nabokov wrote poetry and novels in both the Russian and the English languages, as well as translating Russian writers into English. He died in Switzerland.

NAFANAIL, ARCHBISHOP (b. VASILII LVOV) (1906–86). Born in Moscow (q.v.), he emigrated to Harbin (q.v.), China, following the 1917 revolution. After taking a theological degree, he became a monk. Bishop Nafanail moved to Czechoslovakia, where he lived until the end of World War II (q.v.), when he helped save many Russian refugees from forcible repatriation to the USSR. In 1946 he was elevated to the post of Orthodox bishop of Western Europe, then bishop of Vienna and Austria and, finally, in 1981 to the rank of archbishop.

NAKHIMOV, PAVEL S. (1802–55). A Russian admiral, he circumnavigated the globe between 1822 and 1824, then was given the command of the Russian navy in the Black Sea (q.v.) during the Crimean War (q.v.). Nakhimov died defending the Russian fortress of Sebastopol (q.v.) during the seige by the armies of Britain and France.

NAKHODKA. A Russian port on the Pacific coast southeast of Vladivostok (q.v.), its primary industries are shipbuilding and lumber milling.

NALCHIK. This town was established in 1818 and is now a health resort and capital of the Kabardino-Balkaria Autonomous Area (q.v.), some 100 miles west of Groznyi (q.v.). Its principal industries are meat packing and the manufacture of oil drilling equipment.

NAPOLEONIC WARS. These wars were undertaken by the French in the period between 1799 and 1815. The 1812 campaign against Russia ended in a dramatic defeat when Napoleon, unsatisfied with his success at Smolensk (q.v.) and the terms offered by the Russians, decided to march on Moscow (q.v.). The Russian tactic of destroying or removing anything of value in Moscow left Napoleon with no choice but to sack the city and return to France, allowing the French army to be decimated by hunger, exposure and Russian attack during its long retreat. This defeat and the destruction of the French army signaled the beginning of the collapse of Napoleon's empire.

NAPPELBAUM, MOISEI S. (1869–1958). An apprentice at a photographic studio in 1884, he followed his trade first in Smolensk (q.v.), then in Moscow (q.v.), and eventually in the United States. His first photographs were published in St. Petersburg (q.v.) in 1910. After the October 1917 revolution (q.v.) he photographed such top Soviet political leaders as Dzerzhinskii (q.v.) and Lunacharskii (q.v.) and exhibited his work both in Leningrad (*see* St. Petersburg) and in Moscow. He also photographed Akhmatova (q.v.), Meyerhold (q.v.), Kuzmin (q.v.), and Esenin (q.v.).

NAROD (THE PEOPLE). The term also refers to the lower classes of the population and was frequently utilized by populists in their political appellation "to the people." A *narodnik* was an individual who adhered to the ideology of populism (*see* Narodnichestvo).

NARODNAIA RASPRAVA (PEOPLE'S VENGEANCE). This short-lived student terrorist organization was founded by the terrorist Nechaev (q.v.) in 1869. It was discovered and broken up by the police within a few months of its establishment.

NARODNAIA VOLIA (PEOPLE'S WILL). A terrorist organization that emerged from the collapse of the Zemlia i Volia Party (q.v.) in 1879, its members were primarily junior army officers and urban intellectuals who were dedicated to the establishment of a revolutionary socialist system in Russia. The party aimed at setting off an immediate revolution through the use of individual terror. Ruled by a secret executive committee, it decided on, and carried out the assassination of Tsar Alexander II (q.v.) in 1881.

NARODNICHESTVO. (POPULISM). This ideology was embraced by large sections of the Russian intelligentsia in the second half of the 19th century. It was a political philosophy and a movement that identified itself with the common people of Russia, especially with the peasantry.

Initially, in the early 1870s, the Narodniki attempted to go to the people and to enlighten them as to the true cause of their oppression. After being rebuffed by the peasants, who were suspicious of these educated urbanites, and after arrests by the police, many of them dropped out of politics. A substantial number, however, formed a radical socialist political party, the Zemlia i Volia Party (q.v.), which in 1879 split into two groups, the larger Narodnaia Volia (q.v.) advocated terror as a method of struggle against the tsarist establishment, and the smaller Chernyi Peredel (q.v.) favored a slower process of popular education and politicization. In the 1890s the remnants of Narodnaia Volia participated in the founding of the Socialist Revolutionaries (q.v.) party, which opposed both the Marxist social democrats and the tsarist establishment.

In general, Russian populism as a political tendency has been characterized by the propensity to make appellations to the people, and ever since the 1860s Russian populists have sought a mass base in order to achieve power. Elements of populism also appear in the policies of the political leadership in post-Soviet Russia.

NARODNO-TRUDOVOI SOIUZ (NTS; POPULAR LABOR ALLIANCE). This emigre organization was founded in the early 1930s by groups of young Russian emigres (*see* Emigres, Russian) in Belgrade as a counter-Communist, ideologically based nationalist movement. It was built on the political theory of solidarism first developed in the prerevolutionary writings of Guins (q.v.) and advocated active attempts to overthrow Communist rule in Russia. During World War II (q.v.) many of its members worked with such German-sponsored organizations as the Russian Liberation Army (q.v.) (ROA) in an attempt to establish a political base among the population of occupied Russia. After the end of the war the NTS was very active in Western Europe, publishing a weekly newspaper *Possev*, and broadcasting to the USSR.

NARODNYI KOMMISSARIAT VNUTRENNYKH DEL see NKVD

NATANSON, MARK A. (pseud. BOBROV) (1850–1919). He was one of the leaders of the Narodnaia Volia (q.v.) party. Together with Perovskaia (q.v.) and others, he participated in the assassination of Tsar Alexander II (q.v.). Natanson survived the arrests and executions of the group's other leaders and lived in Western Europe until the February 1917 revolution (q.v.), when he returned to Russia.

NAUMENKO, VIACHESLAV G. (1880–1978). He served as an officer during World War I (q.v.) and as the leader of the Kuban Cossacks (q.v.) in the civil war (q.v.). During World War II (q.v.) he served as commander of the anti-Soviet Cossacks in Austria. After its end, Naumenko moved to the United States, where he published the history of the forcible repatriation of the Cossacks to the USSR.

NAVAL ACADEMY. This educational institution was founded by Peter the Great (q.v.) in 1715 for the training of officers for the Russian navy. During the February 1917 revolution (q.v.) its buildings were the site of meetings of the All-Russian Congress of Soviets.

NAZI-SOVIET NONAGGRESSION PACT. A pact concluded between Germany and the Soviet Union by Foreign Minister von Ribbentrop and the commissar of foreign affairs, Molotov (q.v.), in August 1939, this agreement had a major impact on the subsequent invasion of Poland and its partition between the two signatories. It also enabled Stalin (q.v.) to annex Estonia (q.v.), Latvia (q.v.) and Lithuania (q.v.) in 1940.

NECHAEV, SERGEI G. (1847–82). A notorious terrorist of the 1860s who founded the secret criminal group Narodnaia Rasprava (q.v.) (People's Vengeance). His aim was to create an organization of professional terrorists who would bring about the liberation of mankind through acts of terror. He received support for this scheme from several influential Russian political emigres (*see* Emigres, Russian), including Bakunin (q.v.) and Ogarev (q.v.). Apprehended after murdering a follower, he was deported to Russia, tried and incarcerated for ten years in a military fortress. Some students of the 19th-century revolutionary movement in Russia have found a similarity between Nechaev's theories and those of Lenin's (q.v.).

NEKRASOV, NIKOLAI A. (1821–78). He was the owner and publisher of the highly influential periodical *Sovremennik* (q.v.) (1849), which expressed the viewpoint of the radical intelligentsia of mid-19th-century Russia. He was also a poet and a satirist who focused on the sufferings of the poor and the downtrodden.

NEKRASOV, VIKTOR P. (1911–87). A railroad engineer, he fought in Stalingrad (*see* Volgograd) during World War II (q.v.). After the war, while editing a Moscow (q.v.) newspaper, he displeased the literary authorities and was expelled from the Union of Soviet Writers (q.v.) and the Communist Party (q.v.). In 1974 Nekrasov emigrated and became editor in chief of *Kontinent*, a Russian emigre publication. He died in Paris.

NEMIROVICH-DANCHENKO, VLADIMIR I. (1858–1943). A well-known Russian theatrical figure and cofounder with Stanislavsky (q.v.) of the Moscow Art Theater. He also wrote about the theater in Russia.

NENETS. The Nenets, formerly known as Samoeds, are an Ugric-speaking people who number around 30,000 and live in the Nenets National oblast and adjacent areas. They live by herding reindeer, hunting and fishing.

NEP (NOVAIA EKONOMICHESKAIA POLITIKA; NEW ECONOMIC POLICY). This policy was adopted by Lenin (q.v.) in 1921 and lasted until 1928. It temporarily permitted private enterprise in the smaller sectors of the Soviet economy in an attempt to restore the productivity that had collapsed during the revolution and the civil war (q.v.). By 1928 it had led to a series of economic contradictions that precipitated a renewed factional struggle within the leadership of the Communist Party (q.v.) over which policy alternatives to adopt. It ended with a victory for Stalin's (q.v.) demand for a highly centralized, hierarchically organized command economy.

NEPMEN. This name was used for the successful entrepreneurs during the New Economic Policy (*see* NEP) period in the USSR, which lasted from 1922 to 1928. Such individuals succeeded in enriching themselves and often exhibited conspicuous consumption behavior, thereby provoking the envy of the population.

NERCHINSK, TREATY OF. This 1689 treaty between Russia and China was the first to establish regulated contact between the two empires. It covered boundaries, trade, and diplomatic relations.

NERONOV, IVAN (1591–1670). An archpriest who initiated the religious opposition to Patriarch Nikon's (q.v.) church reforms, he was exiled in 1654 and became the spiritual leader of the Starovertsy (q.v.), or Old Believers, religious sect.

NESTEROV, MIKHAIL V. (1862–1942). Born into a merchant family, he was educated at the St. Petersburg Academy of Art. In 1883 he began painting religious subjects in which he attempted to encapsulate the spiritual aspects of life in Russia. Nesterov was a close friend of Count Leo Tolstoy (q.v.). His first exhibition took place in 1907 in both St. Petersburg (q.v.) and Moscow (q.v.).

NESTOR (1056–1113). A monk of the Peshcherii Monastery of the Caves located near Kiev, he is the reputed author of several hagiographies of early Russian saints, as well as of the Primary Chronicle (q.v.), which renders the early history of Kievan Rus (q.v.).

NEVSKII, PRINCE ALEKSANDR (1220–63). A prince of Novgorod (q.v.) and of Vladimir (q.v.), he led the Russian forces to victory over the Swedish army on the Neva in 1240 and over the Teutonic knights on the frozen waters of Lake Peipus (q.v.) in 1242. He was canonized by the Orthodox Church (q.v.) after his death.

NEVSKII, VLADIMIR I. (b. KRIVOBOKOV) (1876–1937). A member of the Russian Socialist Democratic Labor Party (q.v.) since 1897, he participated in both the 1905 and the 1917 revolutions. He became a member of the Central Committee of the Communist Party (q.v.) in 1917 and was the commissar of communications during the civil war (q.v.). He became a university dean in 1921 and director of the Lenin State Library (q.v.) in 1924. He disappeared during the purges (q.v.) of the 1930s.

NEW ECONOMIC POLICY see NEP

NICHOLAS I, TSAR AND EMPEROR OF RUSSIA (1796–1855). Tsar Nicholas I ascended to the imperial throne in 1825, after the unsuccessful Decembrist (q.v.) rebellion against him organized by a group of guards officers. As the revolutionary movement spread in Western Europe in the middle of the 19th century, he became increasingly more autocratic and adopted the doctrine of "Autocracy, Orthodoxy and Nationalism" as his motto. The Russian secret police, the Third Section (q.v.), was established during his reign (1826) and he helped the Austrian empire crush a rebellion in Hungary (1849). Tsar Nicholas I was responsible for initiating the construction of the first Russian railroads, as well as for encouraging industrial development. He died before the end of the Crimean War (q.v.).

NICHOLAS II, TSAR AND EMPEROR OF RUSSIA (1868–1918). Son of Alexander III (q.v.), Nicholas II succeeded to the throne in 1894 after the sudden death of his father. He married Princess Alix of Hesse and had four daughters and a son by her. During his reign Russia unsuccessfully fought the Russo-Japanese war (q.v.) of 1904–05, and World War I (q.v.). Tsar Nicholas abdicated the Russian throne for himself and his heir, Tsarevich Aleksei (q.v.), in March

1917. After the abdication Nicholas, along with his family, was placed under house arrest, first in Tsarskoe Selo (q.v.), then in the Siberian city of Ekaterinburg (q.v.). Along with their remaining retainers, he and his whole family were shot in the summer of 1918, on orders that are believed to have been approved by Lenin (q.v.).

NICHOLAS ROMANOV, GRAND DUKE (1856–1929). A grandson of Nicholas I (q.v.) and son of Grand Duke Nicholas, who had initiated the reforms of the Russian army after the Russo-Turkish war (q.v.) of 1878. Educated as a military engineer, he graduated from the Academy of the General Staff in 1876 and served as the inspector of cavalry from 1895 to 1905. Grand Duke Nicholas was commander of the St. Petersburg (q.v.) military district during the 1905 revolution and commander in chief of the Russian army at the beginning of World War I (q.v.). An enemy of the monk Rasputin (q.v.), he was disliked by Empress Alexandra, and in 1915 he was replaced in this post by the tsar himself and given command of the Persian/Turkish front. In February 1917 he advised his nephew, the tsar, to abdicate, and in 1919 he emigrated to Western Europe.

NIHILISM. An ideological trend that originated in Russia, its adherents rejected philosophical and moral idealism, advanced positivism and materialism, and advocated revolt against the state and all other authority. Their clearest portrait was given by Turgenev (q.v.) in his novel *Fathers and Sons*, published in 1862.

NIJINSKAYA, BRONISLAVA F. (1891–1972). The sister of Vaclav Nijinsky (q.v.), she graduated from the Ballet School of St. Petersburg in 1908, then began dancing with the Ballets Russes (q.v.) in 1910. She was also a ballerina and choreographer with Diaghilev's (q.v.) Ballets Russes from 1922 to 1924, and then she established her own company.

NIJINSKY, VACLAV F. (1889–1950). A graduate of the Ballet School of St. Petersburg in 1907, he joined the Mariinskii Theater (q.v.) and danced with Kshesinskaia (q.v.) and Pavlova (q.v.). Nijinsky created numerous leading roles at the Mariinskii Theater before becoming a leading star in Diaghilev's (q.v.) Ballets Russes (q.v.). After some ten years of dancing, which brought him international fame, he became mentally ill and spent the balance of his life in a mental institution and in the care of his Hungarian wife.

NIKITIN, ALEKSANDR (1953-   ). Naval officer and volunteer for the Norwegian evironmental group Bellona, which studied the effects of nuclear submarine activity on waters near Norway's coast, Nikitin was arrested at his home in St. Petersburg in 1995 for allegedly divulging state secrets.

NIKODIM, METROPOLITAN (b. BOISROTOV) (1929–78). A son of a Communist Party (q.v.) official, he became a monk in 1947 and graduated from the Theological Academy of Leningrad in 1955. He was a member of the Orthodox Church (q.v.) mission to Jerusalem in 1956 and the head of the foreign relations department of the Moscow patriarchate from 1960 to 1972. In this capacity he promoted the foreign policy of the USSR. He was elected president of the central committee of the World Council of Churches in 1975 and was also made the metropolitan (q.v.) of Leningrad and Novgorod.

NIKON, PATRIARCH (1605–81). After becoming patriarch of Moscow (q.v.) in 1652, he initiated a major reform movement within the Orthodox Church (q.v.), standardizing its ritual and adopting a new prayer book. These measures led to a church schism and to the emergence of the Starovertsy (q.v.), or Old Believers sect. Nikon's measures were condemned by a church council in 1666, and he was deposed and exiled to a monastery.

NIL SORSKII, SAINT (1433–1508). A monk of the St. Cyril monastery, he was the leader of the antiwealth movement within the Orthodox Church (q.v.). He and his followers condemned the accumulation of possessions as being against the teachings of Christ. In 1503 a church council ruled against his doctrines, but later he was canonized.

NIZHINSKII see NIJINSKY

NIZHNII NOVGOROD. Named Gorkii during the Soviet period, this major Russian city is located at the confluence of the Oka (q.v.) and Volga (q.v.) rivers. It was founded in the early 13th century and became famous during the medieval period for its annual trade fairs. Today it is a large manufacturing center with a population that exceeds one million inhabitants.

NIZHNII TAGIL. An industrial city on the Tagil River, some 80 miles north of Sverdlovsk (q.v.), its principal economic base is agricultural production and an aviation machinery and chemical industry.

NKVD (NARODNYI KOMMISSARIAT VNUTRENNYKH DEL). The People's Commissariat of Internal Affairs. It was responsible for the internal security of the USSR and was in charge of the secret police, the border guards, the special army security divisions, and the administration of the concentration camps. It was renamed Ministry of Internal Affairs (MVD) in 1946. *See* SECURITY SERVICES, SOVIET.

NOBILITY see DVORIANE

NOMENKLATURA. This term was used for the Soviet "new class" of high party, state, and cultural officials who enjoyed numerous privileges unavailable to the population at large, such as the right to travel abroad, to send their children to elite schools, and to shop in "closed distributors"—stores that carried provisions and consumer goods unavailable to ordinary Soviet citizens. Technically, they were individuals whose names were placed on a list of candidates eligible to be given responsible party and state positions.

NORILSK. Founded in 1935, this important mining town in the Krasnoiarsk (q.v.) region of the Russian Republic produces copper, nickel and platinum. Its population is just over 200,000.

NORTH OSSETIA AUTONOMOUS REPUBLIC. A part of the Russian empire since the 18th century in the northern Caucasus (q.v.). During the Soviet period it was an autonomous republic with Ordzhonikidze (now renamed Vladikavkaz, q.v.) as its capital. Its population is over 600,000 and consists of native Ossets (q.v.), Ingush (q.v.), and Russians.

NORTH SEA. This part of the Atlantic Ocean is between Great Britain, northern Europe and Scandinavia, an area of 340,000 square miles. It is an important fishery, particularly on the Dogger Bank, and it also contains oil and natural gas deposits.

NORTHERN SOCIETY. Led by Muravev (q.v.), this branch of the Decembrist (q.v.) movement stood for a constitutional monarchy and the emancipation of the serfs. In December 1825 it took part with the more radical Southern Society (q.v.) in an unsuccessful uprising against the coronation of Nicholas I (q.v.).

NORTHERN UNION OF RUSSIAN WORKERS. Organized by Khalturin (q.v.) in 1878, this union sought to undermine tsarism and replace it with a democratic, socialist society. It was suppressed by the government in 1879.

NOVAIA EKONOMICHESKAIA POLITIKA see NEP

NOVAIA SIBIR ISLANDS. This archipelago of islands in the Arctic Ocean was discovered in 1773 by a Russian merchant. It is uninhabited.

NOVAIA ZEMLIA. These Arctic circle islands are found near the Barents Sea (q.v.). During the 1960s and 1970s the Soviet armed forces used them as atomic testing grounds. Their principal industries are fishing and hunting.

NOVGOROD. One of the oldest and most important cities of Kievan Rus (q.v.), it is located on the Volkhov River (q.v.). As a self-governing community in the Middle Ages it prospered because it had never been occupied by the Mongols and because of its strategic location as a fur trading center situated between the Baltic Sea (q.v.) and the Byzantine Empire. From A.D. 1300 to the end of the 15th century, it attempted to fight off the gradual spread of Muscovite power. In 1478 Moscow (q.v.) conquered it, and Tsar Ivan IV (q.v.) suppressed all further resistance by mass deportations and massacres. Today, its primary industry consists of clothing and footwear manufacturing, as well as flour milling. Its population is just under 200,000.

NOVIKOV, LAVRENTII L. (1888–1956). A graduate of the Choreographic School of Moscow in 1906, he danced with the Bolshoi theater (q.v.) troupe in London and the United States. After the 1917 revolutions Novikov emigrated and in 1919 joined Diaghilev's (q.v.) Ballets Russes (q.v.). He then danced with Pavlova's (q.v.) company from 1921 to 1928, and with the Chicago Ballet until 1941. From 1941 to 1945 he was a choreographer for the Metropolitan Opera.

NOVOCHERKASSK. Founded in 1805, this town is located some 20 miles from Rostov-na-Donu (q.v.). It is the center of machine, mining equipment and textiles manufacturing. Its population is just under 200,000.

NOVOKUZNETSK. First established by the Cossack (q.v.) settlers in the early 17th century, this town is located on the Tom River some 100 miles southeast of Kemerovo (q.v.). Its primary industry consists of iron and steel works, and the manufacturing of machinery and railroad equipment. Its population is slightly over 500,000.

NOVOROSSIISK. Established in 1839 on an ancient site, this city on the Black Sea (q.v.) is the center of cement manufacturing, as well as of agricultural machinery. It also serves as the port for shipping exports of grain and petroleum and is the home of the Siberian division of the Russian Academy of Sciences (q.v.). Its current population is close to 160,000.

NOVOSIBIRSK. Located on the Ob River (q.v.) in Siberia (q.v.), it was founded during the construction of the Trans-Siberian Railroad (q.v.) in 1893. An important trade center for agricultural produce, it also manufactures transport machinery, machine tools and textiles. Its population is over 1,300,000. It is also the site of the Siberian division of the Russian Academy of Sciences (q.v.).

NOVYI MIR (THE NEW WORLD) A mass circulation Soviet periodical first established in 1925 in Moscow, it was made famous in the 1950s and 1960s by the editorial management of Tvardovsky (q.v.), under whose direction it published a number of hitherto forbidden works, including Solzhenitsyn's (q.v.) first novel, One Day in the Life of Ivan Denisovich.

NUREYEV, RUDOLF G. (1938–93). Born in Siberia (q.v.), he joined the Leningrad Ballet School in 1955, then the Kirov Ballet School in 1958. While on a tour abroad, Nureev defected in Paris in 1961, became the dance partner of Margot Fonteyn, and soon a ballet star in Western Europe and America. In 1983 Nureev was made the artistic director of the Paris opera, and in 1989 was permitted to dance in St. Petersburg. He died in Paris after a long struggle with AIDS.

O

OB RIVER. This river begins in the Altai (q.v.) and flows north through Siberia (q.v.) for some 2,000 miles to the Kara Sea (q.v.) and the Arctic Ocean. It is a major route for water transport in the summer but remains frozen for almost six months of the year. Its main tributary is the Irtysh River (q.v.).

OBER-PROKUROR SVIATEISHEGO SINODA. CHIEF PROCURATOR OF THE MOST HOLY SYNOD. In effect, minister of church affairs, this post was established by Peter the Great (q.v.) to replace the patriarchate (q.v.), which he had abolished in order to place the Orthodox Church (q.v.) firmly under his own control.

OBKOM (OBLASTNOI KOMITET). The regional committee of the Communist Party (q.v.). These party units played a major role in the management of the affairs of the oblast (regional) territorial units of the Soviet Union.

OBLAST. Region. A territorial administrative unit larger than a *krai* (district) and smaller than a *respublika* (republic). In 1991 there were five autonomous regions within the Russian Republic.

OBLOMOV. The principal character in Goncharov's (q.v.) novel of the same name, he became the stereotype of an individual who led a listless and slothful life of the type that was frequently encountered among 19th-century Russian gentry.

OBOLENSKII, SIR DMITRII D. (1918-   ). Born in St. Petersburg (q.v.) to one of the oldest princely families of Russia, he was educated in Paris and Cambridge and became a specialist in Byzantine history and a professor at Cambridge University.

OBOLENSKII, PRINCE EVGENII P. (1796–1865). A leader of the Northern Society (q.v.), he participated in the unsuccessful Decembrist (q.v.) revolt in 1825. He was condemned to death, but his sentence was commuted to exile in Siberia (q.v.).

OBSHCHESTVO. Society. In late 19th and early 20th century Russia the term became synonymous with the politically active segment of the educated urban classes that strove to curb the power of the monarchy and to obtain a representative parliamentary constitution for the country.

OBUKHOV, ANATOLII N. (1896–1962). Born in St. Petersburg (q.v.), he graduated from the St. Petersburg Theater School, then became a dancer at the Mariinskii Theater (q.v.) from 1913 to 1920. After emigrating to the West, he continued dancing professionally in Berlin and in South America. Obukhov performed with the Ballets Russes (q.v.) from 1935 to 1939, then taught at the New York City Ballet School between 1940 and 1962.

OCTOBER MANIFESTO. The manifesto of Tsar Nicholas II (q.v.) was issued on 17 October 1905 and established the State Duma (q.v.), or Russian parliament. At the time it was issued, this manifesto was greeted by a large section of the Russian intelligentsia (q.v.) as the first step in the realization of their age-old dream of a democratic Russia.

OCTOBER REVOLUTION see REVOLUTION OF FEBRUARY 1917

ODESSA (-1794: KHADZHIBEI). Center of the Odessa oblast in Ukraine and a port on the Black Sea (q.v.), it came under successive Lithuanian and Turkish domination until its annexation by Russia in 1791. It was in Odessa that the crew of the battleship *Potemkin* rebelled during the revolution of 1905 (q.v.). The population is around 1,110,000; in addition to its engineering, shipbuilding, film industry, textiles, and chemical products (including fertilizer), Odessa is a noted resort area.

OGAREV, NIKOLAI P. (1813–77). A life-long friend and collaborator of Herzen (q.v.), Ogarev was a revolutionary and a minor poet. He lived together with Herzen in exile in England.

OGARKOV, NIKOLAI V. (1917-). Born into a peasant family, he graduated from the Kuibyshev Military Engineering Academy in 1941, then served as a military engineer in World War II (q.v.). From 1966 to 1971 he was a member of the Central Committee of the Communist Party (q.v.). In 1977 Ogarkov was elevated to marshal of the Soviet Union and became the chief of staff of the Soviet Army (*see* Armed Forces, Soviet).

OGPU see GPU and SECURITY FORCES, SOVIET

OISTRAKH, DAVID (1908–74). Violinist and teacher at the Moscow Conservatory of Music, Oistrakh studied in Odessa with Petr Stoliarskii before embarking on a career as the leading violinist of his day. He received numerous prizes, both Soviet and European, and was an eager proponent of contemporary Russian and Soviet composers. He played in St. Petersburg (q.v.) (then Leningrad) during the wartime blockade and toured widely after the war; he introduced Shostakovich's (q.v.) first concerto in 1955 in New York at his first appearance there.

OKA RIVER. This river rises in central Russia and flows north to join the Volga River (q.v.) at Nizhnii-Novgorod (q.v.). It is an important inland waterway.

OKHOTSK, SEA OF. A 615,000-square-mile area of the Pacific Ocean, it is partially encircled by Kamchatka Peninsula (q.v.) and the coastline of the Magadan (q.v.) and Khabarovsk (q.v.) regions in the Russian Far East. Though part of the sea is icebound in the winter, it supports significant traffic to ports such as Magadan and Okhotsk and is an important fishery.

OKHRANA. The tsarist department of public security and secret police established by Nicholas I (q.v.), it was abolished by the Provisional government (q.v.) in 1917 but revived under another name a few months later.

OKTIABRIST PARTY. This major political party was formed in Russia in 1905 and lasted until 1917, when it was outlawed by the Soviet government. It was led by Guchkov (q.v.) and Rodzianko (q.v.) and held an overall majority in the last two (the third and fourth) Dumas (q.v.). It participated in the Progressive Bloc (q.v.) that formed, after 1915, the broad center of the Duma's deputies. Its principal political platform was an attempt to ensure that the Manifesto of 1905 was implemented in full by the tsar's government.

Officially named the Union of the 17th of October, it was based primarily on the merchant, industrial and financial bourgeoisie, on large landlords with large agricultural enterprises, and on that part of the Russian intelligentsia (q.v.) that had become integrated into the business world and received high salaries. The leader of this party was the representative of the Moscow mercantile, industrial, and financial circles, Guchkov. The Oktiabrists did not stress parliamentarism, and, with respect to the agrarian question, their main aim was to give the peasantry equality with regard to civic rights. They did not include expropriation of the landlords into their program.

OKUDZHAVA, BULAT (1924–97). Noted poet and song writer, he was one of the first and best-known of the so-called bards. After serving at the front during World War II (q.v.), Okudzhava worked as an editor and joined the Communist Party (q.v.) in 1955; he sang compositions of his own for purely personal entertainment, but the songs became popular at a time when cassette tape recorders began to be more accessible, thereby creating what came to be known (on the model of samizdat [q.v.]) as *magnetizdat*, easily copied and distributed underground cassette tapes. This also popularized the genre known as "guitar poetry," usually a lyric sung to the poet's unobtrusive guitar accompaniment. Although he faced some official criticism, Okudzhava's work was reluctantly accepted toward the end of the 1970s; he began to publish novels and plays around that time. He died of a stress-related heart failure in a military hospital in Paris.

OLD BELIEVERS see STAROVERTSY

OLDENBURG, SERGEI F. (1863–1934). A graduate of the University of St. Petersburg (*see* Universities) in 1885, he became a specialist in

Buddhism and a lecturer at the university. In 1894 Oldenburg became a professor, and in 1900 a member of the Russian Academy of Sciences (q.v.). He was a member of the Kadet (KD) Party (q.v.) and served as minister of education of the Provisional government (q.v.) in 1917.

OLEG. The first ruler of the Russian state for whom there exists clear historical evidence in the Primary Chronicle (q.v.), he became master of the city of Kiev (q.v.) in 882, after which it became the capital of Rus (q.v.). Oleg is known to have led an armed expedition against Byzantium that failed, but that enabled him to obtain a favorable trade agreement with the Greek empire.

OLESHA, IURII K. (1899–1960). A Soviet satirical writer, he began his writing career as a journalist. In the early 1920s Olesha lived in Moscow (q.v.) and together with Ilf (q.v.) and Petrov (q.v.) edited a newspaper. He also wrote several novels and film scripts. Because of Olesha's resistance to the imposition of socialist realism (q.v.) on writers by the Soviet government, he was arrested in 1934 and not released until 1956.

OLGA ROMANOVA, GRAND DUCHESS (1882–1960). A sister of Nicholas II (q.v.), she escaped death at the hands of the Bolsheviks (q.v.) by staying in the Crimea (q.v.) during the revolution and being rescued by a British warship. Together with her mother, the Dowager Empress Maria, she moved to Denmark, then to a farm near Toronto, Canada, where she lived with her second husband until her death.

OLGA ROMANOVA, GRAND DUCHESS (1895–1918). The eldest daughter of Nicholas II (q.v.), she was shot, together with the rest of the imperial family, in Ekaterinburg (q.v.) on orders from Moscow (q.v.).

OLGA, SAINT. The widow of the Kievan Prince Igor (q.v.), she ruled during her son's minority and was baptized in 957. St. Olga is credited with having initiated a gradual conversion of her subjects to Orthodox Christianity.

OLITSKAIA, EKATERINA (1898-?). A member of the underground Socialist Revolutionaries (q.v.) party, she was arrested by the Soviet government and sent to a labor camp in 1924, to be released only in 1930. Rearrested in 1932, she served in the Kolyma concentration camps from 1937 until the early 1950s, when she was released after Stalin's death. Olitskaia wrote her memoirs, which focused on the lives of Socialist Revolutionaries in the Soviet Union during the 1920s and 1930s.

OMSK. A major Siberian city first established in 1716, it is located at the confluence of the Om and Irtysh (q.v.) rivers and is an important industrial and marketing center for western Siberia (q.v.). Its population is just over 1,000,000.

ONEGA BAY. It adjoins the White Sea (q.v.) and the Arctic Ocean. Several of Russia's northern ports are on it, among them Belomorsk, Onega, and Kem.

ONEGA LAKE. Situated in northwest Russia, Onega is one of the largest lakes in Europe. It is connected by a canal to the White Sea and to the Volga River (q.v.).

OPRICHNINA. This organization was created in 1565 by Tsar Ivan the Terrible (q.v.) to aid him in his struggle against the Russian nobility. Its members tortured and executed at the tsar's command.

ORDZHONIKIDZE see VLADIKAVKAZ

ORDZHONIKIDZE, GEORGII K. (1886–1937). A member of the Communist Party since 1903, he took part in the 1905 revolution (q.v.) and then worked in the Baku (q.v.) underground. In 1909 he escaped from Siberian exile, and in 1912 became a member of the Central Committee of the Communist Party (q.v.). That same year, Ordzhonikidze was arrested in St. Petersburg (q.v.) and incarcerated from 1912 to 1915. During the civil war (q.v.) he was a Red Army (see Armed Forces, Soviet) commissar and then, after 1920, one of the leading Communists in the Caucasus (q.v.) and a powerful ally of Stalin (q.v.). He became a member of the Politburo (q.v.), and between 1930 and 1937 served as commissar of heavy industry. His death in 1937 is believed to have been a suicide ordered by Stalin (q.v.).

OREKHOVO-ZUIEVO. A town on the Kliazma River, some 50 miles east of Moscow, its industries consist of cotton milling, metal working, and flour milling. Its population is slightly over 100,000.

OREL. The town was established in 1564 as a Russian fortress on the Oka River (q.v.). It is an important manufacturing center today, producing tractors and textile machinery as well as iron products and footwear. Its population is just over 300,000.

ORENBURG. This town, renamed Chalkov during the Soviet period, is located on the Ural River (q.v.) north of the Caspian Sea (q.v.). Its industrial production consists of flour milling, railroad stock construction and textiles. Its population is just under 500,000.

ORLOV, ALEKSANDR (b. FELDBIN) (1896–1973). In the 1930s he was the chief of the Soviet security police operations in Europe and the organizer of the theft of the gold of the Spanish Republican government by the Soviet Union. In 1938 Orlov defected from his post in France and moved to the United States, where he lived in seclusion until his death in Cleveland.

ORLOV, COUNT GREGORII G. (1734–83). The famed lover of Catherine II (q.v.), Orlov placed her on the Russian throne by helping to overthrow her husband, Peter III (q.v.). He became her trusted advisor and was rewarded by being made a count. Orlov tried hard to modernize the country but did not succeed in freeing the serfs. He left Russia in 1775 and died abroad, insane.

ORLOV, PRINCE ALEXEI F. (1786–1861). Commander of a regiment of cavalry, he helped suppress the Decembrist (q.v.) rebellion. As a reward he was made a count by Nicholas I (q.v.). Orlov participated in the Russo-Turkish war (q.v.), then in 1833 became Russia's ambassador to Turkey, and subsequently served as head of the Third Section (q.v.), the tsarist security police that later became known as the Okhrana (q.v.). In 1856 Orlov negotiated the Treaty of Paris which ended the Crimean War (q.v.). Made a prince, he was also president of the Council of Ministers.

ORTHODOX CHURCH. After the conversion of the East Slavs or Rus (q.v.) to Christianity in the tenth century, the Orthodox Church in Russia remained subordinate to Byzantine ecclesiastic authorities until the 15th century. In 1448 it obtained autocephaly and was placed under the overall guidance of the metropolitan, later patriarch, of Moscow (q.v.). In 1721 Peter the Great (q.v.) replaced the patriarch with a council, the *Sviateishii Sinod* (Most Holy Synod, q.v.). In 1918 the Soviet government decreed a total separation of church and state, simultaneously depriving the Orthodox Church of its previous rights to publicly proselytize and to teach children. There followed many years of persecution, which were somewhat lessened during World War II (q.v.) after its leadership concluded an agreement with Stalin (q.v.) to support the Soviet state.

OSSETIA. An area in the north Caucasus (q.v.) annexed by Russia in the early 18th century, it is inhabited by the Alani people, who are predominantly Christian, and is one of the autonomous republics of the Russian Republic.

OSSETS. A people speaking a language of the northern branch of Iranian and dwelling in the Caucasus (q.v.), they are possibly identifiable with the ancient Scythians and Alans, yet have been ethnically transformed over the centuries through close contact with their Caucasian neighbors. Since the tenth century the Ossets have been Christian; three quarters of the population are Greek Orthodox, the remaining quarter being Sunni Moslem. Their territory was annexed by Russia in 1792.

OSTROVSKII, ALEKSANDR N. (1823–86). A Russian dramatist of the middle of the 19th century, he established a school of dramatic arts in Moscow (q.v.) and organized a society of opera composers.

OSVOBOZHDENIE TRUDA (THE LIBERATION OF LABOR). This early group of Russian Marxists was established by Plekhanov (q.v.) in Geneva. Its other founders were Akselrod (q.v.), Deitch (q.v.) and Zasulich (q.v.). They were firmly opposed to the then prevailing reliance on the use of individual terror among Russian revolutionaries. This group became the ideological predecessor of the Russian Socialist Democratic Labor Party (q.v.) of the 1890s.

OTDEL MILITSII OSOBOVO NAZNACHENIIA (OMON; MILITIA DEPARTMENT FOR SPECIAL ASSIGNMENTS). The "black berets" troops of the ministry of the interior, they were used by the Soviet government to control internal disturbances.

OTECHESTVENNYE ZAPISKI (NOTES OF THE FATHERLAND). An influential Russian literary periodical of the last half of the 19th century, it was edited by Nikolai Nekrasov (q.v.) and took the place of Sovremennik (q.v.) after that journal was closed by the tsarist authorities.

P

PAINTING AND VISUAL ARTS. After the conversion of the eastern Slav tribes in the tenth century to Christianity, religious painting became an important aspect of their life. During the next 200 years, the paintings on icons (q.v.) became increasingly symbolistic, and by the 14th century painting had turned toward a greater focus on the emotional and inner life of human beings. At the end of that century,

Andrei Rublev (q.v.), possibly the greatest of all Russian artists, began his work.

After the second half of the 17th century, etching, woodcutting, and other representational arts began to flourish in Russia. As well, portraiture became very popular. In Moscow a major exhibition was opened of jewelry products and ornamental weapons collected from several Russian cities. In the 18th century a Russian school of sculpture emerged, and in 1757 the Russian Academy of Fine Arts (q.v.) was established. At the end of that century the Hermitage (q.v.) collection was started by Catherine the Great (q.v.), with purchases of a large number of paintings in Western Europe. The 19th century saw the beginning of the development of a Russian school of decorative sculpture and a move among painters to historical themes. At the same time portrait painting gradually turned toward romanticism.

In 1863, young artists who had grown discontented with the conservatism of the Russian Academy of Art initiated a free artistic movement dedicated to the establishment of cooperative traveling exhibitions, aimed at expanding the number of viewers. The majority of their paintings dealt with the life experiences of ordinary people. At approximately the same time an important school of landscape painting emerged in Russia, whose major representative was Repin (q.v.). Wealthy private collectors began to play an important role in the collection and preservation of Russian art. One of them, P. M. Tretiakov (q.v.), gathered a large number of paintings and donated them to the city of Moscow (q.v.) in 1892. At the end of the 1890s an art society was formed in St. Petersburg (q.v.) that rejected academic painting, as well as traveling exhibitions, and reached back to the art of the 18th century. At the turn of the 20th century Impressionism came to Russia from France.

After the October 1917 revolution (q.v.) artists of the representational school organized themselves into an association and attempted to dominate the Soviet artistic scene. By the 1930s, though, the government had begun to require artists to produce paintings that popularized "socialist construction." Those artists who failed to comply were categorized by Soviet officials as "bourgeois decadents." During World War II (q.v.) the major artistic activity was that of poster painting, but then, in the immediate postwar period, the Communist Party (q.v.) initiated an attack on formalism in art. Among the most active proponents of this attack were the leaders of the Academy of Fine Arts (q.v.) of the USSR which had been established in 1947. As late as 1974 an exhibition of avant-garde Soviet artists was bulldozed on orders of the government.

After the beginning of perestroika (q.v.) visitors to art galleries were able, for the first time in several decades, to see a complete history of Soviet art of the 1920s and 1930s. Among the included artists were such world-famous painters as Malevich (q.v.) and Kandinskii (q.v.). The exhibits also featured creations of contemporary Russian artists whose works previously had been banned by the Soviet government.

PALE OF SETTLEMENT (CHERTA OSEDLOSTI). This was a territory in the southern and western part of the Russian empire outside of which Jews were not allowed to settle. Instituted by Catherine II (q.v.) after the first partition of Poland (1772), it grew to include land acquired after successive changes in Russia's imperial territory, finally encompassing more than 380,000 square miles. The purpose was to prevent Jews from establishing themselves in or near the center; during World War I (q.v.), however, the Jews were made to evacuate war zones as possible security risks, and Nicholas II (q.v.) had to allow them to settle outside the Pale, thereby effectively abolishing it.

PALEKH. This village in Russia is famous for its lacquer works. This technique was introduced into Russia in the late 18th century and has since become a major industrial activity in Palekh and several adjoining villages located close to Moscow (q.v.).

PAMIAT (MEMORY). An organization originally established to preserve cultural monuments, it has gradually changed its emphasis to drawing attention to the disproportionate number of Jews at the top of the Bolshevik (q.v.) leadership at the time of the October 1917 revolution (q.v.) and turned somewhat anti-Semitic in its public utterances. In the late 1980s disagreement in leadership caused its membership to decrease, many supporters turning to other groups.

PAN-SLAVISM. A movement strongly supported in Russia, especially during the 19th century, it emphasized the desirability of unity among all Slav peoples and saw its strongest expression in giving support to Serbs and other Slavic Orthodox nationalities against Turkey.

PARIS, TREATIES OF. These treaties, which Russia signed in Paris, vitally affected its relations with Western Europe. The first came after the defeat of Napoleon in 1814–15; the second after the Russian defeat in the Crimean War (q.v.) in 1856.

PASTERNAK, BORIS L. (1890–1960). Pasternak was born into an artistic Jewish family and studied at the University of Moscow (*see* Universities). He graduated in 1913, then began his studies in music and philosophy in Germany, and in 1912 first published his poetry. He remained in the USSR after the October 1917 revolution (q.v.). In the 1930s Pasternak translated Goethe and Shakespeare into Russian and in 1958 published his historical novel *Doctor Zhivago* abroad. For this work Pasternak was offered the Nobel Prize for literature, but was forced by Soviet authorities to refuse it. Pasternak was expelled from the Union of Soviet Writers (q.v.), even though he was considered to be one of the greatest of the 20th century Russian poets.

PATRIARCHATE OF RUSSIA (MOSCOW). This office was established in 1589 to administer the Russian Orthodox Church (q.v.). Before that date it came under the authority of the Patriarchate of Constantinople. In 1720 Peter the Great (q.v.) replaced the office of the patriarchate with the Most Holy Synod (q.v.) to obviate its political power; after the February revolution (q.v.) the patriarchate was restored, with Tikhon (q.v.) elected as patriarch. The current patriarch is Aleksei, who was elected in 1990.

PAUL I (1754–1801). Son of Peter III (q.v.) and Catherine II (q.v.), Paul became emperor in 1796. Having been impressed by the Prussian military, he set about strengthening discipline, tightening censorship, and reining in the nobility; he also restored the system of male primogeniture in the royal succession. Although initially opposed to the French revolution and favoring England, in 1800 he broke with the latter country and signed a treaty with France as a result of the impression made on him by Bonaparte. Regarded as increasingly unstable, he was finally strangled to death in his bedroom by nobles.

PAVLENKO, PETR A. (1899–1951). A student at the Baku Technical School between 1919 and 1920, he joined the Communist Party (q.v.) in 1920. Pavlenko was a member of the Soviet trade delegation to Turkey in 1924, then worked in the film industry in the 1930s. He also wrote the scripts for such films as *Aleksandr Nevskii* and was a war correspondent during World War II (q.v.). Pavlenko was the recipient of numerous decorations from the Soviet government.

PAVLOV, DMITRII G. (1897–1941). He joined the Communist Party (q.v.) and the Red Army (*see* Armed Forces, Soviet) in 1919, and by 1940 had been made commander of the Belorussian military district. Pavlov was commander of the western front in June 1941, when the German army invaded the Soviet Union. He was blamed by Stalin (q.v.) for the initial Soviet rout, court martialed and shot.

PAVLOV, IVAN P. (1849–1936). A graduate of the University of St. Petersburg (*see* Universities) in 1875, he continued his studies in

Breslaw and Leipzig between 1884 and 1886. Pavlov became a professor of physiology at the Russian Academy of Sciences (q.v.) in 1896 and remained at that position until 1924. He was at the same time head of the physiological laboratory at the Institute of Experimental Medicine, where he developed his theory of conditioned reflexes by working with dogs.

PAVLOVA, ANNA P. (1881–1931). A pupil at the Imperial Theatrical School in St. Petersburg (q.v.), she was the prima ballerina at the Mariinskii Theater (q.v.) after 1906, then joined Diaghilev (q.v.) in Paris in 1909. In 1914 she created her own ballet company and settled in London.

PEASANTRY, PREREVOLUTIONARY. By the early middle ages the peasantry formed a distinct social layer of the population in Russia. Most peasants lived in communes, and their main obligation was to pay taxes and fulfill certain specified duties to the local prince. Beginning in the 15th century, the land-owning nobility gradually enserfed the peasantry. By 1497, a decree of the tsar forbade peasants to move from their landlord's land except on one day of the year. This decree also obligated them to pay their landlord with labor for the use of a part of his land. A century later, transfer from one landlord to another was altogether forbidden; in 1649 landlords were given an unlimited right to hunt down peasants who had moved away without their permission. Catherine the Great (q.v.) even permitted them to condemn their serfs to hard labor, to deport them to Siberia (q.v.), and to purchase them publicly. Serfs, on the other hand, were forbidden to lodge complaints against their masters.

At the beginning of the 19th century Tsar Alexander I (q.v.) took some small steps to provide relief for the serfs. In 1803 a decree gave them the right to purchase their freedom, provided that the landlord agreed and that they could pay the heavy price involved, and in 1808 the landlords were forbidden to exile their peasants to Siberia (q.v.).

Serfdom was abolished in 1861 by Tsar Alexander II (q.v.), and 22.5 million peasants were freed by a process that was to take place over a number of years. During the first three years they were to continue in their previous status, after which period they were to be allowed to purchase land from the landlords on payment of 20 percent of the price, the balance being provided by the state on long-term loans. The individual peasants were then obligated to reimburse this sum to the government over a period of 49 years. However, having been freed from their former masters, the peasants still remained tied to their commune, which was collectively responsible for the debts of all of its members. All of the land allotted to the peasants, as well as forests and pasture lands, remained the property of the commune, which it then distributed annually to individual users. Peasants were allowed to leave their commune only if they could pay off their share of these obligations. These communes were governed by village meetings and elected elders. The reforms failed to solve a number of vital agrarian problems.

Among them was the shortage of arable land at the disposal of the peasantry. As well, the availability of agricultural equipment that peasants required to cultivate the land was inadequate for efficient agricultural production. Another unsolved problem was the rapid process of economic differentiation that was taking place in the villages. On the one hand, there were some relatively prosperous peasant households, the "kulaks" (q.v.), which had sufficient capital and farm equipment; on the other hand, there were numerous landless peasants. The 1907 reforms initiated by Prime Minister Stolypin (q.v.) attempted to strengthen the wealthy peasants, as well as to change the previous system of the annual land reallocation. They introduced a system of distributing to individuals adjacent plots of land, instead of the previous multiple strips that were often widely separated from each other. However, the reforms failed to divide up among the peasantry the vast land holdings of the landlords and of the church. They thus left unsolved the basic agrarian problem of Russia right up to the 1917 revolution.

PEASANTRY, SOVIET PERIOD. One of the first decrees issued by the Soviet government after the October 1917 revolution (q.v.) was the Decree on Land. According to this decree, all land owned by the church and the former absentee landlords was to be distributed for use among the working peasantry, all rent payments to former owners were prohibited, and all debts to the peasant banks were cancelled. This decree caused an immediate conflict in the villages because the poor peasants demanded that all agricultural land be divided equally among working adults, including land that belonged to the wealthy peasants, the "kulaks" (q.v.). The latter, on the other hand, insisted that land redistribution should affect only the property of the church and of the aristocracy. After the beginning of the civil war (q.v.) in 1918, the Soviet government established committees of poor peasants in each village and used them to forcibly requisition surplus agricultural produce from the rural population. However, these actions did not sufficiently counteract the peasants' fear of the return of the White Armies (q.v.), which they identified with their former landlords. That is why the majority of them supported, however reluctantly, the Red Army (see Armed Forces, Soviet) in the civil war (q.v.).

In 1921 the compulsory requisitions of farm produce were replaced by a tax in kind, after payment of which the peasants were allowed to dispose of their remaining produce by selling it on the free market. This system, called the New Economic Policy (*see* NEP), rapidly revived Soviet internal trade, and motivated the peasants to produce more than what they required for their own consumption. It also initiated a period of rapid reconstruction of the Soviet economy.

In the following years this process was substantially slowed down by the constant increases of agricultural taxes and by the artificially low price that the government set on foodstuffs. The policy, designed to favor the urban working population, forced the peasants to withhold their surpluses from the market, thereby threatening the cities with hunger. The dominant Stalin (q.v.) faction within the Communist Party (q.v.) had only one solution to the crisis: it abolished the NEP and initiated the forced amalgamation of individual peasant households into collective farms—kolkhoz (q.v.)—from which it was easier to extract taxes and control production. Forced collectivization was strongly but unsuccessfully opposed by many in the top leadership of the Communist Party, including members of the Politburo (q.v.) such as Bukharin (q.v.), Tomskii (q.v.) and Rykov (q.v.), the Right Opposition (q.v.). After their defeat by the Stalin faction, forcible collectivization was carried out with unparalleled brutality, and resulted in a famine that caused the death of millions of peasants, not only in the country's breadbasket—the Ukraine (q.v.)—but also in many agricultural regions of Russia—the Don (q.v.) region, the Volga (q.v.) region, and parts of western Siberia. Hundreds of thousands of the more prosperous peasants, were declared to be enemies of the people and were exiled into the northern wastes.

After Stalin's death, several attempts were made to improve the lot of the Soviet peasantry by lowering the excessively high compulsory delivery quotas imposed on the collective farms, as well as by reducing taxation on the individually cultivated peasant plots. However, these reforms failed to address the basic problems of Soviet agriculture and led to only minor improvements. A new attempt was made to redress some of the deficiencies of the system in 1965. In March of that year reforms were promulgated that were intended to ease the transition from administrative to economic methods of managing agrarian affairs. Despite these efforts, the top-down administrative system of Soviet agriculture was left unchanged, and the number of bureaucrats involved in this sector of the country's economy remained in excess of one million individuals.

The other endemic problem of Soviet agriculture—the price disparity between agrarian produce and industrial goods—was also not solved. It caused many collective farms to operate at a loss and motivated many farmers to leave their villages and move to an urban setting. Between 1967 and 1985 over 700,000 individuals moved from the rural to the urban environment. Attempts to solve these problems at the end of the 1970s through increased capital investment in agriculture failed because of the overly bureaucratized administrative system, as well as a lack of incentives for farmers to make their work more productive.

PEASANTRY, TODAY. At the beginning of the 1990s Russian agriculture was not ready for a major restructuring toward a free market system; it lacked the resources as well as the legal foundations that could support private property relations that are essential to a free market economy. These deficiencies complicated attempts to reorganize Russian agriculture and, as a result, a drop occurred in the gross production levels of both crop cultivation and animal husbandry. A breakdown of trade between different regions of the country, as well as between different sectors of the agrarian economy, has likewise occurred, together with a decrease in capital investments. The combination of these elements has led to a drop in the availability of badly needed inputs of technology and of mineral fertilizers. As well, the disparity of industrial and agricultural prices remains essentially unchanged. As a result, labor-intensive processes are not being mechanized, and production costs continue to rise.

In order to decrease its expenditures of hard currency, the government has lowered its volume of grain imports. This effort has resulted in a significant rise in domestic grain prices, which, in turn, has increased the cost of forage and negatively affected animal husbandry. In addition, independent farmers are experiencing considerable resistance on the part of the existing collective and state farms. The laws that provide for private cultivation of land are mostly ineffective because there are no legal mechanisms to enforce them. Nevertheless, the cost effectiveness of independent farm production is already considerably higher than that of the collective and state farmers.

Collective and state farms have now been reorganized into independent joint stock associations that own the land they cultivate, together with the agricultural equipment and real property located on it. Each member of the association owns a share of the corporation. However, during the process of transforming these units from the Soviet-style kolkhoz (q.v.) into corporate enterprises, some former administrators have managed to appropriate for their own use the best plots reserved for individual cultivation. These plots continue to play an important role in the Russian rural economy. According to the 1992 figures, they produced an aggregate of almost one-third of all wholesale agricultural production of the country.

In October 1993 a presidential decree legalized private property on land. This decree was not approved unanimously in Russia. One reason is that it is conducive to the creation of a speculative market in land, thus permitting its redistribution in favor of the most effective producers. The most enterprising collective farmers have left the villages in order to relocate in urban areas. Those who remain, having in large measure been accustomed to passivity by the previous kolkhoz system, do not want, or even know how to conduct independent farming operations. Many of them are selling their shares of land to speculators and abandoning the countryside.

PEASANTS' UNION. This union of peasants was organized in 1905 and designed to promote the nationalization of land and the distribution of its use among the working peasantry.

PECHORA RIVER. This river flows into the northern White Sea (q.v.) and gives its name to the region of Russia in which numerous concentration camps were established during the Soviet period. The area is rich in timber and coal.

PEIPUS LAKE. It consists of two large connected lakes on the border between Estonia (q.v.) and Russia and drains into the Gulf of Finland.

PENKOVSKII, OLEG (1912–63). A colonel in Russian military intelligence, GRU (q.v.), he approached British intelligence and provided information to both MI6 and the CIA, much of it about Soviet missiles. He was arrested by Soviet authorities in October 1962 and shot after a trial.

PEOPLE'S WILL see NARODNAIA VOLIA

PEPELIAEV, ANATOLII N. (1891–1938). He led a rebellion against the Soviet government in 1918 with the support of Czechoslovak prisoners of war in Russia, who were likewise opposed to the Soviets. After the rebellion he became commander of the White Armies (q.v.) of the Siberian government of Admiral Kolchak (q.v.). In 1920 he was forced to retreat across the Russian border to Harbin (q.v.), China, but returned to Russia in 1922 in support of a new anti-Communist rebellion. In 1923 he was taken prisoner by Soviet forces and sent to a concentration camp, where he died.

PEPELIAEV, VIKTOR N. (1884–1920). A member of the fourth Duma (q.v.) and a leader of the Kadet (KD) Party (q.v.), he was the Provisional government's (q.v.) commissar in Kronstadt (q.v.). After the Bolsheviks (q.v.) seized power in October 1917, he became the interior minister in Admiral Kolchak's (q.v.) anti-Communist government. He was handed over to the Red Army (*see* Armed Forces, Soviet) and shot, together with Admiral Kolchak.

PEREKOP ISTHMUS. A narrow stretch of land that joins the Crimean (q.v.) peninsula to the mainland, it was the scene of a major battle between the Red and White armies during the civil war (q.v.).

PERESTROIKA (RECONSTRUCTION) Launched by Gorbachev (q.v.) in 1985, this was the name given to his attempt to reform the Soviet system without abandoning its fundamental structure. It came to an unsuccessful end with the collapse of the Soviet Union in December 1991. Perestroika's main thrust was the restructuring of Soviet economic foundations, emphasizing the gradual decentralization of management and the involvement of individuals at the lower level of the economic hierarchy in planning, self-financing and self-management.

PERM. Founded in 1780, this industrial town is located on the Kama River (q.v.). Its industries include aircraft and tractor plant manufacturing, the production of fertilizers, and the processing of agricultural products. Its population is just over 1,000,000.

PEROVSKAIA, SOPHIA (1853–81). Daughter of a tsarist general, she became a revolutionary at an early age and joined the terrorist group, Narodnaia Volia (q.v.). As a member of its executive committee, Perovskaia participated, together with her lover Zheliabov (q.v.), in the successful assassination of Tsar Alexander II (q.v.). After the murder, along with most of her fellow conspirators, she was apprehended, tried and publicly hanged in St. Petersburg (q.v.) in 1881.

PERVOURALSK. A railroad junction southwest of Sverdlovsk (q.v.) in the Ural Mountains (q.v.), its industrial production consists of sawmilling and metalwork. It has a population of slightly over 120,000.

PERVUSHIN, NIKOLAI V. (1899–1993). After graduating from Kazan University in 1923, he left for Germany to study German industrial organization. In 1930 Pervushin emigrated to Paris where he lectured on Russian history and economics, then moved to the United States in 1946, to become a senior interpreter at UNESCO. After 1960 he was head of the Russian School in Vermont and in 1962 became a professor at McGill University in Montreal.

PESTEL, PAVEL I. (1799–1826). A guards colonel and leader of the Southern Society (q.v.), he took part in the failed Decembrist (q.v.) revolt in 1826, for which he was tried and executed.

PETER I THE GREAT, TSAR AND EMPEROR (1672–1725). One of the most significant of the Romanov (q.v.) rulers of Russia, from an early age he sought to reform and Europeanize his empire. In 1721 he had himself named emperor. After 1696 Peter spent several years touring and studying Western European ways, including its military organization and shipbuilding in Holland. On his return home he set up special schools for technical and governmental functions and promulgated a table of ranks that placed elevation to the nobility, (*dvoriane*) (q.v.) on a service rather than hereditary basis. His reforms reached into every sphere of Russian life, industry, education, government, and the military. He successfully fought a series of wars with Sweden that enabled Russia to acquire large areas of the Baltic (q.v.) coastline and a window on Europe, on which he built his new capital, St. Petersburg (q.v.).

PETER II, TSAR AND EMPEROR (1715–30). Son of Peter the Great's dead son Aleksei (q.v.), he was proclaimed emperor of Russia in the will of Peter's wife and successor, Empress Catherine I (q.v.). Crowned in 1728, the youth led a dissolute and undisciplined life in Moscow, taking no part in the governing of his kingdom, and died at an early age.

PETER III, TSAR AND EMPEROR (1728–62). Brought up more as a German than a Russian, this rather weak-minded monarch ascended the throne in 1762. His principal impact on Russia was to return to Prussia provinces that Russia had won in the Seven Years' War (q.v.) and to free the noble classes from the obligations of service that Peter the Great had imposed on them. Married to Catherine, a powerful and ambitious woman who had already acquired lovers during their short marriage, he was murdered by one of these lovers. He was succeeded on the throne by his wife, the future Catherine the Great (q.v.).

PETER AND PAUL FORTRESS. This fortress-prison is located in St. Petersburg (q.v.). It was erected in 1703 by Peter the Great (q.v.) to protect his new capital and later served as a prison for political criminals.

PETERS, IAKOV, K. (1886–1938). Born in Latvia, he became a Communist in 1904, and lived as an exile in London until 1909. There Peters joined the British Labour Party and married an English woman. Peters returned to Russia after the revolution of February 1917 (q.v.) and soon became the deputy chairman of the security police (*see* Security Services, Soviet). He was the president of the revolutionary tribunal that prosecuted Bruce Lockhart and Sidney Riley on espionage charges, and he was also instrumental in suppressing the 1918 Moscow (q.v.) revolt organized by the Socialist Revolutionaries (q.v.). Peters commanded the Petrograd (q.v.) military district in 1919 and was chief of the eastern department of the Soviet security police between 1922 and 1928. In 1937 he was commander of the Kremlin (q.v.) guard when he was arrested and shot on Stalin's (q.v.) orders.

PETIPA, MARIA M. (1857–1940). She made her debut in 1875 at the Mariinskii Theater (q.v.) as one of its leading ballerinas, after which she gave numerous performances in Western Europe. In 1917 she emigrated to Paris.

PETIPA, MARIUS (1822–1910). This French dancer and choreographer began working at the Mariinskii Theater (q.v.) in St. Petersburg in 1847, founding the Russian classical ballet tradition with his choreography of *Sleeping Beauty*, *Giselle*, and other works; his training of dancers and choreographers established his approach as a model for the future of Russian ballet.

PETRASHEVSKII, MIKHAIL V. (1821–66). A government official in St. Petersburg (q.v.), he encouraged the development of a circle of the capital's intelligentsia (q.v.) to discuss various sensitive subjects of a literary, political and social nature. Among their number was a young writer, Dostoevsky (q.v.). These individuals met once a week at Petroshevskii's house, for which in 1849 he was charged with plotting the overthrow of the Russian state. He received a death sentence, which was eventually commuted.

PETROGRAD. The Russified name for St. Petersburg (q.v.), which came into use during World War I (q.v.). In 1924 Petrograd was renamed Leningrad, and in 1992 it was returned to its original name of St. Petersburg.

PETROGRAD SOVIET. This was the name of the most influential of the revolutionary councils of workers' and soldiers' deputies, which came into being first during the revolution of 1905 (q.v.), then again in 1917. This soviet played a decisive role during the first year of the Russian revolution, because it was able to command the loyalty of both the garrison stationed in the capital the workers of that industrial city. Its orders were obeyed not only in Petrograd but in the whole of the Russian empire.

PETROPAVLOVSK. Established in 1752, some 800 miles northwest of Alma-Ata (q.v.), this city became an important railroad town when the Trans-Siberian Railroad (q.v.) was built. It is now an industrial city that produces engineering products as well as processing agricultural ones. Its population is just over 200,000.

PETROPAVLOVSK-KAMCHATKA. The major city on Kamchatka (q.v.) Peninsula, its industries include sawmilling and canning of fishery products. It is also an important port for Russian naval and commercial shipping in the Pacific. Its population slightly exceeds 200,000.

PETROV, EVGENII P. (b. KATAEV) (1903–42). As a young man he began publishing short stories and traveled extensively through the United States with his associate Ilf (q.v.) as a *Pravda* (q.v.) correspondent. The two published satirical accounts of their voyages. During World War II (q.v.) he was a war correspondent and died in a plane crash.

PETROVSKII, GRIGORII I. (1878–1958). He joined the Russian Socialist Democratic Labor Party (q.v.) in 1897 and engaged in revolutionary work in Ekaterinoslav. He actively participated in the 1905 revolution, then emigrated to Germany. A member of the fourth Duma (q.v.) in 1912, Petrovskii became its Communist faction leader, was arrested in 1914, and exiled to Siberia (q.v.). He was the commissar of Iakutiia (now Sakha, q.v.) after the October 1917 revolution (q.v.) before returning to Petrograd. He was a member of the first Soviet government and escaped being purged during the late 1930s. After 1940 he served as the deputy director of the Museum of the Revolution.

PETROZAVODSK. Established by Peter the Great (q.v.) in 1702, this town is located on the shore of Lake Ladoga (q.v.). It is the capital of the Karelian Autonomous Republic (q.v.) of the Russian Republic. Its main industry is armaments, but it also produces cement and machinery.

PIATAKOV, GRIGORII (1890–1937). As a young student he joined the Russian Socialist Democratic Labor Party (q.v.) in 1910, then was banished to Siberia (q.v.) in 1912. Piatakov soon escaped and emigrated to Switzerland, where, in 1915, he joined the Bolshevik (q.v.)

faction. He returned to Russia in 1917 and became chairman of the Kiev (q.v.) branch of the Communist Party (q.v.). In 1922 he was elected to the Central Committee of the Communist Party of the Soviet Union (q.v.) where, between 1923 and 1927, he belonged to the opposition group led by Trotsky (q.v.). Expelled from the Communist Party that year, he was readmitted in 1929 and worked as the deputy commissar of heavy industry from 1930 to 1936. In 1937, at the height of the purges (q.v.), he was arrested, forced to make a public confession of being a spy and a saboteur in a show trial (q.v.), and executed.

PIATIGORSK. A spa since the early years of the 19th century, the town is located east of Krasnodar (q.v.), the major city of the Caucasus (q.v.). Besides its resort facilities it also manufactures furniture and clothing.

PIATIGORSKII, GRIGORII P. (1903–76). Cello soloist in the Bolshoi theater (q.v.) symphony orchestra from 1919 to 1921, he emigrated to Western Europe and became a member of the Berlin Philharmonic in 1924. In 1939 he moved to the United States, where he taught music at the Curtis Institute and at Boston University until 1957.

PIATNITSIN, ALEKSANDR A. (1897–1969). Born into a Cossack (q.v.) family, he took part in World War I (q.v.), then became the leader of a White Army (q.v.) detachment on the Don (q.v.) during the civil war (q.v.). He was evacuated from the Crimea (q.v.) after the defeat of General Wrangel (q.v.) and settled in Paris. There he played an important role in the organization of emigre Cossacks.

PILNIAK, BORIS A. (b. VOGAU) (1894–1942). Born into a Volga German (q.v.) family, he became a popular Soviet novelist, known best for his depiction of the civil war (q.v.), and at one time the chairman of the Union of Soviet Writers (q.v.). He was removed from his post in 1929 and arrested in 1938 as a Japanese spy. Pilniak died in prison, probably in 1942.

PIMEN, PATRIARCH OF MOSCOW (b. IZVEKOV) (1910-   ). He became a monk in 1927, was arrested in 1937, and sent to a concentration camp. After his release in 1946 he was ordained a priest, then, between 1947 and 1949, he served as secretary to the bishop of Rostov, after which he became the head of the Zagorsk Seminary, and in 1963 the metropolitan (q.v.) of St. Petersburg (q.v.). In 1971 he was elevated to become the patriarch of Moscow (q.v.). In 1988 Patriarch Pimen obtained Gorbachev's (q.v.) approval to organize the celebration of the millennium (q.v.) of Christianity in Russia. He also presided over the 1988 council that introduced numerous reforms to the Orthodox Church (q.v.) in Russia.

PIONEERS (PIONERY). This was the intermediate age group among the Communist youth organizations (10 to 14 years of age), in between the Young Oktiabrists, aged seven to 10, and the older Komsomol (q.v.). One of its prime functions was to instill Communist ideology in these youths. It also operated a large number of summer camps for its members.

PISAREV, DMITRII I. (1840–68). Educated at the University of St. Petersburg (*see* Universities), he became one of the principal theoreticians of nihilism (q.v.), the intellectual trend that sought to negate most of the prevailing cultural values of Russian society at the time. He was also the editor of a radical St. Petersburg journal.

PLATONOV, SERGEI F. (1860–1933). Professor of history at the University of St. Petersburg (q.v.) and author of an influential textbook on Russian history, he was dismissed from the Academy of Sciences (q.v.) of the USSR by Soviet authorities for his disagreement with official Soviet historiography.

PLEHVE, VIACHESLAV K. (1846–1904). He served first in the ministry of justice, then as director of the police. In 1884 Plehve became deputy minister of the interior and minister in 1902. He was particularly hated by the revolutionaries and was assassinated by them in 1904.

PLEKHANOV, GEORGII V. (pseud. BELOV) (1856–1918). Born into a land-owning family and educated at the St. Petersburg (q.v.) Mining Institute, he was expelled for revolutionary activity in 1876. In the early 1870s he took part in the "March to the People," during which members of the Russian intelligentsia attempted to propagandize the peasantry. Later in the same decade, after the Populists (*see* Narodnichestvo) split into two separate groups, Plekhanov became the leader of the Black Repartition Party (*see* Chernyi Peredel), which denounced as ineffective the use of individual terror for accomplishing political goals. He emigrated to Western Europe in 1880 and remained there until the February 1917 revolution (q.v.). In exile he was introduced to Marxism and became the first major Russian Marxist theoretician. Plekhanov helped organize the Emancipation of Labor group in 1883, but after becoming acquainted with Lenin (q.v.), he criticized him, and remained a bitter foe of the Bolsheviks (q.v.) until his death.

PLEVITSKAIA, NADEZHDA V. (b. VINNIKOVA) (1884–1940). Born into a peasant family, she became a popular singer before World War I (q.v.). In 1921 she married Skoblin (q.v.), a major general of the White Armies (q.v.). As an emigrant to France, she was the idol of the exiled Russians who had settled there after the civil war (q.v.). While pursuing her career as a singer, Plevitskaia simultaneously worked as a secret agent of the Soviet intelligence services and helped them to penetrate the anti-Communist emigre circles. Among her most noted actions was helping to kidnap General Miller (q.v.) from Paris in 1937. She was arrested by French authorities and sentenced to a prison term. She died in prison.

PLISETSKAIA, MAIA M. (1925-   ). A graduate of the Moscow (q.v.) Choreographic School, she joined the Bolshoi Theater (q.v.) in 1943 and became an internationally known ballerina. She appeared in films as well as on the stage.

POBEDONOSTSEV, KONSTANTIN P. (1827–1907). He served from 1880 as the Ober-Procurator of the Most Holy Synod (q.v.) and as the advisor to Tsar Alexander III (q.v.), and was the tutor of the future Nicholas II (q.v.). A man of very conservative political views, Pobedonostsev is believed to have greatly influenced his imperial pupil's political beliefs.

PODOLSK. Located on the Pakhra River some 20 miles south of Moscow (q.v.), this city produces locomotives, steel cables and sewing machines. Its population is just over 200,000.

POGROM. This term denotes a periodic attack by violent disorderly mobs on a peaceful population, primarily Jews, that occurred in pre-revolutionary Russia after some disturbing event for which Jews were blamed by reactionaries or even by the government after the death of Alexander II. Colloquially, it is used for any mass attack on a minority.

POKROVSKII, MIKHAIL N. (1868–1932). A historian with strong Marxist leanings before the revolution, he became the leading Soviet authority on Russian history during the 1920s. He also served as assistant commissar of education and director of the Central Archives of the USSR. Shortly before his death, Pokrovskii's negative rendering of Russian history was challenged by party ideologues and officially repudiated by the government.

POLISH INSURRECTION (1863–64). This was a major attempt by Polish patriots to reverse the decisions of the Congress of Vienna (q.v.), which had allotted a large part of Poland to the Russian empire. The ill-equipped and untrained rebels waged a losing struggle against the Russian army. After their defeat in 1864, the captured leaders were executed. This insurrection was viewed with great sympathy by a large section of the Russian intelligentsia (q.v.), and its suppression by the tsar's government served to further alienate and revolutionize them.

POLITBURO. This acronym stands for the Political Bureau of the Central Committee of the Communist Party of the Soviet Union (q.v.), the highest policy-making and executive body of that party. It exercised overall control of all party activities between meetings of the Central Committee. Its membership fluctuated between 13 and 20 individuals, with some being full voting members and others having the status of nonvoting candidates.

POLK. This term designates a regiment in the Russian army. In the imperial army it consisted of four battalions or 16 companies in the infantry and six squadrons in the cavalry. Its commander usually held the rank of *polkovnik*, or colonel.

POLTAVA, BATTLE OF. Poltava is the site in Ukraine (q.v.) of Peter the Great's (q.v.) most important military victory during the war with Sweden, in which Charles XII of Sweden was defeated and eventually forced to conclude a peace that was favorable to Russia in 1721. The battle was fought on July 8, 1709.

POMESTIE. Originally this meant land granted by the tsar on condition of military service. In the 16th century such landholders constituted the bulk of military and civil officers of the tsar. In the next century their possession of the land was changed from that held for service to a hereditary right.

PONOMARENKO, PANTELEIMON K. (1902–84). He took part in the civil war as a Cheka (q.v.) officer and joined the Communist Party (q.v.) in 1925. He studied at the Moscow (q.v.) Institute of Rail Transport and in 1938 began working under Malenkov (q.v.) in the Central Committee of the Communist Party of the Soviet Union (q.v.). Ponomarenko became a member of the Central Committee in 1939 and head of the Soviet partisan movement during World War II (q.v.). In 1950 he was made minister of supply and then Soviet ambassador to Poland in 1956, to India in 1957, and to the Netherlands in 1959. Between 1962 and 1964 he was the Soviet representative to the International Atomic Energy Commission in Vienna.

POP. This is the Russian colloquial term for priest. There were two categories of priests in the Orthodox Church (q.v.). The *belyi*, or white priests, who were required to marry and had a secular status and usually a family, while the *chernyi*, or black priests, were monks sworn to celibacy.

POPOV, ALEKSANDR S. (1859–1905). He built his first wireless receiver in 1895 and a transmitter in 1896, several years before Marconi. This fact was established after an investigation in 1908.

POPULATION. The population of the Russian empire increased steadily after the beginning of the 19th century. In 1811 it was 36,000,000; by 1897 it had risen to 106,000,000; and in 1915 to 131,000,000. By 1939 the population of the Soviet Union reached 170,000,000 and by 1979 stood at 262,000,000.

After the breakup of the USSR the population of the Russian Federation stood at 148,673,000. The majority of these individuals (80 percent according to the 1979 census) were ethnic Russians. The other 20 percent of the inhabitants of the republic consisted of some 100 different ethnic groups, including Tatars (q.v.), Ukrainians, Chuvash, Bashkir, Volga Germans (q.v.), and Kazakhs, among others, with approximately 90 percent of them having full command of the Russian language.

The European regions of the RSFSR occupy only a quarter of the territory of the country, but are inhabited by over 70 percent of the population. In 1940 only some 40 percent of the population of Russia lived in an urban setting; by 1993 this figure had risen to 70 percent. Of the largest cities, Moscow (q.v.) has eight million inhabitants, and St. Petersburg (q.v.) has over four million. Cities with a population of over one million are Nizhnii Novgorod (q.v.), Novosibirsk (q.v.), Ekaterinburg (q.v.), Samara (q.v.), Cheliabinsk (q.v.), Omsk (q.v.), Perm (q.v.), Kazan (q.v.), and Ufa. There are, in addition, some 18 cities whose population is between 500,000 and one million.

From 1986 to 1992 the number of employable individuals has increased by 0.5 percent, due primarily to a generational effect: since 1986, a larger number of those born at the beginning of the 1970s, when a relative increase in the birthrate occurred, have entered the workforce. The number of individuals who are reaching the retirement age has also continued to increase—since the beginning of 1992 the proportion of pensioners has grown significantly. Until the beginning of the 1980s the number of employed individuals was rising: in 1940 there were 22.2 million employed; by the 1960s this number had increased to 39.5 million; and in the 1980s, 65.6 million. During the 1980s this growth rate began to fall. This is especially true for collective farmers. In 1940 they numbered 16.9 million; in 1970, 6.3 million; and in 1986 less than one million. The number of full-time students has increased from 30.8 million in 1961 to 52.4 million in 1980. In 1992 86.2 million individuals, or 60 percent of the population of Russia, were of employment age.

POPULISM see NARODNICHESTVO

PORT ARTHUR. Russia's easternmost naval base in Manchuria before the Russo-Japanese war (q.v.), it was built in 1898. Without any declaration of war, the Japanese navy attacked and sank many of the Russian naval vessels anchored there. Port Arthur was besieged, taken by the Japanese, and retained by them according to the terms of the peace treaty that ended the war.

POSKREBYSHEV, A. N. (1891–1966). A member of the Communist Party (q.v.) since 1917, he was employed by Stalin (q.v.) as head of his personal secretariat, in charge of gathering information on prominent Communist leaders and in overseeing Stalin's personal security force. Elected a member of the Central Committee of the Communist Party of the Soviet Union (q.v.) in 1939, he was promoted to the rank of major-general during World War II (q.v.).

POTEMKIN, PRINCE GRIGORII A. (1739–93). A favorite, and reputed lover, of Catherine the Great (q.v.), he was instrumental in the annexation of the Crimea (q.v.) to the Russian empire by persuading the khan of Crimea to resign in her favor.

POTEMKIN MUTINY. A rebellion that occurred in 1905 in Odessa (q.v.) on a battleship by that name of Russia's Black Sea (q.v.) fleet. As the mutiny proceeded, two other vessels joined the rebellious sailors of the battleship. Although it occurred quite unexpectedly, its origins go back several years to 1902, when well-organized secret revolutionary cells were set up in the Black Sea fleet's home port of Sebastopol (q.v.). The Russo-Japanese (q.v.) war served only to accelerate the mutiny which eventually failed, with the crew of the *Potemkin* sailing into Constanza, Romania, to seek asylum.

POTRESOV, ALEKSANDR N. (1869–1934). Born into a general's family, he became active in socialist politics in 1890. After graduation from the University of St. Petersburg (*see* Universities) in 1893, he was arrested and exiled. Together with Lenin (q.v.), he founded the newspaper *Iskra* (q.v.) in 1900, then became the leader of the right-wing Mensheviks (q.v.) and a strong opponent of the Bolsheviks (q.v.). Potresov left Russia in 1925 for France, where he continued his political activities by editing a socialist periodical.

POTSDAM CONFERENCE. This conference was held between the United States, the USSR and Great Britain in Potsdam, Germany, in May 1945, at the end of World War II (q.v.). There, Stalin (q.v.), Churchill, Attlee and Truman met to draw up the frontiers of postwar Europe. The conference designated the commanders of the three armies as the supreme authorities in their respective zones of occupation in Germany.

POVEST VREMENNYKH LET see PRIMARY CHRONICLE

POZDNIAKOV, VLADIMIR V. (1920–73). He served in the Red army during World War II (q.v.). After he was captured by the Germans, he became General Vlasov's (q.v.) adjutant. Pozdniakov escaped from Soviet control after the end of the war and emigrated to the United States, where he published several books about General Vlasov and the Russian Liberation Army (q.v.), the ROA.

PRAVDA (TRUTH) The official daily organ of the Communist Party of the Soviet Union (q.v.), it was founded by Lenin (q.v.) in 1912. During the whole of the Soviet period this newspaper had a multimillion circulation and was read with great care by all levels of the Soviet citizenry for its instructions and political line. It is currently published as a privately owned newspaper.

PRAVOSLAVIE. ORTHODOXY. The Russian designation for the Orthodox Church (q.v.), embraced by the early East Slav population of Kiev (q.v.), under the aegis of Prince Vladimir (q.v.) in the tenth century. It was first governed by a metropolitan (q.v.), then, after 1589, by a patriarch until the reforms of Peter the Great (q.v.), which established the Most Holy Synod (q.v.) in 1721 as its governing body. The patriarchate was restored after the February 1917 revolution (q.v.) but was very strictly controlled by the Soviet state until the perestroika (q.v.) policy of the middle of the 1980s.

PREDVODITEL DVORIANSTVA. Marshal of the nobility. Such individuals played a major role in district and provincial affairs after the establishment of the *Zemstvo* (*see* Zemstva) administrations by Alexander II (q.v.) in 1864.

PREOBRAZHENSKII, EVGENII A. (1886–1937). A leading Soviet economist and elaborator of the concept of primary socialist accumulation of capital, he drew up the plan for the industrialization of the Soviet Union, but, having sided with Trotsky (q.v.) in 1927, he was expelled by Stalin (q.v.) from the Communist Party (q.v.) and sent into internal exile. Preobrazhenskii was shot during the purges of the 1930s.

PRE-PARLIAMENT. This is the name by which the temporary council, a consultative body to the Provisional government (q.v.), is sometimes known. It was dissolved after the October Revolution (q.v.).

PRESIDIUM OF THE SUPREME SOVIET. This body acted constitutionally as the head of state, producing legislation and issuing ukases. Its members were elected by the two chambers of the Supreme Soviet (q.v.); it replaced the Central Executive Committee (q.v.) after the introduction of the Stalin Constitution in 1936.

PRESS, PREREVOLUTIONARY. *Vedomosti (News)* was the first newspaper printed in Russia. It began coming out in 1702. Besides foreign news, it featured official notices as well as news items received from a variety of sources. Its circulation varied from a few dozen to several thousand. Initially, the paper was printed only in Moscow; later it began to be published in both Moscow and St. Petersburg. Eventually it was renamed *St. Peterburgskie Vedomosti*.

In 1708 civil orthography replaced the previously used church orthography in all secular Russian publications. By the 1770s there were 16 periodicals in Russia, some of which came out in the provinces. During the 19th century their numbers grew rapidly, so that by 1860 there were more than 500 periodical titles being issued in Russia.

These publications played an important cultural role in the life of the country. Their political slant differed widely but usually coincided with some particular tendency in Russian social thought. In the 1820s and 1830s the democratic tendency was reflected by *The Moscow Telegraph* and, later, by *Sovremennik (q.v.)*. The *Vestnik Evropy* reflected the perspective of the liberal intelligentsia (q.v.) and stood for the inclusion of elected representatives of society in the administrative organs of the government, as well as for local administration reforms. These views were also expressed by *Russkie Vedomosti*, which began publication in 1868 and which was closely tied to groups of progressive university professors.

These publications played an important role in forming a new political consciousness among the educated classes of the country. The views of the radical populists were represented by the periodical *Russkoe Bogatstvo*, which advocated the abolition of the remnants of serfdom and the liquidation of land ownership by absentee landlords, in addition to calling for a redistribution of land among the working peasantry. In 1899 it first published the writings of Chernov (q.v.), who later became the leader of the Socialist Revolutionaries (q.v.) party.

At the beginning of the 20th century weekly periodicals such as *Niva* and *Ogonek* were particularly popular. Besides these social and political journals, there were numerous publications devoted to various art forms, as well as several major satirical periodicals, whose primary focus was a critique of the tsarist autocracy. An important role in the ideological and organizational growth of the Russian social democratic movement was played by the newspaper *Iskra* (q.v.), on whose editorial board Lenin (q.v.) sat.

PRESS, SOVIET. Among the first measures taken by the Soviet government after the October 1917 revolution (q.v.) was the closing of opposition newspapers and the imposition of Marxist ideology on the press. In the RSFSR the press came out not only in the Russian language but also in the many languages of its numerous ethnic groups.

During the 1920s, there still remained some significant differences among the country's leading periodicals, and the ideological struggles that took place during the early part of the decade were to a certain extent reflected in the press. One of the areas of discussion was how to relate to the culture inherited from Russia's past, with some radical advocates asserting that those who were not of working class origin were enemies of the new Soviet culture. Their opponents argued for the desirability of artistic independence from politics. Among the most popular literary periodicals of the 1920s were *Novyi Mir* and *Oktiabr*. They were thick journals that published the works of well-known writers, as well as critical articles, and featured discussions on topics of current interest. However, with the coming to power of the Stalin (q.v.) faction and the beginning of accelerated Soviet industrialization in the late 1920s, all aspects of Soviet society, including the press, were politicized. A new principle was introduced by which literary periodicals were evaluated by the authorities: only that was to be held valuable which directly aided the construction of socialism.

In the 1930s, due in large measure to the spread of literacy among the Russian population, the influence of the press increased significantly. Newspapers, periodicals and books became an important part of the life of both the urban working classes and the rural population. However, the amount of knowledge conveyed in the 1930s by Soviet media was limited by its uniformity in style as well as in content. Publications provided their readers with a minimum of news and understanding and a maximum of propaganda. After the beginning of the purges (q.v.) in the middle 1930s, the press acquired a total uniformity and began the merciless hounding of many artists. In 1936 both *Pravda* (q.v.) and *Literaturnaia Gazeta* (q.v.) published articles in which such writers as Pasternak (q.v.) and Olesha (q.v.), and such film directors as Eisenstein (q.v.), were severely criticized. On the other hand, artists who praised the Soviet government and the Communist Party (q.v.) were lavishly rewarded. The Soviet press of the time was filled with articles about "positive heros" and about individuals who were "actively transforming" Soviet life. Publications that failed to conform to these governmental expectations were placed under suspicion.

During World War II (q.v.), radio broadcasts became very important at a time when many newspapers stopped publication for lack of newsprint, and those that managed to continue had to reduce their size and decrease their frequency.

During the 1950s and 1960s television became available in Russia. In this period one of the characteristic traits of the Soviet mass media was the propaganda of the extraordinary successes of Soviet economic and cultural achievements, as well as of the leading role of Russian science and technology in the last century. The uninhibited praise of Stalin's genius grew to enormous proportions. The 1946 decisions of the Central Committee of the Communist Party (q.v.) concerning the literary periodicals *Zvezda* and *Leningrad* signaled the beginning of a severe tightening of government controls over the Soviet cultural scene.

After Stalin's death and the beginning of Khrushchev's (q.v.) rule, Soviet newspapers and periodicals began, once again, to publish materials that tried to reflect the actual life of the people. Many journalists attempted to show this life without the artificial embellishments that had been previously required of them. During this period two quite different tendencies manifested themselves. On the one hand, there was the tendency represented by the periodical *Novyi Mir* (q.v.) under the editorship of Tvardovsky (q.v.). It was characterized by an effort to avoid the old stereotypes and truthfully report Soviet reality.

On the other hand, there was the tendency represented by the periodical *Oktiabr*. This publication continued to be guided by the former ideological clichés. After the Khrushchev period (1956 to 1964), censorship was intensified once again, and the coverage of news by the press was narrowed. This development led to the growth of unofficial publications, the so-called samizdat (q.v.), or self-publishing, which was done illegally on typewriters and distributed from person to person in secret.

PRESS, TODAY. Since the collapse of the Soviet Union, the termination of press censorship and the inauguration of free public expression in the press has deeply affected the role of the mass media in Russia. Democratic government cannot exist without an open dialogue with the people, and the Russian press today forces the government to see itself through the eyes of its readers. There now exist a large number of newspapers and periodicals in Russia that represent a wide gamut of political and social points of view, many of which are openly hostile to the existing government. Journalists who are close to the government are frequently inclined to offer justifications for its actions, whereas opposition papers concentrate on the darker sides of life and do not notice any thing positive. As a result of such criticism, there are now signs of an attempt by the government to impose some restrictions on the press.

Today, the press in Russia is split not only along political lines, but also by rivalries that at times take on a highly negative tone. Another unwelcome development is the growth of the press's dependence on commercial institutions, a process that seriously undermines its objectivity, since a newspaper depends on advertising for its income. The sudden and total removal of press censorship in Russia has had some undesirable consequences, along with positive ones. Besides news, Russian readers had traditionally looked to the daily press for serious in-depth analysis of current events. Today, however, the flood of commercialized sensationalism and light entertainment is displacing such coverage, at the same time that it has begun to decrease the influence of the literary and artistic periodicals. Even though these periodicals continue publication, their circulation is dropping, as is the public's interest in serious literature.

PRIMAKOV, BORIS (1929-   ). Born in Kiev, Primakov grew up in Tbilisi, Georgia, and graduated from the Moscow Institute of Oriental Studies in 1953. A member of the Communist Party (q.v.) since 1959, he worked as an Arabic-speaking Middle East and Asian specialist for *Pravda* (q.v.) in the 1960s and was engaged in intelligence work. He joined the Soviet Academy of Sciences in 1974, and became director of the Institute of World Economy and International Relations in 1985. He advised Gorbachev (q.v.) on Middle Eastern and Asian matters. From 1991 on he was director of the Russian Foreign Intelligence

Service (SVR) and was appointed foreign minister by Boris Yeltsin (q.v.) in January 1996.

PRIMARY CHRONICLE (POVEST VREMENNYKH LET). This manuscript is said to have been the work of the brethren of the Monastery of the Caves in Kiev (q.v.). It contains legends, hagiography, and accounts of the early battles of Kievan Rus (q.v.), ending at the beginning of the 12th century. Its authorship is attributed to the monk Nestor.

PRIVATE PLOTS. These were the small land allocations given to Soviet collective farmers on which they were allowed to raise their own food. Usually from half to one acre in size, these allotments served as the mainstay of the peasant subsistence economy after the collectivization (q.v.) of Soviet agriculture in the early 1930s.

PROGRESSIVE BLOC. A coalition of moderate deputies in the fourth Duma (q.v.), they were chiefly Cadets (q.v.) and Octobrists (q.v.), whose aim in 1915 was to form a new government, that, on the strength of the popularity of its reforms, could inspire the nation to a successful conclusion of the war. Their project was halted, however, when Nicholas II (q.v.) prorogued the Duma later in the year.

PROKOFIEV, SERGEI S. (1891–1953). A graduate of the St. Petersburg (q.v.) Conservatory of Music, he began composing early in his life, as well as being a concert pianist and a conductor. After emigrating from Russia in 1917, first to England and then to the United States and France, he continued composing and giving concerts. In 1933 he returned to Russia, where he wrote a number of operas, symphonies and ballets. In 1948 Prokofiev was severely criticized, together with several other Soviet composers, by Zhdanov (q.v.), the chief Soviet cultural ideologist, for formalism.

PROKUROR (PUBLIC PROSECUTOR). In the justice system of imperial Russia, as well as during the Soviet period, this office was responsible for making arrests, carrying out investigations of suspects of particular crimes, and looking into complaints made by members of the public.

PROLETKULT. This is a contraction of the name of an organization established after the 1917 revolution, Proletarskaia Kultura (Proletarian Culture), whose task it was to help develop workers' education and culture. It was abolished in 1932 by the Soviet government for not answering the needs of socialist construction as these were defined by Stalin (q.v.).

PROTAZANOV, IAKOV A. (1881–1945). An outstanding Russian filmmaker, his debut occurred in 1909 with a film based on a story by Pushkin (q.v.). Altogether he directed over 80 films. Protazanov emigrated from Russia in 1917, moving first to Paris, then to Berlin, but returned to Russia in 1923. He is considered to have been one of the classic Russian filmmakers.

PROTOCOLS OF THE ELDERS OF ZION. (Also "Protocols of the Learned Elders of Zion"). A forged document purporting to be the record of a Jewish conspiracy, formulated in Basel in 1897, to take over the world by gradually destroying non-Jewish social institutions and seizing control of international finance. In fact cobbled together from a variety of earlier, even unrelated sources, it was published in Russia in 1905 as an addendum to a book about the Antichrist by Sergei Nilus (1862–1930), an official in the Most Holy Synod (q.v.) who wrote other pamphlets of the sort. It became particularly controversial in the years after World War I (q.v.), and occasional editions are still brought out, but it was textually proved to be a forgery in 1921; a court in Berne agreed in 1934.

PROTOPOPOV, ALEKSANDR D. (1866–1918). The last tsarist minister of the interior, he was originally one of the leaders of the Oktiabrist Party (q.v.) in the Duma (q.v.). He led a delegation of Russian parliamentarians to Western Europe in 1916. On his return he suddenly made an about-face and agreed to join the tsar's government as minister of the interior. Protopopov was imprisoned after the 1917 revolution and later executed by the Cheka (q.v.).

PROVISIONAL GOVERNMENT. The street riots, accompanied by the revolt of the Petrograd (q.v.) garrison at the end of February 1917, led to the abdication of Nicholas II (q.v.) at his army headquarters in Mogilev (q.v.) on March 2, 1917. In order to restore order in the capital, members of the Duma (q.v.) formed a provisional committee under the leadership of the Duma's president, Rodzianko (q.v.). This occurred at the same time as the establishment of a left-dominated Petrograd Soviet (council) of Workers' and Soldiers' Deputies. The new government was to put an end to tsarist autocracy and to initiate a transition to a constitutional form of rule. Most of its members came from parties that represented the interests of the mercantile, industrial, and bureaucratic sections of the population and controlled the country's economy as well as its government bureaucracy. However, the real power in the capital at the time rested with the Petrograd Soviet (q.v.), and the Provisional government was forced to enter into negotiations with its representatives, who sanctioned its formation on condition that government decisions had to be approved by the Executive Committee of the Soviet.

The Provisional government consisted of twelve individuals; six belonged to the Kadet (KD) Party (q.v.), one was a socialist, and the rest were members of the Otkiabrist Party (q.v.). The prime minister was Prince Lvov (q.v.), a well-known liberal; the minister of foreign affairs was Miliukov (q.v.), the equally well-known leader of the Kadets. Kerensky (q.v.), the only socialist, was named minister of justice. The program of this government included an amnesty for all political prisoners; the institution of freedom of speech, press, and assembly; and an immediate election by secret ballot to all local governments, as well as to a Constituent Assembly (q.v.) that was to decide on the permanent form of Russia's government.

Shortly after its formation, the Provisional government began encountering economic difficulties among the city's population, and when Foreign Minister Miliukov promised the Allies that Russia would continue the war to a victorious conclusion, protest demonstrations in the streets of the capital again took place. Supporters of the government, consisting mainly of officers, civil servants and students, mounted a counterdemonstration and violent confrontations ensued.

In order to defuse this situation, the ruling parties suggested the formation of a coalition that would increase the representation of left-wing groups such as the Mensheviks (q.v.) and the Socialist Revolutionaries (q.v.). The first coalition government was formed in May 1917 with Kerensky as minister of war. During this time the worsening economic situation of the population, the continuation of the war, and the active propaganda by followers of Lenin (q.v.) began to exert an influence on the city's population. The majority of the participants in the street demonstration of July marched under the slogan of "All Power to the Soviets."

The main reasons why the popularity of the Provisional government fell in the summer of 1917 was that it had failed both to introduce the land reforms that the Russian peasantry was expecting and to grant independence to the national minorities within the empire; and it had not ended the war. The government counted on a successful military offensive against Austro-Hungarian forces to defuse the political situation in the capital, but the Brusilov Offensive (q.v.) of July 1917 proved a failure, and a second coalition government, headed by Kerensky, was formed. He attempted to steer a centrist course, but the rebellion of the conservative General Kornilov (q.v.) against his government in September forced him to seek the help of the extreme left wing of the capital's population, thereby greatly strengthening the influence of Lenin's followers.

Trying to maintain himself in power, Kerensky created a directorate consisting of five moderate left-wingers. The Mensheviks (q.v.) and the Socialist Revolutionaries (q.v.) agreed to support him until the opening of the Democratic Conference (q.v.), which Kerensky summoned for September 14, 1917. At this time the Communists were vacillating between the position of Lenin and Trotsky (q.v.), who were demanding an immediate insurrection and the transfer of all power to the soviets (q.v.), and the more moderate elements led by Kamenev (q.v.), who were inclined to cooperate with other socialist parties and to avoid a forcible overthrow. In October 1917 Lenin finally won approval for an insurrection. In the meantime, Kerensky and his ministers had become completely isolated and were unable to prevent the Bolshevik (q.v.) seizure of power on October 25, 1917 (old style). The ministers of the Provisional government were arrested, and state power was transferred to the soviets, now under the control of the Bolsheviks.

PSKOV. Located on the Velikaia River in the westernmost part of the Russian Republic, it is one of the oldest cities in the country, dating back to the ninth century. Dominated by its neighbor, Novgorod (q.v.), it became a free city-state in the middle of the 14th century and remained so until annexed by Moscow (q.v.) in 1510. It is known for its linen manufacturing, as well as for the production of agricultural machinery. Its population is approximately 150,000.

PUBLISHING. The origin of publishing in Russia is connected with the name of Ivan Fedorov (q.v.). In 1563 he created the first state typography in Moscow (q.v.), and in 1564 published the first book printed in Russia, entitled *Apostol.* Until the reign of Peter the Great (q.v.), all Russian books were printed in the old-style church script, and it was not until 1708 that a new, civil script was introduced. Under Peter the majority of books published dealt with mathematics, warfare and navigation or were textbooks. In 1708 an annual calendar began to be printed, and in 1715 the first private typography was started. Because only a very small minority of individuals were literate, books cost a great deal. In 1721 the government issued a decree forbidding the publishing of any work without the permission of the Most Holy Synod (q.v.), thus introducing the first official censorship in Russia.

By the end of the 18th century, typographies were being established not only in the two capitals, but also in the larger provincial towns, and the number of textbooks also began to grow rapidly. Many of these were created with the participation of members of the Russian Academy of Sciences (q.v.) and of University of Moscow (*see* Universities) professors. In 1773 Novikov, a Russian educator, organized a society of book printers in Moscow, and by 1779 he was printing almost one-third of all books in the country. During this period bookstores had been started in 17 provincial cities, with some 40 of them being located in St. Petersburg (q.v.) and Moscow. The best-known publisher of this period was Smerdin, who specialized in producing a collection of Russian writers. He also published the periodical *Biblioteka dlia Chteniia* (*Library for Reading*).

At the beginning of the 19th century many new private typographies were established in Russia, and there existed a very active book trade. The types of books published consisted in their majority of textbooks, informative books, and books dealing with natural sciences. Artistic literature was issued in considerably smaller editions.

By the end of that century two new major book publishers were particularly active: Suvorin in St. Petersburg and Sytin in Moscow. Suvorin published a series of some 300 titles, called *Deshevaia Biblioteka* (*Inexpensive Library*), which featured the works of Russian writers from the second half of the 18th and the first half of the 19th centuries. Sytin, who published the series *Biblioteka dlia Samoobrazovaniia* (*Library for Self-Education*), featured popular scientific and historical works, as well as popularly written works in economics, geography, and philosophy. These books were distributed by traveling salesmen throughout Russia. They also sold millions of copies of his calendars and textbooks.

In 1919, at the very beginning of the Soviet period, Gosizdat RSFSR, a government publishing house, was established. Through most of the Soviet period the publishing house Sovetskaia Rossiia was the largest publisher in the Russian Republic, specializing in political, popular scientific, and artistic literature. The publishing house Rossikolkhozizdat concentrated on agricultural materials. In 1970 the publishing house Sovremennik began printing classics of Russian literature, as well as the works of contemporary Soviet authors. Childrens' and young adult literature was published by Detskaia Literatura (Children's Literature), and pedagogical literature by Prosveshchenie (Enlightenment). In addition, the major Russian universities had their own publishing houses.

Since the collapse of the Soviet Union, numerous private publishing houses have sprung up. They specialize primarily in commercially profitable translations of such Western literature as detective novels, horror and love stories, and popularly written legal and economic literature.

PUDOVKIN, VSEVOLOD (1893–1953). He studied chemistry and spent several years of World War I (q.v.) in a prisoner of war camp.

He then worked, along with the young Eisenstein (q.v.), under Lev Kuleshev (q.v.); his experiments with montage effects led him to a more literary use of the device. His *Heir of Genghis Khan/Storm over Asia* (1928) attracted the criticism of "formalist indulgence"; he continued to make films, some of them unreleased.

PUGACHEV, EMILIAN I. (1742–75). The leader of a Cossack (q.v.) uprising against Empress Catherine the Great (q.v.), he was finally defeated, captured and executed, but gave his name to peasant uprisings: "Pugachevshchina."

PUGO, BORIS (1937–91). The son of a prominent Latvian Communist, Pugo rose through the ranks of the Latvian Komsomol (q.v.) and the Riga city council to become first deputy chairman of the Latvian KGB (1977–84). Between 1984 and 1988 he was first secretary of the Latvian Communist Party. In 1991 Gorbachev (q.v.) appointed him minister of the interior as a concession to conservatives; in August of that year he took part in the August coup and committed suicide when it failed.

PULKOVO. Site of the foremost Russian astronomical observatory located near St. Petersburg (q.v.), it belongs to the Russian Academy of Sciences (q.v.).

PURGES. These periodic campaigns were organized by the Communist Party (q.v.) within its own ranks, according to Lenin's (q.v.) instructions. Their original aim was to eliminate dishonest or opportunist elements from the party. As developed by Stalin (q.v.), beginning with the late 1920s, they became instruments through which he and his supporters were able to first expel, and then exterminate, all of their political opponents.

PUSHKIN, ALEKSANDR S. (1799–1837). The greatest poet of Russia, he was born into a noble family and educated at the elite Corps of Pages. At an early age he came under the influence of the ideas of the French enlightenment. Exiled twice for radical views expressed in his poetry, he maintained close contacts with the leaders of the future Decembrist (q.v.) rebellion. They, however, shielded him from their activities so as not to embroil him in their conspiracy. So famous did Pushkin become that Tsar Nicholas I (q.v.) personally censored all of his writings. An accomplished literary scholar, Pushkin brought much of Western literary manners to Russia and greatly influenced the development of its literary language. He died fighting a historically controversial duel.

PUSHKINSKOE see TSARSKOE SELO.

PUTSCH OF AUGUST 1991. This effort in August 1991 aimed to forcibly overthrow President Gorbachev (q.v.) and to restore the former Soviet system. Participated in by a very large number of Gorbachev's highest officials, it collapsed after three days of ineffectual and muddled action.

PUTILOV FACTORY. The largest munition factory in Petrograd (q.v.) during World War I (q.v.), it became one of the strongholds of the Bolsheviks (q.v.) during the 1917 revolutions.

R

RABKRIN. The Russian compression of the term for Workers' and Peasant Inspectorate, a Soviet state institution established at Lenin's (q.v.) insistence in 1919 and originally headed by Stalin (q.v.). Its mission was to act as a supervisory organ over the Soviet civil service and to combat bureaucracy, a task which it failed to accomplish.

RADEK, KARL B. (b. SOBELSON) (1885–1939). A member of the German and Polish social democratic parties, he moved to Russia in 1905. During World War I (q.v.) he traveled through Germany with Lenin (q.v.) and became a Bolshevik (q.v.) in 1917. Next year Radek took part in the Brest-Litovsk (q.v.) peace negotiations, after which he helped organize a Communist Party in Germany. Radek was a member of the Central Committee of the Communist Party (q.v.) and of the executive committee of the Comintern (q.v.), as well as being an important Soviet foreign affairs commentator. He was expelled from the Communist Party (q.v.) for supporting Trotsky (q.v.) in 1927, temporarily reinstated in 1929, then rearrested in 1936, when he was tried at a show trial (q.v.) and received a ten-year sentence in a labor camp. Radek is said to have been killed by an inmate of the camp.

RADIO EREVAN. A form of joke that became current in the 1970s, it involved a fictitious "Radio Erevan" that purported to answer listeners' questions with the set phrase, "We don't really know, but it seems to us . . ." followed by a well-meaning, nonsensical reply.

RADISHCHEV, ALEXANDER N. (1749–1802). A Russian author whose liberal opinions brought him to the brink of execution by Catherine II (q.v.), he was sentenced to death for writing a book that exposed the injustices of rural Russia. This sentence was commuted to exile in Siberia (q.v.). Liberated after the empress's death, Radishchev died by his own hand.

RAILROADS. During the second half of the 20th century a period of rapid railroad building took place in Russia. The first major railroad was built under Tsar Nicholas I (q.v.) to link Moscow (q.v.) to St. Petersburg (q.v.) in 1851. This process was accompanied by large-scale construction of train engines and railroad cars, which became an important factor in the development of Russia's metallurgical industry. The growth of a railroad network was greatly assisted by the direct participation of the state in its construction and by the state's covering of the railroads' initial financial losses.

The largest railroad project in prerevolutionary Russia was the construction of the Trans-Siberian Railroad (q.v.), which began in 1891 and which linked western Russia to the Far East as far as the Pacific Ocean port of Vladivostok (q.v.). Other lines were built linking central Russia to the Ukraine (q.v.), the Crimea (q.v.), Central Asia, and Murmansk (q.v.).

During the Soviet period, construction of railroads continued. Railroads received new equipment, and the number of individuals they employed grew. They remained the decisive method of transport in the country. In the period after World War II (q.v.), the total length of the country's rail lines was some 131,000 kilometers, with some railroads, such as those from Moscow to Lake Baikal (q.v.), being fully electrified. In 1984 the construction of the gigantic Baikal-Amur Magistral (q.v.) line was finished.

At the beginning of the 1990s railroad transport was carrying approximately two-thirds of all the freight and three-quarters of all passengers in Russia, with the thickest network being located in the European part of the country. After the collapse of the USSR, railroads were in a particularly difficult situation because many of the factories which constructed railroad equipment, as well as many railroad repair stations, had been located in Ukraine (q.v.) and Belarus (q.v.). An additional cause of difficulties was the fact that, before the collapse of the Soviet dominance in Eastern Europe, Russian railroad needs were largely supplied by Soviet bloc countries, which produced all of the electrical railroad equipment. The volume of railroad transport began to drop and very large stocks of freight accumulated in stations awaiting transportation. These stocks included many perishable materials. The demand for passenger transport also increased, causing delays and long waiting lines. In addition, the number of railroad accidents has increased.

RASKOLNIKOV, FEODOR F. • 255

RAKHMANINOV, SERGEI (1873–1943). A student of Zilot and Zv-
erev, Rakhmaninov trained chiefly as a pianist; his student years at
the St. Petersburg Conservatory and later in Moscow (q.v.) were
fraught with difficulty, since the absorption of virtuoso performance
(in which Rakhmaninov was characterized by planning and precision)
left little time for the composition to which he was drawn. In 1918 he
left Russia for Sweden and emigrated soon thereafter to the United
States, despite the negative impression he had conceived of the country during his 1909 tour. His works include three symphonies, four
piano concertos, other orchestral works including the *Rhapsody on a
Theme of Paganini*, choral works including *The Bells* and a liturgy,
works for piano (one of the earliest pieces, the prelude in C-sharp of
1892, is extremely well known), and a number of songs.

RAKOVSKII, KHRISTIAN G. (1873–1938?). Although born in Bulgaria, Rakovskii migrated to Russia and enlisted in its army in 1907.
A radical from his youth, he joined the Bolsheviks (q.v.) during the
revolution of 1917 and became a member of the Central Committee
of the Communist Party (q.v.) in 1919. He was the Soviet ambassador
to France in 1926 and 1927. As a supporter of Trotsky (q.v.), he was
expelled from the Communist Party (q.v.) in 1927, but later readmitted and allowed to work in the commissariat of health. He was arrested in 1938 and sentenced to 20 years of penal servitude, but died
in a concentration camp.

RAPALLO, TREATY OF. In 1922 Russia and Germany signed a treaty
at this Swiss town to reestablish diplomatic relations and to settle war
damage claims from both sides. This treaty was a major step in breaking down the isolation imposed on these two states by the victorious
Western powers.

RASKOL (SCHISM). The name is used for the dissenters from the
church reforms that had been instituted by Patriarch Nikon (q.v.) in
1654. They called themselves Starovertsy (q.v.), or Old Believers,
and were variously persecuted until a decree of religious tolerance
was issued in 1905.

RASKOLNIKOV, FEODOR F. (b. ILIN) (1892–1939). Head of the
Kronstadt (q.v.) Bolsheviks (q.v.) and leader of the sailors' rebellion
in the spring of 1917, he became the commander in chief of the Red
Navy after the October 1917 revolution. Later, he held several high
diplomatic posts as a Soviet ambassador until the purges (q.v.) of the
1930s, because of which he fled to France in 1939. From there he

wrote a letter denouncing Stalin (q.v.) but was soon found dead, killed presumably by Soviet agents.

RASPUTIN, GRIGORII Y. (1872–1916). He was a major and highly controversial figure in the last years of the Romanov dynasty (q.v.). Originally a peasant from Siberia (q.v.), Rasputin appeared in 1903 in St. Petersburg (q.v.) as a wandering holy man and soon was introduced to the Empress Alexandra, whose young son, the Tsarevich Aleksei (q.v.), suffered from hemophilia. Rasputin succeeded, through his special powers as a hypnotist, in alleviating the child's pain and thereby gained an enormous influence over the empress, who viewed him as having been divinely sent to her. Denounced as an imposter by the Orthodox Church (q.v.) and exposed as a seducer and a degenerate, Rasputin nevertheless maintained his hold over Empress Alexandra and through her was able to obtain nominations to high government posts for his sycophants. His activities antagonized the educated public of Russia, civilian as well as military. In 1916 he was lured by a promise of sexual favors and killed by Prince Yusupov (q.v.) and Grand Duke Dmitry Romanov.

RAZIN, STEPAN (familiarly: STENKA) (1630–71). An important Cossack (q.v.) leader who led a rebellion in 1670 on the Lower Volga, his forces were defeated finally at Arzamas, and the ataman of the Cossacks betrayed his whereabouts in order to avoid further confrontation. He was captured and taken in an iron cage to Moscow, where he was executed. Over time Razin acquired mythic status as a folk hero. He was also popularly credited with magic powers.

RAZNOCHINTSY. This term refers to individuals of various classes who were members of neither the *dvoriane* (q.v.) nor the peasantry.

RED ARMY see ARMED FORCES, SOVIET

RED SQUARE. This was originally a market adjacent to the merchants' and artisans' district east of the Kremlin, known as Kitai Gorod in the 15th century; many of Moscow's main roads converged here. After the burning of Moscow (q.v.) in 1812, it was rebuilt much in its present form. The "Red" of its Russian name (*Krasnaia ploshchad*) originally meant "fair" or "beautiful."

REISS, IGNATII (b. PORETSKII) (1899–1937). He joined the Bolsheviks (q.v.) before 1917, then after the revolution of October 1917 (*see* Revolution of February 1917) worked abroad as an agent of the Cheka (q.v.) in Poland, Germany and Austria. Reiss organized a Soviet spy network in Britain. When ordered back to the Soviet Union in 1937, he refused to return and wrote an open letter denouncing Stalin (q.v.). Shortly thereafter he was assassinated in Switzerland, presumably by Soviet agents.

REMIZOV, ALEKSEI M. (1877–1957). He engaged in revolutionary activity as a student, for which he was exiled from Moscow (q.v.) in 1897. Remizov published his first work in 1902 and soon began exercising a great influence on other modernist authors such as Babel (q.v.) and Bely (q.v.). He emigrated to Berlin in 1921, and from there to Paris in 1923.

RENNENKAMPF, PAVEL K. (1854–1918). A graduate of the Academy of the General Staff in 1882, he commanded a Cossack (q.v.) division during the Russo-Japanese war (q.v.). At the beginning of World War I (q.v.) he was commander of the first Russian army that advanced into east Prussia immediately after the outbreak of the war. His mistakes during this campaign helped cause the Russian defeat at Tannenberg (q.v.). The Cheka (q.v.) executed him after the October 1917 revolution (q.v.).

REPIN, ILIA E. (1844–1930). A portrait painter and sculptor, he studied at the School of Graphic Art in St. Petersburg (q.v.) and at the Academy of Fine Arts (q.v.) from 1864 to 1871, as well as in Italy and France. In 1882 he settled in St. Petersburg, where he spent most of his life.

REVOLUTION OF 1905. In January 1905 in St. Petersburg (q.v.) a peaceful march to the Winter Palace (q.v.) took place, the aim of which was to present Tsar Nicholas II (q.v.) with a petition concerning the needs of the capital's workers. The demonstration was led by a priest, Father Gapon (q.v.) and many of the demonstrators carried icons. They were met by rifle fire and many were killed.

This event was the signal for the start of the revolution of 1905. In the hope of stopping the struggle, the right-wing circles of Russia, among whom there was no unity concerning the events that had occurred, carried out three contradictory actions. In February 1905 an order was issued permitting the inhabitants of the empire to present projects for the improvement of the governmental structure. In a second manifesto the immutability of the autocracy was proclaimed. The third imperial rescript asserted the need for elected individuals to participate in the affairs of state. These three acts initiated work by several governmental commissions, including one that was charged with studying the question of land utilization by the Russian peasantry.

The activity of these commissions was not productive, and the ruling circles of the empire placed their hopes for a peaceful resolution of existing tensions on a successful conclusion of the Russo-Japanese war (q.v.).

The defeat of the Russian Baltic fleet at the Straits of Tsushima (q.v.) in May 1905 created a panic among the country's leadership and served to strengthen the position of those who had advocated concessions by the tsar. In August 1905 Nicholas II (q.v.) issued a new manifesto, summoning an advisory body. This measure failed to put a stop to the social ferment that was disturbing the country. In September 1905 strikes by railroad workers took place, and in October there occurred a political strike that demanded an eight-hour working day, the introduction of democratic rights and freedoms, and the summoning of a consultative assembly. In the hopes of putting an end to the growing dangers of a violent revolution, Tsar Nicholas signed a manifesto on October 17, 1905, proclaiming basic civil liberties, including the untouchability of individuals and the broadening of the country's electorate. This manifesto also promised that all future legislation would have to be approved by an elected Duma (q.v.).

The manifesto was strongly opposed by those sections of the government that had advocated resistance to all demands for concessions. In order to sabotage it, these groups provoked a series of pogroms (q.v.) in provincial cities with a large Jewish population. Their other victims were the liberal intelligentsia (q.v.) and the student youth. The extreme right called their organizations the Black Hundreds (q.v.). They were openly anti-Semitic and preached extreme nationalism, demanding that the ownership of land as well as government services be restricted to those whom they considered to be "truly Russian." In December 1905 a military uprising took place in Moscow (q.v.), which was violently suppressed. After this defeat the revolutionary movement declined rapidly, and the relationship between the left and right forces of the country began to change in favor of the right. Nevertheless, Nicholas II declined to renounce his promises of the preceding October. In April 1906 the work of the first Duma began. In its composition it was quite conservative, having a majority of Kadet (KD) Party (q.v.) members, as well as a large grouping of right-wing Socialist Revolutionaries (q.v.), who represented mainly the well-to-do peasants and the old Populists.

The agrarian projects of the first Duma created wide discontent among the Russian landowning classes. In July 1906 the tsar prorogued it, expecting that the next election would result in a more malleable body. This, however, did not occur. The second Duma began its work in February 1907 and was shortly dissolved, having proven itself to be more radical than the first. This event marked the beginning of an era of conservative reaction.

REVOLUTION OF FEBRUARY 1917. By the beginning of the 20th century Russia had finally begun to accelerate its economic and industrial development, and the Russian middle classes had succeeded in substantially strengthening their economic position. During World War I (q.v.), the tsarist government had demonstrated its inability to handle the many difficult problems exacerbated by a war economy. The ensuing difficulties resulted in a sudden political crisis in the capital during the last days of February 1917, culminating in a series of massive disturbances and a revolt of the Petrograd (q.v.) garrison.

This crisis was provoked by temporary shortages of bread, which created breadlines and stimulated a panic among the working classes. By February 25, segments of the capital's intelligentsia (q.v.) had begun to join the workers in street demonstrations, and on February 26 the government decided to meet these by sending in the army. This occasioned some firing at the demonstrators, who, however, succeeded in turning the soldiers to their side, so that on February 27 the vast majority of the Petrograd garrison had moved to the side of the demonstrators.

At the initiative of members of the workers' cooperatives and the Russian Socialist Democratic Labor Party (q.v.), members of the Duma (q.v.), a Petrograd soviet (council) of Workers' Deputies was established. The majority of its members were either Mensheviks (q.v.) or Socialist Revolutionaries (q.v.). Its first act was to issue Order Number One, which was proclaimed to all members of the garrison in the capital. This order removed all Petrograd troops from the jurisdiction of the high command of the armed forces and placed them directly under the control of the Petrograd soviet.

At the same time that the Petrograd soviet was being formed, the leadership of the liberal parties organized a temporary committee for the reestablishment of order in the capital under the chairmanship of Rodzianko (q.v.), the president of the Duma. During the next few days the tsar's plan to crush the uprising by force failed, and the head of the general staff, General Alekseev (q.v.), convinced the tsar to attempt a political solution. When, after lengthy hesitations, Tsar Nicholas II (q.v.) agreed, his concessions proved to be too late to restore order. Hoping to save the Romanov dynasty (q.v.) as a constitutional monarchy, Rodzianko convinced the tsar to abdicate, which Nicholas did in favor of his brother, Grand Duke Mikhail Romanov. The provisional committee of the Duma, supported by the executive committee of the Petrograd soviet, formed a Provisional government (q.v.) that consisted primarily of members of the Kadets (q.v.) and of the Oktiabrist (q.v.) parties. It was headed by Prince Lvov (q.v.), the president of the all-Russian Committee of the Zemskii Unions. This arrangement resulted in the creation of two parallel centers of state power: the Petrograd soviet, which reflected the interest of workers and soldiers, and the Provisional government, which represented the interests of the wealthier minority of the population.

After the victory of the revolution in Petrograd, Moscow (q.v.) and other cities began to organize their own soviets, as well as to elect local government bodies. It soon became clear, however, that the overthrow of the autocracy and the realization of political freedoms did not suffice to resolve the major questions facing Russia: unemployment, rising prices, speculation, and ending the war. The agrarian question, which was especially pressing, was left until after the convocation of the Constituent Assembly (q.v.), as was the issue of war or peace. This led to growing political instability, which was exacerbated by the existing duality of power. After the euphoria created by the fall of the autocracy in February 1917 and the acquisition by Russian society of democratic freedoms was over, almost all of the layers of the population remained dissatisfied with their situation. The peasants were unhappy because a large part of the arable land remained in the hands of the landlords. The urban workers were dissatisfied because of the continuing disarray in the factories, growing unemployment, and the constant rise of consumer goods prices. With the seemingly endless war continuing, the peasant soldiers began to desert from the trenches and return to their villages. Representatives of the old liberal intelligentsia were troubled by the influx of individuals into the government who appeared motivated more by self-interest than by the desire to solve Russia's problems. Separatism began to grow in the outlying areas of the empire.

The first governmental crisis that occurred after the revolution was produced by Foreign Minister Miliukov's (q.v.) announcement that assured Russia's allies that Russia would continue waging war until a decisive victory over the Central Powers was achieved. Reacting to this declaration, part of the capital's garrison, influenced by the agitation of Lenin's (q.v.) followers, came out in protest. They were supported by the majority of the city's workers, with over 100,000 people demonstrating in the streets and many calling for the transfer of all power to the Petrograd soviet. Supporters of the Provisional government organized a counterdemonstration, and street fighting occurred. In order to stop the disorders, a coalition of political forces from the Kadets on the right to the Socialist Revolutionaries and the Mensheviks on the left, came together. The Bolsheviks, however, refused to participate.

In May 1917, the first coalition of the Provisional government was created. Of the total of 16 ministers, seven were representatives of the moderate socialist parties, and Prince Lvov remained prime minister. This government published a program that proposed the further democratization of the army and the country and preparations for radical land reform and peace negotiations. On June 3 the first All-Russian Congress of Soviets took place. The majority of the delegates of the congress supported the Mensheviks and the Socialist Revolutionaries. The government relied on the success of a planned offensive by General Brusilov (q.v.), hoping that this would enable it to stop the growth of the disintegration that was occurring in the ranks of the army at the front. However, the attack failed. In July a second coalition government of the Provisional government was formed, with the socialist Kerensky (q.v.) becoming prime minister.

However, his policy of moving from left to right created a great deal of dissatisfaction among all the segments of the population, and the strength of Lenin's followers continued to grow. Kerensky tried to find some common ground with the conservative forces led by General Kornilov (q.v.), but the general attempted to take power by force and failed, because of joint efforts of the Provisional government and the Bolsheviks. This signified the final defeat of the right-wing military groups to stop Russia's drift to anarchy, but it also strengthened the position of the Bolsheviks, who soon captured leadership in the Petrograd soviet. The soldiers and workers of Petrograd became increasingly radicalized.

At the same time, the efforts of the Mensheviks and of the other moderate socialist elements to cooperate with the middle-class parties failed to produce any significant results. This led Lenin to demand from his central committee approval for a forcible overthrow of the Provisional government and the transfer of all power to the soviets.

In September Prime Minister Kerensky formed a third coalition government, at the same time that the Bolshevik leader Trotsky (q.v.) was elected chairman of the executive committee of the Petrograd soviet. Under his leadership the Bolsheviks proceeded to carry out an energetic propaganda campaign against the government, and Lenin finally succeeded in obtaining authorization from his central committee to prepare for an armed uprising.

By October 1917 the Provisional government no longer commanded the support of any significant sections of the Russian population and rapidly collapsed. On the night of the opening of the Second Congress of the Petrograd soviet on October 25, 1917 (old style), and November 7, (new style), the Winter Palace (q.v.), where the Provisional government was in session, was captured by armed detachments of Bolsheviks, and the ministers were arrested. Next day, the Soviet congress issued the Decree on Land and on Peace, and formed the Council of People's Commissars (q.v.) under Lenin's chairmanship. Initially supported by the Left-Socialist Revolutionary Party (q.v.) and by the Anarchists (q.v.), the coup soon resulted in a one-party rule by the Communist Party under the chairmanship of Lenin.

REVOLUTIONARY MILITARY COUNCIL (REVVOENSOVET). This collegium of political and military leaders and personnel was established in 1918 to provide political leadership and to expand and develop the newly structured armed forces. It was presided over by the people's commissar for military and naval affairs. It was replaced in 1934 by the commissariat of defense.

RIASAKOV, NIKOLAI I. (1861–81). A member of the terrorist group that carried out the assassination of Tsar Alexander II (q.v.), he was tried and hanged, together with his fellow conspirators.

RIAZAN. Located on the banks of the Oka River (q.v.) some 130 miles southeast of Moscow (q.v.), this industrial city produces refined oil and metal engineering products. Its population is just short of 500,000.

RIAZANOV, DAVID B. (b. GOLDENBAKH) (1870–1938). Riazanov first became an active revolutionary in 1887 in Odessa (q.v.), then moved to St. Petersburg (q.v.), where he joined the Mensheviks (q.v.) in 1903 and began editing the collective works of Marx and Engels. After the October 1917 revolution (q.v.) Riazanov went over to the Bolsheviks. In 1921 he was made director of the Marx-Engels Institute in Moscow (q.v.). Riazanov was expelled from the Communist Party (q.v.) in 1931 and sentenced to internal exile. In 1937 he was rearrested and shot after the murder of his protector, Kirov, the Communist Party boss of Leningrad.

RICHTER, SVIATOSLAV T. (1915–1997). Born into a musical Jewish family, he was a member of the Odessa ballet theater between 1933 and 1937, then a student at the Moscow (q.v.) Conservatory, until 1947. Richter began giving piano concerts abroad after 1950.

RIGHT OPPOSITION. This was an influential group of top Communist leaders in the late 1920s and early 1930s that opposed Stalin's (q.v.) policy of forced agricultural collectivization. It was headed by Bukharin (q.v.), Rykov (q.v.), and Tomskii (q.v.). Its members were expelled from the Communist Party (q.v.) in the 1930s and arrested.

Most of them were condemned either to death or to long terms in concentration camps.

RIMSKII-KORSAKOV, NIKOLAI A. (1844–1908). He was a leading member of the group of 19th-century Russian nationalist composers. Besides teaching composition and instrumentation at the St. Petersburg (q.v.) Conservatory, he was the author of numerous operas, instrumental works, and chamber music.

RIURIK (d. 879). He was the legendary first Varangian (q.v.) ruler of the eastern Slavic tribes and, together with his two brothers, Truvor and Sineus, founder of the dynasty that dominated these tribes until the death of Ivan the Terrible's (q.v.) son Feodor I (q.v.) in 1598.

RODZIANKO, MIKHAIL V. (1859–1924). He was educated at the Pages Cadet Corps and served in the cavalier guards. A leader of the Oktiabrist Party (q.v.) and member of the State Council from 1906 to 1907, he played a major role in Russian politics. He was president of the Duma (q.v.) between 1911 and 1917, then head of the Duma provisional committee during the initial period of the February 1917 revolution (q.v.). During the civil war (q.v.) he was with the White Armies (q.v.) of General Denikin (q.v.). Rodzianko died in Yugoslavia.

ROERIKH, NIKOLAI K. (1874–1947). A graduate of the University of St. Petersburg (*see* Universities) and the Academy of Fine Arts (q.v.), Roerikh first worked as an archaeologist, then began painting, producing a large body of work in a short period of time. Between 1920 and 1923 he toured the United States, where he exerted a strong influence on the Society of Anthroposophists. Roerikh was greatly admired for the mystical content of his art, and after 1928 he lived in the Himalayan Mountains, where he founded the Institute of Himalayan Research. In later life he returned to Russia at the personal invitation of Khrushchev (q.v.).

ROKOSSOVSKII, KONSTANTIN K. (1896–1968). Of Polish extraction, Rokossovskii served as a sergeant in the Russian army during World War I (q.v.). He joined the Red Army (*see* Armed Forces, Soviet) in 1918 and served as a cavalry commander, joining the Communist Party (q.v.) in 1919. After the civil war (q.v.), Rokossovskii graduated from the Frunze Military Academy. He was arrested and imprisoned during the purges (q.v.) of the 1930s but was released at the beginning of World War II (q.v.) and became one of the most competent commanders of the Soviet Army and a marshal of the Soviet Union. After World War II Stalin (q.v.) made him the Polish minister of defense.

ROMA. There are approximately 100,000 Roma, or Gypsies, in Russia. Originally from the south, in particular Ukraine (q.v.) and Moldova (q.v.) (the Ukrainian, or southern, dialect of the Roma is more common than the northern dialect), they are now concentrated in and around large cities such as Moscow (q.v.).

ROMANOV, BORIS G. (1891–1956). After graduating from the St. Petersburg Theater School in 1909, he joined the Mariinskii Theater (q.v.), then choreographed ballets for the Liteinii theater. After the 1917 revolution he continued working in Soviet theaters until 1926, when he emigrated to Western Europe. Romanov worked as a choreographer for the Pavlova Company from 1928 to 1934, as well as for ballet companies in Buenos Aires, Paris, Monte Carlo, Belgrade and Rome. Between 1938 and 1950 he was a choreographer at the Metropolitan Opera in New York.

ROMANOV, GRAND DUKE ALEXANDER "SANDRO" (1866–1933). He was married to Grand Duchess Xenia, sister of Tsar Nicholas II (q.v.), and was the father-in-law of Prince Yusupov (q.v.). Grand Duke Alexander emigrated after the civil war (q.v.) and in 1932 wrote his memoirs, which provide important material on the Romanov family.

ROMANOV, TSAR MICHAEL (1596–1645). He ascended to the throne of Russia in 1613 after being selected by a Zemskii Sobor (q.v.). Tsar Michael restored the authority of the throne and achieved peace in the country after the turmoil of the Time of Troubles (q.v.). He also expelled invading Swedish and Polish armies from Russia.

ROMANOV DYNASTY. The Romanov dynasty ascended the Russian throne in 1613 when young Michael Romanov (q.v.) was selected to be the new tsar by a Zemskii Sobor (q.v.). The family ruled Russia and its empire until the February 1917 revolution (q.v.), frequently intermarrying with members of the German royalty. Its last ruler was Tsar Nicholas II (q.v.), who was assassinated by the Bolsheviks (q.v.) in 1918. Its members who ruled Russia were:

1613	Michael
1645	Aleksei
1676	Feodor
1682	Ivan and Peter I
1689	Peter the Great

1725	Catherine I
1727	Peter II
1730	Anna
1740	Ivan VI
1741	Elizabeth
1762	Peter III
1762	Catherine the Great
1796	Paul I
1801	Alexander I
1825	Nicholas I
1855	Alexander II
1881	Alexander III
1894	Nicholas II

ROMANOVA, ALEXANDRA, EMPRESS (b. ALIX VICTORIA OF HESSE-DARMSTADT) (1872–1918). Born in Germany, she was the granddaughter of Queen Victoria and became the wife of Tsar Nicholas II (q.v.) and Empress of Russia. As empress she was unpopular with the court and became withdrawn and preoccupied with mysticism. Concerned for the health of her hemophiliac son, she fell under the spell of Rasputin (q.v.), a peasant faith healer. Stronger in character than her husband the tsar, she played a major role in Russian state affairs by being able to influence his decisions both as to policy and concerning the individuals he appointed to the highest government positions. After the beginning of World War I (q.v.) she was additionally disliked because of her German origin. Empress Alexandra is frequently blamed for the fall of the Romanov dynasty (q.v.). In the summer of 1918 she was shot by the Bolsheviks (q.v.), along with the rest of her immediate family and several retainers, in Ekaterinburg (q.v.).

ROMANOVA, MARIA EMPRESS (b. PRINCESS DAGMAR OF DENMARK) (1847–1928). Wife of Alexander III (q.v.) and mother of Tsar Nicholas II (q.v.), during the 1917 revolution she was evacuated from the Crimea (q.v.) by a British naval vessel and returned to live in Denmark, where she died.

ROSTOV-NA-DONU. Established in 1749 close to the Sea of Azov (q.v.), this city is an important trade and transportation center for the whole of southern Russia. Its industries include agricultural and railway engineering, textile and chemical works, and shipbuilding. Rostov's population is just over 1,000,000.

ROSTOVTSEV, MIKHAIL I. (1870–1952). He studied at the Kiev (q.v.) and the St. Petersburg (q.v.) universities (*see* Universities), then became professor at the latter from 1901 to 1918. Rostovtsev was a great authority on the history of the classical world and antiquity. In 1920 he accepted a professorship of history at the University of Wisconsin, then in 1925 moved to Yale, where he remained until 1944.

ROSTROPOVICH, MSTISLAV (1927-   ). A noted cellist, he studied at the Moscow Conservatory of Music and went on to perform both in the Soviet Union and abroad. His association with Aleksandr Solzhenitsyn (q.v.) resulted in political difficulties, ultimately causing him to leave the country in 1978. He received an honorary knighthood in 1987.

RUBAKHIN, NIKOLAI A. (1892-1946). Born into a rich merchant family, he graduated from the University of St. Petersburg (q.v.) and early on became involved in revolutionary activity. He emigrated to Switzerland in 1907, and, although he sympathized with the Soviet Union, he never returned there. Rubakhin gained fame for his great library collection and for the system of adult education through books that he developed, which was highly respected by Krupskaia (q.v.), the head of Soviet libraries after the revolution.

RUBINSTEIN, ANTON G. (1829-94). Brother of the founder of the St. Petersburg (q.v.) Conservatory, he was an instructor there. A concert pianist, he was also the author of numerous operas, symphonic works and chamber music.

RUBLE. This unit of Russian currency is like the dollar or the pound sterling. First issued under Peter the Great (q.v.), it is still the name of the basic unit of Russian currency today.

RUBLEV, ANDREI (1360-1430). A famed painter of icons (q.v.), he was born in Vladimir (q.v.), then moved to Moscow (q.v.). Most of his work was executed in the Byzantine style, which he adapted from Greek icons that were brought to Russia from Constantinople in 1422. He was famed for his work in enamel.

RUDZUTAK, JAN E. (1887-1938). A St. Petersburg (q.v.) worker turned Bolshevik (q.v.), he was a close collaborator of Tomskii (q.v.), the head of the Soviet trade unions, but remained loyal to Stalin (q.v.). In 1926 he replaced Zinovev (q.v.) in the Politburo (q.v.) after the latter was defeated in an intraparty struggle at the 14th party congress. Rudzutak was nevertheless accused of treason during the purges (q.v.) of the 1930s, tortured to obtain a confession, which he refused to give, and executed in 1938.

RUMIANTSEV, COUNT PETR A. (1725–96). He served as army commander during the Seven Years' War (q.v.) and the Russo-Turkish war (q.v.) of 1768–74. Rumiantsev then became the governor-general of the Ukraine (q.v.) under Catherine II (q.v.) and was elevated to the rank of field marshal. A famous book collector, his library formed the basis for the Lenin State (now Russian State) Library (q.v.) after the 1917 revolution.

RURIK see RIURIK

RUS. This is the name of the Slavic peoples who occupied the eastern European steppe and forest lands at the end of the first millennium A.D. By derivation, their land, with its principal city Kiev (q.v.), was known as Rus.

RUSSIAN ACADEMY OF ARTS. During the Soviet period it was called Academy of Arts of the USSR. The academy was founded in 1757 and included departments of painting, graphic arts, decorative arts and sculpture.

RUSSIAN ACADEMY OF SCIENCES see ACADEMY OF SCIENCES

RUSSIAN AMERICAN COMPANY (ROSSIISKO-AMERIKAN-SKAIA KOMPANIIA). This Russian company was formed in 1799 to explore Alaska, then known as Russian America. When the territory was sold to the United States in 1868, the company was dissolved.

RUSSIAN ASSOCIATION OF PROLETARIAN WRITERS (RAPP). Founded in 1925, this group of writers was led by Averbakh (q.v.) and Fadeev (q.v.). It claimed to represent the ideology of the proletarian artists, although few if any of its members came from that class of the population. Between 1929 and 1932 it exercised dictatorial powers over Soviet literature, but thereafter it was severely criticized in official party pronouncements and was forcibly integrated into the government-sponsored Union of Soviet Writers (q.v.).

RUSSIAN COMMUNIST PARTY (BOLSHEVIKS) see COMMUNIST PARTY OF THE SOVIET UNION

RUSSIAN FEDERATED REPUBLIC. After the 1917 revolution the Russian empire became known as the Russian Soviet Federated Socialist Republic, (RSFSR) (q.v.). It was the largest and most populous of the 15 union republics that constituted the Soviet Union at the time of its collapse in 1991. After that date it became officially known as the Russian Federated Republic.

Its population is just under 150 million, and its territory constitutes over 70 percent of the former USSR, being some 6,592,812 square miles in size. It produces approximately 70 percent of the total agricultural and industrial output of the former Soviet Union. Its climates range from that of the northern Arctic to subtropical areas in the northern Caucasus Mountains (q.v.). The land is covered by enormous forests, vast steppes and extensive cultivated areas producing a large variety of produce. It is traversed by many rivers that flow generally south to north or north to south. The Russian Republic is bounded on the north by the Arctic Ocean, in the east by the Pacific Ocean, and in the south by the Gobi and other deserts of central Asia, as well as by the Caspian (q.v.) and the Black (q.v.) seas. In the west it borders on the republics of Ukraine (q.v.), Belarus (q.v.), Finland (q.v.) and the Baltic States. It includes 16 autonomous republics, six autonomous krais, and 49 autonomous regions. *See also* ADMINISTRATIVE AND TERRITORIAL DIVISIONS OF THE RUSSIAN FEDERATION.

RUSSIAN LIBERATION ARMY (RUSSKAIA OSVOBODITELNAIA ARMIIA; ROA). This anti-Communist army was established in 1945 in Prague by general and Communist Party member Andrei Vlasov (1900–46), who had been in German captivity since 1942. Its purpose was to liberate Russia from Communism, and it numbered roughly two divisions, composed of Russian prisoners of war, slave laborers and collaborators from German-occupied Soviet zones. It lacked any cohesive ideology and saw little action. Vlasov was captured by the Americans in 1945 and handed over to the Soviets, who shot him and many others.

RUSSIAN MEDIEVAL GOVERNMENT STRUCTURE. The Russian monarchy of the 16th and 17th centuries was based on class. The head of state was the tsar, and below him the rest of the population was divided into social layers whose rights and obligations were defined by law. The class that served the tsar directly was the *dvoriane* (q.v.). It formed the foundation on which the monarch's power rested. This class received land from the tsars for its own use in exchange for providing soldiers in case of war and for participating in civil administration and tax collection. It was also given control over the peasants who lived on the land. These peasants were obligated by law to provide their landlords with labor and military service in exchange for being allowed to cultivate the plots set aside for their use. As early as the 11th and 12th centuries, this upper layer of the tsar's servants began to form itself into a separate social class. By the beginning of the 18th century, it had obtained hereditary ownership of the land that it had previously held only in exchange for service to the state. At the opposite pole was the vast majority of the population—the peasantry. By the middle of the 17th century the peasants had become permanently attached to the land on which they lived and were forbidden by law to leave it—they had become serfs. The craftsmen and the traders who inhabited the urban centers were collectively known as the *posadskie liudi*, or city (*posad*) dwellers. They were unified into communes and were subject to a collective tax obligation, as well as to compulsory performance of specified services.

Another medieval Russian institution was the Zemskii Sobor (q.v.), which was analogous to the West European parliaments, but had fewer powers. It was called together by the tsar (q.v.) only in extraordinary circumstances, when support of the whole population was required. The decisions of these gatherings were not obligatory on the tsar.

The medieval Russian elite was represented in the *boiar* Duma (q.v.), a consultative institution that was subordinate to the tsar. It was responsible for foreign and internal policy, as well as for control over administrative and judicial institutions. In order to weaken this organ of the feudal nobility, the tsars co-opted representatives of the lower-placed members of the ruling class as well as members of the higher service bureaucracy into it, and eventually its role receded until, by the time of Peter the Great (q.v.), it had stopped meeting altogether.

The state administrative structure in medieval and early modern Russia consisted of *prikazy* or departments, of which there were over 40. The most important of these were the land department, the civil service department, the ambassadorial department, and the secret service department.

RUSSIAN ORTHODOX CHURCH see ORTHODOX CHURCH

RUSSIAN REVOLUTIONS. The two successive revolutions that occurred in February and October 1917 (old style) were events long awaited by the radical intelligentsia of the Russian empire and were preceded by a relatively minor revolution of 1905 (q.v.). The two revolutions of 1917 resulted first in the downfall of the Romanov dynasty (q.v.) in February and in the collapse of the democratic Provisional government (q.v.) in October 1917. After their successful coup in Petrograd (q.v.), the Bolsheviks (q.v.) under Lenin (q.v.) and Trotsky (q.v.) consolidated their rule over the rest of the former tsar's empire during a bitter and prolonged civil war (q.v.). *See also* REVOLUTION OF 1905; REVOLUTION OF FEBRUARY 1917.

RUSSIAN SOCIALIST DEMOCRATIC LABOR PARTY. This Marxist party consisted of intellectuals and trade unionists who differed from the populists in concentrating on industrial labor rather than on the peasantry and agricultural questions. The party was founded in 1898 and split into two factions at its second congress in 1903: the Bolshevik (q.v.) faction and the Mensheviks (q.v.). The latter continued to be called the Russian Socialist Democratic Labor Party, but the Bolsheviks disassociated themselves from the name in 1919.

RUSSIAN SOVIET FEDERATED SOCIALIST REPUBLIC (1917–91). The largest of the former Soviet republics, it had an area of 6,693,400 square miles and a population of 140 million. In addition to European Russia, it contained 16 autonomous republics and numerous lesser administrative units. It differed from other union republics in not having its own Communist Party, since, as with many other offices and bodies, the Communist Party of the Soviet Union (q.v.) was also that of the Russian Republic. It was created soon after the October Revolution (q.v.) and became part of the Soviet Union in 1922. At the conclusion of World War II (q.v.), it acquired the Pechenga region from Finland, part of East Prussia, Southern Sakhalin and the Kurile Islands.

The territory of the Russian Soviet Federated Socialist Republic was administratively divided according to ethnic and nationality principles. Each major national group within the Russian Republic had its own autonomous republic. These autonomous republics have remained essentially unchanged since the collapse of the Soviet Union. They were the largest territorial administrative units that existed in Russia during the Soviet period and were designed to provide a measure of local self-rule to ethnic groups large enough to warrant such a designation. Each such autonomous republic had its own constitution, supreme soviet, and representation in the Supreme Soviet (q.v.) of the USSR.

At the time of the abolition of the Soviet Union there were 15 such republics in Russia. Each of these republics was in turn divided into smaller territorial subdivisions: oblast, or region, and *raion*, or district. The term *krai* is equivalent to oblast, the distinction being purely a matter of historical usage. There are also a few *okrugs* within the Russian Republic, a term likewise equivalent to oblast, but reserved for areas that have an ethnic distinction from their surrounding populations. The autonomous *krai* is a district level division, the smallest of the territorial divisions in Russia that have a measure of autonomy from central authorities. It is a component part of an oblast. The autonomous oblast is larger than a *krai* and smaller than a republic. They were introduced under Soviet rule, designed to administer ethnic populations not large enough to warrant the establishment of an autonomous republic, and they were represented in the Council of Nationalities of the USSR.

RUSSIAN STATE LIBRARY (1925–1993: LENIN STATE LIBRARY; GOSUDARSTVENNAIA BIBLIOTEKA SSSR IM. V.I. LENINA; ALSO CALLED THE MOSCOW RUSSIAN STATE PUBLIC LIBRARY). Russia's foremost library, founded in 1862 by Count Nikolai Rumiantsev (1754–1826). Its holdings number over 30 million, with material in over 200 languages. Its Russian and Soviet holdings are virtually without lacunae; foreign holdings are concentrated in the sciences, though by no means exclusively.

RUSSKAIA OSVOBODITELNAIA ARMIIA see **RUSSIAN LIBERATION ARMY**

RUSSO-ASIATIC BANK. Established by the minister of finance Count Witte (q.v.) in 1895 to finance the Chinese Far Eastern Railroad (q.v.), the majority of the bank's shares were owned by French interests. It was the legal owner of the railroad built by Russia to run through Manchuria, from the station Manchuli in the west to Vladivostok (q.v.) in the east.

RUSSO-FINNISH WAR. This conflict raged in 1939–40 between the Soviet Union and Finland over demands made by Stalin (q.v.) for territorial concessions from the Finns. After the Finns were defeated in early 1940, they were forced to cede to the USSR a part of the Karelian Peninsula closest to Leningrad (*see* St. Petersburg), as well as a naval base on the Baltic Sea (q.v.).

RUSSO-GERMAN NONAGGRESSION PACT see **NAZI-SOVIET NONAGGRESSION PACT.**

RUSSO-JAPANESE WAR. The war arose out of the rivalry between the two great Pacific powers in 1904. The Japanese began the war with an unexpected attack on the Russian fleet at Port Arthur (q.v.), sinking much of it. There then followed massive Japanese landings in Manchuria, where the Russian armies were defeated, and the naval battle of Tsushima (q.v.), which resulted in the sinking of Russia's

Baltic squadron, and the capture of Port Arthur. The war was ended through mediation by Theodore Roosevelt and the signing of a peace treaty in Portsmouth, New Hampshire. This treaty gave the Japanese effective control over much of the southern Manchurian territory that had been occupied by Russia before the conflict. The city of Dairen and the military base of Port Arthur were also ceded to the Japanese, as were the southern part of Sakhalin Island (q.v.) and the southern branch of the Chinese Far Eastern Railroad (q.v.).

RUSSO-TURKISH WARS. A series of nine armed conflicts took place between Russia and Turkey, beginning with the first encounter in 1681 and ending with World War I (q.v.).

RUZSKII, NIKOLAI V. (1854–1918). A graduate of the Academy of the General Staff in 1881, he participated in the Russo-Turkish war (q.v.) and the Russo-Japanese war (q.v.). During World War I (q.v.) he was the commander of the northern front and one of the generals who had urged Tsar Nicholas II (q.v.) to abdicate. He was murdered by revolutionary soldiers in 1918.

RYBINSK. Located at the large reservoir fed by the Volga (q.v.), Mologa, Suda and Andoga rivers, some 170 miles northeast of Moscow, this city contains shipbuilding and other industrial plants and is also a trading center for agricultural products and timber. Its population is close to 250,000.

RYKOV, ALEKSEI I. (1881–1938). He joined the Russian Socialist Democratic Labor Party (q.v.) in 1899 and the Bolshevik (q.v.) faction after 1903. An emigre between 1910 and 1911, Rykov returned to Russia but was quickly arrested and exiled. After the October 1917 revolution (q.v.) he advocated a coalition government with other socialist parties, but this proposal was turned down by Lenin (q.v.). He served as chairman of the Supreme Council of National Economy (q.v.) and was also the chairman of the Council of People's Commissars (q.v.) after the death of Lenin. At first an ally of Stalin (q.v.) against Trotsky (q.v.), he later joined with Bukharin (q.v.) and Tomskii (q.v.) to oppose Stalin's agricultural policies. He was dismissed from all his posts in 1929. In 1938 he was arrested, put on trial during one of the show trials, forced to confess to numerous crimes, and executed.

RYLEEV, KONDRATII F. (1795–1826). Poet and editor, Ryleev was a leading participant in the Decembrist (q.v.) rebellion, for which he was arrested and executed.

RZHEV. An industrial city on the Volga River (q.v.), this town manufactures agricultural engineering products, as well as distilled spirits. Its population is just over 50,000.

S

SAGDEEV, ROALD Z. (1932–). A graduate of the University of Moscow (*see* Universities) in 1955, he joined the staff of the Institute of Atomic Energy in 1956 and became a member of the Institute of Nuclear Physics of the USSR Academy of Sciences (q.v.) in 1961. In 1968 Sagdeev was elected a member of the Institute of Cosmic Exploration and made its director in 1973. Sagdeev resigned as the head of Soviet space research in 1988.

STS. CYRIL AND METHODIUS (NINTH CENTURY). Two brothers from Thessaly who became missionaries in Moravia, they worked among the Slavs and translated scripture into Old Church Slavonic and are therefore revered for bringing Christianity to Russia. The alphabet that they developed for the purpose was based on Greek with a few additions from Syriac. It was modified in 1708 to became the modern Cyrillic alphabet used for Slavic languages of Orthodox nations. Its use was also widely extended to languages of the former Soviet Union, mainly those that had no alphabet.

ST. PETERSBURG. The capital of the Russian empire, it was built by Peter the Great (q.v.) in the first two decades of the 18th century. A highly industrialized and cultured city, St. Petersburg has always claimed preeminence as the most Western-oriented city of Russia. It was known as Petrograd from 1914 to 1924 and Leningrad from 1924 to 1991. Its population stands at over 5,000,000.

ST. SERGEI OF RADONEZH (1314–92). The patron saint of Russia, he gave his blessing to Dmitrii Donskoi before the victorious battle of Kulikovo (q.v.) against the Mongols. St. Sergius was the founder of the Troitsa-Sergeyeva monastery, a major center of the Orthodox Church (q.v.).

SAKHA AUTONOMOUS REPUBLIC. Located in eastern Siberia, it has an area of 1,188,300 square miles and a population of 839,000. Part of it is formed by the Lena River basin. The capital is Iakutsk (q.v.), a city of some 150,000. The Iakuts speak a Turkic language. There are important gold, diamond and coal deposits in the region; it was also the location of prison camps.

SAKHALIN ISLAND. A large island lying in the Okhotsk (q.v.) Sea, it was used under the tsars (q.v.) as a place of exile. Its southern half was ceded by Russia to Japan after the Russo-Japanese war (q.v.) but retaken by the Soviet Union after World War II (q.v.). The primary occupation of its settlers is fishing and agriculture.

SAKHAROV, ANDREI D. (1921–89). A graduate of the University of Moscow (*see* Universities) in 1942, he earned a doctorate of physical sciences degree in 1953, then worked at the Lebedev Institute of Physics. Sakharov played a major role in the development of the Soviet hydrogen bomb and was elected a member of the USSR Academy of Sciences (q.v.). In the late 1960s he began to write articles that were disapproved of by Soviet authorities, and in 1970 he joined the human rights movement. Sakharov was awarded the Nobel Prize for Peace in 1975 and soon thereafter was exiled by the Soviet government to Gorkii (*see* Nizhnii Novgorod). In 1986 he was recalled to Moscow (q.v.) by then president Gorbachev.

SALTYKOV-SHCHEDRIN see SHCHEDRIN

SAMARA (1935–1991: KUIBYSHEV). This administrative center of Samara oblast on the Volga River (q.v.) was founded in 1596. It has a population of 1,258,000 and is a center of industry and transportation linking the Urals to the Volga by rail. It produces transportation equipment, aircraft, industrial machinery, chemicals and textiles. The rebellion of Pugachev began here in 1774.

SAMARIN, IURII F. (1819–76). A literary figure and one of the leaders of the Slavophile (q.v.) movement of the 19th century, he strongly supported the emancipation of the serfs by Tsar Alexander II (q.v.), believing that the peasantry and their communal lifestyle represented the true essence of Russia.

SAMIZDAT (SELF-PUBLICATION). The illegal publishing of books and pamphlets, it occurred in the former Soviet Union after the end of the Thaw (q.v.), in the middle of the 1960s. After the onset of perestroika (q.v.), samizdat was no longer necessary and the practice stopped.

SAMOEDS see NENETS

SAMSONOV, ALEKSANDR V. (1859–1914). The commander of the Russian army that entered East Prussia in the early days of World

War I (q.v.), Samsonov was defeated by Field Marshal Hindenburg at
Tannenberg (q.v.) and committed suicide after the battle.

SARAI. This town on the Volga (q.v.) was founded in the 13th century
as the capital of the Golden Horde (q.v.) and destroyed in 1460 by
the Russians.

SARANSK. Established as a fort in the late 17th century, it is now the
capital of the Mordovian Autonomous Republic (q.v.). It processes
mainly agricultural products such as sugar beets and hemp and builds
agricultural machinery. Its population is just under 300,000.

SARATOV. A city of 856,000 situated on the lower Volga (q.v.), it was
founded in 1590 as a fortified river port. It is a center of industry, with
oil refineries and iron foundries as well as machine manufacturing. It
is also the point where Baku oil is delivered to the railway system.

SAVINKOV, BORIS V. (1879–1925). He joined the Socialist Revolutionaries (q.v.) party in 1903 and soon became one of the leaders of
its terrorist wing, participating in the assassination of the minister of
interior, Count Plehve (q.v.), and of the Grand Duke Sergei (q.v.),
governor of Moscow (q.v.). Captured and sentenced to death, he escaped to Western Europe, where he wrote several novels. During
World War I (q.v.) Savinkov served in the French army as a volunteer.
On returning to Russia in February 1917 he became a commissar of
the Provisional government (q.v.) at the Stavka (q.v.). He also served
as the deputy minister of defense under Kerensky (q.v.). After the
Bolsheviks (q.v.) seized power in October 1917 Savinkov attempted
to organize an anti-Bolshevik movement and headed the Russian political committee in Warsaw between 1920 and 1923. He was caught
entering Russia illegally, tried, and sentenced to a prison term, but
died in a Moscow prison under suspicious circumstances.

SAZONOV, SERGEI D. (1861–1927). He began service in the Russian
diplomatic corps in 1893 and rose to become first an ambassador and
then the minister of foreign affairs between 1910 and 1916. As head
of the foreign affairs department in the Denikin (q.v.) and Kolchak
(q.v.) governments, he represented anti-Communist Russia at the
Paris peace conference in 1919.

SCHISM see RASKOL

SCIENCE AND TECHNOLOGY. Before the 17th century in Russia
there was only a small trickle of scientific literature from Western

Europe, and the circle of readers of such literature was extremely limited. The situation began to change during the reign of Peter the Great (q.v.). In 1725 the St. Petersburg Academy of Science, later renamed the Russian Academy of Sciences (q.v.), was opened and unified both scientific and pedagogical functions.

A major role in the advancement of science in Russia was played by Lomonosov (q.v.), on whose initiative the University of Moscow (*see* Universities) was created in 1755. In 1845 the Russian Geographical Society was established, and expeditions by Russian scientists began to play a major role in the exploration of Antarctica, central Asia and Siberia (q.v.). Also, in the first half of the 19th century Russian historiography developed under the influence of Karamzin (q.v.), Sergei Solovev (q.v.) and Granovskii (q.v.). However, Russian science and mathematics continued to lag behind the Western European level, even though there were individual achievements such as the non-Euclidian geometry of Lobachevskii (q.v.).

By the second half of the 19th century this situation had changed, and Russian natural scientists began to receive worldwide recognition. In 1869 Mendeleev (q.v.) discovered the periodical tables of elements, while other scientists investigated the activity of the higher nervous system and established a physiological institute out of which emerged the Pavlov (q.v.) science of reflexology. Pavlov was the first Russian scientist to receive the Nobel Prize. Physicists such as Lebedev demonstrated the push of light.

In the area of philosophy there emerged such important thinkers as Vladimir Solovev (q.v.), Berdiaev (q.v.), and Bulgakov (q.v.). The latter stressed the primacy of spiritual to material values. An important addition to economic science was made by Kondratiev (q.v.), who elaborated the theory of "long cycles."

During the Soviet period, science, as other spheres of life, was heavily influenced by Communist Party (q.v.) ideologists and by government bureaucrats. Especially hard hit were the social sciences: history, philosophy, and political economy. Party leaders actively participated in "learned" discussions, where they laid down mandates as to what was permissible and what was not in an area of scholarship about which they knew very little. For example, Stalin (q.v.) issued a long declaration concerning the science of linguistics that immediately became the only acceptable dogma for Soviet linguists.

The Communist Party also frequently interfered in the natural sciences. In the 1940s a total destruction of Russian genetics took place, with leading geneticists being arrested for supposedly teaching "bourgeois genetics." This was done on the initiative of an agronomist, Lysenko (q.v.), who claimed to have discovered a "Marxist" science of genetics.

At the same time, during the Soviet period there were areas of science—primarily physical sciences closely related to military technology—in which very substantial progress was made. These areas received large financial and organizational support from the government. The Central Hydrodynamic Institute was established, as was the Physical-Technical Institute. The work of Semenov (q.v.) on the kinetics of chain reactions received the Nobel Prize. In the 1930s, colleagues of this institute began active investigations into atomic physics. Their results made possible the creation of an atomic bomb in the USSR in 1949.

In 1934 an Institute of Physical Problems was established with the close assistance of Kapitsa (q.v.), who in 1938 made discoveries in the physics of liquid helium. The theoretical physicist Landau worked at that institute and in 1962 received the Nobel Prize for developing the theory of liquid helium. Investigations carried out by Geldysh and others helped the Soviet Union to be the first country to develop the space technology necessary for orbital flight. Other Soviet scientists contributed extensively to the creation of laser technology. Between 1950 and 1970 the expenditures on scientific research grew by 12 times, and a large scientific center was created in Siberia (q.v.)—the Siberian Division of the Academy of Sciences in Akademgorod, near Irkutsk (q.v.).

However, as a consequence of the rapid growth in the number of individuals entering the field, a large number of less-than-competent persons were admitted into Soviet scientific institutions. Such individuals were better at promoting themselves than in performing scientific work. As well, the Academy of Sciences of the USSR (q.v.) gradually transformed itself into a vast and often inefficient bureaucracy.

In the post-Soviet era government expenditures on science have dropped sharply, and many of the best Russian scientists have left the country or have changed their occupations.

SCISSORS CRISIS. This is the name that Trotsky (q.v.) popularized in order to describe the economic crisis that took place between 1923 and 1925 in the Soviet economy, when industrial prices were rising while agricultural prices were falling. This phenomenon resulted in a substantial drop in the income of the Russian peasantry and contributed to its reluctance to sell its produce to the state for artificially low fixed prices.

SCRIABIN, ALEKSANDR N. (1872–1915). He entered the Moscow Conservatory in 1888. After graduation he taught there until 1903, while gradually becoming immersed in mysticism. Scriabin attempted, with uncertain success, to translate his theosophical ideas into music. Initially intrigued by the work of Chopin, he created tone poems in which he experimented with harmony, even inventing a special chord of superposed fourths; notable among his works is "A Poem of Fire/Prometheus" (1913), which calls for a modest light show. A friend of the Pasternak family, he encouraged the young Boris Pasternak (q.v.) in his musical studies.

SCYTHIANS. This is a general name used by the ancients to mean certain nomadic peoples of the Black Sea (q.v.) coast; they spoke an apparently Iranian language and came to be identified with the Sarmatians and Alans. The height of their influence was in the second century B.C., when they controlled part of the Crimea. Examples of their art, in the form of metalwork, are found in burial mounds. As the word "Scythian" was loosely associated in the ancient mind with barbarism, so the term has been used in this sense in some Russian poetry.

SEBASTOPOL. A city of 301,000 in the Crimea, it was founded in 1783. The natural harbor makes it an excellent port and naval base on the Black Sea (q.v.). There is also a rail terminal linking it to central Russia. The siege of Sebastopol in 1855 during the Crimean War (q.v.) laid waste much of the town. It was also largely destroyed during World War II (q.v.).

SECRETARY GENERAL OF THE CENTRAL COMMITTEE OF THE COMMUNIST PARTY OF THE SOVIET UNION. During the existence of the Soviet Union, the Central Committee of the Communist Party (q.v.) was an organization of enormous power. Each one of its ten secretaries was in charge of a separate department. These departments controlled the totality of all public activities of the country. In 1921, at Lenin's suggestion, Stalin (q.v.) was nominated as secretary general. Soon thereafter Stalin began to accumulate enormous power through his ability to appoint individuals to party posts. By the end of the 1920s this power enabled Stalin to acquire dictatorial control of the Communist Party (q.v.), a power he continued to hold until his death in 1953. After him there followed a succession of secretary generals: Malenkov (q.v.), Khrushchev (q.v.), Brezhnev (q.v.), Andropov (q.v.), Chernenko (q.v.) and, finally, Gorbachev (q.v.).

SECURITY SERVICES, IMPERIAL. The department for the security of order—Okhrana (q.v.)—was established in 1866 with sections in

St. Petersburg (q.v.), Moscow (q.v.), and in Warsaw in 1880. It replaced the Third Section of gendarmes that had been established by Nicholas I (q.v.). In 1903 these departments were consolidated and renamed the security department. Regional security departments worked in close contact with local administrations of the gendarmerie. Their principal tasks were to seek out individual revolutionaries and to expose revolutionary organizations, while the gendarmerie was responsible for implementing the arrests on the basis of materials the security organizations obtained. Security departments were authorized to employ special agents who were instructed to infiltrate the revolutionary groups and to report on their activities and their membership. They usually worked either as passive informers or as agents provocateurs. The security service was divided into several subgroups, each carrying out a specific function, among which was that of conducting censorship of all publications produced in Russia as well as administering the censorship of all mail coming into the country.

The Moscow security department was the principal investigative unit for the whole country. It was headed by Zubatov (q.v.), an official who considered it essential to fight against socialist agitation among the workers by helping to making improvements in their living conditions. Zubatov made an effort to organize workers into trade unions that he was able to control. In this tactic he was supported by Plehve (q.v.), the minister of the interior. In May 1901 Zubatov created an organization called the Society for Workers' Mutual Aid. In the next two years a number of such organizations arose in several Russian cities and began to mount militant strikes, which often expanded from purely economic actions into political ones. This fact led the government to abandon Zubatov's tactic, liquidate his organizations, and retire Zubatov himself. Between 1906 and 1910 more than 26,000 individuals were apprehended by the Okhrana and sentenced to penal servitude. After the February 1917 revolution (q.v.) the security organization was liquidated.

SECURITY SERVICES, SOVIET (1934–40). In 1934 the Soviet security police were incorporated into the People's Commissariat of Internal Affairs, the NKVD (q.v.). Despite hopes for a softening of the role of the secret police, its influence only increased in the Soviet Union. The murder of Kirov (q.v.) in 1934 signaled the beginning of a new period of political repression. It served as the pretext for Stalin (q.v.) to crush his opponents in the Communist Party (q.v.) by enabling him to accuse them of complicity in the murder. A government decree issued shortly after the murder instructed the NKVD to conclude all investigations of political terrorism in no more than ten days.

Such investigations were to be held behind closed doors and without the presence of either the accused or his defense lawyer. Former leaders of the Communist Party who had at one time opposed Stalin, such as Zinovev (q.v.) and Kamenev (q.v.), were accused of involvement in Kirov's assassination, and a massive media campaign was initiated against them. In January 1935 they were condemned to jail terms. Then, a few months later, they were once again accused of political crimes and, this time, of direct complicity in the murder of Kirov as well as of organizing a "United Trotsky-Zinovev Terrorist Center" that was supposedly planning the murder of Stalin and other Communist leaders. Between 1935 and 1938 three major show trials (q.v.) were mounted on evidence provided by the security police. In these trials former high-ranking Communists were placed in the dock and confessed to all charges against them. These confessions had been extorted from them by NKVD operatives, who obtained them by means of political blackmail and threats against their families. The majority of those so accused were sentenced to death and executed.

In September 1936 Iagoda (q.v.), until then the head of the NKVD, was replaced by Ezhov (q.v.), and soon thereafter he, along with the whole of the former secret police leadership, was arrested and executed. After this the investigative personnel of the NKVD were authorized to use all means to extract confessions from the accused, including physical torture. At the same time the media whipped up massive campaigns against foreign spies disguised as Communists, and against individuals who had allegedly attempted to undermine Soviet indusrial growth by sabotage, the so-called wreckers.

In May 1937 almost the whole of the top leadership of the Red Army, including three of its five marshals—Tukhachevsi (q.v.), Iakir (q.v.) and Uborevich (q.v.)—were arrested and executed for treason, along with thousands of generals, colonels and other officers. In March 1938, former leaders of the right-wing opposition (q.v.) to Stalin, such as Bukharin (q.v.), Tomskii (q.v.), and Rykov (q.v.), were also tried for treason. Tomskii succeeded in committing suicide, as did another intended victim, Ordzhonikidze (q.v.), but the others were forced to testify against themselves in open court. All of the accused were executed or sent to labor camps where they died.

This period of 1937–38 is known as the *Ezhovshchina*, after the then head of the NKVD, Ezhov. Terror, lack of trust even among members of one's own family, and mass hysteria swept the country. In September 1938 the commissar of the interior, Ezhov, was himself arrested and replaced by Beria (q.v.), a police chief from Transcaucasia (q.v.). Shortly thereafter the scope of the purges abated somewhat and efforts were made to place the blame for the excesses of the past three years on Ezhov alone.

By the end of the 1930s the commissariat of the interior had acquired authority over all of the concentration camps in the USSR. These camps—the Gulag (q.v.)—held hundreds of thousands of political prisoners and were a gigantic economic and industrial empire in their own right. Using its enormous pool of unpaid prison labor, the commissariat carried out the country's large construction projects, such as building dams and canals and mining for gold and other metals. It also operated the vast timber works using this supply of slave laborers. (See also CHEKA, GPU, NKVD, and KGB.)

SEDOV, LEON (1906–38). The eldest son of Trotsky (q.v.), he was exiled together with his father from the Soviet Union in 1929 and became an active member of the political organization that Trotsky built abroad. In 1938 he died under suspicious circumstances in a Paris hospital.

SELENGA. This river begins in the Khangay Mountains in the Mongolian People's Republic (q.v.) and flows northeast through the Buryatia Autonomous Republic (q.v.) into Lake Baikal (q.v.).

SEMENOV, GRIGORII (1890–1946). A Cossack officer in the Transbaikal Army, he became leader of the east Siberian Cossacks (q.v.) fighting for the White cause during the civil war (q.v.). Semenov both supported and hindered Admiral Kolchak (q.v.), and was criticized for excesses in the field and his narrowness of vision. He had obscure pan-Mongolian ideals, being himself Buriat on his mother's side, as well as having close ties with Japan. In 1921 he left Russia to spend several years in troubled exile. He lived in Manchuria until his arrest there by the NKVD at the end of World War II (q.v.). He was shot in Moscow the following year.

SERAPION BROTHERS. A group of writers in the 1920s, among them were Boris Pilniak (q.v.), Evgenii Zamiatin (q.v.), Iurii Olesha (q.v.) and others who believed that writing need not be dependent on politics or ideological requirements. While not opposed to the Soviet regime, their lack of consonance with party ideals exposed them to censure and persecution. They were eventually absorbed into the Union of Soviet Writers (q.v.).

SERFS. Until the reforms of Alexander II (q.v.), about half of Russian peasants were serfs, belonging to private landlords. Legally, they could not be killed or otherwise mistreated by their owners, but they were permanently attached to a parcel of land and obligated to work for its owners one half of their total work days. The resulting discontent gave rise to numerous peasant uprisings that were always successfully suppressed by force and often with great cruelty. Most of the remaining half of Russia's peasantry lived on crown lands and were governed by often harsh officials. They were known as state peasants.

SERGE, VICTOR (b. KIBALICH) (1890–1947). An anarchist in his youth, Serge emigrated from Russia to France, returning home only after the October 1917 revolution (q.v.). Serge was twice arrested by the Soviet government for his oppositionist activities, in 1928 and again in 1933, but was freed in 1936 thanks to a campaign for his release conducted by left-wing groups in France. Toward the end of his life he became disillusioned with both the Stalinist and the Trotskyist brands of Communism.

SERGEI ALEKSANDROVICH ROMANOV, GRAND DUKE (1864–1905). He fell victim to terrorist assassins during his tenure in the post of governor-general of Moscow (q.v.). Although the actual assassin was Kalaev, the mastermind behind the killing was Azef (q.v.), a double-agent of the Okhrana (q.v.).

SEROV. Founded in 1894 during the construction of the Trans-Siberian Railroad (q.v.), this town in the Sverdlovsk (q.v.) region is a metallurgical industrial center. Its population is just over 100,000.

SEROV, IVAN A. (1905-). Born into a peasant family, he became a Bolshevik (q.v.) activist at an early age and joined the Red Army (*see* Armed Forces, Soviet) in 1923. After 1939 he worked in the ministry of the interior and served as its chief in Ukraine (q.v.) under Khrushchev (q.v.). During World War II (q.v.) he was deputy commissar for state security and supervised the execution of political prisoners during the Red Army's retreat from the advancing Germans. Serov was also responsible for the deportation of numerous Soviet nationals during the war. After the war he was made deputy supreme commander of the Soviet forces in Eastern Europe. In 1953 he helped arrest Beria (q.v.) and in 1954 was appointed chairman of the KGB (q.v.), in which capacity he led the suppression of the 1956 Hungarian revolution. In 1958 Serov was made chief of Soviet military intelligence, the GRU (q.v.), from which post he was dismissed after the exposure of Penkovskii (q.v.), a spy for the CIA and MI6, in 1963.

SERPUKHOV. Located on the confluence of the Nara and Oka (q.v.) rivers, this 14th-century town is today an important trade center for the agricultural produce of the region south of Moscow (q.v.). Its population is just over 100,000.

SEVASTOPOL see SEBASTOPOL

SEVEN YEARS' WAR (1756–63). Russia took part in this dynastic war on the side of France and its allies (Austria, Spain, Saxony and Sweden) against Britain, Prussia and Portugal. A Russo-Austrian victory and the Battle of Kunersdorf in 1759 was decisive, but Peter III (q.v.), who was an admirer of Prussia, made a pact with that country in 1762. The war ended the following year with a British victory, which resulted in Britain's acquiring several formerly French colonies. Russia's rule over Poland was also expanded.

SHAGIN, IVAN M. (1904–82). Born into a peasant family, he began working as a sailor on the Volga River (q.v.) before becoming interested in photography in 1919. He then worked as a press photographer for Soviet newspapers and publishing houses. During World War II (q.v.) he served as war correspondent, then after the war began producing numerous stories illustrated with photographs for Soviet publications.

SHAGINIAN (or SHAHINIAN), MARIETA S. (1888–1982). The daughter of a medical doctor, she graduated from the Higher Women's Courses in 1912 and worked as a journalist from 1906 to 1919. A minor Symbolist (q.v.) poet before the revolution, Shaginian wrote detective stories and thrillers after the revolution.

SHAKHOVSKAIA, ZINAIDA ALEKSEEVNA (1906-). After emigrating with her parents during the civil war (q.v.), Shakhovskaia completed her education at the College de France in Paris. She married the diplomat Sviatoslav de Malevsky-Malevich and wrote for French journals. During World War II (q.v.) she lived in England, and after the Allied invasion of Italy she worked as a war correspondent, covering the campaigns in Greece and Germany and finally the trials at Nuremberg. From 1968 to 1978 Shakhovskaia was the editor of *Russkaia Mysl* in Paris; on retirement she wrote a book about Vladimir Nabokov (q.v.), whom she had known in emigration.

SHAKHTY. A coal-mining town in the Donets basin, its name was given to the first of the major political trials of the Stalin (q.v.) era, which occurred in 1928. During this trial a number of Soviet industrial managers, who had before the revolution been members of the

Menshevik (q.v.) party but who had remained to work within Soviet economic organizations, were falsely accused of sabotage.

SHALAMOV, VARLAM T. (1907–82). Son of an Orthodox (q.v.) priest, he studied law at the University of Moscow (*see* Universities) between 1925 and 1929. Sentenced to prison for counterrevolutionary activity by the Soviet government, Shalamov was released and allowed to work as a journalist. He was rearrested in 1937, but was released in 1953 and fully rehabilitated in 1976. Shalamov wrote numerous stories about life in the Gulag (q.v.) camps, some of which were published in England in 1978.

SHALIAPIN, FEDOR (1873–1938). Considered to have been one of the great bassos of the world, Shaliapin began his career as an opera singer in 1896. His best-known roles were those of Boris Godunov (q.v.) and Ivan the Terrible (q.v.). Beginning in 1901 he toured Europe and America. In 1909, Shaliapin began collaboration with Diaghilev (q.v.) in Paris. He initially supported the 1917 revolution but remained in the West after leaving Soviet Russia in 1921 to raise money for victims of famine. He continued to give concerts until the year of his death.

SHAPOSHNIKOV, BORIS MIKHAILOVICH (1882–1945). A White officer who defected to the Red Army during the civil war (q.v.), he later became a Soviet marshal and head of the Voroshilov Military Academy. A graduate of the General Staff Academy in 1910, he became a colonel during World War I (q.v.), then joined the Red Army (*see* Armed Forces, Soviet) in 1918. Shaposhnikov commanded the Moscow (q.v.) and St. Petersburg (q.v.) military districts from 1925 to 1928 and then became the chief of staff of the Red Army between 1928 and 1931, as well as a nonvoting member of the Central Committee of the Communist Party (q.v.). At the beginning of World War II (q.v.) he served as the deputy commissar of defense and, after 1943, as head of the Academy of the General Staff until 1945. He also wrote several books on military theory.

SHCHEDRIN, N. (1826–89). Also known as Saltykov-Shchedrin, his real name was Mikhail Evgrafovich Saltykov; he is the author of *The Golovlyov Family* (1880) and other works. Shchedrin wrote satirically about the gentry class into which he was born and the provincial life he witnessed as a civil servant in Viatka. He was also keenly interested in social questions and socialism.

SHCHEDRIN, RADION K. (1932–). Born into a musical family, he entered a choral school in 1944 and the Moscow (q.v.) Conservatory in 1950. Shchedrin wrote his first ballet music in 1958 and since then has composed operas, ballets, and symphonies while teaching at the conservatory.

SHCHUKIN, SERGEI I. (1876–1936). Born into a family of wealthy Moscow (q.v.) industrialists, he became a major collector of art, acquiring a large collection of impressionist paintings, including works by Matisse, Cézanne, Gaugin and Picasso. Shchukin was also the founder of the Institute of Philosophy at the University of Moscow (*see* Universities). After the October 1917 revolution (q.v.) his art collection was nationalized and kept in the vault of the Pushkin museum; he emigrated to France.

SHEVCHENKO, ALEKSANDR V. (1882–1948). A graduate of the school of graphic arts in 1907, he lived in Paris between 1905 and 1906, then returned to Moscow (q.v.), where he studied painting in 1908 and 1910. Shevchenko remained in Russia after the October 1917 revolution (q.v.).

SHEVCHENKO, TARAS GRIGOREVICH (1814–61). A Ukrainian poet who was born in serfdom and whose freedom had to be purchased by admirers in 1838, his work is romantic and patriotic. His best-known collection is *Kobzar* (1840), which describes the destitution and injustice of peasant life. Shevchenko was exiled to Orenburg (q.v.) in 1847 for his activity in the underground Brotherhood of Sts. Cyril and Methodius. He returned to St. Petersburg (q.v.) in 1858 and continued to write, developing the Ukrainian literary language. He also painted and wrote novels in Russian.

SHKURO, ANDREI G. (1886–1947). Born into a Kuban Cossack (q.v.) family, he graduated from a Cadet (q.v.) Corps and in 1907 from a cavalry school in St. Petersburg (q.v.). During World War I (q.v.) Shurko served on the Romanian front. After the October 1917 revolution (q.v.) he returned to Kuban, where he waged a guerrilla war against the Soviet government and joined General Denikin's (q.v.) White Armies (q.v.). He emigrated after the civil war (q.v.) and worked as a Cossack (q.v.) rider in a circus. During World War II (q.v.) Shurko joined Cossack forces serving the German army. After Germany's defeat he was first interned in Austria, then turned over to Soviet authorities, who returned him to Moscow (q.v.). There he was tried for treason and executed.

SHLIAPNIKOV, ALEKSANDR G. (1884–1937). A self-educated workman who became one of the early Bolshevik (q.v.) leaders, at the tenth party congress in 1921 he joined Kollontai (q.v.) to lead the Workers' Opposition (q.v.) to Lenin (q.v.). Shliapnikov argued for a larger role for trade unions in the government. During the purges (q.v.) of the 1930s he was executed but received posthumous rehabilitation in 1956.

SHMELEV, IVAN S. (1873–1950). Born into a merchant family, he graduated from the University of Moscow (*see* Universities) in 1898, then began a career in publishing. In 1922 he emigrated to Berlin and then to Paris. Shmelev became known for his descriptions of traditional life in Russia and of Orthodox Church (q.v.) festivals. During World War II (q.v.) he collaborated with a pro-German Russian newspaper in France.

SHOLOKHOV, MIKHAIL A. (1905–84). Born into a Cossack (q.v.) family, he fought on the side of the Bolsheviks (q.v.) during the civil war (q.v.). Between 1928 and 1934 he published a major literary work, *Tikhii Don*. Sholokhov was highly favored by Soviet authorities. He joined the Communist Party (q.v.) in 1932 and was awarded the Stalin (q.v.) and Lenin prizes (q.v.) for literature as well as winning the Nobel Prize in 1965. Sholokhov was a dedicated Communist and a vigorous critic of both Solzhenitsyn (q.v.) and Pasternak (q.v.).

SHOSTAKOVICH, DMITRII D. (1906–75). Born in St. Petersburg (q.v.), he received an early musical education, studying under Glazunov (q.v.) in the Petrograd Conservatory between 1919 and 1925. Shostakovich began composing early in the 1920s and rapidly gained a major reputation in the Soviet Union and internationally. However, his 1934 opera, *Lady Macbeth of Mtsensk,* was banned on orders of Stalin (q.v.). After World War II (q.v.) he was again criticized by Stalin's "cultural tsar" Zhdanov (q.v.) for his formalism. Shostakovich's reputation earned him membership in Italian, British and French musical societies, as well as in the American Academy of Arts in 1959.

SHOW TRIALS. This series of Soviet trials, orchestrated on Stalin's (q.v.) orders, began with the Shakhty (q.v.) trial of industrial managers in 1928 and continued through the 1930s. Their victims were often forced to falsely confess to acts of sabotage and espionage under torture or threats to their families and were invariably condemned either to death or to lengthy terms in the prison camps.

SHTERENBERG, ABRAM P. (1894–1979). Born into an artisan family, he became a professional photographer at an early age, then

joined the Red Army (*see* Armed Forces, Soviet) in 1919. After the
civil war (q.v.) he studied art and design in Tashkent (q.v.), then settled in Moscow (q.v.) in 1922. After the mid-1920s he worked in the
photographic services of various Soviet news organizations, specializing in portrait photography, as well as being a news photographer
for the Soviet press. After 1930 he began exhibiting his work abroad.

SHUB, ESFIR I. (ESTER SHUB) (1894–1959). A graduate of the
Higher Women's Courses in Moscow (q.v.), she became secretary of
the theater section of the commissariat of education and entered the
film industry in 1922. After 1924 Shub worked at the State Film Archives and in 1927 produced a documentary film, *The Fall of the
Romanov Dynasty*, as well as other historical films.

SHUISKII. The name of an ancient noble Russian family that descended
from Riurik (q.v.), one of its members served Ivan the Terrible (q.v.)
until he was suspected of treason and died under torture. Another,
Vasilii Shuiskii, was a *boiar* (q.v.) under Tsar Boris Godunov (q.v.).
After the death of Ivan's son in 1606 Shuiskii was elevated to the
throne. Shortly thereafter he was forced to abdicate and become a
monk.

SHULGIN, VASILII V. (1878–1965). A member of the Duma (q.v.), he
accompanied Guchkov (q.v.) to the imperial headquarters in February
1917 to obtain the abdication of Emperor Nicholas II (q.v.). He fled
abroad after the October revolution (q.v.) and lived in Yugoslavia. In
the 1930s he was lured back to Soviet Russia by the Trest (q.v.), a
Soviet intelligence organization. At the end of World War II (q.v.) he
was captured by Smersh (q.v.) in Yugoslavia and sent to a Soviet
concentration camp. He was released in 1956.

SHUMEIKO, VLADIMIR (1945-   ). A federation council speaker, he
founded the Reform-New Course movement in 1995, that supported
Yeltsin while encouraging an economic path toward decentralization
and some state protectionism.

SHURATOV, MALIUTA (late 16th century). He was a leading member
of Tsar Ivan the Terrible's (q.v.) Oprichnina (q.v.). Said to have murdered the Metropolitan Filip, he was himself eventually murdered by
other *oprichniki*.

SHUVALOV, COUNT IVAN (1727–97). One of the early Russian edu-
cators, he was instrumental in the founding of the University of Mos-

cow (*see* Universities) and a chain of state-controlled high schools. In 1757 he helped start the Russian Academy of Fine Arts (q.v.).

SHVERNIK, NIKOLAI M. (1888–1970). He joined the Bolsheviks (q.v.) in 1905 and was soon arrested and exiled for revolutionary activity. After the revolution he became a trade union leader and, between 1923 and 1925, a member of the presidium of the central control commission, as well as of the Central Committee of the Communist Party (q.v.).

SIBERIA (RUSS.: SIBIR). This part of Russia stretches from the Ural Mountains (q.v.) eastward to the Pacific Ocean, and from the Arctic Ocean to Kazakhstan (q.v.) and the Chinese border in the south, an area of some five million square miles. Geographically, Siberia is divided into three regions: the western Siberian plain, the central Siberian plateau, and a region of complicated mountain chains and river basins in the Russian Far East.

Russians began to colonize Siberia in the late 16th century, but it was only with the completion of the Trans-Siberian Railroad (q.v.) in 1903 that large-scale immigration and industrialization could take place. The population now stands at around 40 million.

Siberia's principle wealth is in its vast deposits of petroleum, coal, natural gas, diamonds, and other minerals.

SIBERIAN KHANATE. In 1582 the Tatar (q.v.) khanate of Sibir was conquered by detachments of Russian Cossacks led by Ermak (q.v.) and Stroganoff, then presented to Tsar Ivan the Terrible (q.v.) to become part of the grand duchy of Muscovy (q.v.).

SIKHOTE ALIN. This mountain range is 1,200 miles long and extends from Vladivostok (q.v.) to Nikolaevsk and parallels the Pacific coast. It is rich in mineral resources.

SIKORSKII, IGOR I. (1889–1972). He graduated from the St. Petersburg Naval Academy in 1903 and from the Kiev Polytechnic Institute in 1907. Sikorskii designed an early version of a helicopter in 1911, as well as the world's first four-engine airplane. During World War I (q.v.) he built warplanes for the Russian army. After the 1917 revolution he emigrated to the United States where he played an important part in the development of the aviation industry.

SIMBIRSK see ULIANOVSK

SIMFEROPOL. A city in the Crimea of 302,000, it was anciently known as Neapolis. It was at one time a Scythian (q.v.) settlement.

The modern city may be said to have been founded in 1784 by the Russians as an administrative capital for their newly acquired Crimean region. Simferopol has a rich fruit and vegetable harvest, and the other industries include fish canning, tobacco processing and relevant equipment manufacturing.

SIMONOV, KONSTANTIN M. (1915–79). He grew up in Russian provincial towns and studied by correspondence in a workers' educational institute. In the early 1930s Simonov worked in the Soviet aviation industry as a production worker. He published his first poems in 1934, then graduated from the Gorky Literary Institute in 1938. After this he joined *Pravda* (q.v.) as a correspondent and traveled abroad. Following World War II (q.v.), Simonov continued to work as a journalist and in 1954 became editor of several major Soviet literary magazines, as well as serving as the deputy secretary of the Union of Soviet Writers (q.v.).

SINIAVSKII, ANDREI (1925-   ). A writer and critic, he began to publish some of his works outside of Russia under the name Abram Tertz, largely as a result of disillusionment caused by Khrushchev's (q.v.) secret speech denouncing Stalin (q.v.) at the 20th party congress and official mistreatment of Boris Pasternak (q.v.). In 1965 Siniavskii was arrested and tried, with Yulii Daniel, for criminal slander of the Soviet government (article 70 of the criminal code); they were convicted and imprisoned, Siniavskii for seven years and Daniel for five. After his release, Siniavskii emigrated to France.

SITKA. A colony in Russian America (*see* Alaska) on Baranoff Island some 100 miles south of Juneau, it was founded in 1799 by the governor of Alaska, Aleksandr Baranov (q.v.), and served as the headquarters of the Russian American Company (q.v.).

SKOBLIN, NIKOLAI V. (1893–1937). Born into a military family and educated in a Cadet (q.v.) Corps, he was decorated for bravery during World War I (q.v.) and commanded a division of the White Armies (q.v.) during the civil war (q.v.). He married Plevitskaia (q.v.), a well-known Russian folk singer. He is rumored to have become involved with German and Soviet secret service organizations and to have participated in a complicated plot to implicate the Soviet Marshal Tukhachevski (q.v.) as a German spy. He is known to have participated in the kidnapping of former White generals Miller (q.v.) and Kutepov (q.v.), after which he fled to the Soviet Union, leaving his wife Plevitskaia to be jailed by the French authorities.

SKRIABIN see SCRIABIN

SLAVIC LANGUAGES. The branch of Indo-European languages to which Russian belongs, it comprises some fifteen languages that can be divided into three groups as follows: Eastern Slavic (Russian, Ukrainian, Belorussian, and Ruthenian); Western Slavic (Polish, Czech, Slovak, and Upper and Lower Sorbian); and Southern Slavic (Old Church Slavonic, used liturgically; Bulgarian, Serbian, Croatian, Slovenian, and Macedonian). Extinct but attested languages are Polabian (Western) and Veliotic (Southern), both of which were spoken by minorities that assimilated into larger, neighboring language groups in the 17th or 18th centuries. The Cyrillic alphabet, derived largely from Greek, is employed for languages historically associated with Orthodox Christianity (Russian, Ukrainian, Belorussian, Bulgarian, and Serbian); the others use Latin letters. An early alphabet of elaborate appearance, known as glagolitic (q.v.) was also initially in use but was dropped in favor of Cyrillic.

SLAVO-GRECO-LATIN ACADEMY. Moscow's first institute of higher learning, it was founded in 1687 by Medvedev and originally styled the Helleno-Greek Academy. It was transferred to the Troitse-Sergieva Monastery and reincorporated as the Moscow Theological Academy in 1814.

SLAVOPHILES. These thinkers tended to counterbalance, or even oppose, Western influence by emphasizing Russia's Slavic, rural and Orthodox base as contrasted to the supposed rationality, secularism and individuality of the West. Notable proponents were Aleksei Khromiakov (1804–60), Konstantin and Ivan Aksakov (1817–60 and 1823–86, respectively) and Ivan Kireevskii (1806–56). Many other writers and thinkers might be said to be *slavophilisant*.

SLAVS. This ethno-linguistic term denotes the Slavic-speaking peoples, the largest linguistic group in Europe. Though today somewhat diverse, an original homogeneous group of Slavs seems to have emerged from Asia in the second millenium B.C., gradually occupying parts of central Europe; by the seventh century they had spread out over Europe and become divided into three main groups, the Western Slavs (Poles, Czechs, and Sorbs), the Eastern Slavs (Russians, Ukrainians, and Belorussians), and the South Slavs (Serbs, Croats, Slovenians, Bulgarians, and Macedonians).

SLOMINSKY, IURII I. (1902–78). He was a student at the St. Petersburg (q.v.) Ballet School, then in the early 1920s he began publishing reviews of ballet performances and giving lectures. In 1932 he became a teacher at the Leningrad Choreographic School and helped to establish its department of choreography. After 1962 he was professor at the Leningrad Conservatory and wrote numerous works on the theory of choreography.

SMENOVEKHOVSTVO. The "change of landmarks" movement, it was a trend among the post-civil war (q.v.) Russian emigres (q.v.) to accommodate themselves to the reality of Soviet power in Russia. They were led by Count Aleksei Tolstoy (q.v.) and General Brusilov (q.v.).

SMERSH ("DEATH TO SPIES"—SMERT SHPIONAM). A wartime division of the security police, it was intended to find and eliminate any enemies of the Soviet regime among the many Russians who had spent any time under German occupation or even in German prisoner of war camps. It also scrutinized the behavior of the Soviet Army for signs of treachery and tried to root out possible opponents in territories held by Soviet forces.

SMOKTUNOVSKII, INNOKENTII, (1925–95). He was an actor who played Prince Myshkin in the Leningrad Gorky Theater's *The Idiot*, based on the Dostoevsky novel, from 1957 to 1960. He also played Hamlet in Kosintsev's 1964 film of that play.

SMOLENSK. An oblast and city on the upper Dnepr River (q.v.), the town dates back to the ninth century, when it served as a commercial stop between Byzantium and the Baltic Sea (q.v.). Acquired by the Lithuanian kingdom in the 13th century, it was eventually restored to Russia. During the invasions by the French in 1812 and the Germans in 1941, it was the site of fierce battles. Its population is just over 300,000.

SMOLNY INSTITUT. A school for girls, it was part of the tsarist educational system for the sons and daughters of the nobility. First established in 1797, it lasted until 1917, when its building was taken over by revolutionaries and then used as headquarters by the Bolsheviks (q.v.).

SNESAREV, ANDREI E. (1865–1937). The son of an Orthodox priest, he graduated from University of Moscow (*see* Universities) in 1888, the Moscow School of Infantry in 1890, and the Academy of the General Staff in 1899. While serving in central Asia, he studied languages and wrote extensively on India, Tibet and Afghanistan. During World War I (q.v.) he commanded a division, then joined the Red Army (*see* Armed Forces, Soviet) in 1918 as commander of the northern Caucasian military district and of the Belarus army group. After the end of the civil war (q.v.) he was elevated to be the head of the Academy of the General Staff. During the Stalin (q.v.) purges (q.v.) of the 1930s, he was accused of being a secret member of a Russian military group of monarchists and executed.

SOBCHAK, ANATOLII (1937–). Reformist mayor of St. Petersburg (q.v.) and founder of the Russian Movement of Democratic Reforms, Sobchak was head of the law faculty at St. Petersburg University (*see* Universities), having specialized in civil law. He left the Communist Party (q.v.) in 1990, and became mayor of St. Petersburg. He supported privatization and led his city in encouraging foreign investment, making it a model for the practice elsewhere in the country.

SOCHI. This city is a major resort on the eastern coast of the Black Sea (q.v.), some 100 miles southeast of Krasnodar (q.v.) at the foothills of the Caucasus (q.v.) Mountains. Its population is almost 300,000.

SOCIAL DEMOCRATS see RUSSIAN SOCIALIST DEMOCRATIC LABOR PARTY

SOCIAL STRATIFICATION, ANCIENT AND MEDIEVAL. By 1400 Russia was becoming a segmented society, divided into social layers whose position in society was fixed by law, with hereditary privileges that belonged to them. Each such social layer in medieval Russia was compelled to carry out a defined set of obligations. The elite of this society consisted of *boiars* (q.v.), and primarily of members of the Boiar Duma. The very top of that society was the court of the tsar (q.v.). This court had its own ranking system that was fixed by law. One's place in this structure of ranks was determined primarily by the status of one's family. The administrative personnel of the tsar's civil and military government were selected from this entourage. In addition to the courtiers, there were also the *dvoriane* (q.v.), or "the servants of the tsar." The legal criteria for belonging to this class was ownership of land and of the peasants who resided on it, as well as the obligation to carry out certain specified services for the tsar— primarily military during times of war and tax-gathering in peacetime.

After the reforms of Peter the Great (q.v.), the primary prerequisite for belonging to the *dvoriane* class was service to the state. Gradually, however, this class obtained the right to hereditary ownership of land and became a closed and privileged layer of society. After the end of the 15th century there began to be formed a service bureaucracy—the deacons of the Duma (q.v.). By the 17th century the power of this bureaucracy in the executive and administrative structures of the government had become very evident.

The most numerous layer of Russian medieval society was the peasantry. After the end of the 15th century there began a process of fixing them into place by limiting their right to move from one landowner to another. The primary agrarian economic system was based on the obligation of the peasants to work the lands of the landowners in exchange for being allowed to cultivate their own allotment of land. By the middle of the 17th century, the process of serfdom had become fixed. This system resulted in massive peasant discontent and in frequent attempts by individuals to escape outside the frontiers of Muscovy (q.v.) to the sparsely populated borderlands—"Ukraine," (q.v.) from the Russian *krai*, or "border." There the runaway peasants amalgamated themselves into semimilitary communities—the Cossacks (q.v.). These remained free individuals who lived in communes that were simultaneously military organizations and civic self-governing bodies. These communes frequently received financial support from both the Russian tsars and from the Polish kings because they guarded the frontiers of both states from raids by Crimean Tatars (q.v.) and Turks.

In medieval Russia the city population included craftsmen and merchants. Generally, the city dwellers were responsible for fulfilling the state's tax assessments by dividing them among the total number of inhabitants. City authorities ensured that no one avoided these obligations. By the middle of the 17th century in Russia there were over 250 towns. At this time new urban layers of the population began to develop: the owners and workers in manufacturing enterprises and also the merchants.

SOCIAL STRATIFICATION, IMPERIAL. The social stratification of Russian society in the middle of the 18th century was characterized by a growth of polarization between the main social layers. The *dvoriane* (q.v.) constituted the ruling class. Their power rested on the ownership of land and of the peasants that worked it. During this period the *dvoriane* received special privileges not available to other classes, such as having full power over their peasants. Those who did not belong to this class were forbidden to purchase land. At the same time the *dvoriane* were permitted to establish manufacturing enterprises on their estates and only they were allowed to have family crests, to organize into their own societies of noblemen, to be free of most taxes and obligations to the state, and to be exempt from corporal punishment.

The peasantry was by far the most numerous layer of the Russian imperial society. It was divided into several groups: state peasants who belonged to the state, free peasants who rented land from the *dvoriane* or the state, and peasants who belonged personally either to the tsar or to the *dvoriane*. According to the 1897 census, peasants constituted 70 percent of the population of the Russian empire. During the 19th century this percentage had gradually fallen as a result of a massive bankrupting of the peasant economy. However, by the middle of the century a new layer of well-to-do peasants began to emerge in Russia.

The reforms of 1861 proclaimed the personal freedom of all peasants. They received the right to own property, to obtain positions in the civil service, to engage in industrial or mercantile enterprises, and to enter into contractual relations with others. The economic dependence of the peasantry, however, was not abolished by these reforms. They remained obligated collectively to the state for the land allocations they received as a result of the state's purchase of land from former owners. After paying 20 to 25 percent of the cost of this land initially, their individual communes were responsible for paying off the balance over a 49-year period, including a six percent interest charge. The peasants were now allowed to carry on with their own individual household economies, but they still remained members of communes that helped individual members during difficult periods. However, they were also taxed by these communes and were subject to strict limitations on their activities. The peasants' dependence on communes was based on the fact that communes allotted the individual plots of land to them and also determined the annual distribution of land among individual households. By the beginning of the 20th century the communes were undergoing a process of differentiation. With the 1906 reforms, individual peasants received the right to leave their communes and to transform their allotments into private property.

By the beginning of the 20th century, a significant proportion of the Russian population was engaged in entrepreneurial or mercantile activities. These were for the most part city dwellers, the *meshchane*, or the middle layer of the population. They were obligated to live in urban areas and it is from this group that the Russian merchant class originated. Merchants enjoyed special privileges, including freedom from certain taxes, from the obligation to render military service, and from corporal punishment. Their principal right was that of engaging in manufacturing and trade activities.

In the middle of the 19th century another layer began to form itself within Russian society: the intelligentsia (q.v.). Before that period, the right to an intellectual occupation was the exclusive prerogative of the *dvoriane* class, but by the end of the century there had emerged a relatively large group of intellectual workers who did not belong to that class. They were primarily professionals: lawyers, journalists, medical personnel, teachers, engineers, civil servants and other professionals. At the same time a new class—the industrial workers—was also forming in Russia. In 1913 there were over three million workers who were employed in factories and mines, as well as another three million individuals who were engaged in small-scale production enterprises. This growth of the industrial working class paralleled the emergence of a commercial and industrial bourgeoisie—the middle class of some 1.5 million individuals. This layer consisted of merchants, manufacturers, and wealthy peasants. At the peripheries of the Russian empire the mercantile groups were most numerous; in Moscow (q.v.) it was the industrialists, and in St. Petersburg (q.v.), the financial bourgeoisie.

SOCIAL STRATIFICATION, SOVIET. The process of class formation in the Soviet Union after the October 1917 revolution (q.v.) and the civil war (q.v.) was influenced by two primary factors. The first was the imposition by political force of an artificial society without antagonistic classes that was supposed to have replaced the previous classes and interest groups of imperial Russia. The second was the nationalization of all financial, land, and real property.

Within this "classless" society there remained, however, occupational and professional groups that were differentiated by their social function as well as by unequal access to political power. Over a period of some 20 years, from 1920 to the end of the 1930s, these groups evolved into sharply differentiated classlike layers. By the later 1930s, a new class structure had become firmly established. It consisted of several groupings: 38.2 percent were industrial workers, 38.5 percent were collective farmers, 18.7 percent were state employees, and 4.6 percent were individual craftsmen and small property owners.

After World War II (q.v.) the number of collective farmers began to shrink rapidly, at the same time that the numbers of industrial workers began to increase, because of an internal migration from villages to the new industrial centers of the country. In addition, because of the massive conversion of collective farms into large state-owned farming enterprises (*see* sovkhoz), the number of rural agricultural workers increased. This urbanization process proceeded at the expense of the villages and without first creating a required social infrastructure. The result was that a large number of farmers were forced to take on the most menial industrial jobs and live, together with their families, in barely adequate communal housing that surrounded the employing enterprises. This infusion into the industrial working class greatly weakened its solidarity as well as its ability to participate in the governance of the country.

At the same time, the constantly shrinking peasant population, herded into collective farms, was deprived of most of the produce that they were creating and, lacking any effective means to participate in the political process, became completely disinterested in the result of their labor and in participating in the political process.

Meanwhile, the proportion of the intelligentsia (q.v.) in the country continued to grow. Between 1939 and 1979 it increased from nine percent to 21 percent of the population. The fastest rates of growth occurred in the industrial intelligentsia, such as engineers, and among the scientific intelligentsia, while the proportion of creative intelligentsia remained approximately constant. The bureaucratic apparatus on the middle and the lower levels of government grew disproportionately, as did the economic bureaucracy. At the same time, the position of the administrative and political elite, the nomenklatura (q.v.), was greatly strengthened. Its growth was based on government policies that flowed out of the state monopoly ownership of the means of production. The de facto owners of this nationalized property were the bureaucrats and higher civil servants whose principal concern was to maintain themselves in power and retain its consequent privileges. The criteria by which individuals gained admission to these privileged spheres were based not on professional or moral qualities, but on political reliability, personal contacts, mutual protection arrangements, and family connections. A major source for recruitment into the nomenklatura was the Communist youth organization, the Komsomol (q.v.).

Toward the end of the 1970s, the low standard of living of millions of people, the impossibility of satisfying even primary needs, the lack of stimulus for work, a feeling of powerlessness and political apathy, and the prevailing culture of materialism all led to a marked degradation of social values in the country that the halfhearted measures undertaken under Gorbachev's perestroika (q.v.) were insufficient to overcome.

SOCIAL STRATIFICATION, TODAY. The social structure of Russian society since the collapse of the Communist rule has undergone serious transformations. It is now characterized by a shrinkage of the number of individuals who participate in any form of production, by the dissolution of the previous class structure, and by a drastic drop in the standard of living of the majority of the population.

The number of working individuals has dropped by some one and a half million persons in Russia alone, with the number of working women having dropped especially sharply. In 1993 only 83 percent of women who were working in the 1980s were still employed. There is a marked growth of unemployed and homeless individuals and of paupers. In December 1993, over one million unemployed persons were looking for work and four million worked only part time. Another difficult problem is that of Russian refugees, who have been forced to leave non-Russian areas of the former Soviet Union. Two million of them have already returned, and another four to six million are expected to do so within the next few years.

All of these changes have caused the former class structure of the country to undergo major transformation, with the old arrangements no longer operating and new ones not yet firmly established. Those who are members of the very small extremely rich layer are primarily former state or party officials who have been able to translate their previous political and administrative power into large economic holdings. In its general outline, the class structure of Russian society that is now emerging is taking on the traits of capitalist societies as they existed some hundred years ago, during the period of primitive accumulation of capital. This period is characterized by the formation of an owning (capitalist) class, by the impoverishment of both the rural and the urban population, and by a general increase in criminal activity. Today, the very rich in Russia constitute only three percent of the population, the well-to-do some seven percent, and the moderately poor 25 percent, while the remaining 65 percent live below the poverty level. At the end of 1993 27 percent of the Russian population had a monthly income under the established poverty level of 42,000 rubles (U.S. $34).

There are significant differences in the incomes and price levels in different regions of the Russian Federation. As of March 1993 the highest real incomes were in the western Siberian region. They were one and a half times the average for all of the country. The northern regions also exceeded the country's average by some 27 percent. There was also a relatively higher level in eastern Siberia (q.v.) the Urals (q.v.) and the Far Eastern regions, at the same time that the averages were lower in the Volga (q.v.) region, the central Russia region, the northern Caucasus (q.v.) region and the region surrounding St. Petersburg (q.v.). This region was the poorest of the whole country, with an average standard of living 40 percent lower than the average.

SOCIALIST DEMOCRATIC LABOR PARTY see RUSSIAN SOCIALIST DEMOCRATIC LABOR PARTY; MENSHEVIKS

SOCIALIST REALISM. The official Soviet aesthetic in literature and art lasted from 1934, when it was adopted by the All-Union Congress of Soviet Writers, until its general demise in the wake of the Thaw (q.v.). It stated that art must be realistic in form and socialist in content.

SOCIALIST REVOLUTIONARIES. These populists shared the goal of socialism in a federal Russia, as envisioned in the program of Viktor Chernov (q.v.) and adopted at their first congress in 1905. They were in reality a diverse group, including both terrorists such as G. Gershuni and legalists. The party split on the issue of World War I (q.v.) and also on their relation to the Bolshevik (q.v.) party. The latter rift at the eighth party congress in 1917 caused M.A. Natanson to form the Left-Socialist Revolutionaries (q.v.); those under Chernov opposed the Bolshevik seizure of power. After the revolution the Left-Socialist Revolutionaries briefly joined Lenin's (q.v.) government, then, a few months later, attempted to overthrow it but were rapidly defeated. After this abortive attempt the Left-Socialist Revolutionaries were suppressed; many of them were either executed or imprisoned for decades.

SOKOLNIKOV, G.Y. (pseud. BRILLIANT) (1888–1939). He joined the Bolsheviks (q.v.) in 1905, then, before the revolution, obtained degrees in economics and law in France. A member of the Politburo (q.v.) in 1917, he commanded the Turkestan (q.v.) front during the civil war (q.v.) and then served as the commissar of finance from 1921 to 1926. Sokolnikov opposed Stalin (q.v.) at the 14th party congress in 1925. In 1933 he lost his membership in the Communist Party (q.v.), and in 1937 he was publicly tried and sentenced to a labor camp, where he died.

SOLOGUB, FEDOR K. (b. TETERNIKOV) (1863–1927). Born in St. Petersburg (q.v.), he became a novelist and a poet of the Symbolist (q.v.) school. Sologub's writings after the revolution were not published because of their pessimistic tone.

SOLOVETSKII MONASTERY. This Orthodox (q.v.) monastery was founded in 1429 on the White Sea (q.v.) islands of the same name. After the 16th century it was also a place of exile and, after 1920, when the monastery was closed, a prison camp.

SOLOVEV, SERGEI M. (1820–79). Author of the authoritative history of Russia and professor of history at the University of Moscow (*see* Universities), he was a Westernizer and a liberal.

SOLOVEV, VLADIMIR S. (1853–1900). As a philosophy student at the University of Moscow (*see* Universities), he rejected the then popular materialism and formulated an idealistic and religious philosophy. Solovev exercised a strong influence on the Symbolist (q.v.) poets of the early years of the 20th century.

SOLZHENITSYN, ALEXANDER I. (1918-   ). This Russian novelist spent the years from 1945 to 1953 in a Soviet forced labor camp. His first novel, *One Day in the Life of Ivan Denisovich*, was published in the Soviet Union in 1962 on the personal authorization of Khrushchev (q.v.) and was the first such work to expose life in the forced labor camps. His later work, *The GULAG Archipelago*, was the result of recalling many of the personal histories with which he had become familiar while in prison; it served as a monument to the repressed. He was subsequently deported from Russia and lived in the United States until 1994, when he returned to Russia. His voluminous writings are heavily focused on the history of the Russian revolution.

SOMOV, KONSTANTIN A. (1869–1939). An artist and illustrator, Somov graduated from the St. Petersburg Academy of Art in 1897, then went on to study art in Paris. In 1913 Somov became a corresponding member of that academy and, in 1918, a professor there. Somov emigrated to France in 1923, where he became well known for his book illustrations, many of which were highly erotic.

SOPHIA ALEKSEEVNA, PRINCESS (1657–1704). The half-sister of Peter the Great (q.v.), she ruled as the regent of Russia after the death of her brother Fedor III (q.v.) in 1682. Sophia attempted to retain power by placing the feeble-minded Ivan V (q.v.) on the throne but was forced to retire to a convent by Peter in 1689.

SOPHIA PALEOLOGUE (late 15th century). The niece of the last Byzantine emperor, Constantine XIII, she married Ivan III (q.v.), the grand duke of Muscovy, in 1472, thereby enabling him to call himself tsar (q.v.), and adopting the Byzantine double-headed eagle as the ensign of Russia.

SORGE, RICHARD (1895–1944). German in origin, he was born in Baku (q.v.) and died a secret Russian citizen. After World War I (q.v.) he became an active Communist in Germany and was dismissed from his teaching post for his political activities. He moved to Moscow (q.v.) in 1924 and there was trained to be a GRU (q.v.) operative. He was actively involved in espionage for the Soviet Union from the 1920s and was a secret member of the Communist Party (q.v.), serving in Shanghai, China, and Los Angeles. After returning to Germany, Sorge joined the Nazi Party as a cover, then moved to Tokyo, where he worked as a reporter and press attaché at the German embassy. This enabled him to provide invaluable information to Soviet military intelligence, including his warning of the impending German invasion of the USSR and of the Japanese plans to attack in the Pacific Islands. He was entrapped by Japanese counterintelligence and shot in 1944. In 1964 Sorge was posthumously proclaimed a Hero of the Soviet Union.

SOROKIN, IVAN LUKICH (1886–1918). A Kuban Cossack (q.v.), he served as an officer in World War I (q.v.) and fought for the Red cause during the civil war (q.v.). He was deputy commander of the southeastern front, commander of the Rostov area, and commander in chief of the North Caucasus Republic. It was in this capacity that his excesses (such as executing members of the North Caucasus soviet) led to his arrest and execution by Red Army (*see* Armed Forces, Soviet) forces.

SOROKIN, PITRIM A. (1899–1968). During his youth, Sorokin worked as a craftsman in northern Russia and attended a village school. At 16 he joined the Socialist Revolutionaries (q.v.) party. Sorokin was actively engaged in underground revolutionary work until he entered the University of St. Petersburg (*see* Universities) as a law student. Sorokin graduated in 1914 and was elected to the Constituent Assembly (q.v.) in late 1917. He worked as a secretary to Kerensky (q.v.) before the October 1917 revolution (q.v.). After the Bolsheviks (q.v.) dispersed the assembly in early 1918, he returned to northern Russia in order to organize resistance to the Communists there. Arrested once again, he escaped execution because of his peasant origin. Sorokin published his first sociological work in 1919. He was expelled from Soviet Russia in 1922 along with many other prominent anti-Communist intellectuals. He lived briefly in Berlin and Prague before being invited to the United States in 1923 to become professor of sociology at Harvard. Sorokin was the founder of the Harvard Center for the Study of Creative Altruism in 1949 and the author of numerous works on sociology and the history of philosophy. He enjoyed a worldwide reputation for his theory of cultural cycles.

SOSLOVIE. This was a class or stratum to which an individual belonged in prerevolutionary Russia that determined the legal status of that individual until the 1917 revolution. It is roughly equivalent to the term "estate," as derived from the French *état* in, for example, the expression *tiers état*.

SOSNOVSKII, LEV SEMENOVICH (1886–1937). Journalist and editor of *Bednota* immediately after the revolution, Sosonovskii had taken part in the 1905 revolution (*see* Revolution of 1905) and aligned himself with the Social Democrats (*see* Russian Socialist Democratic Labor Party). For some years he was active in the labor movement, both in Russia and Azerbaijan. He worked for *Pravda (q.v.)* and was exiled to Cheliabinsk (q.v.) in 1913. Throughout the 1920s he supported Trotsky (q.v.) and, although ejected from the Communist Party (q.v.) in 1927, he was allowed to rejoin in 1935, but was ejected once again in 1936. He was then arrested, tried, and shot in 1937.

SOTSIALISTICHESKII VESTNIK (THE SOCIALIST COURIER). The newspaper organ of the Russian Socialist Democratic Party (*see* Mensheviks), it was published starting in 1922 first in Berlin, then in Paris, and finally in New York until 1966, initially under the editorship of Dan (q.v.).

SOUTHERN SOCIETY. This group was one of the several radical organizations of military officers that sought to reform the Russian political and state structure as an aftermath of their experiences in post-Napoleonic Europe. Led by Colonel Pestel (q.v.), it merged in 1825 with its counterpart, the Northern Society (q.v.), and participated in the failed Decembrist (q.v.) revolt against Tsar Nicholas I (q.v.).

SOVET NARODNYKH KOMMISSAROV see COUNCIL OF PEO-PLE'S COMMISSARS

SOVIET. The Russian word for council (commonly transcribed as *sovet*). After the October 1917 revolution all governmental organizations were ostensibly run by a hierarchy of councils (soviets), starting with local village or neighborhood councils and culminating with the Supreme Soviet (q.v.) of the USSR, hence the designation of the country as the Union of Soviet Socialist Republics (q.v.). Each territorial unit of the Soviet Union had its own council, nominally elected by the populace, but in fact it consisted of individuals nominated by Communist Party (q.v.) officials to run as candidates and then be automatically elected.

SOVIET CONSTITUTIONS. There was no constitution in the Russian empire before the October Manifesto of 1906. The tsar was a sovereign autocrat. The short-lived Provisional government (q.v.) did not have time to implement one. The first constitution for the Russian Republic was adopted in 1918, only to be replaced by a federal constitution in 1924 for the whole of the Soviet Union. In 1936 the so-called Stalin Constitution was adopted after extensive popular discussions: it was billed as the most democratic in the whole world, but most of its freedoms were never implemented. In 1977 under Brezhnev (q.v.), another constitution was adopted, and in December 1993 Russia's President Yeltsin (q.v.) succeeded in having a post-Communist constitution voted in by a national referendum.

SOVIET OF NATIONALITIES. The upper chamber of the USSR's Supreme Soviet (q.v.), it was designed to give representation to the many national and ethnic groupings within the Soviet Union.

SOVIET OF THE UNION. The lower chamber of the USSR, it consisted of elected representatives on the basis of one deputy for every 300,000 eligible electors.

SOVKHOZ (SOVetskoe KHOZiaistvo). A state-run farm, as opposed to a kolkhoz (q.v.), it differed from the latter in that workers were in the direct employ of the state. From the beginning, *sovkhozes* were unpopular and viewed as mismanaged. Khrushchev (q.v.) increased their number and sought to improve their efficiency, but the goal of making them less bureaucratically top-heavy proved elusive.

SOVNARKOM see COUNCIL OF PEOPLE'S COMMISSARS

SOVREMENNIK (THE CONTEMPORARY). Founded by Pushkin (q.v.) in 1836, this literary quarterly soon became the most influential periodical in Russia. Not only did it publish such noted authors as Turgenev (q.v.), but it also became the major voice of political liberalism. It was banned by the government in 1866.

SPERANSKII, COUNT MIKHAIL M. (1772–1839). Liberal minister of state under Alexander I (q.v.), he tried but failed to introduce a constitutional government in Russia. He reformed the administration of Siberia (q.v.) as governer-general, and supervised the first codification of imperial laws.

SPETSFOND. This term was used in Soviet libraries to designate a closed collection of books held in most large libraries. These books were considered unsuitable for mass consumption and were available only to readers with special permits. They were, as a rule, not included in the public catalogs.

SPIRIDONOVA, MARIA A. (1884–1941). Although born into a wealthy family, she became involved in revolutionary activities at a young age. In 1905 she shot a general. After her arrest, she was raped by the general's guards. Her death sentence was commuted to life exile in Siberia (q.v.). She was released by the February 1917 revolution (q.v.) and returned to Petrograd (q.v.) to become a leader of the left wing of the Socialist Revolutionaries (q.v.). After Lenin's (q.v.) government signed the Brest-Litovsk (q.v.) peace treaty in 1918, she organized an anti-Bolshevik (q.v.) uprising in Moscow (q.v.) that was eventually crushed. Arrested once again, she spent the remainder of her life either in Soviet concentration camps or under close police supervision. Allegedly, she was shot by the secret police in 1941, shortly before the arrival of the German army.

SPITZBERGEN (SVALBARD). Largest of a group of Norwegian islands some 600 miles northwest of Murmansk and 300 miles east of Greenland, it covers an area of around 24,095 square miles. Although the islands are difficult to land on, there has been some coal mining there by both Norway and Russia.

SPORT. Contemporary sport began in Russia during the middle of the 19th century, when sports clubs and gymnastic societies were first formed. By the beginning of the 20th century there already were more than 8,000 sport organizations in the country. In 1908 and 1912 Russian sports groups participated in the Olympic games as well as in other international sporting events. At the time the forms of sport most favored were soccer and tennis; the first soccer league was organized in 1901.

During the Soviet period organized sport acquired a mass character. In 1923 the first All-Russian Festival of Physiculture took place, and in 1928 the first All-Union Spartakiad. Numerous organizations, factories and large enterprises set up their own sports groups, and the extension of mass sport received a further impetus after the establishment of the national Ready for Labor and Defense organization.

In the 1950s interrepublic summer and winter games began to take place every four years, involving thousands of participants with the expansion of such forms of sport as aviation, underwater, and automotive events. However, many of the sport events that took place during the Soviet period manifested an exhibitionist character, in which participants were amateurs in theory only. As well, a very large sport bureaucracy was created. For example, in 1976 the number of individuals involved with the administration of various aspects of sport activities exceeded 280,000. In the RSFSR (see Russian Soviet Federated Socialist Republic) alone there were seven institutes of physical culture, 15 sport technicums, as well as a Central School of Trainers. Over 1,500 stadiums were constructed in the Russian Republic alone. Sportsmen continued to participate actively in international competitions, and in 1975 over 300 sportsmen and sportswomen won Olympic medals. However, the tendency to strive above all for the establishment of records, especially in international competitions, led to a number of negative consequences. Physical and emotional pressure on Soviet athletes was such that it often led to sickness and even caused some to become invalids.

At the present time many of these sports facilities have become commercialized. Many other well-equipped sport complexes have been created for those who can afford them. Meanwhile, many more facilities have either been closed or are being converted to other uses, and a large number of the most outstanding Russian athletes are currently working for foreign clubs.

STAKHANOV, ALEXIS G. (1906–77). He was the initiator of a supposedly spontaneous workers' movement to increase industrial production in the 1930s. As a coal miner Stakhanov nearly doubled the daily norm for the extraction of coal and started the Stakhanovite movement, which was highly promoted by the Soviet media.

STALIN, IOSIF V. (b. DZHUGASHVILI, pseud. KOBA) (1879–1953). A Georgian (q.v.) seminary student and son of a shoemaker, he joined the Russian Socialist Democratic Labor Party (q.v.) as a young man. In 1903, after the party split into the Bolshevik (q.v.) and the Menshevik (q.v.) factions, Stalin adhered to the more radical Bolshevik faction. He participated in the party's secret expropriations (bank robberies) and, in 1912, was chosen by Lenin (q.v.) to be a member of the central committee of the Bolsheviks. Stalin was arrested and sent to Siberian exile. After the February 1917 revolution (q.v.) he returned to Petrograd (q.v.) and became editor of the party's newspaper, *Pravda* (q.v.). During the civil war (q.v.) he was commissar of nationalities and the political commissar of the Tsaritsyn (*see* Volgograd) front. After Lenin made him the secretary general of the Central Committee (q.v.) in 1922, Stalin began building this post into the power center of the Communist Party (q.v.).

He briefly shared the leadership of the Soviet Union with Kamenev (q.v.) and Zinovev (q.v.) after Lenin's illness and death, helping them defeat the Trotsky (q.v.) faction. However, in the middle of the 1920s he turned on his allies and, with the aid of the Bukharin (q.v.) faction, defeated them. By 1928 he controlled the majority of the Politburo (q.v.) as well as a majority at all Communist Party congresses. This enabled him to defeat his former ally Bukharin (q.v.) between 1928 and 1930 and to become the sole ruler of the Soviet Union.

During the years from 1930 to 1939 he conducted mass purges of the Communist Party, expelling, exiling and executing all those who had opposed his rise to power. He also forced through a massive collectivization of the Russian countryside and put into action three five-year-plans (q.v.) for the industrialization of the Soviet Union. He led the Soviet Union to victory against the invading Germans during World War II (q.v.) (1941–45), then resumed his policies of forced industrialization and military expansion in eastern Europe and Asia until his death in 1953.

STALIN CONSTITUTION see CONSTITUTIONS OF THE USSR

STALIN PRIZES. Originally called the Lenin prizes and awarded for any important achievement in culture or technology, these prizes were renamed for Stalin in the 1930s. The original name was restored after 1956.

STALINGRAD see VOLGOGRAD

STALINISM. This term is used for the totality of ideological additions made by Stalin (q.v.) to the doctrines of Marx, Engels, and Lenin (q.v.), including such innovations as the proposition that it was possible to build socialism in one country, that the resistance of the former ruling classes would increase the closer a society came to socialism, and the necessity for the state to grow in strength before it could "wither away." The concept is also associated with systematic reliance on brutal employment of force in order to achieve political and social objectives by a ruling party.

STANISLAVSKY, KONSTANTIN S. (1863–1938). The founder of the Society of Art and Literature, he became a major theatrical figure in Moscow (q.v.) after 1888 and created the Moscow Art Theater (q.v.) in 1897. He is famed for his development of a unique method of training actors and as a producer of highly successful plays. Stanislavsky chose to remain in Soviet Russia after the 1917 revolution.

STANKEVICH, ANTON V. (1862–1919). Born to a noble family on an estate near Vitebsk (q.v.), he graduated from an infantry military school in 1880 and commanded an army division during World War I (q.v.). After the Bolshevik (q.v.) seizure of power he joined the Red Army (see Armed Forces, Soviet) as commander. In 1919 he was captured by the White Armies (q.v.) and executed.

STANOVOI RANGE. A mountain chain in the eastern part of Russia, it forms the watershed between the Pacific and the Arctic oceans.

STAROVERTSY (OLD BELIEVERS). In 1653 the reforming Russian Patriarch Nikon (q.v.) was accused by some members of the clergy of heresy for attempting to introduce minor changes in the Orthodox Church (q.v.) liturgy: how to make the sign of the cross and how to spell the name of the Savior. Despite the fact that Nikon was vindicated by a church council, his accusers, who regarded their ancient Russian tradition as sacred, refused to adhere to its ruling and continued their ancient practices. For this they were persecuted, and some committed self-immolation, believing that they were victims of the Antichrist, Peter the Great (q.v.).

In the 18th century the Old Believers separated into two sects: those who insisted on having priests and those who denied the need for a priesthood and abolished all sacraments besides confession and baptism. The Old Believers were persecuted by the government until the 1905 constitution was granted by Nicholas II (q.v.).

STASOV, DMITRII V. (1828–1918). He received his legal education in St. Petersburg (q.v.) and worked until 1861 as an employee of the State Senate. Stasov became influential during the reforms promulgated by Tsar Alexander II (q.v.). Subsequently, he served as a defense lawyer for revolutionaries and even political terrorists such as Nechaev (q.v.). In the summer of 1917, when Lenin (q.v.) was in hiding, he offered his flat to the Bolshevik (q.v.) leader.

STASOVA, ELENA (1873–1966). She joined the Bolsheviks (q.v.) in 1898, was exiled between 1913 and 1916, and then worked as a secretary of the Central Committee of the Communist Party (q.v.) until 1920. Later, she was prominent in the Comintern (q.v.) apparatus. She is buried in the Red Square (q.v.).

STATE COMMITTEE FOR SCIENCE AND TECHNOLOGY. It was established in 1965 to develop the application of new technology for the benefit of the economy and to coordinate the general direction of all branches of scientific work. It also organizes information storage and dissemination, conferences, exchange programs, and international research agreements.

STATE DUMA see DUMA

STATE FARM see SOVKHOZ

STAVKA. This military term designates the supreme headquarters of the imperial Russian and Soviet armies.

STAVROPOL. The main administrative center of Stavropol region, this city was founded in the late 18th century as a fortress and now has a population of around 650,000. It is a center of the grain trade, food processing industries and agricultural machinery manufacturing. There is also an important automobile industry. In 1965 it was renamed Togliatti (spelled Toliatti in Russian) in honor of the recently deceased Italian Communist leader.

STEPPE. This ecological formation consists primarily of grasslands and is located in the cool, temperate zones of Russia. It stretches for thousands of miles from central Russia to Siberia (q.v.).

STEPUN, FEDOR A. (1884–1965). He was born in Moscow (q.v.) but moved to a rural area as a child, where he fell under the influence of the Russian countryside. A graduate of both Moscow and Heidelberg universities, Stepun became editor of a Russian philosophical periodical, then served as an artillery officer in World War I (q.v.). After the February 1917 revolution (q.v.) he was a close associate of Savinkov (q.v.) in the ministry of war of the Provisional government (q.v.). Stepun remained in Soviet Russia after the civil war (q.v.) and was appointed rector of the State Experimental Theater in 1920. In 1922 he was expelled from the country, along with many other philosophers, moved to Germany and became professor of sociology at Dresden University. After World War II (q.v.) he was professor of Russian culture at the University of Munich.

STERLITAMAK. An important river port on the Belaya River in the Bashkir Autonomous Republic of Russia, it manufactures rubber and machine engineering products and processes food. Its population is approximately 225,000.

STOLYPIN, PETR A. (1862–1911). He served as prime minister to Nicholas II (q.v.) from 1906 until his assassination in 1911 at the hands of Socialist Revolutionaries (q.v.) terrorists. During his time in office he introduced a firm but productive series of agrarian reforms. These allowed peasants to leave their village communes, to acquire land of their own, and to settle in Siberia (q.v.) and other areas where land was available.

STRAVINSKII, IGOR (1882–1971). This pianist and composer became associated with Diaghilev (q.v.), producing such influential works as *The Fire Bird* (1910), *Petrouchka* (1911) and *Rite of Spring* (1913). He lived in France after the revolution and subsequently moved to the United States. His area of musical interest was vast; he made forays into a number of idioms, but Russian folk themes were a constant source of inspiration.

STRELTSY. This is the name of ancient Russian armed units, the "shooters," or musketeers, who formed the first permanent regiments of Muscovy (q.v.). These units acquired a great deal of political power but were forcibly disbanded by Peter the Great (q.v.) after their riots of 1698. It was also the name of a famous regiment of the imperial guards.

STROGANOV FAMILY. A family of successful merchants in Ivan IV's (q.v.) time, they ran salt works in the Ural Mountains (q.v.) and were patrons of the arts, commissioning small icons painted in the manner that came to be known as the "Stroganov school." It was the head of their Cossack (q.v.) guard in the Urals, a certain Ermak (q.v.), who began the conquest of the Mongol khanate of Siberia in the 1580s, which led to the eventual annexation of that region.

STRUVE, GLEB (1893–1985). Following the revolution, Struve left Russia and resumed his education in Prague. In London he lectured at the School of Slavonic Studies and moved to the United States after World War II (q.v.) to teach at the University of California (Berkeley). His work has concentrated on 20th-century Russian poets, resulting in important editions of the works of Pasternak, Akhmatova, and others.

STRUVE, PETER B. (1870–1944). One of the original Russian Marxists, he was an economist who participated in the founding of the Russian Socialist Democratic Labor Party (q.v.). He gradually distanced himself from the other Marxists and became the leader of a liberal Duma (q.v.) grouping. Struve joined the Constitutional Democrats (*see* Kadet [KD] Party) after 1905 and participated in the *Vekhi* (q.v.) movement.

STURMER, COUNT BORIS V. (1848–1917). Appointed by Tsar Nicholas II (q.v.) to be prime minister and the minister of foreign affairs, this elderly courtier became a puppet of Rasputin (q.v.) and was finally retired in November 1916.

SUBBOTNIK. The practice, encouraged by Lenin (q.v.), entailed Soviet workers' donating their Saturdays in order to help the country's reconstruction. From a voluntary act, it was transformed into compulsory "volunteering."

SUKHANOV, NIKOLAI N. (pseud. of Gimmer) (1882–1940). He joined the Mensheviks (q.v.) before World War I (q.v.) and was a close friend of Gorky's (q.v.), with whom he collaborated on a newspaper. He also produced extensive memoirs of the 1917 revolution that were published outside of the Soviet Union in the 1920s. Arrested in 1931, he was released and then rearrested in 1939. Sukhanov died a year later in a Gulag (q.v.) camp.

SUKHOMILOV, VLADIMIR A. (1848–1926). A graduate of the General Staff Academy in 1874, he participated in the Russo-Turkish war (q.v.) of 1877, then served as the governor-general of Kiev (q.v.) from 1905 to 1908. Sukhomilov was a controversial minister of war from 1909 to 1915 and was accused of treason in the Duma (q.v.) in 1915. After this charge, he was forced to retire from public life but was never convicted of any crime.

SUPREMATISM. This movement among early 20th-century Russian painters was led by Malevich (q.v.) and included Puni and Klyun. The group sought to deemphasize reproduction of natural objects and produced geometric forms to analyze the dynamics of space.

SUPREME COUNCIL OF NATIONAL ECONOMY. Also known as the Supreme Economic Council, this body was formed in 1917 to organize the country's economy and usher in socialism. With the introduction of NEP (q.v.) in 1921 it was limited to the lesser task of administering industrial affairs. In 1932 it was divided into the commissariats for heavy industry, light industry, and timber. The council was briefly reestablished between 1963 and 1965 to coordinate and reorganize the various branches of industry; however, its importance decreased after Khrushchev's removal and it was dissolved again.

SUPREME SOVIET (VERKHOVNYI SOVET). The Soviet Union's highest state body, it consisted of two chambers: the Soviet of the Union and the Soviet of Nationalities, each containing 600 deputies. These bodies elected the presidium of the Supreme Soviet and the standing committees but did little else. Sessions were only held a few days a year.

SURITS, IAKOV ZAKHAROVICH (1882–1952). A career Soviet diplomat, Surits was active in revolutionary circles in his youth. After a year in the Bund (1902–03) he joined the Mensheviks (q.v.) (1903–14); in 1907 he was exiled to Tobolsk (q.v.) for three years. After the revolution he headed the first Soviet mission to Denmark and held many positions thereafter, notably as Soviet plenipotentiary to Germany (1934–37) and France (1937–40); as representative with the Soviet delegation at the League of Nations; as counsellor in the People's Commissariat for Foreign Affairs; and as the Soviet Union's ambassador to Brazil (1946–47).

SURKOV, ALEXIS A. (1899–1983). A Communist Party (q.v.) poet, during World War II (q.v.) he specialized in patriotic poetry that had mass appeal; he was rewarded by the government in 1954 with the post of secretary to the Union of Soviet Writers (q.v.). In the late 1950s he was removed from this position.

SUSANIN, IVAN. A semi-mythical 17th-century peasant, he is said to have led a troop of Polish invaders astray into a forest in order to protect the youthful tsar, Michael Romanov (q.v.). His legend was used by the tsarist government to enhance patriotic self-sacrifice and served as a title of Glinka's (q.v.) opera on the same theme.

SUSLOV, MIKHAIL A. (1902–82). He joined the Communist Party (q.v.) in 1921, then attended a workers' faculty and the Plekhanov Institute of National Economy. Suslov occupied a high post in the Central Control Committee of the Communist Party and was an active participant in the purges (q.v.) of the 1930s. A member of the Central Committee after 1941, he worked as a high-ranking Security Services (q.v.) officer during World War II (q.v.) and was responsible for mass arrests and deportations in Lithuania (q.v.) in 1944. After World War II he became head of the Party's propaganda department as well as editor in chief of *Pravda* (q.v.). Suslov was a member of the Politburo (q.v.) under Brezhnev (q.v.), responsible for ideological supervision, and was in part responsible for engineering the ouster of Khrushchev (q.v.) and for the suppression of the Hungarian revolution of 1956, and of the attempted Czech reforms of 1968.

SUVORIN, COUNT ALEKSANDR V. (1730–1800). He fought in the Seven Years' War (q.v.) and in the Russo-Turkish war (q.v.). Catherine the Great (q.v.) made him a count for his brilliant command of her armies. Suvorov also successfully put down a Polish uprising in 1794. After Russia allied itself with Austria against revolutionary France in 1799, Suvorov helped expel the French from Italy.

SUZDAL. A city of 15,000 on the Kamenka River some 120 miles northeast of Moscow (q.v.), it has been known since the 11th century. It is now a center of tourism because of the architectural and historical interest of its monastery, cathedral and kremlin. The town was absorbed by Muscovy (q.v.) in the 15th century.

SVERDLOV, IAKOV. M. (1885–1919). He joined the Bolsheviks (q.v.) as a young man, was exiled to Siberia (q.v.) from 1912 to 1917, and then returned to Russia and became the editor of *Pravda* (q.v.) in 1917, together with Stalin (q.v.). Sverdlov was the first president of the Soviet Republic and played an important role in both the revolution and the civil war (q.v.) because of his organizational ability. Before his death from typhus he became a member of the Politburo (q.v.).

SVERDLOVSK see EKATERINBURG

SVIATEISHII SINOD see MOST HOLY SYNOD

SVIATOPOLK-MIRSKII, PRINCE DMITRY P. (1890–1939). The son of a tsarist minister, he left Russia after the October 1917 revolution (q.v.) to live in England, where he was a lecturer in Russian literature at the University of London. He also wrote extensively on literary topics. In 1930 he joined the British Communist Party and returned to Russia in 1932. There, he was denounced as a counterrevolutionary in 1935 and arrested in 1937. He died in a Siberian concentration camp. His fame was that of a literary historian and gifted critic.

SVIR. A river that is a part of the Mariinskii canal system, it starts at Lake Onega (q.v.) and flows southwest to Lake Ladoga (q.v.).

SVOD ZAKONOV ROSSIISKOI IMPERII. The code of laws of the Russian empire, it was promulgated in 1835 and subsequently added to and revised.

SYKTYVKAR. Located on the Vychegda River, this town is the capital of the Komi Autonomous Republic (q.v.). Its main industries consist of timber processing, woodworking and paper making. Its population is just under 200,000.

SYMBOLISTS. Between the 1890s and the beginning of World War I (q.v.), this group of writers, led by Blok (q.v.), Bely, (q.v.) and Briusov (q.v.) strove to convey mystical insights through the "symbolic language of poetry."

SYTIN, IVAN D. (1851–1934). He began as a publisher of inexpensive books for rural readers and in 1884 founded a publishing house in collaboration with Count Leo Tolstoy (q.v.). By the 1890s Sytin was one of the largest publishers in the Russian empire, producing Russian classics, encyclopedias, and a mass circulation newspaper. He also opened over 50 bookstores throughout Russia. After the revolution the Soviet government nationalized his holdings but allowed him to continue working as an employee in one of the publishing houses that he had started.

SYZRAN. Located on the Volga River (q.v.) some 500 miles southeast of Moscow (q.v.), this town is the capital of the Kuibishev region. It produces machinery and clothing and refines oil. It has a population of approximately 170,000.

T

TABEL O RANGAKH (TABLE OF RANKS). It was promulgated in 1722 by Peter the Great (q.v.) and defined the hierarchical structure of the Russian empire into 14 levels, drawing a vertical separation between court, military and civilian service. It conferred either personal or hereditary status of nobility (*dvorianstvo*) to individuals occupying the first eight ranks of the 14 levels of military positions, thus opening access to *dvorianstvo* to all Russians. As such, it introduced merit and service rather than heredity as the defining criteria of status in the empire.

TADZHIKISTAN see TAJIKISTAN

TAGANKA DRAMA AND COMEDY THEATER. A famous Moscow (q.v.) theater, it started in 1964 and had a reputation for liberalism even during the Brezhnev (q.v.) years of reaction.

TAGANROG. The original settlement was destroyed by the Mongol invaders in the 13th century. It was rebuilt in the 17th century as a naval base. Today it is an industrial and manufacturing city producing various types of machinery and aircraft, with a population of just under 300,000.

TAJIKISTAN. A region of 55,250 square miles, it is bordered on the south by Uzbekistan, Kirghizstan and Afghanistan, and by China to the east. The population is around three million; the Tajik language is close enough to Farsi, or Modern Persian, to be readily understood, although it is written with Cyrillic letters. The Tajiks are largely Sunnite Muslim, and cultivate cotton as their neighbors do in Iran. The also grow fruits and grains. The capital is Dushanbe, with a population of 450,000. The former Tajik SSR became independent in 1991.

TAMBOV. Established in the 17th century as a fortress, this town is located some 300 miles southeast of Moscow (q.v.). It now processes agricultural products as well as machinery and synthetic rubber.

TAMM, IGOR E. (1895–1971). A graduate of the University of Moscow (*see* Universities) in 1918, he became a well-known physicist and received the Nobel Prize for physics in 1958. Tamm was a member of the USSR Academy of Sciences (q.v.) from 1953 onward.

TANEEV, SERGEI (1856–1915). Teacher of Rakhmaninov (q.v.) and Scriabin (q.v.), he was a professor at the Moscow Conservatory of Music and from 1885 its director. Taneev was a student of Tchaikovsky (q.v.) and Rubinstein (q.v.). His chief interest lay in counterpoint theory; he composed four symphonies and the opera *Orestea* but is admired mainly for the choral-orchestral work *At the Reading of a Psalm.*

TANNENBERG, BATTLE OF (1914). This battle ended with the German defeat of a superior Russian force in East Prussia in 1914. Russia decided to invade East Prussia at the beginning of World War I (q.v.), but poor communications and misjudgments caused them to lose many thousands of men. The army commander, General Aleksandr Samsonov (q.v.), committed suicide as a result.

TARASOV, NIKOLAI I. (1902–75). A graduate of the Moscow (q.v.) Choreographical School in 1920, he danced with the Bolshoi theater (q.v.) from 1920 to 1935. Subsequently, Tarasov taught ballet in Moscow and wrote a series of ballet manuals.

TARKOV, NIKOLAI (1871–1930). Born into a prosperous Moscow (q.v.) merchant family, he studied art and as a young painter became a member of the Young Muscovite group of painters. In 1899 he went abroad to visit Paris, where he exhibited his work and remained until his death.

TARKOVSKII, ANDREI A. (1932–86). He was a Russian filmmaker whose works were banned in the Soviet Union until the late 1980s. In 1969 his film *Andrei Rublev* won a prize at the Cannes film festival. Tarkovskii's work was heavily criticized and never became well known at home. In 1984 he defected while traveling abroad and was deprived of his Soviet citizenship.

TARLE, EVGENII V. (1875–1955). This is a Russian historian who specialized in the history of the 18th century and especially the Napoleonic era.

TASHKENT. Capital and administrative center of Uzbekistan, it has a population of some 1.5 million. It was founded some time in the second century B.C., but until 1930 the capital of the Soviet republic of Uzbekistan was Samarkand. In the middle ages Tashkent flourished as a trading center between Europe and the East; it was ruled successively by the Arabs and the Mongols and was finally taken by Russia in 1865.

TATARS. This is the alternate Russian appellation for the Mongols who conquered Russia in the 13th century and established the Kazan Khanate (*see* Golden Horde) on the banks of the Volga River (q.v.).

TATARSTAN AUTONOMOUS REPUBLIC. One of the autonomous republics within Russia, its principal ethnic population consists of Tatars (q.v.), a Turkic-speaking people. It is located on the Volga River (q.v.) in the general location of the ancient seat of the Golden Horde (q.v.), which ruled Russia for over two centuries. The capital is Kazan (q.v.), and its population is approximately 3.5 million.

TAUBE, BARON ALEKSANDR A. (1864–1919). A graduate of the Academy of the General Staff in 1891, he served on active duty during World War I (q.v.). In 1918 he joined the Red Army (*see* Armed Forces, Soviet) as one of Trotsky's (q.v.) military experts and served as chief of staff in Siberia (q.v.). After being captured by the White Armies (q.v.) he was condemned to death, but this sentence was commuted and he died in prison.

TCHAIKOVSKY, PETR (1840–93). Originally trained as a lawyer, Tchaikovsky studied music at the St. Petersburg Conservatory and soon joined the faculty of the Moscow Conservatory as a professor of harmony. He became a noted composer and traveled to Europe in 1888 and America in 1891; in composition he was prolific, displaying a mastery of orchestral forms and superb melodic invention, often drawing on native Russian themes. His works enjoyed huge popularity, though a few were met with scepticism, such as the Violin Concerto in D (1878); some of his most notable works were written in his final years, such as the opera *The Queen of Spades* (1890), the ballet *Sleeping Beauty* (1892), and the Sixth Symphony (1893). In life Tchaikovsky was an unhappy man, and may have died a suicide as the result of court scandal.

TECHNICUM. A technical high school, as distinguished from the gymnasium, or classical high school, its curriculum concentrated on engineering, architecture, agricultural and commercial subjects.

TELEGRAFICHESKOE AGENSTVO SOVETSKOGO SOIUZA (TASS; THE TELEGRAPH AGENCY OF THE SOVIET UNION). This worldwide news agency served as the official channel for the Soviet government. It specialized in spot news. Since the collapse of the Soviet Union it has been renamed ITAR-TASS.

TEREK. A river in the North Caucasus, it rises near Kazbek Mountain to flow northeast for 390 miles and empty into the Caspian Sea (q.v.). It runs past the city of Ordzhonikidze (q.v.), and powers a hydroelectric station.

THAW. This term is used for the period of relative leniency coinciding with Nikita Khrushchev's (q.v.) tenure. Partly fueled by the secret speech at the 20th party congress, this relaxation also allowed the publication of Aleksandr Solzhenitsyn's *One Day in the Life of Ivan Denisovich* (1962) and other works; it came to an end with the trial of Siniavskii (q.v.) and Daniel.

THEATER. In the 17th century, the first Russian theater appeared at the court of Tsar Aleksei (q.v.) in 1672. During the reign of Peter the Great (q.v.), the first public theater was opened in Moscow (q.v.). Soon thereafter another started in St. Petersburg (q.v.). The most popular plays at that time were those of Molière. In the 1730s foreign theatrical troupes began arriving in Russia, and in the same century the first theatrical school was organized. It was established in 1738 in St. Petersburg by the ballet master Lande. In 1756 Russian theater acquired an official status when the Yaroslav theater moved to the capital at the invitation of Empress Elizabeth (q.v.). This state theater served primarily the court circles, but soon after a general admissions theater was opened in the capital, intended to appeal to a wider audience.

At the beginning of the 19th century, theatrical drama was dominated by popular comedies, especially satirical ones. Very significant for the Russian theater at the time were the dramas of Griboedov (q.v.) and Pushkin (q.v.). Another stimulus in the development of theater art was brought by Gogol (q.v.), who wrote comedies. In 1824 in Moscow, the Maly Theater was opened in Moscow and soon became one of the most important elements of the country's humanistic culture. In 1832 the Aleksandrovskii Theater was opened in the capital, but it had a rather official character. Numerous provincial theaters flourished during the 19th century, and many troupes of actors moved from one place to another. In the second half of the century productions of plays by Ostrovskii (q.v.) and Chekhov (q.v.) appeared on the Russian stage.

Stanislavsky (q.v.) began his work and Nemirovich-Danchenko (q.v.) formed the Moscow Art Theater in 1898. At the beginning of the 20th century, Kommissarzherskaia formed her own theater in which some time later Meyerhold (q.v.) served as director. In the immediate prerevolutionary period symbolism was a powerful tendency in the Russian theater.

In the first years of Soviet power many theatrical companies were formed, but as a rule they were not professional and did not last long. Some of these theater groups did survive and became the Soviet Russian centers of culture for many years. Among these were the Bolshoi Theater, the Dramatical Theater in St. Petersburg (q.v.) and the Moscow Art Theater (q.v.). During World War II (q.v.), many Soviet artists went to the front to entertain the troops.

In the postwar period the development of the Russian theater was plagued by the constant ideological censorship of the Soviet government, although during Krushchev's Thaw (q.v.), these pressures were lessened and new theater troupes, with original repertoires and new forms of expression, began to appear. In Moscow the theater Sovremennik began its work, and the Taganka (q.v.) theater started under the directorship of Lubimov. These theaters played the classics of Russian and world literature.

During the period of perestroika (q.v.), a number of plays that had previously been forbidden were allowed to return to the Russian stage.

THIRD ROME. According to this belief, Moscow (q.v.) was destined to be the third Rome after the fall of the first Rome to the western barbarians in 476 and that of Constantinople (Byzantium, or the second Rome) to the Turks in 1452. Moscow's Christian Orthodoxy would then spread to other nations and there would be no fourth Rome. The doctrine was formulated by the Pskov monk Philotheus (or Filofei) in the 16th century in a letter to the grand prince of Moscow; its plausibility coincided with Moscow's growing might and domination of other territories, and it owed something to the fact that Tsar Ivan the III (q.v.) had married the niece of the last Byzantine emperor, Constantine XII.

THIRD SECTION. This was one of the six sections of the department of gendarmes under the tsars (q.v.). It was started by Nicholas I (q.v.) in order to act as the secret security service. Its principal function was to supervise political groups that opposed the monarchy and the established order. It also was responsible for the administration of prisons and for censorship of the press. After 1880 it was merged into the ministry of the interior.

TIKHOMIRAEVA, ANNA V. (b. SAFONOVA) (1893–1975). After studying painting in St. Petersburg (q.v.), she married a naval officer. During World War I (q.v.) she met Admiral Kolchak (q.v.), whose lover she became during the civil war (q.v.). After his capture she was arrested and held in various prison camps until she was released and exiled from Russia in 1954. Before her death she wrote her memoirs, which were published abroad.

TIKHOMIROV, LEV A. (1852–1923). A graduate of the University of Moscow (*see* Universities), he joined the underground populist movement at an early age and spent several years incarcerated in the Peter and Paul Fortress (q.v.). He was a leading member of the executive committee of the People's Will (*see* Narodnaia Volia) Party and also the editor of its illegal paper. Tikhomirov emigrated right after the assassination of Tsar Alexander II (q.v.) by his party comrades but soon publicly repented his revolutionary past and received the tsar's pardon in 1888. During the later part of his life he was one of the principal theoreticians of the monarchy and a close associate of Prime Minister Stolypin (q.v.).

TIKHON, PATRIARCH OF MOSCOW (b. BELAVIN) (1865–1925). A graduate of the St. Petersburg (q.v.) Theological Academy in 1888, he became a monk in 1891 and the bishop of Alaska (q.v.) and the Aleutian Islands (q.v.) in 1899, residing in San Francisco and New York. After his return to Russia in 1914 he was elevated to membership in the Most Holy Synod (q.v.) and to the patriarchate of Moscow (q.v.) in 1917. During his tenure of the office he was attacked both by the atheist Soviet government and by the clergy of the Living Church. Arrested in 1922, he was released after promising loyalty to the state, but died two years later.

TIKHONRAVOV, MIKHAIL K. (1900–74). The father of Soviet rocketry, he designed the original liquid-fueled rockets used by the USSR in its space program. He was a member of the International Aeronautics Academy after 1968.

TILSIT (1946- : SOVETSK). A town in the present Kaliningrad oblast of Russia on the river Neman, formerly in East Prussia, it was founded in the 13th century by Teutonic knights. It is a center for the timber and pulp industry and also produces dairy and leather goods. It was ceded to the USSR in 1945, and its German population was almost entirely replaced by Russians, who number some 60,000. It was here that Alexander I (q.v.) and Napoleon met in 1807 to sign the treaty of Tilsit (*see* Tilsit, Treaty of).

TILSIT, TREATY OF. After Napoleon's victory at Jena, Russia and Prussia signed a peace treaty with France at Tilsit (q.v.) that forced Russia to subordinate its trade policies to Napoleonic demands and to join in a continental blockade of England.

TIMASHEV, NIKOLAI S. (1886–1971). A graduate of the University of St. Petersburg (*see* Universities) in 1917, he became a law professor. After the October 1917 revolution, he actively resisted Communist rule and in 1931 was forced to flee to Finland. In 1928 Timashev became a professor at the Paris Institut des Slaves, and in 1936 he accepted an invitation from Pitrim Sorokin (q.v.) to become a lecturer in sociology at Harvard. Timashev was professor of sociology at Fordham University from 1940 to 1957.

TIME OF TROUBLES. This period in Russian history followed the death of Ivan the Terrible's (q.v.) son Fedor I (q.v.) in 1605. During this time a series of pretenders to the throne appeared, and Poland and Sweden invaded the country. The period ended with the accession of Michael Romanov (q.v.) to the throne in 1613.

TIMOFEEV-RESOVSKII, NIKOLAI V. (1900–81). After graduating from the University of Moscow (*see* Universities), he went to Germany for further study of biology. He defected from the Soviet Union in 1937 and remained in Germany until it was captured by the Red Army (*see* Armed Forces, Soviet) at the end of World War II (q.v.). Imprisoned in a special camp for scientists, Timofeev-Resovskii conducted research on the effect of radiation on human beings. On his release in 1954 he was made head of the Obninsk Laboratory of Medical Radiology.

TIMOSHENKO, MARSHAL SEMEN K. (1895–1970). After serving as a soldier during World War I (q.v.) he joined the Red Army (*see* Armed Forces, Soviet) in 1918 and became a member of the Communist Party (q.v.). After the civil war (q.v.), he graduated from the Higher Military Academy in 1927. Timoshenko held command positions during the Soviet occupation of Poland in 1939 and the war with Finland in 1939–40. He became commissar of defense in 1940 and after World War II (q.v.) commanded a military district.

TIOMKIN, DMITRII (1899–1979). A graduate of the St. Petersburg (q.v.) Conservatory in 1925, he emigrated to the United States and become a well-known composer of film music in Hollywood.

TISSE, EDUARD K. (1897–1961). After his graduation from the School of Art and Photography, he filmed military events during World War I (q.v.), then served as a war cameraman in the Red Army (*see* Armed Forces, Soviet) during the civil war (q.v.). Tisse also filmed numerous Soviet leaders, including Lenin (q.v.), and collaborated with Eisenstein (q.v.) on some of his most famous films.

TIUMEN. Located on the Tura River of western Siberia (q.v.), this city of some 300,000 inhabitants is the capital of the Tiumen region of the Russian Federation and produces chemicals as well as sawmill products.

TIUTCHEV, FEDOR I. (1803–73). A graduate of the University of Moscow (*see* Universities), after a brief career in the diplomatic service he became a censor and also began to write poetry. Tiutchev was the forerunner of the Symbolist (q.v.) movement of Russian poets and is often cited for his poem "Silentium."

TKACHEV, PETR N. (1844–85). A literary figure and a member of the political underground, Tkachev was forced to emigrate to Switzerland, where he published a revolutionary periodical. In it he attempted to popularize his conviction that no reforms could be effected in Russia until after revolutionaries succeeded in seizing state power. His ideas greatly influenced Lenin (q.v.).

TOBOLSK. Located at the confluence of the Tobol and the Irtysh (q.v.) rivers, this town was founded in the late 16th century by Cossacks (q.v.) who occupied Siberia (q.v.) during the reign of Ivan the Terrible (q.v.). Its population is just under 50,000.

TOGLIATTI see STAVROPOL

TOKAEV, GRIGORII A. (1910-). Born into a peasant family, he moved to St. Petersburg (q.v.) in 1929 to study mathematics in a workers' academy, after which he attended a higher technical school in Moscow (q.v.). Tokaev became an aeronautical engineer and a lecturer in aircraft design at the Moscow Aviation Institute, specializing in rocketry research. After World War II (q.v.) he worked with former German rocket scientists until he defected to the British in 1947. Tokaev wrote extensively about the underground opposition to Stalin (q.v.) and became a naturalized British citizen. He was first a lecturer and then a professor at the Northampton College of Advanced Technology.

TOLSTOY, COUNT ALEKSEI N. (1882–1945). A prolific novelist and playwright specializing in historical fiction, he emigrated after the revolution but returned to Russia in the early 1920s. His works about Ivan the Terrible (q.v.) and Peter the Great (q.v.) pleased Stalin (q.v.), who rewarded him with numerous prizes and gave him a prominent place among Soviet representatives at international gatherings.

TOLSTOY, COUNT LEV N. (1828–1910). Considered one of the two greatest Russian novelists (together with Dostoevsky, q.v.), he belonged to an ancient Russian noble family. Early in his life he joined the army as an artillery officer and fought in the Caucasus (q.v.) and the Crimea (q.v.). After Russia's defeat in 1856 he moved to his family estate west of Moscow (q.v.), where he began his masterpiece, *War and Peace*. It dealt with Russian life during the Napoleonic wars (q.v.). Tolstoy gradually withdrew from the habitual pleasures of his class, became estranged from his wife, and began publicizing his philosophy of nonresistance to violence, humility, and manual labor. Toward the end of his life he was excommunicated by the Orthodox Church (q.v.) for his theological heresies.

TOMSK. The administrative center of Tomsk oblast in Western Siberia, population 260,000, it was founded in 1604 as a fortified town on the river Tom, which served as a link to Siberian exploration and development; the Tom is also an important tributary of the Ob River (q.v.). Tomsk supports a varied array of industries, among them chemical processing, machine manufacturing, wood processing and metalworking. Its university is the oldest in Siberia, and it is also home to an important technical university.

TOMSKII, MIKHAIL P. (1880–1936). An early and prominent supporter of Lenin (q.v.), this former metalworker became the leader of the Trade Union Council of the Soviet Union and a member of the Politburo (q.v.). He sided with Bukharin (q.v.) and Rykov (q.v.) against Stalin's (q.v.) forced collectivization policy in the late 1920s, for which he was expelled from all his Communist Party (q.v.) posts in April 1929. In early 1938 he committed suicide rather than face arrest by the security services.

TRADE, DOMESTIC. Free trade was completely eliminated in Russia during the 1918–21 period of War Communism (q.v.). After the introduction of the New Economic Policy (*see* NEP) in 1921, commerce between village and town began to revive. In numerous cities, markets were created and trade fairs were held. This helped restore the economic links between different regions of the country.

An important role in this revival was played by cooperative consumer networks that had been established before the 1917 revolutions. Mutual relations between these cooperatives and state-owned industry began to be created through agreements between them. Another favorable factor was the implementation of trade agreements between state enterprises and agricultural cooperatives for the purchase of their harvest at previously agreed-on prices. At the beginning of the New Economic Policy a large part of the retail trade was carried out through private enterprise. In the subsequent years however, private traders were gradually eased out by state trading organizations and by consumer cooperatives.

In the late 1920s and early 1930s, after the wholesale collectivization of the agricultural sector, new collective farm markets arose in which peasants were able to sell at market prices the produce that they were permitted to grow on their individual land allocations. These tiny plots, where private cultivation remained legal, played a very important role in supplementing the produce that was available to consumers through the state distribution networks.

In the 1930s government trade organizations concerned themselves primarily with servicing cities and industrial regions. Cooperative trade, on the other hand, served primarily the rural population. The system of state-administered trade in the Soviet Union was built on a principle of dual subordination: on the sectorial dimension trade was regulated by a hierarchy of state bureaucracies, and on the territorial dimension it was under the control of the local soviets (q.v.).

Reforms that were initiated during the period of perestroika (q.v.) in the late 1980s gave rise to a form of trade where prices were established at auctions, according to the principle of supply and demand. This practice soon evolved into a system of exchanges and, in 1990, the Moscow Trade Exchange came into being. Other agricultural exchanges were also created in order to act as intermediaries between producers and retailers. These exchanges came into being in many regions of the country and served to supply their areas with the needed agricultural produce. Large state enterprises of the region participated in them.

By the middle of 1991 sectorial trade exchanges had come into being. These exchanges helped coordinate the purchasing activities of large industrial and commercial enterprises. Currently, a transformation is taking place of these exchanges into trade associations and investment companies.

During the past three years commercial stores have been established in the larger cities that carry a wide selection of imported goods. The old state stores, on the other hand, although they have been privatized and transformed into publicly owned corporations, still frequently function in a primitive manner, providing poor customer service and offering a limited choice of goods. The other form of retail trade that has come into being since the fall of the Communist regime are the booths that line the streets of the larger cities of Russia. Here farmers can sell their produce to passersby and pensioners and the unemployed sell their personal possessions in order to obtain funds for their basic needs.

TRADE, FOREIGN. The present situation in foreign trade is unfavorable for Russia, and its ratio of exports to imports is substantially below that of other developed countries. Exports for 1993 had dropped by 12 percent relative to 1992, despite substantial increases in the sale of oil, gas, and ferrous metals.

Potentially, Russia has a number of advantages in its competition for foreign markets: it has a highly qualified and inexpensive workforce, a relatively developed infrastructure, and a large and advanced war-production industrial complex that can be transformed into a consumer-oriented sector. Its trade with the former republics of the Soviet Union is also an area of potential growth, because the economy of all of these republics was originally organized into a single unit, and there still exist common production technologies, as well as a common market that has evolved over many decades.

In terms of trade with countries outside of the former USSR, there is a trend developing toward a closer relationship with non-European countries. In 1992, 75 percent of all exports from Russia went to Europe; 21 percent to Asia; and only three percent to America. Increasing trade barriers and sharpening competition for West European markets, as well as the severe ecological safeguards in Europe, are working to lower Russia's export potential to that area. In the past, the Soviet Union was a significant trading partner of several developing countries such as Cuba. Such foreign commerce absorbed as much as 13 percent of all Soviet exports. However, the economic benefits from this trade were small because it was politically motivated, and there was frequently no expectation of repayment of the credits that the Soviet Union extended. In the present circumstances of economic constraint, such trade has rapidly dropped in significance. On the other hand, there is now a growing opportunity for Russia to expand its trade with the newly industrialized countries of southern Asia and the Pacific Ocean regions, such as Singapore, as well as with South America.

TRADE UNIONS. The role of trade unions in the events of October 1917 was secondary compared to the role of other social organizations. In January 1918 the first General Congress of Trade Unions took place with the majority of the delegates being members of the Communist Party (q.v.). At that congress the Menshevik (q.v.) delegates came out for the independence of trade unions from the state, whereas the Bolsheviks (q.v.) insisted that the trade unions should become part of the state organization. In the end, the idea of the independence of trade unions was rejected, and instead, unions were given the responsibility for industrial production. In 1920 a faction calling itself the Workers' Opposition (q.v.) was formed within the Communist Party. Its most authoritative leader was Shliapnikov (q.v.), the president of the metalworkers trade union and a respected member of the Bolshevik (q.v.) leadership. This group demanded that trade unions be placed in complete charge of the national economy. Opposing it was Trotsky (q.v.), who came out for a complete integration of the trade unions into the government. Both propositions were rejected by the party and, instead, Lenin's proposal was adopted. It called for the trade unions to become the school of management of the working class and a transmission belt from the Communist Party to the workers.

By the end of the 1920s a system of social security was created in the Soviet Union in which the trade unions were given an important part to play. In 1928 Soviet trade unions counted some 11 million members and included not only industrial workers but all types of occupations. However, they had been removed from all responsibility for production, which had been given to factory managers and directors of enterprises.

While the numbers of trade unionists continued to grow, the new members came primarily from the collective farms and possessed little if any knowledge about trade unionism, their tasks or traditions. This fact, in part, explains why the quantitative growth of the unions was not accompanied by a similar growth in political influence. Stalin (q.v.) considered the trade unions to be the principal base of the Right Opposition (q.v.) and in the 1930s replaced almost all of the original union leadership with his own appointees. The tasks that remained to the unions were the organization of socialist competitions and the job of ensuring that the annual production plans were fulfilled. The trade unions were also allowed to retain the role of distributing privileges and allocating vacation and other benefits to the most meritorious workers. Membership in a trade union thus provided a measure of social protection.

The fall of the Soviet Union was followed by significant transformations in the Russian trade unions, among which was the rise of

independent trade unions that were critically inclined toward the old
state-sponsored unions. A second development was an attempt to reform the old unions' organizations. This attempt met with only limited success. In most of these old unions the former leadership was
able to retain its position. These unions are still inclined to conform
to management, whereas the newer ones are apt to enter into conflict
with their management. Nevertheless, while experiencing severe financial difficulties, Russian trade unions are, for the first time since
the October 1917 revolution (q.v.), able to participate in strike actions
to defend their interests.

TRAIL, VERA A. (1906–87). The daughter of a minister of war in the
Provisional government (q.v.), she was brought up in Czechoslovakia
and France and became active in the pro-Soviet Eurasian circles.
Later she married a British communist who was killed in the Spanish
civil war. After joining the French Communist Party, she visited the
USSR and helped induce several prominent Russian emigres (*see*
Emigres, Russian), including Prince Sviatapolk-Mirsky (q.v.), to re-
turn to Russia. Arrested briefly in Paris after the start of World War
II (q.v.), she moved to Cambridge, England, where she wrote novels
and film reviews.

TRANSCAUCASIA. These lands, immediately beyond the Caucasus
(q.v.) Mountains in relation to Russia, include Georgia (q.v.), Armenia and Azerbaijan (q.v.).

TRANSPORTATION. The Russian transportation system consists of
several different modes: railroad, sea, river, automobile, and pipeline.
The density of the network decreases as one moves from European
Russia eastward. Although the growth of pipeline and automobile
transport is rapidly increasing, the railroads are still the predominant
mode for moving freight as well as passengers. In 1974 the share of
railroad freight transport was 81.8 percent of the total freight moved;
river transport accounted for 5.9 percent; automobile, 5 percent; sea
transport, 13.6 percent; and pipelines, 13.6 percent. The most important railroads run from Moscow to Povolzhia, the Ural Mountains
(q.v.), and Siberia (q.v.). Railroad transport is used primarily for the
interregional ties of the country and consists of both fuel- and elec-
tricity-driven trains. The electrified railways are located primarily
near cities, in districts with the most intense freight movement, and
in districts with a difficult geological profile. Railroads in general
transport primarily coal, coke, oil products, black metals, wood,
grain, construction material, and mineral fertilizers.
    In the Russian Republic there are several large rivers: the Volga

(q.v.), the Ob (q.v.), the Irtysh (q.v.), Enisei (q.v.), Lena (q.v.), and the Amur (q.v.). These are supplemented by an extensive network of canals: the Belomor-Baltic Canal and the Volga-Don Canal. The primary materials transported on these waterways are wood, oil, and various oil products. Approximately half of all the freight transported by water occurs in the Volga basin.

Sea transport also plays an important role, especially for foreign trade export and import. The most important seaports are Novorossiisk (q.v.), St. Petersburg (q.v.), Kaliningrad (q.v.), Murmansk (q.v.), Arkhangelsk (q.v.) and Vladivostok (q.v.). In order to ensure uninterrupted navigation in the northern waters, large atomic icebreakers have been constructed.

Air transport in Russia consists of a large network of air routes, with hundreds of cities and towns possessing their own airports. Air travel is especially important for passengers traveling long distances.

Automobile transport is primarily concentrated in cities as well as being utilized for regional service. In the past, Russia has had poor quality automobile highways. Even today over ten percent of its roads are gravel. However, in most cities automobile transport exists and takes care of the needs of internal passenger transport, while six cities possess extensive underground metro systems.

Pipeline transport is also growing rapidly. It enables the movement of oil and gas from Siberia (q.v.) and the Far East (q.v.) to be delivered to the European regions of Russia, as well as to East and West European markets.

In the post-Soviet period, because of the sharp drop in production of oil and gas, as well as of the breakdown of economic ties between former regions of the USSR, the general functioning of transportation has worsened, with the total amount of freight transport in 1992 being 22 percent lower than in 1991. A shortage of repair facilities and the frequent lack of adequate servicing of equipment has led to a sharp drop in the quality of urban passenger transport. As a result, in Moscow between 1991 and 1992 many buslines were either closed or had to reduce their service. Nevertheless, despite existing difficulties, the transport system of Russia continues to function, and new transport companies are being formed.

TRANS-SIBERIAN RAILROAD. A railway of almost six thousand miles' length, it links Moscow (q.v.) to Vladivostok (q.v.) on the Pacific. A plan to construct the railway was approved by Alexander III (q.v.) in 1891. Its guiding proponent was Sergei Witte (q.v.), who was appointed minister of ways and communications in 1892 and, later, minister of finance. It was constructed in six steps from west to east. Of these, the penultimate section (from Sretensk to Khabarovsk, known as the Amur section) presented enormous difficulties, necessitating an alternate route through Manchuria. This was to become known as the Chinese Far Eastern Railroad (q.v.) and required a treaty with China before it could be built. The whole project was completed in 1901 and was fully operational by 1903. It was therefore on schedule but, at a cost of some 250 million dollars, it was twice as expensive as foreseen; moreover, in order to meet the deadline, some of the work was poor and entailed numerous repairs. The Sretensk-Khabarovsk section was finally completed in 1916.

TREPOV, DMITRII F. (1855–1906). The chief of police in Moscow (q.v.) from 1896 to 1906, then governor-general of St. Petersburg (q.v.), Trepov was responsible for some of the anti-Semitic pogroms (q.v.) organized by the Black Hundreds (q.v.). As military governor of St. Petersburg, he ordered the illegal flogging of a member of a terrorist organization and, in revenge, one of that group's leaders, Vera Zasulich, shot him, but was judged not guilty at her trial.

TREST. The term, borrowed from English "trust," is used in the legal sense of a financial trust. It was the name of a Soviet security operation that infiltrated Russian emigre groups in the 1920s in Western Europe and the United States.

TRETIAKOV, P.M. (1832–98). A wealthy textile manufacturer, he founded the gallery named for him in Moscow in 1892 on the basis of his private collection.

TRETIAKOV, SERGEI M. (1892–1939). Playwright, journalist and poet, he invented a new "empirical writing" style that was to reflect Marxist materialism. Tretiakov was executed during the purges (q.v.) of the 1930s as a spy.

TRIFON, METROPOLITAN (b. TURKESTANOV) (1861–1934). After graduating from a theological seminary in Moscow (q.v.) in 1895, he became a priest and bishop of Dmitrov. During World War I (q.v.) Bishop Trifon served as a regimental priest, was wounded and retired to a monastery until elevated to archbishop in 1923.

TRILISSER, M.A. (1883–193?). A revolutionary delegate to the 1906 Tammerfors social democratic conference, he became the deputy chairman of the security service (q.v.) in 1926. Subsequently, Trilisser was head of its foreign department. He was executed during the purges (q.v.) of the 1930s.

TROITSA-SERGEEVA LAVRA. One of the three most important monasteries of Russia, located some 40 miles north of Moscow (q.v.), it was started by St. Sergius (q.v.) in the early 14th century and served as a religious center until it was closed by Soviet authorities in 1920. Now it is the seat of the Orthodox (q.v.) patriarch of Russia.

TROTSKY, LEV D. (b. Bronstein) (1879–1940). One of Lenin's (q.v.) principal allies during the October 1917 revolution (q.v.), he was the first Soviet commissar of foreign affairs and headed the Brest-Litovsk (q.v.) peace negotiations with Germany in 1918. Then, during the civil war (q.v.), he was the commissar of war and the principal creator of the Red Army (see Armed Forces, Soviet). Defeated by Stalin (q.v.) in the 1920s in a lengthy factional struggle—a struggle that involved sharply differing perspectives on the future course of the revolution—he was exiled first to Turkey and then to Mexico, where he continued to play an active role as Stalin's severest and most effective critic. In Mexico he founded the Fourth International. Trotsky was assassinated by a Soviet security service (q.v.) agent in 1940.

TRUBETSKOI, PRINCE EVGENII N. (1863–1920). A graduate of the University of Moscow (see Universities), he was the founder of the Moscow Psychological Society as well as professor at the University of Moscow. After the October 1917 revolution (q.v.) he opposed the Bolsheviks (q.v.) and died fighting them during the civil war (q.v.).

TRUBETSKOI, PRINCE GRIGORII N. (1874–1930). After graduating from the University of Moscow (see Universities), he served as a diplomat in Berlin and Vienna and, at the beginning of World War I (q.v.), was the Soviet ambassador to Serbia. He fought with the White Armies (q.v.) during the civil war (q.v.), then emigrated to France, where he wrote his memoirs.

TRUBETSKOI, PRINCE SERGEI N. (1790–1860). A member of one of Russia's most distinguished princely families, he became the leader of the Northern Society (q.v.) in 1823 and participated in the Decembrist (q.v.) rebellion, for which he was banished to Siberia (q.v.) in 1826.

TRUD. The Russian word for work, it was also the name of the official newspaper of the Soviet trade unions, used by the Communist Party (q.v.) as a channel of ideological and organizational influence on the trade union readership of the country.

TRUDOVIKI. A small socialist party faction in the prerevolutionary Duma (q.v.), it represented the relatively conservative wing of the socialist groupings in that assembly. Kerensky (q.v.), the last prime minister of the Provisional government (q.v.), was one of its leading members.

TRUKHIN, FEDOR I. (1899–1946). A member of an aristocratic family and a graduate of a military academy, he became a revolutionary at an early age and joined the Red Army (*see* Armed Forces, Soviet) during the civil war (q.v.). Trukhin rose to the rank of chief of staff of a military district before World War II (q.v.). Captured by the German army in 1941, he joined the pro-German Vlasov (q.v.) movement. At the end of World War II he was taken prisoner by Soviet forces and hanged together with Vlasov.

TRUVOR (mid-ninth century). A semilegendary figure, he was the brother of Riurik (q.v.) and Sineus. Together with his brothers he was invited by the Eastern Slavic tribes to become their ruler.

TSAR. Ruler or sovereign. It is the Russian equivalent of the Roman caesar and the Byzantine basileus. In 1547 Ivan IV (q.v.) was the first to be crowned as the tsar of all the Russias. This title was legally superseded in 1721 when Peter the Great (q.v.) was crowned "imperator" (emperor) but was retained in popular parlance.

TSARITSYN see VOLGOGRAD

TSARSKOE SELO. Until 1917 it was the name of a town some 15 miles from St. Petersburg (q.v.) that was the frequent residence of Russia's tsars. It was founded by Peter the Great (q.v.) in 1718. After the 1917 revolution it was renamed first Detskoe Selo, then Pushkin.

TSCHAIKOVSKY see TCHAIKOVSKY

TSERETELI, IRAKLII GEORGIEVICH (1882–1960). A Georgian Menshevik (q.v.) leader, Tsereteli participated in the second Duma (q.v.) and later in the Provisional government (q.v.) as a minister. With the Bolsheviks (q.v.) in power after the October revolution (q.v.), Tsereteli returned to Georgia (q.v.) to take part in the short-lived Menshevik government of independent Georgia. After the conquest of the country by Soviet forces in 1921 he lived in France and then in the United States.

TSIOLKOVSKII, KONSTANTIN (1857–1935). Known as the father of Soviet cosmic exploration, Tsiolkovskii was born in the village of Izhevsk and, having become partly deaf as a child, devoted himself to the study of science and mathematics. Largely self-taught, he became a math teacher and, later, an important theorist of space flight, manned space travel, and even the long-term colonization of space, long before any of these were remotely possible.

TSUSHIMA, BATTLE OF (1905). The decisive sea encounter of the Russo-Japanese war (q.v.), it was during this engagement that the victorious Japanese navy sank most of Russia's Baltic fleet.

TSVETAEVA, MARINA I. (1892–1941). A Russian poet and friend of Pasternak (q.v.), Mandelshtam (q.v.) and Akhmatova (q.v.), her work, noted for its passion and wordplay, has had considerable influence on poets of later generations. She was married to Sergei Efron, who served in the White Armies (q.v.) while she remained in Moscow (q.v.) until 1922. She moved to Prague and then to Paris but found emigre life uncongenial and the audience for her work meagre. Efron became embroiled in the assasination of an emigre and returned to Russia; Tsvetaeva followed him in 1939, only to find that he had been executed and that her daughter was in a concentration camp. After the outbreak of World War II (q.v.) she was evacuated to the town of Elabuga (q.v.), where she committed suicide in 1941.

TUGAN-BARANOVSKII, MIKHAIL (1865–1919). A noted economist and historian at the University of St. Petersburg (see Universities), he believed that capitalism was unavoidable in Russian economic development. He was minister of finance in the Ukrainian national government, or Rada, in 1917.

TUKHACHEVSKII, MIKHAIL (1893–1937). Born into a noble family, he served as an officer in World War I (q.v.), then in 1918 became a member of the Communist Party (q.v.) and fought with the Red Army (see Armed Forces, Soviet) during the civil war (q.v.). He was commander of the Soviet forces in the Caucasus (q.v.) in the early 1920s, then in 1921 led them in an assault on the rebellious fortress of Kronstadt (q.v.). Tukhachevskii was chief of staff of the Red Army from 1925 until 1928, a marshal of the Soviet Union, and deputy commissar for defense. In 1935 Tukhachevskii was accused of high treason with several other high-ranking Red Army commanders and executed.

TULA. Established in the 12th century, this city is located at the center of Moscow's (q.v.) coal basin. It is an industrial city producing metalworks and is famed for its cannons.

TUMANOVA, TAMARA V. (1919–1996). Born in Shanghai of Russian parents, she studied ballet in Paris and danced with the Ballets Russes (q.v.) in Monte Carlo between 1933 and 1938. Tumanova also danced with Balanchine (q.v.) at the Paris Opera in the late 1940s and 1950s.

TUPOLEV, ANDREI N. (1888–1972). In 1926 he established Russia's first aircraft design bureau, which produced several outstanding aircraft for Soviet military and civilian aviation. Briefly incarcerated during the purges (q.v.) of the 1930s, he was rehabilitated during World War II (q.v.) and designed Russia's first strategic bomber (Tu-4) in 1965–66.

TURGENEV, IVAN S. (1818–83). The son of a noble family, he was educated at the universities (q.v.) of Moscow (q.v.) and St. Petersburg (q.v.) and began publishing his work in 1845. Turgenev was briefly arrested in 1852 and, after his release, moved to Paris, where he became an acknowledged Russian literary figure and associated extensively with European intellectuals of the period. For many years he was involved in a seemingly unsuccessful though perhaps perfectly satisfactory courtship of the singer Pauline Viardot. His novel *Fathers and Sons* is something of a landmark in Russian literature; he is also admired for the story "First Love."

TURKESTAN. This name was formerly in use to denote central Asia, now known by the several names of its constituent parts: Kazakhstan (q.v.), Kirghizstan, Tajikistan (q.v.), Turkmenistan (q.v.), Uzbekistan, and parts of the Afghani and Chinese border area.

TURKMENISTAN. A former Soviet republic covering an area of 187,144 square miles, it has a population of 4,500,000, of whom some 77 percent are ethnic Turkmen; its capital is Ashkhabad. The Turkmen (sometimes "Turcoman") are an Eastern Turkic-speaking, formerly nomadic people. The country was created in 1924 from Russian Turkestan, a dry region that has been successfully irrigated in many parts. In addition to cotton growing and sheep husbandry there are important oil and coal deposits. Turkmenistan joined the CIS in 1991.

TURKSIB. This is the name of the railroad built between 1913 and 1930 that connects the Orianburg line with the Trans-Siberian Railroad (q.v.).

TUVA AUTONOMOUS REPUBLIC. An autonomous republic within the Russian Federation, it is located in southern Siberia (q.v.). Its population is close to 300,000.

TVARDOVSKY, ALEKSANDR T. (1910–71). A poet and the editor of the liberal Soviet literary periodical *Novyi Mir* (q.v.), after Stalin's (q.v.) death he was instrumental in publishing several controversial novels by Russian writers, including Solzhenitsyn (q.v.).

TVER. Established in the 12th century, this city is located some 100 miles northwest of Moscow (q.v.), at the confluence of the Tvertsa and Volga (q.v.) rivers. It acquired early fame for its production of icons and is now a major industrial center producing engineering and textile products. It was named Kalinin during the Soviet period. Its population is just over 400,000.

TYRKOVA-WILLIAMS, ARIADNA V. (1869–1962). Born into a landowner's family, she was educated in St. Petersburg (q.v.), where she became a friend of Krupskaia (q.v.). In 1897 she began working as a journalist while also being active in revolutionary circles. Arrested for smuggling illegal literature, she escaped imprisonment by emigrating to Germany. There she collaborated with Peter Struve (q.v.) on his newspaper. She returned to Russia after the 1905 revolution (*see* Revolution of 1905) and married Harold Williams, an Australian newspaperman. She sided with the White Armies (q.v.) during the civil war (q.v.) and emigrated to England with her husband in the early 1920s, where she was an active anti-Communist. After World War II (q.v.) she moved to the United States and helped resettle Russian refugees there.

U

UBOREVICH, IERONIM P. (1896–1937). Educated at the Konstantinovskoe Artillery Military Academy, from which he graduated in 1916, he served as a junior officer in World War I (q.v.), then in the Red Army (*see* Armed Forces, Soviet) during the civil war (q.v.). In 1922 Uborevich was appointed commander in chief of the Red Army in the Far East. In the early 1930s he became deputy chairman of the Revolutionary Military Council (q.v.) of the USSR and candidate member of the Central Committee of the Communist Party (q.v.). He was court-martialed and shot on Stalin's (q.v.) orders in 1937.

UDMURT AUTONOMOUS REPUBLIC. One of the autonomous republics of the Russian Federation, northeast of Moscow (q.v.), its capital, Izhevsk (q.v.), is an important manufacturing center producing machine tools, locomotives and a variety of consumer products.

UEZD. A territorial administrative unit that first came into use in the 13th century, it was rationalized as a constituent part of a *guberniia* in the 18th century. There were some 500 *uezdy* in the 19th century. In the period from 1923 to 1929 they were turned into the somewhat smaller *raiony* in the Soviet Union but continued in use until the end of the 1940s in the Baltic states and Bessarabia (q.v.).

UFA. A city located east of Moscow (q.v.) at the confluence of the Belaya and Ufa rivers, it is one of the major industrial centers of the Ural Mountains (q.v.), specializing in petrochemical products. Its population is around 1,000,000.

UFA DIRECTORY. After their dispersal by the Bolsheviks (q.v.) in early 1918, members of the Constituent Assembly (q.v.), mostly Social Revolutionaries (q.v.), met in the provincial city of Ufa (q.v.) and organized an anti-Communist government. It was dispersed at the end of that year by forces loyal to the White Armies (q.v.) commander, Admiral Kolchak (q.v.).

UGLICH. This city in the Iaroslavskaia oblast on the Volga (q.v.) was founded in the 11th century. It was here that rumor of Prince Dmitrii's (q.v.) death in 1591 caused a rebellion of the citizenry.

UKRAINE. Independent since 1991, Ukraine is an agriculturally wealthy region of around 231,990 square miles. Although capable of producing enormous amounts of food, its population was decimated by starvation caused by Stalin's (q.v.) collectivization policy in the 1930s. In addition to agriculture, Ukraine has rich deposits of coal and iron ore and two important ports on the Black Sea (q.v.), Odessa (q.v.) and Sebastopol (q.v.).

Kiev (q.v.), the capital, with a population in excess of four million, was historically the cradle of Rus (q.v.) and the Russian Orthodox Church (q.v.). It was the center of medieval culture for the Eastern Slavic peoples until the Mongol invasions in the early 13th century. The current population of Ukraine is around 51,839,000.

ULANOVA, GALINA S. (1910-   ). One of the outstanding Russian ballet dancers of the 20th century, she began her career with the Kirov Ballet Company (q.v.) in 1928. After retiring in 1963, she became ballet instructor at the Bolshoi Theater (q.v.) in Moscow (q.v.).

ULAN-UDE (-1934: VERKHNEUDINSK). Center and capital of the Buryatia Autonomous Republic (q.v.), situated at the confluence of the Uda and Seleng rivers in central Siberia, its population is 300,000, and its industries include glassworks, machine building and food processing. Founded in 1666, Ulan-Ude is an important rail link, being the terminus for the railway from Beijing.

ULIANOV, ALEKSANDR I. (1866–87). Elder brother of Lenin (q.v.), he was executed in 1887 for making the bombs that were to be used by revolutionary terrorists in an unsuccessful attempt to kill Tsar Alexander III (q.v.).

ULIANOVSK. The birthplace of Lenin (q.v.), located between the Sviyaga and the Volga River (q.v.) northwest of Kuibyshev (*see* Samara), this industrial center specializes in sawmilling products and food processing. Its population is close to half a million.

UNGERN VON STERNBERG, BARON ROMAN F. (1886–1921). Born into a family of Baltic barons, he became a Russian army officer in World War I (q.v.) and commander of an anti-Bolshevik (q.v.) military force of Cossacks (q.v.) in Siberia (q.v.) during the civil war (q.v.). He was famous for his extreme cruelty during the period in which he dominated Mongolia. In 1921 he brought his force back to Russia but was captured by the Red Army (*see* Armed Forces, Soviet) and shot.

UNIATES. These are Eastern Rite Catholics, most of whom are found in Ukraine (q.v.), Poland, and those parts of Russia acquired from the partitions of Poland. They are, in effect, Catholics who use the Orthodox (q.v.) liturgy and otherwise adhere to Orthodox practices. In the late 16th century, Orthodox Christians in Poland decided to unite with Rome, largely to avoid excessive Russian influence. The union was made official in 1596 by a synod of Orthodox bishops of Poland at Brest.

UNION OF ARCHANGEL MICHAEL (SOIUZ MIKHAILA ARKHANGELA). A splinter group of the Union of Russian People (q.v.), it shared that group's ultranationalist and anti-Semitic views. Founded in 1908 and led by V.M. Purishkevich, it dissolved after the February revolution (q.v.).

UNION OF RUSSIAN PEOPLE (SOIUZ RUSSKOGO NARODA). An extreme nationalist group promoting anti-Semitism and intolerance, it was founded in 1905 and led by A.I. Dubrovin in St. Petersburg (q.v.). The group dissolved after the February revolution (q.v.).

UNION OF SOVIET SOCIALIST REPUBLICS (USSR). This was the official name for the Soviet Union, which consisted of 12 union republics from its formation in 1921 until 1940, when three formerly independent Baltic countries were brought into the union. The USSR was officially dissolved in December 1991.

The territory of the USSR was divided into administrative units that were based on the principle of nationality. The 15 national republics, designated as union republics until the breakup of the Soviet Union, were: the Armenian SSR, the Azerbaijan SSR, the Belorussian SSR, the Estonian SSR, the Georgian SSR, the Kazakh SSR, the Kirgiz SSR, the Latvian SSR, the Lithuanian SSR, the Moldavian SSR, the Russian RSFSR, the Tajik SSR, the Turkmen SSR, the Ukrainian SSR, and the Uzbek SSR.

Each republic had its own internal governmental structure, its own political and administrative system, and its official language. Each also had within it autonomous republics and/or autonomous regions. All union republics were part of the Russian Empire before the revolutions of 1917, and all had the theoretical right to secede from the Soviet Union. However, under the conditions of an absolute monopoly of power in the hands of the Communist Party of the Soviet Union (q.v.), such rights remained essentially fictitious.

UNION OF SOVIET WRITERS. This government-sponsored organization was utilized by the Communist Party (q.v.) to exercise ideological control over Soviet literature and to impose socialist realism, its officially approved style, on Russian writers. This style was designed to enable the party to transmit its ideology to the population. Expulsion from the union precluded any possibility of publishing one's work.

UNIONS FOR THE STRUGGLE FOR THE LIBERATION OF THE WORKING CLASS. These groups were organized in the cities to promote workers' interests and plan labor actions. They began to appear in the 1890s, usually related to Marxist groups and sharing their ideology. They worked within a network of labor groups and committees in each city. Lenin directed the St. Petersburg (q.v.) union, and its members later formed the nucleus of the Bolshevik (q.v.) party; members of other unions also joined them.

UNIVERSITIES. The first university to open in Russia was the so-called Academic University, created in 1725 in St. Petersburg (q.v.) at the wishes of Peter the Great (q.v.), who died a few months before its inauguration. This institution, staffed principally by German professors, was chronically short of students since noble families at the time sent their sons to military academies. It closed in 1766. Moscow University opened in 1755, under the guidance of Mikhail Lomonosov (q.v.), and eventually gained enough support to sustain itself, becoming Russia's most important institute of higher learning. At the beginning of the 19th century, universities also opened in Kazan (q.v.), Kharkov (q.v.) and St. Petersburg. There are now some 500 universities and institutes of higher learning in Russia.

URAL MOUNTAINS. The mountain chain that separates Europe from Asia and European Russia from Siberia (q.v.), it is almost 1,500 miles in length and runs south from the Arctic Ocean. It is rich in minerals. This wealth of resources has enabled Russia to develop a major industrial center there.

URAL RIVER (-1775: IAIK). This 1,500 mile-long river rises near the Uraltau ridge in the South Urals and flows south to empty into the Caspian Sea (q.v.). It forms a natural border between Europe and Asia and is a source of freshwater fish such as sturgeon. It flows past the cities of Omsk (q.v.) and Orenburg (q.v.), in addition to the ports of Uralsk and Guriev.

USHAKOV, FEDOR F. (1744–1817). An admiral of the Russian imperial navy, he fought the French naval forces in the Mediterranean during the Napoleonic wars (q.v.).

USHINSKII, KONSTANTIN D. (1824–70). A pioneering educational reformer of the primary education system in Russia.

USPENSKII, NIKOLAI D. (1900–87). Born into a priest's family, he was educated at the Novgorod (q.v.) and St. Petersburg (q.v.) seminaries, then became a musicologist and a professor at the conservatory. In 1957 he published a history of liturgical singing in Russia.

USPENSKII, PETR D. (1878–1947). Born into a family of a middle-level government official, he began to work as a journalist but soon became interested in psychology and philosophy. He traveled extensively in the Near East, where he developed his mystical teachings, which were influenced by fellow mystic Gurdjieff. In 1921 Uspenskii moved to England, where he obtained the patronage of several high-society figures and became a popular lecturer on occult subjects. During World War II (q.v.) he lived in the United States, then returned to England in 1947. Uspenskii's writings were very influential among theosophical circles on both sides of the Atlantic Ocean.

USPENSKII CONVENT. This is an example of the Vladimir-Suzdal school of architecture in the town of Vladimir (q.v.) completed in 1160. Later work includes frescoes by Andrei Rublev (q.v.) and Danil Chernyi, dating from 1408.

USSURI. A river in eastern Siberia (q.v.), it becomes the tributary of the Amur River (q.v.) near the city of Khabarovsk (q.v.).

USTINOV see IZHEVSK

USTINOV, DMITRII F. (1908–84). Born into a worker's family, he joined the Communist Party (q.v.) in 1927, then graduated from the St. Petersburg (q.v.) military technical institute in 1934. At the age of 32 he became the Soviet armaments chief, a position he held until 1953. Ustinov was responsible for recruiting German rocket scientists to work for the Soviets after World War II (q.v.) and became a full member of the Central Committee of the Communist Party (q.v.) and the minister of defense from 1953 to 1957, as well as a member of the Politburo (q.v.) in 1976, when he was promoted to the rank of marshal of the Soviet Union.

UVAROV, COUNT SERGEI S. (1786–1855). A conservative education minister under Tsar Nicholas I (q.v.), Uvarov introduced an "Orthodoxy and Nationality" curriculum into Russian education, while at the same time expanding the size of universities and increasing their number.

V

VAGANOVA, AGRIPPINA I. (1879–1951). A student at the St. Petersburg (q.v.) Theater School, she also danced with the Mariinskii Theater (q.v.). In 1916 Vaganova became a teacher at the choreography school in St. Petersburg, where she trained several generations of top Russian ballet dancers such as Makarova and Ulanova (q.v.). Vaganova was also the artistic director of the Kirov ballet (q.v.).

VALDAI HILLS. Located roughly between Moscow (q.v.) and St. Petersburg (q.v.), this system of hills averages around 1,000 feet and forms the watershed of the Volga (q.v.) and numerous other rivers. They are the most signigificant elevation in European Russia; they are wooded and support agriculture and fishing.

VALUEV, COUNT PETR A. (1814–90). He had a major influence on the reforms promulgated by Alexander II (q.v.) as his minister of the interior and president of a ministerial committee studying possible reforms from 1877 until 1881. Valuev advocated an elected assembly and a constitutional government. His plans were nullified by Tsar Alexander's assassination in 1881.

VARANGI. This is the name by which Viking raiders in the Baltic were known to Russia in the ninth century. Possibly invited into the region for protection, they soon established a trade route along the Dnepr River (q.v.) to Byzantium and under their leader, Riurik (q.v.), gave rise to the Ruricid dynasty.

VASILCHIKOV, PRINCE ILLARION S. (1881–1969). A graduate of the University of St. Petersburg (see Universities), after a short service in a guards regiment he became a member of the staff of the State Senate and also served as a government inspector in Turkestan. He was elected to the Duma (q.v.) in 1912 as an Oktiabrist (q.v.). After the 1917 revolution Vasilchikov was appointed by the Provisional government (q.v.) to the Red Cross, then emigrated in 1919 to Paris and Lithuania (q.v.). He moved to Germany after the Soviet annexation of Lithuania in 1940 and remained an active member of the Orthodox Church (q.v.) until his death.

VASILCHIKOVA, PRINCESS MARIA I. (1917–78). The daughter of Prince Illarion Vasilchikov (q.v.), she moved from one European city to another with her parents until settling in Germany in 1940. There she worked in the German foreign office until 1944, when she had to leave Berlin for Vienna in order to escape the Gestapo hunt for acquaintances of the conspirators who had attempted to assassinate Hitler. She married an American intelligence officer after the war and wrote an international best seller, *The Berlin Diaries 1940–1945*.

VASILEVSKII, ALEKSANDR M. (1895–1977). Born into a priest's family, he graduated from the Alekseevskoe military school in 1915, then served in the imperial army as a captain. During the civil war (q.v.) Vasilevskii served in the ranks of the Red Army (see Armed Forces, Soviet). In 1927 he graduated from the General Staff Academy and was appointed a member of the general staff, after which he became the head of the operations department. In August 1941 he was made chief of the general staff. He was commander of the Belarussian front in 1945 and led the occupation of East Prussia, after which he commanded the Soviet forces against Japan in 1945. From 1949 to 1953 he was minister of the armed forces and deputy minister of defense.

VASILIEV, DMITRII (1943-   ). A journalist of conservative views, he helped found and lead the Pamiat (q.v.) group.

VASILII I, GRAND DUKE OF MOSCOW (1371–1425). A cautious prince, he gradually expanded his small Moscow (q.v.) principality but was subjected to an attack by his Mongol overlords in 1408 for failing to pay them tribute.

VASILII II, GRAND DUKE OF MOSCOW (1425–62). He continued the expansion of his Moscow (q.v.) principality but was wounded and taken prisoner by the Mongols. After he was set free by them, he strove to establish in his principality a national state and replace the former feudal system that he had inherited from his Riurik (q.v.) ancestors.

VASILII III, GRAND DUKE OF MOSCOW (1479–1533). The son of Ivan III (q.v.), he strove to further enlarge his principality and forcibly annexed Pskov (q.v.) in 1511, as well as other small independent principalities, including Smolensk (q.v.) in 1514. Under his rule Moscow (q.v.) obtained diplomatic recognition from the Holy Roman Empire.

VAVILOV, NIKOLAI I. (1887–1943). From 1924 to 1940 he was the director of the institute of plant breeding. A world-famous botanist, he fell afoul of Lysenko (q.v.), whose theories of inherited traits he vigorously opposed. He was arrested and died in a concentration camp.

VEKHI ("LANDMARKS"). This symposium was held in 1909 and brought together a number of philosophers and writers, many of whom had passed through a Marxist or Hegelian phase and, influenced by Dostoevsky (q.v.) and Vladimir Solovev (q.v.), had begun to explore Christianity and sought to turn the intelligentsia (q.v.) away from socialism. Preeminent among them were Nikolai Berdiaev (q.v.), Semen Frank (q.v.) and Sergei Bulgakov (q.v.).

VELIKIE LUKI. A town on the Lovat River, it was established in the 12th century near Pskov (q.v.). It manufactures electrical equipment and furniture. Its population is just under 100,000.

VELIKII KNIAZ. Literally, "great prince," it is most frequently translated as grand duke. Under the law, only the direct sons and grandsons of a reigning emperor were entitled to this appellation.

VENGEROV, SIMON A. (1855–1920). He gained fame as a bibliographer, historian of literature, author of a six-volume bibliographical dictionary of Russian writers, and editor of the literary section of the *Brockhaus Efron Encyclopedia.* He was also the founder of the Russian Chamber of Books in 1917.

VENIAMIN, METROPOLITAN OF PETROGRAD (1874–1922). He graduated in 1897 from the St. Petersburg (q.v.) Theological Academy and was elevated to archbishop of Petrograd (q.v.) in 1917. In 1922, as the metropolitan (q.v.) of the city he refused to surrender valuable church vessels to Soviet authorities and was put on trial. After being found guilty of antistate activity he was shot along with several other accused.

VERDEREVSKII, DMITRII N. (1873–1946). Educated at the naval cadet school in St. Petersburg (q.v.), he joined the Russian navy and acted as one of the young reformers before World War I (q.v.). During World War I he served as the commander of Russia's submarine forces, and as commander of the Baltic fleet after the February 1917 revolution (q.v.). He also briefly served as naval minister in the Provisional government (q.v.) until its overthrow in October 1917 by the Bolsheviks (q.v.). He emigrated to France and remained there until his death.

VEREISKII, GEORGII S. (1886–1962). He began his artistic career in Kharkov (q.v.), then moved to St. Petersburg (q.v.) in 1904, where he worked in an art shop until 1915. During his long creative life he did mostly landscape and portrait painting, in addition to lithography and etching.

VERESAEV, VIKENTII V. (b. SMIDOVICH) (1867–1945). Educated as a medical doctor, he turned to writing novels as well as essays on Russian literary figures. He compiled a fairly exhaustive account of the life of Pushkin (q.v.) in several volumes.

VERKHOIANSK. This is a small Siberian town northeast of Iakutsk (q.v.) which is considered to be the coldest regularly inhabited place on earth.

VERKHOVSKII, ALEKSANDR I. (1886–1938). He was a graduate of the Pages Corps School, as well as of the Academy of the General Staff in 1911. After the February 1917 revolution (q.v.), which he supported, Verkhovskii became the commander of the Moscow (q.v.) military region and, in September 1917, the minister of war. A strong advocate of an immediate peace with Germany, he was forced to resign from the Provisional government (q.v.) shortly before the Bolshevik (q.v.) coup of October 1917. During the civil war (q.v.) he joined the Red Army (*see* Armed Forces, Soviet), holding high posts until the war's end, when he became a professor at the Frunze Military Academy. He was shot during the purges (q.v.) of the 1930s.

VERNADSKII, GEORGII V. (1887–1973). A historian of early Russia and the author of numerous books on the subject, he emigrated after the 1917 revolution and lived first in Prague and then in the United States, where he became a history professor at Yale in 1927.

VERNADSKII, VLADIMIR I. (1863–1945). An active participant in local Zemstvo (*see* Zemstva) organizations before 1917, after the revolution he became head of the biogeochemical laboratory of the Academy of Sciences (q.v.) of the USSR.

VERTINSKII, ALEKSANDR N. (1889–1957). After his first appearance in 1915 with a repertoire of songs he had composed, he rapidly rose to fame as a cabaret performer. He emigrated after the revolution and performed before packed audiences. His fellow emigres loved his songs, which were full of nostalgia and melancholy. He returned to Russia with great fanfare during World War II (q.v.) and was awarded the Stalin prize (q.v.) in 1951, continuing to give concerts until his death in Moscow (q.v.).

VERTOV, DZIGA (b. DENIS KAUFMAN) (1896–1954). This influential film director initially studied human neurology and perception before going to work for the Moscow Film Committee in 1918, editing documentaries. While doing this he pioneered montage techniques and began to expand the limits of cinematography. His *Kino Eye: Life Caught Unawares* (1924) was highly acclaimed. Perhaps his best-known work, *Man with a Movie Camera* (1929), a city symphony shot in Moscow (q.v.), Odessa (q.v.) and Kiev (q.v.), was almost too advanced for its time; Vertov found little work in the 1930s and went back to editing documentaries and newsreels until his death.

VESELOVSKII, ALEKSANDR N. (1838–1906). After studying at the University of Moscow (q.v.) and abroad, he became professor of literary history, specializing in folklore and mythology.

VITIM • 341

VINOGRADOFF, PAVEL G. (1854–1925). Professor of history at the University of Moscow (*see* Universities) in 1884, he emigrated to England and became professor of jurisprudence at Oxford in 1903. Returning to Russia to teach at the University of Moscow, he emigrated again after the October 1917 revolution (q.v.). He continued his historical studies and published extensively on the medieval history of England.

VINOGRADOV, ALEKSANDR P. (1895–1970). Graduating from the University of Leningrad (*see* Universities) in 1924 as a geologist, he became in 1947 the director of the Institute of Geochemistry and was elected to the USSR Academy of Sciences (q.v.) in 1953. That same year he became professor at the University of Moscow. A major contributor to Soviet atomic research, Vinogradov also conducted studies of lunar chemistry from samples brought back by Soviet space explorations and was the chairman of the International Association of Geochemistry and Cosmic Chemistry.

VIRGIN LANDS. A vast, semiarid landmass in central Siberia (q.v.) and Kazakhstan (q.v.), it was converted into a wheat-bearing region under Khrushchev (q.v.) through a project of massive irrigation.

VISUAL ARTS see PAINTING AND VISUAL ARTS

VITALII, METROPOLITAN OF EAST AMERICA AND CANADA (b. USTINOV) (1910-   ). Born into the family of a naval officer, his father served with the White Armies (q.v.) and was evacuated to Constantinople at the end of the civil war (q.v.). Metropolitan (q.v.) Vitalii finished his schooling in Yugoslavia, then moved to France in 1923. In 1939 he became a monk. During World War II (q.v.), he served as an Orthodox (q.v.) priest in Germany, ministering to Russian prisoners of war. At the end of the war he became one of the leaders of the Russian church in exile, first in London, then in Brazil. In 1955 he was elevated to bishop of Montreal and head of the Russian Orthodox Church in Exile.

VITEBSK. The administrative center of Vitebsk oblast, Belarus, on the Western Dvina River, it was founded in the 11th century; industries include textiles and furniture. It has a population of around 360,500.

VITIM. This river flows from near Lake Baikal (q.v.) in Siberia (q.v.) to join the Lena (q.v.), over one thousand miles away.

VIZE, VLADIMIR Y. (1888–1954). An explorer who attempted to reach the North Pole in 1912, he organized the polar drift expedition in 1937.

VLADIKAVKAZ. The prerevolutionary name of a city in the Caucasus (q.v.) now named Ordzhonikidze, it was established as a Russian fortress in 1784 and is today the capital of the North Ossetian (*see* Ossetia) autonomous republic. An industrial city, it manufactures metallurgical equipment and processes food. Its population is just under 300,000.

VLADIMIR. The capital of Vladimir oblast some 120 miles east of Moscow, it has a population of 355,600. Vladimir was founded in the 12th century by Vladimir Monomakh. It was absorbed by Muscovy (q.v.) in 1364 and is noted for its cathedrals containing frescoes by Andrei Rublev (q.v.). Its chief industries are machinery, textiles and chemicals.

VLADIMIR, PRINCE (956–1015). The grand prince of Kiev (q.v.), he married the sister of the Byzantine emperor and was therefore baptized in the Orthodox (q.v.) faith. In 988 he made Orthodox Christianity the official religion of Kiev and became Russia's patron saint.

VLADIMIR KIRILLOVICH ROMANOFF, GRAND DUKE (1917–93). A cousin of Tsar Nicholas II (q.v.), he was born during his parents' flight from Russia to Finland in 1917 and educated in Paris and London. He worked in an English factory as a factory hand, then returned to France just before World War II (q.v.). During the war he was interned in Germany together with a group of pro-German Russian soldiers. After the war he lived in Spain and France and inherited his father's claim to the imperial Russian throne.

VLADIVOSTOK. The administrative center of the Russian Far East, it is a port on the Sea of Japan (and home port of the Pacific Fleet) as well as the terminus of the Trans-Siberian Railroad (q.v.). Founded in 1860, Vladivostok is also an important center for shipbuilding, fisheries, food processing, and manufacturing. It has a population of 648,000.

VLASOV, ANDREI A. (1900–46). One of Stalin's (q.v.) better generals during the first months of World War II, he was captured by the German army and became head of an anti-Communist military force that fought on the German side as the Russian Liberation Army (q.v.). He was handed over to the Soviet Army by the Americans in 1945, tried for treason, and executed.

VOLGA GERMANS. These were German settlers, originally numbering around 25,000, who were recruited by the Russian government in Catherine II's (q.v.) time to live in the Volga region. They and their descendants were exemplary farmers who retained their ethnicity; their resistance to Russification caused the government of Nicholas II (q.v.) to consider expelling them. In 1924 a Volga German autonomous republic was created, having as its capital the town of Engelsk (formerly Pokrovsk). In 1941 the republic was abolished amid suspicions that the Volga Germans harbored spies and traitors; around 360,000 of them were resettled in various parts of central Asia and Siberia (q.v.).

VOLGA RIVER. The longest river in European Russia, it flows south to the Caspian Sea (q.v.) for over 2,300 miles from the Valdai Hills (q.v.) northeast of Moscow (q.v.). A canal joins it to the Don River (q.v.) at Volgograd (q.v.). It is one of the major navigational routes of Russia.

VOLGOGRAD. Formerly Tsaritsyn, then Stalingrad, it was there that the German army offensive of 1942 was finally stopped by the Soviet Army. It is a major industrial center for the manufacturing of railroad equipment, tractors, and oil-extraction machinery. Its population is almost one million.

VOLHYNIA. The northwestern part of Ukraine (q.v.), it includes the oblasts of Volyn, Rovno and Zhitomir. In the ninth and tenth centuries it was under Kiev (q.v.), but belonged successively to Lithuania (q.v.) (12th–14th centuries) and Poland (1569).

VOLIA. The Russian word for "will" as well as "freedom," it was used to designate a terrorist political party at the end of the 19th century, the Narodnaia Volia (q.v.), or People's Will.

VOLKHOV RIVER. This river rises at Ilmen Lake (q.v.) and flows north to Ladoga Lake (q.v.), east of St. Petersburg (q.v.).

VOLKOGONOV, DMITRII (1928–95). General and chief of the psychological war department from 1979, he was director of the Institute of Military History until he was expelled after the publication of his controversial books on Stalin (q.v.) and Lenin (q.v.).

VOLKONSKII, PRINCE SERGEI G. (1788–1865). He served in the Russian army as a major general during the Napoleonic wars (q.v.), then joined the failed Decembrist (q.v.) uprising and was sentenced to two decades of hard labor. He was amnestied in 1856.

VOLOGDA. Established by Novgorod (q.v.) merchants in the 12th century, this town is the capital of the region of the same name. It produces agricultural machinery and textiles. Its population is just over a quarter of a million.

VOLOST. Originally a medieval term denoting a small territorial administrative unit, it was reintroduced in 1861 for the administration of village affairs. Roughly the equivalent of a township, it could contain one village or several and was run by village elders who reported to *uezd* officials. By 1929 the *volosts* had been abolished in favor of centralized Soviet control.

VOLUNTEER ARMY. White Armies (q.v.) forces in the south during the civil war (q.v.) under generals Denikin (q.v.) and, initially, Alekseev (q.v.) and Kornilov (q.v.), in 1919 they became the Armed Forces of the South of Russia under Denikin. Largely defeated by the Red Army (*see* Armed Forces, Soviet) in early 1920, its remaining units joined General Wrangel (q.v.).

VORONEZH. Administrative center and capital of Voronezh oblast, it has a population of 895,000 and was founded in 1586. It is about 300 miles south of Moscow (q.v.) near the confluence of the Volga (q.v.) and the Don (q.v.) and is in the center of the Black Earth region. Its chief industries include heavy machinery, chemicals and food processing. It is significant as the place of Osip Mandelshtam's (q.v.) exile and for a spate of UFO sightings in the early 1990s.

VOROSHILOV, KLEMENTII E. (1881–1969). He joined the Bolsheviks (q.v.) in 1903. During the civil war (q.v.), Voroshilov commanded a major Red Army (*see* Armed Forces, Soviet) unit in southern Russia that was defending Tsaritsyn (*see* Volgograd). At this time he formed a life-long association with Stalin (q.v.), who was the commissar for the southern front. Voroshilov participated in the crushing of the Kronstadt (q.v.) revolt against the Soviet government in 1921, then in 1925 was elevated to the post of commissar of the Soviet army and navy. He was the deputy chairman of the Council of Ministers after 1946 and a member of the Central Committee of the Communist Party (q.v.) from 1921 to 1961 and of the Politburo (q.v.)

from 1926 to 1952. Voroshilov was pensioned off by Khrushchev (q.v.) in 1962.

VOTKINSK. An industrial city located some two hundred miles southwest of Perm (q.v.), its products include agricultural and railroad equipment, and its population is just under 75,000.

VOZNESENSKII, NIKOLAI A. (1903–50). A graduate of the Economic Institute of Red Professors, he joined the Communist Party (q.v.) during the civil war (q.v.) and became chairman of the Gosplan (q.v.) in 1938. In 1947 Voznesenskii became a full member of the Politburo (q.v.). After the death of his mentor, Zhdanov (q.v.), he fell foul of Malenkov (q.v.), who had him expelled from all of his party and state posts and executed in the so-called Leningrad Affair (q.v.) of 1950.

VRANGEL see WRANGEL

VYBORG. A Baltic Sea (q.v.) port some 70 miles northwest of St. Petersburg (q.v.) on the Vyborg Bay, it is a manufacturing and a lumber milling town. Its population is just under 70,000.

VYBORG MANIFESTO. After Tsar Nicholas II (q.v.) dissolved the first Duma (q.v.) in 1906 because it was too radical, most of its deputies moved to Vyborg, then in the grand duchy of Finland (q.v.), and issued a manifesto urging Russians not to pay taxes or serve in the armed forces. This measure failed and resulted in the deputies being given short prison sentences and being deprived of the right to stand for elections to the following Duma.

VYSHINSKII, ANDREI Y. (1883–1954). Originally a Menshevik (q.v.), he became a law professor and rector of the University of Moscow (q.v.) in the 1920s. Stalin (q.v.) had him appointed in 1935 as procurator general of the USSR (q.v.). In this capacity he acted as the principal accuser during the show trials (q.v.) of the middle and late 1930s. In 1949 he became commissar of foreign affairs and the Soviet representative at the United Nations in New York, where he died in 1954.

VYSOTSKY, VLADIMIR S. (1938–80). A Russian actor and singer, his death in Moscow (q.v.) provoked a massive funeral demonstration. A leading member of the Taganka (q.v.) theater, he became known throughout the country for his songs, sung to his own guitar accompaniment and circulated widely on cassette tapes. See also GALICH and OKUDZHAVA.

W

WAR COMMUNISM. The newly empowered Soviet government instituted a series of extreme economic policies at the beginning of the civil war (q.v.) in 1918. These were later referred to as War Communism because they sought to implement the basic principles of Communist economic distribution, a nonmonetary, egalitarian economy. After the Kronstadt (q.v.) rebellion of 1920, Lenin (q.v.) saw that such measures were premature and in 1921 urged an immediate reversal of policy, the NEP (q.v.), or New Economic Policy.

WARSAW PACT. This was the name given to the 1955 pact that established a military alliance between the Soviet Union and the East European People's Democracies. It was designed to be a counterweight to the West-sponsored NATO pact. While in theory an agreement between equal sovereign states, it was in fact, completely dominated by the Soviet military.

WESTERNIZERS. One of the two major orientations among the Russian intelligentsia (q.v.) of the 19th century, the Westernizers, as opposed to the Slavophiles (q.v.), looked to the Western industrialized countries (Great Britain, France and Germany) for a model of development for Russia. They admired the reform of Peter the Great (q.v.) and believed that because of the Mongol yoke (q.v.) Russia had missed such important historical stages as the Renaissance. They also held that Western secular and liberal political institutions were the example that Russia should follow. Among the most outstanding representatives of this attitude were Granovskii (q.v.), Herzen (q.v.) and Belinskii (q.v.).

WHAT IS TO BE DONE? This is the title of a novel published by Chernyshevskii (q.v.), which was read very widely by the Russian radical intelligentsia (q.v.) and had a major influence on Lenin's (q.v.) political development.

WHITE ARMIES. This name was given to the anti-Communist military forces during the civil war (q.v.) of 1918–22. Members of these armies, as well as their civilian supporters, referred to themselves as Whites, as against the Reds of the Soviet camp. This White coalition consisted of monarchists, right-wing Social Democrats, most Socialist Revolutionaries (q.v.), and many Cossacks (q.v.). Led by a succession of ephemeral governments and individual military figures, the Whites failed to capture the support of the Russian peasant masses and were eventually defeated.

WHITE SEA. Part of the Barents Sea (q.v.) and the opening for Russia to the Arctic, its chief port is Arkhangelsk (q.v.). It is rich in cod and herring.

WILKITSKII, BORIS A. (1885–1961). After graduating from the Naval Academy in St. Petersburg (q.v.) he served in the imperial navy during the Russo-Japanese war (q.v.), then began the exploration of the coast of northern Siberia (q.v.), discovering numerous islands. He fought with the White Armies (q.v.) during the civil war (q.v.) and later emigrated to Belgium. Later in life he worked as a hydrographic researcher in the Belgian Congo.

WINTER PALACE. A baroque palace facing the River Neva in St. Petersburg (q.v.), it was completed in 1762 by Varfolomei Rastrelli (1700–71). An occasional St. Petersburg residence of the imperial family, it was stormed by workers and soldiers on the night of November 7, 1917, the first action of the October revolution (q.v.). Since 1922 it has housed the Hermitage Museum (q.v.).

WITTE, COUNT SERGEI Y. (1849–1915). As minister of finance from 1892 to 1903, he played a major role in the rapid industrialization of the country and in the building of its railway network. He was the Russian prime minister between 1903 and 1906 and negotiated the Portsmouth peace treaty with Japan at the end of the Russo-Japanese war (q.v.). He also helped persuade Tsar Nicholas II (q.v.) to issue his October 1905 proclamation establishing the Duma (q.v.).

WORKERS' OPPOSITION. This movement of opposition to Lenin's (q.v.) policies arose at the tenth party congress in 1921 and was led by Kollontai (q.v.) and Shaposhnikov (q.v.). It demanded a greater role for the trade unions (q.v.) in the management of Soviet industry.

WORLD WAR I (1914–18). The struggle for markets and geopolitical power between the Tripartite Union—Germany, Austria and Italy—and the Entente—Great Britain, France and Russia—led to World War I, which began in 1914 with a confrontation between Serbia and Austro-Hungary. On August 1, 1914, Germany declared war on Russia, after Russia had begun a full mobilization. Following this event, other countries entered into the struggle. Altogether, 38 governments, with a population of 1.5 billion individuals participated in this war.

During the first days of August 1914, two Russian armies moved against eastern Prussia on the northwestern front. They succeeded in inflicting a series of defeats on the Germans. This advance forced the German high command to move a number of units from its striking force in France, which substantially lightened the pressure on the retreating French army. The advance of the Russian armies ended with their serious defeat, after which the Russians retreated from eastern Prussia, leaving 20,000 dead and over 90,000 prisoners of war. However, they did succeed in obtaining a major military success against the Austro-Hungarian forces in the battle for Galicia. On October 16, 1914, Turkey entered the war on the side of the Germans, and a new Caucasus (q.v.) front was organized. At the same time much of the fighting had stopped on Russia's western front. The Russians were able to prevent a lightning victory that the Germans had counted on at the end of 1914, but a shortage of equipment and ammunition, as well as inadequate training of soldiers, began to be felt by the army. In the summer of 1915 the Russians were forced to evacuate Galicia and also lost Poland, as well as Lithuania (q.v.) and parts of the Baltic states and Belarus (q.v.). The loss of these industrial regions weighed heavily on the economy of Russia. A major crisis was felt in railroad transport. As well, mobilization led to a shortage of labor-capable peasantry. During the first two war years, the overall collection of wheat dropped by 27 percent.

In 1916 a crisis of supply of goods occurred, which forced Richter, the minister of agriculture, to introduce compulsory norms of wheat to be supplied by each province to the market.

Each day of the war cost the Russian government 50 million rubles. In order to cover its expenses, the government resorted to internal as well as external borrowing and to the printing of paper money. By 1917 the value of the ruble had dropped to 27 cents. After 1916 rationing was introduced.

In the spring of 1916 the Russian army on the southwestern front carried out a successful advance. However, other fronts were unable to support it, and by the fall of that year it became clear that there would be no radical change in the war situation. By this time the internal situation in Russia had become particularly strained. From October 17 to 20, 1916, more than 66,000 workers went on strike in the capital. Attempting to cope with the situation, Tsar Nicholas II (q.v.) began to change ministers very rapidly.

At the beginning of the war a feeling of patriotic unity existed among most segments of Russian society, from the most extreme right-wing groups all the way to the liberals and even most socialists.

However, after the prolonged lack of military success, disputes began to break out between these groups and the government of the tsar (q.v.). In August 1915 the general middle-class opposition to the way the government was managing the war led to the creation of the Progressive Bloc (q.v.) of Duma (q.v.) deputies composed of Constitutional Democrats (*see* Kadet [KD] Party) as well as of the Oktiabrists (q.v.). The president of this bloc was the left-wing Oktiabrist Shedlovskii, but its actual leader was Miliukov (q.v.), the leader of the Constitutional Democrats. The extreme right in the Duma also created a bloc of monarchists. The various socialist parties were divided into several tendencies, one being the patriotic defensist tendency, represented by the Mensheviks (q.v.). This group stood for a rapid conclusion of a democratic peace without annexations or contributions. A left-of-center group of deputies, composed primarily of Mensheviks-Internationalists headed by Martov (q.v.), and the Socialist Revolutionaries (q.v.) led by Chernov (q.v.), advocated the conclusion of an immediate peace with "no victories and no defeats."

After the February 1917 revolution (q.v.) this last tendency gave rise to a group of Revolutionary-Internationalists headed by Trotsky (q.v.) and Natanson (q.v.), who tied the outcome of the war to the victory of a socialist revolution in Russia and in Western Europe. The Bolsheviks (q.v.), led by Lenin (q.v.), advanced the slogan of "transforming the imperialist war into a civil war."

In April 1917, the foreign minister of the Provisional government (q.v.), Miliukov, promised the Allies that Russia would seek to conclude the war with a decisive victory. This declaration provoked a major uproar in the country and forced Miliukov to resign his post. The antiwar mood increased as a result of the failure of the Brusilov offensive (q.v.) in the summer of 1917, and by the fall army desertions reached a flood state. When the Bolsheviks seized power in October 1917 (old style), they immediately began peace negotiations with the Germans at Brest-Litovsk (q.v.), where shortly thereafter they agreed to a separate peace, which was signed in early 1918.

WORLD WAR II (1941–45). It is conventional to consider the beginning of World War II for Russia to be June 1941 when German troops invaded the country. However, the Soviet Union factually participated in the war from the first days, from September 1939, because its armed forces began military action against Poland in September 1939 and against Finland in November of that year.

Germany did not act against the invasion of Finland by Soviet troops or against the introduction of Soviet troops into the Baltic countries in 1940. However, despite the nonaggression pact that existed between them, the German army invaded Russia on June 22,

1941, in alliance with Romanian and Hungarian armies. The force that invaded the territory of the USSR was over twice the size of the forces that guarded the western frontiers of the Soviet Union. In order to organize the defense of the country, the supreme command, with Stalin (q.v.) at its head, took a number of extraordinary measures. They immediately declared a state of war, mobilized all of the male population born between 1905 and 1918, and began the transfer of factories from the west of the country to the east. They also organized a total changeover from civilian to military production. Nevertheless, during the first months of the war the German army rapidly advanced hundreds of miles into Soviet territory, destroying over 28 Red Army divisions, with another 72 divisions losing over half of their manpower and equipment. By November 1941 the Germans had occupied territories inhabited by more than 40 percent of the country's population and producing 40 percent of its industrial goods. The reasons for these heavy defeats of the Red Army (*see* Armed Forces, Soviet) lay not only in the might of Germany, but also in the marked drop of the professional level of the Soviet officer corps caused by the purges (q.v.) that Stalin had carried out in the period from 1936 to 1941. These repressions had accounted for the execution or incarceration of over 40,000 experienced military commanders.

Beginning in September 1941 and until April 1942 severe battles took place around Moscow (q.v.). On the October 19, 1941, Moscow was declared to be in a siege situation. By December, leading units of the German army were within 20 miles of Moscow. They failed to advance further as a result of a counterattack by fresh Soviet armies commanded by General Zhukov (q.v.) that had been shifted from the Far East. After fierce battles, the German troops were thrown back in several sectors of the front to the depths of some hundred miles from the capital. This was their first serious defeat. The United States and Britain, which had supported the Soviet Union from the beginning of the German attack, increased their aid to the USSR.

The euphoria of the victory around Moscow led to new mistakes by Stalin (q.v.) in military strategy, as a result of which the Red Army lost a series of very important battles around St. Petersburg (q.v.), in the Crimea (q.v.), and around Kharkov (q.v.). In the summer of 1942 the German army began an advance in the south, with the aim of cutting the central regions of Russia from the Caucasus (q.v.) and central Asia. In September they approached Stalingrad (*see* Volgograd). The resolute Russian defense of this city on the Volga River (q.v.) exhausted the German army. In November 1942 the Russians began a counterattack that succeeded in surrounding the Germans around Stalingrad, and in February 1943 the German Sixth Army Group South was forced to surrender.

In the spring and early summer of 1943 the Germans chose the narrow stretch of the front around Kursk (q.v.), where they concentrated very heavy forces. This operation began on July 5, 1943, but after some initial advances they were stopped on July 12. The battle around Kursk began a general strategic advance by Soviet troops, in the course of which significant territory was regained. During the winter of 1943 and spring of 1944, the Crimea and large parts of the Ukraine (q.v.) were liberated, and the 900-day-long blockade of Leningrad was broken.

In the summer of 1944 the front moved west from within the Soviet Union into Central Europe. The military situation for Germany became even more complicated with the opening of the second front by American and British troops in the west. In the winter of 1944–45 the outcome of the war was already obvious. At the Yalta conference (q.v.) in February 1945 the leadership of the three major allies decided on the postwar organization of Europe and in April and May of 1945 Soviet troops won the Battle of Berlin. On May 8, 1945, Germany capitulated.

After the defeat of Germany the war continued in the Orient. The Soviet Union entered in the final phase of the war against Japan and in September 1945 Japan capitulated.

Although Russia came out victorious, World War II had been a very severe test for the country. More than 27 million Soviet citizens had died, and over a third of the country's wealth had been lost.

WRANGEL, BARON PETR N. (1878–1928). A tsarist general, he took over the command of the White Armies (q.v.) in southern Russia after the fall of Denikin (q.v.). Forced to evacuate the remnants of his forces from the Crimea (q.v.) to Yugoslavia and Turkey, he spent the rest of his life in Western Europe, acting as a leader of the anti-Communist White movement.

Y

YABLONOVY RIDGE see IABLONOVYI KHREBET

YAGODA see IAGODA

YAKUTIA see SAKHA

YALTA CONFERENCE (1945). This meeting was one of the "Big Three" conferences held during World War II (q.v.) between Russia, the United States and Great Britain. Stalin (q.v.), Roosevelt and

Churchill met in the former summer palace of the tsars (q.v.) in the Crimea (q.v.) to map out the final phases of the war against Germany and to lay the foundations of a postwar Europe. Among its major decisions was to establish the United Nations, to share in the administration of conquered Germany, for Russia to join in the war against Japan, and for Soviet refugees to be handed over to the Soviet Union.

YAMAL-NENETS NATIONAL AREA. An autonomous area of Siberia (q.v.) located between the Gulf of Ob and the Kara Sea (q.v.), its principal town is Salehard, and its chief occupations are fishing and reindeer breeding.

YAROSLAV see IAROSLAV

YAROSLAVSKII, EMILIAN see IAROSLAVSKII

YASHCHENKO, ALEKSANDR S. (1877–1934). A graduate of the University of Moscow (*see* Universities), he became a professor of law at the Iuriev University in 1909 and at the University of St. Petersburg in 1913. He was a member of the Soviet delegation to Germany in 1919 and remained there. In the 1920s he participated in the publication of a series of major emigre bibliographical works. Yashchenko organized "Dom Iskusstv" in Berlin, which focused on Russian book publishing and cultural life. He moved to Lithuania in 1923 but died in Berlin.

YASNAIA POLIANA. This is the village where the estate of Count Leo Tolstoy (q.v.) was located, a few miles south of Tula (q.v.).

YAVLINSKY, GRIGORY (1952–). Economist and reformer who supported a market-based economy, Yavlinsky worked in a glass factory in his native Lvov before obtaining a Ph.D. in economics. He worked in several institutes of labor and management, and in 1990 published his "Five-Hundred-Day Program" to revitalize the economy. Unfortunately, his plan was opposed. He continued to work as a respected economist for the council of ministers of the RSFSR (q.v.) and for the Supreme Economic Council of Kazakhstan. After the coup of 1991, Yavlinsky was appointed deputy chairman of the short-lived Committee for Operational Management of the Soviet Economy; he did not appear to have expected the Soviet Union to dissolve, and when it did he became economic counsellor to the Nizhnii Novgorod (q.v.) provincial government. In 1993 he founded the Yabloko bloc, which was composed of like-minded representatives of several parties; the bloc won 6.89 percent of the total party list vote in the 1995 elections, picking up 14 seats in the Duma (q.v.) for a total of 31.

YAZOV see IAZOV

YEFIMOV, MIKHAIL N. (1882–1920). He was one of Russia's first airplane pilots to acquire an international reputation, which he did by winning the 1910 flying prize in Nice. He was an instructor of military aviation during World War I (q.v.). Yefimov was killed by the White Armies (q.v.) during the civil war (q.v.).

YEGOREV, VLADIMIR (1869–1948). Educated at the Alexandrovskoe Military Academy, he also graduated from the General Staff Academy in 1901 and served as a military instructor in Montenegro between 1910 and 1913. During World War I (q.v.) he was a lieutenant general, then became a Red Army (*see* Armed Forces, Soviet) commander and fought against Denikin (q.v.) during the civil war (q.v.). From 1921 to 1926 he was the editor of a Soviet military periodical, as well as lecturing in various military academies.

YEKATERINBURG see EKATERINBURG

YELABUGA see ELABUGA

YELTSIN, BORIS N. (1931-   ). Current president of the Russian Federation and former leading member of the Central Committee of the Communist Party (q.v.), Yeltsin was born in the Ural (q.v.) region and first brought to a high office by Gorbachev (q.v.) in 1985. He was expelled from the Politburo (q.v.) and from his post as head of the Moscow (q.v.) organization of the Communist Party (q.v.), but remained active and eventually won election as parliamentary deputy from Moscow in 1989. The next year, he was elected chairman of the presidium of the Supreme Soviet (q.v.) of the Russian Federation. During the August 1991 coup to overthrow Gorbachev, Yeltsin became the focus of the forces that defeated the attempt. In December 1991 he saw Gorbachev's post as president of the USSR disappear.

   Yeltsin's health and popularity wavered over the next few years. In the December 1995 Duma (q.v.) elections he was threatened by the impressive showing of the Communist Party (q.v.) under Zyuganov (q.v.), but the June 1996 presidential election showed Yeltsin still able to do better than his nearest rivals, with 34.82 percent of the vote; Zyuganov managed to win 32.13 percent, and retired general Lebed surprised observers by winning the important third position at 14.13 percent. In the runoff elections, and with Lebed's backing, Yeltsin was reelected president of Russia and soon after underwent a successful heart operation.

YENISEI RIVER see ENISEI RIVER

YERMAK see ERMAK

YEROFEEV see EROFEEV

YERSHOV, PETR P. (1815–69). Born to an impoverished Siberian family, he was educated at the University of St. Petersburg (*see* Universities) and became a member of Pushkin's poetical circle. He specialized in folktales and wrote a classic rhymed children's tale about a magical hunchbacked horse, *Konek gorbunok.*

YEVTUSHENKO, YEVGENII (1933-   ). A poet of the postwar generation, he was initially attacked in the press for his implied criticism of Soviet society, but was extremely popular and ultimately tolerated by the regime (and published). He has traveled widely and has been translated into many languages. Perhaps his best-known poem is "Babii Iar."

YEZHOV see EZHOV

YUDENICH, NIKOLAI N. (1862–1933). A graduate of the Academy of the General Staff, he served in the army in Turkestan (q.v.) and in the Russo-Japanese war (q.v.). In 1915 Yudenich was promoted to commander in chief in the Caucasus (q.v.). After the October 1917 revolution (q.v.) he moved to Finland (q.v.), where he assumed command of the White Armies (q.v.) in northern Russia. He attempted unsuccessfully to capture Petrograd (q.v.) in 1919, then emigrated to France.

YUROVSKY, YANKEL (1878–1938). A member of the Ekaterinburg (q.v.) soviet, he is believed to have been the commander of the detachment that shot Tsar Nicholas II (q.v.) and his family.

YUSUPOV, PRINCE FELIKS F. (1887–1967). He was the son of Grand Duke Michael (q.v.) and one of the conspirators who participated in the killing of Rasputin (q.v.) in December 1916 at his palace in St. Petersburg (q.v.). Although the murder was discovered, Yusupov was merely exiled to his estate for his role. In 1919 he emigrated to France, where he wrote his memoirs.

Z

ZAGORSK. This is the location of one of the most famous of Russian Orthodox Church (q.v.) monasteries, the Troitsa-Sergeeva Lavra (q.v.), some 40 miles from Moscow (q.v.). It was founded by St. Sergei (q.v.).

ZAITSEV, BORIS K. (1881–1972). A prerevolutionary novelist, he became the president of the Union of Soviet Writers (q.v.) in 1921, but emigrated to the West in 1922. He settled first in Italy and then in France, where he continued to write about the life of the Russian emigration.

ZALESSKII, MIKHAIL N. (1905–79). He served in the White Armies (q.v.) during the civil war (q.v.), was evacuated to Yugoslavia during Wrangel's (q.v.) retreat, and began his studies at Zagreb university. In 1930 he joined the NTS (*see* Narodno-Trudovoi Soiuz) and was sent by them into the Soviet Union during World War II (q.v.) on an intelligence mission. After the war he was employed at the Munich Institute for the Study of the USSR before moving to San Francisco in 1947, from where he directed the NTS until his death.

ZAMIATIN, EVGENII I. (1884–1937). He joined the Bolsheviks (q.v.) at an early age but continued living in England until the 1917 revolutions. Once in Soviet Russia he found that he was unable to accept the Soviet system and wrote a personal letter to Stalin (q.v.) requesting permission to return to Western Europe. Allowed to do so, he moved to France in 1931. His classic novel *We* preceded both Huxley's and Orwell's negative utopias of collectivist societies.

ZASULICH, VERA I. (1848–1919). One of the leading members of the 19th-century Russian terrorists, she shot at and attempted to kill the military governor of St. Petersburg (q.v.). After being unexpectedly acquitted at her trial, she emigrated to Western Europe, where she joined Plekhanov (q.v.) in the founding of the first Russian Marxist group in 1883. She returned to Soviet Russia just before her death.

ZEMGOR. This is the name of the committees established in the summer of 1915 by the Zemskii Soiuz and the Soiuz Gorodov. Its mission was to coordinate assistance to the Russian army and to increase medical and other supplies in wartime.

ZEMLIA I VOLIA. The Land and Liberty Party. It was started in 1876 and consisted of a very small number of dedicated members of the intelligentsia (q.v.) . They believed in the abolition of the monarchy and in the distribution of all land to the peasants who worked it. In order to further their program they mounted demonstrations in St. Petersburg (q.v.) and began to carry out acts of individual terror against the most important tsarist police officials. By 1879 the issue of terror led to an irreconcilable split between those of its members who defended it and those who, like Plekhanov (q.v.), believed this method of struggle to be futile. The two groups organized themselves, respectively, into the terrorist Narodnaia Volia (q.v.) and the evolutionist Chernyi Peredel (q.v.).

ZEMSKII SOBOR. This assembly of representatives of the princes, boiars (q.v.), the Church and other groups occasionally discussed and advised on policy in 16th- and 17th-century Muscovy (q.v.). Through its deliberation the Time of Troubles (q.v.) was terminated in 1612, and the Romanov dynasty (q.v.) was installed in the following year. It was never summoned after the 17th century.

ZEMSTVA. These provincial economic development institutions were created during the reforms of the 1860s. Representatives were elected to the *Zemstva* to administer local economic matters too small to be handled by the central authority. The number of local *Zemstva* grew continually, and legislation was drafted at the same pace to regulate their activity. They were dissolved in 1918 and replaced by local soviets (q.v.).

ZEMSTVO see ZEMSTVA (plural)

ZENZINOV, VLADIMIR M. (1880–1953). Born into a merchant family, he was educated in Germany. He became a member of the Socialist Revolutionaries (q.v.) party and of its terrorist branch in 1906. In 1917 he was a member of the executive committee of the Petrograd soviet (q.v.), and actively opposed the Bolshevik (q.v.) coup in October 1917. After the civil war (q.v.) he emigrated to France and remained a close associate of Kerensky (q.v.), with whom he collaborated in editing a Russian-language newspaper. Toward the end of his life he moved to New York, where he wrote his memoirs.

ZERNOV, NIKOLAI M. (1898–1980). A graduate of the University of Moscow (*see* Universities) School of Medicine, he emigrated to Yugoslavia after the civil war (q.v.) and began studying theology at the University of Belgrade in 1925. He then moved to England and received his doctorate from Oxford in 1932. In 1947 he became a lecturer in Eastern orthodoxy at Oxford, from which university he received a doctorate in theology in 1966. He wrote a number of scholarly works on the Orthodox culture of Russia.

ZHDANOV. Formerly Mariupol, it is a major port on the Azov Sea (q.v.) and an industrial center producing chemicals, steel and heavy machinery. Its population is just over 500,000.

ZHDANOV, ANDREI A. (1896–1948). He joined the underground Bolshevik (q.v.) party in 1915 and was an active propagandist in the army before the October 1917 revolution (q.v.). A close associate of Stalin (q.v.), he was made chief of Leningrad (q.v.) during the blockade (1941–44). After the war he became Stalin's (q.v.) cultural lieutenant. As early as 1934 he delivered a speech at the first Congress of Soviet Writers (q.v.) expounding the doctrine of socialist realism (q.v.). In 1946, on Stalin's instructions, he issued the "Zhdanov decree" on literature. This decree set a pattern for the postwar Soviet repression of writers, composers and artists. In 1947 he organized the Cominform (q.v.), a post-World War II substitute for the Third International (q.v.).

ZHELIABOV, ANDREI I. (1850–81). A member of the executive committee of Narodnaia Volia (q.v.), he prepared the assassination of Tsar Alexander II (q.v.). Arrested and tried, he was hanged together with his fellow conspirators.

ZHELIABUZHSKII, IURII A. (1888–1955). He began working as a film photographer in 1915. During 1917 he filmed numerous revolutionary events, including some public appearances by Lenin (q.v.). He became a film director in 1919, producing "agitation" films and, later fairy tales. After 1927 he concentrated on producing animated films. In his later life he was a professor of filmmaking.

ZHEMCHUZHINA, POLINA S. (1896–1967). She became a member of the Communist Party (q.v.) before the civil war (q.v.) and soon thereafter married Molotov (q.v.). As wife of a high party leader she was intimate with Stalin's (q.v.) wife before the latter committed suicide in 1932. Zhemchuzhina became commissar of the fishing industry and director of the Soviet perfume enterprises. A Jew, she was a high official in the state-sponsored Anti-Fascist Committee of Soviet Jews. Arrested on Stalin's (q.v.) orders in 1949 and tortured in 1953 on charges of being a Zionist spy, she was released after Stalin's death.

ZHIRINOVSKY, VLADIMIR (1946-   ). Born in Alma-Ata, Zhirinovsky studied Oriental languages at Moscow State University and worked as a translator in Turkey. He studied law and was for a time head of the legal department at Mir Publishing. He founded the Liberal Democratic Party, the first congress of which was held in 1990. The party was later renamed the Liberal Democratic Party of Russia and received almost a quarter of the vote in the 1993 Duma (q.v.) elections. In the 1995 elections the party won 11.06 percent of the total party list vote, but picked up only one Duma seat, for a total of fifty-one. Much of his support came from rural areas and from people who rejected mainstream politicians. He also effectively played on xenophobia and regrets at Soviet imperial decline; he published several books and made characteristically extravagant speeches on these themes.

ZHUKOV, GEORGII K. (1896–1974). He fought with the Red Army (*see* Armed Forces, Soviet) during the civil war (q.v.) as a cavalry regiment commander. Then, after graduating from higher military courses, he took command of the Red Army in the Far East and defeated a strong Japanese attack in eastern Siberia (q.v.). He became chief of staff in January 1941 and the outstanding Soviet army commander of World War II (q.v.). Zhukov coordinated most of the successful Soviet army operations right up to the Soviet capture of Berlin. After the end of the war he was made commander of the Soviet occupation troops in Germany and a deputy minister of defense. In 1946 he was transferred to a military backwater on Stalin's (q.v.) orders. After Stalin's death he was partly instrumental in preventing Beria (q.v.) from taking power and helped Khrushchev (q.v.) survive an attempt to overthrow him by Molotov (q.v.), Malenkov (q.v.) and Kaganovich (q.v.). He was nevertheless retired by Khrushchev on charges of "Bonapartism" in 1957.

ZHUKOV, PAVEL S. (1870–1942). He started his career as a portrait photographer in St. Petersburg (q.v.) and took photographs of such outstanding Russians as Tolstoy (q.v.), Chekhov (q.v.), and Tchaikovsky (q.v.). After the 1917 revolution, he became the chief photographer for the Petrograd military district until he was transferred to Moscow (q.v.), where he photographed Lenin (q.v.) and other Bolshevik (q.v.) leaders. He died during the German blockade of Leningrad.

ZINOVEV, GRIGORII, E. (b. Apfelbaum) (1882–1936). A prominent Bolshevik (q.v.) leader, he joined the Bolsheviks in 1901 and stayed close to Lenin (q.v.) in his Swiss exile during World War I (q.v.). After the Bolsheviks overthrew the Provisional government (q.v.) in October 1917, he became chief of the Leningrad party organization and president of the Comintern (q.v.). He was also a member of the Central Committee of the Communist Party (q.v.) and of its Politburo (q.v.). Together with Kamenev (q.v.) and Stalin (q.v.) he formed the triumvirate that ruled the Soviet Union after Lenin's illness in 1922. At the 14th party congress in 1925 he opposed Stalin and was defeated. This led to his removal from all of his posts in the Communist Party (q.v.) and government. In 1927 he joined with Trotsky (q.v.) and Kamenev to form the Left Opposition (q.v.) and was again defeated and expelled from the Communist Party at the 15th party congress. Blamed by Stalin for the murder of Kirov (q.v.) in 1934, he was arrested. In 1935 he was once again tried, together with Kamenev, and condemned to death.

ZIUGANOV, GENNADII see ZYUGANOV, GENNADY

ZLATOUST. Established in the middle of the 18th century, this manufacturing town in the southern Ural (q.v.) region produces steel and machine tools. Its population is approximately 200,000.

ZOE PALAELOGA (d. 1503). She was the niece of the last Byzantine emperor and wife of Tsar Ivan III (q.v.) of Russia, whom she married in 1472.

ZORGE see SORGE, RICHARD

ZOSHCHENKO, MIKHAIL M. (1895–1958). A very popular Russian satirist of Soviet lifestyles of the 1920s and 1930s, together with Akhmatova (q.v.) he was attacked in 1946 by Zhdanov (q.v.), Stalin's (q.v.) cultural lieutenant, for writing "vulgar parodies" of life in the USSR, and expelled from the Union of Soviet Writers (q.v.).

ZUBATOV, SERGEI V. (1864–1917). The Moscow (q.v.) chief of the Okhrana (q.v.), he attempted to create a police-controlled workers' movement and trade union (q.v.). His mutual workers' help society was protected by the police and helped to organize unions that were controlled by his police department. In 1903 the tsar's government decided to abolish this practice and dismissed him.

ZUBOV, PLATON A. (1771–1804). A successor to Potemkin (q.v.) as lover of Catherine the Great (q.v.) and her political advisor, he was involved in the assassination of her son Paul I (q.v.).

ZYUGANOV, GENNADY (1944–). A teacher of math and physics and a member of the Communist Party (q.v.) since 1966, Zyuganov held various posts in local committees in Orel (q.v.) before becoming chairman of the propaganda department of the Central Committee of the Communist Party (q.v.) in the mid-1980s. In 1989 he became vice chairman of the ideology department of the Soviet Communist Party. In 1990 he helped found the KPRF, the Communist Party of the Russian Federation (the RSFSR [q.v.] had no Communist party of its own as distinct from that of the Soviet Union). In 1992 he became secretary of the Central Committee of the KPRF. In the 1995 elections the KPRF won 22.32 percent of the total party list vote and 58 seats in single-mandate constituencies, for a total of 99 seats, or around 35 percent of Duma (q.v.) seats, making it the largest faction in the Duma. He was also supported by the Agrarian Party and some others; his platform favored "peaceful revolution" and the voluntary reintegration of former Soviet republics.

Selected Bibliography

Because of the existence of an enormous number of publications about Russia and the Soviet Union, any bibliography of Russian history has to be very selective indeed. The material included in this volume was based on several strict rules of inclusion: (1) mostly material in the English language that would be accessible to the nonscholarly segment of the reading public was included and (2) emphasis was placed on major scholarly reference works that would be easily accessible to the nonspecialized reading public.

Among the numerous sources that the authors consulted to obtain and cross-check the data contained in this Historical Dictionary, the most useful are marked with an asterisk (*).

Contents

I. Dictionaries, Encyclopedias, and Bibliographies

a. General

American bibliography of Slavic and East European studies. Stanford, CA: American Association for the Advancement of Slavic Studies, 1967.

Andreevskii, I. E., ed. *Entsiklopedicheskii slovar.* St. Petersburg: I.A. Efron, 1890–1907.

Batalden, Stephen K., and Sandra L. Batalden. *The newly independent states of Eurasia: Handbook of Former Soviet Republics.* Phoenix, AZ: Oryx, 1993.

Birkos, Alexander S. *East European and Slavic studies.* Kent, OH: Kent State University Press, 1973.

Brawer, Moshe. *Atlas of Russia and the independent republics.* New York: Simon & Schuster, 1994.

Brown, Archie, ed. *The Cambridge encyclopedia of Russia and the Former Soviet Union.* New York: Cambridge University Press, 1994.

———. The Soviet Union: A Biographical Dictionary. New York: Macmillan, 1991.

Budorowycz, Bohdan. *Slavic and East European resources in Canadian academic and research libraries.* Ottawa, Ont.: National Library of Canada, 1976.

Clendenning, P., and R. Bartlett. *Eighteenth century Russia: A select bibliography of works published since 1955.* Newtonville, MA: Oriental Research Partners, 1981.

Crowley, Edward L., ed. *Prominent personalities in the USSR.* Metuchen, NJ: Scarecrow Press, 1968.

Dewdney, John C. *USSR in maps.* New York: Holmes & Meier, 1982.

Dohan, Michael R. *Traveller's yellow pages and handbook: For Moscow 1995.* Cold Spring Harbor, NY: InfoServices International, Inc., 1994.

Dossick, Jesse John. *Doctoral research on Russia and the Soviet Union.* New York: New York University Press, 1960.

———. *Doctoral research on Russia and the Soviet Union, 1960–*

1975: A classified list of 3,150 American, Canadian, and British dissertations, with some critical and statistical analysis. New York: Garland, 1976.

Dwyer, Joseph D., ed. *Russia, the Soviet Union, and Eastern Europe: A survey of holdings at the Hoover Institution on War, Revolution, and Peace.* Stanford, CA: Hoover Institution Press, 1980.

Eastern Europe and the Commonwealth of Independent States 1992. London: Europa Publications, 1992.

Egan, D.R., and M.A. Egan. *Russian autocrats from Ivan the Great to the fall of the Romanov Dynasty: An annotated bibliography of English language sources to 1985.* Metuchen, NJ: Scarecrow Press, 1987.

*Florinsky, Michael T., ed. *Encyclopedia of Russia and the Soviet Union.* New York: McGraw-Hill, 1961.

Grant, Steven A. *The Russian Empire and Soviet Union: A guide to manuscripts and archival materials in the United States.* Boston, Mass.: G.K. Hall, 1981.

———. *Scholar's guide to Washington, D.C., for Russian, Central Eurasian, and Baltic studies.* Washington, DC: Woodrow Wilson Center Press, 1994.

Grimstead, P.K. *Archives and manuscript repositories in the USSR.* Princeton, NJ: Princeton University Press, 1972–1988.

———. *Recent Soviet archival literature: A review and preliminary bibliography of selected reference aids.* Washington, DC: Kennan Institute for Advanced Russian Studies, 1987.

Horak, Stephan M. *Junior Slavica: A selected annotated bibliography of books in English on Russia and Eastern Europe.* Rochester, NY: Libraries Unlimited, 1968.

———. *Russia, the USSR, and Eastern Europe: A bibliographic guide to English language publications, 1964–1974.* Littleton, CO: Libraries Unlimited, 1978.

———. *Russia, the USSR, and Eastern Europe: A bibliographic guide to English language publications, 1975–1980.* Littleton, CO: Libraries Unlimited, 1982.

———. *Russia, the USSR, and Eastern Europe: A bibliographic guide to English language publications, 1981–1985.* Littleton, CO: Libraries Unlimited, 1987.

*Horecky, Paul, ed. *Russia and the Soviet Union: A bibliographical guide to Western-language publications.* Chicago: University of Chicago Press, 1965.

*Jones, David Lewis. *Books in English on the Soviet Union, 1917–73: A bibliography.* New York: Garland, 1975.

Leadenham, C.A., ed. *Guide to the collections in the Hoover Institution archives relating to Imperial Russia, the Russian revolutions and civil war, and the first emigration.* Stanford, CA: Hoover Institution Press, 1986.

Lewanski, Richard C., ed. *Eastern Europe and Russia/Soviet Union: A handbook of West European archival and library resources.* New York: K.G. Saur, 1980.

Library of Congress. Federal Research Division. *Soviet Union: A country study.* Washington, DC: U.S. GPO, 1991.

Lydolph, Paul E. *Geography of the USSR.* New York: Wiley, 1977.

*Maichel, Karol. *Guide to Russian reference books.* Stanford, CA: Hoover Institution on War, Revolution, and Peace, 1962.

*————. *The Modern Encyclopedia of Russian and Soviet History.* Gulf Breeze, FL: Academic International Press, 1981.

New York Public Library. *Dictionary catalog of the Slavonic collection.* Boston, MA: G.K. Hall, 1974.

Palm, Charles G., and Dale Reed. *Guide to the Hoover Institution archives.* Stanford, CA: Hoover Institution Press, 1980.

Pearson, R. *Russia and Eastern Europe 1789–1985: A bibliographical guide.* Manchester, UK: Manchester University Press, 1989.

Pitman, Lesley, ed. *Russia/USSR.* Santa Barbara, CA: Clio, 1994.

Polovtsov, A. A., ed. *Russkii biograficheskii slovar.* St. Petersburg: Russkoe istoricheskoe obshchestvo, 1896–1918.

*Prokhorov, A.M. (Aleksandr Mikhailovich), ed. *Bolshaia sovetskaia entsiklopediia.* Moscow: Sovetskaia entsiklopediia, 1970.

————. *Great Soviet encyclopedia.* New York: Macmillan, 1973–1983.

Record of World Events. Bethesda, MD: Keesing's Worldwide, 1997.

Russia and Eurasia facts and figures annual. Gulf Breeze, FL: Academic International Press, 1993.

Russia in the twentieth century: The catalogue of the Bakhmeteff Archive of Russian and East European history and culture. Boston, MA: G.K. Hall, 1987.

Schaffner, Bradley L. *Bibliography of the Soviet Union, its predecessors and successors.* Metuchen, NJ: Scarecrow Press, 1995.

Shabad, Theodore. *Geography of the USSR: A regional survey.* New York: Columbia University Press, 1951.

Shukman, Harold, ed. *The Blackwell encyclopedia of the Russian Revolution.* Oxford: B. Blackwell, 1988.

Sullivan, Helen F. *Russia and the former Soviet Union: A bibliographical guide to English language publications, 1986–1991.* Littleton, CO: Libraries Unlimited, 1994.

USSR facts and figures annual. Gulf Breeze, FL: Academic International Press, 1977–1992.

Utechin, Sergej V. *A concise encyclopaedia of Russia.* New York: Dutton, 1964 [c1961].

*Vronskaya, Jeanne. *A biographical dictionary of the Soviet Union, 1917–1988*. London; New York: Saur, 1989.
*————. *Kto est kto v Rossii i byvshem SSSR*. Moscow: Terra, 1994.
Wieczynski, Joseph L., ed. *The Gorbachev bibliography*. New York: Norman Ross, 1995.
————. *The Gorbachev encyclopedia*. Salt Lake City, NV: Charles Schlacks, Jr., 1993.
Zhukov, Evgenii Mikhailovich. *Sovetskaia istoricheskaia entsiklopediia*. Moscow: Sovetskaia entsiklopediia, 1967–1976.

b. Society

Apanasewicz, Nellie Mary. *Education in the USSR: An annotated bibliography of English-language materials, 1965–1973*. Washington, DC: U.S. Dept. of Health, Education and Welfare, Office of Education, 1974.
Fischer, George. *American research on Soviet society: Guide to specialized studies since World War II by sociologists, psychologists, and anthropologists in the United States*. New York: State Education Dept., 1967.
*Hyer, Janet. *Women in Russia and the Soviet Union*. Ottawa, Ont.: Carleton University, 1988.
Katz, Zev, ed. *Handbook of major Soviet nationalities*. New York: Free Press, 1975.
Milner-Gulland, R.R. *Cultural atlas of Russia and the Soviet Union*. New York: Facts on File, 1989.
Movshovich, M.I. *Technical and vocational education in the USSR: A bibliographical survey*. Paris: Unesco, 1959.
Ruthchild, Rochelle Goldberg. *Women in Russia and the Soviet Union: An annotated bibliography*. New York: G.K. Hall, 1993.
Wixman, Ronald. *The peoples of the USSR: An ethnographic handbook*. Armonk, NY: M.E. Sharpe, 1984.
Yedlin, Tova, and J. Wilman. *Women in Russia and the Soviet Union*. Ottawa, Ont.: Carleton University, 1985.

c. Culture

Allworth, Edward. *Nationalities of the Soviet East, publications and writing systems: A bibliographical directory and transliteration tables for Iranian- and Turkic-language publications, 1818–1945, located in U.S. libraries*. New York: Columbia University Press, 1971.
Brickman, William W. *Russian and Soviet education, 1731–1989: A multilingual annotated bibliography*. New York: Garland Publishing, 1992.

Cooper, Henry R. Jr., ed. *The Igor tale: An annotated bibliography of twentieth-century non-Soviet scholarship on the "Slovo o polku Igoreve."* White Plains, NY: M.E. Sharpe, 1978.

Cross, Anthony Glenn. *Eighteenth century Russian literature, culture and thought: A bibliography of English-language scholarship and translations.* Newtonville, MA: Oriental Research Partners, 1984.

De Bray, R.G.A. *Guide to the Slavonic languages.* Columbus, OH: Slavica Publishers, 1980.

Egan, David R., and Melinda A. Egan. *Leo Tolstoy: An annotated bibliography of English language sources to 1978.* Metuchen, NJ: Scarecrow Press, 1979.

Eimermacher, Karl. *Subject bibliography of Soviet semiotics: The Moscow-Tartu school.* Ann Arbor, MI: University of Michigan, 1977.

Foster, Ludmila A. *Bibliography of Russian emigre literature.* Boston, MA: G.K. Hall, 1970.

Garfield, Eugene, ed. *Transliterated dictionary of the Russian language: An abridged dictionary consisting of Russian-to-English and English-to-Russian sections.* Philadelphia, PA: ISI Press, 1979.

Geld, Isidore. *Dictionary of omissions for Russian translators: With examples from scientific texts.* Columbus, OH: Slavica Publishers, 1993.

Harkins, William E. *Dictionary of Russian literature.* Westport, CT: Greenwood Press, 1971.

Ho, Allan, and Dmitry Feofanov, eds. *Biographical dictionary of Russian/Soviet composers.* New York: Greenwood Press, 1989.

Ignashev, Diane M., and Sarah Krive, eds. *Women and writing in Russia and the USSR: A bibliography of English-language sources.* New York: Garland, 1992.

Kasack, Wolfgang. *Dictionary of Russian literature since 1917.* New York: Columbia University Press, 1988.

Katzner, Kenneth. *English-Russian, Russian-English dictionary.* New York: Wiley, 1984.

Macura, Paul. *Elsevier's Russian-English dictionary.* New York: Elsevier, 1990.

Marder, Stephen. *A supplementary Russian-English dictionary.* Columbus, OH: Slavica Publishers, 1992.

Moldon, David. *A bibliography of Russian composers.* London: White Lion, 1976.

Moody, Fred. *Ten bibliographies of 20th-century Russian literature.* Ann Arbor, MI: Ardis, 1977.

Proffer, Carl R., and Ronald Meyer, eds. *Nineteenth-century Russian literature in English: A bibliography of criticism and translations.* Ann Arbor, MI: Ardis, 1990.

Reyna, Ferdinando. *Concise encyclopedia of ballet.* London: Collins, 1974.

Sendich, Munir. *Boris Pasternak: A reference guide.* New York: G.K. Hall, 1994.

Stankiewicz, Edward, and Dean S. Worth. *A selected bibliography of Slavic linguistics.* The Hague: Mouton, 1966.

Weber, Harry B. *Modern encyclopedia of Russian and Soviet literature.* Gulf Breeze, FL: Academic International Press, 1977.

Wheeler, Marcus. *The Oxford Russian-English dictionary.* Oxford: Clarendon Press, 1984.

Zalewski, Wojciech. *Russian-English dictionaries with aids for translators: A selected bibliography.* New York: Russica, 1981.

d. Economics

Birkos, Alexander S. *East European and Soviet economic affairs: A bibliography (1965–1973).* Littleton, CO: Libraries Unlimited, 1975.

Iordanoglou, Alexander. *Partial bibliography of Dr. Vladimir L. Kvint: For the period 1967–1994.* New York: S.n., 1994.

Kazmer, Daniel R., and Vera Kazmer. *Russian economic history: A guide to information sources.* Detroit, MI: Gale Research, 1977.

Loeber, Dietrich Andre. *East-West trade: A sourcebook on the international relations of socialist countries and their legal aspects.* Dobbs Ferry, NY: Oceana Publications, 1976–77.

Moscow business connection. Wayne, PA: Telebase Systems, 1992.

Posadskov, Eugene L., et al. *The Ross register of Siberian industry: A directory to resources, factories, products, mines, banks and stock exchanges throughout Siberia.* New York: Norman Ross, 1995.

e. History

Chew, Allen F. *An atlas of Russian history: Eleven centuries of changing borders.* New Haven: Yale University Press, 1970.

Crowther, P. A., ed. *A bibliography of works in English on early Russian history to 1800.* Oxford: Blackwell, 1969.

De Mowbray, Stephen. *Key facts in Soviet history.* Boston, MA: G.K. Hall, 1990.

Edelheit, Abraham J., and Hershel Edelheit, eds. *The rise and fall of the Soviet Union: A selected bibliography of sources in English.* Westport, CT: Greenwood Press, 1992.

*Gilbert, Martin. *Imperial Russian history atlas.* London: Routledge and Kegan Paul, 1978.

———. *Soviet history atlas.* London: Routledge and Kegan Paul, 1979.

Grierson, Philip. *Books on Soviet Russia, 1917–1942.* Twickenham: Anthony C. Hall, 1969.

Hartley, J.M. *Guide to documents and manuscripts in the United King-

dom relating to Russia and the Soviet Union. New York: Cassell Publishing, 1987.

Hartley, J.M., ed. *The study of Russian history from British archival sources.* London: Mansell Publishing Ltd., 1986.

Jackson, G., and R. Devlin, eds. *Dictionary of the Russian Revolution.* Westport, CT: Greenwood Press, 1989.

Morley, Charles. *Guide to research in Russian history.* Syracuse, NY: Syracuse University Press, 1951.

*Paxton, John. *Companion to Russian history.* New York: Facts on File, 1983.

————. *Encyclopedia of Russian history: From the Christianization of Kiev to the break-up of the USSR.* Santa Barbara, CA: ABC Clio, 1993.

Pushkarev, S.G. *Dictionary of Russian historical terms from the eleventh century to 1917.* New Haven, CT: Yale University Press, 1970.

Shapiro, David. *A select bibliography of works in English on Russian history, 1801–1917.* Oxford: Blackwell, 1962.

*Vernadsky, G., ed. *A sourcebook for Russian history from early times to 1917.* New Haven, CT: Yale University Press, 1973.

*Wieczynski, Joseph L. *The modern encyclopedia of Russian and Soviet history.* Gulf Breeze, FL: Academic International Press, 1976.

f. Law

Feldbrugge, F.J.M. (Ferdinand Joseph Maria), ed. *Encyclopedia of Soviet law.* Dobbs Ferry, NY: Oceana Publications, 1973.

Grabar, V.E. (Vladimir Emmanuilovich). *The history of international law in Russia, 1647–1917: A bio-bibliographical study.* Oxford: Clarendon Press, 1990.

Kavass, Igor I. *Demise of the Soviet Union: A bibliographical survey of English writings on the Soviet legal system, 1990–1991.* Buffalo, NY: W.S. Hein, 1992.

————. *Gorbachev's law: A bibliographical survey of English writings on Soviet legal development, 1987–1990.* Buffalo, NY: W.S. Hein, 1991.

————. *Soviet law in English: Research guide and bibliography, 1970–1987.* Buffalo, NY: W.S. Hein, 1988.

g. Politics and Government

Degras, Jane Tabrisky. *Soviet documents on foreign policy.* New York: Oxford University Press, 1951–53.

Goehlert, Robert. *Reference sources for the study of Soviet politics.* Monticello, IL: Vance Bibliographies, 1980.

McCrea, Barbara P., et al. *The Soviet and East European political dictionary.* Santa Barbara, CA: ABC Clio, 1984.
Russian government directory. Leverette, MA: Rector Press, 1994.
Shavit, David. *United States relations with Russia and the Soviet Union: A historical dictionary.* Westport, CT: Greenwood Press, 1993.

h. Military

Arans, David. *How we lost the civil war: Bibliography of Russian emigre memoirs on the Russian revolution, 1917–1921.* Newtonville, MA: Oriental Research Partners.
*Jones, D.R., ed. *Military-naval enyclopedia of Russia and the Soviet Union.* Gulf Breeze, FL: Academic International Press, 1978.
Lyons, M. *The Russian Imperial Army: A bibliography of regimental histories and related works.* Stanford, CA: Hoover Institution on War, Revolution, and Peace, 1968.
Scott, William Fontaine. *Soviet sources of military doctrine and strategy.* New York: Crane, Russak, 1975.
Sovetskaia voennaia entsiklopediia. Moscow: Voenizdat, 1976–1980.
Soviet documents on the use of war experience / translated by Harold S. Orenstein; with an introduction by David M. Glantz. London; Portland, OR: Frank Cass, 1991.

i. Science

Harris, Chauncy Dennison. *Guide to geographical bibliographies and reference works in Russian or on the Soviet Union: Annotated list of 2660 bibliographies or reference aids.* Chicago: Dept. of Geography, University of Chicago, 1975.
Library of Congress. Science and Technology Division. *Soviet science and technology: A bibliography on the state of the art, 1955–1961.* Washington, DC: Library of Congress, 1962.
Melik-Shakhnazarov, Aram Sergeevich. *Technical information in the USSR.* Cambridge, MA: Massachusetts Institute of Technology Libraries, 1961.

II. General Information

European Communities Staff. *Country profile: The Russian Federation, 1993.* Lanham, MD: Unipub, 1994.
Forbes, Moria. *Jobs in Russia and the newly independent states.* Manassas Park, VA: Impact Publications, 1994.
Sckolnick, Lewis B., ed. *Russia, China, Eastern Europe and world*

place name change directory. Leverette, MA: Rector Press, Ltd., 1994.

Wheeler, Jeff B. *The register: Information directory for the Russian Far East.* Fortville, IN: Dalny Vostok, 1994.

III. Description and Travel

Berand, Henri. *The truth about Moscow as seen by a French visitor.* London: Faber and Gwyer, 1926.

Berry, Lloyd Eason, ed. *Rude and barbarous kingdom: Russia in the accounts of sixteenth-century English voyagers.* Madison, WI: University of Wisconsin Press, 1968.

Binyon, Michael. *Life in Russia.* New York: Pantheon, 1983.

Buettner, Dan. *Sovietrek: A journey by bicycle across southern Russia.* Minneapolis, MN: Lerner Group, 1994.

Cockburn, Patrick. *Getting Russia wrong: The end of Kremlinology.* London: Verso, 1989.

Cook, Thomas. *Russian way.* Lincolnwood, IL: NTC Publishing Group, 1995.

Custine, Astolphe, Marquis de. *Empire of the czar: A journey through eternal Russia.* New York: Doubleday, 1989.

Davies, Joseph E. *Mission to Moscow.* New York: Simon and Schuster, 1941.

Davies, R.W. (Robert William), ed. *The Soviet Union.* London: Allen and Unwin, 1978.

Feifer, George. *Moscow farewell.* New York: Viking Press, 1976.

———. *Our motherland and other ventures in Russian reportage.* New York: Viking Press, 1974.

Flint, David. *Russia.* Chatham, NJ: Raintree Steck-Vaughn, 1992.

Ford, Robert A.D. *Our man in Moscow: A diplomat's reflections on the Soviet Union.* Toronto, Ont.: University of Toronto Press, 1989.

Gautier, Théophile. *A winter in Russia.* New York: Gordon Press, 1977.

Gide, André. *Return from the USSR.* New York: Alfred A. Knopf, 1937.

Greenall, Robert. *An explorer's guide to Russia.* Somerville, MA: Zephyr Press, 1994.

Gregory, James Stothert. *Russian land, Soviet people: A geographical approach to the USSR.* London: Harrap, 1968.

Harris, C.D., ed. *Russian geography: Accomplishments and tasks.* Leverett, MA: Rector Press, 1994.

Kapuscinski, Ryszard. *The soccer war.* New York: Alfred A. Knopf, 1991.

Maier, Frith. *Trekking in Russia and Central Asia, a traveller's guide:*

Urals, Pamirs, Caucasus, Siberia, Lake Baikal, Crimean Peninsula, Kamchatka Peninsula. Seattle, WA: Mountaineers Books, 1994.

Nordbye, Masha. *Moscow-Saint Petersburg handbook: Including the Golden Ring.* Chico, CA: Moon Publications, 1993.

Peskov, Vassily. *Lost in the taiga: One Russian family's fifty-year struggle for survival and religious freedom in the Siberian wilderness.* New York: Doubleday, 1994.

Prince Michael of Russia. *Imperial palaces of Russia.* New York: St. Martin's Press, 1994.

Radishchev, Aleksandr Nikolaevich. *A journey from St. Petersburg to Moscow.* Cambridge, MA: Harvard University Press, 1958.

Russia. Boston: Houghton Mifflin, 1993.

Salisbury, Harrison Evans. *American in Russia.* New York: Harper, 1955.

Sears, Robert. *An illustrated description of the Russian empire* [microform]: *embracing its geographical features, political divisions, principal cities and towns . . . from the latest and the most authentic sources. New ed., rev. enl. and brought down to 1881.* New York: Hurst, [1881?].

Smith, Claude C. *Red men in Red Square.* Blacksburg, VA: Pocahontas Press, 1994.

Smith, Jo D. *Russia: A long-shot romance.* New York: Alfred A. Knopf, 1994.

Tarsis, Valerii. *Russia and the Russians.* London: Macdonald, 1970.

Thubron, Colin. *Where nights are longest: Travels by car through western Russia.* New York: Random House, 1984.

Tips to travelers: Russia. New York: Gordon Press,1994.

IV. Culture—General

Bazanov, V.G., ed. *Kulturnoe nasledie Drevnei Rusi: Istoki, stanovlenie, traditsii.* Moscow: Nauka, 1976.

Blaser, W. *Tomsk: Texture in wood.* New York: Springer, 1994.

Brumfield, William C., and Milos M. Velimirovich, eds. *Christianity and the arts in Russia.* Cambridge: Cambridge University Press, 1991.

Hubbs, Joanna. *Mother Russia: The feminine myth in Russian culture.* Bloomington, IN: Indiana University Press, 1988.

Pyman, Avril. *A history of Russian symbolism.* Cambridge: Cambridge University Press, 1994.

Raymond, Boris. *N.K. Krupskaia and Soviet Librarianship, 1917–1939.* Lanham, MD: Scarecrow Press, 1979.

Stites, Richard. *Russian popular culture: Entertainment and society since 1900.* New York: Cambridge University Press, 1992.

V. Intellectual History

Acton, Edward. *Alexander Herzen and the role of the intellectual revolutionary.* Cambridge: Cambridge University Press, 1979.
Batalden, Stephen K., ed. *Seeking God: The recovery of religious identity in Orthodox Russia, Ukraine and Georgia.* DeKalb, IL: Northern Illinois University Press, 1993.
Berlin, Isaiah, Sir. *Russian thinkers.* London: Hogarth Press, 1978.
Christoff, Peter K. *The third heart: Some intellectual-ideological currents and cross-currents in Russia, 1800–1830.* The Hague: Mouton, 1970.
Fedotov, G.P. (Georgii Petrovich). *The Russian religious mind.* Belmont, MA: Nordland, 1975.
Gasparov, Boris, ed. *Cultural mythologies of Russian modernism: From the Golden Age to the Silver Age.* Berkeley, CA: University of California Press, 1992.
Gershenzon, Michael, ed. *Signposts: A collection of articles on the Russian intelligentsia.* Los Angeles: Charles Schlacks, 1986.
Glazov, Yuri. *The Russian mind since Stalin's death.* Dordrecht: D. Reidel, 1985.
Pereira, N.G.O. *The thought and teachings of N.G. Cernysevskij.* The Hague: Mouton, 1975.
Riasanovsky, Nicholas Valentine. *A parting of ways: Government and the educated public in Russia, 1801–1855.* Oxford: Clarendon Press, 1976.
———. *Russia and the West in the teachings of the Slavophiles: A study of romantic ideology.* Gloucester, MA: P. Smith, 1965.
Rozental, Mark Moiseevich. *Kratkii filosofskii slovar.* Moscow: Politizdat, 1954.
Scanlon, James P., ed. *Russian thought after communism: The recovery of a philosophical heritage.* Armonk, NY: M.E. Sharpe, 1994.
Woehrlin, William F. *Chernyshevskii: The man and the journalist.* Cambridge, MA: Harvard University Press, 1971.

VI. Performing Arts

Abraham, Gerald. *Eight Soviet composers.* London: Oxford University Press, 1943.

Benedetti, Jean. *Stanislavski: An introduction.* New York: Theater Arts Books, 1982.

Benois, A. *Reminiscences of the Russian ballet.* London: Putnam, 1941.

Bland, Alexander. *The Nureyev image.* London: Studio Vista, 1976.

Brashinsky, Michael, and Andrew Horton, eds. *Russian critics on the cinema of glasnost.* New York: Cambridge University Press, 1994.

Buckle, Richard. *Nijinsky.* New York: Simon and Schuster, 1971.

Campbell, Stuart, ed. *Russians on Russian music, 1830–1880: An anthology.* Cambridge: Cambridge University Press, 1994.

Demidov, A. *The Russian ballet: Past and present.* Garden City, NY: Doubleday, 1977.

Duncan, Isadora. *My life.* New York: Liveright, 1955.

Eisenstein, Sergei. *Immoral memories: An autobiography.* Boston: Houghton Mifflin, 1983.

———. *Selected works.* London: BFI Publishing, 1988.

Feigin, Leo, ed. *Russian jazz: New identity.* London: Quartet Books, 1985.

Green, Michael, ed. *The Russian symbolist theatre: An anthology of plays and critical texts.* Ann Arbor, MI: Ardis, 1986.

Hall, Fernau. *Olga Preobrazhenskaya: A portrait.* New York: M. Dekker, 1978.

Jelagin, Juri. *Taming of the arts.* New York: Dutton, 1951.

Johnson, Alfred Edwin. *The Russian ballet.* Boston: Houghton Mifflin, 1913.

Johnson, Vida T., and Graham Petrie. *The films of Andrei Tarkovsky: A visual fugue.* Bloomington, IN: Indiana University Press, 1994.

Kirstein, Lincoln. *Nijinsky dancing.* London: Thames and Hudson, 1975.

Komisarjevsky, Theodore. *Myself and the theatre.* London: Heinemann, 1929.

Kshesinskaia, Matilda Feliksovna. *Dancing in Petersburg: The memoirs of Kschessinska (H.S.H. the Princess Romanovsky-Krassinsky).* London: Gollancz, 1960.

Lawton, Anna (Anna M.). *Kinoglasnost: Soviet cinema in our time.* Cambridge: Cambridge University Press, 1992.

Lazzarini, John. *Pavlova: Repertoire of a legend.* New York: Schirmer Books, 1980.

Leonard, Anthony Richard. *A history of Russian music.* London: Jarrolds, 1956.

Leyda, Jay. *Kino: A history of the Russian and Soviet film.* Princeton, NJ: Princeton University Press, 1983, c1973.

Liven, Petr Aleksandrovich. *The birth of ballets-russes.* New York: Dover Publications, 1973.

Lvov, Nikolai, ed. *A collection of Russian folksongs.* Ann Arbor, MI: UMI Research Press, 1987.

Magriel, Paul. *Nijinsky, Pavlova, Duncan: Three lives in dance.* New York: Da Capo Press, 1977.

Nijinska, Bronislava. *Bronislava Nijinska: Early memoirs.* New York: Holt, Rinehart and Winston, 1981.

Panov, Valery. *To dance.* New York: Knopf, 1978.

Ramet, Sabrina Petra, ed. *Rocking the state: Rock music and politics in Eastern Europe and Russia.* Boulder, CO: Westview Press, 1994.

Ridenour, Robert C. *Nationalism, modernism, and personal rivalry in nineteenth-century Russian music.* Ann Arbor, MI: UMI Research Press, 1981.

Roberts, J.W. *Richard Boleslavsky: His life and work in the theatre.* Ann Arbor, MI: UMI Research Press, 1981.

Roberts, Peter Deane. *Modernism in Russian piano music: Skriabin, Prokofiev, and their Russian contemporaries.* Bloomington, IN: Indiana University Press, 1993.

Roslavleva, Natalia Petrovna. *Era of the Russian ballet.* New York: Dutton, 1966.

Scholl, Tim. *From Petipa to Balanchine: Classical revival and the modernization of ballet.* London: Routledge, 1994.

Schwarz, Boris. *Music and musical life in Soviet Russia, 1917–1970.* New York: W. W. Norton, 1973.

Seaman, Gerald. *History of Russian music: From its origins to Dargomyzhsky.* Oxford: Praeger, 1967.

Segel, Harold B. *Twentieth-century Russian drama: From Gorky to the present.* New York: Columbia University Press, 1979.

Sergievsky, Orest. *Memoirs of a dancer: Shadows of the past, dreams that came true, memories of yesterdays.* New York: Dance Horizons, 1979.

Smith, Gerald Stanton. *Songs to seven strings: Russian guitar poetry and Soviet "mass song."* Bloomington, IN: Indiana University Press, 1984.

Taruskin, Richard. *Musorgsky: Eight essays and an epilogue.* Princeton, NJ: Princeton University Press, 1993.

———. *Opera and drama in Russia as preached and practiced in the 1860s.* Ann Arbor, MI: UMI Research Press, 1981.

VII. Fine Arts

Alpatov, Mikhail Vladimirovich. *Russian impact on art.* New York: Greenwood Press, 1969.

Auty, Robert, and Dimitry Obolensky, eds. *Introduction to Russian art and architecture.* Cambridge: Cambridge University Press, 1980.

Bojko, Szymon. *New graphic design in revolutionary Russia.* New York: Praeger, 1972.

Bowlt, John, E., ed. *The life of Vasilii Kandinsky in Russian art: A study of "On the spiritual in art."* Newtonville, MA: Oriental Research Partners, 1980.

————. *Russian art, 1875–1975: A collection of essays.* New York: MSS Information, 1976.

————. *Russian art of the avant-garde: Theory and criticism, 1902–1934.* New York: Viking Press, 1976.

Brumfeld, William Craft, and Blair A. Ruble, eds. *Russian housing in the modern age: Design and social history.* New York: Woodrow Wilson Center Press, 1993.

Chen, Jack. *Soviet art and artists.* London: Pilot Press, 1944.

Compton, Susan P. *The world backwards: Russian futurist books, 1912–16.* London: British Museum Publications, 1978.

Constructivism and futurism: Russian and other. New York: Ex libris, 1977.

Elliott, David, ed. *Rodchenko and the arts of revolutionary Russia.* New York: Pantheon Books, 1979.

Fauchereau, Serge. *Malevich.* New York: Rizzoli, 1993.

German, Mikhail Iurevich. *Art of the October Revolution.* New York: Abrams, 1979.

Golomshtok, I.N. *Soviet art in exile.* New York: Random House, 1977.

Gray, Camilla. *The Russian experiment in art, 1863–1922.* London: Thames and Hudson, 1971.

Hamilton, George Heard. *The art and architecture of Russia.* Harmondsworth: Penguin Books, 1975.

Jager, Nita, ed. *Russian art of the Revolution.* Ithaca, NY: Office of University Publications, Cornell University, 1970.

Kornilovich, Kira Viktorovna. *Arts of Russia.* Cleveland: World Publishing, 1967–68.

London, Kurt. *The seven Soviet arts.* New Haven, CT: Yale University Press, 1938.

Malevich, Kazimir. *Suprematism: 34 drawings.* London: Gordon Fraser Gallery, 1974.

Myers, Bernard S., and Trewin Copplestone. *Art treasures in Russia: Monuments, masterpieces, commissions, and collections.* New York: McGraw-Hill, 1970.

New Museum of Contemporary Art (New York, N.Y.) *Sots art: Eric Bulatov, Vitaly Komar and Alexander Melamid, Alexander Kosolapov, Leonid Lamm, Leonid Sokov, Kazimir Passion Group.* New York: New Museum of Contemporary Art, 1986.

Nilsson, Nils Ake, ed. *Art, society, revolution: Russia, 1917–1921.* Stockholm: Almqvist and Wiksell International, 1979.
Parker, Fan. *Russia on canvas: Ilya Repin.* University Park: Pennsylvania State University Press, 1980.
Snowman, A. Kenneth. *Faberge lost and found: The recently discovered jewelry designs from the St. Petersburg archives.* New York: H.N. Abrams, 1993.
Valkenier, Elizabeth Kridl. *Russian realist art: The state and society: The Peredvizhniki and their tradition.* Ann Arbor, MI: Ardis, 1977.
Voyce, Arthur. *The art and architecture of medieval Russia.* Norman, OK: University of Oklahoma Press, 1967.
Williams, Robert Chadwell. *Russian art and American money, 1900–1940.* Cambridge, MA: Harvard University Press, 1980.

VIII. Language and Literature

Afanasev, A.N. (Aleksandr Nikolaevich). *Russian fairy tales.* New York: Pantheon Books, c1973.
Aiken, Susan. *Dialogues dialogi: Literary and cultural exchanges between (ex) Soviet and American women.* Durham, NC: Duke University Press, 1994.
Alexander, Alex E. *Bylina and fairy tale: The origins of Russian heroic poetry.* The Hague: Mouton, 1973.
Altshuller, Mark. *Put otrecheniia: Russkaia literatura 1953–1968.* Tenafly, NJ: Hermitage, 1985.
Andrew, Joe. *Writers and society during the rise of Russian realism.* Atlantic Highlands, NJ: Humanities Press, 1980.
Any, Carol. *Boris Eikhenbaum: Voices of a Russian formalist.* Stanford, CA: Stanford University Press, 1994.
Bailey, George, ed. *Kontinent 4: Contemporary Russian writers.* New York: Avon Books, 1982.
Bely, Andrey. *Selected essays of Andrey Bely.* Berkeley, CA: University of California Press, 1985.
Berry, Thomas E. (Thomas Edwin). *Plots and characters in major Russian fiction.* Hamden, CT: Archon, 1977–1978.
Bethea, David M., ed. *Pushkin today.* Bloomington, IN: Indiana University Press, 1993.
———. *The shape of apocalypse in modern Russian fiction.* Princeton, NJ: Princeton University Press, 1989.
Booker, M. Keith. *Bakhtin, Stalin and modern Russian fiction: Carnival, dialogism and history.* Westport, CT: Greenwood Press, 1995.

Bortnes, Jostein. *Visions of glory: Studies in early Russian hagiography.* Atlantic Highlands, NJ: Humanities Press, 1988.

Boyd, Brian. *Vladimir Nabokov: The Russian years.* London: Chatto & Windus, 1990.

Briggs, A.D.P. *Alexander Pushkin: A critical study.* London: Croom Helm, 1983.

Brodsky, Joseph. *Less than one: Selected essays.* New York: Farrar, Straus & Giroux, 1986.

Brown, Clarence, ed. *The portable twentieth-century Russian reader.* New York: Penguin, 1985.

Brown, Deming. *Soviet Russian literature since Stalin.* Cambridge: Cambridge University Press, 1978.

Brown, William Edward. *A history of 18th-century Russian literature.* Ann Arbor, MI: Ardis, 1980.

————. *A history of Russian literature of the romantic period.* Ann Arbor, MI: Ardis, 1986.

————. *A history of seventeenth-century Russian literature.* Ann Arbor, MI: Ardis, 1980.

Browning, Gary. *Boris Pilniak: Scythian at a typewriter.* Ann Arbor, MI: Ardis, 1985.

Burgin, Diana Lewis. *Sophia Parnok: The life and work of Russia's Sappho.* New York: New York University Press, 1994.

Carlisle, Olga Andreyev. *Sozlhenitsyn and the secret circle.* New York: Holt, Rinehart and Winston, 1978.

Chances, Ellen B. *Conformity's children: An approach to the superfluous man in Russian literature.* Columbus, OH: Slavica Publishers, 1978.

Chapple, Richard L. *Soviet satire of the twenties.* Gainesville, FL: University Presses of Florida, 1980.

Cioran, Samuel D. (Samuel David). *Vladimir Soloviev and the Knighthood of the Divine Sophia.* Waterloo, Ont.: Wilfrid Laurier Press, 1977.

Clardy, Jesse V. *G.R. Derzhavin: A political biography.* The Hague: Mouton, 1967.

————. *The superfluous man in Russian letters.* Washington, DC: University Press of America, 1980.

Clark, Katerina. *The Soviet novel: History as ritual.* Chicago, IL: University of Chicago Press, 1981.

Clowes, Edith W. *The revolution of moral consciousness: Nietzsche in Russian literature, 1890–1914.* DeKalb, IL: Northern Illinois University Press, 1988.

————. *Russian experimental fiction: Resisting ideology after utopia.* Princeton, NJ: Princeton University Press, 1993.

Clyman, Toby W., and Diana Greene, eds. *Women writers in Russian literature.* Westport, CT: Greenwood Press, 1994.

Conant, Roger. *The political poetry of F.I. Tiutchev.* Ann Arbor, MI: Ardis, 1983.

Cross, Anthony Glenn, ed. *Russian literature in the age of Catharine the Great: A collection of essays.* Oxford: Meeuws, 1976.

Crouch, Martin, and R.C. Porter, eds. *Understanding Soviet politics through literature: A book of readings.* London: G. Allen and Unwin, 1984.

Curtis, J.A.E. (Julie A.E.). *Manuscripts don't burn: Mikhail Bulgakov, a life in letters and diaries.* Woodstock, NY: Overlook Press, 1992.

Diment, Galya, and Yuri Slexkine. *Between heaven and earth: The myth of Siberia in Russian culture.* New York: St. Martin's Press, 1993.

Dirscherl, Denis. *Dostoevsky and the Catholic Church.* Chicago, IL: Loyola University Press, 1986.

Drage, C.L. (Charles Lovell). *Russian literature in the eighteenth century: The solemn ode, the epic, other poetic genres, the story, the novel, drama: An introduction for university courses.* London: The author, 1978.

Dunham, Vera Sandomirsky. *In Stalin's time: Middleclass values in Soviet fiction.* Cambridge: Cambridge University Press, 1976.

Edwards, T.R.N. *Three Russian writers and the irrational: Zamyatin, Pilnyak, and Bulgakov.* Cambridge: Cambridge University Press, 1982.

Eikhenbaum, Boris Mikhailovich, and Iurii Nikolaevich Tynianov, eds. *Russian prose.* Ann Arbor, MI: Ardis, 1985.

———. *Tolstoi in the seventies.* Ann Arbor, MI: Ardis, 1982.

———. *Tolstoi in the sixties.* Ann Arbor, MI: Ardis, 1982.

Ericson, Edward E., Jr. *Solzhenitsyn and the modern world.* Washington, DC: Regnery Gateway, 1993.

Erlich, Victor. *Modernism and revolution: Russian literature in transition.* Cambridge, MA: Harvard University Press, 1994.

Ermolaev, Herman. *Soviet literary theories, 1917–1934: The genesis of socialist realism.* New York: Octagon Books, 1977.

Feiler, Lily. *Marina Tsvetaeva: The double beat of heaven and hell.* Durham, NC: Duke University Press, 1994.

Fennell, John Lister Illingworth. *Nineteenth-century Russian literature: Studies of ten Russian writers.* London: Faber, 1973.

Field, Andrew. *Vladimir Nabokov: His life in part.* London: Hamilton, 1977.

Finke, Michael C. *Metapoesis: The Russian tradition from Pushkin to Chekhov.* Durham, NC: Duke University Press, 1995.

Frank, Joseph. *Dostoevsky: The miraculous years, 1865–1871.* Princeton, NJ: Princeton University Press, 1995.

————. *Dostoevsky: The seeds of revolt, 1821–1849.* Princeton, NJ: Princeton University Press, 1976.

————. *Dostoevsky: The stir of liberation, 1860–1865.* Princeton, NJ: Princeton University Press, 1986.

————. *Dostoevsky: The years of ordeal, 1850–1859.* Princeton, NJ: Princeton University Press, 1983.

Glad, John, ed. *Conversations in exile: Russian writers abroad.* Durham, NC: Duke University Press, 1993.

————, and Daniel Weissbort, eds. *Russian poetry, the modern period.* Iowa City, IA: University of Iowa Press, 1978.

Goscilo, Helena, ed. *Fruits of her plume: Essays on contemporary Russian woman's culture.* Armonk, NY: M.E. Sharpe, 1993.

————, ed. *Lives in transit: A collection of recent Russian women's writing.* Ann Arbor, MI: Ardis, 1994.

Gumilev, N. (Nikolai). *Nikolai Gumilev on Russian poetry.* Ann Arbor, MI: Ardis, 1977.

Hammarberg, Gitta. *From the idyll to the novel: Karamzin's sentimental prose.* Cambridge: Cambridge University Press, 1991.

Hart, Pierre R. *G.R. Derzhavin, a poet's progress.* Columbus, OH: Slavica Publishers, 1978.

Hayward, Max. *Writers in Russia, 1917–1978.* San Diego, CA: Harcourt Brace Jovanovich, 1983.

Heldt, Barbara. *Terrible perfection: Women and Russian literature.* Bloomington, IN: Indiana University Press, 1987.

Hingley, Ronald. *Nightingale fever: Russian poets in revolution.* New York: Knopf, 1981.

Holmgren, Beth. *Women's works in Stalin's time: On Lidiia Chukovskaia and Nadezhda Mandelstam.* Bloomington, IN: Indiana University Press, 1993.

Hubbs, Joanna. *Mother Russia: The feminine myth in Russian culture.* Bloomington, IN: Indiana University Press, 1988.

Janecek, Gerald. *The look of Russian literature: Avant-garde visual experiments, 1900–1930.* Princeton, NJ: Princeton University Press, 1984.

Jensen, Peter Albert, ed. *Text and context, essays to honor Nils Ake Nilsson.* Stockholm: Almqvist and Wiksell International, 1987.

Kornblatt, Judith Deutsch. *The Cossack hero in Russian literature: A study in cultural mythology.* Madison, WI: University of Wisconsin Press, 1992.

Kropotkin, Petr Alekseevich, kniaz. *Russian literature: Ideals and realities.* Montreal, Que.: Black Rose Books, 1991.

Lawton, Anna (Anna M.), ed. *Russian futurism through its manifestoes, 1912–1928.* Ithaca, NY: Cornell University Press, 1988.

Leighton, Lauren G. *Two worlds, one art: Literary translation in Russia and America*. DeKalb, IL: Northern Illinois University Press, 1991.

Lenhoff, Gail. *The martyred Princes Boris and Gleb: A socio-cultural study of the cult and its texts*. Columbia, OH: Slavica Publications, 1989.

Levitt, Marcus C. *Early modern Russian writers: Late seventeenth and eighteenth centuries*. Detroit, MI: Gale Research, 1995.

Likhachev, Dmitrii Sergeevich. *The great heritage: The classical literature of Old Rus*. Moscow: Progress, 1981.

Losev, Lev. *On the beneficence of censorship: Aesopian language in modern Russian literature*. Munich: O. Sagner in Kommission, 1984.

Lotman, Iu.M. (Iurii Mikhailovich), et al. *The semiotics of Russian cultural history*. Ithaca, NY: Cornell University Press, 1985.

Luker, Nicholas J.L., ed. *From Furmanov to Sholokhov: An anthology of the classics of socialist realism*. Ann Arbor, MI: Ardis, 1988.

Lvov-Rogachevskii, V. (Vasilii). *A history of Russian Jewish literature: Including B. Gorev's "Russian literature and the Jews."* Ann Arbor, MI: Ardis, 1979.

Maegd-Soep, Carolina de. *Chekhov and women: Women in the life and work of Chekhov*. Columbia, OH: Slavica Publishers, 1987.

Maguire, Robert A. *Exploring Gogol*. Stanford, CA: Stanford University Press, 1995.

Mandelshtam, Nadezhda. *Hope against hope: A memoir*. New York: Atheneum, 1970.

Mandelshtam, Osip. *Osip Mandelstam, selected essays*. Austin, TX: University of Texas Press, 1977.

Masing-Delic, I, (Irene). *Abolishing death: A salvation myth of Russian twentieth-century literature*. Stanford, CA: Stanford University Press, 1992.

Matejka, Ladislav. *Readings in Russian poetics: Formalist and structuralist views*. Ann Arbor, MI: Michigan Slavic Publications, 1978.

Matich, Olga, and Michael Henry Heim, eds. *The third wave: Russian literature in emigration*. Ann Arbor, MI: Ardis, 1984.

Matlaw, Ralph E., ed. *Belinsky, Chrnyshevsky, and Dobrolyubov: Selected criticism*. Bloomington, IN: Indiana University Press, 1976.

May, Rachel. *The translator in the text: On reading Russian literature in English*. Evanston, IL: Northwestern University Press, 1994.

Medvedev, P.N. (Pavel Nikolaevich), and Mikhail Bakhtin. *The formal method in literary scholarship: A critical introduction to sociological poetics*. Ann Arbor, MI: University Microfilms International, 1986.

Mirskii, Dmitrii Petrovich. *A history of Russian literature, from its beginnings to 1900*. New York: Vintage Books, 1958.

———. *Pushkin*. London: G. Routledge, 1926.

Moser, Charles A., ed. *The Cambridge history of Russian literature.* New York: Cambridge University Press, 1992.

Nabokov, Vladimir. *Lectures on Russian literature.* New York: Harcourt Brace Jovanovich/Bruccoli Clark, 1981.

Olesha, Iurii Karlovich. *No day without a line.* Ann Arbor, MI: Ardis, 1979.

O'Meara, Patrick. *K.F. Ryleev: A political biography of the Decembrist poet.* Princeton, NJ: Princeton University Press, 1984.

Paperno, Irina, and Joan Delaney Grossman, eds. *Creating life: The aesthetic utopia of Russian modernism.* Stanford, CA: Stanford University Press, 1994.

Paretts, Vladimir Nikolaevich. *Kratkii ocherk metodologii istorii russkoi literatury.* The Hague: Mouton, 1969.

Parthe, Kathleen. *Russian village prose: The radiant past.* Princeton, NJ: Princeton University Press, 1992.

Partridge, Monica. *Alexander Herzen, 1812–1870.* Paris: Unesco, 1984.

Polivanov, Konstantin. *Anna Akhmatova and her circle.* Fayetteville, AR: University of Arkansas press, 1994.

Proffer, Carl R., and Ellendea Proffer, eds. *The silver age of Russian culture: An anthology.* Ann Arbor, MI: Ardis, 1975.

———. *The widows of Russia and other writings.* Ann Arbor, MI: Ardis, 1987.

Propp, V.Ia. (Vladimir Iakovlevich). *Theory and history of folklore.* Minneapolis, MN: University of Minnesota Press, 1984.

Rancour-Laferriere, Daniel, ed. *Russian literature and psychoanalysis.* Philadelphia, PA: J. Benjamins, 1989.

Randall, Francis B. (Francis Ballard). *Vissarion Belinskii.* Newtonville, MA: Oriental Research Partners, 1987.

Robin, Regine. *Socialist realism: An impossible aesthetic.* Stanford, CA: Stanford University Press, 1992.

Rudova, Larissa. *Pasternak's short fiction and the cultural vanguard.* New York: Peter Lang, 1994.

Siniavskii, A. (Andrei). *Strolls with Pushkin.* New Haven, CT: Yale University Press, 1993.

Smith, Gerald S., ed. *Contemporary Russian poetry: A bilingual anthology.* Bloomington: Indiana University Press, 1993.

Sokolov, Iu.M. (Iurii Matveevich). *Russian folklore.* Detroit, MI: Folklore Associates, 1971 [c1950].

Straus, Nina Pelikan. *Dostoevsky and the woman question: Rereadings at the end of a century.* New York: St. Martin's Press, 1994.

Struve, Gleb. *Russian literature under Lenin and Stalin, 1917–1953.* Norman, OK: University of Oklahoma Press, 1971.

Svirskii, Grigorii. *A history of post-war Soviet writing: The literature of moral opposition.* Ann Arbor, MI: Ardis, 1981.

Tavis, Anna A. *Rilke's Russia: A cultural encounter.* Evanston, IL: Northwestern University Press, 1994.

Terras, Victor, ed. *Handbook of Russian literature.* New Haven, CT: Yale University Press, 1985.

———. *A history of Russian literature.* New Haven, CT: Yale University Press, 1991.

Tucker, Janet G. *Innokentij Annenskij and the Acmeist doctrine.* Columbus, OH: Slavica Publishers, 1986.

Wes, Marinus A. *Classics in Russia 1700–1855: Between two bronze horsemen.* New York: E.J. Brill, 1992.

Wiener, Leo. *Anthology of Russian literature from the earliest period to the present time.* New York: B. Blom, [1967].

Wilson, A.N. *Tolstoy.* New York: Norton, 1988.

IX. History—General

Acton, Edward. *Russia.* London: Longman, 1986.

Aleksandrov, Viktor. *The Kremlin: Nerve center of Russian history.* New York: St. Martin's Press, 1963.

Armstrong, Terence E. *The Russians in the Arctic: Aspects of Soviet exploration and exploitation of the Far North, 1937–57.* London: Methuen, 1958.

Aroutunova, Bayara. *Lives in letters: Princess Zinaida Volkonskaya and her correspondence.* Columbus, OH: Slavica Publishers, 1994.

Auty, Robert, and Dimitri Obolensky, eds. *An introduction to Russian history.* Cambridge: Cambridge University Press, 1976.

Bain, Robert Nisbet. *Slavonic Europe: A political history of Poland and Russia from 1447 to 1796.* Cambridge: Cambridge University Press, 1908.

Barker, John W. *Manuel II Palaeologus (1391–1425): A study in late Byzantine statesmanship.* New Brunswick, NJ: Rutgers University Press, 1969.

Bussow, Conrad. *The disturbed state of the Russian realm.* Montreal, Que.: McGill-Queen's University Press, 1994.

Chamberlin, William Henry. *The Russian enigma: An interpretation.* New York: Scribner, 1944.

Conte, Francis, ed. *Great dates in Russian and Soviet history.* New York: Facts on File, 1994.

Czyrowski, Nicholas L. *The economic factors in the growth of Russia.* New York: Philosophical Library, 1957.

Dashkova, E.R. (Ekaterina Romanova), kniaginia. *Memoirs of Princess Dashkova.* Durham, NC: Duke University Press, 1995.

Dmytryshyn, Basil. *A history of Russia.* Englewood Cliffs, NJ: Prentice-Hall, 1977.

Dukes, Paul. *The making of Russian absolutism, 1613–1982.* London: Longman, 1982.

Fennell, John Lister Illingworth. *The crisis of medieval Russia, 1200–1304.* London: Longman, 1983.

———. *The emergence of Moscow, 1304–1359.* Berkeley, CA: University of California Press, 1968.

———. *Ivan the Great of Moscow.* London: Macmillan, 1961.

Florinsky, Michael T. *Russia: A history and interpretation.* New York: Macmillan, 1960.

———. *Russia: A short history.* New York: Macmillan, 1964.

Freshfield, Douglas William. *The exploration of the Caucasus.* London: E. Arnold, 1902.

Gershenzon, Michael. *A history of young Russia.* Los Angeles, CA: Charles Schlacks, 1986.

Goldfrank, David M. *The origins of the Crimean War.* London: Longman, 1994.

Grekov, Boris Dmitrievich. *Kiev Rus.* Moscow: Foreign Languages Publishing House, 1959.

Karamzin, Nikolai Mikhailovich. *A memoir on ancient and modern Russia: The Russian text.* Cambridge, MA: Harvard University Press, 1959.

Kerner, Robert Joseph. *The urge to the sea: The course of Russian history.* Berkeley and Los Angeles: University of California Press, 1942.

Kliuchevskii, Vasilii Osipovich. *A history of Russia.* New York: Russell and Russell, 1960.

Kochan, Lionel. *The making of modern Russia.* London: J. Cape, 1962.

Kurbskii, Andrei Mikhailovich, kniaz. *Prince A.M. Kurbsky's History of Ivan IV.* Cambridge: Cambridge University Press, 1965.

Lawrence, John Waldemar. *Russia in the making.* London: Allen and Unwin, 1957.

Leonard, Carol S. *Reform and regicide: The reign of Peter III of Russia.* Bloomington, IN: Indiana University Press, 1993.

Lewin, Moshe. *Russia—USSR—Russia: The drive and drift of a superpower.* New York: New Press, 1995.

Lieven, D.C.B. *Russia and the origins of the First World War.* New York: St. Martin's Press, 1985.

———. *Russia's rulers under the old regime.* New Haven, CT: Yale University Press, 1989.

Likhachev, Dmitrii S. *Reflections on Russia.* Boulder, CO: Westview Press, 1991.

Lincoln, W. Bruce. *The Romanovs: The autocrats of all the Russias.* New York: Dial Press, 1981.

MacKenzie, David. *A history of Russia and the Soviet Union.* Homewood, IL: Dorsey Press, 1977.

Meyendorff, John. *Byzantium and the rise of Russia: A study of Byzantino-Russian relations in the fourteenth century.* Cambridge: Cambridge University Press, 1981.

Miller, Wright Watts. *Who are the Russians? A history of the Russian people.* New York: Taplinger, 1973.

Mongait, A.L. (Aleksandr Lvovich). *Archaeology in the USSR.* Moscow: Foreign Languages Publishing House, 1959.

Moynahan, Brian. *Russian century: Birth of a nation, 1894–1994.* New York: Random House, 1994.

Nicol, Donald MacGillivray. *The last centuries of Byzantium, 1261–1453.* London: Hart-Davis, 1972.

Nowak, Frank. *Medieval Slavdom and the rise of Russia.* New York: Cooper Square Publishers, 1970.

Obolensky, Dimitri. *The Byzantine Commonwealth: Eastern Europe, 500–1453.* New York: Praeger, 1971.

———. *Byzantium and the Slavs: Collected studies.* London: Variorum, 1971.

Pelenski, Jaroslaw. *The contest for the legacy of Kievan Rus, and related essays.* New York: East European Quarterly, 1993.

Pokrovskii, Mikhail Nikolaevich. *History of Russia, from the earliest times to the rise of commercial capitalism.* New York: International Publishers, 1931.

Ponomarev, V.N., ed. *Istoriia SSSR s drevneishikh vremen do nashikh dnei.* Moscow: Nauka, 1966–1968.

Platonov, S.F. *Boris Godunov, Tsar of Russia.* Gulf Breeze, FL: Academic International Press, 1973.

Rambaud, Alfred Nicolas. *History of Russia from the earliest times to 1882.* New York: AMS Press, 1970.

Riasanovsky, Nicholas Valentine. *Collected writings, 1947–1994.* Los Angeles, CA: Charles Schlacks, 1993.

———. *A history of Russia.* New York: Oxford University Press, 1963.

Rogger, Hans. *Russia in the age of modernization and revolution, 1881–1917.* London: Longman, 1983.

Saunders, David. *Russia in the age of reaction and reform, 1801–1881.* London: Longman, 1992.

Skrynnikov, R.G. *The time of troubles: Russia in crisis, 1604–1618.* Gulf Breeze, FL: Academic International Press, 1988.

Spector, Ivar. *An introduction to Russian history and culture.* New York: Van Nostrand, 1954.

Stephan, John J. *The Russian Far East: A history.* Stanford, CA: Stanford University Press, 1994.

Sturley, D.M. *A short history of Russia.* New York: Harper and Row, 1964.

Thompson, John M. *Russia and the Soviet Union: An historical introduction from the Kievan state to the present.* Boulder, CO: Westview Press, 1994.

Troitskii, S.M. (Sergei Martinovich). *Rossiia v XVIII veke: Sbornik statei i publikatsii.* Moscow: Nauka, 1982.

Ulam, Adam. *Russia's failed revolutions: From the Decembrists to the dissidents.* New York: Basic Books, 1981.

Vernadsky, George. *Ancient Russia.* New Haven, CT: Yale University Press, 1969.

———. *History of Russia.* New Haven, CT: Yale University Press, 1969.

———. *Kievan Russia.* New Haven, CT: Yale University Press, 1973.

———. *Russian historiography: A history.* Belmont, MA: Nordland, 1978.

———. *A source book for Russian history from early times to 1917.* New Haven, CT: Yale University Press, 1972.

Westwood, J.N. *Endurance and endeavour: Russian history, 1812–1986.* Oxford: Oxford University Press, 1987.

Zolkiewski, Stanislaw. *Expedition to Moscow: A memoir.* London: Polonica Publications, 1959.

X. History—Revolution

Acton, Edward. *Re-thinking the Russian Revolution.* London: E. Arnold, 1992.

Avrich, Paul. *The anarchists in the Russian revolution.* London: Thames and Hudson, 1973.

Bradley, John Francis Nejez. *Civil war in Russia, 1917–1920.* London: B.T. Batsford, 1975.

Brovkin, Vladimir N. *Behind the front lines of the Civil War: Political parties and social movements in Russia, 1918–1922.* Princeton, NJ: Princeton University Press, 1994.

Brown, Douglas. *Doomsday 1917: The destruction of Russia's ruling class.* London: Sidgwick and Jackson, 1975.

Chamberlin, William Henry. *The Russian revolution, 1917–1921.* New York: Macmillan, 1935.

Daniels, Robert Vincent. *Red October: The Bolshevik Revolution of 1917.* New York: Scribner, 1967.

Daniels, Robert Vincent, ed. *The Russian revolution.* Englewood Cliffs, NJ: Prentice-Hall, 1972.

Elwood, R.C. *Inessa Armand: Revolutionary and feminist.* Cambridge: Cambridge University Press, 1993.

Ferro, Marc. *Nicholas II: Last of the tsars.* New York: Oxford University Press, 1993.

———. *The Russian Revolution of February 1917.* London: Routledge and Kegan Paul, 1972.

Geifman, Anna. *Thou shalt not kill: Revolutionary terrorism in Russia, 1894–1917.* Princeton, NJ: Princeton University Press, 1993.

Germany. Auswartiges Amt; Z.A.B. Zeman, ed. *Germany and the Revolution in Russia, 1915–1918: Documents from the Archives of the German Foreign Ministry.* London: Oxford University Press, 1958.

Kerensky, Aleksandr Fyodorovich. *The Kerensky memoirs: Russia and history's turning point.* London: Cassell, 1966.

———. *The prelude to bolshevism: The Kornilov rebellion.* New York: Haskell House Publishers, 1972.

Lieven, D.C.B. *Nicholas II: Emperor of all the Russias.* London: John Murray, 1993.

McCauley, Martin. *The Russian revolution and the Soviet state, 1917–1921: Document.* London: Macmillan, 1975.

Pereira, N.G.O. *White Siberia: The politics of Civil War.* Montreal: Mc-Gill-Queen's University Press, 1996.

Reed, John. *Ten days that shook the world.* Harmondsworth: Penguin, 1977.

Schapiro, Leonard Bertram. *The origin of the communist autocracy: Political opposition in the Soviet state, first phase, 1917–1922.* Cambridge, MA: Harvard University Press, 1966.

Shukman, Harold. *Lenin and the Russian Revolution.* London: Batsford, 1966.

Solzhenitsyn, Aleksandr Isaevich. *Lenin in Zurich: Chapters.* London: Bodley Head, 1976.

Spence, Richard B. *Boris Savinkov: Renegade on the left.* Boulder, CO; New York: Distributed by Columbia University Press, 1991.

Sukhanov, N.N. (Nikolai Nikolaevich). *The Russian revolution, 1917: A personal record.* Princeton, NJ: Princeton University Press, 1984.

Trotsky, Leon. *The history of the Russian revolution.* Ann Arbor, MI: University of Michigan Press, 1961.

Warth, Robert D. *The allies and the Russian revolution: From the fall of the monarchy to the peace of Brest-Litovsk.* Durham, NC: Duke University Press, 1954.

Weber, Max. *The Russian revolutions.* Ithaca, NY: Cornell University Press, 1995.

Weinberg, Robert. *The revolution of 1905 in Odessa: Blood on the steps.* Bloomington, IN: Indiana University Press, 1993.

XI. History—Soviet Period

Alliluyeva, Svetlana. *Twenty letters to a friend.* New York: Harper and Row, 1967.

Andics, Hellmut. *Rule of terror: Russia under Lenin and Stalin.* New York: Holt, Rinehart and Winston, 1969.

Bazhanov, Boris. *Bazhanov and the damnation of Stalin.* Athens, OH: Ohio University Press, 1990.

Bortoli, Georges. *The death of Stalin.* New York: Praeger, 1975.

Brook-Shepherd, Gordon. *The storm petrels: The flight of the first Soviet defectors.* New York: Harcourt Brace Jovanovich, 1978.

Brower, Daniel R., ed. *The Soviet experience: Success or failure?* Huntingdon, NY: R.E. Krieger, 1976.

Carr, Edward Hallett. *A history of Soviet Russia.* London: Macmillan, 1950–1978.

———. *1917: Before and after.* London: Macmillan, 1969.

Cohen, Stephen F. *Bukharin and the Bolshevik revolution: A political biography, 1888–1938.* New York: Alfred A. Knopf, 1973.

———. *Rethinking the Soviet experience.* New York: Oxford University Press, 1985.

———. *Voices of glasnost: Interviews with Gorbachev's reformers.* New York: Norton, 1989.

Conquest, Robert. *The great terror.* New York: Macmillan, 1968.

———. *The great terror: A reassessment.* New York: Oxford University Press, 1990.

———. *Stalin: Breaker of nations.* New York: Penguin, 1991.

Dallin, David J. *Soviet foreign policy after Stalin.* Philadelphia, PA: L.B. Lippincott, 1961.

Daniels, Robert Vincent. *The Stalin revolution: Foundations of Soviet totalitarianism.* Lexington, MA: Heath, 1972.

Davies, R.W. (Robert William). *Soviet history in the Gorbachev revolution.* Bloomington, IN: Indiana University Press, 1989.

Deutscher, Isaac. *The prophet unarmed: Trotsky, 1921–1929.* New York: Oxford University Press, 1959.

———. *The prophet outcast: Trotsky, 1929–1940.* Oxford: Oxford University Press, 1980.

———. *Stalin: A political biography.* New York: Oxford University Press, 1967.

Deutscher, Joseph. *Russia after Stalin.* London: J. Cape, 1969.

Dmytryshyn, Basil. *USSR: A concise history.* New York: Charles Scribner's Sons, 1978.

Dukes, Paul. *The emergence of the super-powers: A short comparative history of the USA and the USSR.* London: Macmillan, 1970.

Dziewanowski, M.K. *A history of Soviet Russia.* Englewood Cliffs, NJ: Prentice-Hall, 1979.

Fischer, Louis. *The life and death of Stalin.* New York: Harper, 1952.

Fitzpatrick, Sheila. *The cultural front: Power and culture in Revolutionary Russia.* Ithaca, NY: Cornell University Press, 1992.

Florinsky, Michael T. *Towards an understanding of the USSR: A study in government, politics, and economic planning.* New York: Macmillan, 1951.

Geller, Mikhail. *Utopia in power: The history of the Soviet Union from 1917 to the present.* New York: Summit Books, 1986.

Gusev, K.V. *The USSR: A short history.* Moscow: Progress Publishers, 1976.

History of the USSR: The era of socialism. Moscow: Progress Publishers, 1982.

Hosking, Geoffrey A. *The first socialist society: A history of the Soviet Union from within.* Cambridge, MA: Harvard University Press, 1985.

Iaroslavskii, Emelian. *Bolshevik verification and purging of the party ranks.* Moscow: Cooperative Publishing Society of Foreign Workers in the USSR, 1933.

———. *Landmarks in the life of Stalin.* London: Lawrence and Wishart, 1942.

Kohler, Foy D. *Understanding the Russians: A citizen's primer.* New York: Harper and Row, 1970.

Krylova, Zinaida. *Fostering ideological staunchness: What is Marxism-Leninism? Communist convictions: Education and culture.* Moscow: Novosti Press Agency, 1978.

Lampert, Nick, and Gabor T. Ritterporn, eds. *Stalinism: Its nature and aftermath.* New York: M.E. Sharpe, 1992.

Laqueur, Walter. *The dream that failed: Reflection on the Soviet Union.* New York: Oxford University Press, 1994.

Lieberman, Sandor. *The Soviet empire reconsidered: Essays in honor of Adam B. Ulam.* Boulder, CO: Westview Press, 1994.

London, Kurt. *The Soviet Union in world politics.* Boulder, CO: Westview Press, 1980.

McCauley, Martin. *The Soviet Union since 1917.* London: Longman, 1981.

McClellan, Woodford. *Russia, a history of the Soviet period.* Englewood Cliffs, NJ: Prentice-Hall, 1986.

MacKenzie, David. *A history of the Soviet Union.* Chicago, IL: Dorsey Press, 1986.

McNeal, Robert Hatch. *Stalin: Man and ruler.* Houndmills, Basingstoke, Hampshire: Macmillan, 1988.

Medvedev, Roy Aleksandrovich. *All Stalin's men.* Garden City, NY: Anchor Press, 1984.

Nove, Alec. *The Stalin phenomenon.* New York: St. Martin's Press, 1992.

Pankratova, Anna Mikhailovna. *A history of the USSR.* Moscow: Foreign Languages Publishing House, 1947.

Pethybridge, Roger William. *A history of postwar Russia.* New York: New American Library, 1966.

Pomper, Philip. *Lenin, Trotsky, and Stalin: The intelligentsia and power.* New York: Columbia University Press, 1990.

Ulam, Adam. *A history of Soviet Russia.* New York: Praeger, 1976.

————. *Stalin: The man and his era.* New York: Viking Press, 1973.

Van Laue, Theodore H. (Theodore Hermann). *Why Lenin? Why Stalin? Why Gorbachev?: The rise and fall of the system.* New York: HarperCollins College, 1993.

Volkogonov, D.A. (Dimitrii Antonovich). *Lenin: A new biography.* New York: Free Press, 1994.

————. *Stalin: Triumph and tragedy.* London: Weidenfeld and Nicholson, 1991.

Westwood, J.N. *Russia since 1917.* New York: St. Martin's Press, 1980.

Whitefield, Stephen. *Industrial power and the Soviet state.* New York: Oxford University Press, 1993.

XII. History—Post-Soviet

Adam, Walter, and James W. Brock. *Adam Smith goes to Moscow: A dialogue on radical reform.* Princeton, NJ: Princeton University Press, 1993.

Balzer, Harley D. *Five years that shook the world: Gorbachev's unfinished revolution.* Boulder, CO: Westview Press, 1991.

Belkin, Aron. *Epokha Zhirinovskogo.* Moscow: Print-Atele-Diamant, 1994.

Beschloss, Michael R., and Strobe Talbot. *At the highest levels: The inside story of the end of the Cold War.* Boston: Little, Brown, 1993.

Billington, James H. *Russia transformed: Breakthrough to hope.* New York: Free Press, 1995.

Blum, Douglas W., ed. *Russia's future: Consolidation or disintegration?* Boulder, CO: Westview Press, 1994.

Bremmer, Ian, and Ray Taras, eds. *Nation and politics in the Soviet successor states.* Cambridge; New York: Cambridge University Press, 1993.

Brown, Archie. *The Gorbachev factor.* Oxford: Oxford University Press, 1995.

Clendenin, Daniel B. *From the coup to commonwealth: An inside look at life in contemporary Russia.* Grand Rapids, MI: Baker Book House, 1993.

Colton, Timothy J., and Robert Legvold, eds. *After the Soviet Union: From empire to nations.* New York: W.W. Norton and Co., 1992.

Daniels, Robert V. *The end of the communist revolution.* New York: Routledge, 1993.

Dawisha, Karen, and Bruce Parrott. *Russia and the new states of Eurasia: The politics of upheaval.* New York: Cambridge University Press, 1994.

Dmitrievskii, Iurii Dmitrievich. *Territorialnye problemy sovremennoi Rossii.* St. Petersburg: S-Peterburgskii universitet ekonomiki i finansov, 1995.

Dunlop, John B. *The rise of Russia and the fall of the Soviet Empire.* Princeton, NJ: Princeton University Press, 1993.

Ellman, Michael, and Vladimir Kontorovich, eds. *The disintegration of the Soviet economic system.* New York: Routledge, 1992.

Fish, Steven M. *Democracy from scratch: Opposition and regime in the new Russian revolution.* Princeton, NJ: Princeton University Press, 1994.

Frazer, Graham. *Absolute Zhirinovsky: A transparent view of the distinguished Russian statesman.* New York: Viking, 1994.

Galeotti, Mark. *The age of anxiety: Security and politics in Soviet and post-Soviet Russia.* London: Longman, 1994.

Gillies, John. *The new Russia.* Morristown, NJ: Silver Burdett Press, 1994.

Gleason, Gregory. *Common sovereignty: The politics of change in the Central Asian republics.* Boulder, CO: Westview Press, 1995.

Lambroza, Shlomo. *World leaders: Boris Yeltsin.* Vero Beach, FL: Rourke Publications, 1993.

Lowenhardt, John. *The reincarnation of Russia: Struggling with the legacy of communism, 1990–1994.* Durham, NC: Duke University Press, 1995.

Menges, Constantine C., ed. *Transitions from communism in Russia and Eastern Europe: Analysis and perspectives.* Lanham, MD: University Press of America, 1993.

Parland, Thomas. *The rejection in Russia of totalitarian socialism and liberal democracy: A study of the New Right.* Helsinki: Finnish Society of Sciences and Letters, 1993.

Rowen, Henry S., ed. *Defense conversion, economic reform and the outlook for Russian and Ukrainian economics.* New York: St. Martin's Press, 1994.

Saikal, Amin, ed. *Russia in search of its future.* Cambridge: Cambridge University Press, 1995.

Sakwa, Richard. *Russian politics and society.* New York: Routledge, 1993.

Smart, Christopher. *The imagery of Soviet foreign policy and the collapse of the Russian Empire.* Westport, CT: Greenwood Press, 1995.

Solovyov, Vladimir. *Zhirinovsky: Russian fascism and the making of a dictator.* Redding, MA: Addison-Wesley, 1995.

Steele, Jonathan. *Eternal Russia: Yeltsin, Gorbachev, and the mirage of democracy.* Cambridge, MA: Harvard University Press, 1994.

Volkov, A.G. (Andrei Gavrilovich). *Demograficheskie perspektivy Rossii.* Moscow: Goskomstat Rossii, 1993.

White, Stephen, Alex Pravda, and Zvi Gitelman, eds. *Developments in Soviet and post-Soviet politics.* Durham, NC: Duke University Press, 1992.

XIII. Politics and Government

Allworth, Edward. *Central Asia: A century of Russian rule.* New York: Columbia University Press, 1967.

Avrekh, Aron Iakovlevich. *Stolypin i tretia duma.* Moscow: Nauka, 1968.

Bialer, Seweryn, ed. *Politics, society, and nationality inside Gorbachev's Russia.* Boulder, CO: Westview Press, 1989.

———. *Stalin's successors: Leadership, stability, and change in the Soviet Union.* Cambridge: Cambridge University Press, 1980.

Block, Russell, ed. *Lenin's fight against Stalinism.* New York: Pathfinder, 1975.

Brumberg, Abraham, ed. *Chronicle of a revolution: A western-Soviet inquiry into perestroika.* New York: Pantheon Books, 1990.

Chernukha, V.G. (Valentina Girgorevna). *Vnutrenniaiu politika tsarizma s serediny 50-kh do nachala 80-kh gg xix v.* Leningrad: Nauka, 1987.

Cocks, Paul, et al., eds. *The dynamics of Soviet politics.* Cambridge, MA: Harvard University Press, 1976.

Daniels, Robert Vincent. *The conscience of the nation: Communist opposition in Soviet Russia.* Cambridge, MA: Harvard University Press, 1960.

———. *A documentary history of communism in Russia: From Lenin to Gorbachev.* Hanover, NH: University Press of New England, 1993.

Deutscher, Isaac. *Russia: What next?* New York: Oxford University Press, 1953.

Dumova, N.G. (Natalia Georgievna). *Kadetskaia partiia v period I Mirovoi voiny i Fevralskoi revoliutsii.* Moscow: Nauka, 1988.

Fainsod, Merle. *How Russia is ruled.* Cambridge, MA: Harvard University Press, 1967.

Fischer, George, ed. *Russian emigre politics*. New York: Free Russia Fund, 1951.

———. *Soviet opposition to Stalin: A case study in World War II*. Cambridge, MA: Harvard University Press, 1952.

Fry, Michael G., ed. *History, the White House and the Kremlin*. London: Pinter Publishers, 1991.

Getty, J. Arch (John Arch). *Origin of the great purges: The Soviet Communist Party reconsidered, 1933–1938*. Cambridge: Cambridge University Press, 1985.

Getty, J. Arch (John Arch), and Roberta T. Manning, eds. *Stalinist terror: New perspectives*. Cambridge: Cambridge University Press, 1993.

Goldgeier, James M. *Leadership style and Soviet foreign policy: Stalin, Khrushchev, Brezhnev, Gorbachev*. Baltimore, MD: Johns Hopkins University Press, 1994.

Green, Barbara B. *The dynamics of Russian politics: A short history*. Westport, CT: Greenwood, 1994.

Hunt, R.N. Carew (Robert Nigel Carew). *The theory and practice of communism: An introduction*. New York: Macmillan, 1957.

Larina, Anna. *This I cannot forget: The memoirs of Nikolai Bukharin's widow*. New York: W.W. Norton, 1993.

Lebow, Richard Ned, and Janice Gross Stein. *We all lost the Cold War*. Princeton, NJ: Princeton University Press, 1994.

Lewin, Moshe. *Lenin's last struggle*. London: Faber, 1969.

Ligachev, Yegor. *Inside Gorbachev's Kremlin: The memoirs of Yegor Ligachev*. New York: Pantheon, 1993.

Marcuse, Herbert. *Soviet Marxism: A critical analysis*. New York: Vintage, 1961.

Merridale, Catherine. *Moscow politics and the rise of Stalin: The Communist Party in the capital, 1925–1932*. New York: St. Martin's Press, 1990.

Meyer, Alfred G. *Leninism*. New York: Praeger, 1967.

———. *The Soviet political system: An interpretation*. New York: Random House, 1965.

Millar, James R. *Cracks in the monolith: Party power in the Brezhnev era*. Armonk, NY: M.E. Sharpe, 1992.

Mosley, Philip E., ed. *The Soviet Union, 1922–1962: A foreign affairs reader*. New York: Praeger, 1963.

Penkovsky, Oleg. *The Penkovskiy papers*. New York: Doubleday, 1965.

Pethybridge, Roger William. *The social prelude to Stalinism*. London: Macmillan, 1974.

Raeff, Marc, ed. *Plans for political reform in Imperial Russia, 1730–1905*. Englewood Cliffs, NJ: Prentice-Hall, 1966.

————. *Political ideas and institutions in Imperial Russia.* Boulder, CO: Westview Press, 1994.

Ragsdale, Hugh, ed. *Imperial Russian foreign policy.* New York: University of Cambridge Press, 1993.

Rambaud, Alfred Nicolas. *The expansion of Russia: Problems of the East and problems of the Far East.* Boston, MA: Longwood Press, 1979.

Rigby, Thomas Henry. *Authority, power and policy in the USSR: Essays dedicated to Leonard Schapiro.* London: Macmillan, 1980.

Sakharov, Andrei. *Alarm and hope.* New York: Alfred A. Knopf, 1978.

Schapiro, Leonard Bertram. *The Communist Party of the Soviet Union.* London: Methuen, 1970.

————. *The government and politics of the Soviet Union.* London: Hutchinson, 1967.

————. *Totalitarianism.* New York: Praeger, 1972.

Shevchenko, Arkady N. *Breaking with Moscow.* New York: Alfred A. Knopf, 1985.

Trotsky, Leon. *The basic writings of Trotsky.* New York: Schocken Books, 1976.

Tucker, Robert C. *Political culture and leadership in Soviet Russia: From Lenin to Gorbachev.* New York: Norton, 1987.

————. *Stalin as revolutionary, 1879–1929: A study in history and personality.* New York: Norton, 1973.

————. *Stalin in power: Revolution from above, 1928–1941.* New York: Norton, 1990.

Ulam, Adam. *The Bolsheviks: The intellectual and political history of the triumph of communism in Russia.* New York: Collier Books, 1971.

————. *The communists: The story of power and lost illusions, 1948–1991.* New York: Scribner's, 1992.

————. *Expansion and coexistence: Soviet foreign policy, 1917–73.* New York: Praeger, 1974.

————. *The new face of Soviet totalitarianism.* Cambridge, MA: Harvard University Press, 1963.

Urban, G.R. (George R.). *End of empire: The demise of the Soviet Union.* Washington, DC: American University Press, 1993.

Urban, G.R. (George R.), ed. *Stalinism: Its impact on Russia and the world.* London: Temple Smith, 1982.

Valentina, Jiri. *Soviet intervention in Czechoslovakia 1968: Anatomy of a decision.* Baltimore, MD: Johns Hopkins University Press, 1991.

Van Oudewaren, John. *Detente in Europe: The Soviet Union and the West since 1953.* Durham, NC: Duke University Press, 1991.

Yearbook on international communist affairs. Stanford, CA: Hoover Institution Press, 1966.

XIV. Economics

Antropov, N. *Istoriia profdvizhenii v SSSR*. Moscow: Profizdat, 1961.

Aslund, Anders, ed. *Russian economic reform at risk*. London: Pinter, 1995.

Azhaeva, V.S. *Melkoe predprinimatelstvo v Rossii konets xix-nachalo xx v.* Moscow: Institut nauchnoi informatsii po obshchestvennym naukam, 1994.

Bergson, Abram. *The economics of Soviet planning*. New Haven, CT: Yale University Press, 1964.

Bergson, Abram, and Herbert Samuel Levine, eds. *The Soviet economy: Toward the year 2000*. London: G. Allen and Unwin, 1983.

Campbell, Robert W., ed. *The postcommunist economic transformation: Essays in honor of Gregory Grossman*. Boulder, CO: Westview Press, 1994.

Commander, Simon. *Wage and employment decisions in the Russian economy: An analysis of developments in 1992*. Washington, DC: World Bank, 1993.

Davies, R.W. (Robert William), ed. *The economic transformation of the Soviet Union, 1913–1945*. Cambridge: Cambridge University Press, 1994.

———. *From tsarism to the new economic policy: Continuity and change in the economy of the USSR*. Ithaca, NY: Cornell University Press, 1991.

———. *The Soviet collective farm, 1929–1930*. Cambridge, MA: Harvard University Press, 1980.

Dewar, Margaret E. (Margaret Elizabeth). *Labour policy in the USSR, 1917–1928*. New York: Octagon Books, 1979.

Filtzer, Donald. *Soviet workers and the collapse of perestroika: The Soviet labour process and Gorbachev's reforms, 1985–1991*. New York: Cambridge University Press, 1994.

Dubrovskii, S.M. (Sergei Mitrofanovich). *Stolypinskaia zemelnaia reforma: Iz istorii selskogo khoziaistva i krestianstva v Rossii v nachale xx v.* Moscow: Akademiia nauk, 1963.

Gregory, Paul R. *Restructuring the Soviet economic bureaucracy*. Cambridge: Cambridge University Press, 1990.

———. *Russian national income, 1885–1913*. Cambridge: Cambridge University Press, 1982.

———. *Soviet economic structure and performance*. New York: Harper and Row, 1990.

Holzman, Franklyn D. *International trade under communism: Politics and economics*. New York: Basic Books, 1976.

Hunter, Holland. *Faulty foundations: Soviet economic policies, 1928–1940*. Princeton, NJ: Princeton University Press, 1992.

Jasny, Naum. *Socialized agriculture of the USSR: Plans and performance.* Stanford, CA: Stanford University Press, 1967.

———. *Soviet industrialization, 1928–1952.* Chicago: University of Chicago Press, 1961.

Karcz, Jerzy F. *The economics of communist agriculture: Selected papers.* Bloomington, IN: International Development Institute, 1979.

Lyashchenko, P. *The history of the national economy of Russia to the 1917 revolution.* New York: Macmillan, 1949.

Millar, James R. *The Soviet economic experiment.* Urbana, IL: University of Illinois Press, 1990.

Nove, Alec. *An economic history of the USSR.* Harmondsworth: Penguin, 1976.

———. *The Soviet economic system.* Boston, MA: Unwin Hyman, 1986.

Nutter, G. Warren. *Growth of industrial production in the Soviet Union.* Princeton, NJ: Princeton University Press, 1962.

Schwartz, Harry. *Russia's Soviet economy.* New York: Prentice-Hall, 1954.

———. *The Soviet economy since Stalin.* Philadelphia, PA: Lippincott, 1965.

Spulber, Nicolas. *Restructuring the Soviet economy: In search of the market.* Ann Arbor, MI: University of Michigan Press, 1991.

———. *The Soviet economy: Structure, principles, problems.* New York: W.W. Norton, 1969.

Volin, Lazar. *A century of Russian agriculture: From Alexander II to Khrushchev.* Cambridge, MA: Harvard University Press, 1970.

Von Laue, Theodore H. (Theodore Hermann). *Sergei Witte and the industrialization of Russia.* New York: Cambridge University Press, 1963.

Zauberman, Alfred. *The mathematical revolution in Soviet economics.* New York: Oxford University Press, 1975.

XV. Society

Alston, Patrick. *Education and the state in tsarist Russia.* Stanford, CA: Stanford University Press, 1969.

Anderle, Vladimir. *A social history of twentieth-century Russia.* London: Edward Arnold, 1994.

Andrew, Christopher M., and Oleg Gordievsky. *KGB: The inside story of its foreign operations from Lenin to Gorbachev.* New York: Harper-Collins, 1990.

Atkinson, Dorothy, Alexander Dallin, and Gail Warshofsky Lapidus. *Women in Russia.* Stanford, CA: Stanford University Press, 1977.

Baring, Maurice. *The Russian people.* London: Methuen, 1914.

Baron, Salo Wittmayer. *The Russian Jew under tsars and Soviets.* New York: Macmillan, 1976.

Bernstein, Laurie A. *Sonia's daughters: Prostitutes and their regulation in Imperial Russia.* Berkeley, CA: University of California Press, 1995.

Berry, Ellen E., ed. *Re-entering the sign: Articulating new Russian culture.* Ann Arbor, MI: University of Michigan Press, 1995.

Bloch, Sidney, and Peter Reddaway. *Psychiatric terror: How Soviet psychiatry is used to suppress dissent.* New York: Basic Books, 1977.

Bociurkiw, Bohdan R., and John W. Strong, eds. *Religion and atheism in the USSR and Eastern Europe.* London: Macmillan, 1975.

Boym, Svetlana. *Common places: Mythologies of everyday life in Russia.* Cambridge, MA: Harvard University Press, 1995.

Brook-Shepherd, Gordon. *The storm birds: Soviet post-war defectors.* New York: Weidenfeld and Nicolson, 1989.

Buckley, Mary. *Redefining Russian society and polity.* Boulder, CO: Westview Press, 1993.

Cullen, Robert. *The killer department: The eight-year hunt for the most savage serial killer of modern times.* New York: Pantheon Books, 1993.

Dunstan, John, ed. *Soviet education under perestroika.* New York: Routledge, 1992.

Eklof, Ben. *Democracy in the Russian school: The reform movement in education since 1984.* Boulder, CO: Westview Press, 1993.

Eklof, Ben, ed. *School and society in Tsarist and Soviet Russia.* New York: St. Martin's Press, 1993.

Ellis, Jane. *The Russian Orthodox Church: A contemporary history.* Bloomington, IN: Indiana University Press, 1986.

Elnett, Elaine Pasvolsky. *Historic origin and social development of family life in Russia.* New York: Columbia University Press, 1926.

Fishman, David E. *Russia's first modern Jews: The Jews of Shklov.* New York: New York University Press, 1995.

Fletcher, George R. *The compleat handbook and glossary of Soviet education.* New York: Globe Language Services, 1992.

Forsyth, James. *A history of the peoples of Siberia: Russia's North Asian colony, 1581–1990.* Cambridge: Cambridge University Press, 1992.

Gershunsky, Boris S. *Russia in darkness . . . on education and the future.* San Francisco, CA: Caddo Gap Press, 1993.

Goldman, Wendy Z. *Women, the state and revolution: Soviet family policy and social life, 1917–1936.* Cambridge: Cambridge University Press, 1993.

Holmes, Brian. *Russian education: Tradition and transition.* New York: Garland Publishing, 1995.

Holmes, Larry E. *The Kremlin and the schoolhouse: Reforming education in Soviet Russia, 1917–1931.* Bloomington, IN: Indiana University Press, 1991.

Hyde, Gordon. *The Soviet health service: A historical and comparative study.* London: Lawrence and Wishart, 1974.

International Slavic Conference (1st, Banff, Alta., 1974). *Marxism and religion in Eastern Europe: Papers presented at the Banff International Slavic Conference, September 4–7, 1974.* Dordrecht; Boston: D. Reidel, c1975.

Ispa, Jean. *Child care in Russia: In transition.* Westport, CT: Bergin and Garvey, 1994.

Jakobson, Michael. *Origins of the GULAG: The Soviet prison camp system, 1917–1934.* Lexington, KY: University Press of Kentucky, 1993.

Jancar-Webster, Barbara. *Women under communism.* Baltimore: Johns Hopkins University Press, c1978.

Jones, Anthony, ed. *Education and society in the new Russia.* Armonk, NY: M.E. Sharpe, 1994.

Kaser, Michael Charles. *Health care in the Soviet Union and Eastern Europe.* London: Croom Helm, 1976.

Khardovsky, Michael. *Where two worlds met: The Russian state and the Kalmyk nomads, 1600–1771.* Ithaca, NY: Cornell University Press, 1992.

Kon, Igor, ed. *Sex and Russian society.* Bloomington, IN: Indiana University Press, 1993.

———. *Sexual behavior in Russia: Sexual politics from the age of the czars to today.* New York: Macmillan, 1994.

Kotlyarskaya, Elena. *Women in society: Russia.* New York: Marshall Cavendish, 1994.

Krasnov, Vladislav. *Soviet defectors: The KGB wanted list.* Stanford, CA: Hoover Institution Press, 1985.

Kuzichkin, Vladimir. *Inside the KGB: My life in Soviet espionage.* New York: Ivy Books, 1992.

Levchenko, Stan. *On the wrong side: My life in the KGB.* Washington, DC: Pergamon-Brassey's International Defense Publishers, 1988.

Lewin, Moshe. *The making of the Soviet system: Essays in the social history of interwar Russia.* New York: New Press, 1985.

———. *Russian peasants and Soviet power: A study of collectivization.* London: Allen and Unwin, 1968.

Lewis, Robert A. *Nationality and population change in Russia and the USSR: An evaluation of census data, 1897–1970.* New York: Praeger, 1976.

Mamonova, Tatyana, ed. *Women's glasnost vs. naglost: Stopping Russian backlash.* Westport, CT: Bergin and Garvey, 1993.

Matthews, Mervyn. *The passport society: Controlling movement in Russia and the USSR.* Boulder, CO: Westview Press, 1993.

Mazurkiewicz, Ludwik. *Human geography in Eastern Europe and the Soviet Union.* London; New York: Belhaven Press; Halsted Press, c1992.

Millar, James R., ed. *Politics, work, and daily life in the USSR: A survey of former Soviet citizens.* Cambridge: Cambridge University Press, 1988.

Millar, James R., and Sharon L. Wolchik, eds. *The social legacy of communism.* Washington, DC: Woodrow Wilson Center Press, 1994.

Muckle, James Y. *A guide to the Soviet curriculum: What the Russian child is taught at school.* New York: Routledge, 1988.

———. *Portrait of a Soviet school under glasnost.* New York: St. Martin's Press, 1990.

Murphy, Daniel. *Tolstoy and education.* Blackrock, Co. Dublin: Irish Academic Press, 1992.

Pilkington, Hilary. *Russia's youth and its culture: A nation's constructors and constructed.* New York: Routledge, 1994.

Popov, Nikolai P. *The Russian people speak: Democracy at the crossroads.* Syracuse, NY: Syracuse University Press, 1994.

Popovych, Erika. *The Soviet educational system.* Washington, DC: American Association of Collegiate Registrars and Admissions Officers, 1991.

Posadskaya, Anastasia, ed. *Women in Russia: A new era in Russian feminism.* New York: Verso, 1994.

Prosser, David John. *Out of Afghanistan.* Montreal, Que.: Eden Press, 1987.

Rancour-Laferriere, Daniel. *The slave soul of Russia: Moral masochism and the cult of suffering.* New York: New York University Press, 1995.

Ruane, Christine. *Gender, class, and the professionalization of Russian city teachers, 1860–1914.* Pittsburgh, PA: University of Pittsburgh Press, 1994.

Santa Maria, Phillip. *The question of elementary education in the Third Russian State Duma, 1907–1912.* Lewiston, NY: Edwin Mellen Press, 1990.

Seigelbaum, Lewis H., and Ronald Grigor Suny, eds. *Making workers Soviet: Power, class, and identity.* Ithaca, NY: Cornell University Press, 1994.

Selivanova, Nina Nikolaevna. *Russia's women.* Westport, CT: Hyperion, 1975.

Seregny, Scott J. *Russian teachers and peasant revolution: The politics of education in 1905.* Bloomington, IN: Indiana University Press, 1989.

Shlapentokh, Vladimir, Munir Sendich, and Emil Payin, eds. *The new Russian diaspora: Russian minorities in the former Soviet Republics.* Armonk, NY: M.E. Sharpe, 1994.

Shturman, Dora. *The Soviet secondary school.* New York: Routledge, 1989.

Simmonds, George W., ed. *Nationalism in the USSR and Europe in the era of Brezhnev and Kosygin.* Detroit, MI: University of Detroit Press, 1977.

Sinel, Allen *The classroom and the chancellery: State educational reform in Russia under Count Dmitry Tolstoi.* Cambridge, MA: Harvard University Press, 1990.

Slezkine, Yuri. *Arctic mirrors: Russia and the small peoples of the North.* Ithaca, NY: Cornell University Press, 1994.

Smith, Hedrick. *The new Russians.* New York: Random House, 1990.

Steinberg, Mark D. *Moral communities: The culture of class relations in the Russian printing industry, 1867–1907.* Berkeley, CA: University of California Press, 1992.

Tian-Shanskaia, Olga Semenovna. *Village life in late Tsarist Russia.* Bloomington, IN: Indiana University Press, 1993.

Tomikel, John. *Russia and her neighbours.* Elgin, PA: Allegheny Press, 1994.

Weekes, Richard V. *Muslim peoples: A world ethnographic survey.* Westport, CT: Greenwood Press, 1984.

Wirtschafter, Elise Kimerling. *Structures of society: Imperial Russia's "people of various ranks."* DeKalb, IL: Northern Illinois University Press, 1994.

XVI. Law

Allen, Robert Vincent. *The great legislative commission of Catherine II of 1767.* Ann Arbor, MI: University Microfilms, 1984.

Barry, Donald D., et al., eds. *Contemporary Soviet law: Essays in honor of John N. Hazard.* The Hague: Martinus Nijhoff, 1974.

———. *Soviet law after Stalin.* Leiden: A.W. Sijthoff, 1977.

Bassiuni, M. Cherif, and Valerii Mikhailovich Savitskii. *The criminal justice system of the USSR.* Springfield, IL: Thomas, 1979.

Berman, Harold Joseph. *Justice in Russia: An interpretation of Soviet law.* Cambridge, MA: Harvard University Press, 1963.

Bothe, Michael. *Amazonia and Siberia: Legal aspects of the preserva-*

tion of the environment and development in the last open spaces. London: Graham and Trotman.

Broadus, James M., ed. *The oceans and environmental security: Shared US and Russian perspectives.* Washington, DC: Island Press, 1994.

Butler, William E. *Russian law: Historical and political perspectives.* Leiden: A.W. Sijthoff, 1977.

———. *Soviet law.* London: Butterworths, 1983.

———. *The Soviet legal system: Selected contemporary legislation and documents.* Dobbs Ferry, NY: Oceana Publications, 1978.

Cameron, George Dana. *The Soviet lawyer and his system: A historical and bibliographical study.* Ann Arbor, MI: Division of Research, Graduate School of Business Administration, University of Michigan, 1978.

Daiches, Lionel. *Russians at law.* London: M. Joseph, 1960.

Feldbrugge, F.J.M. (Ferdinand Joseph Maria). *The constitutions of the USSR and the union republics: Analysis, texts, reports.* Alphen aan den Rijn, Netherlands: Sijthoff and Noordhoff, 1979.

———. *Russian law: The end of the Soviet system and the role of law.* Dordrecht: M. Nijhoff, 1993.

———. *Soviet criminal law: General part.* Leiden: Sijthoff, 1964.

Gawenda, Jerzy August Boleslaw. *The Soviet domination of Eastern Europe in the light of international law.* Richmond, Surrey: Foreign Affairs Publishing Co., 1974.

Grzybowski, Kazimierz. *Soviet private international law.* Leiden: A.W. Sijthoff, 1965.

———. *Soviet public international law: Doctrines and diplomatic practice.* Leiden: A.W. Sijthoff, 1970.

Gsovski, Vladimir. *Soviet civil law: Private rights and their background under the Soviet regime. Comparative survey and translation of the civil code, code of domestic relations, judiciary act, code of civil procedure, laws on nationality, corporations, patents, copyright, collective farms, labor, and other related laws.* Ann Arbor, MI: University of Michigan Law School, 1948–49.

Guins, George Constantine. *Soviet law and Soviet society: Ethical foundations of the Soviet structure, mechanism of the planned economy, duties and rights of peasants and workers, rulers and toilers, the family and the state, Soviet justice, national minorities and their autonomy, the people's democracies and the Soviet pattern for a united world.* Westport, CT: Hyperion Press, 1981.

Gureev, Petr Prokhorovich, and Petr Ivanovich Sedugin, eds. *Legislation in the USSR.* Moscow: Progress, 1977.

Hazard, John N. (John Newbold). *Law and social change in the USSR.* London: Stevens, 1953.

————. *The Soviet legal system: Fundamental principles and historical commentary.* Dobbs Ferry, NY: Oceana Publications, 1977.

International Commission of Jurists. *Justice enslaved: A collection of documents on the abuse of justice for political ends.* The Hague: International Commission of Jurists, 1955.

Kaiser, Daniel H. *The growth of the law in medieval Russia.* Princeton, NJ: Princeton University Press, 1980.

Lapenna, Ivo. *Soviet penal policy: A background book.* Westport, CT: Greenwood Press, 1980.

Leites, Nathan Constantin. *Ritual of liquidation: The case of the Moscow trials.* Glencoe, IL: Free Press, 1954.

McWhinney, Edward. *"Peaceful coexistence" and Soviet-Western international law.* Leiden: A.W. Sijthoff, 1964.

Makepeace, R.W. *Marxist ideology and Soviet criminal law.* London: Croom Helm, 1980.

Novikov, Rem Aleksandrovich. *Ekologicheskoe regulirovanie: Mirazhy i realnost.* Apatity, Murmanskaia oblast: Kolskii nauchnyi tsentr im. S. M. Kirova, RAN, 1994.

Oude Elferink, Alex G. *The law of maritime boundary delimitation: A case study of the Russian Federation.* Dordrecht: M. Nijhoff, 1994.

Petrova, Lidiia Ivanovna. *Equality of women in the USSR.* Moscow: Foreign Languages Publishing House, 1957.

Putevoditel po grazhdanskomu kodeksu Rossii. Moscow: Infra-M, 1995.

Quigley, John B. *The Soviet foreign trade monopoly: Institutions and laws.* Columbus, OH: Ohio State University Press, 1974.

Russia (Federation); William Elliott Butler, ed. *Basic legal documents of the Russian Federation.* New York: Oceana Publications, 1992.

Sawicki, Stanislaw J. *Soviet land and housing law: A historical and comparative study.* New York: Praeger, 1977.

Sharlet, Robert. *Soviet constitutional crisis from de-Stalinisation to disintegration.* Armonk, NY: M.E. Sharpe, 1992.

Smith, Bruce L.R., and Gennady M. Danilenko. *Law and democracy in the new Russia.* Washington, DC: Brookings Institution, 1993.

Soviet Union; William B. Simons, ed. *The Soviet codes of law.* Alphen aan den Rijn, Netherlands: Sijthoff and Noordhoff, 1980.

Soviet Union. Laws, statutes, etc. *Fundamental labour legislation of the USSR and the Union Republics.* Moscow: Novosti, 1975.

————. *Fundamentals of legislation of the USSR and the Union Republics on the health service.* Moscow: Novosti, 1975.

———— ; William E. Butler, ed. *The merchant shipping code of the USSR (1968).* Baltimore, MD: Johns Hopkins University Press, 1970.

Szeftel, Marc. *The Russian Constitution of April 23, 1906: Political institutions of the Duma monarchy.* Bruxelles: Editions de la Librairie encyclopedique, 1976.

Wagner, William G. *Marriage, property, and law in late Imperial Russia.* Oxford: Clarendon Press, 1994.

Zakon sudnyj ljudem = Court law for the people. Ann Arbor, MI: Dept. of Slavic Languages and Literatures, University of Michigan, 1977.

Zile, Zigurds L., ed. *Ideas and forces in Soviet legal history: A reader on the Soviet state and law.* New York: Oxford University Press, 1992.

XVII. Military

Bogdanov, Konstantin Aleksandrovich. *Admiral Kolchak: Biograficheskaia povest-khronika.* St. Petersburg: Sudostroenie, 1993.

Boston Study Group. *Winding down: The price of defense.* San Francisco, CA: W.H. Freeman, 1982.

Central Intelligence Agency, Directorate of Intelligence. *Directory of USSR Ministry of Defense and Armed Forces officials: A reference aid.* Washington, DC: The Agency; Library of Congress, 1982.

Deriabin, Peter. *Watchdogs of terror.* New Rochelle, NY: Arlington House, 1972.

Dinerstein, H.S. *War and the Soviet Union.* New York: Praeger, 1962.

Erickson, John. *The Soviet high command.* London: St. Martin's Press, 1962.

Frunze, M.V. *Selected works.* Moscow: Voenizdat, 1965.

Garthoff, Raymond L. *Soviet military policy.* New York: Praeger, 1966.

Grigorenko, P.T. *The Grigorenko papers.* Boulder, CO: Westview Press, 1976.

Heinamaa, Anna, Maija Leppanen, and Yuri Yurchenko, eds. *The soldiers' story: Soviet veterans remember the Afghan war.* Berkeley, CA: IAS Publications, 1994.

Joint Economic Committee of the Congress of the United States. *Economic performance and the military burden of the Soviet Union.* Washington, DC: U.S. GPO, 1970.

Khrushchev, N.S. *On peaceful coexistence.* Moscow: Foreign Languages Publishing House, 1961.

Kintner, W.R., and Harriet Fast Scott. *The nuclear revolution in Soviet military affairs.* Norman, OK: University of Oklahoma Press, 1968.

Knox, Alfred W. *With the Russian army, 1914–1917.* New York: Gordon Press, 1977

Meyer, Stephen M. *Soviet theatre nuclear forces.* London: International Institute for Strategic Studies, 1984.

Newhouse, John. *Cold dawn: The story of SALT.* New York: Holt, Rinehart and Winston, 1973.

Noggle, Anne. *A dance with death: Soviet airwomen in World War II.* College Station, TX: Texas A and M University Press, 1994.

Ofer, Gur. *The relative efficiency of military research and development in the Soviet Union: A systems approach.* Santa Monica, CA: Rand, 1980.

Okhliabinin, S.D. *Chest mundira: Russkaia armiia ot Petra I do Nikolaia II.* Moscow: Respublika, 1994.

Rosefielde, Steven. *False science: Underestimating the Soviet arms buildup: An appraisal of the CIA's direct costing effort, 1960–80.* New Brunswick, NJ: Transaction Books, 1982.

Rowen, Henry S., ed. *The impoverished superpower: Perestroika and the Soviet military burden.* San Francisco, CA: ICS Press, 1990.

Sokolovskiy, V.D. *Soviet military strategy.* New York: Crane, Russak, 1975.

Soviet military power. Washington, DC: U.S. GPO, 1984.

United States. Congress. Commission on Security and Cooperation in Europe. *Implementation of the Helsinki accords: Hearing before the Commission on Security and Cooperation in Europe, One Hundredth Congress, second session: Soviet army defectors and prisoners of war from Afghanistan, March 23, 1988.* Washington, DC: U.S. GPO, 1988.

Vladimirov, Leonid. *The Russian space bluff.* New York: Dial Press, 1973.

Voina v Afganistane. Frankfurt a.M.: Possev, 1985.

Volkogonov, D.A. (Dimitrii Antonovich). *Etika sovetskogo ofitsera.* Moscow: Voennoe izd-vo Ministerstva oborony SSSR, 1973.

Watson, Bruce W., and Susan M. Watson, eds. *The Soviet naval threat to Europe: Military and political dimensions.* Boulder, CO: Westview Press, 1989.

Westwood, J.N. *The illustrated history of the Russo-Japanese War.* Chicago, IL: Regnery, 1974.

———. *Russia against Japan, 1904–05: A new look at the Russo-Japanese War.* Albany, NY: State University of New York Press, 1986.

Wildman, Allan K. *The end of the Russian Imperial Army.* Princeton, NJ: Princeton University Press, 1980.

Yepishev, A.A. *Some aspects of party-political work in the Soviet Armed Forces.* Moscow: Progress Publishers, 1973.

XVIII. Science

Ashby, Eric. *Scientist in Russia.* Harmondsworth: Penguin, 1947.

Bailes, Kendall E. *Technology and society under Lenin and Stalin: Ori-*

gins of the Soviet technical intelligentsia, 1917–1941. Princeton, NJ: Princeton University Press, 1978.

Berry, Michael J., ed. *Science and technology in the USSR.* Burnt Mill, Harlow, Essex: Longman, 1988.

Boss, Valentin. *Newton in Russia: The early influence, 1698–1796.* Cambridge, MA: Harvard University Press, 1972.

Graham, Loren R. *The ghost of the executed engineer: Technology and the fall of the Soviet Union.* Cambridge, MA: Harvard University Press, 1993.

———. *Science and philosophy in the Soviet Union.* New York: Knopf, 1972.

———. *Science in Russia and the Soviet Union: A short history.* Cambridge: Cambridge University Press, 1993.

———. *Science, philosophy, and human behavior in the Soviet Union.* New York: Columbia University Press, 1987.

Holliday, George D. *Technology transfer to the USSR, 1928–1937 and 1966–1975: The role of Western technology in Soviet economic development.* Boulder, CO: Westview Press, 1979.

Joravsky, David. *Russian psychology: A critical history.* Oxford: Blackwell, 1989.

Josephson, Paul R. *Physics and politics in revolutionary Russia.* Berkeley, CA: University of California, 1991.

Kassel, Simon, and Cathleen Campbell. *The Soviet Academy of Sciences and technological development.* Santa Monica, CA: Rand, 1980.

———. *Soviet cybernetics research: A preliminary study of organizations and personalities.* Santa Monica, CA: Rand, 1971.

Kneen, Peter. *Soviet scientists and the state: An examination of the social and political aspects of science in the USSR.* Albany, NY: State University of New York Press, 1984.

Kurakov, I.G. *Science, technology and communism: Some questions of development.* Oxford: Pergamon Press, 1966.

Medvedev, Zhores. *Soviet science.* New York: Norton, 1978.

Melinskaya, S.I. *Soviet science, 1917–1970.* Metuchen, NJ: Scarecrow Press, 1971.

Nalivkin, D.V. (Dmitrii Vasilevich). *Geology of the U.S.S.R.* Edinburgh: Oliver and Boyd, 1973.

Oberg, James. *Red star in orbit.* London: Harrap, 1981.

Riabchikov, E.I. (Evgenii Ivanovich) *Russians in space.* London: Weidenfeld and Nicolson, 1971.

Sager, Peter. *The technology gap between the superpowers.* Berne: Swiss Eastern Institute, 1972.

Shetler, Stanwyn G. *The Komarov Botanical Institute: 250 years of Russian research.* Washington, DC: Smithsonian Institution Press, 1967.

Soifer, Valerii. *Lysenko and the tragedy of Soviet science.* New Brunswick, NJ: Rutgers University Press, 1994.

Vucinch, Alexander. *Science in Russian culture.* Stanford, CA: Stanford University Press, 1963.

Westwood, J.N. *A history of Russian railways.* London: G. Allen and Unwin, 1964.

White, Sarah, ed. *Guide to science and technology in the USSR: A reference guide to science and technology in the Soviet Union.* Guernsey, B.I.: Francis Hodgson, 1971.

Appendix 1:
Administrative Divisions of the Russian Republic

The administrative divisions of Russia are based both on geography and on nationality. The territories of the Russian Federated Republic are: 1 (kray): Khabarovsk, Krasnodar, Krasnoiarsk, Primorie, Stavrapol. 2 (oblast): Amur, Arkhangelsk, Astrakhan, Belgorod, Briansk, Cheliabinsk, Chita, Gorki, Irkutsk, Ivanovo, Kaluga, Kalinin, Kaliningrad, Kamchatka, Kemerovo, Kirov, Kostroma, Kuibyshev, Kurgan, Kursk, Leningrad, Lipetsk, Magadan, Moscow, Murmansk, Novgorod, Novosibirsk, Omsk, Orel, Orenburg, Penza, Perm, Pskov, Rostov, Riazan, Sakhalin, Saratov, Smolensk, Sverdlov, Tambov, Tomsk, Tula, Tiumen, Ulianovsk, Vladimir, Volgograd, Vologda, Voronezh, Yarsolavl. 3—Autonomous Republics of the Russian Federation: Adygeiia, Altai, Bashkir, Buriat, Chechen-Ingush, Chuvash, Dagestan, Kabardino-Balkar, Kalmyk, Karelian, Komi, Mari, Mordovian, North Ossetian, Tatar, Tuva, Udmurt, Iakut. 4—Autonomous Regions of the Russian Federation: Adygei, Karachai-Cherkess, Gorno Altai, Jewish, Khakass. 5—National Areas (okrug): Agi-Buryat, Chukchi, Evenki, Khanti-Mansi, Komi-Permiak, Koriak, Nenets, Taimir, Ust-Orda, Buriat, Yamal-Nenets.

Appendix 2:
Principal Rivers, Lakes, and Mountains

Rivers

Amur: 2,744 miles long; empties into Tatar Strait.
Angara: 1,151 miles long; tributary of Enisei.
Dnepr: 1,420 miles long; empties into Black Sea.
Dnestr: 877 miles long; empties into Black Sea.
Don: 1,244 miles long; empties into Sea of Azov.
Dvina, Northern: 824 miles long; empties into White Sea.
Dvina, Western: 634 miles long; empties into Gulf of Riga.
Enisei: 2,543 miles long; empties into Kara Sea.
Kolyma: 1,600 miles long; empties into East Siberian Sea.
Lena: 2,734 miles long; empties into Laptev Sea.
Ob: 3,362 miles long; empties into Gulf of Ob.
Ural: 1,575 miles long; empties into Caspian Sea.
Volga: 2,293 miles long; empties into Caspian Sea.

Lakes

Aral Sea: 24,904 square miles; greatest depth at 220 feet.
Baikal: 12,162 square miles; greatest depth at 5,315 feet.
Balkhash: 7,115 square miles; greatest depth at 85 feet.
Caspian Sea: 143,244 square miles; greatest depth at 3,363 feet.
Ladoga: 6,835 square miles; greatest depth at 738 feet.
Onega: 3,710 square miles; greatest depth at 328 feet.

Mountains

Cherskii Ridge: extends some 450 miles in northeastern Siberia.
Iablonovyi Ridge: extends 700 miles eastward from Lake Baikal.
Mt. Narodnaia: highest of Ural Mountains, at 6,182 feet.
Pik Pobedy: highest mountain of Cherskii Ridge, at 24,590 feet.

Putoran Mountains: range occupying 60,000 square miles in north central Siberia.

Ural Mountains: extend north-south some 2,500 miles, separating European Russia from Asia.

Verkhoianskii Ridge: extends 600 miles in northwestern Siberia.

About the Authors

Dr. Boris Raymond (Romanov) was born in 1925 in Harbin, China. His father and paternal grandfather had served as officers in the Russian army during both World War I and the civil war with the anti-Communist White armies, until they were forced to leave Russia and seek refuge in China.

Dr. Raymond came to the United States in 1941, graduated from a San Francisco high school, and began university studies at the University of California (Berkeley) in 1943. After serving two years with the U.S. Army in Europe, he returned to the University of California in 1946, earned his bachelor's degree in 1949, and then two master's degrees, in sociology and library science. He then accepted a position as Russian bibliographer at the University of California Library in 1964 and continued working as a librarian at the universities of Nevada and Manitoba. Dr. Raymond earned an additional master's degree in Russian history at the University of Manitoba in 1970 and received his doctoral degree at the University of Chicago in 1972. Since 1974 Dr. Raymond has been teaching at Dalhousie University in Nova Scotia, Canada.

Paul Duffy was born in Gimli, Manitoba. He studied Russian and classics, has worked briefly as a translator, and written a few novels and short stories. He now works at the Killam Memorial Library at Dalhousie University.

For Reference

Not to be taken
from the room.

LONG ISLAND
UNIVERSITY
LIBRARIES